OTHER BOOKS BY Carolly Erickson
The Records of Medieval Europe
The Medieval Vision
Civilization and Society in the West
Bloody Mary

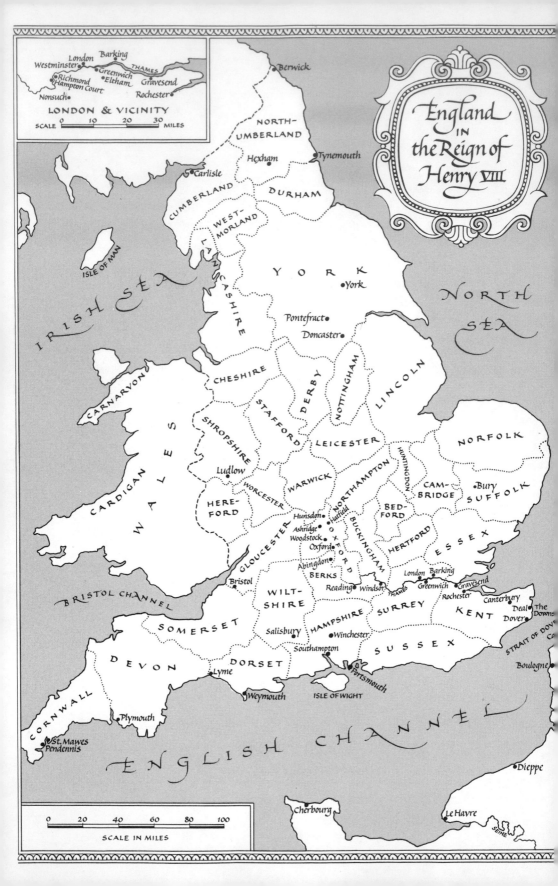

England
IN
the Reign of
Henry VIII

LONDON & VICINITY (inset map)

London Barking
Westminster THAMES
Richmond Greenwich Eltham Gravesend
Hampton Court Rochester
Nonsuch

SCALE 0 10 20 30 MILES

Berwick

NORTH-UMBERLAND

Hexham Tynemouth

Carlisle

CUMBERLAND DURHAM

WEST-MORLAND

ISLE OF MAN

LANCASHIRE

IRISH SEA

YORK

York

Pontefract

Doncaster

NORTH SEA

CHESHIRE DERBY NOTTINGHAM LINCOLN

CARNARVON

WALES

SHROPSHIRE STAFFORD

Ludlow

WORCESTER WARWICK NORTHAMPTON

LEICESTER

NORFOLK

CAM-BRIDGE Bury

SUFFOLK

CARDIGAN

HERE-FORD

HUNTINGDON

BED-FORD

Hunsdon Hatfield
Ashridge
Woodstock OXFORD BUCKINGHAM HERTFORD
Oxford

ESSEX

Abingdon

BERKS London Barking
Reading Windsor Greenwich Gravesend
THAMES Rochester Canterbury

GLOUCESTER

Bristol

WILT-SHIRE

BRISTOL CHANNEL

SOMERSET

Salisbury

HAMPSHIRE SURREY

Winchester

KENT

Deal The Downs
Dover

STRAIT OF DOVE

DEVON DORSET

Southampton

SUSSEX

Boulogne

Lyme

Weymouth ISLE OF WIGHT Portsmouth

CORNWALL

Plymouth

St. Mawes
Pendennis

ENGLISH CHANNEL

Dieppe

0 20 40 60 80 100

SCALE IN MILES

Cherbourg

Le Havre

SEINE

GREAT HARRY

Carolly Erickson

WITHDRAWN

SUMMIT BOOKS
NEW YORK

Published by *Summit Books*
A Simon & Schuster Division of Gulf & Western Corporation
Simon & Schuster Building
1230 Avenue of the Americas
New York, New York 10020
Published in association with Robert Briggs Associates

SUMMIT BOOKS and colophon are
trademarks of Simon & Schuster

Designed by Stanley S. Drate
Manufactured in the United States of America

Library of Congress Cataloging in Publication Data
Erickson, Carolly, date.
Great Harry.

Bibliography: p.
Includes index.
1. Henry VIII, King of England, 1491-1547.
2. Great Britain—History—Henry VIII, 1509-1547.
3. Great Britain—Kings and rulers—Biography.
I. Title.
DA332.E74   942.05′2′0924 [B]   79-21868
ISBN 0-671-40017-7

Contemporary poems and songs quoted as chapter openings are taken from John Stevens, ed., *Music and Poetry in the Early Tudor Court*, 11, 21, 249, 391, 396, 416, 418, 419; Thomas Percy, ed., *Reliques of Ancient English Poetry*, I, 107, 180, 181, 271, 296, 298, 305; II, 61, 139, 222, 244, 270, 273; III, 147, 179, 271, 289, 322; *Lyrics from Elizabethan Songbooks*, 207; *The Portable Elizabethan Reader*, 658; William Chappell, *Old English Popular Music*, 25–26, 61, 74, 76–77; Tucker Brooke and Matthias A. Shaaber, eds., *The Renaissance*, 498; Roy Strong, *Tudor and Jacobean Portraits*, endpapers; Joseph Hall, ed., *The Poems of Laurence Minot*, 110; Kenneth Muir, *Life and Letters of Sir Thomas Wyatt*, 32; Edward Arber, ed., *An English Garner: Tudor Tracts, 1532–1588*, 27; John Stevens, ed., *Music at the Court of Henry VIII*, 50; *Antiquarian Repertory*, III, 263; William Thomas, *The Pilgrim*, 1; Walter C. Richardson, *Mary Tudor: The White Queen*, xiv; Edward Lowinsky, "A Music Book for Anne Boleyn," in *Florilegium Historiale: Essays Presented to Wallace K. Ferguson*, ed. J. G. Rowe and W. H. Stockdale, 181; and G. R. Elton, *Policy and Police*, 137, citing a "vagrant singer" who wandered the Norfolk countryside "with a crowd and a fiddle."

ILLUSTRATION ACKNOWLEDGMENTS

Grateful acknowledgment is made to the following for permission to reproduce the illustrations specified:

Bibliothèque de Méjanes, Aix-en-Provence: 1
By courtesy of the Dean and Chapter of Westminster: 2, 4, 5
National Portrait Gallery, London: 3, 8, 16, 17, 18, 27
Bibliothèque municipale d'Arras, *Recueil de portraits:* 6
From the Woburn Abbey Collection, by kind permission of the Marquess of Tavistock, and the Trustees of the Bedford Estates: 7
Metropolitan Museum of Art: 9, 20
Fitzwilliam Museum, University of Cambridge; reproduced by permission of the Syndics of the Fitzwilliam Museum, Cambridge: 10
By gracious permission of Her Majesty the Queen; copyright reserved: 11, 12, 14, 15
BBC Hulton Picture Library: 13
Copyright The Frick Collection, New York: 19
Kunsthistorisches Museum, Wien: 21, 26
Musée du Louvre: 22, 23
Alte Pinakothek, München: 25
By courtesy of the Society of Antiquaries of London: 24
Staatliche Graphische Sammlung, München: 28

Contents

PREFACE   13

I
Young Harry   19

II
Great Harry   69

III
"The Man Most Full of Heart"   129

IV
"Dieu et Mon Droit"   177

V
The Mouldwarp   247

VI
Old Harry   315

NOTES   373
SELECT BIBLIOGRAPHY   399
INDEX   413

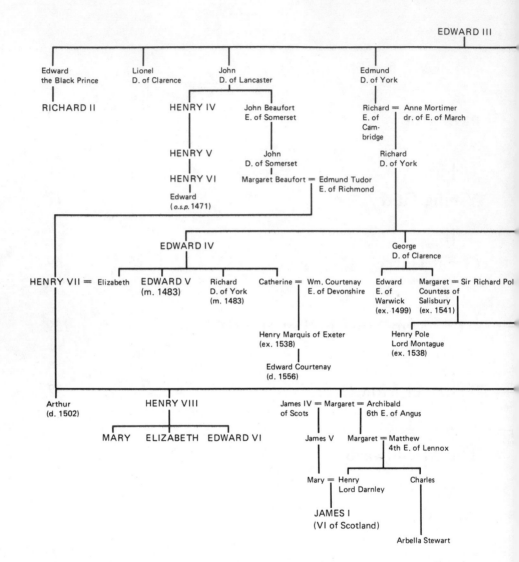

EDWARD III

Edward the Black Prince	Lionel D. of Clarence	John D. of Lancaster		Edmund D. of York	

RICHARD II

HENRY IV — John Beaufort E. of Somerset

Richard = Anne Mortimer
E. of dr. of E. of March
Cam-
bridge

HENRY V — John D. of Somerset

Richard D. of York

HENRY VI — Margaret Beaufort = Edmund Tudor E. of Richmond

Edward (*o.s.p.* 1471)

EDWARD IV

George D. of Clarence

HENRY VII = Elizabeth   EDWARD V (m. 1483)   Richard D. of York (m. 1483)   Catherine = Wm. Courtenay E. of Devonshire   Edward E. of Warwick (ex. 1499)   Margaret = Sir Richard Pol Countess of Salisbury (ex. 1541)

Henry Marquis of Exeter (ex. 1538)

Henry Pole Lord Montague (ex. 1538)

Edward Courtenay (d. 1556)

Arthur (d. 1502)   HENRY VIII   James IV = Margaret = Archibald of Scots   6th E. of Angus

MARY   ELIZABETH   EDWARD VI   James V   Margaret = Matthew 4th E. of Lennox

Mary = Henry Lord Darnley   Charles

JAMES I (VI of Scotland)

Arbella Stewart

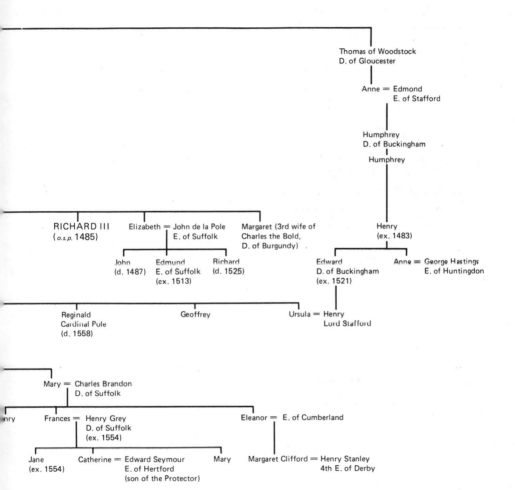

Thomas of Woodstock
D. of Gloucester

Anne = Edmond
E. of Stafford

Humphrey
D. of Buckingham

Humphrey

RICHARD III   Elizabeth = John de la Pole   Margaret (3rd wife of   Henry
(*o.s.p.* 1485)   E. of Suffolk   Charles the Bold,   (ex. 1483)
                                                   D. of Burgundy)

John   Edmund   Richard   Edward   Anne = George Hastings
(d. 1487)   E. of Suffolk   (d. 1525)   D. of Buckingham   E. of Huntingdon
            (ex. 1513)   (ex. 1521)

Reginald   Geoffrey   Ursula = Henry
Cardinal Pole   Lord Stafford
(d. 1558)

Mary = Charles Brandon
       D. of Suffolk

ary   Frances = Henry Grey   Eleanor = E. of Cumberland
                   D. of Suffolk
                   (ex. 1554)

Jane   Catherine = Edward Seymour   Mary   Margaret Clifford = Henry Stanley
(ex. 1554)   E. of Hertford   4th E. of Derby
                          (son of the Protector)

d. — died
m. — murdered
ex. — executed
o.s.p. — died without issue (*obiit sine prole*)

Preface

THERE is a story that in the reign of Bloody Mary, when hundreds of Protestants were being burned for their beliefs, the corpse of Henry VIII was torn from its resting place at Windsor and, by the queen's orders, thrown into the flames and burned to ashes. That Mary Tudor should have taken such bitter and final revenge against her father says much about the passions Henry aroused in others. From his family, his courtiers, his subjects he called forth both staunch affection and undying hatred. Yet an even stronger feeling overshadowed these: a feeling of astounded awe. For Henry Tudor was, as one who knew him wrote, "undoubtedly the rarest man that lived in his time."

Even more than his exalted rank, his towering height, powerful physique and extraordinary handsomeness set Henry apart from his contemporaries. A phenomenal athlete, he seemed to draw on super-human energies as he outrode, outdanced and outfought friends and rivals both in England and abroad. These physical gifts were balanced by unfailing warmth and charm, chivalrous delicacy of feeling, and percep-tive mental endowments that enabled Henry to share fully in the intellec-tual life of the humanists at his court and to win their respect.

Beyond these personal attributes Henry possessed the indefinable quality of majesty, the ensorceling aura of kingly command and fatherly authority that overawed his subjects and gave his enemies pause.

Midway in his reign darker qualities of mind emerged in Henry, growing stronger as he was continuously thwarted in his aims and in the end eclipsing his attractive nature. The radiant hero of the Battle of the Spurs became the troubled, anxious ruler of the mid-1520s, harried in mind by the fear of divine vengeance, then the fearsome murderous king of the 1530s whose wrath was fatal to those about him. The Catholic Church puts at fifty the number of martyrs whose deaths he brought about by execu-tion or starvation. Several wives, at least a dozen blood relatives and a similar number of onetime counselors and friends lengthened the list of victims.

By the 1540s, as Henry entered his fifties, he had become a monstrous figure to his people—an inhuman tyrant of mythic proportions whose valor and integrity had dissolved under the corroding influence of adultery, sacrilege and blood lust. In actuality Henry was by this time an aging colossus plagued by agonizing pains in his legs, soured by domestic misfortunes and overburdened by governmental labors. The inner compass that had guided him to overturn the old order of English society—to break away from the Roman church, destroy the monasteries, and undertake the reshaping of religious belief—had misled him, and he suffered in consequence.

Yet in his last years Henry rose above the limitations of his age and bulk to personally undertake the conquest of France, and displayed again the matchless vitality that all his life made him the envy of younger men. And it was that vitality, which fueled both his hearty bonhomie and his raging irritability, that made Henry the object of helpless fascination. He seemed to know everything, to be everywhere at once. "There is not a single bruit anywhere which he does not hear among the first, be it false or true, even to little private matters which princes care but little to hear," the French ambassador Marillac wrote of Henry. "He speaks as if he knew not only the kings and lords but their servants, forces, places, designs, and occasions, both far and near, as if he had men all over the world who did nothing but write to him."

The Milanese ambassador was more succinct. Henry, he wrote, "wants to have his feet in a thousand shoes."

This is a retelling of Henry's personal story, and as such it is more the life of a man than of a king. As popular history, it makes no attempt to arrive at a fresh assessment of the reign, nor to detail the political accomplishments of Henry or his ministers. My indebtedness to J. J. Scarisbrick's elegant and exemplary political biography of Henry VIII will be evident to informed readers; the bibliography at the end of this book acknowledges many of the other historical works I have used. But my chief resource has been the treasure-house of sixteenth-century letters, dispatches, and official documents collected in the Calendars of Spanish, Venetian and Milanese state papers and in the *Letters and Papers of Henry VIII*. One researcher has estimated that the tens of thousands of pages in these collections contain a million separate details about Henry; to construct a composite image of the king from these slivers of his reality has been my primary task.

Along the way, help has come from several sources: from my ever cheerful, ever competent assistant Brett Cooke and his superlative predecessor Martha Moore; from Decca Treuhaft, Peter Dreyer, Geoffrey Bruun, Gregory Wilcox and other heartening friends, and from readers of *Bloody Mary* whose questions and encouraging letters have buoyed me through a long labor.

One more influence must be acknowledged. When sixteen years ago I applied for graduate study at Columbia University, I hoped to work there with Garrett Mattingly, whose splendidly dramatic account of the Armada I had read with great enthusiasm. Professor Mattingly died before I enrolled at Columbia, but I have been a student of his books ever since, and a passage from his *Catherine of Aragon* has stayed with me during the eighteen months I have spent in the company of Great Harry. In describing him Mattingly referred to "the inwardness of that majestic childishness, that absurd mixture of naïveté and cunning, boldness and poltroonery, vindictive cruelty and wayward almost irresistible charm." As a brief sketch of a multifaceted character, these twenty-three words are unimprovable.

CAROLLY ERICKSON

Berkeley, California
January 31, 1979

Of personage he was one of the goodliest men that lived in his time, very high of stature, in manners more than a man, and proportionable in all his members unto that height; of countenance he was most amiable, courteous and benign in gesture unto all persons, and specially unto strangers; seldom or never offended with anything, and of so constant a nature in himself, that I believe few can say that ever he changed his cheer for any novelty how contrary or sudden soever it were.

Prudent he was in council and forecasting; most liberal in rewarding his faithful servants, and ever unto his enemies as it behoveth a Prince to be; he was learned in all sciences, and had the gift of many tongues; he was a perfect theologian, a good philosopher, and a strong man at arms; a jeweller, a perfect builder as well of fortresses as of pleasant palaces; and from one to another there was no necessary kind of knowledge from a king's degree to a carter's but that he had an honest sight in it.

What would you I should say of him: He was undoubtedly the rarest man that lived in his time.

—WILLIAM THOMAS, writing of
his contemporary Henry VIII
in *The Pilgrim*

I

Young Harry

1

Aboffe all thynge
Now lete us synge
Both day and nyght,
Adew mornyng,
A bud is spryngynge
Of the red rose and the whyght.

ON the morning of June 12, 1497, Elizabeth of York hurried with her five-year-old son Henry from her mother-in-law's house Coldharbour in Thames Street to the Tower of London. Reaching the Outer Ward they entered the White Tower through Coldharbour Gate, then climbed as rapidly as they could the flight of steps that led to the entrance of the great keep. Here, within the massive walls of William the Conqueror's strong fortress, they would be safe.

Outside the city was in panic. A rebel army of Cornishmen, thousands strong, was advancing on London. Armed with bows and arrows, bills and staves the rebels had marched unopposed through Devon and Somerset, to Bristol, then southeastward through Winchester and Salisbury. A general watch was set in the capital, and Londoners were fleeing the city as from a plague.

At first the king, Henry VII, stayed calmly in his palace upriver at Sheen. He had sent urgent word to his captain Daubeney, who was on his way north to meet a threatened invasion on the Scots border, to bring his men south again to head off the Cornishmen. But as the rebels came closer and there was no sign of Daubeney, the king left Sheen for safer quarters, and two days later his wife and second son followed his example. On the day that the queen and prince moved to the White Tower, fifteen thousand of the rebels encamped at Farnham. The next day they were at Guildford, and then, dangerously near, at Blackheath.

The little prince who spent the next uncertain days beside his mother in the Tower apartments was a chunky, round-faced child whose blond hair was bobbed to the ears and combed into long bangs across his forehead. A sketch made of him at about this time shows his alert, interested expression, his face set off by a broad hat with a large feather curled around its brim. His mother, then in her early thirties, was a tall, handsome woman with fair skin and pale gold hair. Londoners called her "the good queen Elizabeth," and Prince Henry, who was rarely alone with her, must have grown closer to her as they waited out the danger together.

At last the royal army arrived, and on June 17 Daubeney and his men confronted the rebels at Blackheath. Two thousand of the Cornishmen were killed that day; the rest, frustrated and beaten, surrendered and then set out for home. All that summer they straggled back to their villages, only to find that their punishment was not yet over. "All Cornishmen who eat grain garnered since the rebellion," the chronicler wrote, "or drink beer brewed with this year's crops, die as if they had taken poison."[1] News of the mysterious deaths spread rapidly. The king's power was indeed awesome, it was said; he was obviously "under the protection of God eternal."

In actuality Henry VII was far from secure on his throne. Within months of the victory at Blackheath the disaffected Cornishmen had joined forces with a stouter rebel, Perkin Warbeck, who had long claimed to be Richard, duke of York, the younger of the ill-fated princes murdered in the Tower many years before. Warbeck's followers were defeated as they assaulted Exeter, and the false "duke of York" was captured, but the king's position seemed hardly more assured in 1497 than it had been when he won the throne by battle twelve years earlier.

The king's insecurity overshadowed the lives of his children, and Prince Henry had never known a time of calm. In the summer that he was born, his father was preoccupied by the threat of invasion from France and was gathering men and money to cross the Channel into Brittany. When the prince was still a babe in arms the king carried out his invasion—the first and only time he commanded an English army. In young Henry's early childhood his father was often away from court on progress, journeying from one town or royal manor to another throughout the areas of discontent, showing himself to his subjects and sending out spies in an effort "to purge his land of all seditious seed and double-hearted fruit."[2] Perkin Warbeck began his six-year campaign to supplant Henry VII when Prince Henry was an infant, and before his misadventure ended he had drawn the French king Charles VIII, the Scots king James IV, and Henry's onetime supporter Sir William Stanley into the conspiracy against the reigning king.

The plots against Henry VII were all the more unsettling in that they were accompanied by murderous intrigues at court. According to a confession written in the year before the Cornish rebellion, several men, among them the archdeacon of London, determined "to kill the king and his children, his mother, and those near his person." Hoping to avoid implicating themselves in the crime, they turned to magic. They went all the way to Rome to find a sorcerer who could provide the deadly charm they needed, an ointment which when spread around a door the king was certain to walk through would somehow compel those who loved him best to become his murderers.[3] Hazards of other kinds intruded on the lives of the royal children. During the Christmastide celebrations in 1497, when the king and his family were in residence at the medieval palace of Sheen, a fire broke out. The flames spread quickly through the wooden structure, destroying the apartments of the king and queen and driving the entire household out into the courtyard. Shivering in the December cold, the servants, the household officials and the royal family watched their possessions go up in flames; "great substance of riches, as well in jewels and other things of riches, was perished and lost."[4]

At Christmas of 1497 there were four children, two sons and two daughters. The eldest, Prince Arthur, was eleven. Princess Margaret, a lively girl who was said to be her father's favorite, was eight. Prince Henry was six and the youngest, little Princess Mary, was not yet two. A fifth child, Princess Elizabeth, had died at the age of three several years earlier.

Of the four surviving children, Arthur took precedence. He was the eldest; he was the best-looking, with skin so fair it was almost pale and curly blond hair; most important, he was heir to the throne. Arthur Tudor incarnated the union of his father's house of Lancaster with his mother's house of York. He was "the rosebush of England," the symbolic joining of the red and white roses, the hope of the Tudor dynasty. At his birth Elizabeth of York, in gratitude for her safe delivery and for the arrival of the hoped-for male heir, founded a chapel dedicated to the virgin in Winchester Cathedral. Her pleasure in her son increased as he grew into a slender boy, admired for his looks and for the rudiments of princely geniality he showed even in childhood. Though unprepossessing in personality, Arthur filled his role well, and gave every sign of growing into a suitable king.

There was always a special bond between Arthur and his younger sister Margaret, but about his relationship with his brother Henry the records are silent. Five years separated the brothers, and by the time Henry was old enough to be a companion to Arthur the latter was sent to hold court on the Welsh border. After this they saw one another only on ceremonial occasions, or when the family gathered for Christmas.

Certainly the king and queen found a second son to be an entirely welcome addition, and when Henry was born on June 28, 1491, preparations were immediately made for an elaborate christening, while extra servants were brought in to help out in the royal nursery. Tradition called for the child to be baptized in the font of Canterbury Cathedral; it was brought up to Greenwich and installed in the church of the Franciscan Observants, high enough so that the nobles and townspeople who crowded into the church could see the ceremony without pressing Bishop Fox, who performed the baptism, too closely. Regulations put out by the king in the "Array of her Majesty's infants" called for the new baby to be "had into the nursery where it shall be nourished with a lady governour to the nursery nurse, with four Chamberers, called Rockers." Lady Darcy, as lady mistress, presided over the entire establishment. Among the rockers were Emily Hobbes and Agnes Butler, and Henry's own beloved nurse, whom he remembered in later years with a generous pension, was Ann Luke.[5]

Shortly before his second birthday Henry received the first of his numerous ceremonial titles, constable of Dover Castle and warden of the

Cinque Ports. Later he was made earl marshal of England and lord lieutenant of Ireland, with competent deputies carrying out the actual duties of these offices. In the fall of 1494, when he was three, Henry was required to undergo a series of ceremonies that would have exhausted an adult. On the first of three days of ritual he was set astride a great warhorse and led to Westminster, where after hours of initiation he was made a Knight of the Bath. The next day he received his spurs, and the day after that, before the king and nobles in the Parliament chamber, he was given the title duke of York. There were still more titles and more ceremonies to come—warden of the Scottish Marches, Knight of the Garter—but this was the most significant. In this year of 1494 a false duke of York was still abroad, and Prince Henry was to be made a living rebuke to his claim. To mark the importance of the occasion there were banquets and tournaments at court, and Princess Margaret, then only five, was allowed to present the prize of honor—a ruby ring—to the most valiant combatant in the lists.[6]

From this time on the duke of York was not only the king's son but a significant, if minor, personage in his own right. As "my lord of York" he appeared more and more frequently in the rolls of the king's expenditures, receiving money to play at dice, to pay his servants, to reward his fool John Goose and his minstrels. A precociously gifted musician, Henry had his own band of music makers, independent of those of his father and brother, from early childhood on.[7] The duke of York was fêted by the city of London when he was seven. The lord mayor and aldermen cleared the streets of beggars before his arrival, and saw to it that the cheering Londoners who lined the roadway where the prince's escort passed were free from disease. In return for the city's official gift—a pair of gilt goblets—Henry made a brief speech of thanks, adding that he hoped to be worthy of the citizens' "great and kind remembrance" in future.

As soon as he was old enough to be out of the nursery Prince Henry began to join in the life of the court. His earliest memories were doubtless of the fools and freaks and entertainers his father loved. In addition to the master fools Scot and Dick, Patch, Diego the Spanish jester, and the "foolish duke of Lancaster" there were traveling dancers and acrobats—morris dancers, dancing children, tightrope walkers and men who did conjuring tricks. On one occasion the king gave a reward to "a fellow who distinguished himself by eating of coals." Monstrosities such as "the great Welsh child," "the little Scotsman," and "the great woman of Flanders" were brought to court for the king's amusement, and when he was not jousting or playing tennis or gambling with his courtiers Henry VII liked to surround himself with human oddities.[8] Long before he was able to join in the sport himself young Henry knew all about the hawks with their hoods and gilt bells, and went often to see the mules and horses in the stables and his mother's greyhounds in their kennels. Later he was brought to see the royal lions and leopards that were kept at the Tower. These he feared, for one of the lions had mauled a man to death earlier in the reign.

At those rare times when Arthur, Margaret and Henry were together they followed their father to the hunt, or watched a bull or bear baited by dogs. Henry taught all his children to shoot with the longbow, and they became proficient archers. At fourteen Margaret shot true enough to kill a buck, and both Arthur and Henry rivaled the archers of the king's guard in their marksmanship.[9]

The royal children were an important part of courtly display, and they took their place in the carefully arranged grouping around the king in the presence chamber whenever important visitors presented themselves. They were spectators at all the great court functions. They stood out of the way in the king's bedchamber on New Year's morning as the usher of the chamber called out from the doorway to announce the bringing in of the gifts. "Sire, here is a New Year's gift coming from the queen," he said, following custom. "Let it come in, Sire." Sitting at the foot of his bed, the king received the gifts of every member of his court, in order of rank, from the queen through the greatest noblemen through the lords and ladies of lesser titles. Afterward the queen received her gifts, and finally the children were allowed to see theirs. Later, on Twelfth Night, they were in the great hall at Westminster when the steward brought in the wassail, giving the traditional greeting "Wassail, wassail, wassail!" after which the chapel singers "answered with a good song." They stayed to watch the disguising that followed, in which a dozen ladies and gentlemen danced in an exotic spectacle; the torchlit hall was always hung with tapestries for the occasion, and benches were erected for the servants and ordinary folk to sit on. After the disguising, confections and spices were served to the king and queen, and then to the courtiers; over a hundred such dishes were served at the Twelfth Night entertainment of 1494. Such magnificence was not confined to holidays. Some eight hundred people dined at the king's table even on ordinary days; when ambassadors or other dignitaries were present the number was even higher, and the dishes—venison, shields of brawn (pickled swine or beef) in armor, swans and peacocks, served tail and all—seemed never to end.

Hand in hand with this splendor went the primitive discomforts of a medieval court. All the royal palaces were perpetually cold and damp. The only warmth came from the fires kept burning in rooms with hearths. The other rooms were warmed, after a fashion, by "fire pans"—round iron pans on wheels, filled with slow-burning charcoal—which were moved from room to room as needed. Carpets of rushes and sweet herbs caught most of the spills and filth that fell on the floor, but even when these were changed as frequently as the king's regulations required the rooms stank after only a few weeks of use, and the household had to move on to another residence. There was no plumbing, only wooden privies kept covered by a "fair cushion" and a green cloth. At night the wardrober brought in a "night-stool and urinal" at need. Cleanliness as we understand it was all but impossible. Expensive tallow or olive-oil-based soaps were available in wealthy households, but the fleas and bugs that lived in the walls and bred in the folds of clothing infested even the cleanest bodies. Mulberry twigs tied in bunches under the bed helped to keep the fleas away at night, but during the day the best that even the king could do was to wear a little piece of fur next to his skin to attract all the vermin to one spot.

The age was unkind to children. Margaret Courtenay, a cousin and companion of the royal children, choked on a fishbone and died at a very young age. Arthur, Margaret and Henry appeared to be strong enough, and the queen's third daughter, Mary, was surviving infancy. But her third son, Edmund, was to live only sixteen months, and by the time she reached her mid-thirties there was some doubt whether Elizabeth of York could bear healthy children in future.

2

Whoso that will himself apply
To pass the time of youth jolly,
Advance him to the company
Of lusty bloods and chivalry

IN the summer of 1499 Erasmus of Rotterdam, soon to become the most celebrated scholar of his age, visited the royal nursery. Erasmus was staying at the Greenwich country house of William Blount, Lord Mountjoy, who that summer had been chosen as companion to Prince Henry; Mountjoy was a former pupil of Erasmus, and as such was well suited to serve as an example of humanist courtesy to the prince. He did not come along, though, when Thomas More visited his friend Erasmus and took him out for a walk to the neighboring village of Eltham.

The largest and finest of Henry VII's country houses, Eltham Palace was set in a forested hunting park where the king liked to hunt stag with his companions. The spacious estate held lists for tournaments and outbuildings for banquets and entertainments as well as the imposing main building with its moated inner courtyard and great hall. In this hall the palace staff and all of Mountjoy's household were assembled, rank on rank, to greet the visitors, and in their midst was a stocky boy whose natural authority gave away his identity.

Recalling the incident more than twenty years later, Erasmus remembered how the eight-year-old Prince Henry had "already something of royalty in his demeanor, in which there was a certain dignity combined with a singular courtesy."[1] Arthur was not present—he was in Wales presiding at his father's court for the Marches—and in his absence Henry was the star of the occasion. Margaret stood at his right and Mary played on the floor beside him, but it was Henry who received all the attention. More bowed to him and presented him with something he had written, and Erasmus, embarrassed that he had nothing to offer, made his excuses and promised to remedy his oversight another time. Caught off guard, Erasmus was angry with his friend for not warning him in advance about preparing a literary gift for the prince; his chagrin was deepened when later that day he received a personal note from Henry "challenging something from his pen."

He went immediately back to Mountjoy's house and sat down to write. Three days later he finished the *Prosopopoeia Britanniae,* which he presented to Henry with a dedicatory letter. "We have for the present

dedicated these verses, like a gift of playthings, to your childhood,"
Erasmus began, in elegant Latin, "and shall be ready with more abundant
offerings, when your virtues, growing with your age, shall supply more
abundant material for poetry."

There is no doubt that Henry, at eight, could read Erasmus' Latin. His
tutor, John Skelton, was a scholar of wide learning—Erasmus called him
"that incomparable light and ornament of British letters"—and he saw to
it that the prince's education was extensive and demanding. He taught
Henry Latin and Greek himself; the boy learned French from Giles
d'Ewes, author of a noted French grammar. Either d'Ewes or one of
Prince Arthur's teachers, Bernard André, taught Henry to write a large,
round hand influenced by the Italian style. Proficiency in Latin and
French was expected of wellborn boys at six or seven; by the time he was
ten Henry was reading the Latin treatise Skelton wrote for both Henry
and Arthur to instruct them in the duties and behavior of a prince.[2]

As his principal tutor Skelton held great sway over the bent of Henry's
mind. His influence was many-sided, for though he was poet laureate and
had recently become a priest Skelton was as ribald and irreverent as he
was sharp-witted. He had not yet begun to write the scurrilous poems that
have made him the most famous poet of his generation, but his biting
sarcasm was already making enemies for him everywhere. He infuriated
other writers, clerics, and especially his bishop, who censured him and
suspended him temporarily from his church. Skelton's parishioners, who
disapproved of his clandestine marriage to a woman who lived in his
house, complained that his sermons were more fit for the stage than the
pulpit, and when in 1502 he went too far with outrageous behavior he was
briefly imprisoned.

Yet it was by design that this colorful personality was put in charge of
Prince Henry's early development; Skelton was much favored by Henry's
grandmother Margaret, countess of Richmond, who acted as his patron
and doubtless chose him as mentor for her favorite grandson. He was
chosen chiefly for his learning, but the countess must have hoped that
something of his wit and irreverence would rub off on Henry too. Both the
prince and his tutor were strong extroverts, and there seems to have been
another natural link between them as well: like Henry, Skelton had a gift
for music, and liked to sing his poems while he accompanied himself on
the lute. In later life Henry loved to sing folk songs with his courtiers; it is
more than likely he acquired the habit from singing with Skelton as a boy.

No record of the order of Henry's school day survives. But outlines
for the education of royal sons in the generations before and after his
childhood describe a pattern of study and recreation that must have
prevailed in the nursery at Eltham.[3] This traditional regimen called for the
boy to rise very early, hear matins sung by his chaplain, and then attend
mass at six o'clock. A light meal of ale or wine and meat and bread
followed, and then the morning's serious study began—Latin, Greek, and
French, penmanship, and perhaps mathematics on one day, logic or law
on another. Chivalry was taken as seriously as the classics, and Henry's
young head was filled with tales of knightly valor, of "virtue and honor,"

and of the prowess of his medieval ancestors. War and mighty deeds became his obsession; naturally he dreamed of fighting the traditional enemy of England's medieval kings, France. Erasmus, who saw Prince Henry a number of times in his childhood, later wrote to a friend that the boy's "dream as a child had been the recovery of the French provinces"—the lost dream of the Plantagenets in the Hundred Years' War.

The morning's studies were cut short at about ten o'clock, when dinner was served, the dishes "borne in by worshipful folk in livery." The tutor presided at the table, watching to see that his pupil ate and drank "mannerly," "after the book of courtesy." Lapses were to be punished with a stout stick. The long afternoons were given over to martial exercises—jousting on horseback at a quintain or at the rings, riding in armor, fighting with blunt weapons both on horseback and on foot. Boys learned to wield a two-handed sword and battle-axe, to thrust with a dagger, and to defend themselves as they would some day do on the battlefield. To strengthen themselves for this far-off contest they ran foot races against other boys, leaped ditches and hurdled fences, and wrestled till they were exhausted. For recreation they hawked and hunted, and practiced shooting with the longbow.

At four in the afternoon, after evensong, there was another light meal of meat and bread and wine, and then came music lessons and "the polite arts of singing, harping, playing the lute and dancing," and practice in courtly conversation. For this feminine company was required; it was normal for boys to be admitted to the women's apartments to play chess or gambling games in the evening. At nine these "honest recreations" came to an end. The palace gates were shut and the children put to bed, their rooms cleared of servants and playmates and the curtains drawn. Made secure by a "sure and good watch," they slept until early the next morning.

This educational plan was not meant to be followed alone, and it was as one of a group of children that Henry received his instruction. Among the members of this little circle were John St. John, nephew of Henry's grandmother Margaret, Edward Pallet, a child whom Elizabeth of York adopted and raised, and the three Courtenay children—Henry, Margaret and Edward—whose mother was Elizabeth of York's sister Katherine. The Courtenays did not live at Eltham; they had their own establishment in Essex near Havering-atte-Bower. But they saw a great deal of their royal cousins, and Henry Courtenay and Henry Tudor were particularly close. Another boy who was constantly in Henry's company was his page William Compton. When Compton became a ward of Henry VII at the age of ten or eleven, he was appointed to serve the infant duke of York, and was continually in his service from then on.

Compton was to remain a lifelong intimate, but another boyhood companion was to be Henry's closest and most enduring friend: Charles Brandon. An orphan, Brandon had been brought into the royal household at the age of seven to be a companion to Prince Arthur. He grew into a strapping, handsome boy, tall and broad-shouldered and fit to race and

ride and joust alongside the prince of Wales and, later, alongside his
younger brother. Brandon's gifts of mind were few, but his splendid
military heritage more than made up for his dullness of intellect. His
grandfather William Brandon had been Henry Tudor's standard-bearer at
Bosworth Field. The elder Brandon had held the Tudor banner aloft until
Richard III sought him out and fought him to the death. This gallant
sacrifice put the king in debt to Brandon's orphaned grandson, and young
Charles Brandon in turn felt the pull of ancestral loyalty to the Tudor
house.

Beyond this, though, a strong affinity developed between Brandon and
the young Prince Henry, who was at least six years his junior. They were
drawn together by a shared physical exuberance—a headstrong delight in
running farther, hunting longer and jousting more tirelessly than any of
the other boys. Weary of his arduous lessons, and of the exalted company
of the scholars, clerics and poets who crowded his father's court, Henry
would turn to Brandon to lead him out onto the tiltyard or into the fields,
where he could serve as an alter ego to Henry's passionate physicality.
The prince grew up in the older boy's shadow, watching him, learning
from him, always stretching his own abilities against Brandon's. In the
end, as Henry approached the threshold of manhood, he began to outdis-
tance Brandon, and eventually overtook him in every sport and skill they
shared. But by this time nothing could shatter the bond that had grown
between them. They would be friends for life.

The lore of the fields and of the tilting ground were of course central to
Henry's education. No gentleman could afford to be ignorant of the
mysteries of the chase. He had to know the nature of the hart and hind and
boar that fed by night and lay in cover in the forest during the day, and of
the buck and fox and roe that hid themselves at night and came out into
the fields in the morning. He had to know too the times and seasons of
each beast, the tricks of scent, weather and wind, the arts of hunting with
hounds. Hunting was more than sport: it was preparation for war, a
toughening of nerve and sinew in conditions not unlike those of the
battleground. "Hunters by their continual travail, painful labor, often
watching, and enduring of hunger, of heat, and of cold, are much enabled
above others to the service of their Prince and Country in the wars," one
treatise declared, "having their bodies for the most part by reason of their
continual exercise in much better health, than other men have, and their
minds also by this honest recreation the more fit and the better disposed
to all other good exercises."[4]

If hunting tempered the body for war, riding was the distinguishing
mark of the gentleman warrior. Noblemen were set apart from other men
by their ability to ride the giant warhorses bred to carry the weight of a
knight in full body armor. Royal sons were expected to excel in horsemanship, for it was understood that no adroitness in diplomacy or at the
council board could compensate for a poor showing in the tiltyard or at
the wars. "No earthly thing bred such wonder to a Prince," an Italian
riding master wrote, "as to be a good horseman. Skill of government was
but a Pedanteria in comparison . . ."[5]

Horsemanship had to be learned young, while the leg muscles were still developing; only then could the child acquire the agility needed to leap onto the horse from either side, or from the back, while he ran free. Once the apprentice rider had learned to mount and dismount without using the stirrup, he tried the same thing in armor, eventually becoming able to grab the mane of a galloping horse and jump into the saddle while burdened with a helmet and breastplate and with heavy cuisses on his legs. Good carriage and a graceful bearing on horseback were essential; with these intact the boy practiced keeping his horse within the lists, running him straight at the ring and not allowing him to swerve aside from an oncoming horse and rider. Management of the lance came next, calling for a coordination of eye and arm needed to avoid running the lance into the post instead of through the ring. Iron-hard courage was needed too, to watch the approach of an opponent and to sustain the violent impact of his lance where it struck the body armor.

All these skills, plus a basic knowledge of horseflesh—of the quality, age and value of a horse, of equine diseases and remedies—were an integral part of what one educational theorist called the "urbanity and nurture of England," the complex of civilizing arts that were the cultural inheritance of the feudal class. The most basic of these arts was civility itself. Politeness, inoffensiveness, courtesy toward superiors and inferiors had to be learned painstakingly through treatises on good behavior. Wipe your nose with a handkerchief—not on your gown, or on the tablecloth— and never look into the handkerchief afterward, these treatises advised. Spit, if you must, on the floor at your feet and tread it well into the rushes. "Belch thou near to no man's face, with a corrupt fumosity," one treatise read. "But turn from such occasion, friend; hate such ventosity." And above all, break wind quietly, and never at the dinner table; only drunk- ards and idiots and senile old men do that.

Among the civilizing arts was that of personal hygiene. Children were taught to clean their teeth with toothpicks and peeled wands, and to rub them with a linen cloth to whiten them. To keep their breath sweet they were told to sleep with their mouths open, and to wear a nightcap— preferably a red one—with a hole in it "through which the vapor may go out." An effort was made to influence eating habits too, though this must have been a vain effort at Henry VII's bountiful court. The stomach is the body's kitchen, young boys and girls were told; everyone knows that if the kitchen is disorderly the rest of the establishment is in chaos. Moderate food and drink will keep the kitchen in order; overeating was hazardous, "lest the belly-God hale you at length captive into his prison house of gourmandise where you shall be afflicted with as many diseases as you have devoured dishes of sundry sorts."[6]

But familiarity with knightly skills and pastimes and civilized courtesy were only the externals of gentlemanly conduct. If Henry was to fulfill his princely office he would have to acquire subtler qualities of spirit. He would have to take on the intangible air of authority that inspired fear and respect in others, and with it the trait the writers of his time called affability—the ability to turn a "gentle and familiar visage" on lesser folk to comfort them and inspire their love. He would have to learn to exercise majesty, that elusive quality "which, like as the sun does his beams, casts on the beholders and hearers a pleasant and terrible reverence."[7] The man of majesty carried himself with dignity, spoke deliberately and seriously, without using coarse language, and accommodated his words and gestures to the occasion. He was an exemplar to those around him, a fatherly yet sainted presence, half man, half angel, whose "countenance should be in the stead of a firm and stable law to his inferiors."

Two other qualities were called for. One was magnanimity, a visionary daring beyond ordinary courage which led the nobleman to challenge himself to perform unimaginable feats. Magnanimity was to honor what valor was to arms—an ennobling, high-minded heroism which lifted every bold act into the realm of legend. The other was grace; not the common grace of elegant movement or graciousness, but an air of effortlessness with which the true nobleman performed even the most difficult test of skill. To make the impossible seem easy, and then to dismiss the accomplishment with nonchalance: that was what every wellborn man strove for, though few achieved it. In Castiglione's words, the consummate sign of nobility was "to use in every thing a certain recklessness, to cover art withal, and . . . to do it without pain, and (as it were) not minding it."

These two characteristics, which were to be so prominent in Prince Henry as he grew older, had already begun to stamp themselves on the boy whose air of royalty so impressed Erasmus on that summer afternoon in 1499.

3

Upon my lap my sovereign sits
And sucks upon my breast;
Meantime his love maintains my life
And gives my sense her rest.
Sing lullaby, my little boy.
Sing lullaby, mine only joy!

IF Prince Henry's tutors instilled in him one set of guidelines for noble conduct, his father supplied a living model for another. Henry Tudor was a remarkable man who had led a remarkable life. Forced into exile at the age of fourteen, he grew to manhood in captivity in Brittany, far from his native Wales and his beloved mother Margaret Beaufort, countess of Richmond. The countess was a great-great-granddaughter of Edward III; by an intricate genealogical calculation this made her son the leading male claimant to the English throne in the Lancastrian line. But the rival Yorkist line held power, in the person of Edward IV, and it was not until Edward's death in 1483—when Henry Tudor was twenty-four—that the Yorkist fortunes began to turn. Richard III became king, and almost immediately Margaret Beaufort, her second husband Lord Stanley, Henry's uncle Jasper Tudor, many Welsh lords and others alienated by Richard's tyranny began to conspire his overthrow.

Their support was essential, but without Henry's own daring their plans would have come to nothing. Borrowing sixty thousand francs from the French king, he assembled an invasion force of two to three thousand Breton and Norman mercenaries and a few hundred English followers. According to one account his soldiers were the worst rabble that could be found—"beggerly Bretons and faint-hearted Frenchmen," Richard III called them—and their arms and equipment too were makeshift. But under the leadership of the tall, slender knight whose blond hair shone in the sun "like burnished gold" and whose blue-gray eyes, "shining and quick," seemed to perceive a hidden destiny, they prevailed over Richard's army at Bosworth Field. To their shouts of "King Harry!" "King Harry!" Richard's crown was put on his head; the throne became his by right of conquest.

When he became king in 1485 few English men and women had heard of Henry Tudor. Within a few years, though, accounts of his majestic appearance and of the splendors of his court had reached to all corners of his kingdom. Ballads told of his heroic struggle for the crown, and chroniclers noted down his looks and manner for posterity. He was not only fairly tall but well built and strong, one of them wrote, and "of a wonderful beauty and fair complexion." He dressed magnificently. A visitor to the royal hunting lodge at Woodstock on an ordinary day found the king wearing a violet gown lined with cloth of gold; around his neck was a jeweled collar, and in his hat a large diamond and an exquisite pearl. His household accounts show a pronounced taste for finery. Silks and satins, furs of many kinds, a stomacher made of "ostrich skin" were among the entries, and in the years between 1491 and 1505 he spent over £100,000 on jewels. When the king outfitted himself to lead his army into France in the seventh year of his reign, he ordered a matchless suit of armor whose helmet was ornamented with a wealth of pearls and jewels bought from the Lombard merchants.[1]

More than anything else about him observers noticed the king's lively, arresting eyes. They lit up his animated face, especially when he spoke, and they seemed to take in everything around him. They betrayed a keen intelligence preoccupied by constant vigilance, learned in his years of captivity, in his months of assembling and holding together a disparate invasion force, in his years as king facing rebels and pretenders and threats against his life. In his youth Henry VII had had the gift of attracting men's loyalty; though he never quite lost that gift, by the second decade of his reign it was overshadowed by other qualities. He was shrewd and cautious in government; he had, the chronicler Hall believed, "the ingenious forcast of the subtle serpent." He brooded over each of his decisions, and became intolerant of even the slightest departure from his explicit orders. He remained an enthusiastic hunter, forcing the ambassadors who sought audiences with him during the hunting season to ride at his heels through the thickets of the New Forest, but in the late 1490s he was more often to be found conducting experiments to turn base metals into gold, or enlarging his collection of relics. In particular he treasured his piece of the holy cross, brought from Greece, and his leg bone of Saint George, whose feast he kept each year with the greatest solemnity.

Henry's growing piety was more superstitious than devout, for events in the spring of 1498 had shaken his confidence badly and made him look for occult guidance. Another pretender appeared, this time a Kentish schoolboy impersonating the young earl of Warwick, son of Edward IV's brother George. The true earl was in prison in the Tower, and the pretender hardly had a chance to make his cause known before the king's spies caught him and hanged him. But the incident haunted Henry's mind, and when he heard of a seer who had foretold the deaths of two of his royal predecessors he determined to learn his own fate. He went to the man and asked him bluntly how his death would come. Without answering directly the prophet replied that his life would be in danger throughout the coming year, adding alarming warnings about future conspiracies against the throne. To make matters worse, though the fortuneteller was sworn to secrecy he proved to be indiscreet, and before long rumors of the royal destiny were widespread. Imprisoning the talebearers did little good. The whisperings continued, and the king saw ill-will everywhere he turned. He spent more and more time hearing masses and carrying out religious devotions. During Lent he was on his knees most of the day, his face anxious and drawn. "He has aged so much," the Spanish ambassador wrote, "that he seems to be twenty years older."

Thus by the time Prince Henry was old enough to begin to take his father's measure the king had begun to decline toward fearful old age. He was in his early forties, but looked much older; his expression had not lost its intensity but his princely good looks had gone long ago. His thinning hair was white, his lined face sallow; the skin hung on his bones, and when he spoke his teeth were "few, poor and blackish." He suffered from gout, and his eyesight was failing. When he tried to write a letter to his mother in his own hand—something he rarely attempted—he squinted and blinked over it for three days. The Englishmen who had once acclaimed him on Bosworth Field now grumbled at his avarice, with those he had specially favored most discontented of all.

Ambassador Ayala summed up the king's predicament. "He would like to govern England in the French fashion"—as absolute sovereign— "but he cannot. . . . He likes to be much spoken of, and to be highly appreciated by the whole world. He fails in this because he is not a great man." An immensely capable ruler, as king Henry Tudor had not lived up to his image as a romantic conqueror. His political and diplomatic achievements were considerable, but in terms of his personal majesty his reign was a long anticlimax. Deprived of the adulation he craved, he withdrew to his relics and his alchemy, and spent his spare time poring over his account books and writing out his expenses in a faltering hand.

At King Henry's side through these changes was his wife Elizabeth, the "good queen" who had shared his fortunes ever since he landed in England. True to her motto "Humble and Reverent," she had borne him six children, three of them male, and had given him no cause to regret having taken her as his wife. She decorated his court, she endured the dominating presence of his mother, and she took a seemly interest in his activities, embroidering his Garter mantle and helping to set in place the pearls and diamonds in his jeweled helmet.

Queen Elizabeth not only shared her husband's piety but exceeded it. Wherever she stayed she sent offerings to all the local shrines. While at Woodstock in the summer of 1502 she sent money "to our Lady at Linchelade," and "to the Rood at Northampton," and paid five priests to say five masses before the statue of the virgin at Northampton church.[2] In time of illness the number of her donations increased, as they did during the major observances of the Christian calendar. During one Lenten season she sent two men on long pilgrimages on her behalf, one to visit the Rood of Grace, the shrine of St. Thomas at Canterbury, and fifteen other churches in Kent, and the other to the chapel of St. George at Windsor, "to the holy cross there," to Our Lady of Eton and the "Child of Grace" at Reading, and to view the Holy Blood of Hales—some sixteen shrines in all.[3]

Her devout piety was not the least of Elizabeth's valuable qualities, but more valuable to her husband was her lineage. Though jealous of the claims of his own bloodline Henry Tudor owed much of his relative security as king to his union with a Yorkist princess. Elizabeth was Edward IV's eldest daughter; the children she bore Henry were thus both children and grandchildren of kings, and shared equally the Lancastrian and Yorkist inheritance. The joining of the two rival houses had been the work of Margaret Beaufort and Elizabeth's mother, Elizabeth Woodville. In the dark months when Richard III ruled and rumor had it that he meant to marry the beautiful young Elizabeth of York himself, the two mothers helped the exiled Henry Tudor and the imprisoned Elizabeth—then a refugee from court living in sanctuary with her mother and sisters—to exchange messages. Before he left France Henry had pledged himself to Elizabeth, and she had sworn to marry this adventurer she had never met. The marriage did not take place, though, until after Henry's coronation, and Elizabeth's own coronation was postponed until after the birth of her first child. Henry Tudor would not have any man say he owed his throne to his wife.

As a young woman Queen Elizabeth was seen as a princess out of legend. She was "the illustrious maid of York, most beautiful in form, whose matchless face, adorned with most enchanting sweetness shines," the girl celebrated in *The Song of the Lady Bessy* as a heroic partner in Henry Tudor's conquest. As queen she seems to have been a gentle and beloved woman, presiding competently in her Council chamber, supervising the auditor of her lands and those who looked after her "matters and businesses," and providing for her several dozen ladies and gentlewomen. Erasmus found her brilliant and witty, but no evidence of her mental accomplishments remains. Richmond Palace, the great house Henry VII built on the ruins of Sheen, was her favored residence. There she joined in the conventional amusements of the court, hunting with her greyhounds, gambling at cards, enjoying the music of her three minstrels and the pranks and jests of her fool William.

If the queen left a somewhat indistinct impression in the records of her age her absorbing preoccupation with family ties may have been to blame. It was said she never appeared in public without one of her sisters at her side, and she gave them all annuities and watched over the welfare of their children as carefully as if they had been her own. She included within the circle of her immediate family her aunt Elizabeth and her nephews Edmund and Richard de la Pole, her cousin Margaret, sister of the imprisoned earl of Warwick, and, of course, her mother, Elizabeth Woodville. The latter bond, though natural enough, was a sensitive one, for the queen dowager had had the indiscretion to involve herself with the pretender Lambert Simnel, and the king had punished her by taking away her lands and forcing her into semi-imprisonment among the nuns of Bermondsey Abbey.

The dominating influence of Prince Henry's childhood, however, was not his mother or his maternal grandmother but Margaret Beaufort, who—the king excepted—was without question the most commanding personality in the royal family. The "Venerable Margaret" had lived through more reigns, with more opportunity to affect their outcome, than any other individual at her son's court. She was, though no one spoke it, rightful queen of England, but she had long since abandoned any thought of asserting her claim. England had not had a queen since the twelfth century, and Margaret's shrewd political sense told her that she could never have seized the throne herself, while her son could. Besides, while Henry ruled she was easily the wealthiest and most powerful woman in the country, with independent control over her extensive lands as "a sole person, not wife nor covert of any husband." In all but name she was queen dowager; she was called "My lady the king's mother," but she was allowed to sign her documents with the regal "Margaret R."

These advantages would have meant little had the Venerable Margaret been a less impressive woman. As it was they gave a naturally dominant woman license to exercise indirect rule. "The king is much influenced by his mother," a court observer wrote in 1498. "The queen, as is generally the case, does not like it."[4] Henry and his mother exchanged "intimate and tender" letters when they were apart, with Margaret addressing her son as "my own sweet and most dear king and all my worldly joy" and "my dearest and only desired joy in this world." More often they were together, for whenever the king wanted to "be merry" he sought out his mother at Coldharbour and "re-created his spirits and solaced himself" in her company. It was during these times, with her women singing and her minstrels playing in the background, that her advice was sought and her wishes made known.

Margaret's formal sphere of authority was limited, but it gave her a degree of control over Prince Henry and his brothers and sisters that was virtually absolute. As mistress of court ceremonial, she was in charge of all procedures to be followed in the royal nurseries. The everyday care of the children was in her hands, and if the wet nurse's food and drink were not carefully tasted, or if the physician neglected to supervise the nurse while she fed the younger children, it was my lady the king's mother who called the guilty servants to account. Of all her charges Margaret favored most her grandson Henry. It is tempting to think that she saw in him some of her own tenacity and vigor, something of the stubborn, cunning will to survive that had carried her through a stormy life. Whatever the reason, by the time he was ten she had singled the boy out as her heir, notifying his father of her intention to keep her tenants free for "my lord of York, your fair sweet son" when he should come of age.[5]

Henry must have feared his grandmother as much as he loved her, for she was both stern and affectionate with him. He had to be wary of everything he did in her watchful presence, and little seems to have escaped her notice. She was a woman of sharp wits, with a trained mind accustomed to scholarly exercise. She kept rooms at Christ's College, Cambridge (endowing a professorship of divinity there whose tenant was called "Margaret Professor"), and had a large library of English and French books; her "holding memory" earned her an enviable reputation among the masters at Cambridge, one of whom, her friend and confessor John Fisher, wrote that she was "of singular wisdom, far surpassing the common rate of women,'' with ''a ready wit to conceive all things albeit they were right dark.''[6]

Growing up under her scrutiny Henry was constantly witness not only to Margaret's intelligence but to the emotional intensity of her world view. Her religious devotion went beyond dutiful observance and heartfelt prayer; she longed to devote her entire life to Christ and his church. If only the kings of Christendom would launch another crusade against the Moslems, she liked to say, she would join them gladly, ''and help to wash their cloths, for love of Jesu.''[7] Even the simplest acts of piety called forth floods of tears. Fisher noted her ''marvellous weeping'' whenever she confessed her sins or took communion, and formal occasions of all kinds left her limp from sobbing. It was an age when tears were more respected than repressed, but Margaret's tears had a special poignancy. Believing that fate had decreed pain and suffering as the price of all happiness, she wept most copiously in times of greatest rejoicing. Thus, ''either she was in sorrow by reason of the present adversities,'' Fisher commented, ''or else when she was in prosperity she was in dread of the adversity for to come.''[8]

Everpresent, ever watchful, masterful yet drained by weeping for unglimpsed tragedies, the figure of Margaret Beaufort haunted her grandson's childhood. Her imprint was indelible; all Henry's life he would be wary of strong women.

4

All is hazard that we have,
There is nothing biding;
Days of pleasure are like streams
Through fair meadows gliding.
Weal and woe, time doth go,
Time is never turning;
Secret fates guide our states,
Both in mirth and mourning.

PRINCE Henry was at the riverside town of Kingston-on-Thames in November of 1501, waiting for the arrival of the Spanish princess who was to be his sister-in-law. With him was the duke of Buckingham, lord steward of his father's household, dressed in his customary splendor and accompanied by a retinue of some three hundred gentlemen-at-arms. Princess Katherine of Aragon was to be Prince Arthur's bride, but as Spanish custom forbade the meeting of bride and groom before the wedding it was Henry who was deputed to accompany Katherine to the capital, and to serve as her escort during the days of celebrations preceding the ceremony. Of course, the king had already offended all the Spaniards in Katherine's suite by refusing to respect the custom; he had presented himself at the house where she was staying at Dogmersfield and asserted his guardian rights over her. He would see the face and form of this sixteen-year-old girl his diplomats had acquired for his son. If she were less than the envoys he sent to Spain had reported her to be, there might be no wedding.

Apparently she pleased him—and Arthur, who also came to Dogmersfield to view his future wife—for the king and his son made themselves at home among the Spaniards, listening to the minstrels Katherine had brought with her and watching her dance. Henry found her manners both agreeable and dignified, or so he wrote to her father King Ferdinand, while Arthur seems to have voiced no complaint. The next day father and son left for London, where they would next see Katherine at the center of a festive procession, making her ceremonial entry with Prince Henry by her side.

Ten-year-old Henry performed his duties well over the following days, riding up to greet Katherine outside Kingston-on-Thames, leading her to her temporary lodgings at Lambeth, and then escorting her the next day as she rode her Spanish mule through the lavishly decorated streets and cheering crowds of the capital. The cheering was lusty and sincere. When she landed at Plymouth the townspeople had gone wild with delight; "she could not have been received with greater rejoicings," one of her attendants wrote, "if she had been the Saviour of the world." Katherine now captivated Londoners no less, riding side-saddle on her mule, her long auburn hair loose under a large round hat tied on with gold lace. She was not a beauty, but she was young and demure, and charming in her quaint Spanish dress. "There is nothing wanting in her," wrote Thomas More, then a law student in the city, "that the most beautiful girl should have."

As he rode along beside her Katherine's boyish companion must have studied closely the foreign being who was about to enter his family. When Arthur became king, she would be queen, though it was hard to imagine this slight girl in such a role. As she spoke no English, her brief conversations with her future brother-in-law must have been limited to Latin; when talk failed, they doubtless resorted to the chivalrous pantomime of courtesy. Henry's attention was in any case divided between Katherine and the street pageants put on in her honor. At London Bridge, Saints Katherine and Ursula recited long poems in her praise, while figures representing "Polycy," "Noblesse," "Vertue" and the Archangel Raphael saluted her at other points along her route. God himself—"a man goodly apparelled representing the father of heaven"—met her in a final spectacular pageant, standing in an elaborate structure painted to resemble the sky and ornamented with seven golden candlesticks.

Two days later Henry, in a suit of white velvet and gold, led Katherine up the nave of St. Paul's to the scarlet-covered platform where Arthur awaited her. As the king and queen, the ambassadors and courtiers and a great crowd of Londoners looked on—the Venerable Margaret weeping copiously—the young couple were married. Prince Henry, who had stood aside during the ceremony, took Katherine's arm immediately afterward to accompany her to her wedding banquet, her husband staying behind to complete the formalities of endowing the princess with one third of the revenues of Wales, Cornwall and Chester. Ten days of feasting, jousting and entertainments followed. During the afternoons the wedding guests disported themselves in the gardens at Richmond, playing chess, gambling, shooting at the butts and watching a Spanish acrobat do "wondrous and delicious Points of Tumbling, Dancing and other Sleights."

In the evenings elaborate disguisings were mounted. In one a huge lantern was unveiled, carrying within it more than a hundred great lights and twelve beautiful ladies of the court. In another, two mountains, "subtly conveyed and drawn upon wheels," were rolled into the banquet hall, one representing England and the other Spain. The mount of England was planted full of greenery, and was complete with "rocks, marvellous beasts and a goodly young lady in her hair pleasantly beseen"; the mount of Spain was barren, a scorched rock out of whose blasted sides grew a wealth of metals and precious gems. Dancing followed the disguisings. Katherine and one of her ladies dipped and bowed in a slow Spanish dance, and Arthur, dancing with his aunt Princess Cecily, trod out an

English measure as the courtiers looked on in respectful silence. But it was Prince Henry whose leaps and kicks astounded everyone. Taking as his partner his sister Margaret, he gave such a lively performance that the onlookers demanded more. The prince and princess started in again, and Henry, "perceiving himself to be encumbered with his clothes, suddenly cast off his gown and danced in his jacket," amid smiles of delight and approval.

The celebrations surrounding his brother's marriage were a high point of Henry's childhood. Now on the sidelines, now at the center of the activities, he had shared in the adulation of the court with none of the strains faced by Arthur and Katherine. Henry could not have foreseen that his exertions had in a way been a rehearsal for a new and more demanding role.

Arthur and his bride had barely settled into their palace at Ludlow when the prince of Wales fell grievously ill. His malady was sudden and inexplicable. If, as some historians believe, he had been tubercular for some time he had shown little or no sign of it; the Spanish ambassador would hardly have allowed Princess Katherine to marry a boy whose health was seriously in doubt, and besides, Arthur had been robust enough on the dance floor only weeks earlier. In any event, plague, or the sweating sickness, or simply fatally low resistance and weak recuperative powers turned the honeymoon into tragedy. Married less than five months, in April of 1502 Prince Arthur died, and his brother, the duke of York, became heir to the English throne.

There was no concealing the severity of the loss. At Greenwich, King Henry and his queen "took the painful sorrows together," consoling one another with assurances that more children might yet be born to them and that all things, even this, were ruled by God's grace. At Ludlow, Katherine lay grieving in her own sickbed, bewildered by a course of events that had turned her from maiden to wife to widow in less than half a year.

Her head had been clouded by recurrent heavy colds and coughs ever since her arrival in England, and as Arthur lay dying she was struck by the same sickness that carried him off. Her recovery took several weeks, giving her time to ponder the odd terms of Arthur's will. Instead of bestowing his worldly goods on his widow, he had left all his personal property—his jewels, plate and wearing apparel—to his favorite sister Margaret. Katherine's mother-in-law at least was solicitous of her welfare, and ordered a mourning litter for her in black velvet fringed with a valance of black cloth. In this grim conveyance she made the journey back to London, where the queen arranged for her to live at Croydon until plans for her future could be made.

Though Henry was undoubtedly next in line for the throne ten months were allowed to elapse before he was declared prince of Wales. Cardinal Wolsey was later to declare that the delay was caused by a widespread belief that Katherine might be pregnant; Arthur's posthumous child by her would inherit his title. But Wolsey's claim was made at a time when the exact circumstances of Arthur and Katherine's marriage had become the greatest issue in the realm, and it is difficult to say what view prevailed in the spring of 1502. Katherine's duenna wrote to Queen Isabella insisting that though she had lived as Arthur's wife the princess was still a virgin, and this judgment coincided neatly with Spanish interests. Arthur died in early April; by May 10 Katherine's parents, the Spanish monarchs King Ferdinand and Queen Isabella, were planning to marry Katherine to Henry.[1] Their daughter must become the next queen of England, no matter how many of King Henry's sons she had to marry in the process.

Of course, before the prince could take his brother's widow as his wife he would have to have a papal dispensation, and to be on the safe side both the dispensation and the marriage treaty drafted by the English and Spanish negotiators stated that Katherine and Arthur had in fact consummated their marriage. King Ferdinand was quick to point out, however, that this was nothing more than a legal fiction inserted to forestall future objections by the disputatious English. "The fact is," he wrote in August of 1503, "that although they were wedded, Prince Arthur and the Princess Katherine never consummated their marriage. It is well known that the princess is still a virgin. But as the English are much disposed to cavil, it has seemed to be more prudent to provide for the case as though the marriage had been consummated, and the dispensation of the pope must be in perfect keeping with the said clause of the treaty."[2] In the end the only unarguable fact of Katherine's marriage was that it produced no child. She did not prove to be pregnant during her time of mourning, and after ten months Henry assumed the title prince of Wales.

His unexpected elevation in status was to bring extraordinary changes in Henry's life, but not before a second family tragedy struck. As if to back up her assurances to her husband that it was not too late for her to bear him more sons, Elizabeth of York became pregnant within months of Arthur's death. She redoubled her usual acts of piety in supplication for the health of her child, and had a special relic—a girdle of the Virgin Mary—brought to her to wear during her delivery. At thirty-seven, the queen faced a considerable risk, and to compound the danger the onset of premature labor prevented her from having the child as planned, in the familiar and comfortable surroundings of Richmond Palace. Instead she was forced to seek refuge in the Tower apartments, within the cold, cramped White Tower whose thick walls had sheltered her and her son from the Cornish rebels nearly six years earlier.

In this provisional setting the queen gave birth to a sickly daughter on February 2, 1503. Both mother and child were wrapped in furs against the midwinter chill, but Elizabeth, who was always subject to ague, became so "alarmingly ill" that the king was desperate. He sent a messenger to Kent, with instructions to ride night and day until he found the best physician in the county, Dr. Aylsworth, and then to bring him back to London. Despite the doctor's ministrations the queen died ten days after her child was born, on her own thirty-eighth birthday.[3] Within weeks her little daughter too was dead.

The king's grief was so profound he was unable to take charge of the funeral. Leaving orders that his wife should be buried in the most splendid fashion possible, he "privily departed to a solitary place to pass his sorrow, and would no man resort unto him." Prince Henry, though, watched as the noblest of the courtiers and household officials "laid their hands to the corpse" and bore the queen's wooden coffin to the Tower chapel. There the chief mourner, the queen's sister Katherine Courtenay, took up her position at the head of the corpse, surrounded by a guard of ladies, grooms and officers of arms.

For thirteen days the death watch continued, the hours of ritual numbing the grief of courtiers and family alike. Finally on February 22 a wax effigy of the deceased, dressed in her royal robes and with a gold circlet on her head, was borne on a raised platform to the church of St. Margaret in Westminster. The banners surrounding the effigy, representing the Christian apotheosis of childbearing—the Salutation, the Nativity of Christ—were painted on a white background to signify that the queen had died in childbed. Along the route thirty-seven virgins, one for each birthday Elizabeth had lived to celebrate, saluted the effigy; they were dressed all in white and carried lighted tapers.

At the church, a final requiem sermon was delivered. Then the grave was opened and the coffin lowered into it.

To Henry it must have seemed one of those sudden reversals of fortune his grandmother Margaret Beaufort lived in dread of. His mother and brother taken from him within the same year, his own safe position as second in line suddenly changed to the awesome status of heir to the throne, the comfortable patterns of his life altered irreparably. In his uncertainty Henry nurtured darker fears—of death itself, and of the killing diseases that could be avoided only by constant vigilance. Four of his brothers and sisters had now died; could he be next? Disturbed by these worries, and still grieving for his beautiful mother, Henry, prince of Wales, embarked on his first lessons in kingship.

5

When I was come to
The age of fifteen yere,
In all this lond, nowther fre nor bond,
Methought I had no pere.

By the summer of 1504 Henry and his father were constantly in one another's company. "It is quite wonderful how much the king likes the prince of Wales," the Spaniard Hernán Duque wrote to Ferdinand and Isabella. "He has good reason to do so, for the prince deserves all love. But it is not only from love that the king takes the prince with him; he wishes to improve him."[1]

At thirteen Henry was being actively instructed in the art of government. The kingdom he was being groomed to govern was in a more peaceful and prosperous condition than it had been for many generations. The pretenders had been put down for good. There was no immediate threat of war, either from within England or from foreign enemies. The king feared conspirators, but none were apprehended, and though their complaints about his inordinate love of money were increasing Henry VII's subjects in fact accepted his rule with far greater docility now than they had in Prince Henry's early childhood. Foreign observers at court concurred in envying the king his calm and orderly kingdom. "England has never been so tranquil and obedient as at present," the Spanish ambassador remarked. "From this time forward he is perfectly secure against Fortune," the Milanese envoy wrote of Henry VII. "His majesty can stand like one at the top of a tower looking on at what is passing in the plain."[2]

In the fifteenth century England had been a country turned in on itself, but the first Tudor king had begun to redirect its energies outward again. Certainly his court had an international and more specifically an Italianate flavor. He surrounded himself with Italian men of letters—his master of ceremonies Silvestro Gigli, his Latin secretaries Carmeliano, Ammonio, and Peter Vannes, the historian Polydore Vergil—and filled his palaces with Italian furniture. He imported Italian cloth of gold and fine damask for his clothes, and ordered sumptuous church vestments sewn by Florentine embroiderers. It was the Italian sculptor Torrigiano who made his most vivid likeness, and who was given the responsibility of carving his tomb. Both Henry and his courtiers kept themselves unusually well informed about Italian affairs, "receiving especial information of

44

every event," relying heavily on the Florentine merchants in London to keep them supplied with news.

The king's fascination with Italy had much to do with the style of rule he had adopted. Like the Italian despots he kept his public presence awesome; he seemed always to be at the center of a spectacle. He hardly entered or left a room without ceremony, and invariably received visitors under his golden cloth of estate. The royal household reflected this personal magnificence. Palace furnishings became more and more luxurious, with rich tapestries and carpets and cushions ornamenting the bedchambers and hangings of cloth of gold covering the walls of the presence chamber. The elaborate regulations for the running of Henry VII's household were unlike any drawn up by his predecessors. Everything the king did had its accompanying ritual; even in his absence the dishes he ate from, the clothes he wore, the bed he slept in were approached with reverent solemnity. The formality was at its height when the court was in residence at Westminster. Here, unlike Richmond or Greenwich, the king slept with his crown beside his bed on a cushion.

In keeping with his exaltation of the monarchy Henry exalted the royal family itself. The matches he made for his children were not merely aristocratic, but royal. Arthur's bride had been a Spanish princess; it looked as though she would one day become Prince Henry's bride as well. The only other immediate candidate to become princess of Wales, Margaret of Angoulême, belonged to the French royal house. And Margaret Tudor, who at fourteen had become a glowing, feisty young woman whose blonde handsomeness matched her brother's, had recently married the Scots king James IV. It had been Elizabeth of York's last happy responsibility to order the utensils and household implements for Margaret to take with her to her new home in Scotland—huge pewter basins, washing bowls, a pair of bellows and a fire pan, "a great trussing basket." Margaret left England saddened by her mother's death and apprehensive about her new life, but what counted in her father's eyes was that she carried the Tudor blood northward, at once ennobling her lineage and cementing relations with a potential enemy.

But what impressed his subjects and foreign envoys even more than Henry VII's majesty and remoteness was his wealth. His riches seemed to grow greater every day; more and more jewels were stored in his jewel house, and more and more heavy gold plate weighed down the display cupboards in his banquet chambers. Once a gold coin entered his strongboxes, it was said, it never came out again, for he paid his debts in depreciated coins only and made large profits from the royal mints. The king's servants, like their master, were said to possess "a wonderful dexterity in getting other people's money"; beyond what their efforts produced, income from crown lands nearly tripled.[3] The king's palace at Richmond became known as "Rich Mount," the repository of all his treasure. "It was spoken to the world's end," the chronicler wrote, "that in this realm was the golden hill."[4]

His wealth, his shrewd mastery of government, his steady enlarging of England's place in European affairs seemed to make Henry an ideal mentor for his son. "Certainly there could be no better school in the world than the society of such a father," the Spanish envoy Hernán Duque wrote. "He is so wise and so attentive to everything; nothing escapes his attention. There is no doubt the prince has an excellent governor and steward in his father." The king's health was slowly failing, but he was only forty-seven; with luck the prince's apprenticeship might go on until he reached adulthood. "If he lives ten years longer," Duque speculated, "he will leave the prince furnished with good habits, and with immense riches, and in as happy circumstances as a man can be."[5]

As he grew out of childhood Prince Henry watched and learned a great deal from his father, absorbing as much about the manner and style of kingship as about its mechanics of politics and ceremony. At the same time, though, he was a constant witness to the king's expanding idiosyncrasies, and confused these with the craft of rule so that at some level of awareness he came to believe that an integral part of ruling was the indulgence of personal obsessions and violent bad temper. It was young Henry's misfortune that his period of training came at a time when his father lapsed more and more into compulsive preoccupations and instability. Henry VII was not able to teach his son the cardinal principle of wise kingship: to discriminate between the use and abuse of power.

The king's ruling passions had by this time grown to consume much of his time. He was less driven by avarice than his critics contended, but was bemused with making gold by alchemy. Hunting out relics became a besetting distraction, and he planned to be surrounded by his relic collection even in death, ordering that his fragment of the holy cross and his leg of Saint George be incorporated into the altar by his tomb. He made frequent pilgrimages to the shrines of the English saints, and arranged that after his death each of these shrines would receive a statue representing the king kneeling in golden armor, holding his crown in his hands. To the Garter chapel at Windsor he pledged a little Saint George in gold, set with diamonds, rubies, sapphires and pearls.[6] Heresy too distracted King Henry. He burned heretics at Smithfield and elsewhere— including one man he personally converted before ordering the fire lit under him—and commanded that those he pardoned wear red crosses and faggots embroidered on their gowns for the rest of their lives.[7]

Once when the prince was fourteen he looked on as his father was confronted with a diplomatic and social crisis. Relations between England and Spain were strained, and a commercial dispute between the two countries had idled eight hundred English sailors. They came in a body to Richmond, "all ruined and lost," demanding to see the king. Henry, taken by surprise, stood before them, his thinning gray hair and squinting eyes giving him the look of an alert old man. After searching their faces and hearing their complaints he turned on the Spanish ambassador de Puebla the full force of his wrath. "The words which came from his mouth were vipers," de Puebla complained, "and he indulged in every kind of passion." Part ungovernable anger, part calculated histrionics, the display of bitter invective reassured the sailors and left the ambassador temporarily speechless. By the force of royal fury a crisis had for the moment been averted. The lesson, which was not lost on Prince Henry, was that bluster and a sharp tongue are a monarch's first line of defense. And he noted too how the king at once astonished and soothed de Puebla by sending him a present of a freshly killed buck a few days after the incident.[8]

In January of 1506 a ship carrying Queen Joanna of Castile and her Hapsburg husband Philip the Handsome nearly capsized in a violent storm and had to take refuge in the English port of Weymouth in Devon. King Henry at once offered them the hospitality of his court. Joanna's sister Katherine was betrothed to his son, and would be eager to see Joanna again. And a meeting with Philip promised to be opportune, for political reasons. Philip was at odds with his father-in-law Ferdinand over Castile, which Joanna had recently inherited on her mother's death. Henry was always glad to see Ferdinand's vexations increase, so when news came of the unexpected visitors he made ready to give them a splendid welcome.

He rode out from Windsor to meet the royal couple as their small retinue approached, their few retainers in somber liveries and Philip himself all in black. The bright gold and crimson and blue gowns of the English lords stood out by contrast, the gold spangles and golden letters hanging on their long striped sleeves glowing dully in the pale winter light. King Henry wore a purple velvet gown and hood, his only ornament a heavy gold chain with a diamond pendant. The hood helped to disguise the signs of recent illness on his face, but the visitors noticed that he dismounted slowly and with difficulty from his magnificent bay.

During the next three months much was accomplished. The two kings struck a bargain. Henry agreed to join with Philip against Ferdinand, and Philip in return handed over to Henry one of the remaining Plantagenet heirs to the English throne—the earl of Suffolk, called the "White Rose," who would spend the rest of his life in the Tower. For Joanna the time was bittersweet. There was much to tell Katherine—about her six children, the eldest of whom, Charles, would some day rule Castile and his father's Hapsburg lands, about their mother's last years, and about her own unhappy marriage. But early in her stay Joanna quarreled so sharply with her husband that they could not be reconciled, and she left as suddenly as she had arrived. Much distressed, Henry would have intervened, but his councilors advised him not to.

In his wife's absence Philip continued to make himself agreeable to the king, and was particularly attentive to his son. It was apparent that the sunny, strapping fifteen-year-old Prince Henry would not have long to wait before becoming king, and Philip hoped that English support for his interests would endure into the next reign. He cultivated the prince's friendship, and invested him with the highest honor in his gift, the Order of the Golden Fleece.

The visit of Philip and Joanna would have been no more than a minor incident had it not been for its consequences. The king seems to have been much taken with the beautiful and spirited Joanna, and when her husband died suddenly the following fall Henry looked seriously into the possibility of marrying her himself. As always his political interests were primary. He wanted Joanna less than he wanted her kingdom of Castile, and if he could not acquire it by marrying her he was prepared to gain it by marrying his daughter Mary to Joanna's heir Prince Charles. But no matter how calculated his offer—and he was currently involved in at least two other sets of marriage negotiations—Henry's personal interest in Joanna was considerable, and he took it badly when he learned that there was a bizarre impediment to her remarriage.

Ever since Philip's death his widow had kept his corpse with her, ordering the coffin carried from place to place along with the other furnishings of her household. No one, not even Ferdinand, could persuade her to give the dead man up for burial; finally Ferdinand concluded that, like her grandmother before her, Joanna had lost her mind. Her affliction made marriage unthinkable. According to the Spanish ambassador de Puebla the English were willing to overlook Joanna's insanity as long as she retained her fertility, but Ferdinand's answer proved final.[9]

His affections thwarted, King Henry took out his anger on Joanna's sister. Katherine of Aragon (who for as long as she lived continued to spell her name "Katerina") was now twenty-one, and though she was hardly acclimatized to English ways she was trying her best to make herself useful at court in an effort to better her unfortunate situation. She had begun to serve as an informal representative of Spanish interests in England; by 1507 she had received formal diplomatic credentials, and was writing to her father that she had managed to decode the Spanish diplomatic cipher unaided.

Katherine still clung to Spanish ways. "I do not understand the English language," she wrote to Ferdinand in 1506, "nor know how to speak it." She had only Spaniards around her, and never saw the courtiers or the king's children as she had once had. For a year or so after her betrothal to Prince Henry Katherine had been taken into the life of the court, hunting with the prince and his sister and traveling with the princess and the ladies of the court. She had not been able to adapt well to the English diet and climate, however, and had suffered recurrent "derangement of the stomach" and chills. The king had been solicitous, sending her messages, offering to visit her and, if necessary, to call together all the physicians in the kingdom to effect a cure.[10]

But this royal gallantry evaporated once King Henry decided not to let the marriage proceed. According to the treaty, Prince Henry was to marry Katherine when he reached the age of fourteen; his fourteenth birthday came and went, and no wedding preparations were discussed. Unknown to Katherine, he was being instructed to make a formal protest against the treaty, sworn in secret before the bishop of Winchester in a private chamber of Richmond Palace.

From 1505 on Katherine was little more than a diplomatic hostage. Worsening relations between England and Spain, Ferdinand's obstinacy in the matter of Queen Joanna's remarriage and, above all, his unwillingness to pay what remained of Katherine's dowry all increased Henry's resentment. He turned Katherine out of the house she had been living in, cut off the allowance he had been giving her, and made plain to her that she would enjoy neither his money nor his favor until her father honored his obligations.

The princess saw her situation as desperate. Her creditors came every day to insult her, she wrote. She had no money to give them, or to pay the wages of her five remaining Spanish serving women. They had seen Katherine faithfully through years of changing fortune; all they had to show for their loyalty and sacrifice were the ragged clothes she had not been able to replace. They were so wretched they were "ready to ask alms," the princess complained to her father, while her own state was hardly better. "About my own person, I have nothing for chemises," she wrote, "wherefore, by your Highness' life, I have now sold some bracelets to get a dress of black velvet, for I was all but naked."

Katherine's pride and self-esteem had been grievously assaulted. "I have suffered martyrdom," she said simply, and went on to describe how she had appeared before King Henry and all his Council, in a plain dress she would not have allowed her maid to wear five years earlier, pleading with tears that he would pay her debts. The king had taken no notice, and she had been forced to leave his presence deeply humiliated.

But there was a worse cause of anxiety. By 1507 Henry was tormenting Katherine by keeping her away from his son. "The most difficult thing for me to bear," she told her father, "was to see the prince so seldom. As we all lived in the same house, it seemed to me a great cruelty that four months should have passed without my seeing him." Her only hope was that somehow a way would be found for her to marry Henry. He was her future, and the daily sight of him must have heartened her in her misery. Deprived even of this she was in despair, a despair deepened by the probability that she was already in love with him.

For his part Prince Henry took little notice of the unfortunate princess he had forsworn before Bishop Fox. She hovered uncertainly in the background of his life, hardly able to speak with him unless they spoke Latin, shabbily dressed, and with the cast of chronic sickness darkening her complexion. She was a pitiable, alien creature, but her misery was so much a fixture of the court it was almost invisible. When he thought of her at all the prince associated her with mistreatment and neglect, and when he thought of his own future she held no place in it.

6

For they wold have hym hys libertye refrayne
And all mery company for to dysdayne;
But I will not so whatsoever thay say,
But follow hys mynd in all that we may

"THERE is no finer youth in the world than the prince of Wales," de Puebla wrote to Ferdinand of Aragon in 1507. The blond, apple-cheeked prince was sixteen; he was already taller than his father, and was developing an extraordinary physique. "His limbs are of a gigantic size," de Puebla remarked; along with his uncommon dimensions and strength the prince had the coordination and dexterity of a gifted athlete. In features he resembled his dead brother Arthur, with Arthur's close-set eyes, thin brows and pretty, bow-shaped lips. The oldest of his father's courtiers said he resembled his grandfather Edward IV even more. King Edward had been nearly six feet four inches tall, a striking knight "of visage lovely, of body mighty, strong," and in Prince Henry he seemed to live again.

The exuberant child had grown into an energetic young man. Though he did not neglect his music or his learning he seemed always to be in the tiltyard, riding up and down its length lance in hand, or throwing himself against another boy until he wrestled him to the ground. In the summer months the prince and his companions rarely missed a day of this exercise; a visitor to Richmond in July of 1508 joined the king and his mother in watching young Henry ride in a mock tournament, "the prince excelling over all the others."[1]

What only a few of the most intimate courtiers and household servants knew was that the prince's exercise was all the more precious to him as a release from the close confinement in which he was living. The Spanish envoy Fuensalida, who came to the English court in the spring of 1508, found that young Henry was kept "as locked away as a woman," in a room just off the king's bedchamber. The king or his guardsmen watched everyone who entered and left the prince's room, and allowed only a few attendants to see him. For recreation he was permitted to go through a secret door into a park, where he practiced jousting with his carefully chosen companions, but even then he was never out of sight of his bodyguard.[2]

Young Henry was kept in almost total isolation, seeing and speaking to no one outside his small circle. He appeared beside his father on ceremonial occasions, but seemed oddly reticent and retiring. "He is so subjugated," Fuensalida wrote, "that he doesn't speak a word except in response to what the king asks him."

What kept Henry silent was fear of his father's uncontrollable temper. The king's frequent outbursts of anger were the talk of his court. Fuensalida found out from certain women who claimed to "know all his secrets" that King Henry was prone to childish spites and monumental rages, and a recent incident left no doubt of this. The arrival of a letter had triggered his wrath. His servants scattered; he sent for his daughter Mary and "fought with her for no reason." Nearly beside himself by this time, he sent for his son, and fought with him as violently "as if he sought to kill him" before shutting himself away for several hours to let his seizure pass.[3] The king's fits were clearly pathological. They sent him into a trancelike state—"his eyes closed, neither sleeping nor waking"—and they were not the only sign of a disturbed mind. Every night, it was said, the king got up out of bed, dressed himself, and went walking in his sleep.

Evidently King Henry's good relations with his son had gone sour as the boy grew into a towering, muscular youth. According to Reginald Pole, a kinsman of the prince who was in a good position to know, Henry VII disliked his son intensely, "having no affection or fancy unto him."[4]

In a sense the physical restrictions imposed on the prince were no more than a logical extension of his strict upbringing. Great care had always been taken to guard him from harmful influences of all kinds, to ensure that "all the talk in his presence [was] of virtue, honour, cunning, wisdom and deeds of worship, of nothing that shall move him to vice." There were more pressing reasons for keeping him isolated. One was the sweating sickness. A lurking danger every spring and summer, in 1508 the sweat became an epidemic. It was a disease of the lungs accompanied by influenza, and it struck its victims without warning. They broke out in a heavy sweat; then, stinking horribly, they turned red all over and developed a high fever. In the last stage an infected rash appeared, and death soon followed. Only a few hours elapsed from the onset of the disease to the moment of death, and many of those who staggered through the London streets clutching their heads were dead soon after they reached their doorsteps.

The sweat had first appeared at the start of Henry VII's reign, and his critics said the disease was God's punishment for his harsh rule. Certainly the affliction did not spare the courtiers or royal servants, and fear of the sweat kept the king moving at intervals of only a few days from one country house to another throughout the summer of 1508. Driven from Wanstead when some of his servants showed the dread symptoms, he went on to Berking; again some of those around him fell ill, and he had to ride in haste to another house. He could not return to Greenwich or Eltham, for the household staff at both places had been infected. So from mid-August until, with the first frost, the danger of infection was past the king stayed in the homes of his nobles, giving strict orders that no one from London was to come near him or his son. Several of Prince Henry's servants were stricken with the sweat, and did not survive. For them, "flight was not possible," the chronicler wrote, "since death conquered all."[5]

The other cause of the prince's seclusion was the king's health, and his councilors' preoccupation with the succession. For at least three years Henry VII had been outliving the pessimistic prognostications of his courtiers. "The king's grace is but a weak and sickly man, not likely to be a long-lived man," they had been saying, but until this year of 1508 he had continued to force himself into his litter to appear before his subjects on ceremonial occasions. He took longer and longer to recover from the attacks of illness that came every spring, though, and his capacity for mental effort was declining. His appetite was nearly gone; no matter what the cooks prepared the dishes came back to the kitchen nearly full. Finally his "disease of the joints" made even the shortest rides impossible, and his public appearances ended.[6]

A change of rulers could not be far off. The prince of Wales' life was the realm's most precious asset, Henry's advisers warned. He should be guarded securely against harm, and if possible married to a foreign princess—possibly Queen Joanna's daughter Eleanor, or the daughter of Duke Albert of Bavaria—so that he could beget a son. Cautious, befuddled, possibly fearful, the king did nothing. One court observer, the Spaniard Miguel Pérez de Almazán, was to say later that Henry "was always beset by the fear that his son . . . might during his lifetime obtain too much power by his connexion with the house of Spain."[7] If the thought of the Spanish marriage did indeed alarm him, probably any marriage for young Henry would have seemed threatening. The prince remained closeted in his chamber, restive and impatient in his enforced idleness.

Finally in March of 1509 the king sank into his last illness. He took the customary step of proclaiming a general pardon for criminals—thieves and murderers excepted—and in other ways put his affairs in order to end his reign. By March 24 he was reported to be *in extremis*. Prince Henry was at his bedside in the following weeks, until at the end the king struggled for some twenty-seven hours, "abiding the sharp assaults of death." He still hoped to strike an ultimate bargain with God. "If it pleased God to send him life," he swore aloud, he would be "a changed man." The plea went unheard. Henry VII died in his palace at Richmond on April 21, 1509.[8] Prince Henry, Henry VIII, was king.

7

My hart she hath and ever shall
To by deth departed we be;
Happe what wyll hap, fall what shall,
Shall no man know her name for me.

SEVEN weeks after the old king's death the new king went to the church of the Observant Friars at Greenwich to be married. His bride was Katherine of Aragon.

What prompted him to marry Katherine—the nervous councilors, the existing treaty with Spain, or simply the immediate availability of a girl of suitable rank and acceptable appearance—is unknown. The only explanation Henry gave came in a letter to Margaret of Savoy, daughter of the Hapsburg emperor Maximilian. According to the letter, on his deathbed Henry VII had urged his son to fulfill his old agreement with Ferdinand and take Katherine as his wife; in accordance with these last wishes, Henry obeyed.[1] A more plausible account, written by Fuensalida, told how the dying king had assured his son he was free to marry any woman he liked; this had so disheartened the Spaniard that he had already ordered Katherine's belongings packed when news of the planned marriage reached him.[2]

It would be interesting to know what, if any, influence Margaret Beaufort had on the new king's choice of a bride. Katherine was just the sort of girl she would have found acceptable. Learned, highly intelligent, like the Venerable Margaret herself she had preserved her dignity while enduring years of exasperating torment. Margaret's approval would surely have carried weight with her grandson. So too would the opinion of Archbishop Warham, however, whose view of the proposed marriage was unfavorable. His objection revived the issue of Katherine's previous marriage to Arthur, questioning the validity of the papal bull of dispensation. Katherine's confessor objected too, and the theological point was too well known not to have caused some raised eyebrows at court.

Katherine, who toward the end of Henry VII's reign had begun to believe that she would become queen after all once his son became king, was silent about the theological propriety of her remarriage.[3] She renounced her dowry in favor of Henry, receiving from him in return a long list of lands and rents including the London palace of Baynard's Castle, and prepared for her wedding day. She was only too happy to smooth the way for the marriage any way she could. It did not disappoint her that the .

ceremony was to be a modest one, unlike the crowded spectacle of her first marriage. That it was held in the church of her favorite Observant Friars surely pleased Katherine, and as she looked up at the tall, handsome youth who stood beside her before the altar on the appointed day she must have thanked God that all her troubles were ending in joy.

All the bells of the hundred churches of London were set ringing on the day before the coronation. By custom the new king and queen rode in splendor from the Tower to Westminster on this day, through the narrow streets choked with shouting onlookers and brightened with tapestries and embroidered hangings and cloth of gold. Girls in white dresses holding branching wax candles stood in front of each of the dozens of goldsmith's shops, and members of each craft and guild stood rank on rank along the procession route, with the lord mayor and aldermen. All the clergy of the city arrayed themselves in their richest copes and had their great jeweled crosses borne before them; when the king and queen passed they swung their silver censers and blessed them.

There was no mistaking the king. Amid all the cloth of gold and silver, the embroidered velvets and the gorgeously caparisoned horses in the royal procession he stood out most resplendent of all. Like his gentlemen and household officers he wore scarlet robes, but his were of the richest velvet and furred with ermine. Sewn into his jacket of raised gold were diamonds, emeralds, pearls and other precious stones which flashed and sparkled in the sunlight, and across his chest he wore a baldric of outsize rubies. Even without his finery, though, Henry would have been unmistakable. His great height, his striking beauty and gracious manner betrayed his identity beyond question. "The features of his body, his goodly personage, his amiable visage and princely countenance" were known to all his subjects, the chronicler Hall wrote enthusiastically, adding, "I cannot express the gifts of grace and of nature, that God hath endowed him with all."[4]

Katherine too looked very splendid this day, drawn in her gleaming litter and dressed in white satin. Her most notable adornment was her thick red hair, "of a very great length," which hung to her waist; crowning it she wore a jeweled circlet. She was surrounded by the great ladies and gentlewomen of the court, some riding and some sitting in chariots, those of highest rank dressed in cloth of gold and silver, the others in velvet.

The following day the people crowded around the palace gate, watching for Henry and Katherine to come out for the walk to the abbey. When they appeared the crowd gave ground before the royal couple, whose way was marked by a rich carpet of cloth leading to the cathedral. Once the cloth had served its purpose the people tore it to shreds, and waited for the sovereigns to emerge again into view.

They had many hours to wait. The coronation ceremony, enriched through generations of tradition, unfolded in layer upon layer of ritual— prayers, oaths, the anointing with holy oils and the crowning itself, the ceremony of homage from the clergy and nobles and the celebratory mass. At one point the spectators were asked whether they would take

Henry to be their king, and the fervent cheer of "Yea, yea" that went up in response left no doubt of their "reverence, love and desire" for him. They cheered again when late in the afternoon he came back to Westminster Hall for the coronation banquet, and they listened outside the hall for the trumpets that announced the arrival of each of the "sumptuous, fine and delicate" courses.

Crowning their anticipation were the jousts and tourneys held at Westminster to mark the opening of the new reign. A miniature castle had been built in the tiltyard where the king and queen would sit to watch the mock battles. Supported by gilded arches and turrets, the little castle had a fountain and, set into the low roof, a large plaster crown imperial, painted and gilded and surrounded by an intricate design of roses and pomegranates and the intertwined letters H and K. Gargoyles at the sides of the castle began to spout forth red, white and claret wine as Henry and Katherine took their places. The king did not take part in the jousting, but his friend Charles Brandon—whom he had recently rewarded by making him warden and chief justice of all the royal forests and marshal of the king's bench—was among the defenders, along with Edward Howard, lord admiral, and his brother Thomas Howard, heir to the earl of Surrey. The challengers, wearing gold helmets with huge feather plumes, included Edward Neville, a tall, strong courtier very like the king in build and coloring, and two other favorites, Edward Guildford and John Pechy. The defenders were declared to be knights of "Dame Pallas," the challengers knights of the huntress Diana, and on the second day of the tourney a hunt was staged in Diana's honor in the tiltyard, within an artificial park. Fallow deer were released, which were chased into the miniature castle by greyhounds; the dogs killed the deer, and their carcasses were trussed on poles and presented to the ladies. A dispute broke out among the knights over whether or not the victors in the combat should be awarded the greyhounds, but the king intervened with a solution that satisfied them all, and the jousts went on to their conclusion.

8

Time to pass with goodly sport
Our sprites to revive and comfort;
To pipe, to sing, to dance, to spring
with pleasure and delight
To follow Sensual Appetite.

"Hunt, sing and dance," Henry wrote in one of his songs soon after becoming king, "My heart is set,/All goodly sport/To my comfort/Who shall me let?" It was as if he had pledged himself to make up for all the restraint and confinement his father had made him suffer in his last years. He threw himself vigorously into hunting, hawking, shooting and archery. He rode up and down in the tiltyard and practiced at the barriers and wrestled with the strongest opponents he could find. He ordered his revels master to arrange elaborate spectacles for the entertainment of his court, and hundreds of craftsmen and laborers were kept constantly at work at Blackfriars, where the revels stuff was built and stored, molding and painting and gilding the props and pageant gear. Thousands of yards of cloth were cut and sewn for costumes, and fashioned into trees and flowers; carpenters worked steadily constructing the wooden platforms on which the scenery was mounted, and the pavilions and castles which held the maskers.

The king made himself the gaudy center of these entertainments, ordering his Flemish tailor Stephen Jaspar to make him doublets in rich stuffs that shone "like beaten gold" and robes of shimmering bawdkin and Venetian brocade. Clothing at Henry VII's court had been medieval; his son brought in the swaggering magnificence of the Renaissance. The old style gave way to a dozen new styles, each more exotic than the last. At one banquet Henry danced with fifteen others in German-style jackets of crimson and purple satin, at another in crimson velvet doublets open and laced with silver chains, with cloaks and hats trimmed in pheasant feathers "after the fashion of Prussia." At a feast for the ambassadors in the spring of 1510 Henry ordered long "Russian" gowns of yellow and white satin for two of his gentlemen. With them they wore gray fur hats and boots that turned up at the ends, and they carried hatchets in their hands. That same night the king and the earl of Essex appeared dressed as Turks in long gowns of bawdkin, with high turbans "with great rolls of gold" and armed with two scimitars.

In addition to these planned spectacles Henry delighted in impromptu disguisings and parties at odd hours. One morning the queen and her ladies were frightened when their chambers were invaded by twelve men dressed in the short cloaks and hoods of outlaws and armed with swords and bows. They demanded to dance and "make pastime" with the ladies, despite the early hour and the queen's condition—she was nearing the end of her first pregnancy—and would not leave until their whim had been satisfied. Had the leader of the band been anyone but the king the intrusion would have been unforgivable; as it was Katherine and her dismayed attendants swallowed their offended dignity and partnered the outlaws with a good grace.

All day and evening Henry kept himself surrounded by melody. Besides the dozens of household musicians—the "styll shalms," Blind Dick, the harper, the king's trumpeters, the sackbut and shalm players of the privy chamber—there were always traveling minstrels and other performers to amuse him. The names of foreign musicians appear often in the lists of payments—forty shillings to "Bonitamps, Petie John, Cokeryn and Baltasar, minstrels," eight pounds six shillings to "two women out of Flanders that did pipe, dance and play before the king"—along with those of entertainers whose skills were more obscure. In April of 1510 a reward of six pounds thirteen shillings was paid to "a long gentleman of Picardy."

Henry himself was the foremost amateur musician, and when he was not hunting or riding in the tiltyard he occupied himself with singing and dancing and playing the recorder, flute or virginal. He set poems to music too, and wrote masses and ballets in the Italian style for several parts. And with a candor characteristic of him Henry wove into his songs the thoughts that weighed on him in these years.

His songs defended the carefree, good times of youth—the recreations and innocent sport of a boy and his friends. They were fresh, bracing songs, vigorous and direct. But at the same time they sounded a cry of the heart.

> Youth will needs have dalliance,
> Of good or ill some pastance;
> Company me thinketh best
> All thought and fancies to digest,
> > For idleness
> > Is chief mistress
> > Of vices all;
> > Then who can say
> > But pass the day
> > Is best of all?

Behind the rousing verses was a plea for freedom and pleasure, and the argument, endlessly repeated, that innocent, "honest" pastimes counteracted the vices bred by idleness.

In part, this plea was a response to a chorus of critical voices. Although Henry himself insisted that his good times did not keep him

from attending to affairs of state, and there is considerable evidence this
was true, his principal advisers saw him as little more than an overgrown
child. "He is young, and does not care to occupy himself with anything
but the pleasures of his age," the Spanish ambassador Caroz wrote a year
after Henry's accession. "All other affairs he neglects."[1] Richard Fox,
bishop of Winchester, lord privy seal and the leading power in the
Council, concurred. Fox, who had been a trusted adviser to Henry's
father for more than twenty years, was at the head of things; to Badoer his
authority was so great he seemed almost a king himself.[2] Henry trusted
Fox, but confided to Caroz that he did so "at his risk." "Here in
England," the king told the Spaniard, "they think he is a fox, and such is
his name."[3] Thomas Ruthal, bishop of Durham, was another councilor
who made his disapproval of Henry's behavior known. With Fox he sent a
message to Henry's father-in-law Ferdinand of Aragon asking him to urge
the boy to take more notice of his political responsibilities.

Of Henry's potential critics one voice had been stilled. Margaret
Beaufort, who at sixty-eight was still active enough to serve as principal
executor of her late son's estate, took to her bed during the festivities
surrounding her grandson's coronation. She lived long enough to advise
him, as she lay on her deathbed, to take as his mentor her confessor and
close friend John Fisher. Fisher's destiny was indeed to be bound up with
Henry's, but in a way the Venerable Margaret would have shuddered to
hear. She foresaw only that the thoughtful, learned Fisher could help to
guide her eighteen-year-old grandson through the trying transition to high
authority now that she herself could not. Comforted by this she died, and
was buried in Henry VII's chapel in Westminster Abbey, where her
bronze effigy shows a lined but handsome face, full of resigned tolerance.

Henry had not forgotten his grandmother when he began his reign. In
his first month as king he granted her a manor in Surrey, and had
smoothed her way as his father's executor. Now he served as her
executor in his turn, dividing her extensive lands and houses among the
household officers, many of whom had been her servants. Her London
house of Coldharbour went to the steward of the household; another
London residence, "The Royal," was given to Roger Radclyf, a former
servant of Margaret's who joined Queen Katherine's staff. One Gryffyn
Richards, another of Margaret's household who became clerk of the
signet to Katherine, was made keeper of Margaret's manor of Collyweston,
while John Pechy, one of Henry's favored companions, became steward
for all her holdings in Kent.[4]

The passing of the Venerable Margaret broke Henry's last link to his
childhood. The two dominant figures of his past, his father and grandmother, were swept from his life within months of one another. He was his
own master. He might face the disapproval of his councilors, but whatever they thought of him, he was still their king. And the king's word was
law.

It was this awesome realization, coupled with his awareness of his
immaturity, that ran in Henry's thoughts at the outset of his reign and
found expression in his verses. "With good order, counsel and equity,/

God lord, grant us our mansion to be!'' he wrote. "For without their good guidance/Youth should fall in great mischance.''[5] He was unsure of himself; he was finding his way, a young man of firm conscience but slight experience set over sophisticated courtiers of uncertain morality and unmistakable inclinations to vice. "God and my right and my duty,/From them I shall never vary" Henry sang, insisting "I hurt no man, I do no wrong;/I love true where I did marry.'' But he knew as well as anyone that, if he chose, he could let his duty go, hurt whom he chose and cultivate wrongdoing, and betray Katherine with any woman who appealed to him—all without hindrance.

> For youth is frail and prompt to do,
> As well vices as virtues to ensue;
> Wherefore by these he must be guided
> And virtuous pastance must be therein used.

Any of a number of activities might have driven out the temptations Henry faced. But one pastime more than any other furthered the political and personal aims of the young king while keeping him on the path of virtue. Feats of arms—tourneying, tilting, fighting at the barriers—not only absorbed his idle time and kept him from idle thoughts but allowed him to demonstrate his remarkable physical virtuosity and his eagerness for battle. These were the preoccupations of a king bent on war, and on disheartening his enemies.

Though he trained almost daily Henry did not enter the lists himself until one day in January of 1510, when he heard that some of the courtiers were preparing a joust in secret. Someone gave the secret away, and the king, with his closest intimate William Compton, had himself and his companion armed in the little hunting park at Richmond and rode onto the tiltyard "unknown to all persons, and unlooked for.''[6] The two strangers acquitted themselves well, breaking many staves and coming away the winners in encounter after encounter until Compton, running against Edward Neville, caught a crippling blow and was so severely injured he was not expected to live. His partner disabled, Henry turned to leave the field. But he had been recognized: a voice cried out, "God save the king!'' and he had to take off his helmet and disclose himself to the cheering spectators.

Once Henry began to compete formally in the jousting he seemed never to miss a tournament. With Compton (who recovered), Brandon, Buckingham or Neville he challenged all comers, often hurling his spear farther than the others and giving more telling blows with his huge two-handed sword. The king and his aides often took the prize, though their opponents were "divers valiant and strong persons,'' but even when he lost Henry remained the most enthusiastic and hardy of all the contestants, never missing a day of exercise and attending every joust. "The king of England amuses himself almost every day of the week running the ring, and with jousts and tournaments on foot,'' Caroz wrote to Ferdinand during a series of jousts in the late spring of 1510. "Two days in the week are consecrated to this kind of tournament, which is to continue till the Feast of St. John, and which is instituted in imitation of Amadis and Lanzilote, and other knights of olden times, of whom so much is written in books."[7]

The jousts played out Henry's childhood dreams of knighthood, dreams built on medieval tales of romance and courtly adventure. But if the mock combats honored the enchanted chivalry of the Round Table their practical utility was always kept in view. In the document proclaiming these jousts the king explained their purpose. In the summer season, his proclamation read, it was customary for gentlemen to pass the time in hunting or hawking or other such diversions; but "because such sports be not ready in May and June, to eschew idleness, the ground of all vice, and give honorable and healthy exercise," five weeks of jousting would be held.[8] Another tournament summons reminded the court that the king was "not minded to see young gentlemen inexpert in martial feats." Several months earlier Henry had taken a first step toward making the young men of his court fit to serve him in arms. He instituted a special armed guard to be drawn from noblemen's sons, especially those "unexercised in the feat of arms, and in the handling and running of spears." The recruits were to be turned into skilled fighting men, outfitted with armor and ready to be put into the field, each with two horses, a page, a full panoply, and two good archers well horsed and harnessed.[9]

Henry's intentions were clear: he meant to go to war. And his intended enemy was equally evident. "The new king is eighteen years old, a worthy king and most hostile to France," a Venetian diplomat wrote, adding "it is thought he will indubitably invade France." To remove any doubt about the object of his belligerence Henry took the earliest opportunity to display his hostility toward the French. In the first summer of his reign an ambassador arrived from France, a corpulent cleric who in addition to his diplomatic services to Louis XII was abbot of Fécamp. Henry invited the abbot to his palace at Westminster, but almost as soon as the Frenchman entered his presence he became enraged. The abbot had been instructed to acknowledge King Henry's letter to his master requesting friendship and peace. The letter had in fact been written by Henry's councilors, and was in itself little more than a gesture of protocol at the opening of a new reign. The king chose to take it as a betrayal of his true feelings, however, and exploded in rage when the abbot announced he had come to England to confirm the good relations between the two countries.

Glaring at the courtiers around him, Henry shouted, "Who wrote this letter? I ask peace of the king of France, who dare not look me in the face, still less make war on me!"

Without waiting for anyone to reply he stormed out of the audience hall, leaving Fox and the others to placate the ambassador. But there was more to the insult. Henry saw to it that the injured abbot was invited to watch the afternoon's sport of tilting at the ring, giving careful orders that once he arrived no seat was to be provided for him. Now it was the ambassador's turn to walk off the tiltyard in anger, but before he got far a royal messenger called him back, offering him a cushion to sit on. Thoroughly affronted, he eased his great bulk onto the cushion and watched in silence as Henry rode back and forth across the field, putting his lance through the metal ring time and time again. To all appearances Henry had forgotten the abbot entirely; his boyish face was as free of concern as if the incident in the presence chamber had never happened.[10]

Throughout the following year the talk of war continued. "The report is that he means to attack France, and to send troops across," Badoer wrote. Three men had been sent on a special mission to Italy to buy horse armor and other military accouterments, and the French were more suspicious than ever of Henry's intentions. To prevent the true state of affairs from becoming known—the English were in fact hampered by the lack of a military ally—the English ambassador in Rome had to send his dispatches home hidden in the cover of a book, as the French searched all passengers crossing the Channel. French diplomatic efforts intensified in the spring of 1510 when the disgruntled abbot of Fécamp came to England again, this time bringing with him two other emissaries and eight carts, "said to contain chests full of silver to give to the king."[11]

But if they thought they could bribe him they misjudged both his character and his treasury. Henry VII had left his son a treasury full enough to keep him free from financial worries for a while at least—making him, temporarily, richer than any of his fellow monarchs on the continent.[12] More than this, though, Henry was not likely to be swayed from any aim he sought merely by riches. "This king of ours is no seeker after gold, or gems, or mines of silver," Mountjoy wrote of his former protégé. "He desires only the fame of virtue and eternal life."

No group was as delighted with the new king as the men of learning. Mountjoy spoke for the entire humanist circle in writing rapturously of Henry's "extraordinary and almost divine character." A "new star" in the firmament of English government, he was to Mountjoy that rarest of men: a bold hero who was also an earnest seeker after goodness and justice; a strong ruler who valued knowledge as highly as he did power.

Henry had shown his regard for scholarship by inviting Erasmus to come to live in England, offering him everything he needed to ensure his comfort and asking nothing in return "save to make our realm your home." In his letter to Erasmus Henry had called himself "your constant friend and admirer" and recalled the stages in their acquaintance. Erasmus had met Henry a second time when he stayed in England from 1505 to 1507, and though they cannot have spent long stretches of time in one another's company in these years they did share their thoughts more than once. Clearly they impressed each other, Erasmus finding in Henry the same gifted uniqueness and charm he had noted when they first met, and Henry, now able to take the measure of this celebrated scholar, listening to Erasmus talk of his interests and his travels with the keen eagerness of an avid student. It must have been during this time that Henry confided his military ambitions to his friend, and Erasmus, looking toward his future, wondered aloud whether he might settle in England when he became too old to travel any longer.

"I recollect," Henry now wrote him, "that you once said that when you were tired of wandering you would make this country the home of your old age." He urged Erasmus to act on this intent now, without waiting for old age or any other consideration beyond the one Henry himself saw as critical. In defining it he disclosed another of the imperatives: to safeguard the welfare of Christendom. "It has been and is my earnest wish to restore Christ's religion to its primitive purity, and to employ whatever talents and means I have in extinguishing heresy and giving free course to the Word of God," Henry wrote. Through his enlightened scholarship Erasmus was a bulwark against heresy and impiety; in protecting and supporting Erasmus Henry would be preserving the purity of the faith. Come then, he concluded, "you and we together, with our joint counsels and resources, will build again the Gospel of Christ."[13]

Henry took the same deeply serious tone in a conversation he had with Mountjoy. He expressed regret at his own ignorance, and nothing the nobleman said could comfort him. His subjects did not expect him to be learned himself, Mountjoy protested, only that he encourage learning in others. But Henry responded with a dutifully pious epigram. "Without knowledge," he informed the overjoyed courtier, "life would not be worth our having."[14]

That Henry was saying what he knew Mountjoy wanted to hear in no way deflated the latter's enthusiasm. "The heavens laugh, the earth exults, all things are full of milk, of honey and of nectar!" he wrote to Erasmus. "But when you know what a hero he now shows himself, how wisely he behaves, what a lover he is of justice and goodness, what affection he bears to the learned, I will venture to swear that you will need no wings to make you fly to behold this new and auspicious star."

9

Adew, adew, le company,
I trust we shall meet oftener.
Vive le Katerine et noble Henry!
Vive le prince, le infant rosary!

IN the last days of January, 1510, Queen Katherine went into labor with her first child. Because the birth was premature there had been no time for the formal ceremony of withdrawal, the ritual preliminary to the final month of waiting during which the queen was closeted with her women, the physicians and midwives. Her labor was prolonged, and agonizing. Hour after hour she struggled with the pains, her chamber emptied of all but one physician, two Spanish women, and her cherished confessor, Diego Fernández. A day and a night passed, and into the second day, at the height of her ordeal, she cried out to the Franciscan Saint Peter the Martyr to ease her suffering, vowing to send to his shrine one of her richest headdresses if he would bring her safely through her ordeal.

Hours later the child was born, a stillborn girl. Katherine wept from exhaustion and disappointment, but remembered to send one of her maids to the shrine of Saint Peter with the jeweled headdress. The midwives lowered their eyes and crossed themselves against the evil omen and hoped the king would not take out his anger on them.

Henry had to be told, of course, but not at once. Only the five people in the birth chamber knew what had happened, and they were sworn to secrecy. Publicly it was said that the queen was still pregnant, with the birth expected in May, and the king, looking forward eagerly to the arrival of a son, ordered new coverings for the steps of the baptismal font and linen napkins for the servants who were to assist at the ceremony. A special upholstered cradle of estate was made ready to hold the royal infant, lined in crimson cloth of gold and embroidered with the king's arms. All the accouterments of the birth chamber were ordered too—sheets and bearing panes for the bed, swaddling bands for the newborn infant, beds for the nurse and two rockers who would sleep by the queen in her labor, and the "groaning chair" where she would sit for the delivery itself, trimmed like a seat of honor in cloth of gold and equipped with a bowl of copper and gilt to catch the blood.[1]

In the first weeks after the stillbirth a biological enigma helped to sustain the delusion that she was still pregnant. Her uterus swelled to a prodigious size—"larger than ever was seen in a pregnant woman"—and her physicians made ready for another birth. Katherine herself half believed there might be another child in her womb, though there were indications to the contrary. Then, as suddenly as she had swelled up, the queen deflated. But by now the pretense had been carried to its final stage, and Katherine had formally withdrawn to await the birth. Henry and his closest advisers had learned the truth, and the awkwardness of the situation was not altered by the fact that sometime in March or April Katherine actually did conceive a second child.

By the end of May messengers were arriving from foreign courts asking why the birth had been delayed. King Ferdinand was particularly insistent, and Katherine, who had feared to anger her father by her failure to bear a healthy son, finally confessed the truth to him, begging him to accept the misfortune as God's will and to spare his anger. She added a distressing note. The maid to whom she had entrusted her jeweled headdress—a trustworthy and pious girl who hoped to become a nun— had been kept from fulfilling Katherine's vow. Her father had confiscated the headdress and had sworn before a notary that it belonged to his daughter and not to the queen. The man's want of respect offended Katherine, as well as thwarting her act of piety, and she begged Ferdinand to punish him however he could.[2]

The bizarre course of the queen's pregnancy had disrupted Henry's smoothly running court. The privy councilors, who had to live down the daily embarrassment of Katherine's continued withdrawal, openly blamed her bedchamber women for the error but privately accused the queen. She had put them in an impossible position; "they find it so difficult," Caroz wrote, "that they do not know what to say." Their indignation weighed heavily on Henry, who had already had to resign himself to the disappointment of the stillbirth and had found Katherine's ever changing condition increasingly hard to tolerate. He was frustrated by the timid physicians and midwives who feared to tell him anything displeasing, and hence said nothing, and annoyed by Katherine's confessor, who confused everyone he met with farfetched explanations of Katherine's behavior in an effort to protect her from ridicule. He was ill at ease with Katherine, whose fear of new disorders and of his anger made her reluctant even to tell him the good news of her second pregnancy until long after she was certain of it. She knew the councilors blamed her for making fools of them—and of the king. More than this, she knew she bore direct responsibility for assuring the succession.

"I know," Caroz wrote to Ferdinand, "that many of the privy councilors and other persons are murmuring, and they presume that because the queen is not pregnant she cannot conceive." Rumors of Katherine's inability to bear healthy children increased as her confinement was prolonged, fed by the courtiers' irritation with her as well as by her curious cycle of symptoms. She looked healthy enough. Fernández described her as very fit, "and the most beautiful creature in the world, with the greatest gaiety and contentment that ever was," and Caroz too found her to have "a pretty and most healthy color in her face." Yet the aftermath of her first pregnancy had been anything but normal, and according to Caroz she suffered from an irregularity in her menstrual periods—one cause of the continuing uncertainty about her condition, and perhaps a hindrance to conception. The ambassador attributed this to nothing more serious than poor eating habits, and thought that if Katherine could be taught to take more care for what she ate the problem would disappear. But the rumors continued, even after the queen came out of confinement and the ambassadors and courtiers were told she had suffered a miscarriage. A shadow of doubt had been cast over the marriage, a shadow that lengthened with the king's first infidelity.

Anne Stafford came to Henry's court when she married Sir George Hastings some time during the first year of the new reign. She had been a very young girl when she married her first husband, who left her a widow in her teens; on her second marriage she became one of Katherine's ladies of highest rank. Her sister Elizabeth was already in Katherine's service, and was one of her favorites; as sisters to the duke of Buckingham both women were given places of prominence at banquets and entertainments, and Anne quickly became known to the king and his companions.

It was William Compton, Henry's former page and groom of the bedchamber, who acted as the king's go-between when he made Anne Stafford his mistress. Compton made a habit of coming to Anne's private chamber, talking with her, and arranging her meetings with Henry, and while this plan worked well for a while, eventually Elizabeth Stafford guessed the truth and confided her suspicions to her husband and brother. The duke, the greatest peer in England and a hot-tempered man given to "rail and misuse himself in words," determined to intervene. Waiting in Anne's chamber, he confronted Compton the next time he came in. The groom of the bedchamber could say little in reply to the sulphurous duke, who "severely reproached him in many and very hard words." But once he escaped from Lady Hastings' chamber Compton went at once to the king, who sought out Buckingham and shouted at him until he left the palace.

Henry's anger was boundless. There was little he could do to Anne's husband Lord Hastings, who had ridden off in terror immediately after the confrontation between Buckingham and Compton. Anne herself had been packed off to a convent sixty miles away, but her sister remained to face the king's extreme displeasure. If Elizabeth Stafford thought the queen would protect her she soon found out how powerless Katherine was. She and her husband were ordered in the harshest terms possible to leave the palace and not to return, and for a time Henry swore he would dismiss a good many others as well. "Believing that there were other women in the employment of [Elizabeth Stafford], that is to say, such as go about the palace insidiously spying out every unwatched moment, in order to tell the queen," Caroz wrote in his version of the incident, "the king would have liked to turn all of them out, only that it has appeared to him too great a scandal."[3]

He had had his fill of women—of his wife and her malfunctioning womb, of the network of watchful females who spied on him, of righteous court ladies who interfered in his private affairs. For weeks his conscience and the queen's angry silence made him pay for what he had done, though, and "almost all the court knew that the queen had been vexed with the king, and the king with her, and thus this storm went on between them."[4]

In public Katherine continued to take her place as Henry's ever smiling, ever gracious queen, but she carried out her duties with a heavy heart. Henry's affection for her had been strained. He still jousted in her honor, wearing her symbol, the pomegranate, embroidered on his horse trappings; he gave her gifts, and spoke frequently of her in her absence, and in time the bad feeling between them lessened. Yet the gift she treasured most now made her sad. It was Elizabeth of York's missal, in which Henry had written "I am yours, Henry R. for ever." He was no longer hers alone. She could no longer be sure that, as he wrote her father shortly after their marriage, "if he were still free he would choose her in preference to all others."[5]

Amid the young beauties of the court Katherine seemed plain. That her confessor saw her as beautiful only made their relationship suspect, for if others noted her "lively and gracious disposition" and her clear, glowing complexion no one but a lover would have called her pretty. A candid Venetian described the queen as "rather ugly than otherwise," though it was generally agreed that she excelled at the courtly diversions of dancing and music-making. Katherine's excellent education helped to compensate for her foreigner's English; she spoke and wrote more accurately than many of the carelessly educated ladies of her suite.[6] Her piety too was exemplary. She often got up at midnight to say matins, and then again at five for mass, dressing hurriedly and telling her maids that any time spent in adorning herself was time wasted. On Fridays and Saturdays she fasted all day; she read the Office of the Blessed Virgin daily and, after dinner, read a saint's life to her women. It was said that when she knelt to pray, she denied herself the comfort of a cushion.

These virtues would have counted for little had Katherine proved to be barren. But she was pregnant again, and before long she found the courage to inform Henry. In September of 1510 the "King's Nursery" was fitted out once more. New hangings were ordered for the rooms where the lady mistress would superintend the birth, and later watch over the infant's nurse and rockers; a new bearing pane with a long train was sewn in purple velvet. Everything was ready for the birth of a prince.

Henry's second Christmas as king was celebrated more joyously than any feast yet seen. The court was at Richmond, for the queen had chosen to be delivered there and had already retired to her apartments. On New Year's Day, just after midnight, she gave birth to a son. When the news reached London bonfires were made and wine was set out in the streets for the rejoicing Londoners to drink. They cheered for the king, for the queen, and for the New Year's Boy, who was called Henry after his father. They came to see him christened, marveling at the precious golden gifts his illustrious godparents Margaret of Savoy and Louis XII of France presented. And they cheered for the midwife, proud and relieved that the birth had been successful, as she took her place in the church. Around her neck she wore a gold chain worth ten pounds, the gift of the grateful king.[7]

As soon as he had appointed the officers of his infant son's household —a sergeant at arms, a clerk of the signet, yeomen of the beds and wardrobe, and of course a nurse, Elizabeth Poyntes—Henry made a pilgrimage to the shrine at Walsingham to give thanks for the safe arrival of his son. This done, he called for a solemn joust at Westminster in honor of the queen.

Leaving the little prince in the care of his nurse at Richmond the entire court moved to the great palace where day after day pageants and feats of arms were held. The king was the star performer, making his entry onto the tiltyard under a pavilion of cloth of gold adorned with golden letters. He rode as Sir Loyal Heart, sharing the prizes with Thomas Knevet and Edward Howard, and after the joust had formally ended he ran extra courses with Howard and Charles Brandon "for the king's lady's sake."

In all, the banquets, costumes and pageant finery cost Henry as much as sixteen new ships of war, but the expense was justified. His eldest son, his heir, deserved to be ushered in with splendor.

But as the spectacles went on the baby weakened, and toward the end of February he died. No one was blamed. Elizabeth Poyntes, "late nurse unto our dearest son the prince," was given her twenty pounds annuity, and the keeper of the great wardrobe, who had so recently fitted out the nursery, now provided the hearse. Four hundred pounds of wax candles burned around it night and day in the monastery of Westminster until the New Year's Boy was laid to rest.

II

Great Harry

10

Pray we to God that all may gyde
That for our kyng so to provid,
To send hym power to hys corage
He may acheffe this gret viage:
Now let us syng this rownd all thre;
Sent George, graunt hym the victory!

AT midday on June 30, 1513, the waters off Dover teemed with ships. Three- and four-masted warships with huge emblazoned banners flying from their masts rode at anchor side by side, while rowboats wove in and out among them, bringing aboard the last loads of bowstaves and flour and beer. Twenty-five thousand oxen had been killed and salted down to feed the soldiers—causing the local price of beef to triple—and twelve thousand suits of armor had been ordered from the arms merchants of Flanders for them to fight in. "Certain secret engines" made for the king by a joiner were locked securely in the hold, along with two special large field guns, demi-culverins, which he affectionately called his "minions," and the giant "Twelve Apostles," heavy guns with figures of Saint John, Saint Thomas and the others cast on their barrels.[1] The crews of the ships had been outfitted in coats of green and silver-white, the Tudor colors— made in damask for the captain, camlet for the pilots and masters, and for the mariners, good woolen cloth. They stood at their posts now, waiting for the signal from the flagship to draw up anchor.

Finally Henry, who had said his goodbyes to Katherine at Dover Castle, was rowed out to his ship. Only three weeks earlier it had been reported that she meant to cross with him to France, despite her condition—she was pregnant for the fourth time—but he had decided to leave her behind as his regent. Pride overwhelmed her disappointment as she watched him embark, standing in the bow of the rowboat in gleaming armor, his polished steel headpiece crowned with a rich coronal. Over his armor—a new and more flexible type made with overlapping plates which slid on rivets—he wore the tunic of a crusading knight, a simple fall of white cloth of gold with a large red cross sewn on the front. With a jeweled Saint George on his crown, the cross of Christ on his breast and the arms of the pope on his banners, the crusader Harry the Eighth was off to war.

Exactly a hundred years earlier England's greatest hero, Henry V, had asserted his right to the French throne. Two years afterward he too had

sailed to France with an army, and had met the French on a field sewn
with winter wheat near the village of Agincourt. Like his sixteenth-
century namesake, Henry V had been an athletic young king who
dreamed of restoring the French lands that had been England's centuries
before, and then of capturing Jerusalem. And at Agincourt, his thousand
men-at-arms and six thousand archers had resoundingly defeated the
twenty-five thousand heavily armed Frenchmen who came against them,
slaughtering the encumbered enemy until they lay in heaps of dead and
dying, "taller than a man's height," as a chronicler wrote with exuberant
inaccuracy. The English, he went on, climbed these walls of dead "and
butchered the adversaries below with swords, axes and other weapons."
So great was the victory that nothing could darken it in the memories of
the English—not even the king's unchivalrous order that all captives be
killed in cold blood, a command which led to the incineration of wounded
French prisoners in the cottages which sheltered them. After all, the
command had been rescinded in time to spare the noblest and richest of
the French, and no one objected to the dishonorable treatment of the
dead, whose corpses were ransacked for valuables before being buried by
the thousands in pits dug by the peasants of Arras.[2]

After Agincourt Henry V had made his name even more illustrious by
conquering Normandy, besieging town after town and in the end winning
the right to the French throne. He had died, still a hero, at thirty-five, and
the dented helmet he had worn at Agincourt was hung on his tomb in
Westminster Abbey, a symbol of renown for the young Henry VIII to
dream on.

As the new reign went forward and the king's determination to fight
the French grew greater and greater the image of Henry V was often
conjured to inspire his ambition. Courtiers and foreign visitors alike
predicted that he "would now renew the name of Henry V," and noted
that like his predecessor Henry was devoted to the joust and to other
military skills, and was beguiled by schemes of conquest on a vast scale.
To the knights at Henry's court war meant valorous deeds and feats of
arms, the exploits of Edward III during the Hundred Years' War and the
chivalrous triumphs described in Froissart's *Chronicles*; one of these
knights, Lord Berners, "a martial man, well seen in all military discipline," translated Froissart at the king's request. Another Englishman
anonymously translated an Italian life of Henry V, hoping that King
Henry, seeing the "virtuous manners and victorious conquests" of his
namesake would be inspired to "conform himself to his life and manners."[3]

At least one court observer had no doubt the young king would
surpass all his predecessors. The Venetian ambassador Badoer looked
forward to hearing that Henry had marched straight through to Paris to be
crowned king of France, "which result may God grant, he being the true
king of France, and deservedly so, as within the last thousand years there
never was a king more noble and more valiant."[4]

No one expected more of Henry than he did of himself. He was "not
unmindful," he told his councilors, "that it was his duty to seek fame by

military skill,'' and alarmed them by announcing that he was not only eager to make war on the French but to lead the army into battle in person. Englishmen fight more bravely and fiercely when led by their king, he explained, though he had a strong personal motive as well. He hoped ''to create such a fine opinion about his valor among all men that they could understand that his ambition was not merely to equal but to excel the glorious deeds of his ancestors.''[5]

Glory, military glory, culminating in a famous name and a permanent place in the annals of chivalry had been Henry's coveted aspiration since boyhood. He knew by heart the stories of the Holy Grail, of Lancelot, Galahad, Tristram and Percival; he longed to enter into their world, where all else was forgotten in the selfless quest for the unobtainable. And he knew that, though the chivalric tradition was ebbing, it was not quite out of reach. Only a generation earlier the earl of Warwick, Richard Beauchamp, had lit all Europe with his shining renown. Brilliant in the tiltyard and on the battlefield, he had been proclaimed the "Father of Courtesy"; should all knowledge of true knighthood be lost, it was said, it could be recovered again in him.

Henry's tutor Skelton had given his pupil's hunger for glory a fixed purpose: the conquest of France. His reading—Malory, Caxton, Froissart and the tales of Henry V—was all of English kings waging war on French lands. He knew how the English had taken Thérouanne after the great victory of Crécy, how Edward III had besieged Tournai for many weeks, how Henry V, inexhaustible, had ridden around his camp in the pouring rain, exhorting his sodden soldiers to take heart and defeat the French. And as the prince's young body had developed its heroic proportions, his dreams too had widened to encompass the hallowed, almost mystical vision of the sublime moment of triumph—when, for an instant outside time, all odds were overcome, all physical limitations transcended, and a mortal knight was exalted to immortal fame.

By the time he reached early manhood these ideals had taken a deep and compelling urgency for Henry. England in the early sixteenth century was at a cultural crossroads. The influence of Renaissance Italy was already bringing about change in English statecraft, while the social order of the middle ages was rapidly giving way to newer and less settled forms. In the popular mind the old images of heroism and knight-errantry, of Arthurian ideals and enchanted adventure held firm, but the better edu-cated, more sophisticated of Henry's subjects were adopting the non-chivalric outlook of the English humanists. To the humanists the glories of war did not compensate for its butchery and misery, while personal honor, as an end in itself, was a highly suspect goal. In scholarship as in music Henry was a prodigiously gifted amateur, and men of learning were very much at home at his court. But by temperment he belonged to the chivalric past; the high principles that ruled him were drawn from the time-honored code of his medieval ancestors.

Oddly enough it was Erasmus who gave a name to this quality in the king. He called Henry *cordatissimus*—of all men "the man most full of heart."[6] Even more than high-heartedness and cheerful high spirits the

word connoted courage, magnanimity, unsullied integrity. Henry appeared to incarnate all the ardent vitality of Christian knighthood, the
dauntless zeal for the right that could outbrave all dangers. Here the
expectations of Henry's fellow-soldiers and the scholars he patronized
came together, for both saw in him an example of virtue to his subjects.
"A king's command goes far," Erasmus wrote, "but the king's example
goes further." As he explained in a letter to Henry written in 1519, "By
their monarch's character realms are ennobled or depraved. Future ages
will tell how England throve, how virtue flourished in the reign of Henry
VIII, how the nation was born again, how piety revived, how learning
grew to a height which Italy might envy, and how the prince who reigned
over it was a rule and a pattern for all time to come." England was
becoming another Camelot; in coming ages, Erasmus dreamed, it would
be told "how a king once reigned there who in his own person revived the
virtues of the ancient heroes."[7]

The most revered of heroes was the crusader, and Henry had long
seen himself in that role. When he set off for France in the garb of a
crusading knight he was in fact fulfilling a long-held desire of his father's,
who, as he told the emperor Maximilian, had discussed the matter of a
crusade "very seriously," though circumstances prevented him from
undertaking it. He cherished his father's ambition as an heirloom, Henry
said; since the start of his reign he had thought of nothing else but taking
the cross.[8]

Not long after he went to France a genuine call for help came from the
Holy Land itself. Friar John of St. Martin, guardian of his order in
Jerusalem, wrote to Henry urging him to send help to protect the holy
places from being defiled. A Turkish captain, abetted by his Christian ally
the king of Georgia, had destroyed the altar of the Latin Christians on
Mount Calvary. The friars built it up again, but had to pay the Turkish
sultan more than a thousand ducats for the privilege. The safety of
pilgrims visiting the holy sepulcher of Christ had been threatened; to
guarantee it the Christians had had to bribe the emir of Jerusalem, the
caliphs of Gaza and other Saracen officials with robes of silk and velvet.
All the shrines were costly to maintain, the friar told Henry, and whereas
in the past he and his brethren had been supported by many of the
European sovereigns their only income now was an inadequate legacy
from the late Queen Isabella of Spain. Another letter was even more
poignant. The monks of Mount Sinai informed Henry that, though they
continued to live their religious life as best they could, they were so poor
they had had to pawn their sacred vessels and furniture in order to buy
food. Eventually he helped them in some way, for in another letter they
thanked him gratefully for his succor.[9]

Henry's crusading dream merged with his hostility toward France
when shortly after his accession the French king and the pope renewed
their enmity. The armies of Louis XII besieged the papal forces at
Bologna, while assembling at Pisa a schismatic church council meant to
depose the pope and replace him with a pontiff more amenable to French
interests in Italy. The pope, Julius II, was even more warlike than his

French adversary. Erasmus caught sight of him in the midst of a triumphal procession at Bologna, a noisy spectacle of "troops under arms, generals prancing and galloping, lovely boys, torches flaming, spoils, shouts that rent the heavens, trumpets blaring, cannon thundering," and over it all the pope carried aloft in a gorgeous litter.[10] In October of 1511 Julius proclaimed the formation of a Holy League to "defend the unity of the church" and drive the French out of the Italian lands. Henry, who saw in the papal League both a holy cause and an opportunity for military renown, joined Julius' camp. Fighting under the papal banner, he explained to the emperor in the following year, was certain to prove as acceptable to God as fighting against the Turks; to confirm his assertion Henry procured for his soldiers the time-honored papal indulgence, granted since the eleventh century to crusaders who died in battle against the infidel.

"We live in evil times, and the world grows worse instead of better," Henry wrote sadly at the outset of his reign. Fighting on the side of good against the forces of evil was where his duty lay, and from time to time he checked the splendid extravagance of his court when he thought self-denial would further the cause of the right. He issued sumptuary laws forbidding all those below the rank of lord or knight to wear silk, and even the highest nobles were expected to adopt a less sumptuous mode of dress. The talk of the court turned periodically to saving money on clothes so that it might be spent on arms and horses, and in these times the Genoese and Tuscan cloth merchants suffered for want of English business. The king put aside his jeweled caps and velvet doublets for more modest garb, and his counselors and companions followed his example. In December of 1511 Henry and the entire House of Lords dressed themselves frugally in long gowns of gray cloth cut in the Hungarian fashion.[11]

Sobriety and restraint in dress were paralleled by a deepened reverence for the highest symbols of the faith. A number of relics arrived from Italy at this time, sent by the bishop of Famagosta: a stone from the tomb of the martyr Saint Katherine, along with some of the oil which flowed from her body, a fragment of the holy sepulcher, and another of the column at which Christ was scourged, part of Christ's sponge, and a piece of the vessel in which he washed his apostles' feet.[12] Henry's piety had just been rewarded with a special mark of papal favor. Julius II had taken back the title "Most Christian King" from the schismatic Louis XII and conferred it on Henry VIII; this, coupled with the pope's gift of the French throne itself, seemed justification enough to order the royal painter John Brown to "paint divers of the pope's arms in divers colors" on the banners and streamers the king would one day carry into battle.

The campaign of 1513, then, was the culmination of years of eager cultivation of the mood of war. While the knights assembled their panoplies and bought warhorses and armor the king was ordering guns cast by the master gunners of Flanders. As early as January, 1510, he sent specifications to Hans Popenruyter, a gunmaker at Malines, for twenty-four thousand-pound curtolds—later to be christened with such dynastic titles as Rose, Crown, York, and Lancaster—and an equal number of thousand-pound serpentines for his ships. Thousands of handguns were ordered as well, along with saltpeter, gunpowder and gun frames. Wooden chests had to be built to store the arms, and carts without number to carry the chests, supplies and provisions to the seacoast and, after the crossing, to the battleground itself. All these things Henry looked to, leaving the day-to-day management to his able almoner Thomas Wolsey and devoting his energies to convincing his contrary Council that he would not be thwarted in his purpose.

The councilors, chosen for Henry by his father before his death, were for the most part skeptical of the young king's zeal for battle. His principal advisers, a trio of ecclesiastics who had served Henry VII for years, were unsympathetic to war as a costly adventure offering at best more risk than profit. William Warham, archbishop of Canterbury and chancellor, Erasmus found to be "witty, energetic and laborious" beneath a quiet exterior, but his long years of diplomatic and legal experience and his own weariness—he wanted nothing more than to retire to his church and parishioners—left him no stomach for war. Richard Fox, bishop of Winchester and lord privy seal, "a lord of extreme authority and goodness," had worked too long in the previous reign in the interests of peace to endorse Henry's military policy, while Thomas Ruthal, bishop of Durham and the king's secretary, narrowly devoted all his energies to the everyday drudgery of administration and the continuing accumulation of the vast lands and rents that made him the richest prelate in the realm. But if these three spoke out against war others in the Council stood with the king, notably Wolsey and Thomas Howard, earl of Surrey, whose son Edward was lord admiral. And Henry's resident envoy in Rome, Cardinal Bainbridge, like Pope Julius a warlike cleric with an inveterate hatred of the French, supported the plans for war with unvarying passion.

Bainbridge was in constant touch with the court through Queen Katherine, who was herself the chief advocate of war next to the king. She sent the cardinal all the political news, writing with the judicious and informed tone of a seasoned stateswoman. Her views and influence were important enough to merit inclusion in the dispatches of the resident ambassadors; the Venetian Badoer reported tersely in November of 1512 that "the king is for war, the council against it, and the queen for it."[13] Katherine's consuming interest in military affairs extended to specific points of naval strategy. When Henry was preparing to send his fleet against France she became "very warm" about the enterprise and strongly recommended that he acquire four great galleasses and two smaller ones from Venice, as she had information that the French were building two small galleasses of their own. She spoke long and earnestly to Badoer about this, asking the cost of the ships and soliciting his involvement in the conflict with France.[14]

As war preparations gained intensity the French protected their interests by paying spies to send them news of English military preparations and to sabotage them whenever they could. A French merchant living in London was paid to write daily reports on English affairs, sending his letters to his brother in Rouen, routing them by way of Antwerp because

English couriers were barred from French ports. A French gunner in the service of the English Lord Penys agreed, in return for a large sum, to set fire to the stores of gunpowder on an agreed signal. There were reports that one of Henry's secretaries had been won over to the side of the French and was passing on valuable information to his employers. And a Norman priest living at the English court who was able to travel regularly to his home region in the Argentan without arousing suspicion was making himself particularly useful to Louis XII. This relatively inconspicuous cleric, "of brown visage, having his left brow higher than the other," was being employed to carry messages from Louis to members of the de la Pole family—representatives of the men the French upheld as the rightful heirs to the throne of England.

Edmund and Richard de la Pole, sons of Edward IV's sister Elizabeth, had an unarguably good claim to the throne. In one view, it was a better claim than Henry's, for the legitimacy of Henry's mother Elizabeth of York had been called into question.* According to a document produced in the reign of Richard III, Elizabeth's parents had not been validly married; all their children were bastards. This put the descendants of Edward IV's brother and sister in line for the crown—first his brother George's grandchildren, Henry, Geoffrey and Reginald Pole, and then his sister Elizabeth's surviving sons Edmund and Richard de la Pole. The elder son Edmund, earl of Suffolk, had been imprisoned in the Tower since 1506; his wife Margaret was one of Katherine's ladies in waiting. The younger son Richard was a captain in Louis XII's service. Through the Norman priest the de la Poles were kept in communication with one another during 1512 and the early months of 1513, and with the French court.[15]

The war strategy of the Holy League took final shape early in 1513. Each of the allies was to harass the French from a different quarter—the pope in Provence or Dauphiné, Ferdinand of Aragon in Béarn, Languedoc or Aquitaine, Henry in Picardy and Normandy, and Emperor Maximilian in another region still to be determined. The pope was to fulminate ecclesiastical censures on any power which opposed the League, while Henry bound himself to aid Maximilian with a payment of 100,000 crowns.

Now that a definite timetable had been agreed to—the simultaneous assaults were to be under way by June—Henry sprang into action. His first concern was his fleet. Throughout February and March he went to the docks nearly every day to encourage the sailors and the shipwrights and carpenters who were making ready the *Mary Rose,* the *Peter Pomegranet,* the *John Hopton's* and the other large and small warships. Writs went out to all the royal vassals to supply the king with "tall persons to serve on the sea," and a special guild of masters and mariners was founded "for the reformation of the navy, lately much decayed by

---

*Of course, Henry's title rested not only on his mother's Yorkist pedigree but on his father's admittedly weaker Lancastrian claim. His paternal grandmother Margaret Beaufort was a great-great-granddaughter of Edward III.

admission of young men without experience, and of Scots, Flemings and Frenchmen." Ships of all sizes were subject to royal conscription for use in the war, and as the trade in military stores and equipment escalated all other business ceased.[16] According to a list painstakingly drawn up by Henry himself in February of 1513, some twenty-six ships had been hired to supplement the existing fleet of twenty-three. The king noted the names and tonnages and captains of all the royal ships, changing five of the captains' names as adjustments in their assignments were made. The flagship he renamed, with a symbolic name he would use later for a much larger and more powerful ship: the *Great Harry Imperial*.

In Holy Week of 1513, two months before the king and his army embarked from Dover, the fleet sailed down the Thames and out into the Channel. There were eighty ships in all, including one little boat named for Erasmus, and a number of long, low vessels manned by hundreds of oarsmen and reputed to be more effective than galleys in Channel waters. In addition to a double complement of sailors the fleet carried, according to one account, as many as sixteen thousand picked soldiers; when battle was joined the warships were coupled by means of grappling hooks and the soldiers poured over onto the enemy's deck, fighting there as if on land. By April 23 the English had won a major encounter at sea. Word arrived from Admiral Howard in Brittany that four French ships had been captured, and inviting the king to come in person to celebrate the victory. Henry gave an extravagant reward to the sailors who brought the news and declared himself ready to set off at once, but his councilors held him back; it was risk enough, they said, for him to accompany the army.[17]

If all went well for the fleet at first, by the end of the month its fortunes had soured. Admiral Howard wrote at length to Henry praising the performance of each of his ships—the king had asked him to send word "how every ship did sail"—but his letters told of misfortunes and hindrances. He had never seen such storms; food was growing scarce; he had word that a hundred French ships were sailing toward him, but though he trusted in God and Saint George to "have a fair day on them," he could not be sure of victory. Some of the men were sick, or wounded from the first encounter. Many had died of measles. And one of his great ships, the *Katherine Fortileza,* was sinking slowly. "Bedell the carpenter bored so many holes in her," he confided to the king, "that she leaks like a sieve."[18]

The worst blow came when Howard and sixteen others boarded a French ship and, after a furious fight, all save one were killed. The survivor, wounded in eighteen places, lived to tell how in his final moments of life the admiral had flung his gold whistle of command into the sea lest it should fall into the hands of the French. It was a gesture befitting a hero's death, but other testimony contradicted the story. The French captain who found Howard's body left no doubt that he was still wearing his admiral's whistle. Among those who mourned Howard's loss the most were the king and Charles Brandon, his closest friends. To Henry he left one of his ships and one of his two bastard sons—whichever of the two he might choose—to be his servant when he reached full age.

To his "special trusty friend" Brandon, Howard bequeathed his other ship, "praying him to be a good master unto him," and his ceremonial chain of office made from three hundred gold coins.[19]

Undeterred by his admiral's death Henry made his final arrangements to cross to France. To enhance his personal magnificence he ordered his goldsmiths to fashion the harness and trappings for his horse, spending enough on these sumptuous adornments to buy twenty heavy brass field guns.[20] He spent another thousand pounds on little chains, branches, buttons and aglets of solid gold to fasten onto his doublets when he laid his crusader's tunic aside. His weapons were as gorgeously appointed as his armor; among them was a silver crossbow sent to him by the emperor, mounted in an elaborately worked silver-gilt case.

A series of last-minute frustrations threatened to delay the embarkation. A huge band of thieves attacked the train of wagons bound for the coast carrying the royal money chests; eighty of the robbers were caught and, on the king's order, hanged on the spot.[21] "Some lewd persons" burned and broke apart many of the little boats used to convey men and provisions from the shore out to the larger ships, hampering loading. And a crisis developed over the soldiers' beer. Brewhouses had been set up at Portsmouth to brew a hundred tons of beer a day, employing dozens of brewers, millers, beer-clerks and coopers. Deep trenches had been dug, covered with boards and turf, to store the filled barrels and protect them from the heat, but the soldiers complained that the country beer of Portsmouth soured too quickly for their taste and could not be compared to that made in London with barley malt. The London beer proved to be no better. "Much of it is as small as penny ale," the new admiral, Thomas Howard, grumbled, "and as sour as a crab."

Their holds full to bursting with men and horses and sour beer, the ships of the fleet were ready at last. Henry gave the order to weigh anchor, confident that he had enough troops and equipment and cannon to conquer hell.

11

Owre Kynge went forth to normandy
With grace and myght to chyvalry:
Ther god for him wrought mervelusly.
Wherfore englonde may calle and cry
Deo gratias.
Deo gratias anglia redde pro victoria.

WHEN they landed at the English-held town of Calais the king and his army were given a joyous welcome. Charles Brandon, recently created Viscount Lisle and marshal of the army, and Thomas Wolsey, whose signature on thousands of orders and receipts and authorizations had been largely responsible for bringing the army together and seeing it safely transported across the Channel, now supervised the unloading of the ships. As the king rode into the town amid the cheering citizens of Calais to give thanks for his safe journey Brandon and Wolsey watched the sailors lead ashore the oxen and mules and great Flanders mares that would pull the carts and ordnance. Alert to each detail, Wolsey counted every chest, barrel and box that came out of the holds to make certain nothing was missing or lost.

For the next three weeks the army stayed in Calais while the English and imperial diplomats worked out a joint strategy and the mercenaries Henry had hired assembled. In his spare time the restless king, eager to leave for the battlefield, practiced shooting with the archers of his guard. Standing among them in a garden one afternoon he was conspicuous for his height and bearing, an observer wrote, and surpassed them as far in skill as in appearance, taking such sure aim that he hit the target squarely in the middle.

Archery was waning in England in the early sixteenth century, and Henry was attempting to promote it by example and by statute. English archers had formed the core of the fighting force in the Middle Ages, though in Henry's reign a new archery technique had reduced their effectiveness. A well-aimed arrow could still penetrate sheet steel, how-ever, and the recent advent of handguns had not yet made the bow obsolete. Even at extreme bowshot, some two hundred and fifty yards, trained archers shot far more accurately than men armed with ar-quebuses, who could be relied on to hit their targets only at point-blank range. What was more, archers could shoot six times a minute, ar-quebusiers only once in two or three minutes.

And firearms were heavy, awkward and unreliable. Soldiers who

80

used them tired quickly, and only the most experienced of troops had the presence of mind to load them carefully under fire, remembering to put wadding between powder and ball and then again on top of the ball, making certain the fuse stayed lit long enough to fire the gun while keeping it clear of the reserve gunpowder. Handguns were delicate mechanisms which broke or malfunctioned frequently, and could be repaired only by gunsmiths; bows, on the other hand, never clogged or fouled and were equally reliable in all weathers.[1] Both archers and arquebusiers were needed, though Henry's backward-looking battle array relied too heavily on the former in an age of artillery, heavy cavalry and massed pikemen.

Whatever the drawbacks of the English forces they were destined to carry on the work of the Holy League virtually alone. Emperor Maximilian upheld the commitment to make war, joining Henry's army and fighting alongside his fellow sovereign of England—albeit with few troops, and for pay. And his daughter Margaret of Savoy, ruler of the Netherlands, continued to defy the French king, daring him to "spit out all his venom and do his worst, for she was safe under the English arrows."[2] But the other allies fell away before the campaigning began. The papal assault that was to have come through Provence or Dauphiné was never launched; indeed it was said in Venice that the pope was neutral. And Ferdinand of Aragon, far from leading an assault from the south, had made a truce with the French even before his son-in-law set sail from England.

Ferdinand, now an asthmatic sixty-two, was reportedly "too old and crazy to endure war." Publicly he justified his betrayal of his allies by explaining that, feeling himself to be near death, he was reluctant to leave his lands to his heir in a state of discord.[3] Privately he thought himself well rid of the expense of war, and of allies who, except for his idealistic son-in-law, would not hesitate to desert him whenever it served their interests.

This was not the first time Henry had been given reason to distrust Ferdinand's diplomatic integrity. A year earlier it had been arranged that England and Aragon would campaign jointly against the French. The English force arrived on schedule in Navarre, only to find that Ferdinand had abruptly decided not to wage war after all; stranded among the hostile peasants near Fuenterrabía, the Englishmen sickened, mutinied, and finally took themselves home without striking a blow. Ferdinand's reputation for duplicity was well established. He made a practice of representing his motives and actions differently to everyone he dealt with, and rarely if ever told the simple truth. To the pope he complained that Henry was insincere in his desire to make war on France, and had made a truce with Louis XII; to Louis he denounced Henry as a warmonger who refused to sign the truce that he, Ferdinand, had worked so hard to arrange. Nor was he modest about his accomplishments in deceit. Overhearing that one of his victims had accused him of cheating him twice, Ferdinand denied the charge vehemently. "He lies," insisted the king. "I cheated him three times."

Ferdinand followed Henry's every move with shrewd vigilance, glad enough to profit from the younger man's undertakings but skeptical about their likelihood of success. He wrote at length giving Henry military advice—that he must rely on the pike and musket, and not on archers, who alone could not resist the stoutest mercenaries in a pitched battle—but confided to a friend that he "had no great confidence in any of the enterprises of the king of England." He was careful not to involve himself in the campaign of 1513, though to the end he kept Henry half convinced he might join in. Yet he kept himself minutely informed about the course of the fighting, about Henry's behavior and appearance and his relations with Maximilian, through fast ships that sailed continuously between Calais and Guipúzcoa, bringing him news.[4]

To the pope, the emperor and the king of Aragon—all of them mature men of the world—war was one of a variety of diplomatic alternatives to be pursued or abandoned as political expediency dictated. To Henry it was a holy cause and a sacred duty. And he made certain his fellow sovereigns understood that, once pledged, he meant to go to war with or without their aid. Within the hearing of the Venetian ambassador he affirmed his belief that Ferdinand and the pope would never desert him, but added pointedly that if they did "yet he would never withdraw from this war until that schismatical sovereign"—Louis XII—"be made an end of."[5] Besides, the French campaign was only a beginning. Frenchmen were easily disposed of; the Swiss contemptuously called them "hares in armor," and they were known to fear meeting the English in battle. Once they were crushed, Henry boasted to the Venetians, he would take his army into Italy to win further glory. There was no end to his dreams of conquest. A military memorandum drawn up at this time contained the breathtaking pronouncement that "to win a battle against a whole world only twelve thousand footmen are requisite," provided they were armed with huge brass "pomegranates" which spewed stones and fire.[6]

With projects such as these churning in his head Henry led his men out of Calais in late July into the hostile territories of France. The army strung itself out for miles along the narrow road in three long "wards" after the medieval fashion. In the "king's ward" rode, first, Henry with his attendants and pages, his spears and six hundred guardsmen, his clerks, secretaries, heralds and pursuivants, and his thirty-one physicians and surgeons. His personal bowyer and fletcher rode near him, as did his trumpeters and minstrels and the thirty-five artificers who forged his armor and kept it and his weapons in good repair. The two hundred and fifty officers and servants of his stable and his chapel came next, and the grooms and pages and menials of his household, nearly a thousand strong. Directly behind them lumbered the great guns, each pulled by teams of a dozen or more oxen or tall draft horses. A small army of twelve hundred accompanied the ordnance—gunners and blacksmiths, miners and pioneers and "toyle setters" to raise the tents, masons, armorers, trench-makers and carpenters. Last of all came the great nobles and royal favorites whose honor it was to ride with their retinues in the king's ward: the duke of Buckingham with his five hundred men, William Compton with his six hundred, Fox and Ruthal with their hundred-odd and Wolsey with his two hundred and fifty, and, grandest of all, the marshal Charles Brandon with fifteen hundred archers and billmen and armored knights.[7]

Shortly after the march got under way it started to rain, and by midafternoon great sheets of rain were making progress difficult. The soldiers took shelter in their tents, but as the storm grew more violent gusts of wind overturned the tents and men, beasts and equipment were drenched. It was an inauspicious beginning, and Henry, who had read how in adverse circumstances Henry V rode around his camp encouraging his men, was determined not to let the weather dishearten his troops. Through most of the night, as the storm raged on, the king rode in full armor from one miserable cluster of men to another, calling out to them to remember that better luck was sure to follow. "Now that we have suffered in the beginning," he told them, "fortune promises us better things, God willing," and the sight and sound of him cheered the men and bound them to him more strongly than ever.[8]

A few days later the first brief encounter with the French roused them further. On the march toward St. Omer the English vanguard caught sight of several thousand French troops leaving the cover of a wood. After a minor skirmish the French withdrew, leaving the English eager to engage them again. Henry, who longed for a pitched battle, was very pleased, though he would have preferred to meet Louis XII in person. Louis, for his part, was attempting to stir himself into activity, but according to Henry's informants he "had a better heart than legs" for warfare as his gout was painfully acute. The small-scale encounters continued. A party of French attacked an English contingent carrying supplies from Calais to the main English force, and three hundred English were killed; French raiders captured a hundred and fifty English wagons and killed many of the English who were escorting them, with the rest fleeing to take refuge in a nearby castle. And after a skirmish near Ardres the French gathered up all the enemy corpses they could find, stripped them, and mutilated their faces beyond recognition.[9]

It was Thomas More's melancholy observation that "the common folk do not go to war of their own accord, but are driven to it by the madness of kings." What were the thoughts of Henry's troops as they followed him, admiringly yet surely somewhat reluctantly, toward the dangers to come? Immediate preoccupations aside (their soaking clothes, aching legs, and general discomfort), explicit and undefined fears must have tormented them. Rumor had it there was plague at Brest, brought there by sailors; English sailors, it was said, were certain to bring the sweating sickness to Calais, where it would spread to Henry's army. The king had brought fourteen wagons loaded with gold and silver coins on this expedition, but there was always the chance they might not be paid their sixpence a day—eightpence for the archers and artisans, four shillings for the captains—or that, once paid, the money might be stolen or gambled away.

Even the most stalwart of fighting men knew and dreaded the hazards of battle. Sword or lance wounds, they knew, if not fatally deep would heal in time. Broken arms or legs could be set and splinted. But an arrow in the chest or abdomen meant certain death, if not at once then within a few agonizing days; the doctors could do nothing for severe blows to the head, or for men who broke their backs falling from their horses in full

ENGLAND

●Reading

London
THAMES
Gravesend

THE
Pale of Calais
and Vicinity
EARLY IN THE
Reign of
Henry VIII

SCALE IN MILES
0   10   20   30   40   50   60

ENGLISH
CHANNEL

Diep

●cherbourg

●Le Havre

FRANCE

NORTH SEA

The Hague

Margate
Canterbury
Dover

Antwerp

Ostend
Bruges

Ghent

Dunkirk
Calais
Gravelines

Brussels

Guînes
Ambleteuse
Ardres
Marquison

Boulogne
St.Omer
Thérouanne

Lille
Tournai

Guinegate

Montreuil

Crécy

THE PALE OF CALAIS (English)

Ostend
Bruges

Ghent

Rysbank
Dunkirk
Gravelines

FLANDERS

Calais
Guînes
Ardres

COUNTY OF
FLANDERS
(Autonomous)

Ambleteuse
Marquison

St.Omer

Lille

Boulogne
Thérouanne

Tournai

Guinegate

F
R
A
N
C
E

Agincourt

PICARDY

Montreuil

BURGUNDIAN

Crécy

| 0 | 10 | 20 | 30 | 40 | 50 |

SCALE IN MILES

armor. Camp fevers and other epidemics were an everpresent concern, diarrhea a universal aggravation. It would not be long, they knew, before the collective miseries of constant rain, filth, continual ill-temper and the cold fear of death would make them wish for the moment of truth, just before battle, when by custom all soldiers went down on their knees before a priest and took earth into their mouths in token of the death and burial they faced.

On August 1 the English arrived before the walls of Thérouanne, known as "La Chambre du Roi," "The King's Treasury," and the key of Picardy, and began to bombard it with their great siege guns. The bombardment continued day and night while the laborers set up camp— hundreds of tents and pavilions arranged "like a castle or little town." Each tent had a name: for the royal treasurer, "The Gold Ring," for the master of the armory, "The Gauntlet," for the chaplains, "The Chalice," and for the carpenters, a tent the size of a long hall called "The Hammer." The king had eleven tents, connected by covered walkways, including one for his master cook and one for his kitchen, "new made at Guinegate in the field." The royal tents were of blue waterwork and cloth of gold so fine the emperor's tailor estimated it to be worth thirty-three florins an ell. Inside, the grandest of Henry's pavilions was lined from floor to ceiling with money—gleaming ducats and golden florins—and displayed a huge gilded sideboard where wine and English beer were dispensed in golden drinking cups.[10]

Henry also had a specially built wooden house with an iron chimney where he could take refuge from the answering fire of the besieged garrison of Thérouanne. The precaution was justified, for if the incessant pounding of the "Twelve Apostles" was breaking down the walls and houses of the city the French guns were doing their share of damage to the English camp. Talbot, captain of Calais, lost a leg to the French fire, and other English knights were killed as they sat or walked about the city of tents. A Devonshire knight, Edward Carew, was hit by a French bullet as he sat in council in Lord Herbert's pavilion and died before the eyes of his dismayed comrades. "This is the chance of war," Herbert told them once the shock passed. "If it had hit me you must have been content; a noble heart in war is never a feared of death."[11]

Certainly the king appeared to have no fear, disdaining to keep cover and riding in the open in his golden crusader's tunic wearing a rich jeweled cap and "a red shaggy hat with many red feathers" in place of his helmet. He was more energetic than ever, practicing with his archers, entertaining the emperor in his pavilion and giving him valuable presents, and, following the older man's advice, getting up hours before dawn to adjust the positions of his men and artillery for maximum effect. Everywhere he went he was escorted by fourteen young boys in golden coats, wearing scarlet mantles over them to keep out the rain; their horses were trapped in silver and adorned with silver bells which jingled sweetly as they rode. Bells of pure gold hung from the harness of the king's horse, and Henry liked to make his mount leap and bound until the bells flew off and the watching soldiers scrambled for them in the mud.

When the siege had been under way for ten days a herald arrived in the camp. He brought word from Henry's brother-in-law James IV, king of Scotland and ally of Louis XII. Henry listened, "standing still with sober countenance, having his hand on his sword," as the herald recited King James' message: Henry should withdraw from Thérouanne; he should leave French territory entirely; in defense of his French allies, James summoned his brother-in-law home. It was nothing short of a challenge to battle, a clear warning that the perpetual fighting along the Scots border was about to erupt into full-scale war.

Henry's reply was thorough and defiant. "It becometh ill a Scot to summon a king of England," he began. "Tell him there shall never Scot cause me to return my face." James had been bribed with French coins to make this challenge, Henry added, and did ill to threaten the sovereign who was his natural ally by marriage. Growing more and more indignant, Henry sent the herald off with a challenge of his own. "Recommend me to your master," he concluded, "and tell him if he be so hardy to invade my realm or cause to enter one foot of my ground I shall make him as weary of his part as ever was man that began any such business."[12]

Katherine and the captains who looked to her as regent would deal with the Scots; the immediate problem was the French. Thérouanne was holding out too long. Helped by the persistent storms, the defenders were succeeding so well on their own that the French army besieging the nearby imperial town of Hesdin had not even bothered to send relief troops in force, only raiding parties which seized two of the great Apostles and managed to sink one of them in a deep pond. On August 16 the French commander Vendôme decided to try to draw the English away from Thérouanne and sent two companies of knights toward the town. Among their number were two men well known to the English: the Chevalier Bayard and his friend Richard de la Pole, "the great traitor of England." (As a precaution against rebellion in his absence Henry had ordered the execution of de la Pole's captive brother Edmund just before leaving for France.)

Contemporary accounts greatly exaggerate the numbers involved on both sides, but there were probably about eleven hundred English knights who rode up to meet some two thousand of the French near the town of Guinegate. By the time the French saw the English approaching it was too late to avoid an encounter, and the skirmishing began. According to one account, the English charged, sending one body of French horsemen back into the others and causing a panic. Within minutes all the French were galloping madly across the fields the way they had come, shedding their standards and lances and even the bardings of their horses as they rode. Henry, who at first had wanted to join the English charge, was restrained by his councilors and busied himself with the artillery. When the chase began, though, he threw aside all caution and set off, surrounded by his bodyguard, after the retreating French in the distance.[13]

The exhilaration of that hour was unique. Never again in Henry's life would he savor the excitement of a breakneck chase after a hopelessly defeated enemy, knowing that total victory was his. For a brief span of moments all his dreams of chivalric conquest took on form and substance; he entered the timeless realm of knighthood proven, of valor undisputed—the realm of legend.

A French eyewitness reported later that, had Henry stayed with his footsoldiers instead of dashing ahead of them, and reformed his horsemen for a fresh charge, he might have routed the entire French army. But his mind was on the glory, not the scale, of victory. And the glory of it was very great—nine standards taken, over a hundred notable prisoners seized for ransom, along with a fortune in forfeited arms and accouterments. Men would speak for hundreds of years of what the English had won that day, and they would credit Henry VIII with the triumph.

The remaining weeks of the campaign passed smoothly and swiftly. The English took Thérouanne, then went on to Lille, where, after a minor alarm—it was reported that three gunners with handguns had sworn to assassinate Henry, but they were never found—the king enjoyed three days and nights of gallant amusements in the company of Margaret of Savoy, playing every musical instrument brought before him, demonstrating his archery, and dancing until morning in his shirt and stocking feet. From there they went on to besiege and reduce the "great, handsome and powerful" city of Tournai, the "Unsullied Maiden" whose thick double walls and ninety-nine fine towers made it an even richer prize than Thérouanne. In all, seven walled towns were taken before the campaigning season ended and Henry and his army left for home in October, a respectable achievement to set alongside the memorable day at Guinegate that was coming to be called the "Battle of the Spurs."

Only once during the campaign had there been a few hours of uncertainty. It was on the misty night the king left Lille, intending to make his way with a relatively small escort to the camp where the rest of the army awaited him. The camp had been moved during his three-day stay in the town, but he must have assumed that someone among his attendants knew where it was. About a mile outside the town he happened to ask which way the camp lay, and discovered that no one knew. None of his men had been given directions; there was no guide, and the night was so dark and foggy they could easily pass the sea of English tents without realizing it. Returning to Lille was impossible, for the town gates had been shut and secured for the night. Going on was dangerous; they could only become more hopelessly lost, and there might be French raiding parties in the area. Not knowing what else to do, the gunners shot off the loudest of the artillery pieces again and again, but they went unheard. "Thus the king tarried a long while," a chronicler wrote, "and wist not whither to go."

At last a figure emerged from the mist—a lone victualer bringing his cart from the English camp to Lille to fetch provisions. When he got over his astonishment the carter was persuaded to put aside his errand and lead the king safely to the camp.

12

He was lyvely, large, and longe,
With shoulders broade, and armes stronge,
That myghtie was to se:
He was a hardye man, and hye,
All men hym loved that hym se,
For a gentyll knight was he.

NEWS of King Henry's victories in France spread quickly, until stories of his bravery, his prowess in arms, his chivalrous treatment of his enemies and his glittering person could be heard in every tavern and marketplace. Men to whom the English king had been only a shadowy name now spoke familiarly of him, telling one another how he won the day at the Battle of the Spurs, how he walked fearlessly in the open at the siege of Tournai, heedless of danger, for hours at a time, how when his men hesitated to ford a swollen river he jumped off his horse and waded in, shaming the others into following him. Tales of his scrupulous chivalry were eagerly told. After taking Thérouanne, it was said, he returned to Guinegate and awaited a challenge to do battle for the town, as the laws of arms required. He had shown the greatest courtesy to his French prisoners, allowing some to ransom themselves for a token payment and subsidizing the ransoms of others out of his own money. To the captured duc de Longueville, a noble of the highest rank, he gave a gown of cloth of gold, forcing the duke, despite his objections, to dine at the royal table. And though Henry had shown himself a fearsome adversary, declaring through his Garter King of Arms to the citizens of Tournai that if they did not yield he would "put them and their city to sword, fire and blood," in fact he treated the conquered population magnanimously. There was little destruction, and no plundering; instead he turned the town into an arena for spectacular entertainments and pageantry, with torchlit processions and tournaments held in the open in the market square.

Those who saw in Henry another Henry V were entirely satisfied. The resplendent English king had not only repeated many of his predecessor's feats but had done them at a younger age, and earlier in his reign. To be sure, he had not shown the generalship of the fifteenth-century ruler, nor had he actually won the French crown. But he did not have Henry V's stern and arrogant nature either, and his campaign had none of the brutality of medieval combat. The behavior of Henry's soldiers had in fact been one of the minor wonders of the campaign. Sixteen hundred copies of "statutes of war" had been printed and distributed among them, statutes in which Henry's concern for virtue and good repute were unmistakable. The fighting men were enjoined against robbery, pillage and sacrilege; they were not to burn houses, or to gamble (except with the king, who looked on gambling as a form of largesse and seemed to enrich everyone who played with him); they were not to "murmur or grudge against the king or the officers of his host."[1] Camp followers were outlawed, and all other women were to be treated with consideration. The soldiers were not even to enter, much less to raid or occupy, a house where a woman lay in childbed; the "marvellous fair, well fed and clean washen" girls of the region were to be left strictly alone. No such precautions could protect women against the incidental harms of war, however. During the siege of Thérouanne the English artillery destroyed a large house, possibly a convent or a beguinage where lay women lived and worked in common, and when it fell, "many dozen fair young women" were killed.[2]

Foreigners who passed through the English camp in France took back stories which augmented the king's reputation still further. They confirmed the unheard-of order and clean living observed by his soldiers, and recounted at length the scenes of splendor they had witnessed: the surrender of Thérouanne, when the bedraggled townspeople filed out one by one, their possessions on their backs, through the ranks of English horse and foot ranged on either side of them, and later the razing of every wall and house until only the cathedral was left standing; Henry's triumphant entry into Lille, wearing his crown, a doublet of cloth of silver over his jeweled armor; the girls of Lille running out to offer him little crowns and scepters and garlands of flowers while the criminals of the town reached out to him with white rods in their hands begging for pardon; the elaborate jousting at Tournai in the pouring rain, with Henry taking the prize and riding round the circle acknowledging the cheers of the spectators in his wilted, ruined doublet of multicolored velvet.[3]

Before he left for France Henry had been a crowned boy, a "youngling." Now English men and women spoke of him as "our great king," not just King Harry but Great Harry. Soon the entire world would talk of him, a Venetian envoy wrote. Already he had no equal among the kings of Christendom for gold, silver and soldiers.[4] Who could say what glory his next campaign would bring?

There was no doubt in Henry's mind that he would go to war again, and soon. Even before he left France he assured Pope Leo that he would return as quickly as possible with a larger army, and resume his conquest of France.[5] He thrived on challenge, and war was the most thorough and most unrelenting of challenges. Lesser men might pale or quake under the endless strains of campaigning, but Henry seemed to grow stronger, not weaker, as the weeks went by. The Milanese ambassador Paolo da Lodi reported how at Tournai, when he should have been resting from his exertions, Henry chose instead to join in the tilting. He ran course after course, striving to outdo the best of the jousters, Charles Brandon and the emperor's champion Guillaume de Guislain, until in the end "without flattery" the spectators had to admit that he had "done excellently and broken many lances." To the ambassador's astonishment, the king showed not the least sign of being winded or fatigued. "He was fresher after this awful exertion than before," he wrote. "I do not know how he can stand it."

What made the effort all the more amazing was that Henry had had little if any sleep the night before. Days in the tiltyard and at the gambling table alternated with nights of banqueting, courtly flirtation and dancing—such dancing as no king had done in recent memory. From late evening until dawn Henry hopped and dipped and bowed, "dancing magnificently in the French style," partnering Margaret of Savoy and each of her women in turn. "He does wonders and leaps like a stag," the incredulous Milanese wrote. He seemed never to tire, but went straight into the next day's round of arduous exercise, bright-eyed and "wonderfully merry."[6]

Along with his tough, untiring physique Henry had a superabundance of nervous energy which urged him on from one diversion to another and which put a keen edge on his every movement. Idleness was foreign to him; "he is never still or quiet," da Lodi remarked. When no pastime presented itself he created one, usually turning for amusement to the people around him. With the courtiers he joked and teased and played matchmaker, promising to reward his favorites among the younger women with extravagant sums when they married. At least one of them held him to his promise afterward. One Étienette de la Baume sent Henry a letter reminding him that when he had flirted and bantered with her at Lille, calling her his page and "telling her many pretty things . . . about marriage and other things," he had also said he would give her ten thousand crowns when she took a husband. Her father had now found one for her; Henry must pay up.[7] To his soldiers and captains the king was bellicose and full of boast. "He is as eager for war as a lion, and greatly desires to fight the French," da Lodi noted. But even as he spoke of battle the spirit of play would overtake him and he would rush out, leap on his horse and challenge his companions to a race. A foreigner staying in the English camp saw the king riding from the town one evening, surrounded by about twenty-five mounted attendants, racing and playing games and tricks with them, as carefree as any young squire with his companions.[8]

It was this quality in Henry—this ability to cast aside the aloofness of monarchy and show the lively familiarity of a good companion—that won him affection as well as admiration. The towering magnificence of his person made him overwhelming. He was literally earthshaking; "when he moves," it was said, "the ground shakes under him."[9] He was awash in splendor; to the ordinary folk of Flanders he must have seemed, as he did to the Venetian Bavarin, "a being descended from heaven."[10] But if he was godlike, he was a god made flesh, approachable and even eagerly friendly, and the weight of his presence was counteracted by the warmth of his camaraderie.

"He is very popular with his own people," the Milanese envoy remarked, "and, indeed, with all, for his qualities." The nobles of Flanders flocked to see him, and many of the common people as well. They found him to be "merry, handsome, well-spoken, popular and intelligent." They took note too of the "two obstinate men who governed everything" for the king, Charles Brandon and Thomas Wolsey. Brandon, Henry's hulking shadow, appeared to be a "second king" with the power to "do and undo" at will.[11] Wolsey was slightly less conspicuous but equally indispensable, directing the provisioning, transport and communications of the army in the field. The king's subtler political and even domestic duties were left to Wolsey; it was he who remembered that Queen Katherine had entered the last months of her pregnancy and had begged for frequent letters, as she was without any other comfort in Henry's absence. When he neglected to write her Wolsey wrote for him, soothing her fears and assuring her quite inaccurately that the king was being careful "to avoid all manner dangers."[12] Katherine took heart. She was glad her husband was coming safely through his "dangerous passage"; she believed him to be invincible. "With his health and life nothing can come amiss to him," she wrote buoyantly, adding that she was now preoccupied with war herself, supervising the campaign against the Scots.

From a purely military standpoint Henry's war had been little more than a costly chivalric adventure. In taking Thérouanne and Tournai Henry had damaged French interests but had brought little direct benefit to England. The emperor Maximilian, who had taken Thérouanne nearly thirty-five years earlier and then lost it, had the most to gain from the campaign; taking the two fortress towns out of French hands not only made the borders of the empire more secure but temporarily distracted the French from fighting the imperial armies in Italy. Even the English had to admit that Henry was neglecting his own advantage; one English ambassador compared him to the heroic Athenian King Codrus, who was so preoccupied with the welfare of his neighbors and friends that he forgot to look out for himself.[13]

Henry could not even take full credit for the success of his undertaking. There had been imperial and Swiss troops engaged as well, and they had won victories in Burgundy as the English were taking the first of their prizes. (Ferdinand too gave every appearance of joining in the war, sending messengers to his son-in-law declaring his intention to assist him as soon as a new treaty was signed, meanwhile arranging for the signing to be delayed until the campaigning season was past.[14]) Critics disparaged the fall of Tournai to the English as a hollow victory. To be sure, the town was fortified, and occupied by the French, but it was encircled by the neutral Netherlands territories of Prince Charles and had no garrison; the English had faced only feeble citizen resistance, and could not have won the town more easily.

If only they had known it, these same critics could have charged the king quite accurately with impoverishing his kingdom. Slightly less than a million pounds had been spent on military preparations and on the campaign itself. When all was over the treasure in jewels and plate that had been Henry VII's legacy to his son was spent. One of the last things the king did before leaving for France had been to secure the jewel house in the Tower, ordering a new brick wall, stronger bars and windows, new doors set in secured with "hanglocks" and keys. By the time he returned there was little left to guard.[15]

In a way, Henry had missed the main campaign entirely. For if the Battle of the Spurs had won the admiration of contemporaries the English victory over the Scots at Flodden inspired their awe, eclipsing every other event of the summer. It was a great victory. The Scots king had sold all his plate and gold chains to buy ordnance, and brought up seven huge guns—the "Seven Sisters"—against the English. His nobles stood by him in the field in full strength, and many churchmen too, excusing their collaboration in slaughter by arguing that they only set off the guns that did the killing, they did not kill with their own hands. Thomas Howard, the doughty, septuagenarian earl of Surrey, led the English. The battle went on for three hours, and when it was over the Scots king and his clerics lay dead on the field, plundered by the Northumberland folk who drove off their hundreds of horses and by the armorers who swarmed over their corpses and sold their armor.[16]

Queen Katherine had been on her way north with a large army when the news of Flodden reached her. Probably she expected to lead her men into battle, bearing her child, if need be, in the military camp the way her mother had borne her three decades earlier. According to one account Katherine harangued the captains "in imitation of her mother Isabella," telling them "to be ready to defend their territory, that the lord smiled upon those who stood in defense of their own, and that they should remember that English courage excelled that of all other nations."[17]

Katherine sent the news of Flodden to Henry with as much pride as if she had won the battle singlehandedly, though she was careful to attribute both this and the successes in France to her husband's piety. She had shown no less prowess than he, she wrote. Her infantry had defeated the mounted, heavily armed Scots. The valor of her knights, especially Surrey, and of an unnamed "English lady" who captured three Scottish horsemen unaided, was without parallel.[18] And if he had taken captive a duke, her men had killed a king. To prove it Katherine sent him James' plaid tunic bearing the royal arms of Scotland, torn and stained with his lifeblood.

13

They cast on their gownes of grene,
And tooke theyr bowes each one;
And they away to the greene forrest
A shooting forth are gone.

WHEN the two Venetian envoys Giustiniani and Pasqualigo arrived at Greenwich to celebrate May Day of 1515 with the king and his court they were met by a smiling Queen Katherine. She was richly dressed in the style of Spain and mounted on a white horse, and was attended by a number of footmen and twenty-five waiting maids whose gold-trimmed gowns and pure white palfreys were nearly as splendid as her own. The secretary of the Venetian embassy, Niccolo Sagudino, observed later that the "sumptuous appearance" of her women made Katherine seem rather plain, but her manner was cheerful and gracious as she rode alongside the ambassadors the mile or so to Shooter's Hill, and she took pleasure in the first of the sights they came across—a triumphal car, or float, drawn by griffins with human faces and filled with singers and musicians. A little farther on the king came riding toward the company on a prancing bay Frieslander. His appearance, though traditional on May Day, was arresting: he was dressed entirely in Lincoln green velvet, from his cap to his shoes, and as soon as he came in sight of the foreigners he made the bay bound and leap as he approached them, "performing such feats," Pasqualigo wrote, "that I fancied myself looking at Mars."[1] With Henry accompanying them the group then rode to the top of the hill, where they came upon two hundred or more archers of the royal guard, dressed all in green like the king and carrying bows and arrows. At their head was one who called himself Robin Hood, with Maid Marian by his side. (Which of Henry's courtiers impersonated Robin Hood is unclear, but the part of Maid Marian was taken by one "Mr. Villiers," who wore a woman's frontlet and red kirtle and covered his head with a kerchief.)

With the king's permission, Robin Hood signaled his men to shoot their arrows all at once. The arrowheads were made to whistle as they flew through the air; with several hundred shot at once the noise was "strange and great," and pleased the king. Then Robin invited all the nobles present to "come into the greenwood, and see how the outlaws live," and Henry turned to Katherine and her women and asked "if they durst adventure to go into the wood with so many outlaws." "If it pleased him," Katherine answered, "she was content," and at that the trumpets

94

sounded and the green-clad archers led the way to where a banquet chamber had been created in the midst of the wood, made of boughs and branches and covered with flowers and sweet herbs. Songbirds had been loosed within it, and long tables were laid for a feast.

"Sir," Robin Hood told the king, "outlaws' breakfast is venison, and therefore you must be content with such fare as we use." Henry and Katherine sat down to eat, and the others joined them, served with venison and wine by the archers and serenaded by flute and organ music and songs sung to the lute.

As the banquet progressed Henry came over to Pasqualigo and addressed him familiarly in French.

"Talk with me awhile!" he said good-naturedly. The ambassador had recently been at the French court, where Henry's old enemy Louis XII had died and a new, young king—Francis I—had come to the throne. Courtiers were comparing the handsome, athletic Francis very favorably to his brother monarch of England; he was younger, and if anything even more avid for the hunt, the joust and the battlefield. Henry wanted to assure himself that his pre-eminence in personal magnificence among the European sovereigns had not been challenged.

"The king of France," he asked Pasqualigo, "is he as tall as I am?"

The ambassador answered tactfully that there was little difference in their heights.

"Is he as stout?"

Again the ambassador replied that Francis' girth was less than Henry's.

The king grew more insistent. "What sort of legs has he?" Here the ambassador ambiguously conceded Henry's advantage, calling Francis' legs "spare." At this, Henry tore open his doublet to expose his tight-fitting hose and slapped his thigh. "Look here!" he asserted. "I also have a good calf to my leg!"

Henry talked expansively on, assuring Pasqualigo that he was "very fond" of Francis and that he regretted not having seen him when he was campaigning in France two years earlier. He had come very close to encountering him three times, Henry added, but Francis "never would allow himself to be seen, and always retreated." Having insulted his rival's courage the king went on to tell the Venetian the entire story of his campaign in detail, leaving out nothing that pertained to his glory, before rejoining Katherine and the others.[2]

In comparing the two sovereigns in Henry's presence Pasqualigo spoke with guarded tact. When writing to the Venetian Signory, however, he allowed his sincere admiration for Henry free rein. "His majesty is the handsomest potentate I ever set eyes on," he stated simply. He is "above the usual height, with an extremely fine calf to his leg, his complexion very fair and bright, with auburn hair combed straight and short, in the French fashion, and a round face so very beautiful, that it would become a pretty woman, his throat being rather long and thick." He had seen all the kings in Christendom, Pasqualigo concluded, and so had grounds for comparison. Henry stood out among them all.[3]

The Venetian had formed this impression when he first saw the king at Richmond a week or so earlier. It was Saint George's Day, the day when the Garter Knights were installed and the order's anniversary celebrated. The court was at its most splendid and solemn, and when the ambassadors arrived they were ushered into the royal presence through room after room of gorgeous display. Each chamber they entered was hung with richer tapestries than the one before, the shadowed texture of the hangings highlighted by gold and silver threads. Halbardiers of the king's bodyguard lined the way, armed with pikes and wearing silver breastplates. They had been chosen for their height; "and, by God," Pasqualigo wrote, "they were all as big as giants."

Finally they entered the throne room, where the notables of the court had taken their places around the king as if posed for a portrait. Ranged along an aisle leading to the throne were dozens of noble men and women in cloth of gold and silk. Ten heralds wearing the arms of England on their gold tabards and six officers bearing golden scepters surrounded the king, while to his right were eight of his fellow Garter Knights and to his left a number of bishops in their linen rochets and miters. The king stood under a heavily embroidered canopy of golden cloth—"the most costly thing I ever witnessed," Pasqualigo said—leaning casually against his gilded throne. He was dressed in his Garter robes, his slashed hose and striped doublet in tones of scarlet and crimson and white. A purple velvet mantle girt with a thick rope of gold hung from his shoulders and ended in a train four yards long. His ornaments were a dagger, a gold collar with a round cut diamond, "the size of the largest walnut I ever saw," Pasqualigo noted, a necklace with a pendant Saint George in diamonds, and his garter of knighthood. His fingers, the Venetian wrote, "were one mass of jeweled rings."[4]

After the May Day banquet of venison on Shooter's Hill huge pasteboard figures representing the giants Gog and Magog were brought out and placed on wheeled cars. Another car held Lady May and Lady Flora, who sang duets to the king before joining the long parade back to the palace at Greenwich. The guardsmen led the way, after them the decorated cars and musicians "sounding the trumpets and other instruments," and then the king bringing up the rear "in as great state as possible," an observer recorded, "being followed by the queen, with such a crowd on foot, as to exceed, I think, twenty-five thousand persons."[5] Not twenty-five, but several thousand persons may well have followed Henry back to Greenwich that day, jumping and straining to catch a glimpse of the tall king in his Lincoln green on his capering horse.

It is likely many in this crowd were palace servants. The life of the royal court was sustained by a shifting, conglomerate population of serving men and women thrown together into a tiny kingdom of their own. They staffed the enormous assemblage of coordinated operations that made up the royal household. Taken separately, each function in the aggregate was an extension of a personal service done for the king himself—cooking his food, looking after his clothes, his furnishings, his family, his entertainments and his treasure. But because the king lived magnificently, and because his person was the focus of a crowd of attendants, officials, suitors and bearers of public business, serving him became a colossal task to be divided among some five hundred ushers, yeomen, grooms and their servants.

Below the principal household offices of steward, treasurer, and comptroller were the heads of the major categories of service. The gentlemen ushers saw to it that the rooms and halls of the palace were cleaned and properly furnished, walking through every chamber early in the morning and ordering fresh rushes here, a carpet there, a fire laid or a warming brazier provided. When the king stayed as a guest in a noble-man's house—as he often did when hunting, or on progress—it was the duty of one of the gentlemen ushers to go before him and make certain the roofs and floors of the strange house were strong and sure, that no rain could leak into his bedchamber, and that any back doors were locked or boarded shut. The assigning of rooms was of special importance to Henry; it was the responsibility of his gentlemen ushers to see that none but his preferred companions had the rooms below his bedchamber. Gentlemen ushers also allotted quarters to the servants, two to a bed (always "a gentleman with a gentleman and a yeoman with a yeoman"), and were in charge of arranging meals at the times the king requested.

Ordering meals meant, first, notifying the ewerer of the character of each meal and the number to be served, so that he could have the table laid with either fine damask or diaper table linen or plain canvas or holland cloth. Next came a meeting with the sewer, who arranged the dishes at the table, and the carver, who cut the meat; both were "armed" with their towels of office, the sewer's around his neck and the carver's around neck and arm, baldric-wise. Finally the gentlemen ushers watched to make certain the seating arrangement was perfect, with the king seated exactly in the middle of the table, "a little above the salt, his face being to the whole view of the chamber," and the other diners ranged in rank on either side, their importance indicated by their nearness or distance from the towering gold saltcellar that sat beside their lord.

Between five hundred and a thousand people ate from King Henry's bounty every day; on special occasions the number could rise to fifteen hundred. Feeding them required nearly as much planning, provisioning and scheduling as feeding an army on campaign. Try as they might, though, the household officers could make only an approximate estimate of how much food would be needed. When the vast hall or great chamber was filled for dinner or supper, and the diners removed their caps to shouts of "Room for the sewer!" as the dishes were brought in, there were nearly always more mouths to be fed than anyone had foreseen. Idlers and vagabonds usurped the places laid for court officials and visiting nobles. Thieving servants reduced the available portions still further, and the dogs which made off with scraps from the alms tubs that held the leavings of the meal occasionally took food from the tables as well. Grooms armed with whips and bells patrolled the dining hall in vain in an effort "to fear them away withal," but there were too many; courtiers often brought their hunting dogs with them when they attended on the king, and the sound of their snarling and fighting with the pets and mongrels of the palace was a familiar annoyance at dinner and supper.

Large quantities of food and other stores were kept in readiness for the needs of the cooks and kitchen staff. Perishables such as fresh meat, fish, poultry, cheese, vegetables and eggs were stored in the acatery, a general storehouse for the foodstuffs bought daily at the palace gates by the clerk of the market. Non-perishable foods were bought in much larger quantities a few times a year, thousands of bushels of wheat at Michaelmas, dozens of barrels of oil, honey, and salted meat and fish, verjuice and vinegar, brewed liquor and spices—hundreds of pounds of pepper, ginger, cinnamon, nutmeg and "grains of paradise." These, along with many cauldrons of sea coal and charcoal, stacks upon stacks of logs and kindling, thousands of pounds of candlewax and yards of cloth, were stored in the bakehouse, brewhouse, buttery and scullery and a dozen other household departments.

Beyond the servants and officers of the household itself there were falconers, huntsmen, fewterers to keep the greyhounds, rat men and mole men to control house and garden pests. Aveners and squires and ordinary stableboys fed and brushed the king's horses, farriers shod them, and a special category of "the king's riding boys," or "boys which run the king's geldings" exercised them. Particular keepers were assigned to each of Henry's favorite horses. A large complement of laborers of many kinds—carpenters, bricklayers, joiners, plumbers, plasterers and masons—were kept constantly employed in building and repairing the palaces, while a crew of gardeners and women listed in the account books as "weeders in the king's garden" kept up their grounds. Still another group of servants attended to the moving of the highly itinerant household from one palace to another. Furniture, kitchenware and other heavy fixtures were not transported, but all personal effects were. Hundreds of chests were packed for each removal, loaded onto carts or strapped to the backs of horses or mules tended by sumptermen with specialized functions. Moving the queen's goods alone required, in addition to saddlers, yeomen of the litter, gentlemen of the "chair" and yeomen of the "close chair," an array of sumptermen for the bottles, beds, robes, and closet.

A high proportion of the household staff was occupied with personal service to the king. Yeomen of the chamber made the fire in his bedchamber and cleaned his chamber pot. Yeomen of the ewery supplied his chambers with basins and candlesticks; yeomen of the wardrobe looked after his bed furnishings, replacing the decorative quilts on his bed with warmer furs or "Irish rugs" at night. His plume-maker, Gerrard Van Arcle, ornamented his hats and his armor. His laundress Ann Harris took charge of the two chests kept in his chamber, "the one to keep the clean stuff, the other to keep the stuff that has been occupied," and provided the sweet herbs needed to keep the clothing entrusted to her freshsmelling. Caring for the king's clothing was a full-time task for a staff of skilled wardrobe servants. The wardrobe itself was equipped with racks, trunks, presses, brushing tables and a variety of covering- and carryingcloths to protect the costly garments. Wardrobe servants had to be able to look after the dozen or so kinds of velvet used by the royal tailors, and had to know how to brush up the raised pile on the cut brocades and how to treat the precious cloth of gold and silver. Folding and "laying up" doublets and robes was an art in itself, and moving the entire elaborate operation from one palace to another took many hours of preparation.

The king's day began when his pages, who had already dressed and eaten, entered his apartment at seven o'clock to bring firewood. They woke the esquires of the body, two of whom slept on straw pallets in the "pallet chamber" outside the king's bedchamber itself. The esquires then dressed and presented themselves at the bedchamber door at eight. A yeoman usher took up his station there to keep out everyone but the esquires and gentlemen of the privy chamber. Then, one by one, the royal garments appeared, brought to the bedchamber door by the yeoman of the wardrobe, received at the door by a groom of the chamber, handed through the door to one of the six gentlemen of the chamber who passed them to the other five in turn and finally given to the king.

The men privileged to serve in the privy chamber had a responsible yet delicate office. They had to have the reverence and sensitivity to wait on their master's intimate needs while keeping "a convenient distance from the king's person, without too homely or too boldly advancing themselves thereto." They needed to have a "vigilant and a reverend respect and eye to his Majesty, so that by his look or countenance they may know what lacketh or is his pleasure to be had or done." While he was present they had to anticipate his every wish; in his absence they guarded his rooms, keeping strangers out and passing the long hours until his return in dicing and gossiping. With his going and coming their sole focus of attention inevitably they speculated—perhaps even wagered—on his activities, much to his annoyance. Henry complained that his chamber men were given to inquiring where he was, where he intended going, and how long he meant to stay, mumbling about his pastimes and shaking their heads over the late hours he kept.[6]

In the evening, whether he was present or not, his bed was made with extraordinary ceremony. The exacting ritual called for a yeoman or groom of the wardrobe to bring in the clean sheets, pillows and blankets. Then, with gentlemen ushers holding the curtains at the sides and foot of the bed out of the way, two esquires of the body took their places at both sides as a yeoman leaped onto the bed and "rolled him up and down" to try out the straw, incidentally making certain there were no weapons concealed in it to the king's harm. Next the featherbed was laid on, and beaten well, then a yeoman placed the first blanket on the bed, and the esquires smoothed it and tucked it in, "laying it straight upon the bed without any wrinkles." The same procedure was followed with several more layers of sheets and blankets, and coverings of marten and ermine, and then, the bed turned down, the yeomen took the pillows, fluffed them, and tossed them to the esquires to set in place. Finally a gentleman usher closed the bedcurtains and an esquire sprinkled them with holy water, and the whole group retired to a corner of the room to reward themselves with bread, ale and wine.

The household thrived on such rituals, and on minute differentiations of function. Each servant knew exactly where his or her duties began and ended, and if those limits were not observed, conflicts arose. The yeomen in waiting knew well that they were to appear, their livery well ordered and their persons clean and groomed, at the door of the king's great chamber at seven o'clock each morning to relieve their counterparts who had the night watch. They knew that persons who insisted on seeing the king or bringing him messages were to be referred to the huissiers, who would relay the information to the chamberlain, who would pass it on to the king. They understood their obligations to summon the carver and sewer, to serve at supper when needed, to bring the king torches, or water to wash his hands if necessary, and to carry his messages. And if theirs was the night watch, they expected to remain alert throughout the night, listening for suspicious noises, ejecting suspicious persons, and guarding against the sudden fires that flared up in candlelit bedrooms and menaced the wooden interiors of the palace.

Service to the king or queen was both an honor and an opportunity for enrichment. The men who dressed the king and held the basin and napkin in which he washed and dried his hands at dinner were all lords and gentlemen with household servants of their own. The king's yeomen, grooms and pages served in hope of earning preferment in the ladder of service and, eventually, the reward of lands and modest titles. To be sure, service had its ugly side. A sixteenth-century proverb advised all servants to cultivate "an ass's back, a pig's snout, and a cow's ears"—an ass's back to bear the burden of constant hard work, a pig's snout to be able to eat cold leftovers and sour wine, and a cow's ears to be oblivious to the master's abuse.

And if the gentlefolk who held the more important posts in the household would have resented this treatment, the hundreds of menials below them had never known any other. As a group, they had not been bred to civility. They had to be taught how to behave in polite company—how to stand quietly in attendance without clutching at their backs or heads as if after a flea, without picking their noses or blowing them loudly into their sleeves, without spitting, belching, "clawing their cods" or "casting stinking breath" on their lords. They had to learn how to keep their faces set in an expression of agreeable repose, without gaping or pouting or "squirting with their mouths," while cultivating a soft voice and a quiet tread. Once these lessons were mastered advancement in the household was assured. Longtime servants could even become loved and cherished friends. John Colet, a humanist at Henry's court, told a friend how he was called to his mother's country house to console her in her extreme grief. A serving man whom she had loved like a son had just died; it was weeks before she was restored to herself again.[7]

The affection of a kind mistress was only one compensation for faithful service. Discards and valuable scraps were always the perquisites of servants. The yeomen of the horse were given old saddles and bridles; huntsmen were allotted the skins of beasts killed in the hunt; wine lees and empty casks went to the yeomen of the cellar, and candle ends to the yeomen of the ewery. In the kitchen, the clerks were allowed to take the heads and skins of lambs and calves, and the grooms and children who turned the spits shared the bones, necks and giblets of fowl and the savory drippings from roast meat.

If Henry's palace officers and servants recognized the benefits to be gained from faithful observance of their duties, they were also quick to sense that the young king was inclined to be a lax taskmaster where his household was concerned. For if he often insisted on decorum in his surroundings, and had immense personal dignity, he also liked noise and uproar. He liked the constant coming and going of retainers and messengers; he liked crowds. There is good evidence that during the earliest years of his reign his court was a bedlam.[8]

The strict rules of service were sometimes kept, sometimes flouted. The good order to be observed on the king's arising was ignored. The esquires who slept in the pallet chamber refused to get up on time, and snored on until long after the energetic king was dressed and gone. People of every description burst in on Henry in his private bedchamber, asking for favors, complaining of injustices and simply urging recognition of their charm and merits. In the corridors and galleries of the palace servants of the nobles who lived at court or came there on business crowded one another and started fights, and the king's own retainers, overburdened and insulted, grew careless in their work and surly to one another.

Large retinues were the most obvious index of status, and every great personage who came to court brought with him as many servants as he could, complete with wardrobe chests, liveries, cartloads of baggage and horses for travel, hunting and the tilt. Some gentlemen brought not only their hounds but their hawks and caged ferrets, and filled their rooms with hunting gear and rabbit nets. They seemed determined to extort from the king every conceivable advantage due to their station. They squandered his food, especially his wines and ale. They used up his firewood and candles at a tremendous rate, and brought in their relatives and retainers to dine at his table uninvited. When they went with him to his country hunting lodges they trampled all the planted fields in the neighborhood and took the best fish in all the ponds. And when they left the steward complained that they had taken with them tables, cupboards, trestles and forms, and even the locks off the doors.

Among the worst abuses of court demeanor was that the courtiers were not satisfied to make use of their salaried underlings, but gave tips and odd jobs to a rabble of hangers-on who held horses, carried loads, delivered messages and fetched things from shops and inns outside the palace gates. Every smartly-dressed groom or guardsman was followed by a pack of little boys eager to touch his velvet coat or hold his poleaxe or run his errands. The men of Henry's personal guard, their numbers swollen by the recent military campaign, now jostled for space at the already overcrowded court. Some three hundred strong, they lounged and joked and quarreled throughout the palace when they were not standing at attendance in the great chamber, and each of them had several meanly-dressed attendants who slept at his feet and cleaned his boots. These, and the "vagabonds and vile persons" who enticed, accosted and occasionally robbed servants by offering to supply them with stolen goods or women, added to the existing "annoyance, infection and confusion" of court life and were left behind to cause trouble whenever the court moved.

Regulating vice and petty criminality was the duty of the marshal and provost marshals, who rode herd on the "vile persons"—beggars, cutpurses, drunkards, prostitutes—who followed the king's household. Misbehaving servants too were brought before them: those absent from court for too long, those who were caught repeatedly wiping their hands on the tapestries, or carelessly laying dirty dishes down on the embroidered bedcoverings, or boys caught drawing huge phalluses on the walls. Swearing, fighting, drunkenness or "haunting bad houses" were punishable by public humiliation, loss of wages, or possible dismissal. The marshal could imprison any household employee who committed a more serious crime, but most wrongdoing could be kept under control by less drastic measures. Stealing food could be prevented by ordering the yeomen and grooms to serve without their cloaks; stripped to their coats, they were "the easier to be seen if they carried forth any meat that they ought not to do."

In 1525, when Henry was thirty-four, he tried to take firmer control of the uncontrollable population of his court. Ordinances drawn up in that year referred to the "abuses" which had "crept up in his household" during his wars, which, "now that peace is established, he was determined to reform." The vice-chamberlain and others were hereafter to aid the marshal in assuring the "sufficiency and demeanor" of all servants; only "honest persons of good stature, gesture and behavior" were to be tolerated. Disobedience and incompetence were to be severely punished, with incorrigibles ordered to leave the palace at once. To prevent the "insufferable disorders" of the past, limits were put on the numbers of retainers visiting nobles could bring with them, and the king's guardsmen, also reduced in numbers, were forbidden to keep servants of their own. All animals but ladies' spaniels were outlawed, and the motley corps of boys and vagabonds were to be kept outside the court gate.

The ordinances were issued, read and, perhaps, enforced. Or perhaps they stood as sterile embodiments of the royal will, noted or ignored at random by each of the men and women who served the king.

14

To spend the daye with merry cheare,
To drinke and revell every night,
To card and dice from eve to morne,
It was, I ween, his hearts delighte.

To ride, to runne, to rant, to roare,
To always spend and never spare,
I wott, an' it were the king himselfe,
Of gold and fee he mote be bare.

"WITHIN the past few days," the Venetian ambassador wrote to his superiors in May of 1519, "King Henry has made a great change in his court." He had dismissed some of his chief companions, "who had enjoyed very great authority in the kingdom, and had been the very soul of the king." Other officials had also been replaced by older, more experienced men. The incident was thought to be as vitally important as any that had taken place for many years, and as soon as the news became known all the ambassadors scurried to their usual sources of court gossip to try to uncover its deeper meaning.

Dionysius Memo, Henry's favorite performer and close friend, told the Venetian ambassador that the courtiers were sent away because they had become partisans of the French and of French ways during their recent embassy to the court of Francis I. The same view prevailed at the French court itself. The French ambassador in England, relying in part on information from compatriots who were hostages at the English court and much in favor with the king, was convinced that Wolsey was behind the dismissals; Wolsey feared the power that Henry's intimates had over him, the hostages said, and thought they might use it to his detriment. That the men who replaced the ousted favorites were Wolsey's men lent weight to this view, but there was a third conjecture. The septuagenarian Thomas Howard, created duke of Norfolk for his valor at Flodden, offered the explanation that the favored courtiers had led their master into incessant gambling which left him thousands of pounds poorer. "Resolving to lead a new life," Norfolk maintained, Henry had put them from him.[1]

According to the chronicler Hall, the six men—Francis Bryan, Nicholas Carew, John Pechy, Edward Poyntz, Edward Neville and Henry Guildford—were guilty of nothing more than overexuberant playfulness.[2] "Not regarding his estate nor degree," they were "so familiar and

103

homely" with the king that they forgot who they were, and who he was. They failed to observe that deferential remoteness that served as a barrier between the anointed monarch and ordinary mortals. They behaved, in fact, the way they had at the French court, where every day King Francis had ridden with them through the streets of Paris, throwing eggs and stones and other things at his long-suffering subjects. In France they learned to admire French food, French wine, French gowns and French women; when they returned to England "they were all French," and found everything English, including their sovereign, ludicrously inadequate. Henry endured their disrespect patiently, Hall wrote, until his Council implored him to put an end to these "enormities and lightness." Then he gave his councilors permission to banish the six from court—which "grieved sore the hearts of these young men, which were called the king's minions."

In itself the banishment of Bryan, Carew and the others was of only passing interest. All six were back at court within a year or so, and none permanently lost his standing with the king. But the excited reaction of court observers and the explanations advanced to account for the event are of the greatest interest, for they reveal the power that went with personal attendance on the king, and the difficulty of unriddling the shifting images of that power in the records of contemporaries.

The court was a shadow-world of hidden motives, ambiguous gestures and elusive confrontations. Personal jealousies and rivalries took subtle forms; illusions of deference and domination, of calculation and ingenuousness were everywhere. The king, his nobles and officials were like carved pieces on a chessboard, their moves and countermoves forming an intricate puzzle often unfathomable to outsiders. Thus where the Venetian diplomat saw shrewd political awareness in the banished "minions" the chronicler perceived only puerile misbehavior. The royal councilors were dismayed by what they looked on as rowdy impropriety in the young men, while the French laid everything to the charge of the man they most feared and respected at court, Wolsey. These shifting views make it hard to see the king clearly amid the circles of his courtiers in the first decade of his reign.

He was perhaps fondest of his minions, the dozen or so boon companions who made it easiest for him to forget he was a king. Of the six who were temporarily exiled, Poyntz and Pechy—the latter a knight in whose hunting parks Katherine loved to ride and hunt—appear infrequently in the records. Henry Guildford was both controller and master of the revels, much sought out by Henry and Katherine for the fairytale entertainments he designed and produced. With the tall, athletic Edward Neville Henry felt the shared bond of royal blood. Neville was of the Plantagenet line, like the Courtenays and de la Poles; though he and Henry were only distantly related they closely resembled one another, not only in height and build but in facial appearance as well. Having Neville at Henry's side was like having a twin brother, and the resemblance was put to good use to baffle the court at disguisings and other entertainments. Beyond this the king, with whom exact gradations of nobility counted very much, thought of Neville as a particularly suitable as well as enjoyable companion for his leisure hours, and suitable too to fill the high office of sewer.[3]

Nicholas Carew and Francis Bryan came to prominence as "young gentlemen" whom Henry chose to "set forth" and encourage in feats of arms by lending them horses and armor in the spring of 1515. Bryan went on to become a very capable jouster, Carew an extraordinary one, and the ties between them were strengthened when Carew married Bryan's sister Elizabeth. Both men were to enjoy long careers in the royal service, Carew as a soldier and Bryan as a cipherer, trusted diplomatic envoy and eventually ambassador to France. A clever, versatile and eagerly dissolute man, Bryan looked like a pirate; he had lost an eye in a tilting match, and wore an eyepatch to hide it. He had in fact been at sea, serving under Admiral Thomas Howard in the *Margaret Bonaventure* in 1513, and this combined with his skill at the tilt made him very popular with Henry. More than any of the other minions Bryan knew the art of retaining the king's favor, altering his loyalties as his master did and never allowing friendship or family ties to bring him into conflict with the king. He kept himself constantly at Henry's side, playing shovel board, bowls, primero and tennis with him while at the same time carrying out his duties as cupbearer, gentleman of the bedchamber and master of the toils. Bryan was a poet as well, an admirer of Erasmus and a chosen companion of Wyatt and later of Surrey—in short, a many-sided, highly capable man like the king himself, though without the king's charisma or brilliance.

Others in the privileged circle of Henry's companions included Henry Norris, gentleman waiter and, in these years, the only man permitted to enter the royal bedchamber, and William Compton, once Henry's page and since risen to become, among a variety of offices and appointments, chief gentleman of the bedchamber and "usher of the black rod" at Windsor Castle. Knighted for his service in the campaign of 1513, Compton had begun to amass a large fortune, though his bid to gain the hand and wealth of the widowed Margaret Pole, countess of Salisbury, was unsuccessful. Compton was thought to have great influence with Henry in the earliest years of his reign. The Venetians, the French and representatives of papal interests in England all showered pensions and valuable gifts on him, and he was certainly noteworthy for the stature of his enemies. Wolsey was his rival, and Queen Katherine and the duke of Buckingham still resented him for his role in the affair of Anne Stafford. Buckingham too was frequently at Henry's side, though much less frequently than Compton. The duke's popularity, coupled with his fierce pride in his royal ancestry, made the king wary; it was said that if Henry died without a male heir Buckingham might easily take the throne.[4]

These were the leading favorites, though there were background figures around the king waiting for fate or luck to cast them within his chosen circle: Thomas Boleyn, William Brereton, Henry's cousin Henry Pole, Henry and Anthony Knevet, Thomas and William Parr. All held enviable court offices, and lacked only the right opportunity to bring them into prominence. Then too there were the transient favorites such as the duc de Longueville, lodged elegantly in the Tower along with his personal retinue of six attendants ever since his capture at the Battle of the Spurs. Another group of Frenchmen—the young and spirited hostages sent to England as pledges of Francis' good faith—found themselves constantly in Henry's company for as long as their visit lasted. And there were passing infatuations such as the king's great delight in a young lutenist brought to court by Memo in 1517. Henry could not hear the boy play often enough, and "never wearied of listening to him"; until the king's amazement at his skill wore off all the other lutenists were thrown into the shade.[5]

These chosen companions were at the heart of the larger society of the court. The members of that society were drawn to the palace by obligations of service and rank, by political interests, family attachments and simple ambition, by a love of finery and gluttony and spectacle. Whatever their own motives, however, the courtiers existed primarily to serve particular functions for the king. They kept him company. They served as a vast pool of companionable associates, always eager to accompany him anywhere, to be his playfellows, partisans or friendly rivals in any of a dozen pastimes. They hunted with him in summer and fall, rising before dawn and joining him in the fields by five, then riding by his side until nine or ten at night. They kept up with him largely without complaint, though the exhausting regimen led some to sigh in agreement with Wolsey's humanist secretary Richard Pace that Henry "spared no pains to convert the sport of hunting into a martyrdom." They kept themselves in readiness to follow his every whim—to shoot, to run races, even to slip away from court, if invited, to join the king in a distant residence and share his solitude. He seldom craved solitude, though; more often he relished a great concourse of people to share his amusements and to serve as occasional targets of his bemused silliness. At banquets many hours long, when there was no dancing or music-making or masking to divert his boredom, he entertained himself by throwing sugarplums and comfits at his guests.[6]

Banqueting at the court of Henry VIII was of gargantuan proportions. Nowhere was the food so plentiful and varied as in England. It was said English stomachs had need of more food than others, and the distinctive English habit of shameless belching at table was eloquent testimony to their capacity. Sumptuary laws passed in 1517 limited the number of courses a great noble or churchman could serve his hundreds of guests to seven or fewer, but as each course called for perhaps a dozen dishes, restraint was easily mistaken for excess. And the king himself was exempt from these restrictions. In one day of feasting his courtiers consumed eleven entire carcasses of beef, six sheep, seventeen hogs and pigs, forty-five dozen chickens, fifteen swans, six cranes, thirty-two dozen pigeons and fifty-four dozen larks, nearly six dozen geese and four peacocks. Three thousand pears and thirteen hundred apples went to flavor the meat and fowl, while the bakers provided three thousand loaves of bread and the buttery nearly four hundred dishes of butter.[7]

Each of the dishes at a royal banquet was brought before the king in a setting of unparalleled magnificence, amid displays of gold and silver plate that not only conveyed an impression of wealth but served as a dazzling source of illumination. Candles were often set in the center of silver plates hung along the walls; the reflected light blazed out over the diners and shone on the dishes and goblets and cutlery. The heaping trays of meat and fish were served according to a strict order and following culinary and gastronomic traditions centuries old. First the sewer and his assistants brought in the large, whole-footed birds such as swans, geese and drakes, then the smaller birds, then baked meats and fish in their proper order, then fruit and sweets. Apprentice serving men memorized the names and serving order of hundreds of dishes, a task made complicated by the variety of names used for a single creature at different stages of its growth. Among fish, conger eels were called such only at maturity; if caught very young they were called griggs or sniggs; if half-grown, scafflings. Youthful sparlings were sprats, baby cods whitings; shrimps grew into sprawns and eventually into crevices.[8]

Once the names were mastered, complex carving techniques had to be learned—which portions of each animal were to be discarded as inedible and which were delicacies. A skilled carver learned to slice brawn, splat a pike, unbrace a mallard and barb a lobster. He had to know that bitterns were not carved like turtledoves or plovers, and that there was a correct sauce for every meat—garlic for beef and goose, ginger for fawn, salt and cinnamon for woodcock and thrush, verjuice for veal and mullet, exotic sauces of amber, musk and rosewater for other dishes. With elegant meals a commonplace the demand for greater and greater delicacies grew. The royal cooks prepared minnows, sea-hogs (porpoises), green, dried or marinated neat's tongue, calves' heads and mugget (veal's entrails made into a pie). They salted the sweet-smelling livers of sturgeons and dolphins, and crowned their banquets with carefully spiced whale meat, whaleflesh being known as the "hardest" and most unusual of all foods.[9]

Between courses came pageantry in food. Subtleties—confectionery miniatures sculpted in sugar and wax—were made in the shape of figures, buildings, even elaborate natural landscapes, and were set in the middle of the table to round off each segment of the endless feasting. Often they were biblical: Gabriel greeting Mary, an angel announcing Jesus' birth to three shepherds, wise men from the East bringing gifts. Some were classical or literary, as with one cake made to resemble a mountain from which a poet emerged to recite verses. Others were metaphorical. At one English banquet four subtleties represented the four seasons and ages of mankind: the age of pleasure (a young man called spring, playing the pipes on a cloud), the age of quarreling (a man of war called summer, red-faced and angry), the age of melancholy (a tired man with a sickle, called harvest), and the age of aches and troubles (a gray-haired old man called winter, sitting on a stone).[10]

Wines in endless variety washed down every course and dish. By the end of the sixteenth century more than five dozen kinds of "small wines"—French and Rhenish—were known in England, and nearly as many sweet wines. All were new, harsh and very heady, but the courtiers drank copiously, disregarding the warning of physicians that too much wine made for black teeth, sagging cheeks and sodden brains. The English of Henry's time were especially fond of sugared wine—believed to be an aphrodisiac—and of dessert wines such as malmsey and hippocras, mixed with honey and spices. Named, according to one fifteenth-century writer, for the spice bag called ''Hippocrates' sleeve'' with which it was flavored, hippocras was a tempting blend of red wine spiced with cinnamon, ginger and sugar or sugar candy, strained through a fine cloth and served with wafers.[11] When the feasting was over and the last of the scraps had been distributed among the servants, the food dealers and the alms tub, the weary courtiers took to bed a thick warming posset of sugared ale curdled with hot milk, eggs and grated biscuit.

Henry was very partial to banquets on shipboard. In 1515 he launched a new galley, the *Virgin Mary,* named in honor of his sister. It amused him to play the role of ship's master that day, striding the decks in a sailor's coat and trousers made from cloth of gold. Ruthal, bishop of Durham, hallowed the ship with a mass and Princess Mary christened it, but the king attracted more attention than either of them. Engraved on the broad gold chain he wore around his neck was the device *''Dieu est mon droit,''* an altered version of his motto, and attached to the chain was a large whistle whose shrill blasts sounded almost as loud as a trumpet. The king blew his whistle again and again as he showed his guests the great brass and iron guns the ship carried and led them around her capacious decks built to hold a thousand fighting men.[12]

Knowing his liking for dining on shipboard the Venetian ambassador entertained Henry and his attendants aboard his city's flagship in 1518. Some three hundred courtiers were rowed out to the galley in little boats, and came aboard to find the decks transformed into a banqueting hall complete with a raised platform for the king and four rows of long tables for the other diners. Tapestries and silks were hung from the masts, and the tables held an abundance of sponge cakes and other confections and wine served in goblets of Venetian glass. The cleverness of the arrangements led Henry to praise the captain and masters again and again, and the unique entertainment that followed the feasting caused even more comment. Sailors appeared high above the heads of the courtiers, hanging from slack ropes suspended from the mast; they turned and twisted in the air, entangling and disentangling themselves in the rigging and performing amazing feats of balance and acrobatics. Though the banquet was a great success what interested Henry most was the galley's artillery. The next day he returned and asked to have all the guns fired one by one, watching each to note its range and trajectory and praising the gunners' skill.[13]

Henry's courtiers were constantly called upon to wager with him. Bets were made on everything from wrestling matches to tournaments, and every gentleman or lady was expected to have the courage to play coolly for high stakes. The knight marshal of the household took charge of the official wagering that accompanied jousts and other competitions, and sent the king dice and cards in a ''fair silver bowl'' when he called for them. Fortunes changed hands at the king's gambling tables. The privy purse accounts list hundreds of pounds lost from day to day, and thousands allotted for "playing money" in general.[14] But the wagering was not confined to games of chance. Because of the betting that accompanied it tennis was condemned by the cautious as "dangerous for the body and for the purse"; indeed the excitement of risk was added to every courtly pastime. Buckingham's day-to-day losses in 1519 included sums of fifteen and forty pounds lost at dice to his brother and Lord Montague, fifty-one pounds lost "to Suffolk and others since coming to the king," another thirty-one lost to Suffolk at shooting and fourteen "lost to the king at tennis" and seventy-six pounds lost at dice "in my new place with the duke of Suffolk and the Frenchmen."[15] Sums an ordinary householder would have thought princely were casually gambled away in an hour's leisure; according to Giustiniani, the amounts the king himself risked were incalculably higher, reaching six to eight thousand ducats in a single day. Henry could not after all allow his nobles to appear to be wealthier or less concerned about their losses than he was, with the result that he made himself an easy mark for the really skilled gamblers among his gentlemen and for the professional gamesters they brought to court to cheat him.

In the second year of his reign Henry was reportedly "much enticed to play at tennis and at dice, which appetite, certain crafty persons about him perceiving, brought in Frenchmen and Lombards, to make wagers with him, and so he lost much money."[16] He eventually saw what was happening and drove the cheaters out, or so he thought, but there were others to take their place. London was said to be full of professional gamblers; there were "half an army" of dicers alone, a contemporary wrote. Their trade flourished. Boundlessly wealthy, they dressed splendidly, "always shining like blazing stars in their apparel." They spent their days despoiling naïve noblemen of their inheritances, their nights in the company of prostitutes and tavern keepers.

The best among them were masters of an art as "complex and perfected" as any in the medieval trivium or quadrivium. Equipped with false dice which always rolled high or low (provided, for a fee, by prisoners in the King's Bench or the Marshalsea), or with an accomplice who posed as an onlooker and betrayed the victim's card hands by signs, the expert chose a target and, in time, took all he had. Even the most suspicious player, who was on the lookout for cards marked with fine spots of ink or nicked at the corners, or for weighted dice, could be outwitted. Wary of playing another man's game, he could be beaten easily at his own, where he had the reckless confidence to wager "God's cope" itself. Careful not to let anyone he suspected see his hand, he could be cheated by a female accomplice sitting demurely beside him and sewing; by the speed of her needle she signaled his cards to her associate.[17]

Henry's attempts to rid his court of gamblers only led them to seek dupes elsewhere in his domains. In 1514 three such men, Peter Roy, Peter le Negro and Bartholomew Costopolegrino, were accused at Calais of cheating at cards and dice. In denying the charge they tried to establish their good reputations by assuring their accusers that they had played with many noblemen in England—a claim that may well have led to further charges.[18] Of course, not all card and dice play meant gambling; some was for fortunetelling. Playing cards could be used to predict the future, with the numbers on the cards corresponding to good or ill luck and the picture cards read according to their color symbolism. Dice were cast to make predictions too, and especially to foretell the future in matters of love.

If the courtiers were expected to keep Henry company and to share his amusements they were also an appreciative audience for his performances. They listened attentively while he sang and showed his virtuosity on the virginal, recorder, gitteron-pipe, lute-pipe, cornet and organ. They applauded his informal concerts on the organ and harpsichord—instruments he was said to practice on day and night. They sang the melodies he wrote to French verses about sorrowful partings, lovers' sufferings, and true love and overlooked the awkward rhymes he wrote himself:

> The daise delectable,
> The violett wan and blo;
> Ye ar not varyable;
> I love you and no mo.
>
> I make you fast and sure;
> It ys to me gret payne
> Thus longe to endure,
> Tyll that we mete agayne.

They were proud of his skill as an amateur composer whose best-known song, "Pastime with Good Company," became a popular classic. His songs were sung in inns and alehouses as well as at court, and preachers incorporated them into their sermons. In 1521 servants in the royal household heard the king's almoner speak, taking as his text "Pastime" and another of Henry's songs, "I love unloved." His masses and motets, no worse than many others written by professional musicians, were sung in his chapel and elsewhere, and his instrumental music was played at banquets and as an accompaniment to court pageantry.

In Henry's time music went with every significant event and many mundane ones; in the intervals between events it filled the hours of idleness. A German traveler to England in Henry's childhood was delighted at the musical receptions he was given everywhere he went. When he stopped at an inn for the night invariably the host or hostess would come out into the street to welcome him, accompanied by the entire household, all of them singing as they approached.[19] At court the king's bands—shalms and oboes for outdoor entertainments, lutes, rebecs and pipes for indoors—played for many hours each day. The children of the Chapel Royal sang at the frequent daily masses and for vespers and compline when required. The pre-eminence of his choral musicians was important to Henry; when he suspected that Wolsey's choirboys were more capable than his own, he pointedly complained of the fact to his choirmaster William Cornish, with the result that "young Robin," one of Wolsey's best singers, thereafter lent his "sure and cleanly singing" and "good and crafty descant" to the royal choir.[20]

Of course, the king's virtuosi had no rivals: Blind More, his principal harper who recited long poems of "old adventures" in the medieval fashion, the anonymous Brescian lutenist who was paid the remarkable wage of three hundred ducats a year, the organists Dionysius Memo and Benedict de Opitiis, appointed in 1516 "to wait upon the king in his chamber." Foreign musicians hoping to enter Henry's service arrived at court every month, counting heavily on his renowned patronage.

The sad story of one of these visiting artists, Zuam da Leze, reached his native Venice sometime before 1520.[21] A gifted clavicembalist, da Leze had no doubt that he belonged at the court of Henry VIII, and that once he heard him play the king would make a place for him and reward him as his talent deserved. Ordering the finest clavicembalo he could afford from the Venetian instrument builders, da Leze had it carted overland across Europe, worrying that any bump in the road or change in the weather might damage the delicate soundboard or sour the strings. Finally he arrived in England, brought his instrument to court, and played for the king—only to be sent away with polite thanks and a purse of twenty nobles, far less than the cost of the instrument alone. The Venetian was at first stupefied; then he despaired. At dinner, surrounded by courtiers indifferent to his disappointment, he took his knife and plunged it into his breast. Servants hurried him away from the table and into bed, dressing his wound and calming him, but once they left him alone he hanged himself with his belt. No one recorded what the king said or did when he heard the news, or what became of the beautiful clavicembalo.

Most court players had less tempestuous careers. They were minstrels, general-purpose entertainers recruited at the schools of minstrelsy held each year during Lent and valued for the variety of their talents. "Harping and carping"—music and speech—was their usual offering, but some combined skill on the lute or rebec with acrobatics, storytelling, or acts with trained animals. They were sometimes interchangeable with fools. "Sir, what say ye with your fat face?" was a standard line, thrown out along with mimicry and rapid-fire insults interspersed with songs and dance tunes.[22]

At least one of Henry's minstrels, Hans Nagel, combined skill in music with a more unsavory talent: spying. He served as a courier for the pretender Richard de la Pole in France, delivering messages to de la Pole's adherents in England and Scotland and reporting on the state of the English court and government. Nagel's dual identity was known to the English, but he was allowed to carry out his secret errands unimpeded; his movements and contacts were noted with care, for it was rumored that de la Pole was preparing to invade England with fifteen thousand German mercenaries in the pay of Francis I. Other information from English spies in France suggested that de la Pole might be taken to Scotland to raise rebellion there, or that the French might try to recover Tournai.[23]

Throughout the winter of 1516 Nagel sang and joked for Henry and his courtiers, unaware of the shrewd intelligence that lay behind the king's affable smile and of the use being made of his activities by the king's ministers.

Musical ability was all but indispensable in servants. A list of the men and women employed in the household of the marquis of Exeter described all their talents in detail, giving special prominence to music. William Perpoynte the compiler noted as "aged twenty, unmarried, goodly stature, can play well upon sundry instruments." Anne Browne was listed as "not married, good with the needle, and can play well upon the virginals and lute." William Boothe could "sing properly in three-man songs," and Thomas Wright, aged thirty-eight, could "play well with a harp, sing, juggle, and other proper conceits and make pastimes." One of the men in the list was a skilled musician, perhaps a professional, who played four or five instruments, while another, who had served the marquis as master of the musicians, played only indifferently himself but was able "to teach men to do things in music which he himself cannot express nor utter, and yet he can perfectly teach it."[24] When Henry bought children, as he did in December of 1516, paying a stranger forty pounds for a child, it is tempting to think that he purchased them for their musical gifts.[25]

All the carefully orchestrated ceremony, fantasy and fairytale pageantry of court life came together in the spectacles called mummeries or disguisings, or masks. Here the courtiers were sometimes audience, sometimes participants; they frequently played themselves, though in idealized roles, and the king joined them in their role-playing.

Henry's former tutor John Skelton, William Cornish and others were called upon to create these entertainments, loosely organized around an allegorical plot and set on movable stages. Singers and musicians figured prominently in the overall scheme, but the principal feature of the mask was virtuosic dancing by the disguised couples. The dances were intricate and demanding; they took many hours to learn, and more hours to polish. The king was a superb dancer, agile, graceful and light on his feet, and the mask might have been invented to show off his skill. At a mummery in 1518 twelve couples danced before the assembled company, dressed alike in suits of fine green satin overlaid with cloth of gold tied with golden laces. Masking hoods covered their heads, and the ladies wore elaborate headdresses. When they had finished their dances they took off the hoods; Henry and his sister Mary were found to be the leading dancers, with Brandon, Neville, Bryan, Poyntz, Norris, Henry Guildford and Nicholas Carew among the others.[26]

A much more elaborate mask was held at New Year's of 1516, when the court was at Eltham. Fifty people took part, in addition to the children of the Chapel Royal, who began the evening with a comedy featuring Troilus and Pandarus. A "castle of timber" was wheeled into the hall, out of which came three knights ready to do battle with three challengers. They fought with "punching spears," then with naked swords; after they left the scene a queen and six of her ladies came out of the castle, recited their parts, and listened to a "melodious song" from seven minstrels perched on the battlements. Finally the maskers appeared, six couples dressed in green and white Bruges satin, trimmed in spangles and brooches and ornamented with the letters H and K in yellow. They danced again and again to the music of the minstrels, the entire entertainment lasting many hours.[27]

Masking was so frequent a pastime at Henry's court that large storerooms and even houses were rented to accommodate the "revels stuff" that accumulated. Catalogues of these costumes many pages long record their character: "seven masking hats, Tartary fashion, of yellow and red sarcenet, with eight hairs curled to serve them," "eight satin mantles trimmed with silk, Irish fashion," "for the Palmer's mask, eight short cloaks of scarlet with keys embroidered on the shoulders, eight hats of crimson satin with scallop shells embroidered in front, eight palmer's staves, clapdishes and beads."[28] Props and stage settings took up at least as much space—bushes and trees with green satin leaves, silk flowers in all colors of the rainbow, made so cleverly "that they seemed very flowers," antique pillars, gilded arches, arbors and lattices, and an occasional oddity such as the "image of Hercules, made of earth" constructed for a pageant in 1511.[29]

The masks were entertainment, spectacle, stage settings for a special sort of royal performance. But they were at the same time a mirror of court life, a narcissistic reflection of its artificiality and its exaggerated emphasis on finery. A kind of mania for elaborate dress infected all the European courts in this period. Diplomats, soldiers on campaign, traveling merchants and entertainers took foreign styles with them wherever they went, until Italian, Greek, German and Turkish fashions were as familiar in France and England as they were in their own lands. Styles changed rapidly, with the cut of men's trousers and doublets shifting even more often than that of women's gowns and kirtles. There were constant innovations—low bodices, very wide sleeves, very narrow sleeves, trousers "divided off like a chessboard" and costly to make. Drapers made available an ever increasing array of velvets and silks and brocades and metallic fabrics of gold and silver, as valuable as coin or plate made into cloth. Once bought they were cut and sewn by battalions of expert tailors, embroiderers and seamstresses, who were often called upon to work with unbelievable efficiency. One of Louis XII's courtiers planned to wear a splendid gown at the king's marriage ceremony in 1514. He sent a messenger to Italy to buy a bolt of the most sumptuous cloth of gold available, at a cost of 116 crowns a yard. The messenger made the return journey at top speed, arriving on the eve of the festivities. Overnight the gown was designed, stitched and lined with sables—all at a cost of two thousand crowns. When the resplendent courtier made his appearance the following day he was pronounced the most superbly dressed man in the room.[30]

The English courtiers were no less affected by the fascination with adornment. Though another "act against costly apparel" was passed in 1515 they continued their passionate interest in the newest trimmings and the prevailing taste in gown colors—Lady blush, gosling, marigold, Judas color, peas porridge tawny or popinjay blue. In the early years of Henry's reign gentlewomen wore velvet caps with lappets hanging down over their shoulders, or white caps or kerchiefs. Though this headgear covered their hair completely they were accused of spending hours arranging it; "I am certain," a preacher harangued his parishioners in the early sixteenth century, "that it would take less time to clean out a stable of forty-four horses than it takes you to pin up your hair."[31] The men wore their hair short with bangs across the forehead, "like the priests in Venice," and covered it with caps in a variety of continental styles. Their fine lawn shirts were bordered with lace and lavishly embroidered at the neck and wrists while the coats, gowns and doublets worn over them were of velvets and damasks lined in satin or velvet of a contrasting color. The wealthiest lined their gowns with fur—often sable or lynx—or with the rarest and most precious of all linings, egret's down. The wardrobe inventory of the duke of Buckingham, a man of opulent taste, listed one gown of white damask cloth of gold lined in crimson velvet and another "laid with silver and gilt, and a girdle of green riband silk, with a great knot thereto." In all, the duke's wardrobe list included fourteen gowns, twelve doublets and jackets, nine pairs of hose and eighteen pairs of shoes.[32]

Foreigners found Henry's courtiers magnificent, and wrote at length about their finery. The handsome gold chains the men wore, thick links of gold as much as a hand's breadth wide, and so long they were sometimes looped several times around the neck, were especially impressive. At a ceremony in 1514 the Venetian ambassador Badoer was struck by the display of these imposing ornaments. All the English nobles present, he wrote, "bore such massive gold chains that some might have served for fetters on a felon's ankles, and sufficed for his safe custody, so heavy were they, and of such immense value."[33]

In their gorgeous array the courtiers formed a spangled, bejeweled backdrop against which the figure of the king moved in majestic splendor. Encompassed by their elegance he shone all the more brilliantly, his suits more luxuriant, his jewels more dazzling, his person more exquisite in every way than those around him. He dripped gold. Gold ornaments hung from his doublets and caps and sleeves; gold aglets and roses trimmed his gowns. His buttons were of gold with inset pearls, the embroidery on his sleeves was of damask gold. His goldsmiths wasted more of the precious metal in satisfying his requests than most men saw in their lifetimes. In 1516 two of these metalworkers, Amadas and Rowlet, were paid nearly eight pounds "for the waste of gold"; sometimes garments of cloth of gold would be begun, then permanently laid aside "as the king's purpose changed," the glittering fabric spoiled.[34]

The smallest details of his raiment were works of art: the embroidered branches on his doublets bearing flowers made of pearls; the "Morisco work" on his sleeves trimmed in knots of Venice gold; the ship pendant he wore at his throat, its masts and decks outlined in diamonds. The overall effect, observers agreed, could hardly have been surpassed. Impressed as he was with the English courtiers Badoer was taken aback completely on one occasion by the breathtaking beauty of the king posing regally in their midst, his gown a dramatic fall of white damask closely studded with diamonds and rubies.

15

KING Henry, his close friend Thomas More once wrote, had the rare gift of making everyone around him believe he was speaking to him or her alone. While remaining the center of every circle he entered he adapted rapidly to the interests and preoccupations of that circle, showing different sides of his protean temperament and varied talents to different groups of courtiers. To his minions he was the carefree, fun-loving companion who on a snowy day in January, 1519, rushed outside to join his nobles in a snowball fight, borrowing a cap from a boy to keep his ears warm. To the gentlemen of his chamber he was the high-spirited amateur musician who sang "By the bank as I lay" and "As I walked the wood so wild" and other two-part songs with Peter Carew by the hour. To his French hostages he was a serious gambler, to his ship captains an amateur pilot who loved ships and the sea. And to More, Erasmus and the dozen or so men of profound learning who knew him well and observed his mind and thoughts at close range, he was a man of brilliantly keen intellect who took deep pleasure in the exercise of his wits.

An elite of the learned surrounded the king, less conspicuous than his other favorites but no less prized. They provided the special sort of companionship his own restless intelligence craved—the communion of minds and the exchange of ideas. They came to his court gladly, not only because, as More wrote, "the king's majesty our sovereign has himself more learning than any English monarch ever possessed before him," but because, after a decade as a king, he was more than ever their ideal ruler made flesh. Neither the burdens nor the temptations of his office had dissuaded him from his commitment to learning, or from the respect for the life of the mind he had expressed to Mountjoy soon after his coronation. Henry brought to his studies the same effortless talent, the same grace and natural excellence which made him admired as a musician and dancer. Since boyhood he had had the sort of mind that learned almost anything quickly; once he was conversant with a subject he moved about with ease within it, shifting nimbly from one argument to another and fastening eagerly on controversial points.

The range of his linguistic accomplishments was wide. He spoke excellent French, and understood Italian well. Latin was so comfortable a

medium of expression for Henry that he used it in all his diplomatic
discussions with foreign ambassadors, and had the fluency even to make
impromptu speeches. When in August of 1518 Cardinal Campeggio came
to England to preach a crusade against the Turks, he made a long Latin
oration before the king and his assembled courtiers. Henry listened with
interest, standing before his throne while the cardinal unraveled his
carefully prepared discourse. When he had finished the king replied at
length in equally elegant Latin, omitting none of the rhetorical nuances or
elaborate turns of phrase in the humanist lexicon.[1] His written style was
equally well developed, and distinctive; whether he wrote in English,
French or Latin, the result invariably betrayed his own unmistakable
stamp.

Beyond this, he was exceedingly well read, not only in the works of
literature and piety appropriate to a cultivated gentleman but in the thorny
treatises and summas of the medieval scholastics. Erasmus called attention
to the depth of his reading, and the theologians against whom he tested his
knowledge were often forced to concede his superiority in citing texts. He
kept himself surrounded by books of every sort; the "highest library" at
Greenwich contained well over three hundred volumes, and he was soon
to add to their number an important work of his own.[2]

Henry was happiest, though, in bringing the weight of his learning to
bear on a dilemma of philosophy or theology, preferably in an informal
discussion. He found the battle of wits as stimulating as the breaking of
lances in a joust, and prepared himself to meet his intellectual opponents
as carefully as he did his partners in the lists. As often as he could get
away from the affairs of state, Erasmus said, the king either read or
engaged in debate. He often arranged "little combats"—
conflictatiunculae—and shut himself away with the works of Aquinas or
Scotus or Gabriel Biel to make ready for them. No matter how impassioned the contest he never grew heated, however; "amazingly
courteous and calm," he maintained the tone of a friendly rival and never
of a sovereign.[3]

One of these disputations pitted Henry against a well-known churchman. They argued the proposition "Whether a layman is obliged to say
his prayers in words," and one of the courtiers who was present found the
encounter worthy of record. At other times the issue was more
controversial—the correct understanding of transubstantiation, a point of
canon law or the meaning of a passage from the decretals. Often the king
served as arbiter in the disputations of others. On one occasion a court
preacher turned his sermon into a raging diatribe against humanist
studies—chiefly against Greek, which had recently come under attack at
Oxford as harmful to piety—and against Erasmus, denouncing him by
name. As the harangue continued Richard Pace gave the king a significant
look; Henry laughed quietly in reply. After the sermon the theologian
found himself summoned into the royal presence to debate his opinions
with Thomas More. Henry joined in the disputation on More's side,
"speaking most eloquently in defense of the study of Greek." When it
came time for the offending theologian to reply his nerve broke, and he

went down on his knees, begging to be forgiven for having been so "carried away by a spirit" that he misspoke himself.

"Nevertheless," Henry told him, "that was not the spirit of Christ, but of foolishness." As for his condemnation of Erasmus, had he read any of the great man's works? The theologian acknowledged that he hadn't. "He is an evident fool," the king concluded, "who condemns what he hasn't read."

In a last effort to redeem himself the churchman said he had read Erasmus' satire *The Praise of Folly*—"Which has a great deal to do with the case, your majesty," Pace broke in sarcastically—and admitted, on second thought, that Greek might not be so dangerous to piety after all, since it was derived from Hebrew. This final absurdity brought the interview to an end. Henry sent the man away, with instructions never to preach before his court again.[4]

Katherine played a conspicuous role in the king's intellectual life, if not in the "little combats." In her knowledge and "excellence" the queen was a match for her husband, "a rare and fine advocate" of the New Learning, according to Erasmus. Like Henry she had been an apt pupil as a child, and had never lost her taste for letters. She had even asked the great Erasmus himself to be her teacher, and though his itinerant life made that impossible—he had left England in 1514—he saluted her as "miraculously learned for a woman." Katherine was as outspoken as she was learned, and did not hesitate to challenge Erasmus' scholarly activities. Talking with another of the court scholars one day she questioned Erasmus' greatest undertaking: his edition of the Latin New Testament, the first such effort since the Vulgate of Saint Jerome in the fourth century.

"Was Jerome not a learned man?" she asked.

"Yes, certainly," the scholar told her.

"And is he not in heaven?"

"Indeed," came the reply.

"Why then," the queen insisted, "does Erasmus correct Jerome? Is he wiser than Jerome?"

The question was often posed. The most distinguished humanist associated with the English court, Erasmus nonetheless made enemies readily and was attacked by critics wherever he went. Those who were put off by his work *The Praise of Folly* were enraged at his New Testament. Many condemned it unread—or so the author claimed—on no better evidence than a tavern rumor that a new work had been published "which was to pluck out the eyes of theologians like crows."[5] Others found the attempt to improve on the age-old version of Jerome presumptuous and possibly heretical. Once the accusation of heresy was made it became widespread among his critics. "Heresy is held a deadly crime," Erasmus wrote to a friend, a canon at Bruges. "So if you offend one of these gentlemen they all rush on you together, one grunting out 'heretic,' the rest grunting in chorus, and crying for stones to hurl at you."[6] Assaulted from all sides he longed to return to England, to the friends who appreciated and sheltered him, to the king who wrote him affectionate letters and the queen who, despite her championing of Jerome, wanted Erasmus for her tutor. Above all he wanted to make his home amid the "galaxy of distinguished men" that surrounded Henry VIII, making his court "a very museum of knowledge.

Erasmus' letters describe a court populated by earnest thinkers serving a philosopher king. In place of the uproar of dogs and servants and the babble of gossip the humanist heard only "grave and modest conversation on points of morals or knowledge" in Henry's halls. The king himself sought out companions who shunned the dissolute pastimes dear to other courtiers, he claimed, preferring their society "to that of silly youths or girls, or the rich, or the dishonest, who might tempt him to foolish indulgences or injurious courses."[7] So great was his desire to avoid the dissolute life and improve his mind that he all but coerced the most capable men in his realm to live at court, "that they may be in a position to watch all that he does, and share his duties and his pleasures." There were enough men around him who praised his every act; he relied on men such as More, Pace and Colet to speak their minds plainly, and enjoyed the give and take of their exchanges. In their midst he gained new stature; he joined that elite company of rulers remembered for their civilized virtues. He became "Ptolemy Philadelphus in his enthusiasm for good letters, Alexander the Great in felicity, Julius Caesar in force of mind, Augustus in sane judgement, Trajan in mildness, Alexander Severus in integrity, Antoninus Pius in doctrine, and Theodosius in piety."[8]

The humanists who lent such luster to the king included Mountjoy, once his informal tutor in the gentlemanly arts and now head of Queen Katherine's household, the aged ex-chancellor Warham, John Fisher, bishop of Rochester, to whose enlightened care Margaret Beaufort had entrusted her grandson on her deathbed, Pietro Carmeliano, an old-fashioned versifier ridiculed by Erasmus for mixing up his long and short syllables, Henry's Latin secretary Andrea Ammonio and the latter's kinsman Peter Vannes. One of Henry's physicians was a noted humanist: Thomas Linacre, whom Erasmus called "as deep and acute a thinker as I have ever met with"; John Stokesley, a theologian and Hebraist, was a politician who sat on the Privy Council along with More.

In the constellation of brilliance around the king three figures stood out. One was Richard Pace, a winsome, ingenuous and thoroughly likable young courtier taken from Wolsey and employed as a royal secretary and diplomatic envoy. For wit and sweetness of disposition he bore comparison with More; much in demand by Wolsey and the queen, Pace was even dearer to Henry, who looked on him "as his very self." Educated at the University of Padua, a lecturer at Oxford and an exceedingly promising Greek scholar, Pace became a valued negotiator at foreign courts. Before he was forty it was being said that, if the king lost Wolsey to Rome, Pace would be the one to fill his offices, becoming the most powerful man in England next to Henry himself.[9]

The dean of St. Paul's, John Colet, also stood out from the others. Tall, handsome and utterly absorbed in his learning—he never went walking without a book in his hands—Colet was conspicuous for the neatness and austerity of his dress. Where other priests went in purple gowns of costly fabrics he wore plain gray wool, and surrounded himself with only the simplest of furniture, food and books. He used his large inherited fortune to found a school for boys, disapproving of the English universities as encouraging idleness rather than scholarship, and refused to follow the conventional practice of giving to monasteries. The religious houses did not deserve his charity, Colet said; on the whole he found clerics to be more prone to dishonesty and avarice than laymen, with monks and bishops worst of all.

Colet's "immensely learned earnestness" was offset by his sunny nature and laughter, but when he lectured or disputed his words carried unparalleled authority. "When Colet speaks, I might be listening to Plato," Erasmus said. He described his friend sitting among his colleagues, speaking "with a sacred fury" about the book of Genesis while they listened in rapt attention.[10]

It was a measure of Henry's respect for Colet—and of his tolerance for views which conflicted sharply with his own—that when on the eve of the military campaign of 1513 the dean had the temerity to preach against war the king listened attentively to his sermon. The immediacy of war was upon the entire court; Colet's impassioned denunciation could not have been more pointed. Yet Henry followed his arguments one by one, hearing him contrast Christ's teachings of gentleness and brotherly love to the butchery and fratricide of warfare. Better to imitate the Prince of Peace than Caesar or Alexander, the preacher concluded in a final challenge directed to the king himself.

The sermon caused a furor. Colet's episcopal colleagues, already incensed at him for condemning their overly comfortable lives, now denounced him as a traitor to the cause of the Holy League. It was feared that the soldiers might lose heart, or be confused about where their Christian duty lay. Henry too was slightly bewildered: he believed Colet to be a man of sound doctrine, yet this doctrine condemned the pope's own crusade, a fight to which the king was wholeheartedly committed and which he had undertaken not out of sheer battle lust or greed but from the most sincere motives. He sent for the dean and called him into the garden at Greenwich. Sending everyone else away he talked with Colet quietly and earnestly, admitting that the sermon had brought on inner doubts he needed to work through.

"I have summoned you," Henry said, "in order to resolve my scruples of conscience, so that guided by your counsel I can fulfill my office rightly." Nearly two hours later, their private disputation at an end, they rejoined the waiting churchmen and other courtiers. A solution had been found. War was unchristian, but some wars were justified by a higher ethic. Henry embraced Colet in front of his mortified colleagues, calling for wine to pledge him with a toast. "Let every man choose his own doctor," he said exuberantly. "Dean Colet shall be mine!"[11]

The approval of men such as Colet was important to Henry. He wanted badly to believe that he was doing the right thing; he wanted that belief reinforced by others untainted by fear or flattery. He sought unfeigned consent to his undertakings, and was willing to spend whatever time it took to earn it.

Henry valued no one's approval more than Thomas More's. A highly successful lawyer, More was unpretentious and kindly in manner, though his adroitness in argument was unsurpassed. It was said he could annihilate theologians even when debating the subjects they knew best, and his skill in weighing and judging complex issues made him especially valuable in the Council chamber.

More was the most reluctant of courtiers. The velvets and gold chains of high office left him indifferent; intrigue he found tiresome and the labor of government a continual burden which robbed him of his peace and kept him from his family. According to Colet, More had more genius than any man in England, yet his preferred pastimes were modest. He liked to walk along the riverbank at his country house—sometimes the king walked with him—and he enjoyed watching his tame ferret and weasel and fox. His principal labor was the leading of a sane and balanced life; his principal companions were his wife and four children, who lived together in extraordinary harmony. "His whole house breathes happiness," declared his frequent houseguest Erasmus.

Henry and his privy councilor had much in common. Both were complex, quick-witted, able to command respect and loving obedience from others. ("If he bade me dance a hornpipe," Erasmus said of More, "I should do it at once just as he bade me.") More made the king an ideal foil, valuable and in time indispensable. Despite his pleas for a quiet life Henry would not part with him, and as the years went by he came to rely on More so heavily that he scarcely let him out of his sight.[12]

16

Eighth Henry ruling this land,
He had a sister fair,
That was the widow'd Queen of France,
Enrich'd with virtues rare;
And being come to England's Court,
She oft beheld a knight,
Charles Brandon nam'd, in whose fair eyes,
She chiefly took delight.

ONE man stood even above More in the king's affections: Charles Brandon. Closer to Henry than his roistering minions, Brandon shared his sovereign's innermost life and concerns in a way the king's scholarly companions could never do, and to a degree that Wolsey, no matter how powerful he became, could never approach. The things Henry cared about most—manly things such as his military ambitions, his jousting and his love life—were the things he shared with Brandon. Theirs was the special, unaccountable bond of friendship, a bond no hindrance or breach of faith could sever for long.

A gentleman by birth, Brandon became one of the two highest peers of the realm in 1514, when Henry made him duke of Suffolk. The title rewarded his valor in the French campaign, where as marshal of the army he had been Henry's second in command and had taken possession of one of the city gates at Tournai unaided. It also made him eligible to marry a highborn woman, overlooking the minor drawback that he already had three wives.

Henry had rewarded Brandon by giving him wardship of an heiress, Elizabeth Grey, in 1512. Elizabeth was the only child of the late John Grey, Viscount Lisle, and Brandon lost no time in laying claim to her title and fortune. A marriage contract bound her to marry him when she came of age—she was only eight years old when the contract was signed—and in 1513 letters patent were issued naming Brandon Viscount Lisle and referring to Elizabeth as his wife. But in Henry VII's reign he had acquired two earlier wives, one of whom, Anne Browne, had borne him a daughter. A church court had declared his marriage to the second wife, Margaret Mortimer, invalid, but even so his marital status was by no means beyond dispute. None of this prevented Brandon from claiming the title of Viscount Lisle in right of his child bride-to-be, however, and the king had even higher aspirations for him.

During the French campaign Henry had prepared the way for two royal marriages. One was the long-awaited union of his sister Mary with Queen Katherine's nephew Charles, the future Emperor Charles V. The other was to join Brandon with the emperor Maximilian's daughter Margaret of Savoy, regent of the Netherlands for Charles. The first betrothal had been arranged years earlier; all that remained was to schedule the wedding. A new treaty called for Mary and Charles to marry no later than May of 1514, with heavy money penalties to be exacted from the imperialists if it were delayed.[1] The second proved more difficult to conclude, and showed Henry's ineptitude as a matchmaker. It was not that Margaret found Brandon displeasing. On the contrary, she much approved of "the virtue and grace of his person, the which me seemed that I have not much seen [any] gentleman to approach it." Seeing how much Henry favored him she went out of her way to pay attention to Brandon, but could hardly take seriously Henry's half-playful, half-earnest hints at a betrothal.

Could she not give Brandon some "promise of marriage," he coaxed, "seeing that it was the fashion of the ladies of England, and that it was not there holden for evil." Such a thing was impossible, she told him, as "it was not here the custom, and I should be dishonored, and holden for a fool and light." Neither her father nor her subjects would permit such a promise, she said, adding that she had no inclination to marry anyone ever again, having been unfortunate in her past husbands.

This should have settled the matter, but both Brandon and the king were persistent. One night at a banquet at Tournai Brandon went down on his knees before Margaret, took her hands in his, and so distracted her with his amorous conversation that he was able to slip a ring off her finger without her noticing it. When he showed it to her later and refused to return it she was dismayed, for the ring was easily recognizable as hers and might be misinterpreted as a pledge of love. At another time, when she was entertaining Henry and his friend in her chamber late at night, Margaret was again pressed to give Brandon her hand. No argument would satisfy the king this time—not the imminent departure of the English for home, not Brandon's lowly status, not her determination "not to again never to put me where I have had so much of unhap and infortune," in a state of matrimony. In the end Henry forced out of her a promise not to marry anyone until the English returned the following year; Brandon, for his part, vowed not to marry without Margaret's consent, and the agreement was reiterated on another day.

Margaret had all but forgotten this bargain when she suddenly found herself the object of international gossip the following spring. Brandon received his ducal title in February; in the first week of March Henry was busy stirring up rumors about his friend's impending marriage in Flanders. Brandon proudly displayed Margaret's ring to substantiate the rumors, and before long the "unhappy bruit" of their betrothal had spread throughout the Low Countries and the German principalities. Wagers were made on the date of the wedding, jokes were made about the difference in their ages—Brandon was still in his twenties, while Margaret was a twice-married, matronly thirty-four—and there was nothing Margaret could do to correct the false impression Henry was doing his best to create. "I have had one marvellous sorrow," she wrote to the English ambassador Wingfield, and in her humiliation she fled into the country, ostensibly for a pleasure trip with her nieces and nephew but in fact to escape all the talk.[2]

In the end a sudden shift in English diplomacy put a stop to the rumors, though Brandon's marital prospects were not dimmed for long. As it turned out he was to wed still higher.

In 1514 Henry's sister Mary was a glowingly beautiful girl of eighteen, with the fairest of complexions and delicate, perfect features. She was short in stature but very graceful, and in her lively disposition she was very like her ebullient brother. "There is nothing gloomy or melancholy about her," as a Flemish diplomat wrote, and indeed Mary was not only high spirited but strong willed, and when she agreed to accommodate Henry by making a marriage of state it was on condition that she could choose her next husband herself. And it was no secret her choice would fall on Charles Brandon.

The marriage Henry arranged for her in the spring of 1514 surprised everyone. The imperial alliance was abandoned; the coalition against France had dissolved and, if Henry's personal belligerence remained strong, his diplomatic interests called for a rapprochement with his former enemy. The aged, gouty widower Louis XII still reigned in France, and he had no son. He needed a wife. Mary Tudor's engagement to Prince Charles was broken off and she dutifully became queen of France, taking with her forty new gowns and a household of several hundred officers and servants.

Though he suffered from flux and gulped his spittle when he talked Louis was a generous husband to her. He showered her with gifts, and spoke of taking her to Venice, which she had always wanted to see. The jewels he gave her were magnificent. Before she left England he sent her a matchless diamond "as large and as broad as a full-sized finger," known as the Mirror of Naples. With its pendant pearl, the size of a pigeon's egg, the jewel was estimated at sixty thousand crowns in value. There were others nearly as splendid: table diamonds, a "marvellous great pointed diamond" worth ten thousand marks, a ruby two and a half inches long.[3]

After less than three months of marriage Mary's pampered life as queen of France ended abruptly when Louis collapsed and died. All at once the court revolved around Louis' son-in-law and successor Francis I, who made no secret of his interest in the beautiful young queen dowager. For the time being at least Mary was his captive, and could not count on any of her English friends for aid. Wolsey sent her a heartening letter, swearing "to the effusion of his blood and spending of his goods" that he would never forsake her, but all he could do was to warn her not to allow herself to be forced into a hasty second marriage, and to urge her to wait patiently until her future was arranged. She found the waiting painful. Rumor had it she would be forced to enter a convent, or to marry a French nobleman, or that she was to be taken to Flanders to fulfill her original contract to Prince Charles. More agonizing still, the man she really wanted was at the French court on a diplomatic mission. Charles Brandon's arrival could not have been more opportune. Mary determined to stake her future on his chivalry and affection.

Brandon described their interview afterward in a letter to Henry. Mary was beside herself, he said. She seemed not to know whom to trust and whom to fear. Two English friars had recently been to see her bringing frightening news and a dark warning. Though Henry had given his word that she could marry freely, they said, he would never keep it; furthermore, she must stay away from the duke of Suffolk, who was known to have traffickings with the devil. In her frustration Mary accused Brandon of coming to France to betray her.

"You are come to take me home to the intent that I may be married into Flanders," she said, "which I will never, to die for it." She would rather be torn in pieces than make another diplomatic match, Mary added, and burst into tears.

"Sir, I never saw a woman so weep," Brandon wrote to Henry. No reassurances, no endearments could dam the flood of her tears. There was only one way he could convince her he was truly on her side, and that was to marry her himself.

Moved by her tears and befuddled by her arguments, Brandon hedged. She must get Henry's written consent first, he said. He had his own conscience to reckon with, after all. Before leaving England he had met with the king at Eltham, and in the gravest possible manner, with Wolsey as witness, he had sworn he would not act on impulse once he got to France and marry his sweetheart. Henry promised in turn that, "with good order and saving of his honor," Brandon could have her after a suitable delay.[4]

None of this had the slightest effect on Mary. She became more and more unreasonable, until in the end she risked all. Either he married her right away, she told him, or he could "look never after this day to have the proffer again." "And so," he confessed, "she and I was married."[5]

Six weeks later the newlyweds found the courage to inform Henry of what they had done. Brandon explained himself by making it look as though his wife had put him in an indefensible position; Mary, in letters edited by her good friend Wolsey before they reached the king, took full responsibility on herself. She addressed Henry as "the King's grace, me brother," but assured him she had always found him to be "both a father and a brother" to her. She trusted to his clemency; she reminded him of his promise to her, and of his well-known reputation for keeping his word. And to soften his anger she sent him a diamond and a huge pearl from among her French jewels, vowing to give him first choice from among them all as soon as Francis returned them to her.[6]

The king took the news "grievously and displeasantly." Mary's irresponsible behavior might be put down to womanly hysteria, but Brandon's was hard to forgive. "He would not believe he would have broken his promise had he been torn with wild horses," Henry told Wolsey. Together the couple had disappointed and embarrassed him, and cost him a good deal of money as well. Her marriage to an English husband had given Francis the legal right to confiscate Mary's dowry; even the gifts Louis had given her, including the much coveted Mirror of Naples, were now his. Mary had cost him the expense of her royal wedding, Henry reasoned, while Brandon still owed him the three thousand pounds he had borrowed as a loan on his plate to pay for his mission to the French court.[7]

But the king's displeasure was mild compared to the reaction of his Council. To a man (Wolsey excepted) they called for Brandon's execution, or imprisonment at least. For a gentleman's son to marry the king's sister was outrageous, even if he had been made a duke.[8] The French were equally angry. It was said Brandon hardly dared to walk the streets of Paris for fear he would be mobbed as the hated Englishman who had married Mary Tudor.[9] Finally Mary and Brandon struck a bargain with Henry, and once he was placated the irate councilors had to swallow their wrath. The erring couple bound themselves to pay the enormous sum of twenty-four thousand pounds in yearly installments, and even though Henry gave them estates and lands enough to earn in rents what they owed him, still the burden was a heavy one. Long after the scandal had died down the king continued to look for these payments, complaining loudly when they were overdue yet conspicuously squandering the money once he received it. Each year he took the purses of coins to Katherine's apartments and poured them out into the eager hands of her waiting maids, leaving enough to distribute to his minions to play with at cards. It was ransom money, he told them, paid in token of his domination of France.[10]

After his marriage observers looked in vain for Brandon's standing with the king to change. Henry indicated his full approval of what had happened by attending a second wedding ceremony of his sister and brother-in-law in Grey Friars Church, and by accepting the compliment graciously when the couple named their first child after him. The Venetian ambassador thought in the summer of 1516 that Brandon was "not in so much favor with the king as heretofore," but the minor shift in influence was only temporary, and was part of a broader political alteration. Power in the royal Council was becoming concentrated in the hands of Wolsey, Ruthal and Norfolk; along with the other councilors, Brandon was eclipsed for a while.

In fact the friendship between Brandon and Henry was far too strong to be interrupted for long, and there was something else too that bound them together. Since boyhood Brandon had been Henry's preferred jousting partner. Next to warfare, tourneying was Henry's principal arena of personal glory. And if jousting was indispensable to Henry's reputation, Brandon was indispensable to the joust.

For a decade and more Brandon and the king had ridden side by side at every tournament, often wearing identical suits of cut velvet or cloth of gold, alike in strength and valor. Chroniclers described again and again how the two men dominated the field, fighting at the barriers or defending at the tilt against all comers until they won the prize. When they fought against one another it was a battle of titans. The Venetian ambassador Giustiniani witnessed one such combat toward the end of his stay in England. The skill and resilience of both jousters was magnificent, and they were so well matched they stretched each other's abilities to the limit. All who saw them, the ambassador wrote, imagined they were watching, not the king and his duke, but Hector and Achilles.[11]

Giustiniani omitted to record who won the contest, but very likely it was the king. It was among Brandon's most valuable qualities that he enhanced Henry's celebrity without overshadowing him. Other jousters who possessed more skill than Brandon lacked this essential attribute. Nicholas Carew, for example, perfected himself in the joust by constant practice. A special tilt was kept for him at Greenwich, and a shed to arm in; he ran there daily, preparing the unique feats he often performed to complement the traditional exercises at a joust of honor. His stunts were prodigious. Once, after all the courses had been run, Carew entered the lists alone. Both he and his tall horse were covered entirely in blue satin, and the horse was blindfolded to prevent him from rearing in terror at what his master was about to attempt. Three men then carried onto the field a young tree nine inches around and twelve feet high, and fastened it into Carew's lance rest with forked poles. He rode steadily forward, bearing the weight of the tree "most stoutly" without flinching and keeping it upright, until he nearly reached the opposite end of the lists, "to the extreme admiration and astonishment of everybody."[12]

Spectacular feats such as this were fine for star performers, but the king's jousting partner had to be a complementary figure like Brandon. There could be no margin for doubt in the spectator's minds that Henry was the most brilliant jouster of all.

That he was able to shatter many lances, to hurl his opponent to the ground, mount and all, to fight equally well with battle-axe or sword or hand to hand Henry's admirers had known for years. That he made as splendid a figure on horseback as any king living or dead no one doubted; he looked "like Saint George in person," one man wrote who saw him at the tilt in 1515.

But his great distinction was his Italianate riding, and in this art, new to England and cultivated with enthusiasm by the king and his horse masters, Henry surpassed even the spectacular Nicholas Carew.

The Italian art of the manage, or handling, called for highly skilled riding and highly trained horses. Using his calves, his voice and a wand or rod to touch the horse on his shoulder or flank—the best riders rarely used their spurs—the rider put his mount through a variety of maneuvers. The horse came suddenly to a full stop from a full gallop. He made half turns, full turns, and double turns in place, "keeping his body in one staye, writhing neither head, neck, nor any part of his body." He wove at a gallop in and out of barriers, in a serpentine pattern. And he reared up on his hind legs, jumped in place, and performed the "goat leap," or capriole, raising his forelegs together and then bounding up with his rump, kicking out with his hind legs before his forelegs touched the ground.

A gorgeously clad rider exercising such perfect control over a magnificent horse was a beautiful sight, and Henry knew how to vary his mount's turns and leaps to create endless enjoyment. Both he and his horses were trained by the finest riding masters he could recruit in Italy, and by Englishmen who had studied the manage at Naples or Ferrara or Mantua where the best riders were. Horses brought to the English court from Italy were accompanied by grooms who were skilled riders and trainers; in 1519 several horses arrived with their groom, Giovanni Scaticia, esteemed by the Ferrarese who chose him to be "the most skilled rider in Italy."[13] At every joust Henry exhausted many horses in the rigors of the manage, tiring out one after another by making them perform "a thousand jumps in the air," until they were worn down and delighting his audience with his horsemanship.

To indulge this pastime he needed a large supply of horses, and the stables at Eltham were enlarged in 1513 to accommodate them. Good horses were scarce in England, however. Compared to Italians the English trained their horses too young and worked them too hard; to find suitable mounts the king had to send agents to the continent to bargain for the swift barbs, high-stepping Neapolitans, bounding Frieslanders and Spanish jennets he required. When young and well fed, and free of lameness, windgall, the staggers or "running imposthumes," riding horses were costly. Buyers such as Jacotyn de Bornemacker, empowered to acquire horses in Flanders for Henry's stable, had to pay thirty or forty pounds for choice mounts. No gift pleased the king more than the gift of a horse, and European sovereigns who hoped to win Henry's good will always sent fine animals to his stables. Ambitious courtiers did the same thing. In 1520 Edward Guildford gave Henry a handsome black pied horse and a young bay called "Byard Hays," with his grooming boy Jacquette. Byard Hays he kept; the black horse he gave to Carew to ride at the tilt.[14]

Henry treasured his horses as he did his companions, and arranged special care for his favorites. Ammonio wrote a poem about one of the king's best-loved horses, Canicida; another, the "Barbaristo" or Barbary horse, was a prized Arabian with its own keeper and its own account in the records of the stables. According to these records, Henry paid seven shillings for each "bath for the barbary horse."[15] As often as he could the king visited his horses, riding them for hours at a time and training them to respond to his commands. "Ha traitor! Ha villain!" he cried to correct them, "holla, holla, so boy, there boy" to encourage them and show his approval. They learned to jump at his "hey" and "now," to "fetch the capriole" when he clicked his tongue or cried "hup" and pressed his calves into their flanks. Following the Italian practice he taught them to seek his "cherishing" rather than to fear his spurs. When they did well he scratched their necks and withers with his riding wand, patting them and speaking softly and admiringly.

One of Henry's happiest days was the day the Mantuan barb Gov-ernatore arrived at his court.[16] He came, with three brood mares, as a gift from the marquis of Mantua, a renowned horse breeder whose stables were famous all over Europe. Their keeper and trainer Giovanni Ratto presented the horses to the king on a spring day in 1514, as he and

Katherine and some of the courtiers were walking through the stables. As soon as he saw them Henry exclaimed with delight, and wanted to try them out at once. Ratto rode the mares for him, one by one, saying as he did so that if they were less good than he deserved, he might choose any others from the marquis' stables, "together with his territories and children, and his own person."

Henry could not have been more pleased if the marquis had given him a kingdom, an observer wrote. He went from one courtier to another asking "What think you of these mares? They were sent to me by my cousin the marquis of Mantua," and announcing that he had never seen better animals. The duc de Longueville spoke up to say he was certain the French king had no horses to compare with these, and the others agreed they were extraordinary. Then, for Katherine's sake, Ratto brought out Governatore, a bright bay of incomparable beauty, and rode him "in the Spanish fashion." The marquis had been offered his weight in silver for this horse, it was said, but had preferred to send him to his brother monarch in England. Katherine and the others were unrestrained in their admiration, but the king was suddenly quiet. Here was the horse of his dreams. He went up to Ratto as he dismounted.

"Is not this the best horse?" he asked. The trainer assured him he was. The king smiled in pleasure and nodded his head, and reached out to stroke Governatore's neck. "So ho," he said softly. "So ho, my minion."

III

"The Man
Most Full of Heart"

17

It chanc'd the king upon a day
Prepar'd a sumptuous feast:
And there came lords, and dainty dames
And many a noble guest.

IN the hot summer of 1520 officers of arms were dispatched to ride throughout England and France and even to the faraway courts of Flanders and Spain to summon all who claimed mastery of arms to a great tournament. Harry of England and Francis of France had pledged to meet on the windswept fields of Flanders to show their brotherly good will and test their prowess. Jousts would be held between the gentlemen of the English and French courts, "for the honor and pastime" of the ladies, and all the knights of Christendom were invited to join in the feats of arms. Throngs of workmen were already turning the barren landscape of the Val Doré, the Golden Valley, into a fairyland of castles and pavilions, and crowds were gathering to watch them at their work and to anticipate the spectacle to come. Before the summer was over, accounts of the knightly splendor of this meeting of the kings at the Field of Cloth of Gold would be carried to every court in Europe, and those who had witnessed it would be calling it the eighth wonder of the world.

The site of this celebration of Anglo-French brotherhood had only recently been a place of slaughter. The Golden Valley lay between the English-held town of Guînes and the French town of Ardres, and it was a scant four years since English soldiers had sacked Ardres and burned it to the ground. Now the silken tents and pavilions of the French jousters were being raised on its blackened ground, but French and English alike were skeptical of the newfound harmony between their sovereigns. To be sure, English merchants and sailors had made themselves at home in Bordeaux and its surrounding regions by the thousands, and their close and constant fraternization with the local population made Francis uneasy. If war broke out, his subjects in Bordeaux might forget their loyalty and let the English ships go on landing as they always did. But these good relations were exceptional; in other coastal regions the English raided and burned villages as they had Ardres, and French merchants in London were despised and cheated. Their movements severely restricted, French cloth merchants were not allowed to attend the English cloth fairs, and were imprisoned as spies if found walking the streets of London at night without a candle. Before leaving for home they were subjected to the humiliation of a search, stripped to their shirts and examined for concealed valuables.[1]

Certainly the English seemed prepared for war, if war came. Since 1514 German armorers had been working in London, in hired houses and cellars and in a newly built armory at Greenwich, forging arms and armor from iron imported from Innsbruck. Some of what they made was jousting armor, but not all, and they were forging guns as well as harness. One new gun, the Basilisk, was an immense project in itself. Many laborers were required to cast its iron shot, still more to cast the huge gun, working in a rented tenement that was nearly wrecked in the process. The building's owner, John Rutter, was paid thirty-three pounds as compensation for "hurts and damages by him sustained" while the king's armorers toiled under his roof.[2] Thousands of pounds were paid out to armorers in the years following the English campaign of 1513, and thousands more to the shipbuilders who were enlarging the royal fleet. Should France attack, Wolsey boasted to the Venetians, "I tell you, that we have ships here in readiness, and in eight days could place sixty thousand men on the soil of France." As for Francis, "we are able to thwart any of his projects at our pleasure," Wolsey said curtly.[3]

Wolsey's pronouncements were invariably heard and recorded, for it was he, many believed, who was the deciding voice in war and peace. No one stood higher in government or in the church; no one had greater ability. In the king's shrewd estimation, Wolsey's "singular diligence and high wisdom" were unmatched. Through the cardinal's unique powers, Henry said, he had accomplished more than all the kings of England before him.

From royal almoner and junior Council member Wolsey had risen to become, successively, bishop of London, archbishop of York, chancellor and cardinal of the church—all in less than two years' time. The old powers in the royal Council, Warham and Fox, gave way before Wolsey and his deputy Thomas Ruthal, bishop of Durham, who when Wolsey became chancellor took the office of lord privy seal. In 1518 the pope made Wolsey papal legate, but even this lofty office did not cap his ambition: he wanted to be pope.

Boundless ambition was certainly the mainspring of Wolsey's character, but it was his capacity for tireless, exacting labor and above all his awesome powers of mind that gave him strength and force. Admirers and enemies alike acknowledged his "wonder wit," and trembled under the penetrating scrutiny of his intellect. Impatient with lesser minds, grave and often pensive, Wolsey took a sardonic delight in bringing his vigorous intelligence to bear on a knot of problems and cutting through to a solution. "His chief study," a contemporary wrote, "yea, and all his felicity and inward joy, hath ever been to exercise that angel's wit of his."[4]

And he had the unflagging discipline to focus his attention for many hours at a time, heedless even of his bodily needs. A member of his household, his gentlemen usher George Cavendish, told how on a diplomatic mission in France Wolsey rose at four in the morning and immediately sat down to write urgent letters to the king and others in England, stopping only to order his chaplain to prepare himself to say mass. Twelve hours later he was still at his desk, "all which season," Cavendish wrote, "my lord never rose once to piss, ne yet to eat any meat but continually wrote his letters with his own hands, having all that time his nightcap and keverchief on his head."[5] Finally toward evening he dispatched his correspondence, heard mass and took a little walk, then went right to bed after a light supper, ready to resume his labors the next day.

The cardinal's hard work might have won him praise had he been a different sort of man. But he was arrogant, harsh and violent. He struck the papal nuncio Chieregato and bullied him in "fierce and rude language." He was haughty with ambassadors, and demanded from nobles and commoners alike the kind of deference usually reserved for royalty. He boasted of his wealth, and took every opportunity to display it, wearing ermine-lined cloaks and cardinal's robes of red silk, "the best that he could get for money," with sables at the neck. His cardinal's hats came from France, and were dyed with a special brilliant scarlet dye unobtainable in England. Gilt cardinal's hats adorned the bedsteads in his palaces, where hundreds of liveried servants reflected his magnificence; the master cook of his privy kitchen, it was said, "went daily in damask, satin, or velvet with a chain of gold about his neck."[6]

Wolsey's grandiloquent vanity, along with his evident mastery of affairs, created the dangerous impression that he had taken over the government from the king. The unparalleled pomp that accompanied his comings and goings, the careless assurance with which he confused the royal will with his own, the near-regal fury of his displeasure convinced foreign envoys that the cardinal had become *"ipse rex"*—the king himself—and caused them to shift their diplomatic focus accordingly. "This cardinal is king," Giustiniani said simply, "nor does his majesty depart in the least from the opinion and council of his lordship."[7] Henry spoke only through Wolsey's mouth, it was said, and Fox spoke for the other English councilors when he told Giustiniani that "We have to deal with the cardinal, who is not cardinal, but king."[8] By 1518 Wolsey was so thoroughly in command, it seemed to More, that he was acting without Henry's full knowledge, while the Venetians had begun to address all correspondence to Wolsey first and then to the king, "lest he [Wolsey] should resent the precedence conceded to the king."[9]

Narcissistic, ostentatious, outrageously presumptuous, Wolsey had few admirers. But there was more to him—and more to his relationship with the king—than his enemies and diplomatic colleagues saw. For if Wolsey was proud and disdainful, he was also capable of "rare and unheard-of affability." A bitter opponent called him "a gay finder out of new pastimes," and it was widely known that one of his strongest bonds to Henry was the extravagant hospitality he offered him, marked by lavish entertainments and imaginative diversions. Wolsey needed diversions, in fact, to offset the brooding preoccupations of high office, for he approached his work with the greatest seriousness, and found it hard to relax. Giustiniani caught a glimpse of him one day in 1517, deep in thought, his features troubled and his forehead furrowed in "mental perturbation"; it was this reflective, untiring servant and not the offensive egotist that Henry saw in Wolsey, and made good use of.[10]

Those who confused the servant with the master were deceived largely by a difference of style; it was hard to believe that the boyish, jovial king was in command of the middle-aged, authoritarian churchman. Henry liked to hide the fact that he too worked hard, that like the cardinal he too had a taste for detail and exacting precision. It was Henry, not Wolsey, who went over the specifications for a new citadel at Tournai item by item, looking for ways to save money. He noted with care which towers and gates were to be completed and which abandoned, recommended the optimum thickness of the walls—fifteen feet thick at the top—and found a way to economize by letting many of the full-time soldiers go and hiring others who could double as laborers.[11] It was Henry too who scrutinized the accounts of all his ships and the lists of their crews, and kept clearly in mind from day to day the locations and dispositions of his soldiers. He was capable of guiding by letter the course of a legal dispute between rival ecclesiastical sees while conducting a military campaign, and of instructing his ambassadors—who ought to have known such things far better than the king did—on the exact natural boundaries and political jurisdictions of the European states.[12] Clearly the often-quoted statement of Louise of Savoy's envoy Baltasar Tuerdus, a hostile witness, that Henry "cared for nothing but girls and hunting," distorted the truth.[13]

The exact nature of the partnership between Henry and his chancellor was elusive, but there can be no question that all major governmental decisions were the king's, and that his inclinations governed the minor ones. If management of the day-to-day continuity of affairs was left to Wolsey it was not without close royal supervision. Henry customarily read word for word all the long letters Wolsey sent him when he was away from court, sometimes more than once, and was always eager for news from Flanders and France. If he was hunting he read them as soon as he returned, letting his supper get cold while he sat and pored over his servant's daily reports. After supper Henry kept his secretaries and advisers up for hours reading dispatches to him and taking down his reactions, his plans and his directives to Wolsey and others.[14]

Pace described the way he and the king worked, with Henry calling Pace to bring pen, ink and Wolsey's letters into his privy chamber. Then Henry would read the letters through three times, marking every passage he meant to answer, and finally he would dictate his reply to the secretary. Often he ordered Pace "not further to meddle" with the replies to make certain his meaning was not diluted by secretarial rewording.[15] When fear of the plague made it necessary for the king to be away from court for many weeks in 1518, he made certain this written dialogue with Wolsey would continue without delays. A special post was set up between the two men, with riders standing by to carry messages back and forth every seven hours.[16]

Ambassadors found Henry to be minutely, indeed embarrassingly, well informed. When French envoys tried to boast to him that ten thousand Swiss mercenaries had been killed at the battle of Marignano in 1515, he observed that the figure was remarkable, since there were no more than ten thousand engaged.[17] He was always ready to take foreign envoys aside, to talk to them with disarming earnestness about his desire for peace, his sorrow over the bad faith of other princes and his concern for the welfare of Christendom. Not infrequently he out-talked even these professional talkers; one Venetian complained that the king held him in conversation for so long that he finally had to go away with a pain in his side.[18]

Now in the summer of 1520, however, Wolsey appeared briefly to eclipse his master as, almost singlehandedly, he carried forward the monumental exercise in logistics that made possible the Field of Cloth of Gold.

The meeting between the two sovereigns called for planning on an unprecedented scale. Henry and Francis were eager to outdo one another in every detail, but their rivalry had to be controlled; for the meeting to take place at all French and English negotiators had to agree on the size of the two royal retinues, how and where they would be lodged, where the kings would meet and, when they did, which of them would enter the building first. The numbers of nobles and their ladies, gentlemen, servants and guardsmen were set at over five thousand for the English and nearly as many for the French. Francis would bring, beyond his personal house-hold, four dukes, fifteen counts, several princes and the king of Navarre, plus four hundred archers of his personal guard. Henry would have with him, besides Cardinal Wolsey and his immense retinue, the archbishop of Canterbury and five bishops, two dukes, one marquis, ten earls, and twenty barons; two hundred of his household guard would attend him. Katherine's following, which was nearly half the size of Henry's, included a duchess, ten countesses, twelve baronesses, and twenty knights' ladies, plus an earl, three bishops and four barons.

The challenging task of reproducing the comfort and grandeur of a royal court on the barren coast of Flanders was sizable enough for the French but even greater for the English, who had to bring every horse-shoe, tent stake and cushion to the Val Doré by ship. A mutual problem was the near-total lack of building materials in the area—the Golden Valley was a treeless waste—and both the English and the French had to import from elsewhere the huge tree trunks which, lashed together, held up the high tents and Francis' gorgeous, ill-fated pavilion.

Supplying some ten thousand courtiers, their servants and their horses with fresh and well-prepared food would have been difficult enough in the vicinity of London or Paris; the little towns of Guînes and Ardres were hardly able to supply a fraction of the needed foodstuffs. Thousands of cows and sheep, lambs and chickens, pheasants and herons would have to be brought to huge temporary cookhouses to be slaughtered, cleaned and dressed, and served with the heavily spiced sauces that both the English and the French loved. Fish too would have to be brought in in large quantities, thousands of loaves of bread baked by a cohort of bakers, thousands of pounds of sugar and nuts and spices and fresh cream supplied to the pastrycooks who would make the cakes and comfits for the kings' tables. Oats for the horses and straw for their stalls were an additional burden, and both royal retinues included more grooms of the stable than guardsmen at arms.

These complications mattered less to Henry and Francis, though, than the points of precedence and time-honored usage that governed the jousts themselves. The tiltyard had to be built at a point equidistant from the kings' camps—otherwise one side or the other would appear to have the advantage. The shields and banners of the combatants had to be displayed with meticulous attention to their ranks and nations, again without favoritism, and their arming stations assigned with the same care. How and where each knight would enter and leave the lists had to be decided in advance, to prevent collisions and to ensure that no combatant would have to yield the right of way to an equal or an inferior. The all-important matters of weaponry and the rules of combat were settled by a combined contingent of French and English knights who determined that no "sharp steel" or two-handed swords would be allowed, and that the use of heavy swords would be severely limited. All swords and lances would of course be blunted.

These precautions were intended to prevent injuries, but they also served to disguise a sensitive point: the English were, man for man, taller and heavier than the French, and in the use of the heavy medieval weapons they would have held an overwhelming advantage. Precise sizes and weights for all weapons were agreed on along with the number of courses each knight might run and the number of strokes he might deliver. Fighting at close range was disallowed unless the parties themselves desired it, and jousters were not to be fastened into their saddles, to ensure that they could mount and dismount with ease. Finally rules governing mishaps—knights disarmed, bolting or wounded horses, jousters who missed their turns—were decided on and published, and the business of forging and garnishing arms began to preoccupy both courts.

They preoccupied the two young kings as well. For months before the meeting at the Golden Valley Henry and Francis carried on a running exchange of information, through their diplomatic intermediaries, about the finer points of arms and armor. Through the new English ambassador at the French court, Richard Wingfield, Henry sent Francis an unusually heavy sword. Wingfield explained to the French king that Henry was able to wield it by means of a gauntlet made according to a certain design, and Francis eagerly asked Henry to send him one, promising in return to have his armorers make Henry the newest kind of cuirass which took much of the weight of the armor off the shoulders and allowed easier movement of the arms.[19]

Both Henry and Francis made a great show of concern about each other's panoply, but in fact the entire exchange was little more than an exercise in politeness, intended to cover the intense desire of each man to overthrow and ridicule the other in the lists. Both nations conceded the general superiority of the English in combat; the ferocity of English knights was legendary, and an unbiased observer, Giustiniani's son Merino, remarked that any ten Englishmen were a match for twenty Frenchmen.[20] But when it came to the kings themselves the issue was less clear, for they were well matched in size and skill, and at twenty-six Francis had the advantage of being three years younger than Henry. The two men had never met, but there had been plans for a meeting between them for years. In the first months of Francis' reign they had agreed to meet at Calais, and Henry had immediately sent messengers to Florence for great quantities of silk and cloth of gold, "so as to meet this most Christian king with honor."[21]

Five years were to pass before the costly stuffs were used, years which saw Francis gain diplomatic and military stature—though Henry still referred to him as "this youth"—and which brought about a comprehensive, if precarious, settlement of their political disputes. Wolsey had brought together all the continental states in a treaty of universal peace in the fall of 1518; as part of those negotiations England and France came to terms over Tournai, the "Unsullied Maiden" still in English hands. The town had been in a miserable state ever since Henry took it, blemished by destruction, its population made wretched and rebellious by plague and high debts imposed by the English conquerors. Much the worse for its years under English rule, Tournai was finally sold to the French for 600,000 crowns.[22]

If it did nothing else the meeting of the two kings would satisfy Henry's curiosity about his rival. Francis was reputed to be flamboyant, ambitious, magnificent in his dress and bearing—in short, much like Henry himself. His portraits show a handsome man with a habitually sanguine, slightly disdainful expression. In person he was said to look like the devil; his courtiers called him "Long-Nose" and were wary of the fire in his eyes. Detractors remarked that Francis had an overly large belly, and was "much inclined to corpulence," but even the most hostile observer found him kingly, especially in his coronation crown of uncut rubies and sapphires and his massive gold scepter and tall royal staff of beaten gold surmounted by its orb and cross.[23] Certainly the women of his court found Francis irresistible. Heedless of his wife, the "impotent, halt and naturally deformed" Queen Claude, the French king gathered beautiful women around him and wooed them untiringly. In the words of one courtier he was "of such slight morals that he slips readily into the gardens of others and drinks the waters of many fountains."

Francis was as renowned a hunter as he was a lover. Devoted to his dogs (when his favorite hound Hapeguai died he mourned for days and then ordered the dog skinned and the skin made into gloves to remember him by), he cherished his horses as greatly as his brother monarch of England. It was said that no nobleman in France rode with such incredible speed as the king did when he galloped headlong across country in pursuit of a deer or stag, crossing hills and rushing through thick forests with nothing but his upraised arm to protect him from low-hanging branches.

As mighty as Orion himself in facing the deadly wild boar, Francis had proven his unparalleled bravery before the entire court at Amboise early in his reign. The royal huntsmen were commanded to capture a ferocious boar and bring him to the castle so that the king could "fight him, man against boar, in front of the ladies." Francis' mother, Louise of Savoy, was horrified at the risk to her son, and to please her the king had the castle courtyard filled with life-sized mannequins and the boar released among them instead. The beast charged the statues one after another, running madly around the enclosure in ever-widening circles while the king and his courtiers looked on from overhanging balconies. Suddenly the boar rushed up one of the stairwells leading to the balcony where Francis stood surrounded by a number of ladies. Lowering his head, he charged straight for the king; five or six gentlemen ran to help Francis but he waved them aside, drawing his "good strong sword" and sweeping the ladies into a terrified huddle behind him. His sword poised, his features composed, he watched the oncoming boar "with as complete an assurance as if he had seen coming toward him a demoiselle." Just as the sharp tusks were about to tear into his thigh he leaped to one side and thrust his sword through the beast's heart. The bleeding boar fell heavily back down the stairway and died, as the relieved courtiers cheered and clapped for the king.[24]

Francis showed the same unruffled confidence in the face of his English enemies. "He is young, mighty, insatiable," the English ambassador Wingfield wrote. He talked constantly, and always of his plans for military glory. His continual preoccupation was to restore to France the possessions and rights squandered by his "ignoble predecessors," Wingfield said, and he boasted he would not rest until "the monarchy of Christendom shall rest under the banner of France, as it was wont to do." As always, Henry's talk was equally bellicose. He took delight in telling all who came to his court that it was Francis' dread of English arms that kept the French king from venturing beyond his own borders. Francis hated Henry and all other Englishmen, he explained, but kept up an appearance of cordiality out of fear. Walking hand in hand with Giustiniani and Sagudino one day in the spring of 1518 Henry spoke of Francis' ill-disguised enmity. "I know for certain that he wishes me worse than he does the devil himself," Henry confided to the envoys, "yet you see what kind of friendly language he employs toward me. I prefer peace," he added, "but I am so prepared, that should the king of France intend to attack me, he will find himself deceived. He will fall into his own pit."[25]

Henry had good evidence of Francis' murderous intentions toward him. The bishop of Worcester, traveling on the continent, sent back to England an account of his visit to an astrologer Francis consulted; while they talked, three tall men—English, as he supposed—came into the astrologer's chamber on some mysterious errand, stayed there briefly, and then left by a secret way. Later he heard that they went to Francis and offered to kill King Henry for him.[26] The following year a spy sent a report to the English court describing how he had seen the pretender Richard de la Pole with the French king at Lyons, both men riding together on a mule, deep in conversation. According to the best intelligence the man could piece together, Francis had determined to send four assassins to Henry's court "to set fire by crafty and cautelous means within the house wherein his grace shall be abiding, to the intent (which God forbid) to destroy his most noble person and all other there being present." De la Pole had promised the evildoers a reward of four thousand francs.[27]

It was amid this atmosphere of hostility and secret treachery that that most spectacular gesture of good will, the Field of Cloth of Gold, was planned. Many on both sides believed that the mock combats to be held in Flanders would turn into a real battle through perfidy. The English sent more spies than usual to watch the movements of the French captains and munitions, and the stories they sent home were alarming. John Pechy reported from Paris that his informers had definite evidence of a planned French attack at the Golden Valley. Francis, they said, was sending some fifteen thousand men toward Ardres and had already dispatched nine ships full of gunpowder to supply them there.[28] This account, and others like it, were more than enough to convince Queen Katherine that the royal meeting was an ill-fated mistake. Early in April of 1520 she called her Council together to discuss it, leading the discussion herself and putting forward, in cogent detail, a list of excellent arguments against it. By the time Henry arrived and inquired what was going on she had persuaded her councilors of the folly of the undertaking. They in turn made fresh protestations to the king, but planning for the Field proceeded. For her display of adroit reasoning Katherine was thereafter "held in greater esteem by the king and his Council than ever she was," the imperial ambassador reported, though her reasoning fell on deaf ears. Though most of the nobles and the majority of her subjects agreed with Katherine, the king did not.

The one hope of opponents of the meeting lay in another royal meeting: between Henry and his nephew by marriage, the Holy Roman Emperor Charles V.

The most resolute and most potent enemy of the French, the twenty-year-old Charles had been emperor only a year (he had been king of Spain for nearly four) but was already showing the intelligence and grasp of affairs which were to mark his long and astonishing reign. His appearance was against him. A prominent, misshapen jaw and irregular teeth disfigured his features and detracted from the considered judgment he showed in his speech. With his pale blue eyes and dead-white complexion he was far short of handsome, but he had finally managed to grow a beard and was said to possess the vigor of a grown man.[29] To the English, who held none of his imperfections against him, Charles V was the nephew of their beloved queen, master of the Low Countries—chief entrepôt for English goods and a major source of English wealth—and nominal over-lord of Christendom. It was impossible to describe their delight, Thomas More wrote, when the news came that he was on his way to England.[30]

Charles was convinced that a visit to England could only advance the imperial cause. Henry had been a reliable ally of the empire for the first ten years of his reign, but his recent rapprochement with France left room for doubt about the future. The emperor did not hope to disrupt the upcoming meeting between Henry and Francis, only to disquiet the French and ingratiate himself with his royal uncle. A personal visit could serve the invaluable purpose of strengthening his most enduring ties to England: ties of blood.

Toward the end of May, amid the confusion and activity of last-minute packing and boarding of the ships that would take Henry and his courtiers to Flanders, Charles landed at Dover, where Henry waited to embrace him. The following three days were crowded with feasting and dancing and, for a few hours, serious diplomacy. But for the young emperor the emotional high point came on the second day, when for the first time he saw his mother's sister, Queen Katherine.

He went early that morning to Canterbury, to the archbishop's palace, to meet her.[31] Twenty-five of her loveliest ladies greeted him at the door of the palace, and escorted him inside and down a long corridor guarded by twenty of her pages dressed in gold brocade and crimson satin. Finally he came to a wide marble staircase and, looking up, saw the smiling queen seated on the landing halfway up. She wore robes of cloth of gold lined with ermine, with a beautiful string of pearls wound around her neck. Katherine was not as comely as his mother Joanna; she was plump and matronly, though her face was glowingly alive and her eyes bright and keen. Next to his mother and his sisters, Katherine was his nearest relative, and as soon as he saw her Charles took her to heart. Her sweetness and charm won him over completely as, "not without tears," they embraced one another tenderly and walked arm in arm up the stairs to breakfast.

18

Saint George he was for England;
Saint Dennis was for France.
Sing, Honi soit qui mal y pense.

KING Henry set sail for Flanders in his grandest ship, the *Great Harry,* on the last day of May, 1520. The *Great Harry*—familiar name of the thousand-ton warship *Henry Grâce à Dieu*—was "admiral ship," or flagship of the "king's great army on the sea," and had been built some seven years earlier to the king's exacting specifications by twelve dozen shipwrights working on eighteen hundred tons of timber. It took nine hundred mariners to sail the great ship, and many gunners to man her heavy guns, so formidable it was doubtful "whether any fortress, however strong, could resist their fire." The *Great Harry* was newly fitted for the journey, with banners and pennants flying from every mast and sumptuous sails of cloth of gold. Henry's pleasure in his impressive namesake was enhanced by his knowledge that Francis had nothing like her in his navy, and he was only sorry that the French king would not be in Calais to see him disembark.

On June 11 the two kings installed their households and courtiers on opposite sides of the Golden Valley—the French in some four hundred tents pitched beside a small river at Ardres and the English in some twenty-eight hundred tents stretching away behind Guînes. Francis' huge gold brocade tent, some sixty feet around, had a canvas roof decorated with astrological motifs and stars made from gold foil. Ivy bushes and freshly cut tree branches were fastened around the interior walls of the pavilion, which was crowned with a large gilt statue of Saint Michael that shone brightly in the sun. Several ship masts had been lashed together to form the central support of this structure, which one French observer called "the most beautiful tent ever seen."

The elegance of Francis' pavilion was more than matched by the festive Italianate palace built by six thousand English and Flemish masons, carpenters, bricklayers, glaziers and tilers over a period of months for Henry and his party. A long rectangle of stonework supported by tall brick columns and decorated with battlements, crenellations and a band of ornamental tilework, the compact structure was dignified yet gay, with its fan-shaped stone and ironwork ornaments and its life-size statues of antique heroes posturing in every niche. Large heraldic animals in stone adorned the corners of the roof, from whose center rose a six-sided cupola surmounted by more animals and a gilt angel. All who saw the exquisite palace praised its proportions and design—one Italian remarked that Leonardo himself could not have made a finer one—and admired in particular the high arched windows which lined the length of the upper floor and, at night, turned the entire building into a blazing landmark. Thousands of feet of glass had been imported to Guînes for these windows, which "lumined the eyes of beholders" and contrasted with the narrow slits in the walls of the old castle of Guînes nearby and the windowless tents of the French.

Inside the palace every surface was decorated, the windows framed in gold inlay, the walls lined in silk hangings and tapestries, or studded with the roses of the Tudor livery, the corridors filled with warlike busts with "images of sore and terrible countenances." Henry's most beautiful tapestries and carpets were brought from Greenwich and Richmond to cover the walls and floors of this palace, and to give it the air of an authentic court. Its little chapel was furnished with candlesticks and chalices brought from Westminster Abbey, and its altar cloths were of cloth of gold tissue embroidered with pearls. Golden statues of the twelve apostles as large as small children astonished the guests who came to hear mass in the palace, but even more astonishing were the two fountains in its courtyard, which poured forth claret, hippocras and beer for all who cared to drink.

Henry and Francis were only a cannonshot apart in their temporary quarters, but they did not meet. Instead each notified the other of his presence by messenger, with Henry sending Wolsey and his entourage to Francis to arrange the time and place for the two sovereigns to meet in person. Wolsey's retinue caused a great stir. He had far more attendants than did the dukes of Suffolk and Buckingham and the archbishop of Canterbury combined. Fifty mounted gentlemen in crimson velvet preceded him, with fifty ushers bearing gold maces "as large as a man's head." His standing gold cross with its jeweled crucifix was borne solemnly before him, and the richly trapped mule he rode was surrounded by dozens of lackeys and guards wearing his device. Bishops and other ecclesiastics rode behind the cardinal, among them the grand prior of the Knights of Saint John of Jerusalem, and a hundred mounted archers of the king's guard, their bows bent at the ready, brought up the rear.

Wolsey's display was only partly meant to impress the official participants in the festivities. He had in mind too the watching townspeople of Guînes and Ardres, the local farmers and shepherds whose animals continued to graze undisturbed in the fields as the royal tents were erected and the tiltyard constructed, and the growing crowd of curious spectators who camped on the hills around the Golden Valley and came to drink the king's wine in the courtyard of the English palace. Francis had turned back some ten thousand of these idlers who followed him on his initial journey to Ardres, and the provost marshal of the Field tried in vain to enforce the joint royal command that persons with no business in the valley should leave it within six hours "on pain of hanging." But the crowds grew unchecked, eager for the sight of finery and wealth and eager, too, to search the faces of men and women who always had enough to eat and who could spend the long summer days in knightly pastimes. Beggars appeared at the tents of the courtiers, and peddlers from the towns and fairs tried to sell them pies and trinkets; minstrels followed them playing for coins, while from a distance laborers, villagers and poor travelers stopped on their journeys to enjoy the spectacle, and memorized its details to tell their children.

Two days after the royal parties arrived came the first great event of the Field of Cloth of Gold, the face-to-face meeting of the two kings. They left their respective camps late in the afternoon, at the sound of a cannonshot from Guînes Castle. Henry and his train approached the meeting place from one side, Francis and his from the other, and when both parties reached artificial hillocks built up at opposite entrances to the valley they halted to allow the kings to go on alone. A little pavilion had been erected at the exact center of the valley, furnished with chairs, cushions and refreshments, for the first conversation between the two monarchs, and it was toward this pavilion that they now rode, slowly at first and then, after taking off their hats in token of greeting, at a fast gallop "like two men of arms going into combat at spearpoint." They had in mind to embrace one another while still on horseback, but Henry's splendid bay proved too lively, and they had to dismount before beginning a lavish display of heartily feigned affection. An Italian eyewitness swore they threw their arms around each other more than twenty times, thrilling the French and making them weep for joy.

Inside the little pavilion—which they entered together, arm in arm, to avoid the issue of precedence—the two kings were joined by Wolsey and the French admiral Bonnivet. The articles governing the meeting were read out, and when Henry's titles were read, including the time-honored phrase "King of France," he characteristically made light of the matter and suggested in very good French that Francis' presence obviously invalidated it. When the kings had conversed for a while and drunk a great quantity of wine, the initial meeting ended, and Henry and Francis rode back to their waiting retinues to the sound of the English oboes and sackbuts and the drums and flutes of Francis' hired Switzers. Wolsey and Bonnivet reported that the good feeling at the meeting was boundless, with Francis calling Henry his brother and friend, and Henry swearing that "he never saw prince with his eyes, that might of his heart be more loved."

Three weeks of feasting, jousting and fierce competition followed. Francis gave banquets for Henry's knights, Henry for Francis' knights; the two kings dined together in a hall lined with pink brocade; Queens Katherine and Claude feasted one another; Francis feasted Katherine, and Henry Claude; and Wolsey entertained the French queen dowager, Louise of Savoy. According to one account, an inexhaustible supply of dishes were served at each of these banquets, with the food and wine so abundant that the courtiers choked themselves, but another observer noted that the guests of honor did nothing but converse, having eaten before they came.[1]

Each day the order of the jousting was arranged by heralds standing at the foot of a huge artificial "tree of nobility," nearly a hundred and thirty feet high and forty feet wide, which bore the escutcheons of the combatants and celebrated famous tournaments of the past. Both the French and English bands tilted furiously, breaking hundreds of lances (the English brought fifteen hundred with them) and fighting valiantly at the barriers. For the French, Francis, St.-Pol, Fleuranges and a dozen other knights won prizes, while Henry, Suffolk, Dorset, Francis Bryan, Anthony Brown, William Carey, John Neville and Richard Jerningham—who was nearly unhorsed in the last week of the jousting—gained prizes among the English knights. In all, the weapons forge that was brought from Greenwich and set up at Guînes repaired as many swords for William Kingston, Giles Chapel, Nicholas Carew and Anthony Knevet as for Henry himself.

It could not be said, though, that the subjects outdid their sovereigns. Francis, an observer wrote, "shivered spears like reeds, and never missed a stroke," while Henry lived up to his unparalleled reputation as a jouster and expert horseman, tiring six horses in rapid succession one day in the exercises of the manage, "laughing the whole time, being in truth very merry, and remaining in the lists for upwards of two hours."[2] To be sure, Francis went down to defeat to one of the English knights, Weston Brown, and suffered a slight wound and a great momentary humiliation, but he got his revenge: he challenged Henry to an impromptu wrestling match and quickly threw his burly rival to the ground. Both men surpassed themselves in fighting at the barriers, dealing blows "with such force that the fire sprang out of their armor," and in the final tally neither went away the loser.

The royal ladies were appraised as carefully as the kings. Francis' mother, Louise of Savoy, a great beauty in her youth and an extremely powerful figure at her son's court, eclipsed her pregnant, retiring daughter-in-law Queen Claude. When Francis was not dressing or dining or hunting or keeping a rendezvous, he was nearly always to be found with his mother, who looked on him as her crowning achievement and a fitting consolation for the indignities of her earlier life. In her eyes Francis was "my glorious son and triumphant Caesar," and she spurred on his ambitions for conquest with all the enthusiasm of a matron of ancient Rome.[3]

The English Queen Katherine too stood out, riding in her gilt-columned open litter upholstered in cloth of gold and trimmed in crimson satin. Wearing a becoming Spanish headdress that left her long auburn hair hanging free over her shoulders and gown, she made "a very beautiful sight," and it was easy to forget—from a distance at least—that she had already reached the advanced age of thirty-five.[4] "The beautiful Lady Mary, the king's sister," was also conspicuous among the English women. Though she was now Charles Brandon's wife Mary still kept the title and heraldic symbols of a queen of France; the fleur-de-lis and the monogram L and M, for Louis and Mary, decorated her litter, along with Louis XII's symbol, the porcupine.[5] Among Katherine's ladies, Anne Brown, sister of his nemesis Weston Brown, found favor with Francis.

Her handsomeness was widely remarked, and the French king chose her as his dancing partner and dinner companion several times.[6] The drinking of the English ladies scandalized a Venetian diplomat, who saw them pass flasks and then large cups of wine from hand to hand as they watched the tilting, draining more than twenty of the cups and sharing them freely with the French lords.[7]

Miraculously, there was no recorded treachery, no brawling, and none of the practical jokes for which both Henry's minions and Francis' playful companions were famous. There were constant disputes: over the English markers torn down by the French, over the location of the tiltyard and the poor view of it from the ladies' scaffold, over the one-sided wrestling contest held when the powerful Breton wrestlers were absent.[8] But none of these arguments erupted into violence and both French and English confined their volatile passions to the jousts. The weather was a hindrance. At best it was uncomfortably hot—"hotter than St. Peter's in Rome," an Italian wrote—and at worst the winds were so high the jousters "could not couch their lances," and dust blinded the horses and parched the throats of the spectators. The high wind blew Francis' great pavilion away toward the sea and damaged the smaller tents. Injuries to the combatants were unavoidable. Francis emerged from the tiltyard with a black eye, and had to wear a rakish eyepatch for a few days, and later a fiery English knight sliced the plume clean off his helmet. Henry sprained his hand. A French knight, tilting against his brother, was hurt so badly he died of his wounds.

But overall the thousands who attended the celebrated meeting behaved as if their cordiality was real, and did credit to their genteel upbringing. The amity between the two sovereigns and their courtiers was symbolized by exchanges of lavish gifts. Henry gave Francis a jeweled collar with a great pendant ruby in the shape of a heart. Claude gave Katherine a gorgeous litter, with its mules and pages; in return she received beautifully trapped riding horses. Francis made a present of gold vases worth twenty thousand crowns to Wolsey, and his mother presented the cardinal with a jeweled crucifix; Wolsey's gift to the French king was not recorded, but to Louise he offered a relic of the true cross, set with precious stones.[9] Of all the gifts befitting royalty the noblest were fine horses, and both kings received their share. Henry admired the mount of one of the French knights; later, after he had run his courses, the man dismounted, kissed the king's hand, and made him a present of it. Henry gave a number of valuable horses to Francis, but in the opinion of a Mantuan who saw them all, the finest horses at the Field were those Francis gave Henry—a splendid sorrel mare, Mantellino, a high-stepping jouster who ran twelve courses without swerving, and the prize of them all, Dappled Mozaurcha.[10]

After three weeks of guarded sociability it could almost have been said that the English and French were able to get along well together. At the elaborate concluding ceremonies, where Wolsey officiated at mass (a rare event) in a temporary chapel built overnight in the tiltyard, the two kings vowed to dedicate a permanent church to "Our Lady of Friendship" and to return to the Golden Valley often with their courtiers. High-spirited as ever, Henry seemed "as well pleased with this interview as if he had gained a great realm," and Francis was equally satisfied. But though the sovereigns parted with effusive displays of sorrow their followers were eager to return home, and were hardly out of earshot before they began to heap insults on one another. "If I had a drop of French blood in my body," Lord Leonard Grey was overheard to remark to a companion, "I would cut myself open to get rid of it." "And so would I," was the reply.[11] When he heard of this Henry had both men arrested, but no amount of royal wrath could wipe away the ill feeling between the English and French, an echo of hatreds centuries old and soon to be rekindled. And besides, it was hardly out of consideration for his brother monarch Francis that Henry traveled immediately to Gravelines, where he and Charles V set to work to undermine French interests.

The eighth wonder of the world came and went too quickly to leave a lasting memorial. The church to Our Lady of Friendship was never built, and it is doubtful whether either sovereign seriously considered meeting the other again soon, except in battle. The French and English disliked and distrusted each other even more than before, and the meeting stirred old fears of invasion and conquest on both sides.

Still less did the Field of Cloth of Gold touch the lives of the French and English people. To the thousands who came to gape at the spectacle at first hand it was a shimmering vision never to be forgotten, but to most people it was only an evocative name. For while the Field was in progress, the citizens of London spent their days and nights as they always had, heedless of the marvels across the Channel.

By an odd chance we know what some Londoners were doing on a summer night at about the time of the Field.[12] Because apprentices and others in the city had recently rioted against London's foreign craftsmen, threatening to rise up and kill them all, searches were made from time to time in the suburbs for "suspected persons." A document has survived which tells us, on one July night, what the searchers found.

In Paddington, a tailor and his servant, a servant of the abbot of Westminster and his son, and another man "played all night till four o'clock in the morning" at cards and dice, at which time the game was broken up and the players reported to the constable. In St. Martin's, Southwark, Lambeth and Stepney, many "masterless men" were found in shabby rooms, though few of them were judged to be the sort of "vagabond and misdemeanored persons" the searchers were looking for. Ten Germans were seized in Southwark, in the parish of St. Woloff's, and seven Frenchmen along with them in a house in a neighboring street; five mariners lodged in victualing houses were questioned, but were found to be honest crewmen of a ship called *The Christ*.

The stews yielded fifty-four men and women to be detained under suspicion, though many houses were merely crowded with their ordinary tenants in varying states of discomfort and mundane vice. Two women, "an old drab and a young wench," were found lying huddled together on a dirty sheet on the bare ground in the cellar of a house; upstairs were Hugh

Lewis and Alice Ball, "taken in bed together, not being man and wife." John à Park, a brewer, and one Agnes Cotes were taken "in like manner," while Philip Humphrey, who claimed to be a royal servant, was found "in a house by himself in a chamber, and a woman in a chamber underneath, without shutting of doors." In the Rose tavern at Westminster the officers questioned Anne Southwick, "late dwelling within the bars of Westminster," and released her. In Tothill Street, at the buckler-maker's house, they detained Elizabeth Hammond, who said she had been brought there by one John Thomas of Brondwood, whose child she was carrying.

In all the number of undesirables was small. Most of the inns and lodging houses of Knightsbridge, Kensington and Hammersmith were filled with honest craftsmen and laborers—"mowers, haymakers, makers of tile and brick." There were four countrymen at the sign of the Katherine, and at the White Hart, two men bringing oxen to Wolsey at court. Two carters were found snoring side by side at the sign of the Plough; other lodgings yielded a tailor, a parish clerk, an old man without work and four men of the west country who had a suit at Whitehall before the dean of the chapel. At Chelsea, toward morning, the king's servants found only two men sent to clean a house for their lord, and in a barn, a beggar and his wife.

19

But alas! what a griefe is this
That princes subjects cannot be true,
But still the devill hath some of his,
Will play their parts whatever ensue;
Forgetting what a grievous thing
It is to offend the anointed king?
Alas for woe, why should it be so,
This makes a sorrowful heigh ho.

IN the same year that the Field of Cloth of Gold celebrated the glory and majesty of Henry VIII, the king confided to Wolsey a haunting suspicion of the men around him. ''I would you should make good watch on the duke of Suffolk, on the duke of Buckingham, on my lord of Northumberland, on my lord of Derby, on my lord of Wiltshire and on others which you think suspect,'' he wrote, adding that the reasons for his mistrust were so secret he was disclosing them to ''none other but you and I.''[1] No record remains of the exact nature of Henry's suspicions, though they were very likely associated with accusations brought against the duke of Buckingham in the following year. The letter belied the apparent concord surrounding the king and brought to the surface, perhaps for the first time, dangerous undercurrents of conflict and potential rebellion that ran far below the smooth surface of court life.

This was not the first shadow to fall across the reign. In the spring of 1517 the hatred of foreigners that had been building among London apprentices erupted into large-scale violence. Isolated attacks on foreign artisans and merchants gave way to mass assaults on the quarters where the French and Flemish workers lived, and on the embattled houses of the Florentines and Genoese. Closing the city gates to prevent the king's soldiers from reinforcing the city guard, the rioters temporarily took control; in Richmond, the king was roused from his bed at midnight by stories of mayhem in the capital and made ready to lead his soldiers against the thousands of apprentices and the ne'er-do-wells and criminals who had joined them. In a matter of hours royal forces under Norfolk and his son the earl of Surrey had fought their way through into the city and eventually restored order, and overall the damage was found to be light.

Henry's judgment against the captured rebels was swift and spectacular, however. Some four hundred of the malefactors were brought before the king and his chief lords in the great hall at Westminster, ''all in their shirts and barefoot, and each with a halter round his neck,'' and heard him condemn them to death. They cried for mercy; Wolsey and several of the other lords urged clemency, and at length, after keeping them for some time in fear of their lives, Henry relented. The pardoned men leaped for joy, tearing the halters from their necks and throwing them in the air, and making a great impression on the spectators. The quartered bodies of forty others, denied pardon, made another sort of impression. "At the city gates one sees nothing but gibbets and the quarters of these scelerats," a visitor to London wrote, "so that it is horrible to pass near them."[2]

Just after the "Evil May Day" frightened Londoners were subjected to a second panic. The sweating sickness returned with frightening virulence, striking nearly every household and setting the church bells tolling endlessly for the dead. "In some one town half the people died," the chronicler Hall wrote, "and in some other town the third part, the sweat was so fervent and infectious."[3] By August most of the country lay in dread of death, with victims being "borne to their graves in every direction," and fresh graves dug every day. But the alarm was nowhere greater than in the capital, where some were so terrified, the Venetian Chieregato observed, "that they suffered more from fear than others did from the sweat itself."[4] Masters and servants joined in taking daily preventives, and in nursing those who succumbed despite them, wrapping the victims sometimes to the point of suffocation in warm clothes and blankets in an effort to prevent air from reaching their swollen armpits.

In the royal household the king's own preventive made from sawge of vertue, herb of grace and elder leaves was employed, but to little effect. One by one the servants began to sicken and die—young Lord Grey, then an unnamed German servant, then dozens among the kitchen staff and in the stables, and finally even some of those who waited personally on the king. To save his life the royal secretary Ammonio made hasty plans to leave for the countryside with a friend. The arrangements were made; riding horses were sent for, and the two men packed their belongings and celebrated their deliverance with a hearty dinner together. Three days later Ammonio was dead of the sweat, and his relatives and fellow-churchmen were petitioning to be given the benefices left vacant by his death.[5]

Henry left London at the first sign of infection, moving from place to place with a greatly reduced household, zigzagging from one untainted village to another as the summer months passed. By fall disease had reduced his household further, and had made many in it easy marks for healers and miracle-workers of all sorts. In October a Spanish friar came to court, esteemed for his wonder-working powers as a saint. The courtiers listened eagerly as he told how he had escaped the peril of the sea in a violent storm, ordering the waves to calm and the wind to cease, "the heaven itself, at his protest, shutting its windows." Some may have availed themselves of the friar's blessings, but the king, as eager as any to find a cure, remained skeptical. After an hour's interview with the man he sent him on his way, pronouncing him to be more a friar than a saint, and returned to his hawking.[6]

In November the royal servants were still dying, and in desperation

Henry sent them all away and settled down to wait for the sweat to pass in the company of the queen, three favorite gentlemen, and the musician Memo. For the first time since the start of his reign he made no plans to spend Christmas in state. None of his palaces was free of infection, and those near London were at additional risk. In the absence of the king and cardinal—Wolsey, stricken with the sweat in August, was roaming the countryside with the remnant of his decimated household—public order had once again been menaced. The London apprentices had rioted against the foreigners a second time, and the city was in arms for its defense.[7]

The approach of Christmas found Henry and his tiny retinue near Southampton, waiting anxiously for the arrival of the Flanders fleet, intending to buy their winter provisions as the goods came off the ships and before they could circulate in the disease-plagued countryside.[8] Bad weather delayed the fleet, and day after day passed without news of it, though there were dozens of stories of fishing boats and even galleons lost in the stormy seas. One way and another Henry and his companions came by what they needed, but it was January before they returned to London, and even then their stay was to be brief. In March Henry was startled into fear when he learned that three of the pages who slept in his chamber had been struck down suddenly, and just as suddenly died, their bodies whisked away before the sight of them could unman their master completely.[9]

He took his councilors and left the capital again, finding refuge at Abingdon where, as he said, he could be at ease "where no man cometh to tell him of the death of any person, as they were wont daily." Despite the inconveniences—the lack of space, the shortage of foodstuffs and of horse meat, the difficulty of getting news from Wolsey at Westminster— the king settled in at Abingdon, with his advisers, his sister Mary, whose presence pleased him so much he urged her to stay on, and his wife, who told him in no uncertain terms what a mistake it would be to return to London. "Although she was no prophet," Katherine said, "yet she would lose her finger if some inconvenient should not ensue unto the king's person if he should at this time repass towards London."[10] Gradually, as the dying became less frequent, the routines of the court were cautiously re-established, and Henry's fear of sickness and sudden death receded out of consciousness once again.

His fear of over-mighty courtiers, though, was growing, and in April of 1521 he struck out against the most conspicuous of them, Edward Stafford, duke of Buckingham.

High steward of England, a proud, pugnacious lord in the medieval mold, Buckingham had served Henry from the time the latter was prince of Wales. As king Henry had tolerated the duke's hot temper, his profane raillery and his open hatred of Wolsey, leaving him in possession of his vast estates—he was said to be the greatest landholder in England—and relying on him as a soldier and a stern governor of his lordship on the Welsh border.

By 1520, however, his trust in the duke had dissolved. Wolsey had "made a good watch" on Buckingham, as the king asked, and he and his agents had learned much from the duke's servants. They told how

Buckingham had gathered and armed fighting men, ostensibly in the name of the king but in fact to be used to overthrow him. He had bought hundreds of pounds' worth of cloth of gold and silver and silks, they said, to bribe the royal guard and ensure their support when the moment of action came. He had consulted a treasonous Carthusian monk, Nicholas Hopkins, who prophesied that the king would have no son and that Buckingham himself would one day be king. And he had the monstrous daring, so his surveyor Charles Knevet swore, to conceive of murdering the king, coming into his presence, "having upon him secretly a knife, so that when kneeling before the king he would have risen suddenly and stabbed him."[11]

For this catalogue of offenses Buckingham was seized, along with his brother-in-law Lord Abergavenny and two of the Poles. (Reginald Pole, whom the king had sent to Italy to study, was not implicated and wrote to England at once asserting his loyalty.[12]) As alarming as the duke's criminous improprieties was the public sentiment in his favor. He went to his trial under heavy guard, amid fear that he might be rescued "by reason of his numerous followers in London." Convicted of plotting to kill Henry and take the throne, he was not greeted with the jeering contempt a traitor deserved. Instead, the crowds who gathered to watch the duke on his return to the Tower found his fate distressing. His death was "universally lamented by all London," the Venetian ambassador wrote; all men grieved for him, and many wept at his execution. "Our Italians," he added, "had not the heart to see him die."[13]

The king had not the strength to watch Buckingham's death either. He was in bed with a high fever and chills, unable to eat and worried over by his physicians. It was left to Wolsey to remind him that a callous etiquette obliged him to write consoling letters to the widow and son of the man he had condemned to death, and to send drafts of these letters for the royal signature.[14]

That the people should mourn a man accused of imagining their king's death confused and dismayed Henry, though the duke's trial had already brought to light much that was dismaying. Discontent had begun to temper the affection Henry's subjects still felt for him—discontent with his high-handed treatment of his nobles, with his choice of associates in power, with the course and nature of his rule.

To take Buckingham's word for it—the word of a condemned man, convinced even as he spoke in his own defense that "he knew it was the king's will that he should die"—the nobles greatly resented Henry's strong mastery over them. Their ancestral place in government was being disregarded, their ancestral prerogatives overlooked. Instead of ruling alongside the king they were overruled by him, while men of lesser rank served him in the work of governing. He "wished the nobles would break their minds," the duke complained to one of his officers, revealing the extent of their displeasure, "for few of them were contented, they were so unkindly handled." For a great aristocrat to keep his grievances silent was an intolerable humiliation. Buckingham roared out his feelings, speaking his fate: "he would rather die than be ordered as he was."[15]

What the English nobility of the 1520s saw as an affront to their personal status was in truth part of a shift in governmental power that had been under way for more than a generation. Ideas of honor and precedence formed in feudal times persisted, but in reality men such as Buckingham were not the prepotent lords they had once been. They still kept barrels full of suits of armor in their castles, ready to arm their fighting men as their medieval ancestors had done, but their old power was waning. Comfort and luxury more than the need for defense now determined the structure of their castles; they thought less often of enforcing their rights through warfare than of displaying their rank through fine clothes, a costly table, and splendid entertainments. And as their tastes shifted toward grandeur their incomes—derived from fixed rents in a time of rising costs—declined, enfeebling them still further and making the kind of stalwart opposition Buckingham wished for even more remote.

Henry could not afford to take comfort from these changes, though, for he had to confront not abstract forces but arrogant, lordly men, men bred to violence whose family histories were scarred with tumult and local warfare. Provoked too far, such men could become disloyal; if they should rebel there was little enough to stand between them and their sovereign. Though he boasted to foreign envoys that he had "more money and greater force and authority" than his ancestors had ever possessed, Henry had no standing army and was not well prepared for internal lawlessness. His coastal and border fortresses were barely satisfactory, but few other royal castles were in condition to be used. Many were in ruins, their fallen walls and crumbling battlements plundered for building materials. Others, though usable to some extent, were in severe decay; only a handful were "metely strong" to resist assault. Henry could not afford to risk a baronial rebellion, and the dissatisfaction now spoken of made him uneasy.

Angered at their displacement from power, the nobles were infuriated to see their places filled by mere "boys"—the king's minions—and other inferiors. The fees and offices that should have gone to Henry's great lords were squandered on men such as William Compton, an orphan raised at court, or the young scholars of humble family whom the king favored for their capability. Though created a nobleman of the highest rank Charles Brandon was looked on as one of these inferiors, envied for his influence and feared for his ambition. His grandiose, pinnacled mansion in Southwark gave credence to rumors that he had high hopes of the crown in right of his wife, and since his restoration to favor he had resumed his old role at Henry's side, meeting foreign visitors to court, discussing matters of state "very earnestly" with ambassadors and conducting himself as second only to Wolsey in power.

But it was Wolsey who rankled most. Buckingham's hatred of him was so great it was at first rumored that the duke was imprisoned for plotting his assassination and not the king's.[16] The cardinal's middle-class origins were an insult to all men of rank; his aristocratic arrogance and disdain were too much for real aristocrats to bear. There was a warfare of style between Wolsey and the peers of the realm, and it was irksome that the king should favor Wolsey. Emboldened by the royal favor the cardinal lashed out venomously at the nobles, in language preserved by another of his enemies, Henry's old tutor Skelton. "He regardeth lordes/ No more than pot shordes," Skelton wrote. He called them "doddy pates," rainbeaten beggars, ruffians and recreants.

> He hath despite and scorn
> At them that be well born
> He rebukes them and rails
> Ye whoresons, ye vassals
> Ye knaves, ye churls' sons
> Ye ribands, not worth two plums . . .

So Wolsey reviled the men he surpassed in pride and ostentation, galling them by his insults yet relying on his unequaled power to protect himself from their revenge. Everything about the cardinal was offensive to the nobility. He kept them waiting, refusing to see callers until they had tried three or four times to get in to see him; he thought himself the equal of royalty, and sat down to dinner with the king and queen, forcing Buckingham and Suffolk to serve him as they did their royal master. He sat in state to receive his New Year's gifts from the courtiers just as the king did, and entertained them at Hampton Court in a fashion that put their own magnificence to shame.

Guests at the cardinal's great palace of York Place walked through eight elegant rooms to reach his audience chamber, rooms hung with tapestries and adorned with costly gifts from foreign sovereigns. In an era when sour-smelling rushes covered the floors of hovels and palaces alike Wolsey's palace of Hampton Court was furnished with sixty large damascene carpets—a gift from the Venetian Signory, made at Wolsey's demand. (After some debate the Venetians decided to satisfy the cardinal by selling the gold chain Henry had given their ambassador Giustiniani to pay for the carpets.[17]) As a cardinal the sumptuary laws allowed Wolsey to serve nine courses at his banquets—even a duke was limited to seven—and his cooks and pastry chefs were regularly called upon to turn out dozens of ingenious dishes in quantities to satisfy hundreds of diners. At one feast well over four hundred guests consumed pies baked in the shape of St. Paul's Cathedral, and puddings sculpted to represent dancing courtiers, all as real-looking as a painting.

Through this splendor Wolsey strode like one born to wealth, his robes flowing in elegant folds to his feet, his wit flying, pressing to his nose from time to time a pomander filled with "confections against the pestilent airs" which blocked out the odors of the crowded hall.

Embittered by the cardinal's prosperity the disappointed courtiers told stories about the hidden foulness of his life: how he had fathered a bastard son and daughter, and made the girl a nun and endowed the boy with church livings worth many thousands of pounds; how he encouraged churchmen to flagrantly abuse their vows of chastity, following his example; and how "he was the king's bawd, showing him what women were most wholesome, and best of complexions."[18]

Hatred of Wolsey was not confined to court circles. From the time he became cardinal, the chronicler Hall wrote, "all men almost hated him, and disdained him."[19] Rioting apprentices on the Evil May Day threatened to kill Wolsey, and in the taverns of the capital it was said that "the cardinal would destroy this realm, and set all the nobles in the king's top."[20] Merchants accused him of lending money from the royal treasury to foreigners for profit, and every unpopular act of Henry's was laid to Wolsey's charge.[21]

So profound was Wolsey's impact on the popular imagination that he began to figure in the obscure occult pronouncements the people confided to one another over their pots of ale. A brewer, so Wolsey's spies reported, claimed to "see by prophecy that a great man being bishop, should ride upon a high horse and should have as great a fall as ever had man." Another man, Thomas Gyldon, predicted in 1520 that "within this two year he the said cardinal would have the shamefullest fall that ever chanced in England," and added that he would give a hundred pounds from his own purse to see that time come soon.[22]

These and other murmurings carried hints that among Henry's subjects were some who no longer saw in him the gifted, all-powerful young king who had won glory in France and Flanders. A counter-image had arisen—of a ruler vulnerable to sinister forces, ruled by others and seemingly unable to break his dark bonds.

"It is a wonder to see the king how he is ordered nowadays," a Lincolnshire man told a group of his fellow-townspeople, "for the cardinal and the duke of Suffolk, which the king hath brought up of nought, do rule him in all things even as they list." He was not certain of the source of their power, whether it arose from "necromancy, witchcraft, or policy," but others were ready to swear that both Suffolk and the cardinal trafficked in black magic. The duke, it was said, had used magic to cause the leg of his rival William Compton to become diseased, while Wolsey was rumored to worship satanic powers, "taking council of a spirit how he might continue to have the king's favor."[23] Together they "meddled with the devil, and by puissance of the said devil kept their master subject."

Henry counted on the lords in the Star Chamber to take quick action to silence these rumors, but he brooded for days in his sickbed over the treachery of Buckingham, and over the perplexing problem of an heir.

20

O waly, waly, gin love be bonny,
A little time while it is new;
But when its auld, it waxeth cauld,
And fades awa' like morning dew.

BY far the most disturbing of the revelations to come to light at Buckingham's trial was that Henry's subjects were actively, vocally worried that he had no son. In 1521, twelve years into the reign, the problem of the succession was becoming acute. The queen had borne three sons, but none survived. The New Year's Boy had lived less than two months. The son born in 1513 either was stillborn or died just after birth. And the eagerly awaited son born prematurely in 1514 was also born dead, "to the very great grief" of a king and court hoping fervently that this time the odds would be in Katherine's favor.

It was almost an anticlimax when in February of 1516 Katherine gave birth to a liveborn daughter who instead of dying, kicked and screamed her way into healthy infancy. The baby, Princess Mary, was welcome enough—chiefly as living proof that the queen was capable of motherhood—but a daughter could not fill the need for a male heir. Katherine's physician, Ferdinand de Victoria, was paid handsomely for his part in the queen's success, yet even as they congratulated the new father Henry's subjects were thinking ahead to the possibility of a son. "Beseeching our lord to send you as much rejoicing of my lady princess, and make you as glad a father as ever was king," Mountjoy wrote to Henry, "and after this good beginning to send you many fair [children] to your grace's comfort and all your true subjects'."[1] When a month after Mary's birth Mary Brandon was delivered of a healthy son it must have pained his royal uncle to attend his christening and to give the boy his own name.

Two years later, though, hopes rose once more as Katherine again became bountifully, enthusiastically pregnant. As soon as her condition was suspected it became the most absorbing topic of conversation at court. In hushed tones the king's officials and household staff exchanged gossip about her prospects for a safe delivery, listening for scraps of news from Dr. de Victoria and watching the queen's face for signs of strain. Once again the doctor became a very important man; he had long since settled in as Katherine's chief physician, and to make him more comfortable his wife had been brought from Spain to join him, at some considerable cost.

No physician could have been more solicitous of Katherine's well-being than Henry, though, who as her pregnancy continued to go well kept her with him on his hunting progresses and let her needs govern his itinerary. Pace recorded the king's delight the night he rode to Woodstock to meet Katherine "and the queen did meet with his grace at his chamber door, and showed unto him, for his welcome home, her belly something great, declaring openly that she was quick with child." Henry officially informed Wolsey at once, and gave orders for the quickening to be celebrated with a solemn singing of the Te Deum in St. Paul's. In a secret letter to the cardinal written at about the same time he made his hopes plain. He trusted that Katherine was indeed carrying a living child, he told his chancellor, and he meant to make certain she came to no harm. For her sake he would not return to London, "because about this time is partly of her dangerous times, and because of that I would remove her as little as I may now." Henry's letter revealed his guarded excitement. He had been disappointed too often not to restrain his optimism, but after all the last child had lived and this one gave signs of life. Nothing was certain, Henry wrote, all was in God's hands, but the queen's condition was "a thing wherein I have great hope and likelihood." God might well bring to completion that which he had begun.[2]

Again the hopes proved to be vain. The child, a girl, was stillborn. It was to be Katherine's last.

Now in 1521 only the most resolute optimist could envision the birth of a son to Katherine of Aragon, and in the absence of such a prospect there was much anxiety about who the king's heir would be. Buckingham had been an alarmingly likely possibility. The Carthusian who had encouraged the duke with his treasonous revelations was far from alone in thinking he might one day rule; his popularity had been undeniable. Richard de la Pole, though he lacked Buckingham's popular support, had an impeccable bloodline and the somewhat fitful backing of the French king; his claims could hardly be ignored. Of Henry's own blood, there was the surviving son of Margaret Tudor and James IV, Prince James, whom some already spoke of as the natural heir, and Henry Brandon, the young earl of Lincoln who had been born just after Princess Mary.[3]

More distant relatives of the king were thought to have at least some chance of succeeding. In 1519 Henry and Wolsey were somewhat startled to hear that Charles V's minister Chièvres had proposed a match between his own niece and Henry Courtenay, Henry VIII's first cousin and close confidant. A princely dowry of fifty thousand gold crowns was being offered with the girl, and the emperor indicated he would add even more. For some reason—perhaps the same reason he had tried to arrange a marriage between Charles Brandon and Margaret of Savoy—Henry seems to have favored the match, but Wolsey was highly suspicious of it. He saw to it that inquiries were made to discover just what Chièvres' motives were, and asked pointedly whether the offer was based on an expectation that Courtenay might succeed to the throne.[4]

Though spoken of only in whispers—for to debate the question of the king's heir was treason—the matter was much in the air in the early 1520s, and weighed heavily on Henry. What had gone wrong? Evidently a large part of the problem lay with Katherine, whose checkered history of stillbirths, miscarriages and odd female phenomena—unexplained swellings and deflatings, menstrual irregularities—put her record of failure far outside the norm, even in an age when perhaps half of all infants died within their first year.[5] A series of physicians and midwives, of which Dr. de Victoria was only the most prominent, had been unable to cure the queen's disorders, and she was rapidly reaching the end of her childbearing years.[6]

Publicly at least no one said that Henry was to blame. Even if such a suggestion had not been treasonous it would have been all but unthinkable, for as he reached his late twenties the king was no less virile and vigorous than he had been at the start of his reign. His agile, admirably proportioned body was still a match for most opponents in the joust; the angelic beauty of his face had become more striking with the years, and he still had a boyish air, though his red-blond hair was now complemented by a thick, manly red beard which "looked like gold."[7] Long hours of riding, either in the tiltyard or through the grounds of his hunting parks, kept Henry exceedingly fit; the quick laugh which punctuated his speech, the hearty way he clapped his hands on men's shoulders when he talked to them, his frequent, ringing oath "By St. George!" all betokened high spirits and abundant health.

Yet if the problem was entirely Katherine's, why had one of her children lived? At five years old, Princess Mary was proving to be a reasonably hardy, precociously gifted little girl who had her father's blonde hair and gray eyes. Henry appeared to be very pleased with his daughter. He enjoyed carrying her in his arms, showing her to each of his courtiers in turn and calling her his "pearl of the world." She was quick-witted and musical, as he was, and she charmed ambassadors with her smiles and her accomplished playing on the virginals; they agreed with one another that she would grow into a beautiful woman. Henry saw little of Mary, however. She had her own household, her own servants and tutors and furnishings, her own miniature throne covered in cloth of gold and velvet. Henry's relative Margaret Pole presided over Mary's establishment, and Katherine saw to it that the princess was prepared for her future role as a serious, devout wife.

Mary was thriving; Katherine was vindicated. There must be another explanation for the troubled succession. Evidence given at Buckingham's trial had shown that there was. It was said God was punishing Henry for his tainted marriage. Two sins, incest and murder, befouled the union of Henry and Katherine. Theologians had questioned the lawfulness of Henry's marriage to his brother's widow; the king's subjects recalled the execution of the earl of Warwick in 1499 and said that a marriage— meaning the marriage of Katherine and Arthur—made in blood must be accursed.

Buckingham's chancellor had heard the duke say that Warwick's death still rankled, and that God was exacting punishment for it "by not suffering the king's issue to prosper, as appeared by the death of his son"—in this instance, the son born in 1511.[8] To sixteenth-century men and women the idea of divine vengeance at work in human affairs was natural, indeed unavoidable. Superhuman explanations for earthly events came to mind more readily than human ones, and they worked with particular force on Henry's alert imagination.[9]

Haunting, vexing, perhaps insurmountable, the need for a son made itself felt in every area of Henry's life. His least indisposition gave rise to inordinate concern. When fevers laid him low, or pains in the head with "rheums falling out of the same," the court officials fretted and feared the worst until he was well again. Every time he entered the tiltyard his councilors prayed he would not emerge battered or maimed, and that the ringing blows his opponents aimed at his head and neck would not scramble his brains or unravel his wits. Having no son made it hazardous for the king to lead his men into battle, either against other nations or against rebels at home. From a diplomatic standpoint Henry and England were at a particular disadvantage. With a son he would have been able to arrange a match with the daughter of almost any European ruler he chose, demanding a large dowry and a military alliance in addition. With a daughter he might still gain a military alliance along with a betrothal, but the large dowry would have to be paid out, from his own coffers. And in addition there was the serious question of whether the princess' husband would in time become king of England.

When Mary was betrothed to the French dauphin in 1518 and, after that alliance was set aside, to Charles V in 1522, the marriage treaties named the princess as Henry's heir in the event he had no son. "It is to be considered that she is now our sole heir," Henry instructed his imperial envoy Tunstall to say in 1521, "and may succeed to the crown."[10] But under English law women's property, titles and incomes passed to their husbands. If she became queen would Mary's husband become king? And wouldn't she, as a dutiful wife, defer to his judgment in matters of state, or perhaps even give the entire kingdom into his keeping? Sometime in the early 1520s Henry called together his chief justices and questioned them at length on these issues. Because no precedent existed, there were no certain answers, yet it seemed clear that Mary's husband would not be able to claim the throne by right. Whether he might obtain it by force or by intimidating his wife was another matter.

Long before this Henry had begun in a roundabout way to seek another sort of solution to the succession problem. If his wife could not give him a son, perhaps a mistress could.

Henry's liaison with Anne Stafford had not been renewed following her abrupt departure from the court early in the reign, yet there were many other girls to choose from. English girls were exceptional: "divinely pretty," soft, pleasant, gentle and charming, "as bright as a breast of bacon," in one contemporary description. "They have one custom [in England] which cannot be too much admired," Erasmus wrote. "When you go anywhere on a visit the girls all kiss you. They kiss you again when you arrive. They kiss you when you go away; and they kiss you again when you return. Go where you will, it is all kisses."[11] To outsiders the

English habits of love seemed odd. The women appeared to be highly passionate, while the men, though lustful, seemed impervious to romance. Heedless of medical warnings that excessive lovemaking brought on gout, anemia, dyspepsia and blindness Englishmen were "somewhat licentious in their dispositions," yet they rarely fell prey to passion. "I never have noticed anyone," a visiting Venetian remarked, "either at court or amongst the lower orders, to be in love; whence one must necessarily conclude, either that the English are the most discreet lovers in the world, or that they are incapable of love."

Though he was hardly incapable of love, none of Henry's mistresses stirred his feelings to any great degree. The earliest of them, Jane Popyngcort, left few traces of her place in the king's affections—if indeed she was his mistress.[12] A maid of honor to Queen Katherine who lost her good reputation when she became the mistress of the hostage duc de Longueville, Jane became a lady in waiting and close companion of Henry's sister Mary, and a lively participant in court revels and disguisings. Henry's involvement with her came in the final months of 1514, when Mary was in France as wife to Louis XII and the duke was in attendance on her, leaving Jane behind in England. Before long Jane left for Paris to resume her place at de Longueville's side, and when she did Henry sent her off with a reward of a hundred pounds.[13]

By the time Jane left England in May of 1516 Bessie Blount had been the court beauty for several years. A relative of Lord Mountjoy, Bessie sang and danced beautifully and was a favorite of Charles Brandon and of the king's minions, especially the lecherous Francis Bryan. By her "goodly pastimes," wrote the chronicler Hall, Bessie "won the king's heart," and by summer or fall of 1518 she had become his mistress. As Henry was taking care to guard Katherine's health that summer, and writing to Wolsey of his hopes for her child, he was almost certainly keeping company with Bessie Blount as well; his bitter disappointment at Katherine's stillbirth was softened somewhat by news of Bessie's pregnancy.

Ironically, Bessie's child not only lived, it was a boy. He was christened Henry Fitzroy, in acknowledgment of his royal paternity, and was assigned a princely household like that of the king's legitimate daughter. Bessie made way for her successor as royal mistress, Mary Boleyn Carey, content to be unofficially honored with the title "mother of the king's son" and content, too, with Henry's generosity toward her. Manors in Lincoln and York were given her, and a marriage was arranged with one of Wolsey's retainers, Gilbert Talboys. Both Talboys and his father, a madman in Wolsey's custody who had once been a soldier in Henry's armies, benefited from the marriage; Henry rewarded them with great sums of money, and in addition, Gilbert Talboys was knighted and became sheriff of Lincoln in 1525.[14]

Of Henry's next mistress surprisingly little is known. Thomas Boleyn's older daughter Mary married one of the king's favorites, William Carey, in 1520 and Henry attended their wedding and made an offering.[15] With Carey's indulgent complicity his wife served the king's sexual needs over the next several years, though neither she nor her husband received rewards on the scale of those given to Bessie and Gilbert Talboys. Henry christened one of his ships the *Mary Boleyn;* that was all.[16] By the mid-1520s the liaison had ended and instead of installing a new mistress right away Henry began to turn his attention more and more to his unsatisfactory marriage.

Sometime in 1524 Henry expressed a keen desire to see Erasmus and talk with him. He had recently been given a copy of the great humanist's treatise on the freedom of the will, and a passage in the work spoke to his thoughts in an especially satisfying way. In it Erasmus urged his readers not to be too curious about the ways of God, but to leave them as divine mysteries. As Henry had been pondering these mysteries intensely, Erasmus' insights may have offered some sort of release; in any case they made him wish for a visit with his boyhood friend, very possibly to confide to him the unsettled state of his mind about his marriage.

Several things weighed on him. The gravest of them, the succession, was still unresolved. Mary was officially the heir; Henry Fitzroy, though he might prove useful in time, had not yet been designated to succeed, and his illegitimacy posed a problem. The uncertain succession thwarted the king at every turn; it was becoming intolerable. Then there was the indeterminate state of his marriage itself. Judging from a remark Henry made years later to a visitor at court, it was just at this time that he and Katherine ceased to live together as man and wife.[17] Soon afterward she reached menopause, and the diplomats authorized to discuss the matter at foreign courts openly acknowledged that though "God might send her more children," it would be nothing short of a miracle if he did.[18]

Henry was in a quandary. What should he do? The church taught that the purpose of marriage was procreation, yet his marriage would be fruitless from now on. It was a king's Christian duty to provide a male heir to the throne, for the safety of the kingdom, yet so long as he stayed with Katherine there would be no son. If he persisted in this marriage Henry would leave these clear moral obligations unsatisfied. Finally there was the all too persuasive idea that God himself disapproved of the union, and would be placated only if it were dissolved.

These and similar themes ran through Henry's mind in the middle years of the 1520s like the arguments and counter-arguments in the debates he loved to arrange. There were hints about a divorce, though outwardly the king and queen preserved an amicable, comfortable companionship that offered many shared pleasures to them both.[19]

"I love true where I did marry," Henry sang in his early years with Katherine. Probably he still loved her; the deaths of their children, the ventures he had undertaken with her avid support, the triumphs and common dangers they had faced bound them together in default of passion. The initials "H & K" were still woven into Henry's jousting finery and revels costumes, sometimes intertwined with trueloves and hearts, and he still enjoyed planning surprises for his wife. One day early in 1520 Henry and Katherine were in her chamber, when suddenly to the queen's amazement four masked gentlemen entered the room unannounced, along with a wheeled cart. A lady sat in the cart, with jousting armor beside her. The gentlemen challenged the king to a joust; he entered the challenge, and the little ceremony came to an end.[20] Henry and Katherine rarely spent more than a few hours in one another's company, but they saw each other often. The king was frequently reported to be "taking his pleasure as usual with the queen"; ambassadors and officials often found him in her chamber, discussing books or politics or religion. They hunted together, went on pilgrimages together—though sometimes to separate shrines—and met at the end of the day for supper and vespers when there were no banquets or entertainments to attend in the great hall.

Henry was accustomed to visit Katherine after the midday meal, accompanied by whichever of the courtiers were in attendance on him. The bishop of Lincoln described in a letter how when he was at Eltham in January of 1525 he went to Katherine's apartments and was met there by the king and queen.

"Madam," Henry said to his wife, "my lord of Lincoln can show you of my lord cardinal's college at Oxenford, and what learning there is and shall be, and what learned men in the same."

Bowing to the bishop, Henry left him with Katherine, and she listened graciously as the churchman went on to explain to her Wolsey's plan for the new college he was building, how it would draw students from all over Europe and how the students and masters alike would remember to pray for her welfare.[21]

With Thomas More Henry and Katherine were more relaxed. He came to them on business but stayed on long after the business was done to talk and laugh and enjoy their company. In November of 1524, when there was war on the continent and the old enmity between England and France had been rekindled, More brought Henry the latest dispatches with news of European affairs. The king talked with More awhile, then read the papers with close attention, making comments to Katherine as he went along. She listened with informed interest, saying she was glad to hear the Spanish troops were acquitting themselves well in Italy and smiling to hear of the bad fortunes of the French. Henry and More laughed over the predicament of King Francis, halted on his way into Italy and in need of help to extricate himself and his troops.[22]

Such hours were precious to the king. No matter how great the pressures that weighed on him, Henry realized his familiar happiness with Katherine was not to be put aside lightly.

Besides, the imponderables of his marriage seemed trifling matters compared to the scandalous and outlandishly complex married lives of many of the men around him. The least offender was William Compton, who had recently been cited in the ecclesiastical courts for living openly with a married woman.[23] Thomas Howard, earl of Surrey who became duke of Norfolk on his father's death in 1524, was the center of a more sordid triangle. After living for some years with a woman he chose "for love," his second wife Elizabeth, he suddenly became enamored of a woman of the court, Bess Holland, and with her as his mistress he shunned and abused his wife and cut off her income, cursing her when she complained. Even though Elizabeth Howard was a woman of notable virtue—"the king's grace shall be my record how I used myself without any ill name or fortune," she wrote in her defense—her husband subjected her to humiliation and eventually to torture when she refused to accept his new love. Good-hearted courtiers sympathized with the duchess and condemned Norfolk for what he was doing, but he seemed not to care. "He knows it is spoken of far and near to his great dishonor and shame," the aggrieved wife wrote, yet he was "so far in doting love" with Bess Holland "that he neither regards God nor his honor."[24]

Though less scandalous than Norfolk's, Charles Brandon's tangled marital history was currently giving him no peace. In October of 1524 a long legal treatise was drawn up defending the validity of his marriage to Mary Tudor and the legitimacy of their daughter Frances. Evidently questions had arisen about his past marriages and betrothals, and possibly about his continuing ties to his first wife Margaret Mortimer.[25] Brandon had his hands full managing his current wife's affairs, in particular her dowry, yet he was forced to involve himself in a bitter dispute between Margaret Mortimer, her husband, and her daughter and son-in-law. The issue was Margaret's inheritance, and the conflict became so heated it led to blackmail and attempted murder; finally, after a year of writs and lawsuits and injunctions, with Wolsey's help Brandon seems to have resolved matters.[26]

The irregular marital histories of lesser royal subjects came to the king's attention from time to time, and made his own domestic troubles seem idyllic by contrast. Early in 1525 the case of one Robert Constable of Flaymburgh in Yorkshire was discussed by the Privy Council. The case concerned his "riotous taking and carrying off of Anne Grysacre, daughter of Edward Grysacre, and the king's ward under age," and Henry and his councilors had to sit in judgment to resolve it.[27] At about the same time another man—this time a royal servant—sought Henry's pardon for two similar crimes. As a young man William Hetherington, "in youth a very evil-disposed person," had carried off a woman who was about to marry someone else, taken her to a "forbidden place," and married her. Later, finding that either his bride or his conscience pained him, Hetherington felt remorse and had his situation examined in an ecclesiastical court. Meanwhile he came across a woman who pleased him better than his first bride, and obtained from the royal court a letter of request for her hand. This woman proved to prefer another man, however, and went to live with him "for her pleasure," becoming pregnant with his child. Despite her condition the infuriated Hetherington kidnapped her, "partly against her will," and took her to live with him. It was left to the king to decide whether Hetherington's eighteen years of faithful service to the crown mitigated his offenses.[28]

Katherine too was concerned about her marriage, and like Henry, she seems to have turned to Erasmus for guidance. She asked him to write her a treatise "On Preserving Marriage" (De servando conjugio), having admired another work of his on the comparative states of virgins and martyrs. Vives had dedicated to the queen his disquisition on virgins, wives and widows; now she wanted to read what Erasmus had to say about the married state.[29]

Erasmus did not find time to write his book on marriage for nearly a year. When he did it was all but superfluous, for Katherine had long since come to terms with her situation and made up her mind to persevere in it. She saw clearly enough that her role as Henry's wife was changing, but instead of abandoning it she looked on her new circumstances as a challenge to her piety. Her devout belief, her deep conservatism, her duty to Mary demanded that she go on, even though she could not give Henry the son he needed. She would be true to her marriage vows, ignoring her husband's mistresses and treasuring his companionship, and devoting her sorrows to God.

Two incidents in these years frightened Henry into a strong awareness of his mortality and brought the succession sharply into focus. While jousting with Brandon he narrowly escaped death when wooden fragments from a shattered spear flew into his unprotected face; he had forgotten to lower his visor. He blamed no one but himself, and ran six more courses afterward to prove he was unhurt, but the entire court knew how close he had come to fatal injury. Soon after this he had another accident. Following his hawk across the muddy fields he came to a ditch full of water, too wide to jump. In trying to vault across he slipped and fell head first into the water. His head stuck fast in the mud at the bottom of the ditch, and he would have drowned without help, but fortunately an alert footman saw what had happened and rescued him.

There was no time to delay; an heir had to be designated, before fate or hazard deprived the realm of a sovereign. Nine-year-old Princess Mary was given the title Princess of Wales and sent to hold court at Ludlow in the Welsh Marches. More significantly, six-year-old Henry Fitzroy was brought to court and elevated to such prominence that the king's intentions for him were unmistakable. In every way possible, Bessie Blount's son was being marked as heir to the throne.

A huge concourse of people gathered at Bridewell in June of 1525 to attend the ceremonies. As they mingled in the gardens and antechambers of the palace they talked of little but the meaning of Fitzroy's sudden advancement, and of the intolerable heat and dust that kept them in constant discomfort that day. First the boy was created earl of Nottingham in a lengthy ceremony. Then he was made duke of Richmond and Somerset—the titles Henry had held as a boy. As More read out his patent of nobility Fitzroy knelt before his father, who solemnly invested him with the robe and sword, cape and circlet of a duke. Other men were advanced to new titles at the same time, among them Henry Courtenay, created marquis of Exeter, and Thomas Boleyn, created Viscount Rochford. But Fitzroy's status put him ahead of every other nobleman in the kingdom, and ahead of the princess; as the Venetian ambassador Orio wrote, "he is now next in rank to his majesty."[30]

Henry himself drew the design for Fitzroy's arms, and had ducal robes made for him in crimson and blue velvet. He rode in a litter upholstered in cloth of silver—a gift from Wolsey—and his riding horse was trapped in black velvet with gilt reins. His household was now increased to nearly two hundred officers and other servants, and some eighty manors came to him with his new titles.[31] There was good reason to believe, as Orio said, that Henry loved his little son "like his own soul."[32]

The king had made his decision. Bastard or not, Fitzroy would succeed him, unless he found an alternative. And for the moment, there was none in sight.

Katherine reacted angrily to Fitzroy's advancement. "It seems that the queen resents the earldom and dukedom conferred on the king's natural son, and remains dissatisfied," an observer noted. She kept up her objections until the king lost his temper. He blamed her obstinacy on three of her Spanish ladies—as he had done once before, when she objected to his affair with Anne Stafford—and took the extreme measure of sending the three women away from court. Katherine continued to fume, to show her resentment in every way she could, and privately to question her daughter's future. But her anger made no difference, and in the end "she was obliged to submit and have patience."[33]

21

Nought is more honorable to a knight,
Ne better doth beseem brave chivalry,
Than to defend the feeble in their right,
And wrong redress in such as wend awry.

WHEN Cardinal Campeggio came to England to preach a crusade in 1518 his message reanimated Henry's ideal of chivalric service to the pope. Two years earlier the Ottoman Turks under Selim I the Grim had taken the Holy Land; now as in medieval times the knights of the West were called on to liberate the sacred places of Christendom. Henry, it seemed, was to be foremost among them, and to show the burning sincerity of his resolve he wrote a letter to Leo X eloquently pledging his aid.

His highest aim had always been to defend Christendom against the infidel, Henry wrote, and now that the call had come he was ready to answer it with all his heart. With "ardor of soul" he promised an army of twenty thousand men and a navy of fifteen thousand, in seventy ships; everything else he possessed—his royal authority, his wealth and treasure, his realm itself—was the pope's to command. He did not spare his own safety. Pledging his life blood to the holy cause, he vowed to lead his army in person if his wife should bear a son before the expedition got under way.

The Field of Cloth of Gold temporarily banked the fires of Henry's crusading ardor, but the idea was too ingrained in him to be put aside for long. Several years earlier he had spoken of conquering Jerusalem with an army of only twenty-five thousand men, and had asked the Venetians to provide him with four galleys to transport them in.[1] Campeggio's visit had set him burning again, and his spirits rose to meet the challenge.

Henry's crusading ambitions, though extravagant, were not unique: Emperor Maximilian had envisioned a much more improbable offensive in which the Turks would be defeated by the imperial armies allied with the emperor of Abyssinia, the king of Georgia and the Persian shah. But where Maximilian had been carried away by a thirst for glory Henry saw a larger obligation. For him undertaking a crusade was among his prime duties as the pope's champion, chief defender of the Holy See among the European sovereigns. Since the start of his reign, encouraged by Wolsey but even more by a sincere if archaic devotion rooted in medieval chivalry, Henry had aligned England's interests with those of the papacy. Time and again the course of diplomacy had been set to benefit the pope;

over the years Henry had fought the pope's enemies, joined his allies, and avenged his injuries, growing more and more certain with each campaign that because England sided with Rome, God and right must be on England's side.

In 1521 this conviction was sealed when the pope conferred on Henry the title Defender of the Faith. Julius II had earlier given the same title to the Swiss, but as none of the proposed alternatives—King Apostolic, Orthodox, Defender of the Holy Roman Church—met with Leo's approval, it now went to Henry.[2] The title crowned his reputation for virtue, a reputation he made every effort to expand. Of all the European princes, he told the Venetian ambassador Giustiniani, he alone kept faith; "and therefore," he added, "God Almighty, who knows this, prospers my affairs."

For the pedestrian, tortuous realities of sixteenth-century diplomacy Henry had an enlightened contempt. Its intricacies must be respected, its treacheries forestalled. Yet when he came face to face with dissimulation Henry recoiled in exasperation. The Venetians, who had been sworn enemies of the French, changed sides abruptly in 1516, leading the king to lecture Giustiniani on the ethics of statecraft. "There could be no necessity soever for making you have recourse to such perfidy," he said indignantly, "becoming rather pale in the face."[3] That duplicity was the norm of politics never ceased to perturb him, no matter how clearly he perceived his opponents' designs or how effectively he averted them. "Do you not perceive that the potentates first make peace and confederacy with a state, and then negotiate its destruction with others?" he asked Giustiniani. "How would you possibly have me place reliance?"[4]

Other states were in truth no more devious or calculating in their dealings than England, and Wolsey was certainly capable of as much guile and dishonesty as any of his counterparts at foreign courts. Yet somehow Henry felt himself to be above all that. His ambassadors and his chancellors might dissemble; he did not.

Pure in his intentions, unsullied by bad faith and guided by his loyalty to the pope Henry saw himself as all but invincible in the treacherous arena of European politics. More dangerous still, he imagined, like crusaders before him, that he had divine protection in battle. After the Battle of the Spurs he wrote to the pope saying he "attributed all his victories not to himself but to God alone. As God gave Saul power to slay a thousand and David strength to kill ten thousand enemies," he boasted, "so he made him strong."[5]

Henry's high-minded courage set him apart from his brother monarchs in France and the empire. Though he had become "the eldest prince in Christendom," older than Francis I by three years and older than Charles V by nine, Henry retained the ideals of his youth long after the others had shed their naïveté. Wolsey called Francis "the Christian Turk" for his shrewd deviousness; according to the cardinal he was more to be dreaded than the real Turk.[6] As for Charles, though he had barely reached adulthood Wolsey found him to be very wise for his age, "and well understanding his affairs, right cold and temperate in speech, with assured manner, couching his words right well and to good purpose when he does speak."[7] Prophecies were circulating about the young emperor, predicting, as part of a grander scheme of conquest, that he would subjugate England. Though unsettling, these predictions could easily be discounted, however. The family ties between the Tudors and Hapsburgs were strong; if England came to the emperor it would be by marriage, not conquest, when Charles married Princess Mary and made her empress of all his domains.

As he embarked on his second decade of European politics Henry saw his future clearly and quite inaccurately. With imperial support he would defeat the French and be crowned in Paris. He left it to Wolsey to prepare the way.

No one knew better than the cardinal the strength of his master's vision. The full force of his determination had been loosed. "He is a prince of royal courage and hath a princely heart," Wolsey wrote, "and rather than he will miss or want part of his appetite he will hazard the loss of one-half his kingdom." Throughout the fall of 1521 Wolsey negotiated with the imperialists at Calais, working out the details of a treaty binding Henry to declare war against France in the following year and to send his armies across the Channel a year later. His health suffered under the strain of overwork and, at one point, from fear of poison, but in the end he obtained Henry's aim. The king felt the challenge of war move closer; he was convinced, Pace wrote, that "great war is toward," and he made ready for it with his usual urgency.

Armor was ordered, ships newly fitted and soldiers mustered to arms. Every royal subject and every foreigner living in the capital was ordered, under threat of heavy penalties, to collect all their storage barrels and wine casks and to set them out in the streets for the king's purveyors to buy. Anything that might be of use to the army, no matter how small or great, was subject to confiscation. In an effort to force Venice into the war on England's side Henry seized the Flanders galleys—part of the Venetian fleet—and stripped them of their heavy guns for use against France. The Venetians tried in vain to get the ships released, first by means of a bribe paid through Wolsey's physician and then through the intervention of the pope. After many months Henry finally let the ships go—though he kept their heavy guns—and ignored the hint from the aggrieved ambassador that he might at least recompense the innocent shipmasters and mariners for the pay they had lost. Damaged and undermanned, the fleet limped out of port at last and made for Venice, armed with ordnance borrowed from Wolsey for protection against pirates and Turkish sea rovers on the return journey.

The campaign was launched in force in August of 1523. Charles Brandon was in command of some fourteen thousand men, plus another four thousand landsknechts and an allied contingent of three thousand horse.[8] At first his objective was to be Boulogne. He would besiege and capture this Channel port, then take his army back to England before the onset of bad weather, gaining a foothold to be used by a larger invading army in the spring. But Boulogne held out for weeks, and while Henry waited eagerly for news of the war Wolsey, it seems, rethought the military situation and envisioned a bold new plan. Brandon would break off the siege and march toward Paris, with the aim of "winning some great part of France or at the least wise all that is on this side of the water of Somme."

The cardinal's scheme worried Henry. He knew well what it meant to march an army thousands strong through the "wet weather and rotten ways" of Picardy, dragging the huge guns and heavily laden carts across the swollen rivers, always fearful that supplies might be cut off or that the enemy might appear in force.[9] The French were fighting in Italy, far enough away to put the minds of the English somewhat at ease, but Francis was determined to drive back any assault they made. He had been heard to swear "on the faith of a gentleman" that he would defeat Henry come what may, and he had reportedly equipped Richard de la Pole—the "White Rose" still in France awaiting his opportunity to seize Henry's throne—with twelve thousand men to put into the field against his royal cousin.[10]

Wolsey's view prevailed, and late in September Suffolk and his men set out southward, headed for Paris. To the king's surprise they advanced without serious hindrance, meeting and defeating two French companies and winning "free entry into the bowels of France" before the end of the month. Brandon sent word to Henry from his camp at Compiègne that there was "good likelihood of the attaining of his ancient right and title to the crown of France to his singular comfort and eternal honor"; four weeks later the English were only fifty miles from Paris.[11]

Then all at once the hazards of weather closed in. A frost so severe it crippled the entire camp prevented all movement for days. A hundred men froze to death in forty-eight hours, and many who escaped death lost their fingers and toes, the nails dropping off their frostbitten hands. Suddenly the air turned warmer, leaving the half-dead soldiers to founder in a sea of mud and to long mutinously for home. Brandon sent word to Henry "that his people which were in the French ground abode much misery, for the weather was wet, the ways deep, long nights and short days, great journeys and little victual, which caused the soldiers daily to die." Without waiting for a reply he broke up the camp and let his men return home, and when he and his captains followed them they "came not to the king's presence a long season, to their great heaviness and displeasure."[12]

Henry was irritated at this souring of his hopes, but soon convinced himself it was nothing more than a temporary setback. Brandon and the others regained the royal favor, and the king laid his plans to renew the war in the spring. First, though, he had to fill his empty coffers, and there was reason to think his subjects already grudged having paid heavily for a war which had brought no victories.

Villagers complained of high taxes, and told one another the king meant to take half of every man's possessions. "And if every man would do as he would do," a Norfolk man was heard to say, "he would take him by the head, and pull him down." When asked whom he meant to pull down he said fearlessly, "Harry with the crown." Others named such talk treason, and spoke in the king's defense, but the voices of the dissatisfied were louder. "Better to take against king Harry," they said, than to pay what his tax commissioners asked.[13]

It was not only the amount of the tax that led to resentment: it was the use to which the money was put. One of Wolsey's agents received a report of a disturbance in Shaftesbury, where one John Brody called John Williams a "vagabond and thief." When Williams protested that he was no vagabond but a soldier in King Henry's armies, Brody's answer was sharp.

"A, sir, have ye been with Master Henry King? A noble act ye did there! Ye spent away my money and other men's, like a sort of vagabonds and knaves!"

Brody suffered for his "unfitting words," punished by two justices of the peace and the mayor of the town, yet no coercion could change his harsh judgment of the king's wars, and there were many who felt as he did.[14]

Parliament too resisted paying for the war. When two shillings in the pound was asked from the Commons, the issue was debated for over two weeks before assent was given; though the members were urged to consider the king's necessity, they took their own poverty more to heart, and said they could not remember ever giving half as much before at one grant.[15] No matter how high the rate was set, the amount actually collected was invariably much lower—too low to fill the king's needs. Something more than half of what was assessed was in fact paid, though the men who paid it were as bitter as if they had given their full share.

Despite this opposition money was found to launch a spring campaign, and in the first weeks of 1524 a merchant was bribed to smuggle sacks of coins to mercenaries on the continent who were to fight for the English. The money was sewn into "coats of brigandines fashion"—light body armor—and carried on men's backs across several borders undetected, the merchant having been paid well "not to meddle with it."[16] At the same time plans were made known for a unique double offensive. Henry meant to send two armies to France this time, one a vast force of twenty thousand which he would lead himself and the other a smaller, secret army with an undisclosed destination.

Yet even as his plans matured his Council and his chancellor undercut them. Wolsey was secretly negotiating with the French, while the Council members tried to restrain Henry's eagerness to prolong the war. Beyond the obvious hazard of battle for a king who had no son, they argued, they could see no clear advantage to be gained from another season of costly adventuring in France. Apart from Henry's idiosyncratic zeal for combat, it was difficult for outsiders to understand his aims. An Italian in the service of the bishop of Capua wrote to his employer in March of 1524 analyzing the motives and interests of all the European sovereigns. He found the aims of the emperor and the French king plain enough, but those of the English monarch baffled him. Why should he fight the French, a futile undertaking all but valueless even if successful? Did he want revenge against the allies of the Scots? Was it a personal vendetta against Francis? Had Henry been so deluded by the flattery of Charles V that he would do anything the emperor asked? Or did he cling to the vain hope that, if he fought the emperor's enemy, he might claim a part of France from him as a reward? There was no satisfactory answer; the Italian concluded that Henry "had no clear object in view."[17]

So far removed were Henry's true aims from the comprehensible logic of power. The locus of competition in Europe in the mid-1520s was not France but Italy, a fact Wolsey took full account of but which failed to arouse Henry's interest. As the Italian situation moved nearer to reaching a critical point he continued to look for the mounting of his dual assault on France, and as late as September of 1524—too late in the year for full-scale invasion—he was rousing the nobility to stand ready to aid him in the taking of France.[18]

In the following February the French suffered a disastrous defeat—but at the hands of Charles, not Henry. A French army led by Francis himself besieged Pavia, then held by the imperialists, and did not retreat at the approach of troops commanded by Charles' ablest general Pescara. In the battle that resulted the French were crushed, and their king, dazzlingly and conspicuously dressed in a doublet of cloth of silver, was captured by the enemy.

With Francis in captivity, his fighting men in leaderless confusion, the moment seemed ripe to fulfill Henry's desires. Among the demands the emperor made of his royal captive was that he surrender Normandy, Guienne and Gascony to the English; now all they had to do was to take possession of what had once been theirs.[19]

Once enough money was raised the assault could begin—an assault, this time, that could not fail. Wolsey could not go to Parliament again. He had just asked them for the unprecedented sum of four shillings on the pound, and to ask for more was futile. He would try a broader appeal. In medieval times kings had gone directly to their subjects for aid when they led their armies into battle in person. Making much of the fact that Henry meant to do this now, Wolsey asked Henry's subjects to make their king an "Amicable Grant" of one-sixth of their incomes. Clergy were to contribute one-third. Within weeks of the victory at Pavia royal commissioners were dispatched throughout the country to collect the grant, and Henry, released at last from the frustrations of nearly eighteen months of peace, threw himself one last time into preparing his ships and men.

Imperial envoys who called on him during these weeks found him in the highest spirits, his face lit with anticipation, his talk full of his hopes.[20] "Now is the time for the emperor and myself to devise the means of getting full satisfaction from France," he told them animatedly. The opportunity had arrived, the host was gathering, the means were all in hand. Speed was what counted, the king insisted. "Not an hour is to be lost!"

22

Fortune my foe, why dost thou frown on me?
And will thy favour never better be?
Wilt thou I say for ever breed my pain,
And wilt thou not restore my joyes again?

In the same week that Wolsey sent out his commissioners to collect the Amicable Grant the emperor Charles V sat down to compose his response to his eager uncle in England. He sat a long while in thought before beginning it, his brow furrowed and his pale blue eyes squinting in a frown, his ungainly chin cupped in his hand. He had before him a letter from the imperial ambassador in England, the Flemish nobleman de Praet, warning him that further neglect of his commitments there would seriously harm his interests. Pensions promised to English noblemen close to the king had not been paid for several years; worse still, the princely pension of nine thousand crowns promised to Wolsey was long in arrears, and Wolsey more than most men could be counted on to resent the slight. What made for even more urgency was that the cardinal was negotiating secretly with the French, and any further insult might send him irrevocably into their camp.[1] For good relations to be restored, the emperor must give prompt attention to English affairs without delay.

Charles had another letter before him as he wrote—from Henry, who addressed his wife's nephew as "my most beloved son" and signed himself "your good father, brother and uncle." This miscellany of styles conveyed affection, deference and paternalism all at once, and in fact Henry was in some confusion about just how to address his precocious young in-law. At twenty-five, Charles had just defeated Henry's archenemy in battle; he had come a long way in the five years since he first came to England and appealed to Henry as his "good father" for advice. Charles had long since outgrown Henry's tutelage, if not his alliance, and his recent startling victory called for a reconsideration of their difference in status.

As he thought over how to inform his impassioned kinsman in England that he meant to make peace, not war, Charles gave passing consideration, in his methodical way, to his aunt Katherine. He had been neglecting her too, causing her to complain in letters to him that she could not imagine any reason for his silence, and to remind him bluntly that "love and consanguinity both demand that we should write each other oftener." She could say little, for Wolsey read her letters and looked on her with suspicion, as he would a foreign agent at court. But her feeling of abandonment was plain. "Nothing indeed would be so painful to me as to

171

think that your highness had forgotten me,'' she wrote, adding an entreaty that, at the very least, her nephew should send her occasional news of his health.[2]

Fondness for his aunt may have drawn Charles' attention away, momentarily, from the task at hand, but if so his concentration was quickly restored. The idea of Wolsey surely restored it—Wolsey the arrogant alter ego of the king, the shrewd diplomat and ceaseless intriguer who even as he wrote assuring the emperor of his undying loyalty was conniving against him with the wily Genoese Giovacchiono, or Joachim, an agent of the French. Bad feeling between the emperor and the cardinal had been growing at least since 1521, when at the Anglo-imperial conference at Bruges and Calais Wolsey spent three terror-stricken days in bed, believing the emperor's cook had poisoned him. (At the same conference Charles himself had feared poison. A small bladder filled with hair and foul-smelling powders and potions was discovered hidden in a platter of meat. The cook and four others were arrested, but released when the noxious mixture was found to be nothing more dangerous than a love charm.[3])

And there were other grievances. Beyond the emperor's failure to pay Wolsey's pension, there was his failure to use his influence in raising the cardinal to the papal throne. Twice Charles had promised to support Wolsey's candidacy for the papacy, in 1521 and again in 1523, and twice he had at the last moment betrayed him. Though he protested that he had no interest in governing the church and was glad the elections had gone as they did Wolsey felt duped nonetheless; his ambition was not to be trifled with, certainly not by a boy nearly thirty years his junior, no matter what his title.

Wolsey would be the first to shout betrayal now, Charles realized as he began to set down his instructions to de Praet. Yet his course of action was as clear and logical to his mind as Henry's expectations of aid were in his. The French were beaten. Pavia was in the hands of his generals, and the rest of Italy lay open to the imperial forces. He had no interest in conquering France, and no need of English aid in conquering the remainder of Italy. What troops he could spare from campaigning there would in any case be sent to the German states, where furious peasants unsettled by the apocalyptic preachings of the former friar Martin Luther were massing to attack their masters. He ordered de Praet to tell Henry, as diplomatically as possible, that if the English meant to go to war they would have to fight alone.[4]

Henry was stunned when the message was delivered. Just as his hopes reached their zenith the inconceivable was happening. His staunch friend, the man he had chosen to be his son-in-law, the ally he had supported with nearly half a million crowns in loans, was going back on his word and turning against him. Bad faith of every kind—broken promises, violated treaties, even simple changes of mind invariably wounded Henry. In his chivalrous imagination every shift of purpose was recreancy, every equivocation disparagement. It made no difference that Charles sent assurances that despite his peace efforts he would not disarm, and that if he failed to make peace he would go to war as originally planned. To

Henry the insult was as final and dishonorable as the repeated affronts of Charles' grandfather Ferdinand of Aragon more than a decade earlier. Spaniards, Flemings, Hapsburgs—none of them could be counted on to keep faith.

Wolsey gave vent to his anger in a sweeping repudiation of the emperor and all his lands. All hope of future "amity and good feeling" between the two courts was dead, he announced to two Flemish envoys. "I know full well that we shall never get any assistance from you; but we shall do our best, either by contracting alliance with the Turk, or making peace with the French, by giving the princess' hand to the dauphin, or otherwise declaring against the emperor." Everything that could harm the imperialists would be done, he swore, "so that the war between us may last a whole century!"[5]

It only remained for the last link—the dynastic link—to be broken. Now that Charles V no longer needed the English there was no reason for him to take an English bride, especially when a more attractive candidate was available. Whereas Mary Tudor was a fragile girl of nine, Isabella of Portugal was a marriageable nineteen, with a dowry of a million crowns besides. The betrothal to Mary was broken off, and Charles, in a letter that referred to the "almost indissoluble tie" between himself and Henry, now loosed that tie with a stroke of his pen.[6]

Henry was still red-faced and reeling from the emperor's rebuff when he was startled by reports of rebellion against the Amicable Grant. Instead of eager generosity in support of the king's war the commissioners sent to collect the grant found wretchedness, ugly recalcitrance, and open criticism of royal policy. In Kent Thomas Boleyn was assaulted when he tried to collect what was owed; in Suffolk, Charles Brandon and his fellow commissioners had to defend themselves against hundreds of rioting villagers who rang the alarm bell and swore they would kill anyone who tried to take their money. Another collector recorded meeting a group of four hundred ragged men on the high road near Bury, many of them dressed only in their tattered shirts, who knelt before him and begged him, for the sake of the king's mercy, to relieve them of the tax. Elsewhere, taxpayers tried to clear their obligation by paying in goods instead of the scarce coins, bringing the royal commissioners cartloads of wheat and caged chickens and lowing cows; others told stories of how their barns and houses had burned to the ground, leaving them destitute, or how cattle disease had killed their herds and made them penniless.

"It would have made a man sorrowful," one collector wrote, "though he had a right hard heart, to hear their lamentation—not only of the poor, but of those who were thought rich. Those who were before valued at £100 or £200 now make twenty nobles in ready money, and some scarcely forty shillings."

Unquestionably there was much real poverty in England, and a shortage of coins so widespread that goods were selling for half their worth in silver. One reason the villagers preferred to pay their tax in cows and wheat was that they could not sell either in the local markets, no matter how low the price they asked.[7] But genuine scarcity was one thing, and articulate, determined opposition to royal policy another, and what alarmed the commissioners and dismayed the king was not the excuses and pleas for money but the obstinate, violent resistance of those who refused to pay on principle.

Archbishop Warham, now a septuagenarian retired from court and looking after his parishioners in Kent, wrote down the arguments of those who grudged the tax in his county and sent them to London. Cursing the author of the tax, Wolsey, as vehemently as they did its misguided purpose, the men and women of Kent taunted the commissioners and reminded them that the last "loan" advanced to the king had never been repaid, and that too much English coin had already been exported abroad in the wars to the enrichment of the Flemish and French. With unassailable logic they harangued the royal servants sent to tax them, arguing that all the money paid toward the conquest of France in 1523 had not led to the capture of a single foot of ground, and that even if the coming campaign succeeded it would only mean more loans and grants to pay for the defense of the newly acquired territories. In their boldness the people went on to criticize the soundness of their king's judgment in seeking to conquer France at all, comparing him unfavorably to his father Henry VII, "who lacked no riches or wisdom to have won that kingdom if he had thought it expedient."[8]

Such harsh words soon gave way to violence, and by May reports of assault and organized resistance were reaching the court from throughout the countryside. The most adamant of the resisters, having attacked and harassed the commissioners, began to turn on their fellow-villagers. Terrified of being "hewn in pieces," those country people who had not yet paid what they owed refused to, while those who had already pledged money or goods to the king took them back again.[9] The exasperated commissioners did what they could, arming their household servants to patrol areas where opponents of the tax were massing, and riding many miles each day to confer with one another, but they were too few in number to contain the spreading disturbances. They sent urgent dispatches to the court, asking advice and complaining that the situation was beyond their power to control. If nothing was done, Norfolk and Brandon wrote jointly, the isolated rioting might grow into full-scale rebellion. And then "God knows what ill spirits might put in their minds."[10]

The nightmare image of a peasantry out of control, turned loose to avenge generations of high taxes and subservience was no fantasy. In the territories of Charles V it was already coming true. At first groups of a few dozen angry villagers had taken to arms in many different areas. Then in only a few weeks' time the scattered rebels had joined together into regional armies thousands strong, marching unopposed against the forces of local rulers and eventually against imperial troops. Armed with pikes and firearms, they roved in bands through Swabia, Franconia and Thuringia and even through Alsace and the German-speaking Swiss lands, demanding time-honored manorial rights they felt they had lost and citing Luther's doctrines of Christian freedom and scriptural authority in justification of their revolt.

To European aristocrats whose world view was grounded in the idea of an ordered society, with lords and gentlefolk above and farmers and peasants below, the reports of the German revolt were deeply disturbing. There had been rural uprisings for centuries, but never anything on this scale. In the past the murder and mayhem had been confined to at most a few dozen square miles, and the perpetrators had been quickly annihilated. But this conflagration covered huge areas of the imperial lands, and swept into itself tens of thousands of rebels; in Frankfort alone they destroyed thirty fortresses and sacked eighty monasteries, and every region had its share of the far-ranging devastation.

Accounts of the anarchy in the German regions reached every European court by May of 1525, along with rumors that similar catastrophes would soon engulf other realms. As they gathered strength some of the German peasants began to envision an apocalyptic transformation of Europe into a community of equals in which all distinctions between master and servant, king and subject would be abolished. Panic-stricken rulers glimpsed the same horrifying possibility, and in their eyes events in England were bringing the dreaded cataclysm closer. A Swiss cleric who had seen the rebels at their work at close range wrote to the imperial ambassador in Venice likening the rioting in England to the German rebellion. He had letters from English friends, he said, telling him that King Henry's subjects were everywhere turning against him and that no one could say where the unrest might end.[11]

Such accounts of the protest against the Amicable Grant were exaggerations, yet they show the fear the tumult inspired. As it was happening no one could foresee its end, or judge its true scale. And in fact, had Henry decided on a harsh policy toward his impoverished, cantankerous and turbulent subjects instead of on leniency, large-scale rebellion might well have been the result.

As it was, collection of the grant proceeded, unsatisfactorily, for a while longer; the commissioners retreated when they were threatened and proceeded, through blandishments and coercion, to gather up at least some of what was owed as often as they could. "Fair words and the rough handling of one or two" villagers did yield some return, though in many places the amount owed had to be lowered or remitted altogether. Taken aback by the loss of his subjects' faith and esteem, and uncertain of his aims in the light of Charles V's defection, Henry gave orders that, if possible, his agents should "proceed doucely, rather than by violence" to bring the recalcitrant to pay.[12] Eventually he capitulated entirely, withdrawing the Amicable Grant and insisting that from the first he had known nothing about it. In place of the heavy burden of one sixth of all their goods he now asked only "such as his loving subjects would grant to him of their good minds," and did not punish those who had risen against the tax.[13]

Henry's clemency appeared to win back what favor he had lost, and the people went back to vilifying Wolsey as the true originator of the Amicable Grant. "In conclusion," the chronicler Hall wrote, "all people cursed the cardinal and his coadherents as subversors of the laws and liberty of England," and muttered to one another that Wolsey was secretly sending all the king's money to Rome.

1 The future Henry VIII as a child, sketched by an unknown artist.
(Bibliothèque de Méjanes, Aix-en-Provence; photo H. Nicollas)

2 Henry VIII's paternal grandmother Margaret Beaufort, a strong influence throughout his childhood and youth. Tomb sculpture by Torrigiano. (By courtesy of the Dean and Chapter of Westminster)

3 Henry VII in 1505, by Michael Sittow. (National Portrait Gallery)

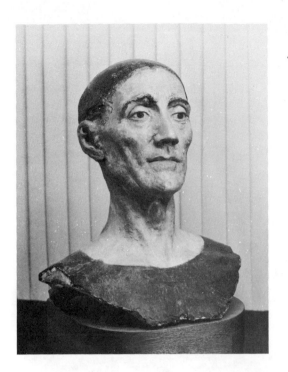

4 Death mask of Henry VII. (By courtesy of the Dean and Chapter of Westminster)

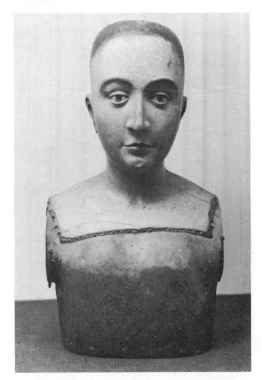

5 Funeral effigy of Henry VIII's mother Elizabeth of York. (By courtesy of the Dean and Chapter of Westminster)

6 Cardinal Wolsey, Henry
VIII's chancellor and
dominant figure of the
first twenty years of his
reign. Drawing attributed
to Jacques le Boucq of
Artois. (Bibliothèque
municipale d'Arras, *Recueil de
portraits,* ms. 266; photo
Giraudon)

7 "Wedding picture" of
Mary Tudor and Charles
Brandon, by Jan
Mabuse. (By kind permission
of the Marquess of Tavistock,
and the Trustees of the Bedford
Estates)

8 The young Henry VIII, date and artist uncertain, perhaps c. 1520.
(National Portrait Gallery)

9 Torrigiano's bust of the young Henry VIII, giving him an Italianate air. (Metropolitan Museum of Art)

10 Miniature of Henry VIII at thirty-five.
(Fitzwilliam Museum, University of Cambridge;
reproduced by permission of the Syndics of the
Fitzwilliam Museum, Cambridge)

11 Henry VIII, attributed to Joos van Cleeve. Date uncertain, but conventionally dated 1536. (Reproduced by gracious permission of Her Majesty the Queen; copyright reserved)

12 Mary Tudor, daughter of Katherine of Aragon and Henry VIII; succeeded to the throne in 1553. Sketched as a young girl, perhaps by Holbein. (Reproduced by gracious permission of Her Majesty the Queen; copyright reserved)

The Lady Mary after Queen.

13 Henry VIII's natural son Henry Fitzroy. (BBC Hulton Picture Library)

14 Elizabeth Tudor, daughter of Anne Boleyn and Henry VIII; succeeded to the throne in 1558. Painted at age fourteen by an unknown artist. (Reproduced by gracious permission of Her Majesty the Queen; copyright reserved)

15 Edward Tudor, son of Jane Seymour and Henry VIII; succeeded to the throne in 1547. Artist unknown. (Reproduced by gracious permission of Her Majesty the Queen; copyright reserved)

16 Anne Boleyn by an unknown artist. (National Portrait Gallery)

17 Katherine of Aragon in middle age, by an unknown artist. (National Portrait Gallery)

18 Miniature of Katherine of Aragon in later life, attributed to Horenbout.
(National Portrait Gallery)

19 Thomas More in 1527.
(Copyright The Frick Collection, New York)

20 Torrigiano bust of an
English ecclesiastic
traditionally said to be
John Fisher, bishop of
Rochester, executed in
1535. (Metropolitan Museum
of Art)

21 Jane Seymour, third wife
of Henry VIII, by
Holbein. (Kunsthistorisches
Museum, Wien)

22 Anne of Cleves; a portrait based on the famed likeness which brought about her marriage to Henry VIII. (Musée du Louvre)

23 Francis I of France, painted by Titian in about 1538. (Musée de Louvre)

THE ENCAMPMENT OF KING HENRY VIII AT MARQUISON, JULY MDXLIV.

ENGRAVED FROM A COEVAL PAINTING, AT COWDRAY IN SUSSEX, THE SEAT OF LORD VISCOUNT MONTAGUE.

24 Engraved sketch of Henry VIII's encampment at Marquison, near
Boulogne, in 1544; eighteenth-century copy of an original painting. (By
courtesy of the Society of Antiquaries of London)

25 The Emperor Charles V
a year after Henry VIII's
death, by Titian. (Alte
Pinakothek, München)

26 Portrait of John Chambers, one of
Henry VIII's doctors, by Holbein.
(Kunsthistorisches Museum, Wien)

27 Portrait of Charles Brandon, duke of
Suffolk, by an unknown artist. (National
Portrait Gallery)

28 Chalk drawing of Henry VIII in old age, by Holbein. (Staatliche
Graphische Sammlung, München)

IV

"Dieu et Mon Droit"

23

Youth must have some dalliance,
Of good or ill some pastance;
Company methinks then best
All thoughts and fancies to digest,
     For idleness
     Is chief mistress
     Of vices all:
     Then who can say
     But mirth and play
     Is best of all?

THE torchlit presence chamber of Hampton Court had never been more resplendently decked than on the night of January 3, 1527, when a great feast was held there to celebrate the new year. At the long tables set up against one wall the chief nobles of Henry VIII's court were being served course after course of meats and fish and fowl. They were seated, as always at Wolsey's banquets, lord next to lady and gentleman by gentlewoman; the Venetian ambassador wrote afterward that he felt out of place beside his dinner partner, a "very beautiful damsel," until he realized that each of the diners had been assigned a companion as radiant as his. It was said there was never a shortage of alluring young women at the cardinal's entertainments, and this, plus the choice wines and gorgeous spectacles he offered his guests, made them glad enough to put aside their thorough hatred of him and enjoy themselves for an evening at his expense.

The cardinal had taken his usual pains with the banquet, sending his household officers out weeks in advance to search for the finest and most costly provisions and ordering carpenters and joiners and painters to repair the rooms of the palace and its furnishings. When these had finished, the yeomen and grooms of the wardrobe hung new hangings in the halls and put fresh silk coverings on the beds, while the sewer and his staff polished all the plate and displayed it in a massive cupboard that filled one entire wall of the presence chamber.

In the kitchens below, new cooks, the most expert to be found in the realm, had been working night and day alongside Wolsey's own excellent chefs to create subtleties, "strange fabrics in paste, towers and castles, which are offered to the assault of valiant teeth." The sixteenth-century cook addressed his calling with lusty vigor. In his long bespattered apron he stood by his pots, chopping and slicing and stirring and attending to a dozen things at once, bawling out orders to his servants and swearing at them when they worked too slowly to please him. It was said that a good chef needed a choleric temperament, with curses "the very dialect of his calling." "The kitchen is his hell, and he the devil in it," a contemporary wrote, and in the sweltering kitchens of Hampton Court an army of devils labored over their turning spits and shining platters on the night of Wolsey's great banquet, "interlarding their own grease to help the drippings."

Upstairs the cardinal, oblivious to these exertions, dined apart from his guests at a high table in the center of the hall, under his rich cloth of estate. His portly form was all but hidden from view by the heaping platters of delicacies spread out before him on the perfumed tablecloth. All around him stood serving men to refill his goblet and hold his napkin while he ate; still others waited attendance at his side and behind his chair, imposing reminders of his status.

Cardinal, legate, chancellor and indispensable servant of the king, Wolsey had reached the pinnacle of his power and wealth. Advancing age and sickness now weighed down his fleshy body, but had not dulled his mind; he was as capable as ever, and still transacted business with the single-purposed intensity that had first brought him to Henry's notice nearly fifteen years earlier. He had his wits about him tonight, as he was soon to play a central role in a little drama devised by the king to enliven the evening.

In the midst of the dining the guests were startled by the sound of many small cannons being fired all at once just outside the palace, "which made such a rumble in the air that it was like thunder." As they turned to one another in astonishment, asking what it might mean, Wolsey called on the royal chamberlain William Sandys and the revels master Henry Guildford to see what was happening. Looking out the window onto the river, they reported seeing some noble foreigners, possibly the envoys of a distant prince, arriving at the water stairs.

"I shall desire you," Wolsey then told Sandys and Guildford, "because ye can speak French to take the pains to go down into the hall to encounter and to receive them according to their estates, and to conduct them into this chamber, where they shall see us and all these noble personages sitting merrily at our banquet, desiring them to sit down with us and to take part of our fare and pastime."

The two men descended to the lower floor, accompanied by torchbearers, and returned shortly afterward escorting a large company of curiously dressed maskers and their attendants, who came into the hall to the raucous sound of drums and fifes. They were dressed in garments with the simple cut of shepherds' tunics, though they were made of alternate stripes of crimson satin and fine cloth of gold; visors hid the maskers' faces, and artificial beards and hair of fine gold wire or black silk covered their heads completely. There was no sound but that of the drums and fifes as the mysterious visitors filed solemnly, two by two, past the banqueters and down the length of the chamber toward the table where

Wolsey sat alone. Even after they reached him and the musicians stopped playing the strangers did not speak, but merely bowed low in reverence.

Sandys spoke for them, explaining that they knew no English yet hoped to be admitted to the banquet to make the acquaintance of the many "excellent fair dames" in the hall, and to gamble and dance with them. Wolsey consented, and then a lengthy pantomime began. The maskers walked up and down the hall a second time, greeting each of the women in turn and appraising each for her beauty. Then, having decided which one was the loveliest, they returned to her and, placing a cup of gold coins before her, cast the dice. After a single cast they moved on to another of the women, and cast again, then to another and another until each had had her turn to win or lose against them.

Throughout the play the maskers continued to keep silence, with the only sound in the vast room the clatter of the dice and the clinking of coins into the cup as it filled with their winnings. Finally, when the last wager had been won, the strangers returned to the cardinal's table and poured out the coins before him, indicating that it was his turn to play. He bet them all on a single cast, and won.

At once the banqueters burst into noisy applause, sighing with relief and breaking the tension in the room. When the tumult had subsided Wolsey spoke.

"I pray you," he said to Sandys, "show them that it seems to me there should be among them some nobleman, whom I suppose to be much more worthy of honor to sit and occupy this room and place than I, to whom I would most gladly—if I knew him—surrender my place according to my duty."

Wolsey knew that the king was among the maskers, though when asked to point him out he had to scrutinize them all carefully and finally chose the wrong man—Edward Neville, the tall gentleman of the privy chamber who was Henry's near-double. When he saw the cardinal's mistake the king could not contain himself. He burst out laughing, pulling off his mask and reaching over to pull off Neville's as well. At the sight of his merry face the banqueters broke into delighted applause a second time, and Wolsey at once rose heavily to his feet and made his obeisance, motioning for Henry to take his chair. Instead of sitting down, though, the king left the room and went straight to Wolsey's bedchamber, explaining that he wanted to change his clothes. While he was gone every sign of the banqueting—every plate and goblet, every cloth and piece of cutlery—was removed and a new one put in its place. By the time he returned a second banquet was under way, more lavish and more sumptuous than the first.

That Henry made himself at home at Hampton Court was to be expected, for though Wolsey continued to use the splendid palace from time to time it had in fact belonged to the king for several years. Since the start of the reign, when the royal palace at Westminster was destroyed by fire, Henry had not had a residence befitting his majesty. He used the apartments in the Tower, the old Norman fortress of Baynard's Castle, and his new palace of Bridewell, but all were too restricting. Every year as Henry's household grew larger his palaces came to seem smaller, while by contrast Wolsey's monumental establishments at York Place and Hampton Court loomed princely and vast. In time the contrast became too sharp to be borne, and in 1525 Wolsey, ever eager to retain his master's good will, made Henry a present of Hampton Court.

The huge red brick structure had many advantages beyond its spaciousness and its imposing exterior. There were five large courts and two hunting parks, an herb garden where the king could grow his medicinal plants and a tennis court where he could wager with his courtiers. Fine Italian craftsmen and sculptors had been brought in to design the unique plumbing system that brought drinking water to the palace in leaden pipes and drained off wastes through brick sewers.

As remarkable as Hampton Court was, Henry had no difficulty devising ways to improve it. He added a tiltyard and ordered work begun on an elaborate great hall—an undertaking so large it took five years to complete. Still more marvellous was the large astronomical clock he added in 1540, designed by the German astronomer Nicholas Kratzer and built by the French clockmaker Nicolas Oursian. The intricate dial of this twenty-four-hour clock indicated not only the time of day (approximately, for sixteenth-century clocks had no second hand) but the positions of the moon and the constellations of the zodiac as well. In an age when the accurate calculation of time was an obscure art the great clock of Hampton Court was a monument of precision. Time was told differently in different parts of Europe. In England and Flanders, noon and midnight marked the beginning of two cycles of twelve hours each, but in Germany a single daily cycle of twenty-four hours began at sunrise. In Italy the twenty-four-hour cycle began at sunset, and as both sunrise and sunset varied from one town to another no regional synchronization of times was possible. But in the Hampton Court clock the English hours were brought into harmony with the heavenly bodies, an accomplishment so rare it never ceased to amaze visitors to the palace.

Wolsey, his staff and his guests waited while their king put off his masking costume and arrayed himself in his kingly velvets. Then when he returned and took the place of honor under the cloth of estate—"commanding no man to remove but sit still as they did before"—the new banquet began. Two hundred different dishes were set before the king and his sated courtiers, "of wondrous costly meats and devices, subtly devised," and excellent wines in great variety. When they had eaten so much they could scarcely walk they made their way to another hall where a Latin comedy, Plautus' *Menaechmi,* was performed, and then returned once again to the banqueting chamber.

Here a final entertainment was offered. On a platform stage Venus and six beauteous attendants appeared, looking as radiant "as if she and they had really come down in person from heaven." Then at the sound of trumpets Cupid was brought in on a cart, dragging behind him six old men who were his prisoners. Love bound these aged victims hand and foot; their sweethearts, who were Venus' attendants, had wounded them by failing to return their love. Cupid made an eloquent Latin oration to his mother on their behalf, causing her to take compassion on the sufferers. She ordered her attendants to end their lovers' torment at once, "commanding them to afford them all solace and pastime, and requite them for past pangs." The pageant ended with an intricate dance, after which the king and his minions took partners and danced on and on until daybreak.[1]

The agile dancing, elaborate masking and general enthusiasm and energy Henry showed that night at the cardinal's banquet belied the oppressive mood that had preoccupied him and disturbed his thoughts for many months. The outward change was slight; inwardly, though, he had reached an impasse.

The besetting dilemma of the succession seemed insoluble. The thought of it filled him with frustration and sadness, and time and again he wore down his wits in a self-defeating effort to think it through. In his role as king, much that had been knitted together favorably in the first decade of his reign had come unraveled. The vision of conquest that had sustained his military ambitions had faded when, with bewildering finality, his enemy had been defeated by another power. The French king was no longer a strutting rival, but an enfeebled captive in the emperor's custody; the grand campaign Henry had determined to launch against France had been undercut by the emperor's obstinacy and the recalcitrance of his own subjects. He had been given reason to fear his courtiers, and to note with concern his loss of popular favor. He had, in fact, been thwarted in nearly all that he undertook, and the more he turned this dispiriting realization in his mind the more his self-confidence was eroded and his natural resiliency impaired.

Worst of all, Henry was losing his sense of mastery. Once accustomed to sweeping aside all obstacles to his desires he had now grown accustomed to rebuffs. He was repeatedly, consistently overmatched by circumstances, and if he seemed to make headway one day he met with reversals the next. To struggle on in unseemly battle with all the odds against him was humiliating for a king, bred since boyhood to dominate; defeat was beginning to eat away at Henry's assured manner, shadowing his sunny nature on occasion and making him short-tempered and curt.

Since the spring of 1525, when his hopes for the conquest of France had collapsed amid the alarming advance of popular rebellion, Henry had stepped back from his responsibilities, allowing himself to be carried through the days by diversions rather than purposeful activities. In the winter months he read in his library, or called in the scholars at his court to debate with him. He busied himself concocting possets and preventives and medicinal salves, and in looking after his dozens of keyboard instruments and seeing that they were kept properly strung and tuned. He exercised his horses in the afternoons and, in the evenings, looked at the moon and stars through "speculative glasses" with his companion Thomas More. And when the "grass season" came, the warm months when there was game in the woods and long hours of daylight to chase it in, he abandoned himself in isolated fury to the hunt.

From mid-May well into October he was on the move from one hunting lodge or country estate to another, now accompanied by his large "riding household," now only by the queen and a few dozen servants and companions. Ten-year-old Princess Mary, who headed a large establishment of her own on the borders of Wales, joined her father occasionally, though he saw as little of her as he did of the ambassadors who often had to wait from morning till nightfall for him to come in from the fields.

The hart and falcon and stag, not his family or his courtiers, ruled Henry's schedule during the hunting season. An official who approached him with a packet of letters one day in July of 1526 was brushed aside and told to wait; "he was going out to have a shot at a stag," Henry said to the man, and asked him to keep the letters until the evening.[2] Other officials were given the same reception. The king was hawking with his Flemish falconers, they were told, or harboring a stag with his keen-scented lyam hounds, or going after harts his huntsmen had gathered for his sport, so that "he must needs hunt them."[3]

In September of 1526, after he had been released from captivity and was moving toward an alliance with England, King Francis sent Henry a shipload of wild swine. He heard they were scarce in England, he wrote, and thought Henry might enjoy the challenge of their ferocity, as "the hunting of them was very pleasant, and a king's game."[4] "The high enterprise and dangerous hunting of the perilous wild swine" was indeed a challenging sport, and one at which Francis had excelled ever since his famous exploit against the runaway boar at Amboise at the start of his reign. The frenzied beast, a ton of lumbering madness, was driven into a wide net. The hunters, stripped to their doublets and hose and armed with sharp spears, then turned their dogs on him; as he charged the dogs, wounding many and goring others to death with his tusks, the men inched closer until the boar began to lunge at them as well. The fainthearted backed off then, but the most intrepid of the hunters stayed on, keeping just out of reach of the great tusks while watching their chance to move in for the kill. Eventually the moment came; the sinews were slashed and the spear thrust to the heart, and the raging beast staggered and fell. The hunter who killed him was accorded great honor, and accounted as valorous "as though he had slain a man of arms."

Where and when Henry dispatched the French boars Francis sent him is not recorded, but it is certain they filled out his sporting calendar in the late summer of 1526. He followed a leisurely itinerary during these months, staying at one country estate for a week or so and then moving on, traveling ten or twelve miles in a day, to the next. With him went a footman with a purse full of coins, for charity along the way. For amusement he took his fools and jesters, and for safety a locksmith who installed new locks and bolts on the chamber doors of each residence he occupied.[5]

The king's route in August led from Arundel in Sussex, where the earl of Northumberland's officers presented him with six oxen and forty wethers for his cooks to serve and where he "had good game for his recreation," to Thruxton, Ransbury, Compton and Langley. He was reportedly "merry and in good health," and appeared to have no other care but for how much venison he could present to his host and to the patient secretaries and men of affairs who met him in the evenings, dispatches in hand. But he was seldom able to throw off for long the dark musings that confounded him, and his moods became more intense as day after day of unseasonal rain spoiled his hunting in September. He moved to Bycester, then to Buckingham, then to Ampthill and Grafton, everywhere encountering the same dripping foliage and leaky roofs, everywhere housebound and irritable.

The rain did not stop when Henry gave up his hunting later in the fall, but continued to descend in torrents. Rivers and streams overflowed their banks and flooded fields and villages. The panicked villagers hoisted their children onto their backs and set off to seek higher ground, leaving their corn to rot under water and their sheep and cows to drown in the inundated pastures.

Once back at court, in the intervals between public business the king returned to his indoor pastimes, emerging from time to time to address ambassadors and other visitors and to learn from them news of continental affairs. He kept himself well informed, as always; the Milanese ambassador Scarpinello admired the range of his understanding and his eloquence, "worthy of a great orator rather than king."[6] Observers still noted in him that unique blend of guileless candor and high aspiration he had shown at the outset of his reign; the king is "simple and candid by nature," Scarpinello wrote, yet at the same time he burned to be at the center of every undertaking, to join every expedition and govern every negotiation. As the Milanese explained to his superiors, Henry "wants to have his feet in a thousand shoes."[7]

Two influences were working to revitalize Henry and to lift him out of his pensive mood in the fall of 1526. The first was an alchemy of personality. As he reached his mid-thirties Henry's resemblance to his father began to be more pronounced.

Erasmus had noted long before how alike they were. The son resembled the father "not in name and likeness only," he said, "but with all royal gifts so representing his father that the latter seems rather to have renewed his youth than died." The two terracotta busts Torrigiano sculpted of Henry VII and Henry VIII show little likeness of features, yet in manner and mental address Henry was very much his father's son. It was his keen alertness, the bright and wide intelligence that lay behind his "quick and penetrable eyes," and his air of self-assurance more than any physical resemblance that led Erasmus to observe how like his father Henry was. Now other characteristics were emerging, qualities which enabled Henry to regain a conviction of mastery and to begin to assault his besetting dilemmas head on.

He was taking on for the first time the full weight of princely authority, an overriding majesty of presence which aroused both terror and awed respect. Henry had always been a formidable, outsize figure; now he was becoming a fearsome one. His father had known, to a fine degree of accuracy, when to check and when to unleash his wrath. Now Henry was beginning to master this art, and to use it to increase his sense of command. In time this new consciousness of sovereignty worked to counteract the concerns that oppressed him, until eventually he moved forcefully to seize and maintain control of his own and England's future.

But there was an even stronger influence at work on the king as the year 1526 drew to a close and the new year, celebrated by the cardinal's banquet, began. While his head was clouded and his emotions in disarray, he had fallen helplessly, exhilaratingly in love.

24

Joy, dearest lover, thine shall be
And I shall lead thee tenderly
Where hope would have thee seek thy pleasure;
Alive I shall not part from thee,
And still when death has come to me
My soul its memories shall treasure.

ANNE Boleyn was already a ripening, self-aware girl when she was brought to the court of Henry VIII in late 1521 or 1522. She may have been no more than fourteen or fifteen years old—the date of her birth is uncertain—when her grandfather, the octogenarian duke of Norfolk, and his close-lipped, ungentle son obtained a place for her among Katherine's maids of honor.[1] But already she was distinctive. She wore her thick black hair long, letting it fall unbound to below her waist. Her skin complemented her hair; she had an olive complexion, though her critics called it dark or sallow. In later years they made much of Anne's other singular physical attributes: a tooth that was out of line with the others, a large mole on her neck, a double nail on one hand where a sixth finger had begun to grow. These blemishes were more than eclipsed, though, by the elegance of dress and grace of movement she displayed at court functions, and by her ability to attract and fascinate men.

Anne was always full of life, creating excitement and tension wherever she was. The fact that she was a nubile young girl, "likely enough to have children," gave that excitement a strong sexual edge. All Anne's vitality and magnetism seemed to center in her large, almond-shaped dark eyes—"black and beautiful"—which quickly took in the subtle cross-currents of court society while remaining outwardly coquettish and captivating. As she matured she grew more and more provocative; at nineteen she had become, to Henry and others, a woman of infinite allure.

It was no small part of that allure that Anne had spent the formative years of her early adolescence at the French court. At age twelve she had gone to France with her father, Henry VIII's ambassador Thomas Boleyn, and had joined the large suite of girls in the household of Francis I's queen Claude. There, under the tutelage of the ill-favored but virtuous queen—Claude limped and was afflicted with a squint, and was described as "very small and strangely fat"—Anne became fluent in French, acquiring a taste for the literature and art of King Francis' gilded Renaissance court. Her pronounced musical gifts too were developed; she

187

became a skilled singer and lutenist, and may have met the reigning luminaries of French music, Josquin des Prés and Claude Mouton. Poets dedicated books and poems to her, saluting her charm and confirming the judgment of other observers that, in subtle ways, she had become a Frenchwoman. In the language of one poet, she was such a graceful maidôn that no one would have believed she was English.

Anne's idea of the relations between men and women were also formed at the French court. Here, in contrast to the atmosphere surrounding Henry VIII, a sort of relaxed decadence prevailed. In England even the most companionable of the king's courtiers observed an outward show of respect for his person; in France the courtiers lounged casually near their sovereign, "some leaning upon his chair, and some upon his table, all much more familiarly than is agreeable to English manners." Rakish in their silk doublets and hose, earrings glittering in one or both ears, the courtiers of Francis I were equally familiar in their treatment of women. The king himself set the tone for their eager voluptuousness. "Alexander the Great saw women when there was no business to be looked after," a contemporary wrote; "Francis I looks after business when there are no women."

Anne Boleyn arrived in France shortly after the king took the first of his official mistresses, the dark, strapping Françoise de Foix. Françoise maddened her royal lover with her infidelities, while he found solace reveling until morning with his "little band" of lesser favorites and the officially appointed prostitutes and their madam, "la dame des filles de joie." The entire court was privy to the quarreling of Francis and Françoise, which grew to be as predictable as the king's neglect of his pathetic wife.

Between the ages of twelve and fifteen Anne became habituated to the spectacle of stormy amorous liaisons, erotic adventures and the living of private lives in public. The experience made her worldly before her time, as did another influence: the example of her sister Mary. By the time Anne joined Queen Claude's household Mary Boleyn, who had been in France for five years, had become a full participant in the sensual pastimes of the French court. She not only lost her innocence but became known for her sexual complaisance; long after she had returned to England Francis kept her in memory as a "hackney" or "English mare" he and others had often ridden. Still later, looking back across nearly twenty years, he called Mary "a great prostitute, infamous above all."[2]

No doubt her sister's chosen path of compromising dalliance swayed Anne. To countervail it she had only the example of the lonely queen and the more upright of her ladies, who hastened to cross themselves whenever they heard an obscenity and remained closeted with their needlework while the king made merry.

"Rarely or never did any maid or wife leave that court chaste," Brantôme wrote. Whether Anne's sojourn in France tarnished her reputation as it did her sister's is not recorded, but it seems certain that Thomas Boleyn and his brother-in-law Thomas Howard, duke of Norfolk, looked on both girls as useful pawns in the dangerous game of court politics. Norfolk intended to use them to advance himself at the expense of the all-powerful Cardinal Wolsey and his other rival, Charles Brandon, while the handsome, coolly observant opportunist Thomas Boleyn stood to gain even more.

Oddly enough, Anne Boleyn's father is among the most obscure figures at the court of Henry VIII. His imprint on the records of the time is tantalizingly slight: a quarrel with Wolsey in the early years of the reign, close ties with his Howard relations and with William Compton, a revealing comment by a French diplomat that Boleyn "would sooner act from interest than from any other motive." Erasmus praised his love of learning and sent him one of his works. The rest is evidence from silence. As adroitly as he made his way to power he outlasted its backlash, deflecting the fate that brought his son and second daughter to the block and dying calmly in his bed.

"Thy niece, thy cousin or thy daughter," the poet Thomas Wyatt wrote in a satire of court life,

> If she be fair, if handsome be her middle,
> If thy better hath her love besought her,
> Advance his cause and he shall help thy need.

Wyatt's words describe the Boleyns perfectly. Mary Boleyn was brought to England, married to the king's esquire of the body, William Carey, and installed as informal royal mistress. Within months her father had become treasurer of the household, a Garter Knight, and keeper of several manors and parks—a lucrative list of offices that was to grow still longer in the years to come. By 1525 he had been created Lord Rochford, the only commoner to hold such a title; more significant was his assured place in the innermost circle of power around the king. Ambassadors and foreign rulers now reckoned with his influence, and tried to make use of it. In 1525 he was receiving a pension of a thousand crowns a year from the imperial court—as high as that paid to Norfolk and Brandon.

But Boleyn was to rise still higher by trading on his younger daughter's charms. While she was still in France he put her at the king's disposal, and Henry's first reaction was to try to marry her to the Irish chieftain James Butler, to settle an old rivalry between the Boleyns and Butlers over the earldom of Ormond. The negotiations came to nothing, and Anne came back to England marriageable and unattached. She made herself conspicuous among Katherine's maids of honor, kept an observant eye on her sister's interesting situation as wife and royal mistress, and, for her pastime, lent her decorative looks to court pageants. With her sister, Mary Brandon, and four others Anne took part in an entertainment called "Le Château Vert" soon after her arrival, wearing a white satin gown and jeweled bonnet and pretending to defend the castle with missiles made of sugarplums. Among the knights who assaulted the castle was the king, but if he was attracted then by his mistress' sister he did nothing to indicate it.

Instead it was left to Wolsey to guide Anne's destiny over the next few years. The cardinal's entry into Anne's affairs was an abrupt one, and left a painful scar. Anne and young Henry Percy, heir to the earl of Northumberland and a member of Wolsey's household, fell in love. In his infatuation Percy, a sensitive though somewhat violent youth, chose to forget that he was already promised to a daughter of the earl of Shrewsbury, Mary Talbot. Wolsey remembered, however, and shouted at Percy for becoming enamored of "that foolish girl yonder in the court." The young man had no choice but to give in, though his marriage to Mary Talbot proved to be miserably unhappy. At the time Anne's punishment must have seemed even more severe. She was sent away to Hever, the Boleyn country house, where for some three years at least her sophistication and allure were wasted on the rural gentry. Used to gaiety and variety, Anne had to accustom herself to a dull, uneventful existence made humiliating by the stigma of disgrace. At once heartsick, angry and resentful, she blamed all on Wolsey. "If it ever lay in her power," she swore, "she would work the cardinal as much displeasure."

Finally in 1525 or 1526 Anne came back to court, now a beauty of eighteen or nineteen. Possibly at this time, if not earlier, she had another love affair—with her longtime admirer, the poet Thomas Wyatt. There is reason to think that Anne became Wyatt's mistress, and that years later the poet confessed this to the king and his privy councilors. But whatever the truth of their involvement, Anne and Wyatt could never have indulged their feelings for long—he because he was married (though separated from his wife) and she because she soon became the object of a more commanding passion.[3]

Sometime in 1526, it would seem, Henry was, in his phrase, "struck with the dart of love" for Anne. His comfortable liaison with Mary Boleyn had come to an end perhaps a year earlier, and for a time, no single favorite took her place. There were certainly women in his life. Looking back on this period some six years later, Norfolk told the imperial ambassador that Henry was "always inclined to amours"—a tendency the imperialists were only too eager to exploit. According to one French report, Charles V was attempting to influence English foreign policy "by means of women who he thinks are favored by the king."[4] But before too many months had passed he had begun to prefer one above the others, and for the second time his choice fell on a daughter of his councilor Thomas Boleyn. Characteristically, Henry signaled the course of his affections in nautical terms. Some years earlier he had christened one of his ships the *Mary Boleyn;* now in 1526 payment for a new ship, the *Anne Boleyn,* was made from the royal military accounts.[5]

There were other signs that the king was in love. He ordered his goldsmiths to make him four gold brooches, one of Venus and cupids, one of a lady holding a heart in her hand, a third of a gentleman lying in a lady's lap, and a fourth of a lady holding a crown. It is tempting to think they may have been made for Anne.[6] In addition to his ever resplendent dress—a visitor to court in October of 1527 saw him in an elegant suit of black velvet lined with sables, his studs and buttons made of diamonds and pearls—Henry now doused himself often with a perfume of his own invention, a pungent concoction of musk, ambergris, sugar and rosewater.

That the restless, vital king should have been attracted to a fascinating, dark-eyed girl sixteen years his junior poses no mystery. The course their long, eventful passion took is somewhat harder to account for. Perhaps because she resisted repeating her sister's thankless fate, perhaps because from the start Henry hoped to provide her with a higher destiny, Anne at first became the king's love without becoming his mistress. For years unfulfilled longing bound Henry to Anne with a force more potent than the most powerful aphrodisiac; in his chivalrous imagination she remained the unattainable maiden, the worthy locus of all hope and worship.

Most important, Henry's love for Anne became linked in a unique way to his need for a son. Unlike her predecessors Bessie Blount and Mary Boleyn, Anne came to embody, not merely a distraction from the besetting dilemma of the succession, but an answer to it. She would become not his mistress but his wife. The new marriage would have none of the frustrations or tragedies of the old. No whispered rumors of a curse would overshadow it; there would be no deadborn children, only strong, vigorous sons to carry on the Tudor line.

Once he began to see his way past the snares of his fruitless marriage, the other vexing preoccupations that had so perplexed the king in recent months began to seem less daunting. His passion for Anne renewed and emboldened him to take up the struggle against the forces thwarting him at home and abroad—against the emperor, whose lukewarm allegiance had darkened Henry's vision of conquest in France, against his critical subjects and his intriguing courtiers, against that inner sense of defeat that dispirited him and drained him of energy.

To Londoners it seemed as if the early months of 1527 were devoted to nothing but days of jousting and pageantry and nights of banquets and disguisings. The revelry was misleading; behind the scenes envoys from the French court were meeting in long bargaining sessions with English diplomats, working out the terms of three treaties that would bind the two realms into an alliance sealed with the betrothal of the Princess Mary to the second son of the French king. Though busied with the negotiations Henry found time to give special attention to the celebrations that accompanied them, setting nineteen tailors and five fabric cutters to work fashioning jousting costumes of purple Florentine velvet trimmed in gold fringe and gold lace. He ordered the Flemish and German workmen of his armory to make a suit of armor for the French comte de Turenne, copying as exactly as they could armor made for Henry himself shortly before, said to be the safest design ever invented.[7]

To judge from the scale of the rejoicings, the newfound amity with the French surpassed all previous diplomatic accords in importance. At Hampton Court the envoys feasted in luxurious abundance, marveling at the edible sculptures served between courses. Culinary artists had been brought in to prepare these masterpieces, in the lifelike forms of beasts, birds and inhabited castles. Jousting courtiers in full armor, soldiers battling with guns and crossbows, leaping knights dancing with ladies—all were brought to life in gilded confections rising above the heavily laden dining tables. At one point a chessboard, complete with chessmen, was set before the guests, made entirely of sweetmeats. In acknowledgment of his skill as a chess player Wolsey gave it to one of the Frenchmen, ordering a special case built to carry it to France. Every effort was made to overwhelm the visiting diplomats, in order "to make them such triumphant cheer as they may not only wonder at it here, but also make a glorious report in their county to the king's honor and of this realm."[8]

Crowning the festivities was a great celebration in a new hall and theater built on the tiltyard at Greenwich. Here in a magnificent setting made splendid by the work of dozens of foreign artisans the king entertained the French envoys. The children of his chapel sang for them, and two companies of maskers, among them Henry and nine-year-old Princess Mary, danced an intricate measure. The little princess, her slight form weighed down by her heavy gown and abundant jewels, was shown off afterward to the representatives of her future husband. As they looked on Henry unbound her fair hair, letting it fall becomingly around her shoulders while he stood back in pride at their approval of his daughter.

As usual, efforts were made to share the spectacle with the people of London. The hall and disguising house were left standing for three or four days after their usefulness ended, their gorgeous contents intact; "all honest persons" were welcomed in to gape at the cupboards of gold and silver plate, the silken carpets and fantastic carvings that decorated the walls. But while a great number of people came, many grumbled at what they saw. The alliance with France greatly disturbed Londoners, who were always predisposed to favor the emperor. Merchants whose businesses depended on uninterrupted trade with Flanders—certain to be ruptured once England and France became allied against the imperialists—joined with the German merchant community in the capital in condemning the negotiations, while the poorer citizens swore "they would have no Frenchman to be king of England."

In the streets and taverns of the city the story of an unwitting clash between the French envoys and two unfortunate apprentices aroused more interest than the gilded banqueting hall and all its furnishings.

One evening several members of the French delegation were going from Blackfriars to the Tailors' Hall. Their way led them past a house where two apprentices were cleaning a gutter and throwing the accumulated sludge into the street; unintentionally the boys hit a French lackey with a clod of filth. The man was unhurt, but the Frenchmen took the incident badly and complained to Wolsey. The cardinal's formidable anger flared and, "too hasty of credence," he sent for the lord mayor and ordered him to imprison everyone in the house from the master down to the meanest servant. The apprentices were locked away in the Tower to await their punishment. It was a full six weeks before the unfortunate householder and his family and servants were allowed to return home. One of the apprentices was in time released from the Tower, lamed by the fetters which had bound his legs and ankles; the other died before he could be freed. "Of the cruelty of the cardinal, and of the pride of the Frenchmen," the chronicler Hall wrote, "much people spake, and would have been revenged on the Frenchmen, if wise men in the city had not appeased it with fair words."[9]

With the approach of May Day, traditionally the occasion for assaults on foreigners, Wolsey put the city on guard. Nightly watches were set at some half-dozen points throughout the capital, manned by householders and their servants; at Westminster soldiers stood ready to break up any commotion that might arise, backed up by heavy guns charged to fire. May Day came and went, but still the unrest in the city grew. Handbills critical of the king's Council and especially of Wolsey circulated nightly, warning against the French marriage and threatening the cardinal with punishment as "an enemy to the king and the realm." The authors of these attacks were impossible to apprehend because they were impossible to find; their campaign of slander escalated until by mid-May it was rumored the king meant to relieve Wolsey of his share in the government—a rumor made plausible by the cardinal's withdrawal from court.[10]

In truth Wolsey was ill, and had been for weeks. The stress of the negotiation, the fear that his French allies might betray him at the last moment (or so the imperial ambassador believed), the strain of his frequent "high words" with Norfolk and Tunstall, his chief opponents in the Council, all had taken their toll. When not laid low by indigestion or fever he stormed through his working days, lashing out at those around him and leaving them bewildered by his inconsistent orders. One day his talk would be of nothing but war; he would command all ships taking on goods for Flanders and Spain to be seized and detained in port. The next day, fearful of a popular rising, he would take back these orders in even stronger terms.[11] Hearing that he had been ridiculed in a disguising staged by the law students of Gray's Inn he threatened the actors "in a great fury," and had the author of the work imprisoned in the Fleet. He insisted it was the king who was "sorely displeased," but there could be no doubt whose displeasure had in fact been aroused.[12]

As rapprochement with the French proceeded the few remaining ties between England and the empire grew frayed. Communications between the two courts broke down, and after the imperial ambassador de Praet left England in the spring of 1525 the emperor waited more than a year and a half before sending another. By the time Mendoza arrived in December of 1526 events had moved too far to permit the breach to be healed. The king met the ambassador with an annoyed recital of his nephew's grievous shortcomings as an ally: he had accepted English money and used it against English interests, he had negotiated a separate peace with the pope and the French, neglecting his uncle and ally, he had not kept faith. Charles had nothing but words for him, Henry said heatedly; deeds he kept for others.[13]

Clearly Henry had passed the point where he would listen to reason. When told that he had not always kept his own obligations he replied "rather in a passion" that the accusation was totally false; he would answer for his honorable conduct "against whomever contradicted him." Each meeting with Mendoza grew more heated, with the king abandoning words for gestures, gesticulating in frustration and "showing his anger even more in manner than in words."[14] By mid-March the interviews had reached a quarrelsome stalemate, and the ill feeling was not directed to the ambassador alone.

Queen Katherine's awkward and anxious situation in the spring of

1527, Mendoza afterward observed, was entirely the result of her close identification with the interests of her nephew Charles V. She had been out of touch with him for years, yet she continued to look upon herself as his agent at the English court. Her letters to him were full of reproaches for his neglect, but she never failed to assure the emperor of her "readiness for his service"; if he would only send his orders, she wrote, she would do her best to carry them out.[15]

By now Katherine had lived nearly two thirds of her life in England, yet according to one English witness she still spoke her adopted language haltingly. Her spelling revealed her heavily accented pronunciation; like the Spanish envoys who came and went from the imperial court she spelled Greenwich "Granuche" and Hampton Court "Antoncurt." Surrounded by her Spanish women and household servants, she preserved a cultural distance between herself and the English, whose peculiarities she noted with the detachment of an outsider. "A small advantage renders them overbearing, and a little adversity makes them despondent," she once remarked of her husband's diplomatic advisers, and it was just this sort of shrewd objectivity, combined with her clearheaded loyalty to her Hapsburg relatives, that made Katherine seem dangerous to Wolsey.

What Wolsey did not see was that in recent years Katherine had paid dearly for her isolation. Hers was a narrow world, enlivened too infrequently by messages or gifts from the outside. One winter a letter came from the faraway lands in America, from Hispaniola, describing curiosities to be sent to her: a ceremonial native gown and a chair or saddle of the kind the island women rode in. He decided against sending parrots, Katherine's correspondent in the New World said, as he feared they would not survive the long sea journey.[16] Surprises such as this were rare, and did little to alter the austere regimen of Katherine's day, a regimen built around unfailing observance of religious services and meditations. On many days she fasted and, having become a professed sister of the Third Order of Saint Francis, wore a Franciscan habit under her court robes. The queen's devotions made her a "mirror of goodness," yet they brought more resignation into her life than joy. As she advanced more deeply into middle age her troubled marriage weighed her down and occasionally made her morbid. Writing to Wolsey about the proposed marriage of one of her waiting maids, Katherine said that she was concerned to provide for her attendants while she still could, "before God called her to account."[17]

Katherine's one unalloyed source of pleasure was her daughter. Everything about the little princess—her demure good manners, her quick mind and well-behaved diligence in learning, her graceful dancing and agile musicianship—gave the queen reason to hope that Mary would some day sit on her father's throne. More and more, though, the king appeared to favor his bastard Henry Fitzroy as his heir. Currently there was talk of adding to Fitzroy's titles unprecedented authority as king of Ireland, with vast estates to support his rule in that untamed region. Henry was hoping to make an important marriage for his son as well, and even as he railed in anger at Mendoza he proposed a match for Fitzroy with the emperor's niece Maria.[18]

What talk she heard of Fitzroy's advancement distressed Katherine, not only for her daughter's sake but, increasingly, for her own. She was becoming exceedingly uneasy about her position. Wolsey was tightening the ring of suspicion he had thrown around her some years earlier. In addition to maintaining informants among her servants and reading every letter that came and went from her desk he now refused to let her see the imperial ambassador in private, insisting that he be present at their meetings and even then interrupting their conversation on the pretext of an urgent communication from the king. Henry too seemed altered. Once he had listened to his wife's advice; now he turned from it. His passion for Thomas Boleyn's dark-haired daughter was taking an unexpected course, one which threatened much greater harm than a conventional court dalliance.

Sometime in March of 1527 Katherine formed a darker conviction. In one of his brief visits with the queen Mendoza brought her a welcome letter from her nephew, and she sent an immediate reply. To avoid Wolsey's spies her message had to be a verbal one, carried by her physician Ferdinand de Victoria. Through her envoy she told the emperor that her husband was secretly attempting to divorce her.

25

Alas, what shall I do for love?
For love, alas, what shall I do?
Sith now so kind I do you find,
To keep you me unto.

IN April the ceaseless rains returned. Not a day passed without showers or a storm; often the rain continued falling through the night, and farmers who went to sleep to the sound of a gentle drizzle awoke to thunder and a downpour. In May a torrential shower flooded southeastern England for nearly thirty hours without letup, causing rivers and streams to overflow and destroying the newly sown corn. Rain such as this had ruined the king's hunting the previous summer and fall; now it drove him off the tiltyard and spoiled his maying, and sent the French envoys who joined him in his outdoor pastimes scurrying for cover.

Katherine waited out the stormy season in somber anticipation. What she feared most in the world—that her beloved husband would discard her and take another wife—was indeed happening. Her world was shaking around her, yet she went on, concealing her distress and gathering what news she could of the steps the king was taking.

Much was hidden from her, but she managed to find out a good deal. She knew that leading churchmen and theologians were being asked to give opinions on the validity of the marriage, and that Wolsey—whom she blamed for the entire affair—was using his office as papal legate to expedite the case. She may even have heard something of the secret proceedings held in May at Wolsey's house at Westminister, where at Henry's request an inquiry into the marriage was held "to the tranquillity of consciences and the health of his soul."

Thus she was less surprised than stunned when toward the end of June Henry confronted her with the announcement that, as far as he was concerned, their marriage was at an end. Indeed, he said, there was no need to end something which had never been. And there was no marriage, only an illusory union based on a misunderstanding of scripture and a papal misapplication of canon law. For eighteen years these errors had gone unheeded, the king admitted, but now that they had been brought to light by learned opinion they weighed down his conscience intolerably and impelled him to leave Katherine's bed and board once and for all. It only remained for her to choose where she would live from then on, and to retire there as quickly as possible.

Henry's concise, direct message loosed all the emotion Katherine had kept inside for months. She wept long and piteously, and was too distraught to reply. Without appearing to grasp the enormity of his words Henry urged Katherine to keep the matter secret for the time being, adding the feeble consolation that "all would be done for the best."[1]

How Henry came to his decision has long been a matter of debate. Of course, the succession had preoccupied him for years and, with it, the troubling rumors of an accursed marriage. From time to time throughout the early 1520s he had discussed with churchmen the theological questions raised by the marriage of a man with his dead brother's wife, partly because he was intrigued by the intellectual puzzles they presented, and partly as an indirect way of approaching his personal dilemma. Had Erasmus been in England Henry would surely have raised these issues with him, seeking spiritual counsel as much as understanding. In the absence of his boyhood friend he hounded his confessor John Longland, bishop of Lincoln—or so Longland told his own chaplain later—becoming so insistent on the subject of the divorce that he "never left urging him until he had won him to give his consent."

In the years to come Longland would often be accused of leading Henry to question his marriage, and of suggesting a divorce. The imperial ambassador called him "the principal promoter of these practices," and in fact Longland was among the most zealous advocates of the king's cause. The weight of his influence is clear from a remark he made long afterward, when what had begun as a marital dispute had mushroomed into an epoch-making controversy. He would rather be the poorest man in the world, the bishop said, than ever have been the king's councilor and confessor.[2]

In discussing with the king the ending of his marriage Longland was only articulating what was, at least by 1524, accomplished fact. Henry and Katherine no longer lived together as man and wife, and their situation was no secret. The idea of a formal separation between the king and queen must have crossed the minds of court officials, diplomats and courtiers alike, especially in view of the uncertain succession. By the time the proceedings actually began in 1527, many at Henry's court may have wondered why the king had waited so long.

Why, then, did Henry choose to act decisively when he did? What was it that, after years of talk, finally converted a vague notion into a plan of action?

Here two things confuse the matter. One is that the surviving evidence is less concerned with the actual progress of ideas and motivations in the king's mind than with what he and others wished people to believe about his motives. Henry offered different explanations for his actions at different times, depending on which seemed most useful in the circumstances. At bottom these explanations are not so much conflicting as complementary, which leads to the second source of confusion. Henry VIII was an exceedingly complex man, and was capable of maintaining several parallel rationalizations for what he thought and did at the same time. These two obstacles to simple interpretation must be kept in mind as the influences that triggered the divorce are sought.

To begin with, there was the king's conscience, always an active organ of discrimination for Henry and increasingly the locus of his discontents. As he explained it, at the start of the new year of 1527 the full weight of Leviticus 20:21, "If a man shall take his brother's wife, it is an impurity: he hath covered his brother's nakedness; they shall be childless," became clear to him. Consultations with learned men reinforced his newfound certainty, until he could no longer restrain himself. His long overburdened conscience goaded him, for the sake of his soul, to set right what he had done in error at the outset of his reign, and cease to think of Katherine as his wife. To be sure, the pope had given a dispensation permitting the marriage. But no earthly authority, not even the pope, could justify to Henry what was surely abominable in the sight of God.

Then too there were the French. In the course of negotiations between English and French diplomats—either in England or in France, depending on which version of the account is read—over the betrothal of Princess Mary to the second son of Francis I the issue of Mary's legitimacy arose. Was Henry certain no claim could ever be made that his marriage was invalid, thus disinheriting the princess? Because Henry told this story in several different ways, and eventually instructed his diplomats to drop it entirely, it has been looked on with suspicion as a justification invented after the fact. Yet it is not implausible. Diplomatic records are full of queries about inheritance rights, and there is no reason to doubt the possibility that the matter was raised at some point during the long weeks of deliberations. If it was, then the question may have provided the king, if not with an urgent motive, at least with a statesmanlike excuse for carrying through something he had been contemplating for other reasons.[3]

Finally there is the suggestion that it was Anne Boleyn and her chaplains who played on Henry's religious scruples and frightened him into putting Katherine aside. Reginald Pole, a resolute opponent of the divorce and of the religious changes that grew out of it in the 1530s—and an inveterate enemy of Henry and Anne—wrote that "the first origin of the whole lying affair" lay with Anne. Having learned from her sister's example how fleeting the king's affections were, Pole wrote to Henry, Anne resolved to keep secure her position by becoming his wife. To this end "she herself sent her chaplains, grave theologians, as pledges of how ready her will [to marry] was, not only to declare to you that it was lawful to put [Katherine] away, but to say that you were sinning mortally to keep her as your wife even for a single moment, and to denounce it as a high crime against God unless you straightway repudiated her."[4]

None of these explanations rings false. If Henry's motives were not entirely idealistic, they were not entirely opportunistic either, and the protean character of his reasoning often baffled the men around him. One thing seems certain: Henry rarely perceived his "great matter" as others did, and he maintained his idiosyncratic viewpoint throughout its tortuous course.

In thinking he could keep his proceedings secret he was particularly deceived. By mid-June, Mendoza wrote, the affair had already become "as notorious as if it had been proclaimed by the public crier," and few Londoners were without an opinion on the merits of the king's case. At Rochester Bishop Fisher, to whom Katherine appealed for advice in her trouble, had heard what was afoot from his brother in the capital. Not long afterward the news reached Spain, carried by Katherine's sewer Francisco Felipe. He had served the queen for nearly thirty years, and his fidelity had never counted for more than in this crisis. Though the king gave him a passport allowing him to travel to Spain via France he never meant Felipe to arrive at the imperial court, knowing full well the message he carried. The French were asked to cooperate in waylaying the aging messenger. But Felipe was more wily than his would-be captors, and before he could be found in France he had reached Spain and delivered his news to Katherine's nephew at Valladolid.

Probably Henry thought the entire issue would be settled, and his troublesome marriage set aside, in a matter of months. After all, in point of law he was not seeking a divorce at all—which the church disallowed—only confirmation of the inherent invalidity of his marriage. Strictly speaking, his case was a nullity suit, and Wolsey, whose legatine powers made him, in one historian's phrase, "a kind of vice-pope for England," appeared to have the authority to rule on it. Besides, what Henry was attempting to do was hardly unprecedented. For centuries European rulers had discarded unsatisfactory spouses; accommodating popes had evolved dispensations to fit virtually any marital situation, just as they had always found ways to permit marriages between persons related by blood. Far from being writ in marble papal pronouncements on royal marriages seemed grounded in quicksand; it looked as if canon law could always be bent to bind or dissolve at will.

In recent months the dissolution suits of Henry's sister Margaret and his closest friend Charles Brandon had given fresh evidence of this. Margaret Tudor asked the pope to free her from her second husband Archibald Douglas, earl of Angus. Even if she had not aroused suspicion by living with another man—Henry Stewart, who had divorced his wife in order to marry her—Margaret would have had an exceedingly weak case. Of the two claims on which it rested, one (that her first husband James IV had not been killed at Flodden) was unquestionably false and the other unproven. Yet despite all she won her suit, and was declared free to marry again in March of 1527.

Her brother in England could not have been more outraged. Margaret had gone against the advice he had given her earlier, and had disregarded the "divine order of inseparable matrimony"; in departing from her husband she had sinned grievously, he said with indignation, for during his lifetime she could "have none other by the law of God." "The behavior of my sister sounds openly to her extreme reproach," Henry declared. "She is more like an unnatural and transformed person than a noble princess or a woman with a sense of wisdom and honor." Like all adulterers, she would surely suffer in hell, while the officials in Rome who had handed down the "shameless sentence" deserved to be punished along with her. Henry's fulminations were sincere enough, though even as he spoke them he must have noted the obliging temper of the papal court, and kept his own plea in mind.

Charles Brandon's tangled case was of greater interest to his royal brother-in-law. He had put aside one wife, outlived another, and married

a third, not without recurring complications. Many years earlier, when he
sought his dissolution, Brandon had felt some of the same pressures
Henry now felt: the need for a son and heir (at the time he had only
daughters), worry over an invalid papal dispensation, the sting of conscience. Like Henry, Brandon had ceased to live with his wife, so the bull
of dispensation said, because in doing so he imperiled his soul. And like
Henry, he had appealed to the ever capable Wolsey to conduct the
legalities. Though the circumstances of Brandon's divorce were long past
the case was fresh in Henry's mind, for Wolsey was currently working to
obtain a bull for Brandon supplementing and overriding all earlier
ecclesiastical pronouncements and punishing anyone who challenged
them. If Wolsey had been able to unravel Brandon's case and bring it to a
satisfactory conclusion, there was every reason to think he could confirm
Henry's simple, unarguable reason for leaving Katherine.

That was, in fact, just the procedure Henry seems to have had in
mind—a solemn court convened in England, with Wolsey presiding as the
pope's delegate, a ruling against the dubious dispensation, a quick
confirmation from Rome, and finally a quiet separation of king and queen.

And so it went—for two weeks. Wolsey convened his court, and
summoned Henry before it to answer the charge that he had been living in
sin. The king made his response, in person and then through a proctor,
and witnesses were produced to support the contention that because
Katherine and Arthur had been man and wife her subsequent union with
Henry was unlawful. Wolsey's court met four times in all, then adjourned,
abruptly, for the last time. Possibly the competence or finality of the court
had come in doubt; more probably the extraordinary news from Italy had
eclipsed all other undertakings, and set Wolsey working on a larger and
more desperate task.

On the first of June news reached England that Rome had been
captured by the German and Spanish troops of Charles V, and that for
weeks the churches and palaces of the ancient city had been plundered
and befouled by the lawless soldiers. The relics of the saints, shrines
sacred to the pious for a thousand years and more, holy treasures of every
kind had been destroyed or dishonored, while the monks and nuns who
tended them were brutally beaten and tortured. Many clerics were killed;
as the nightmare went on many of the plunderers died too, victims of the
famine and disease that followed in the wake of the destruction.

The despoiling of Rome was more than a monstrous sacrilege: it was a
breach with the past. Rome was the citadel of medieval faith, and the
imperial invasion symbolized the onslaught of the newer doctrines—the
teachings of Luther, Zwingli, and dozens of lesser-known sectaries—that
were assaulting that faith with growing success. Rome was also the city of
the pope, and when it fell his power fell with it. Pope Clement VII
and his cardinals escaped with their lives, taking shelter in the Castel
Sant'Angelo, yet for the indefinite future the pope would have only such
authority as his captor, the emperor, allowed him to have.

Wolsey saw at once how fateful events in Rome could be for the
successful progress of the king's nullity suit. He wrote to Henry the day
after the news arrived, pointing out the harm that could be done if the

pope were killed or captured before he could release the king from his present difficulties.[5] The cardinal knew well what was in the forefront of his master's mind, but there were vaster issues at stake. With the pope in the hands of a secular power the church was in need of a rescuer. Wolsey would be that man. He would go to France—where the queen mother Louise of Savoy was suggesting that all the sovereigns of Christendom should withdraw their allegiance from the bishop of Rome until the imperial captivity ended—and would summon all the other free cardinals to join him there. Acting on Pope Clement's behalf he would then take over the spiritual government of Christendom.

No man in Europe was more fitted for the task. Wolsey lived like an emperor, with one third of the English church under his personal rule. More princely than any prince of the church, he thought of himself in regal terms. When he died he intended to be buried, like the king, at Windsor; his tomb, commissioned from the Florentine sculptor Benedetto da Rovezzano, was to be as splendid as that of Henry VII. A black marble sarcophagus would hold the carved bronze figure of the cardinal lying in repose. Kneeling angels bearing the symbols of Wolsey's dignities—his cross and cardinal's hat—were to guard his head and feet, while four more angels carrying candlesticks were to be perched atop thick bronze pillars nine feet high.

Wolsey's grandiose egotism was continually reinforced by court precedent and diplomatic flattery. It had long been customary for visitors at the English court to kiss the cardinal's hand before kissing the king's—an acknowledgment of the higher respect due to the divine office, but in practice as much a bow to Wolsey the man as to his cardinalate. The pope himself claimed to look on Wolsey not merely as a brother, but as a colleague; the cardinal relied on this collegial sentiment now, as he organized his retinue for the journey to the coast and the crossing to France.[6]

As he threw himself into this most ambitious venture of his long career Wolsey struggled to quiet his inner apprehensions. He was surrounded by enemies: burly Suffolk, shrewd Norfolk, clever Boleyn, now more and more the man at the king's right hand, Boleyn's friends and relatives at court and, most annoyingly, his mercurial, dark-haired daughter Anne. The common people of England hated him almost without exception, or so it seemed. He could bear the combined animosity of the entire kingdom without complaint as long as he kept the king's trust and favor, but now that too had begun to erode. He hoped, desperately, to regain Henry's reliance on him—to return to the deferential partnership that had marked their early years. In the privacy of his gardens he brooded on these things, giving orders that no one was to approach him in his musings. Suitors who came to him there were told to wait at a suitable distance, "as far as a man will shoot an arrow," until the cardinal was ready to take up the threads of government affairs again.

Before leaving for France Wolsey consulted with his astrologer, and chose a favorable day for his departure. On the appointed day his attendants formed their ranks and set off for Dover, spreading themselves out along the narrow road for three quarters of a mile. Hundreds of

gentlemen and yeomen in black and tawny liveries rode in the vanguard, along with the closely-guarded carts and carriages loaded with
the cardinal's traveling furnishings. As always, Wolsey himself rode on
muleback, his rich cardinal's robes blending with the red velvet trappings
of his mount. Seven attendants rode before him bearing his tall silver
crosses and pillars, the Great Seal of England, his cardinal's hat and the
gold-embroidered bag that held his scarlet cloak.

At Canterbury he paused to join in a special litany for the captive
pope. "Saint Mary, pray for our Pope Clement," the monks intoned,
while Wolsey knelt and "wept very tenderly" from sorrow. Two other
errands delayed his departure. One was a visit to Archbishop Warham.
There was reason to think that Warham might be taking Katherine's part
in the marital dispute, and Wolsey needed to assure himself this was not
so. The cardinal explained the king's position to the aging archbishop,
stressing the fact that what Henry sought was nothing more than an
inquiry into the truth. Warham's words were reassuring. "However
displeasant it may be to the queen," he told Wolsey, "truth and law must
prevail."

Heartened by Warham's expression of support Wolsey called on
Bishop Fisher, whom he knew to be opposed to the king's suit. Like
Warham Fisher was an old man, nearing seventy, a relic from the old
century and the old reign. Contented with his modest episcopal see of
Rochester, he spent his time in "his paradise"—his library—whose high
windows let in more wind and fog than they did light, giving him head
colds. In a well-reasoned written opinion on the divorce he had already
informed Wolsey that he considered the papal dispensation authorizing
the marriage to be valid, and further inquiry needless. Without trying to
change Fisher's mind the cardinal merely explained Henry's view to him
more fully, adding that Katherine had spoken harshly to her husband—
which Fisher condemned—and urging him not to take any further action
of any kind without the king's authorization. The interview was not free
from tension—Fisher was Katherine's partisan, and Wolsey knew it—but
at least he offered no overt objection to what was asked of him.[7]

Weighing carefully how he would conduct his embassy, and believing,
however obtusely, that the fate of the church was in his hands, Wolsey
took ship at Dover early in July. As he was boarding a farewell gift arrived
from Henry—a "great, goodly and fat hart" killed by the king's crossbow
and sent for Wolsey's table in token of his royal master's love.[8]

26

Wherefore now we
That lovers be
Let us now pray
Ones love sure
For to procure
Without denay.

SOMETIME in the spring or summer of 1527 Henry wrote the first of his love letters to Anne Boleyn. "My mistress and friend," he wrote, "I and my heart commit themselves into your hands, beseeching you to hold us recommended to your good favor, and that your affection to us may not be by absence diminished."

He missed her, "more than he would ever have thought." He could not bear their separation, except that he had a "firm hope" that his affection was returned. To keep himself constantly in her thoughts he sent her his picture, set in a bracelet, adding the awkward sentiment that he wished himself in its place around her wrist.[1]

Henry was on his summer hunting progress, traveling with a larger entourage than usual. The indispensable Norfolk and Suffolk were with him, as were his cousin Henry Courtenay and Anne's father Thomas Boleyn, Lord Rochford. At least four other titled courtiers rounded out the company, along with three of their wives. Katherine traveled with the hunting party too, though Henry no longer came to her chamber when his long day in the fields was over. Instead he sought out the company of the men, and dined alone with them in seclusion.

In the dark stillness of the forest the high matters of politics and government, the bruits of the London streets, the clamor of the court seemed far away and the king could lose himself in the joy of the chase and the still greater joy of thinking about his love. He was not entirely out of touch. News came of reactions to the nullity suit—called in diplomatic dispatches "the king's great matter"—of Wolsey's mission to France, of the French king's new mistress Hély, "whose beauty," Anthony Browne wrote from the French court, "is not highly to be praised." Yet these reminders of outside events rarely intruded on Henry's thoughts, and if they did he had only to call to his side his hunter John Yardeley or Humphrey Rainsford, master of the privy hounds, to talk to them about the next day's sport. The king was in good health, a clerk wrote to Wolsey from the traveling household. His "merry visage" had returned, and with it his usual high spirits. He even remembered to show a certain chivalry toward Katherine, whose bed and board he had so pointedly renounced. When he left Hunsdon for Beaulieu toward the end of July "though he was ready to depart by a good space, he tarried for the queen, and so they rode forth together."[2]

If he sensed Katherine's pain Henry did not show it. Armored by the conviction that the step he had taken was right in God's eyes, buoyed by his growing infatuation for Anne, he shrugged off the evidence of Katherine's unhappiness and looked ahead to the day, not far off, when his new queen would be crowned.

Not long after Henry sent his letter and portrait bracelet to Anne he received a gift in reply. It was an ornament of some sort, perhaps a piece of jewelry, with a beautiful diamond and a miniature ship with a tiny passenger, a "solitary damsel." It charmed him completely, and called forth fresh declarations of love. By her gift Anne had shown her "great benevolence and goodwill" toward him, giving such warm evidence of her affection that he could not help but pledge her all his honor, love and service; in her alone his hope "hath set up his everlasting rest, saying *aut illic aut nullibi,*" either there or nowhere. He ventured now to write of his greater hope, that soon he could dedicate his body to Anne as well as his heart, "as God can bring to pass if it pleaseth him, whom I entreat once each day for the accomplishment thereof, trusting that at length my prayer will be heard."

That she should become his body and soul was Henry's all-encompassing desire, yet her eagerness did not match his. Many years later Anne confessed that, at the start of their affair, she had "never . . . in her heart, wanted to love the king." She may well have been more wary of him than fond. She may have been confused in her feelings, uncertain whether the mastery she was slowly conceding to him sprang from romantic passion or from the dutiful response of a young girl to her breathtakingly handsome king. Anne certainly had more than enough sophistication to resist Henry, and the discernment to know what the effect of her resistance would be. Yet her response may have been more hesitant than calculating. And, of course, her response may not have been hers at all. Quite possibly her letters, at least in the beginning, were dictated by parents and relatives unwilling to leave in the hands of a girl of twenty a matter that concerned their own futures so directly.

For a time Anne's letters sent Henry into despair. Having said one thing she informed him she meant to do another. She seemed to waver in her emotions, now sounding ardent, now formal and detached. He was unable to reconcile the differences between these passages, and asked her, "in great distress," once and for all to say unambiguously what she felt. With all his heart he begged her to "expressly certify me of your whole mind concerning the love between us two." He had loved her for more than a year; now he had to know whether she rejected or favored his suit. However expressed, the positive answer she finally gave—none of Anne's letters has been preserved—made Henry's hopes soar again, and turned his thoughts more keenly than ever to securing his divorce.

Meanwhile Wolsey's efforts to accommodate his king went forward. He arrived in France in early July, prepared to undertake an extraordinary array of diplomatic tasks. The grandest of them, the assumption of headship of the church, would come last. As a preliminary he was to finalize the Anglo-French treaties agreed to in England three months earlier, and to arrange for a splendid meeting between Henry and Francis, on the model of their triumphant encounter at the Field of Cloth of Gold seven years before. Wolsey hoped to achieve nothing short of a European peace—his old dream—climaxed by a three-way accord with the emperor. Once peace treaties united England, France and the Hapsburg empire, the pope might be freed. If not, Wolsey would don the papal authority—and use it, if need be, to hasten the favorable outcome of Henry's suit.

From the start the inflated aims of the embassy were punctured by petty annoyances. In Boulogne the mule Wolsey was riding shied at the sound of cannonfire and nearly threw him to the ground. Insulting graffiti were found in his lodgings; in one place a cardinal's hat was carved into a stone windowsill, with a gallows over it. Thieves broke into his chamber many times, stealing gold and silver ornaments and other things he kept for his personal use. Finally at Compiègne he lost something truly indispensable: the silver and gilt inkpot he used when he wrote his dispatches to Henry in England. A search was made, and a ragged boy of twelve or thirteen—a "ruffian's page," servant to a professional thief in Paris—was found hiding under the stairwell. The boy confessed he had taken not only the inkpot but everything else the cardinal had missed, and had delivered all to his master.[3]

An even more bizarre incident marred the banqueting that followed the diplomatic meetings. Accompanying the cardinal as part of his traveling household was a company of highly skilled minstrels, one of whom, a shalm-player, excelled all his peers. King Francis was so taken with the musicians that he borrowed them from Wolsey and kept them in constant attendance on him wherever he went. One night he dined away from court, at a nobleman's house, and as usual the English minstrels went along and performed for the banqueters. They played on and on throughout most of the night, outdoing themselves and so captivating their audience that they were declared to surpass the king's own musicians in virtuosity—the shalm-player in particular. Two days later the shalm-player was dead, "either with extreme labor of blowing or with poisoning." It was rumored the man was given poison out of envy, though he may simply have played his heart out for the king.[4]

The talks with the French went smoothly. Francis ratified the marriage contract binding his younger son to the Princess Mary, and had only the most gracious words for England and the English. He could ill afford even the shadow of a quarrel with the least of his allies; his sons were still hostages in imperial hands, and the outcome of his longstanding dispute with Charles V was far from certain.

Everywhere Wolsey went he was saluted as Cardinalis Pacificus, Cardinal Peacemaker, yet his hopes to erect a broader European peace were soon abandoned. The emperor was at present ill disposed to make

peace either with Francis or his errant uncle in England, though he was far
too shrewd a statesman to allow a domestic quarrel to block his political
advantage. He was moving with deliberation to prevent the divorce,
writing in affronted moderation to Henry and assuring Katherine of his
loyalty and concern. He sided with her in "this ugly affair," as he termed
it, and took her plight as much to heart as if she were his mother. "Nothing
shall be omitted on my part to help you in your present tribulation," he
told her, and to back up his words he followed her suggestion and urged
the pope to revoke Wolsey's legatine power, leaving him without authority to deliver a judgment in the nullity suit.[5]

In the end Wolsey's self-important vision of rescuing the church faded
as well. With the majority of the cardinals captive in Rome he could
gather little support for his scheme to take on the headship of the church.
Three French and one Italian cardinal joined him in a declaration refusing
to obey Pope Clement while he remained in the hands of the emperor's
troops, but in the absence of more extensive support there was little he
could do.

The months of wearisome travel wore Wolsey down. He had been
rushing from city to city, he wrote Henry, making the best time he could,
traveling as fast as his "old and cracked body may endure." He had put
up with French roads, French heat and French impudence, and with the
annoying French habit of ignoring foreigners' ignorance of the French
language. He had warned his serving men and attendants about this before
they left England. "Now to the point of the Frenchmen's nature," he told
them, "ye shall understand that their disposition is such that they will be
at the first meeting as familiar with you as [if] they had been acquainted
with you long before and commune with you in the French tongue as
though ye understood every word they spoke." He urged them not to be
disconcerted by this custom, but to return it in kind, answering pleasantly
in English and carrying on their side of the mutually incomprehensible
dialogue.[6]

News from London and the English court nagged at Wolsey. In the
capital his embassy had won him greater disfavor than ever, with the
people calling him "all French" and weaving what they knew of the
divorce and French diplomacy into their own curious explanation of
current events. The king's confessor Longland, they said, and "diverse
other great clerks" had advised Henry to take as his wife Francis I's
sister, the duchess of Alençon. Thomas Boleyn had gone to France to
fetch the duchess' picture; now Wolsey had gone to get the bride herself,
and to bring her back to England.[7] (The gossip was not entirely preposter-
ous. The duchess had been married the previous January, but another
member of the French royal house, Louis XII's daughter Renée, did loom
large in Wolsey's thoughts as a potential wife for Henry.) At the court
itself the king's favorite councilors were taking advantage of Wolsey's
absence to undermine his power; in an effort to counteract their influence
he tried to convince Henry that even in the midst of other matters his
mind was ever on the divorce.

"Daily and hourly musing, and thinking on your grace's great and secret affair," he wrote from Abbeville, "and how the same may come to good effect and desired end," he had at length become convinced that a papal judgment on Henry's behalf was the only sure way to settle the matter, since Katherine might appeal any judgment handed down by a lesser court convened in England. A few weeks earlier the cardinal had managed to discover a crucial argument in the king's favor. In discussions of the theology and canon law of the nullity suit much weight had been given to the issue of Katherine's virginity. If, as she claimed, her marriage to Arthur was never consummated, then, so she and her supporters insisted, her former marriage was no impediment to her union with Henry; hence that union was irreproachably valid. Wolsey pointed out that the mere fact of the public marriage of Katherine and Arthur was sufficient in canon law to present an impediment to the queen's remarriage—the so-called "impediment of public honesty."[8] Her disputed virginity was irrelevant; her case crumbled.

Thus far Wolsey's work on the king's great matter had been beyond criticism. At one blow he had knocked down the strongest defense Katherine could boast, and his further efforts promised to be equally effective. Yet for a variety of reasons Henry was pursuing the case in his own way, unknown to the cardinal. His confidence in his longtime servant had declined somewhat, though it was probably the urgency of his desire for Anne as much as any loss of faith in Wolsey that led him to carry through a secret strategy of his own. Adopting more than one approach, he reasoned, would improve the odds in his favor, and he meant to have his will no matter how high the obstacles that stood in his way.

At Henry's order two draft bulls were prepared to be taken to Rome by a special royal envoy, William Knight. The first permitted him, once he was free from Katherine, to marry any woman he chose, even one who would normally be forbidden him because of a prior connection with one of her relatives. (As opponents of the divorce never ceased to point out, through Henry's affair with Mary Boleyn Anne had become "related" to him in the same way that Katherine had by marrying Arthur.) Significantly, this bull looked ahead to the possibility that Anne might consent to become Henry's mistress before marriage; this too was to be no hindrance. The second bull was startling: quite simply, it sanctioned bigamy. If no way could be found to declare Henry's marriage to Katherine invalid, this document read, then the pope was to permit him to take a second wife.

In turning to Rome for aid Henry was putting his future happiness in dubious hands. The ways of the pope and the Roman Curia in the early sixteenth century were not those of sanctity and equity; corruption underlay every spiritual transaction, bribery every judgment of the papal court. To outsiders the cardinals and other officials seemed to view their posts as sinecures to be enjoyed in profitable splendor, neglecting all but their own aggrandizement. Vice and criminality of many kinds flourished in the papal city. It was widely believed that among the cardinals were some willing to use poison against one another and even against the pope. To the humanist Richard Pace the Eternal City appeared to be a perversion of everything holy, a monstrosity "full of shame and scandal." There "all faith, honesty and religion seem to have vanished from the earth." With few exceptions Englishmen visiting Rome found the ways of the Curia a disillusioning mystery. Some managed to acclimatize themselves in time, but most accomplished little. The English in Rome, one cardinal wrote in 1517, did nothing but eat and drink, run riot and abuse each other.[9]

Presiding over this profane milieu was Giulio de'Medici, Pope Clement VII, a quick-witted, hard-working man of inoffensive life with an unfortunate tendency to deceive and betray almost everyone who approached him. He gave way easily under pressure, promising publicly to fulfill whatever was asked of him, then working in secret to undermine the agreement; an English ambassador called him another Judas, while a Spanish diplomat declared he had never encountered anyone whose words were more opaque. Despite his flaws Clement was not devoid of humor or intelligence, and had the makings of a capable pope. Yet overwhelmed by the responsibilities of the papacy and the shattering events of his pontificate, he failed. "He endured an enormous labor," one historian has written, "to become, from a great and respected cardinal, a small and little-esteemed pope."[10]

When confronted with Henry's envoys, letters and arguments in favor of his nullity suit—and Charles V's rigorous messages of opposition to it—Clement found himself in a multiple predicament. Shaken to numbness by the wrecking of his city, he was in no condition to arbitrate even a dispute between petty princelings, let alone a highly consequential issue dividing the Defender of the Faith in England and the powerful emperor whose troops now held him captive. Even after his escape from the Castel Sant'Angelo in December—he walked out past the Spanish sentinels disguised in a long false beard, wearing the tunic and slouched hat of a household servant—he could not breathe free. He settled in among his cardinals in the tumbledown bishop's palace at Orvieto a day's journey from Rome, and began the complex, drawn-out and often baffling series of maneuvers that were his response to the nullity suit.

According to his intimate associate Paolo Giovio, the chief aim of Clement's response was delay. The longer he waited to make a definite judgment, the more the two parties in the dispute would be compelled to treat him with deference.[11] To be sure, fear of further imperial reprisals broke in on this strategy from time to time. Yet that fear also worked to Henry's advantage, driving the pope into the arms of his erstwhile English allies and turning him against the cause of Charles V and his aunt. Pulled by these conflicting forces, Clement acted as both his temperament and his strategy dictated: he vacillated. As he waited for a decisive judgment Henry soothed his impatience by writing more and more impassioned letters to Anne.

Through the fall and winter of 1527–28 he wrote her time after time, pouring into his letters all the ardor, all the longing, all the exasperation and insecurity of a lover. He wrote in French and in English, at length and in brief. He wrote of the monumental upheaval that loving her had worked in him—"my great folly," he called it—and of his fear that, having committed his heart to her, she might after all turn away in indifference. Hunting, he sent her his trophies—"a hart for Henry," a buck "killed my hand late yesternight," and other game. Along with them he sent messages of how he missed her, and wished she and not her brother George were there to ride beside him through the forests. He suffered such heartfelt pain at her absence that "neither tongue nor pen can express the hurt," he wrote; his only compensation was the thrill of anticipating their long-awaited meeting, which he "more desired than any earthly thing." "For what joy in this world," he added, "can be greater than to have the company of her who is the most dearly loved, knowing likewise that she by her choice holds the same, the thought of which greatly delights me."[12]

These were neither the foolishly effusive letters of a man besotted by love nor the purple outpourings of a self-conscious stylist. They had all the fresh, vigorous openness of Henry's speech and manner; they were sincere and engaging, and they would have won any woman's heart.

In February the letters began to take on a new tone. "Darling," Henry wrote excitedly, "you and I shall [soon] have our desired end, which should be more to my heart's ease, and more quietness to my mind, than any other thing in the world."[13] New envoys were being dispatched to Italy, two young lawyers Edward Foxe and Stephen Gardiner, men with the ambitious toughness to sweep the negotiations with Clement VII through to a conclusion. Gardiner was particularly able, quick-witted and adroit in argument and with the subtlety to throw an opponent off guard and maneuver him in unexpected directions. Together the two negotiators were under orders to convince the pope to agree in advance to support the judgment of a legatine court in England, to be conducted jointly by Cardinal Wolsey and the erudite canonist Cardinal Campeggio. Foxe would bring the written arguments back to England right away; Gardiner would remain to accompany Campeggio when he made his journey later in the year.

Anticipating his envoys' success Henry wrote to the pope, thanking him in advance for his support in the nullity suit. He and all his kingdom would be eternally bound to Clement for what he was doing, the king wrote; he was sure there would be no objection to the strategy Gardiner and Foxe would put forward.[14] As if in celebration of a final settlement Henry arranged for a vast impromptu picnic at Windsor. It was held in the lodge of the little hunting park adjoining the castle, a site so ill equipped for large-scale entertainments that all the kitchen equipment had to be brought in by water and the trestles and tables borrowed from the town nearby. The dozens of plovers, partridges, larks and rabbits for the diners came from the surrounding fields, the beef, bacon and oxen from the local purveyors. The park keeper's wife supplied the cream.[15]

The following weeks were happy ones for Henry, with his sweetheart beside him and good news about their future apparently in the offing. Anne made herself at home at Windsor, joining the king when he rode out hawking or walked in the park in the afternoons, and dining in the evenings with Thomas Hennage, a servant of Wolsey's. Henry and his love had little to occupy themselves but each other. There were few household servants in residence, and fewer courtiers; beyond attending to his master's correspondence Hennage had little to do but to convey to Wolsey Anne's requests for dinner—carps, shrimps, and other delicacies.

Anne's status was changing. She had not yet displaced Katherine— Henry still acknowledged Katherine's rank by conducting visitors to court to greet his wife and daughter—but she had risen greatly in influence. The most conspicuous sign of that influence was her new relationship to Wolsey. Anne had come a long way since the day the cardinal had separated her from Henry Percy and sent her in disgrace to Hever Castle. Then he had commanded her; now she commanded him, at least in small matters, and Wolsey was quick to shift his ground.

Their relative places in the king's esteem had become clear on Wolsey's return from France. He had come to Richmond, bringing all the news of his embassy and of the rich gifts he had received from King Francis—a golden chalice and paten, gold silk altar cloths, tapestries worth thirty thousand ducats. As usual he sent a message to the king asking to be received, expecting a joyous private welcome from his master. This time, though, Anne was waiting along with Henry, and she had the insolence to answer on the king's behalf. She cut short the cardinal's opportunity for a private audience, and peremptorily summoned him. "Where else is the cardinal to come?" she said to the servant who approached her. "Tell him that he may come here, where the king is."[16]

When Gardiner and Foxe reached Orvieto they found Pope Clement in a state of appalling wretchedness. He had liberated himself from captivity only to enthrone himself amid squalor. Surrounded by his hungry and ill-clad retainers he was shut up in the foul-smelling episcopal palace, whose "naked and unhanged" chambers stood open to the weather where the roof had fallen in. A shabby retinue of some thirty officials and hangers-on made up the papal court in exile, waiting aimlessly for their sorry master to gain possession of himself amid his calamities. In their midst he paced up and down, sighing and wiping his eyes and be- moaning his fate. The Spaniards were practically at his doorstep; he was, he said, "in the power of the dogs."[17]

The English envoys had little regard for Clement's misery. They were there to persuade, argue and, if need be, threaten him into cooperation. First, though, they had to disabuse him of a dangerous misapprehension: that the nullity suit was prompted solely by Henry's "vain affection and undue love" for Anne Boleyn. He had heard, Clement told Gardiner and Foxe, that the English king wanted his divorce for "private reasons" only, and that the woman he loved was far below him not only in rank but in virtue. Rumor had gone even further. It was said at the papal court that Anne was pregnant, and that Henry urgently wanted to make her child his heir.[18] On the contrary, the Englishmen assured him, Anne was a model of chastity (though assuredly "apt to procreate children"), impressing all who saw her with "the purity of her life, her constant virginity, her maidenly and womanly pudicity, her soberness, her chasteness, meek- ness, humility, wisdom, descent of right noble and high thorough regal blood," and so on. The pope need have no doubt that of all the women in England, Anne was the fittest to become queen.

As for Katherine, she would be treated with all the honor and love due to a sister, "with all manner of kindness." (Wolsey had convinced Henry to put the bigamy proposal aside.) It would be best for her to withdraw her opposition to the king's suit and acknowledge the invalidity of her marriage; if she did, Henry would treat her more liberally. Gardiner and Foxe asked Clement and his cardinals to write to Katherine and urge her compliance, then turned to the more weighty matter of the divorce itself.

The lawyers argued Henry's case from all sides, bringing to bear every point they had found in theology and the canon law. Clement listened attentively, evidently grasping all that they had to say yet hesitating to pronounce on its merit. "He sees all that is spoken better and sooner than any other," Gardiner remarked, "but no man is so slow to give an answer." The pope was in fact at a disadvantage, as he had little or no knowledge of canon law. Yet his ignorance served his purpose, in allowing him an excuse to postpone judgment. He needed the advice of his most trusted councilors, he said; to act without it would be to risk their dissent from his opinion later. The envoys pressed their arguments; the pope shook his head and said there was nothing he could do for the present. They "spoke roundly" to him, but he only sighed repeatedly and wiped his eyes.

Clearly they had reached an impasse. Only threats remained. Before leaving England Wolsey had instructed Gardiner and Foxe to tell the pope that, if Henry got no satisfaction at the papal court, he would find other means of satisfying his conscience and ridding himself of his present wife. They said this now, adding that, should he look for a judgment elsewhere, the king might be forced to "live out of the laws of holy church."

27

Syck, sicke and totowe sick
and sicke and like to die,
the sikest nyghte that ever I abode.
good lord have mercy on me

IT was in April that the sweating sickness began to break out once again in London. Without warning, men and women were struck down where they stood, bent double by gripping intestinal pains and throbbing headaches, violent chills and dizziness, then a stinking sweat and a fever so high it burned them to the point of collapse. Death came within hours; those who lived through their agony for an entire day had good hope of survival.

Just before the physical symptoms appeared the sufferers experienced a curious mental disorientation—a sense of apprehension and fear, a foreboding of pain and death. At least one contemporary, the royal secretary Brian Tuke, believed this fear to be a sort of psychological contaminant which terrorized the healthy into illness. Tuke himself combatted the disease directly by working himself into a natural sweat each night, but others who withdrew in panic fell victim to their fearful imaginations. Carried away mentally by the "disposition of the time," Tuke wrote, they brooded on the inevitability of infection even as they struggled to avoid it. Every rumor of a renewed outbreak sent them into agitated alarm. "One rumor causes a thousand cases of sweat," Tuke insisted. "Thousands have it from fear who need not else sweat, especially if they observe good diet."[1]

It was precisely this link between fear of the sweat and the onsetting symptom of the disease that made the epidemic so frightening. Panicked citizens could not distinguish between their dread of infection and the infection itself, and the more they shut themselves away in fainthearted isolation the more surely illness seemed to come. By one estimate, forty thousand contracted the sweating sickness in London alone in the early weeks of its appearance. Of these many thousands died, while those who recovered remained weak and were often burdened with secondary infections. The disease had scoured England three times before—most recently in 1517—yet this visitation was the most severe by far. It was as if each fresh outbreak was a stronger sign that the English were at odds with God and were being punished in consequence. At root, the mass apprehension that unmanned Londoners in the spring of 1528 was less the fear of death than the fear of hell.

212

There was little help to be had from the doctors. They could account for the disease, after a fashion, but they could not cure it. The poison entered the body through the heart, liver or brain, they believed. Bleeding the patient from the arm, or from between the thumb and first finger, or possibly from between the shoulders could draw off some of the toxin; otherwise the fatal fever would set in along with a "pricking or flakering of blood." Physicians and apothecaries disagreed over remedies, with the latter recommending exotic medicines compounded of treacle and herbs, sapphires and sometimes pure gold. Many doctors agreed, though, that what mattered most was to keep the afflicted person awake, lest he fall into a fatal sleep.[2]

Panicked city-dwellers tried in vain to purge the atmosphere of its poisons by burning spices and perfumes, but as the sweat moved through the streets and households of the capital in May and June, striking down most of those who stood in its path, all who could fled to the countryside to escape it, leaving their goods and livelihoods behind.

In the country folk medicine prevailed. Preventives first compounded four decades earlier when the disease entered England were revived now, their recipes passed by word of mouth in every village and hamlet. Proved medicines of many kinds circulated. Great quantities of vinegar were consumed. It was an essential ingredient in many preventives, and was also used to cleanse the stale air. Mixed in sauces, vinegar aided digestion and was thought to increase resistance to the sweat; for the same reason it was mixed with drinking water and drunk instead of white wine. Throughout the spring and summer of 1528 the strong smell of vinegar hung in the households of Tudor England like a malodorous fog, its taste choking the appetite and its fumes crowding out even the overpowering stink of unwashed floors and unswept streets.

The sweating sickness descended upon a population already plagued by severe economic malaise. There had been widespread famine since the previous fall, brought on by a meager harvest and made worse by an unusually harsh winter. Wheat flour became so scarce it had to be mixed with beans; even then it sold for many times its normal price—an imponderable quantity in any case, given the alarmingly rapid inflation of the 1520s. Heavy snows and "frozen seas" made it impossible for relief supplies of grain to be imported from across the Channel, and in one week when the scarcity was particularly acute the king sent six hundred quarters of his own grain into the capital to help prevent starvation. What made matters worse was that meat was equally unobtainable. Murrain had killed off many cattle and sheep; those still to be seen in the fields were scrawny from lack of hay. Many fewer lambs and calves were born to these unhealthy beasts, and the newborns were "hunger-bitten and worthless." Most of the pigs had been slaughtered; the peas and beans they would otherwise have eaten had to go to keeping the horses alive. Poultry and freshwater fish were sold in the shrunken markets, but at prices few of the hungry could afford.[3]

"Either the people must die for famine," the lord mayor and aldermen told Wolsey, "or else they with strong hand will fetch corn from them that have it.'' The threat of popular violence was severe enough to frighten the substantial householders of the capital, who hesitated to bring grain into their cellars to feed their families and servants. The cardinal assured the petitioners that relief was on its way from France, and that the French king had sworn that if he had only three bushels of wheat in his storehouses he would send two to his beloved allies in England. But the weeks passed and no French wheat appeared, while by late January grain ships from Flanders had begun to arrive regularly at the docks. Without their precious cargoes, the Venetian ambassador wrote, the people would have died of hunger.[4]

It was a dismaying paradox to the hungry English to find themselves at war with their Flemish benefactors. Economic ties between the English wool industry and Flemish clothmakers had always been essential to English prosperity, and any dispute between Henry VIII and Charles V threatened to result in a drastic disruption of trade. In reaction to the scandal of the nullity suit several Flemish towns had begun to refuse admission of English cloths in the summer of 1527; in January of 1528 England and France went to war with the Hapsburg empire, and overnight merchants, clothiers and woolworkers found themselves without employment. Outraged villagers erupted in protest. There was a rising in Wiltshire. In Norfolk the duke was able to persuade the clothiers to continue to employ their workmen for at least a while longer; had he failed, he wrote, he would have had to face a crowd of women hundreds strong, begging him to make the clothiers put their husbands and children to work again. And in Kent the clothworkers, long past the point of merely complaining over the threat to their livelihoods, took more drastic action.

They blamed the war and its evil results entirely on Wolsey, and they meant to punish him for the harm he had done. Four clothmakers, joined by a fuller and a fiddler—and by a hundred and fifty of the men of Frikynden and Cranbrook, "ready to rise"—conspired to kidnap Wolsey and drown him. The plot called for the villagers to break into neighboring manor houses and steal the arms and armor stored there, then, taking the masters of these houses as hostages, to seize Wolsey. "We will bring him to the sea side," one of the conspirators explained, "and there will put him in a boat, in the which shall be bored four great holes." Once the boat was launched in the sea the holes would be unplugged and the victim would sink from view, boat and all.[5]

A solution to the intolerable economic strain was soon found. Henry and Charles agreed to overlook their mutual hostility where trade was concerned. Workshops were reopened, and the clothmakers and their employers resumed their occupations—at least until the warm weather set in, and with it the dreaded sweating sickness.

Toward the end of June, as Londoners were making general processions and offering prayers for relief from the worsening pestilence, the king left hurriedly for the countryside. His servants and courtiers were sickening and dying, and he was surrounded by news of mortality and hazard. His young namesake Henry Brandon, earl of Lincoln, was dead.

All of his chamber servants had been struck down, and three had died. One of his apothecaries was sick, and his mason Redman died—a matter of urgent annoyance to the king, who was eager to see the completion of the repairs Redman had been making at the manor of Tittenhanger. Norfolk was among the first to be afflicted, and recovered imperfectly. Even after the major symptoms passed he still suffered a "sore fit" every week, and had difficulty walking, "the fume did so arise in his head."[6]

So many of his gentlemen fell sick that Henry feared to enter his own apartments, and he must have become, if not habituated, at least resigned to receiving news of their sudden deaths. The king was at Hunsdon—a country house he had bought for its "wholesome air" in time of plague—when he heard that William Compton had succumbed to the sweat. The news was bitter, as carelessness had hastened Compton's death; he had been "lost by negligence, in letting him sleep in the beginning of the sweat."[7] Indignity followed on tragedy. Compton had been an immensely wealthy man, and once he was dead his goods were plundered by thieving servitors and others before his executors could protect them. The other courtiers went after his offices like crows descending on carrion; their letters of entreaty soliciting a share in the spoils of Compton's estate fill many pages in the court records. Of what was left after the thieves and opportunists took their booty, much went to Compton's common-law wife Anne Hastings, while to Henry he bequeathed his "little chest of ivory with gilt lock" (and its contents of jewels and treasure), a chessboard and a pair of tables.[8]

Of greater concern than Compton was William Carey, whose death drew on a double tragedy. Carey's widow was Mary Boleyn, whose welfare was of some concern to her sister Anne as well as to her former lover King Henry. For some reason Thomas Boleyn broke with his daughter and all but disowned her in her widowhood, until at Anne's request Henry wrote to him telling him to take her into his house again and resume her support.[9]

Always in the forefront of the king's fears was the safety of his son. Henry Fitzroy was at Pontefract when the epidemic broke out, and within days of its first appearance people in the villages surrounding the castle had begun to die and the boy's council ordered the household removed. Eventually an uncontaminated lodging was found, and there Fitzroy remained throughout the late spring and summer, attended by only a handful of servants. As a precaution one of his councilors wrote to the king asking him to send a physician to attend his son should he fall ill. No doctors at all were to be found in the remote areas of the north—only wise women and gentlewomen who knew enough of folk medicine to care for their children and servants. Henry did not send a physician, but he did send preservatives of his own making for the boy to take, and read with relief the letters that came informing him that Fitzroy continued well throughout the dangerous season.[10]

During much of June the royal household—reduced through illness, death and the king's scrutiny to "a small and clean company"—changed residences every day or two in an effort to outrun contagion. To lighten his troubled mind Henry busied himself with inquiries about the nature and course of the sweat, what remedies were found to be most efficacious against it and, above all, what reasons might be found for optimism. "Little danger was in it, if good order was observed," he insisted to his secretary Tuke. Many of those who fell ill recovered, he reminded the surviving courtiers; his own physician Dr. Butts had managed to shake off the disease, as had his beloved Anne and her father. First Anne's maid had been affected, then others of the household at Hever. Both Anne and Thomas Boleyn had been taken seriously ill, but were recovered a week later, thanks in part to the efforts of the enfeebled Dr. Butts.

Wolsey obliged his master by sending him what news he had of proven remedies, some concocted for use in his own household and others in use elsewhere. The dowager duchess of Norfolk acquired a particular reputation as a healer during the sweat season, and the cardinal wrote about her at length. She had saved many who came to her *in extremis,* having received the sacraments and prepared themselves for death, and her remedies and advice were much sought after. The duchess was convinced that those who died of the sweat succumbed "through default of keeping," and that adequate care, combined with bed rest and the right medicine, would restore any sufferer to health again. She dosed those with pains around the heart or in the groin with treacle and "imperial water"; those with stomach cramps she gave an herb to purge the swelling and refused them all food and drink for sixteen hours. To keep well, she advised Wolsey to wrap a mixture of vinegar, wormwood, rosewater and crumbs of brown bread in a linen cloth, and to keep the cloth before his nose whenever he came near an infected area.[11]

Henry too was full of advice and remedies, sending Wolsey "manus Christi," an efficacious herb, and instructing him to eat lightly and drink very little wine, and to take "pills of Rasis" to fortify himself. He showed much solicitude toward Tuke, who suffered from a painful bladder complaint; one by one he explained to the secretary all the remedies he knew of, as knowledgeably "as any most cunning physician in England could do."

Henry had given up the frantic itinerary which had kept his servants packing and unpacking daily, and settled in at Tittenhanger. There seemed to be nowhere else to go; there was sickness at Eltham, Hunsdon had proven to be as pestilential as any other country house, and Greenwich was full of the sweat. (An attempt to purify Greenwich by ordering the mass emigration of the town poor proved futile; perhaps as a penance Henry ordered his marshal afterward to divide some eighteen pounds among the longsuffering townspeople displaced at his whim.[12])

Everything possible was done to make Tittenhanger safe from disease. The rooms were purged daily with fire. The courtiers and household servants were given regular doses of the best preservatives to be found. The king, always a believer in the health benefits of fresh air, ordered the small window in his private room greatly enlarged, and spent many hours walking briskly through the grounds of the estate, breathing deeply as he strode through the gardens and park.

To some extent the exhilaration of survival seems to have kept Henry's spirits up even as the fear of death threatened to unnerve him. In his own words he was "of good heart" despite all, and communicated his own hopefulness to those around him. To them he appeared "very merry," both when working with his secretaries and when walking abroad. He began his day with Katherine, then sought out Hennage for news about the divorce. The "great matter" and other letters and dispatches kept him busy until dinner time, after which he went out to hunt and shoot until supper. The hunting so drew him that he found the work of government tedious; Tuke wrote how, as he read aloud the letters of greatest importance, the king grew restless and "seemed to think them long," and impatiently sorted stacks of papers as he listened.[13] The work finished, Henry was off to the fields, and before too many weeks passed his favorite companion joined him in his pastimes. Anne returned to court toward the end of July, and rode out with the king in the long summer afternoons, equipped with a bow and arrows and a shooting glove made especially for her.

Though outwardly cheerful Henry did daily battle with his inner fears. The sickness and death that encircled him triggered old terrors left from his earliest childhood, and the very mention of the contagion filled him with dread. The mere name of the sweat, Gardiner wrote, "is so terrible and fearful to his highness' ears that he dare in no wise approach unto the place where it is noised to have been."[14] Years later a French ambassador called Henry "the most timid person in such matters you could meet with," and indeed it would be hard to overestimate the traumatic impact of the 1528 epidemic on the king. Prevailing common sense dictated that he should isolate himself from all but a few companions, and it became his practice to shut himself away for long periods, sometimes in his chamber and sometimes in a high tower which he used for a variety of purposes. He often took his supper there, alone, or at other times consulted there with his physician Dr. Chambers.[15]

Seclusion was appropriate to Henry's deeper moods, when he was "much troubled" by fears and when his faith in his own powers of survival waned. At these times he feared to sleep alone, and ordered Francis Bryan to sleep in the privy chamber with him. The hours of concentrated reading and writing he undertook during these months gave him headaches, and the country air brought on head colds; these infirmities, combined with the everpresent danger of the sweat, forced him into a constant state of spiritual preparedness for death. He confessed daily and received the eucharist, as did Katherine; he put his conscience in order; and he made his will. His tomb—a towering structure to be built in white marble and black touchstone—he had commissioned nearly ten years earlier. Whether he gave further thought to it now is unclear.

Certainly he gave deep thought to the larger issues of life and death, destiny and chance, and to his longed-for future with Anne. Surrounded by uncertainty, he resigned himself to destiny, recognizing that, as he wrote to his beloved, "whoso will struggle against fate at such a point is full often the further off from his desire." Every time he took the sacrament he felt more secure, and announced himself to be "armed towards God and the world."

He drew even more security from the unsullied state of his conscience, believing that its purity ensured him God's favor. In the letters he wrote the word conscience appeared again and again: he would not "clog the conscience" of his correspondent; he forbore to "distain his honor or conscience"; "good conscience" must rule, "conscience can be best judge." The "exoneration of conscience before God" he held to be of pre-eminent importance, conscience being, in his view, the instrument by which people accounted for themselves in God's eyes.[16]

His own conscience could not have been more clear. He had begun to compose a book on the subject of his invalid marriage, and spent his evenings poring over theological volumes and extracting texts to support his position. The work went well. "I am right well comforted," he said, "in so much that my book maketh substantially for my matter." Probably Henry expected his treatise to have the same impact as his book against Luther; certainly he expected it to offset the halfhearted response his diplomats had received from the pope in Rome. Some nights he devoted as much as four hours to this labor, and the more writing and reading he did the more entrenched his view of the issues became. By August the king was so committed to his cause, the French ambassador Du Bellay declared, "that none but God can get him out of it."[17]

One at least tried. Wolsey was far from sanguine about the eventual outcome of the nullity suit. With shrewdness acquired over many years of skilled diplomacy he assessed Pope Clement's position and concluded, rightly, that no definite answer was likely to be forthcoming—at least not in the near future. The king was bound to be disappointed, and his disappointment might be turned to rage by Wolsey's enemies. The cardinal tried to make his master see what he saw, and to retreat from his position. But Henry only "used terrible language" to Wolsey and went on with his book, leaving Wolsey anxious and distraught. Should the king's suit turn out as he expected he would bear much of the blame. It would take "a terrible alchemy and dexterity," he told Du Bellay, to overcome the assaults of those ranged against him.[18]

As the summer advanced the sweat receded, until by the end of August "little or nothing was heard thereof in any place." Henry and Anne were apart once again—a nod to discretion in honor of the coming of the papal legate Campeggio who, the lovers hoped, would clear the way for their union. Henry sent Anne news of Campeggio's progress on the long journey from Rome. "The legate which we most desire arrived at Paris on Sunday or Monday last past," he wrote, "so that I trust by the next Monday to hear of his arrival in Calais; and then I trust within a while to enjoy that which I have so longed for, to God's pleasure, and our both comforts."[19]

Henry was writing at the end of a day of hunting in the forest, in the closing days of the season he loved best. He had come through a dangerous time unscathed, and better days seemed to lie ahead. He was tired, yet his letter, though brief, was full of fervor and hope:

No more to you at this present, mine own darling, for lack of time, but that I would you were in mine arms, or I in yours, for I think it long since I kissed you.

Written after the killing of an hart, at eleven of the clock (minding, with God's grace, to-morrow, mightily timely to kill another) by the hand which I trust shortly shall be yours.

Henry R.

28

My welth is health, and perfect ease;
My conscience clere my chiefe defence;
I never seeke by brybes to please,
Nor by desert to give offence:
Thus do I live, thus will I die;
Would all did so as well as I!

As it turned out Campeggio did not arrive until the first week in October—a circumstance which set a pattern for delays and obstructions that was to continue throughout his stay in England. The significance of his tardy arrival was lost on Henry and Anne, who had begun to look on their joint future as assured, and could not perceive that Campeggio's lateness was part of a broad papal policy designed to frustrate the conclusion of the nullity suit for as long as possible. Optimistic reports from the negotiators Foxe and Gardiner had raised their hopes, while Clement himself had sent Henry word that he would do his best to satisfy him, no matter how difficult it might be.[1] Petitioners at court had begun to look to Anne, as they had once looked to Katherine, to help them gain the king's favor. She was not yet queen, of course, but she seemed a sort of queen-to-be, continually at Henry's side, evidently important to him, the prime focus, when he was not preoccupied with the business of government or his engrossing pastimes, of his interest and attention.[2]

From being infatuated friends Henry and Anne had become, in some sense, lovers; they did not yet share the same bed, but they were on the most intimate terms. "Wishing myself (specially an evening) in my sweetheart's arms," he wrote to her at the end of a letter, "whose pretty dukkys [breasts] I trust shortly to kiss."[3] Passion bound them now, as well as joint expectations, and in addition a new note of cozy domesticity had entered their relationship. Anne wrote to Wolsey saying she "longed to hear from you news of the legate, and hope they will be very good," and at the bottom of the letter was another paragraph in Henry's hand. "The writer of this would not cease till she had called me likewise to set to my hand," he said. "Both of us desire to see you."[4]

Though not living together they were rarely far apart, and as Campeggio reached the last stages of his journey new lodgings were being prepared for Anne at Greenwich under Wolsey's direction, separate enough from the king's apartments to avoid open scandal yet close enough for easy access. The arrangements were certain to be temporary in any case; according to the Spanish ambassador Mendoza, Henry and Anne saw the favorable papal judgment as all but in hand, and were already making plans for their wedding.[5]

The man on whom they relied to make it possible had to be carried slowly and painfully into London on a litter. Excruciatingly crippling gout prevented him from either walking or riding; it was all he could do to sit in his litter and endure the shocks and jars of the journey without crying out in complaint. Curious villagers who caught sight of him along the way saw little but a shrunken figure hunched in pain with a long untrimmed beard—the latter, rumor informed them, a sign of mourning for the state of the English church.[6]

Cardinal Campeggio was a great master of the canon law. No less a giant of erudition than Erasmus called him "one of the best and most learned men living," and he was universally held to be one of the least prejudiced as well. He held the counterbalancing offices of cardinal protector of England and cardinal protector of the Holy Roman Empire. He was by title an English as well as an Italian prelate—Henry had made him bishop of Salisbury four years earlier—and though he was clearly bound to represent the pope (and therefore to avoid alienating Charles V) he was ambivalent in his attitude toward Hapsburg interests. His house had been ransacked by imperial soldiers during the recent plundering of Rome, and he had been forced into a possessionless exile. In his gout-ridden condition even the most minor dislocation in his life caused extra pain, and the violent disruptions in the papal city had taxed his endurance to its extreme limits.

Campeggio had one further advantage as arbiter in the king's divorce: he was a married man himself. Before taking holy orders late in life he had been a professor of canon law at the University of Bologna; in secular life he had a wife and three children. He was not unsympathetic to domestic quarrels, and was capable of weighing the issues involved with his own experience as well as the canon law to guide him.

He was to need all the expertise he could summon to settle Henry and Katherine's embattled situation. The authorization and instructions he brought with him to England were at once sweeping and exceedingly restricting. With Wolsey, Campeggio was to preside over a court inquiring into the validity of the dispensation of Pope Julius II permitting Henry and Katherine to marry, and to pronounce on the validity of the marriage itself in consequence. The judgment—if in fact the case ever came to judgment—would rest with Campeggio rather than his colleague, for Wolsey was no canonist and was even ignorant of the basic procedures to be observed in a legatine court. And the judgment was to be final; neither Henry nor Katherine was to be allowed subsequently to appeal the case to Rome.[7]

So ran the official instructions. Unofficially Campeggio brought with him a long list of counter-instructions intended to undermine the outward purpose of his legacy. His primary directive was to delay the convening of the court for as long as possible. Henry and Katherine were to be presented a number of alternative solutions, any one of which would

circumvent the need for a papal judgment rendered in England. Henry
was to be urged to follow the example of Charles Brandon and obtain a
judgment of nullity from an English church court. Once he had it the pope
could confirm it, with relatively little blame. Or Katherine was to be
persuaded to enter a convent, thus leaving Henry free to remarry—at
least in theory. (The most learned of Clement VII's lawyers eventually
advised the pope that he could not grant Henry a dispensation to marry if
Katherine took the veil.[8]) Other proposals were more ingenious: that
Henry Fitzroy should marry Princess Mary, thus becoming unarguably
the heir to the throne, and satisfying the king's need for a legitimate male
heir; that children of Henry and Anne born out of wedlock be made
legitimate by papal decree; that, as Henry first suggested, he be allowed to
have two wives.

Unknown to anyone but the king and Wolsey, Campeggio brought
with him a document prejudicing the impartiality of the legatine court
beyond recall. It was a secret commission which in essence weighed the
legalities of both sides in advance and affirmed Henry's cause to be the
stronger. This "decretal commission" would seem to have reduced the
entire proceeding to a dishonorable pretense, except for two things. First,
it might never be needed, and second, it rounded out a papal strategy in
which each of the parties affected by the suit was given an equal measure
of false hope. Henry and Wolsey had reason to expect that the court
would rule in their favor. Anne had Henry's reassurance, if she did not
share his exact knowledge, that his cause and hers would prevail.
Katherine could console herself that a learned, ethical man was to preside
over the case in the pope's name. And all the imperialists, from Charles V
on down, could take comfort from the continually delayed settlement and
the discomfiture of the English king.

Campeggio took in Henry's mood of excessive eagerness at once. His
desire for a settlement was "most ardent," the legate wrote a week after
his arrival. No argument could dislodge his feeling of certainty about the
nullity of his union with Katherine. After four hours of conversation with
the king Campeggio was stunned by his erudition. "His majesty has so
diligently studied this matter," he concluded, "that I believe in this case
he knows more than a great theologian or jurist." (Du Bellay confirmed
Campeggio's judgment. "He talked to me at great length about the
matter," he said of Henry, "and I promise you he requires no advocate,
he understands it so well.")

Henry had begun to train all the faculties of his powerful intellect on
the nullity suit—an effort which greatly reinforced his certainty. Self-
confidence, logic and learning all convinced him that he was in the right.
"I believe that an angel descending from heaven would be unable to
persuade him otherwise," Campeggio wrote, and despaired of shifting the
king's judgments by reason alone.[9]

Meanwhile Henry was at work trying to muster support for his
position among his subjects. He drew up a document indicating assent to
the nullity suit and had it circulated among his courtiers and the other
"principal men" of the kingdom, expecting to find their signatures ap-

pended to it. To his dismay only three men lent their names in support—Anne's father and brother and her uncle the duke of Norfolk.[10] Among the common people opinion ran even more heavily to Katherine. Some favored a compromise—bigamy—but many, particularly the women, blamed Henry vociferously for following lust instead of duty. "The king would for his own pleasure have another wife," they said loudly whenever any defense of the divorce was offered. They gathered outside the palace and cheered lustily for Katherine whenever she appeared, shouting messages of encouragement and wishing her victory over her enemies. Campeggio had encountered a group of these women as he made his way to London. Accusing him of opposing the queen, they hurled abuse at Anne, chanting "No Nan Bullen for us! No Nan Bullen for us!" until the old man was out of sight.

The popular view was in fact not far from that of the Spanish ambassador Mendoza, who saw in Henry a lovesick fool led astray completely by his passions. According to Mendoza, the month after Campeggio arrived Henry abandoned all propriety and rode off into the countryside to be with Anne, intending never to return. He came to his senses again, the ambassador said, but not before he had sent Katherine away to another palace and dispersed his household to an unprecedented extent. "He is so blindly in love with that lady that he cannot see his way clearly," Mendoza concluded, "and though the connection is so abominable that it may lead to the worst consequences, he is so determined upon this divorce that all his subjects are greatly afraid of his ultimately carrying his plans into execution."[11]

Mendoza was not the best judge of the king's feelings or intentions, and where he saw in Henry a man of unbridled willfulness and dangerous appetites, "fond of extreme measures," others perceived a more temperate personality. "His majesty will not go to extremes," Campeggio wrote when the nullity suit was first opened, "but act considerately in this matter, as he is accustomed to do in all his actions."[12]

More significant than Henry's self-indulgence or moderation was the arresting authority he communicated in his first public speech on the divorce in November of 1528. Henry had always been an imposing figure in large-scale settings, and at thirty-nine he was at the height of his heroic good looks. "In this eighth Henry God has combined such corporeal and intellectual beauty as not merely to surprise but to astound all men," the Venetian ambassador Falier wrote. "His face is angelic, rather than handsome, his head imperial and bold, and he wears a beard, contrary to English custom." Falier's secretary was even more impressed. Seeing the king in his presence chamber, regally posed under his canopy of cloth of gold and wearing a gown of gold brocade trimmed with lynx's skins, the secretary found Henry quite simply the handsomest man he had ever seen, "a perfect model of manly beauty in these times." To judge from his looks alone he was "in favor both with God and man," and as he addressed the assembled Londoners his compelling beauty added weight to his words.[13]

"Our trusty and wellbeloved subjects," he began, "both you of the nobility and you of the meaner sort, it is not unknown to you how that we, both by God's provision and true and lawful inheritance, have reigned over this realm of England almost the term of twenty years.'' He reminded them of the peace they had known under his rule, undisturbed by invasion or conquest, and of the ''victory and honor'' he had brought to England in his two decades as king. ''But when we remember our mortality and that we must die,'' he went on, ''then we think that all our doings in our liftetime are clearly defaced and worthy of no memory if we leave you in trouble at the time of our death.'' Without a true heir to succeed him, he said, he would fail in his duty toward them. Thus when he found that, in the opinion of the ''greatest clerks in Christendom,'' his marriage was wrong in God's eyes and his child a bastard, his distress was unbearable.

''Think you my lords that these words touch not my body and soul?'' he asked his subjects. ''Think you that these doings do not daily and hourly trouble my conscience and vex my spirits?'' Knowing the devotion his hearers felt to Katherine, he praised her good qualities at length, calling her ''a woman of most gentleness, of most humility and buxomness''—in short a peerless wife, if only their union were valid. As it was, he was forced to depart from her, and to lament not only his long adultery with her but the divine displeasure that adultery had occasioned. ''These be the sores that vex my mind,'' the king confided to his subjects in conclusion. ''These be the pangs that trouble my conscience, and for these greves I seek a remedy.''[14]

It was an effective speech, and one that foreshadowed a new and powerful political alliance between the king and his subjects. It failed to satisfy the queen's partisans, however, who knew full well that Katherine was no longer the cherished partner the king described, but a misused woman sinking under the weight of her sorrows.

Queen Katherine was forty-three when Campeggio came to England, but to him at least she looked much older—''nearly fifty''—and others noticed that the lines on her face had deepened and her eyes had grown more careworn in recent months. Even now her everpresent smile did not desert her, save when she sat with the theologians and legists concerned with her case, consulting with them in grave earnest as Henry did with his advisers. She had put on weight; her face had become fleshy and jowly, and her figure stout. Beside the spirited Anne Boleyn Katherine was almost grotesque, and by keeping both women near him Henry invited the unflattering comparison.

Katherine's depression deepened as, one by one, those who supported her showed how little they were willing or able to do. Warham deserted her out of fear of the king; Vives left England, insulted by Wolsey and dismayed by Katherine's evident self-reliance. Mendoza tried to obtain imperialist lawyers from Flanders to argue for her, but they never arrived. Bishop Fisher was infinitely helpful and resourceful, though a sole champion could do little against the forces ranked on the king's side. Charles V promised the greatest assistance. In letters he swore that he considered Katherine's cause his own, and assured her that ''everything in his power would be most willingly done." Yet he preferred to use his influence indirectly, relying on Clement VII's fear and Campeggio's sense of justice to rescue Katherine from an unjust fate. And Campeggio, the queen feared, had been so led astray by lies that he could not be relied on to help her. Her informants told her that the legate had been misled into thinking the divorce would be accepted by everyone concerned—the emperor, Katherine herself, even the English people. This misinformation, coupled with pressure from Henry and Wolsey, might make the difference between justice and inequity.[15]

Katherine's determined cheerfulness and Henry's bluff insouciance hid the sordidness of their domestic life. "Looking at the two together," Du Bellay wrote, "one could perceive nothing, and to this hour they have but one bed and one table." The royal couple continued to keep up appearances even after Katherine was ordered to leave Greenwich so that Anne could take up residence there in luxurious apartments adjoining Henry's. In private, though, their sharing of bed and board had become a painful ordeal for the queen. Henry had made it known that, "for marvellous great and secret" reasons, he was "utterly resolved and determined" never to sleep with Katherine again.[16]

Yet he continued to give every appearance of cohabiting with her, having been advised by his lawyers that to do otherwise would be to give occasion for a countersuit; if he neglected her her lawyers, it seemed, could allege that he was acting in defiance of her conjugal rights.[17] The tension caused by this pretense was made worse by Henry's continual suggestion that out of misplaced loyalty one of Katherine's Spanish servants might try to do him harm, and by the even more outrageous insinuation that Katherine herself had been plotting to kill him.

Was it true she had attempted the king's life in order to free herself and her daughter to marry whomever they pleased? Tunstall and Warham asked the queen in November. Aghast at the suggestion, Katherine managed to stammer out a denial. She could not believe that the king, her lord, had said such a thing; he knew full well that she valued his life more than her own. Well, then, the prelates said, if she was not conspiring against the king, others in the kingdom were, and should they attempt anything against him she would be punished along with them. They stopped just short of warning Katherine that in case of rebellion she would be executed as a traitor, but the meaning behind their words was clear.[18]

Warham and Tunstall were not the only royal envoys sent to pressure Katherine and wear her down in the months after the legate's arrival. Wolsey, Campeggio, and the king himself all confronted her, now pleading with her and appealing to her piety and compassion, now assaulting her dignity, now resorting to blunt language and threats. In each case the result was the same. The queen refused to pave the way for Henry's marriage to Anne by entering a convent, giving her tormentors "to understand that all efforts to move her from her purpose will be in vain." In desperation Henry used the sharpest weapons at his disposal. He accused Katherine of heartlessness and hatred, and threatened to keep her away from their daughter. Tunstall and Warham were instructed to tell Katherine that Henry could no longer persuade himself that she loved him. She appeared rather to despise him, and since it was not safe for him to come into the presence of such animosity he would see little of her in the future, and would keep the princess away, too, for the same reason.[19]

Henry's attitude to Katherine had more behind it than his impatient desire to begin a new life with Anne. Katherine deserved punishment, for she had done the unforgivable: she had gotten the better of Henry by means of a legal stratagem. Soon after Campeggio arrived she announced that she possessed a document overturning all of the king's arguments against the validity of their marriage and establishing once and for all that they were man and wife. Henry's case turned on the terminology and legal arguments made in the papal bull of dispensation; the document Katherine now produced, a papal brief supplementing the bull, made good many of the defects in the bull and contained language the king's lawyers were hard put to assault. The royal forces tried their best to invalidate the brief, insisting that the copy in Katherine's possession counted for nothing, and that only the original in Spain could be considered seriously. Besides, the brief contained errors, they claimed, and was probably a forgery; imprecise legal formulas, an unusual computation of the date and "false latinities" suggested deception.

Finally after much wrangling efforts to bring the original of the brief to England ceased, but not before the issue had caused months of delay. Another unforeseen occasion of delay was the fragile health of the pope. Early in the new year of 1529 Clement became violently ill, with a raging fever, severe head pains and stomach cramps. He vomited up all of the medicines his physicians gave him, until he grew so thin there were "great apprehensions" about his recovery. One night he lapsed into a comatose state and his anxious attendants, unable to find his pulse, gave him up for dead. By the time he opened his eyes weakly the next morning couriers had been sent out with the news of his death, and within two weeks Henry heard that the man who had frustrated his divorce for nearly two years would not impede it any longer.[20]

For months after the false news of his death was corrected the pope's life remained in danger, and Henry, sensing his opportunity, wrote to his envoys in Italy instructing them to use whatever influence was needed— "promises of spiritual promotions, offices, dignities, rewards of money"—to ensure that Wolsey was elected as his successor. (Should Wolsey prove unacceptable to the other cardinals, Campeggio should be suggested.) That the occupant of the papal throne be favorably disposed toward Henry was of the utmost importance; the choice of a new pope was "that on which depends the making or marring of the king's cause."[21] Of course, in the event of Clement's death the two legates in England could judge the nullity suit *sede vacante,* even before the new candidate was chosen. In either case Clement's passing would put an end to the endless postponements which, as the months passed, made Henry more and more anxious. "At present there is nothing that annoys this king so much as the idea of not accomplishing his purpose," Mendoza remarked on the eve of Campeggio's arrival. The longer the final settlement was delayed, the greater his annoyance grew, until finally on May 30 he issued the license to Campeggio and Wolsey to begin their proceedings, and they in turn convened the legatine court the following day.

The Parliament Chamber at Blackfriars was arranged "like a solemn court" for the occasion, with carpets on the floor and tapestries on the walls. There were two chairs for the presiding churchmen at the head of the hall, and on their right and left chairs for the opposing parties, the king's covered with a rich canopy of estate. Neither party appeared at the opening sessions, and it was not until June 18 that the dramatic confrontation between the king and the queen began. On that day Katherine's defense was to be made, and her partisans crowded the great hall in order to make their voices heard in her behalf. Katherine had eleven advocates in all, seven English ecclesiastics—of whom only Fisher carried out his assignment competently—and four foreigners, Vives, her confessor Jorge de Athequa, and two Flemish canonists. The two Flemings, sent to England at last by Margaret of Savoy after much delay, had gone back when they found the trial had not yet begun; the imperialists believed they had been ordered out of the kingdom.[22]

To the astonishment of the entire assemblage it was not Katherine's lawyers but the queen herself who entered the great hall on the day appointed for her defense. She bore herself with the greatest dignity, leaning on the arm of one of her oldest servitors, Griffith ap Rhys, who by an irony of lineage happened to be Anne Boleyn's uncle. (The aging ap Rhys had served Katherine and Arthur Tudor at Ludlow during their brief marriage; he was a living link with the queen's unhappy past.) In default of more able defenders Katherine had determined to argue her own case, which so delighted her supporters that as soon as she came into view they burst into loud applause and cheers of encouragement.

"Good Katherine! How she holds the field!" they shouted. "She doesn't care a fig. She's afraid of nothing!"

The queen walked past the noisy spectators without breaking stride, but she smiled and nodded her head in acknowledgment of their words in what the French ambassador called "a display of Castilianisms."[23] When she reached the appointed place she read a prepared statement, attacking the competence of the legatine court to try her case. The judges were biased, she claimed, and besides the matter was already in the hands of a higher authority, the pope. As to the substance of the nullity suit, she had only one argument to put forward. As she had remained a virgin throughout her first marriage—indeed, as she told Campeggio, she had slept by Prince Arthur's side only seven nights in all—her second marriage was unarguably valid. The papal brief in her possession gave the second marriage the sanction of approval from Rome. And twenty years of married life with Henry lent it a time-honored legitimacy no legal argument could assault.

Katherine's eloquence proved ineffective. When the court resumed next both the king and queen were present, and after Henry made a long speech the legates rejected Katherine's objections and prepared to go ahead with the gathering of evidence on the validity of the marriage.

Without waiting to hear more Katherine made a dramatic appeal. Rising from her chair she crossed the room and knelt before Henry. In a clear, strong voice she made a moving plea for clemency and justice.

"Sir, I beseech you for all the loves that hath been between us and for the love of God, let me have justice and right." "I have been to you a true, honorable and obedient wife," she went on, "ever conformable to your will and pleasure." She had never grudged him anything, she swore, or shown as much as a fleeting sign of discontent with him. If she was culpable in any way, she would gladly undergo the punishment she deserved. But if there was no fault in her, she begged him to restore her to her rightful place at his side, and to deal justly with her.

Lastly she appealed to his sense of right and wrong. "And when ye had me at the first (I take God to be my judge) I was a true maid without touch of man; and whether it be true or no, I put it to your conscience."

Her plea over, the queen waited in silence for an answer that never came. Then she got to her feet and made her way slowly to the door of the great hall. Henry signaled the court crier to call her back.

"Katherine queen of England," he shouted, "come into the court!" She refused to acknowledge the summons, even when it was repeated and her escort, the faithful Griffith ap Rhys, urged her to turn back.

"On, on," she said to him, "it makes no matter, for it is no indifferent court for me. Therefore I will not tarry, go on your ways."

Nothing that came afterward could match the intensity of that moment, though weeks of detailed testimony dulled the courtiers' memories of the queen's defiant stand. Every incident of that faraway wedding night in 1501 was brought to light again—how Katherine had lain under the sheets when Arthur was escorted into the bedchamber, her face veiled out of modesty as the clerics blessed the bed; how the two had remained together all that night; how Arthur, early the next morning, had called lustily to his gentlemen for a cup of ale, saying he had "been this night in the midst of Spain." "Masters, it is good pastime to have a wife," he had told them, and some among them still remembered remarking to one another that the prince's decline in health set in just after his wedding night; at the time they concluded that his weakness came about "because he lay with the lady Katherine."[24]

None of this was conclusive. Much of what the courtiers and servants said was as irrelevant as it was embarrassing, and even the best evidence was only circumstantial. Yet except for Fisher Katherine's lawyers defended her poorly, and by mid-July Campeggio realized that when the time came he would have no choice but to rule for the king. Caught between the weight of the king's case and the pope's directive to avoid judgment Campeggio made an anguished decision. When on July 23 the king's proctor made his formal request for judgment the legate rose and announced that, as all the courts in Rome were in recess at this period, he was obliged to recess his court as well, to reconvene in October.

After months of hopeful effort Henry had been tricked. Wolsey too had been fooled, for as legate he had it in his power to pronounce a definitive judgment and he had let his opportunity slip. No document records the king's reaction to the announcement; rage, dismay, above all a wave of monumental impatience must have swept over him.

Suffolk's response spoke for him. As soon as Campeggio announced the adjournment the nobleman rose to his feet and, clapping his hand furiously down on the table in front of him, swore an oath.

"By the mass, now I see that the old said saw is true, that there was never legate or cardinal, that did good in England!"[25]

With that all the nobles got up together and swept out of the room, "leaving the legates sitting one looking at the other sore astonished."

29

Long time I lived in the courte,
With lords and ladies of great sorte;
And when I smil'd all men were glad,
But when I frown'd my prince grew sad.

THE drama at Blackfriars in the summer of 1529 closed the first stage of the king's struggle for his divorce. For the next few years, though efforts to bring about a definitive judgment continued, the mood of almost compulsive urgency surrounding the king's great matter gave way to the settled expectation that, in time, King Henry would have his way.

Slowly the courtiers adapted themselves to the new tone of court society, learning to amuse themselves at "Pope July," the game whose points were called matrimony, intrigue, and the pope and whose tacit object was to make a light matter of the king's divorce. They followed their sovereign's example and arrayed themselves more magnificently than ever, parading through the galleries of Hampton Court as if in disdain of all troublesome thoughts, and paying extravagant attention to the king and his lady.

Henry had begun to show Anne such husbandly devotion—even in Katherine's presence—that disapproving visitors to his court were outraged. He caressed her "openly and in public as if she were his wife"; he gave her Katherine's seat of honor at banquets. When he went riding he lifted Anne into the saddle in front of him and together they galloped over the fields. "Her will is law to him," a visiting Italian wrote, while the shrewd Du Bellay warned in his dispatches that Anne might soon be pregnant with the king's child.[1]

The relationship between Henry and Anne, never without turbulence, had now taken on the atmosphere of a stormy marriage. Anne had long since begun to anticipate her future status as queen, and was unrestrained in her sarcasm for her rival Queen Katherine. In the presence of one of Katherine's ladies Anne remarked that she wished all the Spaniards in the world were in the sea, and when the woman protested that Anne should not abuse the queen's honor with such language Anne replied sharply that she cared nothing whatever for Katherine, and that she would rather see her hanged than acknowledge her as her mistress.[2]

Such exchanges were a mild embarrassment to Henry, but he was hesitant to complain about Anne's behavior. To chastise her would mean adding to the store of grievances she nourished, and giving her added

230

reason to burst into tears and bewail her fate. She often lamented her condition to Henry, alternately sobbing and regretting the loss of her youth and honor and angrily accusing him of failing to promote the nullity suit as vigorously as he might. More than once she threatened to leave him, playing on his complete devotion to her and reducing him to a state of fearful anxiety. When Anne was in these moods, it was said, "the king had much trouble to appease her," even though he begged her, with tears in his eyes, not to speak of leaving him. After one severe quarrel in January of 1531 he was again at his wits' end, and turned in his tearful extremity to Anne's relatives, pleading with them to intercede and to try to bring about a reconciliation.[3]

Henry attracted a good deal of criticism by his deference to Anne. He "showed himself so forgetful of what is right," an imperialist wrote, "and of his dignity and authority, that everybody thinks little of him, as of a man who is acting against his truth, honor and conscience."[4] To show such overanxious concern toward a wife would have seemed inappropriate enough; to be so disquieted over a mistress was little short of ridiculous.

Certainly Henry provided Anne with luxuries worthy of a queen. She had gowns of purple velvet and scarlet satin, and a court dress of crimson cloth of gold worth the price of a small jewel. There were expensive furs to trim these gowns, and diamonds and pearls in abundance to adorn them. There were purses of coins for playing money and spending money, and large sums of a hundred pounds or more as New Year's gifts. When she went riding Anne could choose from four French saddles Henry ordered for her, upholstered in black velvet fringed with silk and gold; each had a matching footstool for mounting and dismounting and matching harnesses and gilt bits.[5] Anne's lodgings were filled with elegant furnishings—costly hangings and soft rugs, embroidered cushions, a beautifully worked desk "garnished with paten and gold." In 1530 Henry ordered a new bed, elaborately carved and fitted with rich testers and counterpane. It may have been for his private bedchamber, or it may have been the bed he shared with Anne.[6]

Late in 1530 Henry disconcerted his courtiers by creating a place for Anne among the nobility. The Boleyn ancestry was not inherently distinguished. Anne's great-grandfather Geoffrey Boleyn had risen from rural origins to become a prosperous merchant dealing in silk and wool—and lord mayor of London. Her grandfather had married a noble heiress; her father was an influential courtier linked by marriage to one of the most powerful men in England, the duke of Norfolk. But recent connections contracted by marriage were nothing compared to a noble claim centuries old. Now Henry discovered two Boleyn forebears—one a twelfth-century Norman lord, the other a fourteenth-century Picard—whose aristocratic blood shed luster on Anne and her family.[7]

Among the courtiers Anne's newfound nobility gave occasion for jokes, and to those who took Katherine's side, secret outrage. Among the common people it nourished a hostility that erupted into murderous violence.

According to a report reaching Venice from France, a mob of from seven to eight thousand women—and men disguised as women—gathered in London and marched to the riverside house where Anne was staying alone. It was said they intended to kill her, and they might well have succeeded had word not reached Anne of their approach. She escaped across the river in a boat and made her way to safety, doubtless vowing to stay closer to the king from then on, and to trust her future subjects less.[8]

Terrifying though it must have been to Anne, this incident evoked little official response; being "a thing done by women," it seemed relatively slight, or so the French report claimed. What notice Henry took of it is unrecorded. Outwardly at least his interests seemed to narrow somewhat in these years; his privy purse accounts reveal a preoccupation with finery and amusement reminiscent of his first decade as king.

His costumes more than matched Anne's in splendor. His gowns were of silver tissue and cloth of gold, his doublets of crimson tissue furred with sables. One doublet cost twice the value of a small farm, while the value of the gold and jewels used to trim others surpassed many a nobleman's annual income. One day in October of 1530 Henry bought a thousand pearls. The royal milliner Christopher, who supplied a variety of ornaments of dress, brought the king velvet caps and gold buttons and yards of yellow lace—and perhaps his scarlet nightcap embroidered in gold. Looking ahead to a long life of splendor, in 1529 Henry undertook to buy from the cloth merchants of Florence more than ten thousand pounds' worth of velvets, satins and precious metallic cloths, with payment to be made over twenty-six years.[9]

Dressed in the fruits of his extravagance, his robes gleaming and jewels shining from his cap and throat and chest, the king was awesome, and he knew it. In order to admire himself at full length he ordered a large looking glass, and stood before it, perhaps, as his attendants perfumed his clothes and person with lavender and orangeflower water.[10]

The interstices of his working days were filled with a variety of amusements. He liked to watch his guardsmen shoot at targets, and to listen to plays put on by the children of the Chapel Royal or the boys of St. Paul's. He wagered with anyone and everyone: with his treasurer, his pages, and the sergeant of his cellar, with Anthony Knevet at tennis and Thomas Boleyn at a shooting match at Hampton Court. Acrobats, freaks and wandering entertainers—such as "the fellow with the dancing dog"—held his interest and amused his courtiers, and when other pastimes failed the king went boating on the Thames in his barge and filled the bargemen's pockets with drinking money afterwards.[11]

The accounts of Henry's activities show an unusually varied and energetic life. One day he supervised workmen building a bridge at York Place, and advised them on its finishing; another day he inspected one of his fortifications, discussing its defense with the captain and gunners. At other times he went down to the docks and boarded his warships, or to the stables, where his favored mount the Barbary horse was living out his old age. Often he looked in on his horse keeper Hannibal Zinzano to talk over the state of his horses' health. Payments for "drink and other medicines" for the royal horses, or for their healing, were a recurring entry in the king's personal accounts, though his riding was now confined chiefly to travel and the hunt. He no longer astonished his courtiers with the acrobatics of the manage, and jousted infrequently. In March of 1531 he rode two matches in the lists against his redoubtable old partner Charles Brandon, but as Brandon was forty-six and the king in his fortieth year their combat must have lacked a good deal of its onetime fire and fervor. Henry's military ambitions were dormant too for the time being, though he continued to pay the armorer of Windsor Castle to "keep clean the king's harness there."

As ever, the woods and fields lured Henry out of doors at all seasons. He began to devote more time to hawking than in the past, and went fishing with the "angling rods" provided for him at Hampton Court. To improve his hunting in summer and fall Henry oversaw the replenishing of his hunting parks with deer and other game brought from elsewhere, and ordered his park keepers to set out hay and oats for the beasts in the winter months when food was scarce.

A substantial part of the king's attention went to looking after his numerous dependants. There were aging relatives and retainers to be supported. Annuities went to Katherine, countess of Devonshire, sister of Elizabeth of York and Henry's aunt (who styled herself proudly "daughter, sister, and aunt of kings"), to Henry's old nurse Anne Luke, to a retired "footman and tumbler," to an elderly gentlewoman of Elizabeth Woodville's who lived to be nearly ninety.

But his generosity also extended to his subjects at large. Small knots of needy men and women gathered wherever the king went—along the roadway when he traveled, before the door of the church where he heard mass—hoping to be noticed and rewarded with a few coins. Occasionally they brought him gifts: roots and herbs, green geese, live foxes, and every sort of food, from apples and orange pies to pheasants and pomegranates and cooked salmon, and the baked lampreys of which he was especially fond.[12] But more often they asked his charity, "for the love of Saint George," and sometimes they told him their stories. William Kebet, "late sumpterman of the ward," had lost his living and was "fallen in poverty and decay." The king gave him a hundred shillings, and when Kebet came again for assistance the following year, he received four pounds. To another wretched man in need and "like to be lost" went another hundred shillings, and to the destitute father of thirteen children, three pounds six.[13]

The momentum of Henry's thinking and working increased as he approached his forties. In the aftermath of the inconclusive legatine trial—which even before it was recessed became superseded when Pope Clement advoked the case to Rome—the king turned with renewed intensity to studying the theological issues in the nullity suit. Always fascinated by the stuff of intellectual debate, Henry now attacked the complexities of his divorce with the fervid intelligence of a committed participant. He read and reread the pertinent passages from the Bible, the works of the Church Fathers, the writings of the scholastics and great teachers of the canon law. He read all that his own library held, then went on to exhaust the libraries of the religious houses. The abbots of Ramsey, Reading, Gloucester, Evesham and Spalding all sent him books, and when he traveled the books he was using were transported from palace to palace along with his wardrobe and other personal furnishings.

Once he mastered the accessible texts Henry went on to seek out the more obscure works which defended his side of the suit. He sent the humanist Richard Croke to Italy to search for little-known manuscripts he hoped would be available there, writing out detailed notes for Croke to follow and giving him lists of specific treatises to find and passages within them to consult.[14] Whenever a rare treatise came to light nearer home he ordered its pertinent passages transcribed for his library, and oversaw the transcription himself.[15]

By 1530 the evidence on both sides in the nullity suit had been sifted for three years and more, and the arguing points had become exceedingly minute. From the outset the queen's defenders had built their case on the passage in Deuteronomy allowing marriage with a brother's widow, whereas the king's lawyers had cited the Levitican admonition against it. But over the years the issue had become much finer: in the original Hebrew, so Henry's supporters claimed, the term translated as "brother" in the two texts was not the same. (The word used in Leviticus meant "male sibling," that in Deuteronomy "relative.") Katherine's supporters denied this, and added the scholastic argument that the good arising from beneficial treatment of the widow by her second husband canceled out whatever transgression might be inherent in the new union.

Relatively abstruse points such as these eventually grew to be familiar knowledge to Henry, and the more adroit he became in wielding the weapons of theological argument the more sanguine, even cocksure, he seemed. When the imperial ambassador Chapuys attempted to pin him down on a statement he had made sometime earlier about Katherine's virginity he immediately found a way to slip out of the verbal trap and robbed Chapuys of his triumph. Having eluded his opponent, the ambassador wrote, Henry "as if he had won a very great victory, or discovered some great subtlety for gaining his purpose, began to crow, telling me, 'Now have I paid you off? What more would you have?' "

As important in increasing Henry's confidence as his skill in argument were the treatises, commentaries and collective opinions he was gathering from scholars throughout Europe. Though the most learned and esteemed churchmen of the time argued for Katherine—Cardinal Cajetan, Robert Bellarmine, the highly respected Fisher and Vives—Henry was amassing judgments in his favor, hoping to outmatch in sheer bulk the weight of all counterargument. In June, 1530, the canonists of Padua determined that no man could legitimately marry his brother's widow. The scholars of Bourges agreed, as did fifty-seven doctors and "other learned men" of Verona, Venice, Brescia, Bologna and other Italian cities. The Spanish universities of Alcala and Salamanca ruled for Katherine, as expected, but the greatest center of learning of them all, the University of Paris, judged for Henry.[16] When the news of the Parisian endorsement arrived the king ordered the text of the determination read out in the streets and marketplaces, and made no secret of his delight.

Katherine was unimpressed. "I do not hesitate to say," she told the king to his face, "that for each doctor or lawyer who might decide in your favor and against me, I shall find a thousand to declare that the marriage is good and indissoluble."[17] But Henry was as undaunted by the queen's bravado as he was unmanned by Anne's threats and pleadings. In his own mind, he was right. He knew he was right. And "there was nobody in this world capable of turning the current of his passion or fancy in this particular case."[18]

Henry was in fact at an extraordinary peak of creative power, not only intellectually but artistically. His mind ranged widely, and illumined everything it touched. He drew up visionary architectural plans. He commissioned painters, sculptors and master craftsmen to decorate his palaces and guided their work with craftsmanlike taste. He endowed colleges and patronized students and scholars. He returned with renewed fervor to composing love songs and instrumental pieces, writing two motets—"O Lord the Maker of All Things" and "Quam Pulchra Es"— that entered the enduring canon of English church music.

As a composer and performer Henry was a part of a broad transition in court music, from the highly professional and traditional style of the late Middle Ages, with its chivalrous basse-dances, its set forms and preference for the harp to a newer, more fluid Italianate style. Amateurs and professionals performed together the lively Italian pavanes and galliards, the amateurs learning from music-masters to read written notes and to follow the intricate patterns of part songs. The king had long been the most illustrious amateur musician in the country, and in Anne Boleyn he found a talented companion to share his enthusiasm.

Musicians continued to be an important group in the royal household. Under the leadership of Hugh Wodehouse, "marshal of the king's minstrels," dozens of players were kept on the household rolls to provide entertainment at all hours. A corps of sixteen trumpeters, their instruments hung with banners and tassels, attended the king; his minstrels Pero and Nowell, Peter Taberet and John Bolenger sang and spun out their patter as he dined. Francis Weston was one of the royal lutenists; another musician (and incomparable dancer) was Mark Smeaton. The destinies of both men were to be closely linked to that of Anne Boleyn. The king and his players performed on a vast collection of instruments, many of them precious works of art. Among Henry's hundreds of recorders, lutes, and keyboard instruments was a silver organ with gold ornaments; some of the other pieces were gilded and studded with jewels.[19]

The waxing of Henry's creative powers may have owed something to circumstances, for after 1529 he found himself for the first time in sole command of government.

Cardinal Wolsey, who had for so long been the unshakable pillar on which English government rested, had been swept from the scene. Soon after his colleague Campeggio left the country Wolsey was indicted for exceeding his legatine authority and was stripped of his secular offices and most of his incomparable wealth. Thomas More became chancellor; Wolsey was ordered to go north to York, to the archbishopric he had never seen, if he hoped to avoid worse punishments. His fall was the king's decision, influenced by Anne and her Norfolk relatives. Norfolk himself could not restrain his spite toward his old enemy. When the cardinal was slow to leave the capital the duke sent word to him that "if he go not away, I will tear him with my teeth."

Heavy-hearted and ill with worry, Wolsey started out on his journey, leaving behind for the king's agents an immensely long inventory, carefully written out in his own hand, of all that he possessed. He had been given the humiliating and tedious task of compiling this document without assistance, under strict instructions to leave nothing out. At the same time, watches were set at the port cities to make certain he did not try to leave the country with his treasures.[20]

In his fear and uncertainty Wolsey was haunted by the prophecy he had held in mind with dread ever since the king's infatuation with Anne Boleyn had become his central passion.

> When the cow rideth the bull,
> Then, priest, beware thy skull.

For years the people had recited this verse in dark anticipation of Wolsey's loss of favor, and the cardinal had long believed "that a woman should be his confusion." Throughout his agonizing months at York he alternately cursed Anne as the cause of his downfall and mused over how he might gain her clemency, never doubting that she was responsible for his fate.

Henry had allowed his former servant to retain not only his bishopric but a pension of three thousand angels and personal furnishings adequate to keep up appearances—eighty horses and their trappings, six mules, enough tapestry and plate to equip five rooms, £300 in clothing and more than enough fish, salt, oxen and muttons to feed his immense, bloated body for many months.[21] These provisions proved to be insufficient: the portion of his pension the king had advanced to Wolsey was soon spent, and he was left without enough money to repair the decayed episcopal residence waiting for him at York. He had lost most of his servants, and, temporarily, his baggage; for months he camped helplessly under the leaking roof of his shabby mansion, "wrapped in misery and need on every side, not knowing where to be succoured or relieved."[22] To compound his distress the cardinal's illness worsened, and he had to be treated with leeches—"very hungry ones," his doctor prescribed—and with "vomitive electuary." He had never in his life been so wretched. In a letter to Gardiner Wolsey signed himself "Thomas the miserable, Cardinal of York."[23]

It was Wolsey's physician, Augustin de Augustinis, who betrayed him in the end, supplying his enemies with the testimony they needed to destroy him. Wolsey had sought the help of the French king against Henry, the physician said, "singing the tune as they wished him"; afterward de Augustinis was lodged in Norfolk's house "like a prince," while his patient was accused of high treason and seized by another old enemy, Anne Boleyn's former love Henry Percy.

The moment he had feared most had come. In desperate anguish

Wolsey tried to starve himself, refusing food for days "hoping rather to finish his life in this way than in a more shameful one." Unsuccessful in his attempt he finally began the journey southward, but the final stages of his illness overtook him on the way and he died among the monks of Leicester. He was buried in a place of infamy, in the church the people called "the tyrants' sepulchre," alongside Richard III.[24]

"Oh, the slippery turns of this world!" Erasmus exclaimed when he heard of Wolsey's fall. Others were less philosophical in their reactions. Courtiers the cardinal had abused for so many years gloated noisily over his fate, while the common people cursed his memory. Wolsey's former servant Thomas Cromwell heard a countryman say that the cardinal "was not worthy to wipe his horses' feet," and other things too harsh to preserve in writing, while in every village tavern men and women reminded one another that the old prophecy had been fulfilled, and the cow had ridden the bull at last.

At first Henry did nothing but complain about the monumental chaos Wolsey had left behind. Governmental affairs were in such great confusion, the king told Katherine, that it was all he could do to restore order, even though he worked at it night and day.[25] As the months went by, however, Henry came to realize the immensity of the task his chancellor had grappled with for so many years, and to appreciate as never before Wolsey's uncomplaining efficiency. Compared to the late cardinal, his councilors seemed like blundering novices, and he told them so. When they displeased him he shouted at them in a rage that Wolsey had been "a better man than any of them for managing matters," and, repeating himself for emphasis, he stormed out of the Council chamber.[26]

Dissatisfied with his councilors, preferring to fill Wolsey's role himself, Henry bent under the burden of a greater workload than he had ever known. And as he struggled with it, amid the frustrations and occasional excitements of the controversy over his divorce, amid extraordinary domestic tensions and personal stress, Henry felt from time to time the assaults of age, the cutting edge of his own mortality.

The headaches and "rheums"—catarrhs—that had given him such pain while he was writing his treatise on the divorce continued to attack him in these years, along with sore throats and occasional hoarseness. In 1532, at forty-one, a severe sinus attack and toothache laid him low, and from time to time another affliction not only gave him torturous pain but hampered his movement until his impatience turned to rage.

He developed a varicose ulcer on his thigh, an angry red inflammation that no physician could cure for long and that he tried to treat himself with the "posset for swelling of the legs" listed in the records of his medical remedies.[27] The ulcer was chronic; from an angry local infection it would from time to time spread outward and downward, causing the lower leg to swell and throb with acute pain. More and more of the veins became inflamed, then thrombosed; the exposed nerve endings sent stabs of pain up and down the entire leg, and led to dangerously high fevers.[28]

If his increasing physical ills unsettled Henry his mental stress was at least as troublesome. He had clearly determined the course he meant to take, to divorce Katherine and marry Anne, and he believed in the

rightness of his decision under divine judgment and human logic. Yet the
years had passed and rightness had not yet prevailed. There were too
many forces inimical to divine judgments, too many voices eager to
confound human logic. Relativist arguments pulled at Henry from many
sides, shaking (though not dislodging) his confidence and forcing him to
rethink, reformulate and defend his position time and again. As in his
youth, he worked into the words of his songs the thoughts that weighed on
him.

> But love is a thing given by God,
> In that therefore can be none odd,
> But perfect in deed and between two;
> Wherefore, then, should we it eschew?[29]

His desire to make Anne queen seemed on one level such a simple and
natural thing; why was it that so few others saw it as he did? The candid,
boyish man in Henry grew more and more bewildered even as the shrewd,
perceptive politician in him weighed his opponents' motives and plotted
his counter-moves. His strategy did not falter. The pope issued threats
against him; he responded by calling Clement ignorant or guilty of
simony, and by threatening to settle the nullity suit within England in
despite of papal authority.[30] The emperor spoke of war in defense of
Katherine; Henry announced he was displeased with Charles' haughti-
ness and was thinking of recalling his ambassador from the imperial court.
The powers of Catholic Europe stood against him; he sought allies among
the forces of religious opposition, the followers of Martin Luther.

Yet his resolute belligerence masked an underlying tension. When he
learned that Luther had decided to support Katherine, Henry began to
suffer from insomnia. He was reported to be wakeful at night, even more
tormented than usual by headaches and restlessness. For some days he
was "ill in bed in consequence of the grief and anger he had lately gone
through."[31]

Henry's body was betraying the torment of his mind, a torment he
revealed to Du Bellay in January of 1530. The king took the ambassador
into his cabinet, "where his books are," and kept him there for more than
four hours, talking over his situation. What Henry revealed to the
Frenchman was not free from calculation, but the impression he made
was authentic. "In substance," Du Bellay wrote afterward, "he plainly
confesses that he finds himself in such perplexity that he can no longer
live in it."[32]

30

Thus pray all the citizens, wife, child, and man,
God save King Henry, and his Spouse Queen Anne!

ANNE Boleyn's coronation procession wound its way through London in May of 1533 to the sound of glorious music. In her open litter of shimmering white cloth of gold, under a golden canopy hung with silver bells Anne was carried through the streets of the capital amid singing and playing sweeter than any within memory. At Gracechurch Apollo and the nine muses, seated in a pageant as if "among the mountains, sitting on the mount of Parnassus," played sweetly to her on their instruments. At the Leadenhall a child sang a long ballad in her honor as another pageant unfolded, in which an angel descended from the "heavenly roof" of a castle to crown a white falcon—Anne's device—while Saint Anne watched nearby. Choirs saluted Anne with "great melody" at several points throughout the city, and there was "marvellous sweet harmony both of song and instrument." On the roof of St. Martin's Church a large choir of men and boys sang new ballads written in praise of Anne, while at the conduit in Fleet Street the air was filled with "chimes melodiously sounding." Here too a spectacle had been erected, a town with four turrets, from each of which came such music "that it seemed to be an heavenly noise, and was much regarded and praised."

The lavish outpourings of songs and pageantry were more than matched by the visual spectacle—the houses and shopfronts hung with velvet and cloth of tissue and rich tapestries, the resplendent blue and violet and scarlet liveries of Anne's attendants, the bright clothing of the Londoners who choked the streets and crowded balcony windows to see the new queen pass. The center of attention was Anne herself, resplendent in white robes bordered with royal ermine, her luxuriant black hair crowned with a coif and a circlet of rare jewels.

To the Londoners who came to gape at her on that May afternoon the sight of Anne Boleyn paraded past them as their rightful queen must have been little short of amazing. Rarely if ever in English history had a knight's daughter risen to such an eminence so quickly. Never had a royal mistress, no matter how beloved of the king, supplanted a reigning queen. And no queen within memory had worn to her coronation festivities the loose gowns and broad stomachers of a woman with child.

Seen in retrospect Anne's exaltation had proceeded by logical steps—first her assumption of precedence over Katherine at court functions, then in 1532 her creation as marquess of Pembroke, and her presence at the king's side as his consort on his excursion to Calais to meet the French king. To be sure, there had been talk of marriage between them for six years. Norfolk told Chapuys that only his opposition and that of Anne's father had prevented the king from marrying Anne early in 1532; many believed the wedding would surely take place once the couple was in France, where no popular uprisings could mar the celebration. As it happened, the marriage was celebrated, in the utmost secrecy, late in January of 1533, with only Anne's immediate family, two of her intimate women friends and a priest from her diocese present.[1]

It was nearly three months after her marriage that Anne first appeared in public in royal state. On Easter morning trumpeters heralded her as she went to mass, dressed in cloth of gold and decked with a rich freight of jewels—Katherine's jewels. Norfolk's daughter held the long train of her regal gown as she entered the church, and sixty young ladies attended her, and if all this pomp were inadequate to indicate her new status the king's preachers provided the ultimate proof. In their prayers for the king and the queen they substituted Anne's name for Katherine's, acknowledging in the sight of God a transition about to be completed in law.[2]

Just at this time Henry's new archbishop of Canterbury, Thomas Cranmer, was beginning proceedings which were meant to put an end to the controversy over the king's relationship to Katherine once and for all. On May 23 their marriage was pronounced invalid, and shortly afterward a second judgment held that Henry's marriage to Anne was legal and binding. A papal judgment had, after all, been circumvented. Henry had determined to let his English archbishop stand as final arbiter of his conscience.[3]

It was one thing to change Anne's legal status; it was another to wring respect for her from courtiers who for years had shown, at best, an insincere deference to Anne for her royal lover's sake. At her Eastertide appearance Henry was reported to be "very watchful" of his courtiers' reactions, searching their faces for signs of disapproval, and afterward he "begged the lords to go and visit and make their court to the new queen."[4] In the next weeks he went ahead to complete the outward changes marking Katherine's dispossession, appointing Anne's household officials and hearing their oaths of loyalty to the new queen, ordering Katherine's arms stripped from the royal barge so that it could be readied for Anne to ride in to her coronation, even ordering Katherine's arms removed from the stone gate of the great hall at Westminster—an ignominy heretofore reserved for traitors to the crown.[5] But at every stage Henry paused to read the temper of his court, for there were many who privately frowned on his second marriage, and some whose disapproval took forthright and even violent form.

In her years as Henry's sweetheart Anne had alienated most of the leading men and women of the court, and was frequently at odds with the blood relatives who at one time had been her staunchest supporters. Her insults drove Henry Guildford to resign his offices. She failed to gain the loyalty of her aunt, Norfolk's wife, who remained so staunch a defender of Katherine's rights that she refused to attend Anne's coronation. Anne's sarcasm and hauteur so offended Norfolk and her father that they exchanged harsh words with her more than once, but it was Suffolk who proved to be the most bitter opponent of Anne and her faction.

Charles Brandon had long opposed Henry's plan to make Anne his queen, and in 1530, after bringing the king a story about Anne's illicit relations with another courtier, he was sent away to his country estates. Anne fumed and nursed her anger against Brandon for a long time, then relented and allowed Henry to send for him again. But the enmity was renewed in April of 1532, this time because of "opprobrious language" spoken against Anne by Brandon's wife Mary. Norfolk took it upon himself to avenge Anne's honor and, calling together some twenty of his hired followers, he ordered them to assault Suffolk's men within the sanctuary of Westminster. It was all Henry could do to restrain Suffolk from joining in person the brawl that resulted, and for weeks afterward the courtiers talked of little but the spectacular clash of factions. As often happened, Anne had the last word; she accused Brandon of seducing his own daughter.[6]

That the woman who had so brazenly put not only the royal household but the entire court in turmoil should actually become queen seemed almost beyond belief. Against the advice of his councilors, in despite of Katherine's rights, heedless of the views of his subjects and of the threatened menace of the pope, King Henry had made Anne his queen, and meant to have her crowned. "All the world is astonished at it, for it looks like a dream," a contemporary wrote, "and even those who take her part know not whether to laugh or cry."[7]

To those of Anne's subjects who lined the streets to watch her coronation procession the dream seemed a nightmare. How could they pay the king's harlot the homage due a queen? They ridiculed her dress, her person, the litter in which she rode and the unbecoming crown with which Archbishop Cranmer crowned her. Not a few laughed aloud as she passed, though many more greeted her with cold stares. The customary cry of welcome, *"Dieu garde la reine"*—"God save the queen"—was heard not at all, and when one of Anne's servants asked the lord mayor to teach his citizens better manners he answered sharply that he could not command people's hearts, any more than the king could. It was left to Anne's fool—a witty woman who was much traveled and spoke several languages—to defend her mistress with sarcasm. Seeing how few of the onlookers took off their hats to the queen, she called out, "I think you all have scurvy heads, and dare not uncover!"[8]

The popular disfavor shown at Anne's coronation climaxed years of persistent public disdain for the king's favorite. If Henry's courtiers held Anne in low esteem his commoners roundly hated her. In private and sometimes in public they referred to her as "a common stewed whore," "a goggle-eyed whore," "a whore and a harlot." Laborers, tradespeople, housewives and clerics spoke with equal vehemence against the "scandal of Christendom," with the women crying out loudest of all.[9] Royal representatives who came to Oxford to advance the nullity suit were driven away by angry women armed with large stones. A preacher in Salisbury who spoke in favor of the king's suit was hissed and shouted down by his parishioners, and had to be rescued before he "suffered much at the hands of women."[10] In St. Paul's in London a woman delivered a pointed response to a sermon in favor of the divorce. The preacher was in error, she said. Worse than that: he lied. The king's bad example in casting off his true wife would destroy the healthful and restraining bonds of matrimony among his subjects; he ought not to be encouraged but chastised.[11]

The popular view of the king's proceedings was rooted in common-sense rationality. What Henry did his subjects might be expected to do; his morality defined the moral bounds for others. His claim to be acting according to the dictates of his conscience was not taken seriously, Chapuys wrote. Instead the people hinted at the king's "evil destiny," and told one another that he was impelled by forces far stronger than conscience to act against his own best interests.[12]

Here rationality ceased and popular lore asserted itself. Prophecies foretelling the fate of England in allegorical language had been preserved among the common people since the Middle Ages. Books of such prophecies were cherished possessions among the literate, to be brought out and read aloud to friends around the hearth fire. The meaning of these densely obscure texts was rarely evident at first hearing, but self-appointed interpreters were always at hand. Thus when a prisoner in Colchester jail was questioned in 1532 about the prophecies he was spreading he explained that they came from one William Harlock (who got them from his employer, a "doctor of physic and astronomy") and that he had easily found help in deciphering their messages.

"The White Hare shall drive the Fox to the Castle of Care," the prisoner learned from Harlock, "and the White Greyhound shall run under the root of an oak, and there shall be such a gap in the West that all the thorns of England shall have work enough to stop it." A Somerset man told the prisoner this plainly meant there would be a great battle among priests. A Taunton goldsmith had another interpretation, relating this prophecy to another concerning the Dreadful Dragon who was coming to land with the Bare-legged Hens. Both messages foretold an Irish invasion, the goldsmith said. To others the saying indicated "much trouble" in the years to come, possibly even the death of the king.[13]

In about 1530 one prediction was creating much concern among the people. At about this time, the prophecy ran, the kingdom was to be destroyed by a woman. The story gained greater credence as Anne's status rose, until by the time of her coronation in 1533 the people were said to be "greatly agitated" at the prospect of her reign.[14]

A series of recent marvels on earth and in the heavens gave occult confirmation to their fears. A dead fish of a size and kind never before seen—a monstrosity some ninety feet long—was beached on the northern coast. Next, on the day Henry and Anne embarked for Calais, a second wonder occurred. The tide flowed in for nine straight hours, and the Thames rose higher than ever before, to the very steps of Greenwich

Chapel. Shortly afterward a ball of fire "the size of a human head" was seen to fall from the sky near Greenwich, while for weeks a comet, its long tail "in the form of a luminous silver beard," was visible for two hours before daybreak. "The English consider these things prodigies," the Venetian ambassador noted; certainly they created an unsettled climate for the installation of the new queen.[15]

In the weeks following Anne's coronation Henry was exultant. For better or worse he had taken his destiny into his own hands, ending the unendurable cycle of false hopes, fresh starts, and endless delays in Rome. He had made the woman he loved his queen, and within months the greatest desire of his adult life would be fulfilled. His queen would bear his son.

"I never saw the king merrier than he is now," John Russell wrote from the country house where Henry and his attendants were staying, "and there is the best pastime in hunting red deer." Everywhere the royal party went in that summer of 1533 the hospitality seemed lavish, the talk bright and the good cheer inviting. Anne was in excellent health, and past the time when she might miscarry. Her child was alive within her, and gave promise of a timely and safe birth. To protect Anne from strain Henry did no business in her presence, often meeting with his advisers at some distance from the house where he was staying. When bad news arrived from Rome at the end of July he arranged a division of the household, leaving Anne comfortably settled at Windsor and taking his remaining followers to a smaller house. He told Anne he was going hunting; in fact he summoned his councilors and theologians and held hours of talks, setting them to work on the issue of his worsening relations with the pope.[16]

Clement VII issued a sentence of excommunication against Henry on July 11. The document was final and unconditional, but the pope held out one last opportunity for reconciliation. If the king changed his mode of life and took Katherine back the sentence would not be declared, he wrote; he waited in vain for a response from England.

The excommunication was not the only dark cloud on the horizon. The sweating sickness broke out near where the royal party was staying. Two of Henry's household officers died, and his physician and several others fell ill. At once the king and his chamber servants moved to a private house, where fortunately no sign of the sickness appeared.[17] There were other annoyances as well. Dispatches from abroad carried news of Henry's changed image in the imaginations of foreigners. In Flanders he was pictured as a pathetic dupe, deceived by "diabolic illusions" and shackled by the unworthy object of his passion. "The king is abused by the new queen," the Flemish said, "and his gentlemen goeth daily a-playing where they will, and his grace abides by her all the day long, and dare not go out for the rumor of the people."[18]

In fact the Flemings were wide of the mark, for Henry and Anne had quarreled. She had complained of his flirtations, and he had answered harshly. He had made her what she was, he said, and he could break her again. She had better accustom herself to his infidelities, "as her betters had done"—a stinging reminder that Katherine, despite her loss of status, was of higher birth and more genteel manners than her successor.

Katherine had by now become an echo of the past. Henry had come to terms with his continued mistreatment of her in the only way he knew: by erecting barriers of distance and silence and indifference between them. She was kept far from court, in remote and uncomfortable quarters, with only a few of her most loyal servants to attend her. Henry never spoke of her unless compelled to in the course of a diplomatic audience; in his presence she was referred to now as "princess dowager," the title appropriate to her as the king's widowed sister-in-law. (Throughout her life Katherine refused to renounce her title of queen.)

Henry appeared to care nothing for Katherine or her welfare, yet he went out of his way to avoid a final meeting with her. Once he resolved to separate himself from her permanently in July of 1531, he sent word to the palace where she was staying ordering her to move elsewhere in anticipation of his arrival. They never met again. (Later that year the king and queen occupied the same country estate for a time, but dined in separate chambers.[19]) In a similar way Henry had avoided a final meeting with Wolsey. The cardinal came to see him for the last time at Grafton in September of 1529. Wolsey was told, on Henry's orders, that the king was out hunting and would see him later, in London; the two never met again. In both cases the outwardly tough, inwardly emotional king spared himself the anguish of saying goodbye.

Queen Anne formally "took her chamber" in August to await her delivery. After hearing mass on the appointed day she was escorted to her apartments by the principal courtiers, who left her in the hands of her women to face her ordeal. From now until her labor was over Anne would see only women; the male butler, sewer, ushers and yeomen of her household were temporarily replaced by women who busied themselves about the dark chambers readying all for the birth of the king's son.

According to ordinances written by Henry's grandmother Margaret Beaufort decades earlier the queen's birth chamber was to be thickly carpeted, with all the windows save one covered by opaque hangings. The mother was to lie between sheets of soft lawn, resting her head on down pillows, while the bed was to be covered with scarlet counterpanes bordered with ermines and cloth of gold. Two cradles were made ready for the royal infant, one of wood gilded with fine gold, the other a cradle of estate, upholstered in cloth of gold with blue velvet furnishings.

Henry had provided the most beautiful bed in the kingdom for his son to be born in. Once given for the ransom of the duc d'Alençon, it was one of the "richest and most triumphant" beds ever seen, a masterpiece of carving and embroidery and elaborate ornamentation. Henry had less luck in providing christening robes for the child. He ordered Katherine to give up the robes Princess Mary had worn at her christening, but she refused, and the demand was not pressed. A new christening mantle was made for Anne's child of crimson cloth of gold, its long train and furred collar symbols of the infant's regal status.

As he waited out the final days of Anne's pregnancy Henry consulted with the astrologers and physicians he had brought to court. They all reassured him again and again that the child would be a strong, healthy boy, and approved the names he had chosen for the prince—either Edward or Henry. The birth of a prince called for jousts of celebration, and Henry ordered his horse master and armorers to spare no expense in arranging a lavish spectacle. Anne's friends and relatives, hoping to make a brave showing at these festivities, sent to Flanders for strong warhorses and bought new finery for the banquets and masques.

To the king's annoyance, a minor scandal surrounding Charles Brandon threatened to overshadow the arrival of the heir to the throne. Brandon had become a widower in June, and almost before his mourning robes were ready he announced his intention to marry again. His bride was to be none other than fourteen-year-old Catherine Willoughby, an heiress until recently betrothed to his son. The shameful haste of his remarriage, the age and past attachments of the bride all gave rise to gossip, and as they listened for an announcement from the queen's apartments the courtiers whispered over Brandon's gallantry and looked forward to his wedding.

On the morning of September 7, as Anne Boleyn lay in labor in her high carved bed, Catherine Willoughby became duchess of Suffolk. That afternoon, between three and four o'clock, the child Henry had waited nearly seven years to see and hold was born. To his great surprise, it was a girl.

V

The Mouldwarp

31

The hunt is up, the hunt is up.
The masters of art and doctors of divinity
Have brought this realm out of a good unity.

A YEAR and a half after the birth of Anne Boleyn's child a young Middlesex priest, Robert Feron, recalled in great detail a conversation he had with the vicar of Isleworth John Hale. The two men met frequently to talk over the state of the church and the country, and one afternoon, as they were "walking to and fro," Hale delivered himself of a thundering indictment against King Harry.

"Since the realm of England was first a realm, was there never in it so great a robber and piller of the commonwealth read of nor heard of as is our king," Hale said with vehemence. "And not only we, that be of the spirituality, by his wrongs be oppressed and robbed of our livings as if we were his utter enemies, enemies to Christ, and guilty of his death, but also thus ungoodly he doth handle innocents, and also highly learned and virtuous men—not only robbing them of their livings and spoiling them of their goods, but also thrusting them into perpetual prison, so that it is too great pity to hear, and more to be lamented than any good Christian man's ears may abide."

In his heretical cruelty Henry was clearly bent on destroying the church utterly, Hale went on, while at the same time he impoverished the nobility, using their wealth to build the towering palaces in which he "enjoyed and used his foul pleasures." The king's private life was mired in vice. "If thou wilt deeply look upon his life, thou shalt find it more foul and more stinking than a sow, wallowing and defiling herself in any filthy place," the vicar insisted. "For how great soever he is, he is fully given to his foul pleasure of the flesh and other voluptuousness." The king had violated nearly every woman in his court, neglecting his wife and tarnishing the sanctity of marriage; to crown his offenses he had "taken to his wife of fornication this matron Anne, not only to the highest shame and undoing of himself, but also of all this realm."

Hale not only denounced his king's behavior, he condemned Henry's very conception of his royal power. "In a marvellous fashion he boasteth himself to be above and to excel all other Christian kings and princes," the vicar said. The king's manifold sins called for contrition and humility; instead Henry was "puffed with vain glory and pride," and persisted in his crimes even though, as Hale believed, three out of four of his subjects had turned against him, and he faced imminent invasion from Ireland and Wales.

A tyrant's death was the only fitting end to such villainy, Hale told Feron, and he wished on Henry the fate of King John of evil memory, who died as his rebellious barons seized his lands, or of Richard III, "sometime usurper of this imperial realm," killed ignominiously in battle on Bosworth Field. "Until the king and the rulers of this realm be plucked by the pates," Hale concluded, "we shall never live merrily in England; which I pray God may chance and now shortly to come to pass."[1]

The first of Hale's accusations—that Henry was robbing the clergy and destroying the church—was one few clerics would have quarreled with, at least privately. A recent series of statutes had radically altered the shape and nature of the English church, severing its time-honored ties to Rome and to the pope and making the clergy subject to the king in spiritual as well as secular matters. In 1532 the First Act of Annates forbade the English prelates to send to Rome the first year's income from their sees, a practice in force for hundreds of years, while in the following year the Act in Restraint of Appeals denied that the bishop of Rome had any more authority in England than any other foreign bishop. The autonomy of the clergy in making laws, judging spiritual cases and electing bishops and abbots was abolished; in the Act of Supremacy the king's absolute, unchallenged headship of the church was declared. Henry became "the only supreme head in earth of the church of England," with "full power and authority over all such errors, heresies, abuses, offenses, contempts and enormities, what soever they be."

Inseparable from these sweeping changes was the final legal settlement of the succession. With papal power nullified Parliament passed the Act of Succession making Anne Boleyn's child heir to the throne and requiring all royal subjects to swear an oath to uphold the new dynasty. Narrowly defined, the Succession Act called for nothing more than a simple affirmation of loyalty to the royal line. Yet the oath meant more than this: implicitly, those who swore loyalty to the offspring of the Boleyn marriage denied the pope and accepted royal headship of the church.

That the transformation of the church became intertwined with dynastic interests was a fact of great import for England's future as well as for the future of the reign. In England, religious reform and the security of the monarchy were henceforth one. Henry VIII's subjects had to choose between pope and king, and the few who sided with the pope had to be sacrificed, for to side against the king was treason.

The roots of these changes ran back at least to 1531, when in the wake of Wolsey's fall the entire body of the clergy was accused of violating medieval laws restricting papal power to appoint churchmen and to judge cases in canon law. Even earlier than this Henry had not only spoken out strongly against the clerical establishment but had begun to formulate a new concept of his role within it. During 1530 and 1531, as he supervised the work of the scholarly emissaries he sent to gather texts on the nullity suit from continental libraries, the king carefully studied another collection of passages. These texts, compiled by a group of court scholars perhaps headed by Edward Foxe, provided support for the argument that England was an autonomous realm and, on that account, immune from papal authority. This theory buttressed two companion ideas that were much in Henry's thoughts during these years: that as king he had a God-given responsibility for the souls of his subjects, and that inhering in his crown was an ultimate, ultra-royal sovereignty—an imperial power—which made him supreme in both church and state within his domain.[2]

For several years these notions went no further. Henry continued to hope for a papal judgment nullifying his marriage to Katherine, and held back from precipitating an irreversible breach with Rome. He did, however, advance to power in his service a man whose thoroughgoing ideas of reform reflected his own impatient urge for a radical solution to his dilemma.

Thomas Cromwell rose swiftly to hold a succession of court offices after 1530, becoming master of the jewels, then privy councilor, master of the king's wards, chancellor of the exchequer and finally, in 1534, principal royal secretary—his preferred fulcrum of political leverage. By this time it was being said that the king's new chief servant had been granted as much authority as Wolsey once possessed (though Cromwell never achieved Wolsey's degree of influence with Henry), and his role in drafting the key reform statutes of the 1530s made him the central figure in the politics of that momentous decade.

Save in his expanding girth and phenomenal intellect, Cromwell was in fact unlike his former master Wolsey in every respect. Where Wolsey had been carefully schooled Cromwell was self-taught, with a voracious eagerness to learn that drove him, despite his governmental labors, to learn Italian, French, Latin and a little Greek. On a long journey to Italy he diverted his mind and edified his spirit by memorizing the entirety of Erasmus' Latin New Testament. Cromwell had none of Wolsey's dazzling ostentation; though Henry rewarded him with abundant wealth he lived during the early years of his power in a large house more suited to a successful merchant than a royal secretary.[3] Where Wolsey had been a worldly churchman in the medieval mold, Cromwell was deeply, resolutely anticlerical, though along with his hatred of the clergy went a profound piety that had much in common with the teachings of Luther and the other reformers.

Of greater immediate importance to the king was that Cromwell brought to the tasks of government the dispassionate, calculating eye of an accountant and lawyer. Wolsey's policies had cost Henry countless sums; Cromwell was responsible for even more far-reaching innovations, but made the solvency of the royal treasury a paramount concern.

The stolid, almost porcine portraits of Thomas Cromwell reveal his shrewd intelligence but do scant justice to the many-sidedness of his personality. By his own admission he had been a wild and unruly youth—a "ruffian," he called himself—and carried a residue of tough, hearty unconventionality into adulthood. Expecting Cromwell to stay at his house in York in 1537, Norfolk offered him every comfort. "And if ye lust not to dally with my wife," the duke wrote, he had "a young woman with pretty proper tetins" to offer the royal secretary.[4] Cromwell spoke well, and pointedly. His banter was admired by an exacting judge of wit, Chapuys, and the ambassador noted how Cromwell's normally controlled features would come alive during a conversation, his eyes adding subtleties of expression to his words.

Cromwell was indeed an excellent foil for his royal master—an individualist who shared Henry's physicality as well as his view of affairs. Though he worked so hard that his friends warned of illness from "overmuch paining his body and cumbering his wits," the secretary enjoyed a good deal of recreation, taking particular pleasure in his hawks. He hunted with the king in summer and fall—he was an excellent shot with the longbow—and played bowls and gambled with him at other times. They took mutual pleasure when events were to their liking. In October of 1534 news reached the English court that Clement VII, Henry's longtime nemesis, was dead. The king and Cromwell reacted with immense satisfaction, and the secretary could not restrain himself from saying publicly "that this great devil was dead," and looking as if he would gladly have used a more insulting term than devil.[5] (The people of Rome, whose own view of the pope was even more bitterly hostile, refused to let Clement's corpse rest in peace. They broke open his tomb and stabbed his lifeless body, dragging it along the ground by a hook.)

If Henry held in mind ideas of clerical reform, immunity from papal jurisdiction, and personal headship of the church long before Cromwell's tenure in power began, still it was Cromwell who brought these ideas clearly into focus and translated them into policy. It was an outgrowth of the secretary's genius that the strictly religious changes in the Reformation statutes were embedded in a broader general theory of sovereignty, and that both were brought into being in a way that redefined the governmental role of Parliament as the natural arena of royal legislation. A new bond was formed between king and Parliament in the 1530s, a bond fateful for the direction of English government and for the growth of the monarchy. Much that was old remained, but the transformation to which Cromwell was midwife revitalized the Tudor state and exalted Henry to unprecedented authority.[6]

The scope of these events was hidden from Vicar Hale, who saw in them nothing more than criminal tyranny and equated them with the king's other enormities. Prominent among these was Henry's fleshly appetite and taste for "foul pleasures." By the mid-1530s the scandalous circumstances under which Henry had ended his first marriage had long since lent him a reputation for amorous excess. His infidelity to Anne increased this reputation, until references to the king's fondness for women became as much a commonplace of diplomatic correspondence as it was of court gossip. Henry "caused a number of beautiful ladies to come to the court" in honor of the French admiral's visit in 1534; he was "more given to matters of dancing and of ladies than he ever was," Chapuys reported shortly afterward; it was well known, Charles V wrote to his ambassador, that Henry was "of amorous complexion."[7] The mere mention of a girl's name in the king's presence called forth a comment on her fairness or plainness; that this indicated more than a heightened aesthetic awareness seems probable from Norfolk's testimony that Henry was "continually inclined to amours."[8]

Fear or discretion must have made Henry's subjects reluctant to commit to writing what they may have known of his royal lust, but there were whispered hints at wholesale lechery. Hale heard from the porter at Syon that "our sovereign lord had a short of maidens over one of his chambers at Farnham"—perhaps a royal brothel.[9] And a sanctuary man (almost certainly a criminal) of Westminster told of hearing one William Webbe swear that the king had abducted his mistress in broad daylight.

Webbe was out riding near Eltham, his "pretty wench" behind him. They encountered Henry, who "plucked down her muffler and kissed her, and liked her so well that he took her from him." It was said the girl was still with the king, and Webbe, who had sworn vengeance on his sovereign, was desperately telling his story to anyone who would listen.[10]

How much Hale exaggerated in condemning Henry's sexual sins must remain conjectural, given the slenderness of the surviving evidence. Another of his criticisms, though, touched a central theme in the king's character in these years. In saying that Henry saw himself as exalted above other rulers and was "puffed with vain glory and pride," the vicar put in crude terms a significant shift in personality.

In his thirties Henry had begun to take on the lineaments of mature kingship, showing more than a hint of his masterful father's sense of command. Now in his forties he had gained a new plateau of authority, all the more formidable in that it drew its strength from a unique font of inner conviction.

In the crucible of the divorce years Henry had developed an unshakable faith in the reliability of his own intelligence and judgment, a sense of certitude that enabled him to stand firm against the opposition that encircled him. While he never lost sight of the weight of expert opinion—hoping, as he said, to "conquer by numbers as well as by justice and truth"—still he placed greatest reliance on his personal discrimination. He was right, he declared, "not because so many say it, but because he, being learned, knoweth the matter to be right."[11] An inventory of Henry's jewels in 1535 listed a gold bracelet bearing the enameled inscription *"plus tôt morir que changer ma pensée"*—"to die rather than change my mind."[12]

This certitude matured during the era of the breach with Rome—just at the time Cromwell was drafting the ringing preamble to the Act in Restraint of Appeals with its reference to England's "one Supreme Head and King having the dignity and royal estate of the imperial Crown." The act accorded Henry "plenary, whole, and entire power, pre-eminence, authority, prerogative, and jurisdiction." From one standpoint it put him on a level of unquestionable, all but infallible power—an aggrandizement unique in English history.

The exaltation of the monarchy, the assumption of headship of the church, the vocabulary of imperial dignity set a special seal on Henry's inner certainty, as if God and Parliament were backing his sense of rightness. Buoyed by these heady supports, he thought more and more of his place in the world and in history, envisioning both in grandiose terms.

In discussing with Chapuys his grievances against Charles V, Henry took the tone of an injured giant consoled by the assurance of vindication on a Europe-wide scale. The recollection of these grievances "caused him great trouble and almost illness," Henry said, yet "it was enough for him that the world knew his wrongs." Not long afterward he gave a lavish banquet, and as he ate and drank, surrounded by his courtiers and foreign visitors, he boasted of the amazing religious changes he was bringing to the realm. "He would make such a reformation," Henry said exultantly, "that in the end he should be eternally remembered in all Christendom."[13]

The more expansive he became the more Henry distanced himself from those around him. Convinced that he was by nature different from other men, endowed with insight and discernment far beyond the common, Henry heeded less the voices of his councilors and allowed his kingly instincts to guide him. "God has not only made us king by inheritance," he wrote in 1536, "but has given us wisdom, policy, and other graces in most plentiful sort, necessary for a prince to direct his affairs by to his honor and glory."[14]

Yet if in his own eyes the king was sublimely purposeful and rational, to others he was increasingly bewildering, full of contradictions and inclined to caprice. His conscience seemed to follow a logic all its own. His policy toward other rulers was a puzzling amalgam of chivalrous boast and shrewd inaction. Francis I, on good terms with Henry in the mid-1530s, called him "the hardest friend to bear in the world—at one time unstable, at another time obstinate and proud, so that it is almost impossible to bear with him." At the height of his impatience Francis dismissed Henry as a self-satisfied dupe who "thinks himself very wise, but is nothing more than a fool." In sum, though, the French king found Henry a baffling enigma, quite simply "the strangest man in the world."[15]

Cromwell was occasionally exasperated to the point of collapse by his master's childish irrationality. When in the spring of 1536 prolonged discussions of relations between England and the empire failed to lead to enlightened policy-making the secretary "took to his bed from pure sorrow," and pronounced a wistful judgment on all royal personalities. "Princes have spirits or properties," he said, "which are hidden and unknown to all others."[16]

Reginald Pole, a longtime supporter of the king turned opponent by England's repudiation of the pope, saw well his royal cousin's dilemma. What Henry needed was to listen to the forthright criticism of well-meaning advisers, Pole said. Henry must be shown his faults, clearly and without regard to his pride or his power of revenge. Pole himself had undertaken the task of undeceiving the king in a harshly critical treatise attacking Henry's policies and personal life; had he not done so, he remarked despairingly, who else would have?

That Pole's treatise went unheeded was cause for concern, for as Henry went ahead it became more and more clear that his inner compass had gone awry.

32

These blodye dayes have brokyn my hart;
My lust, my youth dyd then departe
And blynd desyer of astate;
Who hastis to clyme sekes to reverte.

ON the morning of the twenty-second of June, 1535, crowds gathered at the Tower in the courtyard where, fourteen years earlier, the duke of Buckingham had been executed. They had come to witness another death, one many of them found impossible to imagine. John Fisher, the frail, seventy-six-year-old bishop of Rochester, was to give up his life by the king's command.

Workmen were still erecting the scaffold when Fisher rode into view, a shrunken figure in a black cloth vest and cap, withered with age and so emaciated from his months in the Tower that he seemed "more like a shadow than a man." He had awaited the day of his execution in dread ever since Cromwell informed him of it, telling him at the same time that the pope had made him a cardinal. Now he had still longer to wait, for the workmen were at their task for another hour, and the old man was kept sitting astride his mule, watching in heavy silence as they prepared the arena of his suffering.

This day would bring to an end more than two years of painful imprisonment. During his tenure in the Tower Fisher had endured the dual agonies of age and confinement. His delicate stomach refused the rank food the jailer brought him; he shivered even at midday in the damp and cold of his cell; ill-fed and weak from exposure he "fell into decay and diseases of his body," and could not care for himself. "I have neither shirt nor sheet nor yet other clothes that are necessary for me to wear," he wrote to Cromwell in his wretchedness, "but that be ragged and rent too shamefully. Notwithstanding, I might easily suffer that if they would keep my body warm."[1]

If he shivered now in the cold morning air the bishop disguised it well, for his voice was clear and bold as he spoke to the crowd after mounting the scaffold. He told them to love the king and obey him, "for he was good by nature," though mistaken in his religious policies. Of his own deeds he said little but that he was condemned to die for wishing to preserve the honor of God and the Holy See. Looking out over the upturned faces of the men and women below him—many of them the same people who had come "in great grief" to demand his blessing when he first entered the Tower—Fisher asked for their prayers. He was only flesh, he told them, and feared death as any man would. He had long since

255

made up his mind to die, if need be, for Christ and his church, yet now that the moment was at hand his body rebelled in terror.

The death Fisher faced was a traitor's death, its fearsomeness compounded by humiliation and butchery. After the headsman finished his work the headless corpse of a traitor was slit open, his bowels drawn out and burned. His remains were then hacked into quarters and hung in the sun to rot, and before his blood dried on the scaffold the makers of charms and potions crowded around to gather it into vessels for safekeeping.

Had he thought of these things Fisher might have lost his nerve, yet he seemed to find the courage to "suffer cheerfully his approaching punishment," as he had hoped. As the onlookers prayed he knelt down with the difficulty of an elderly man, and laid his head on the block, and died.[2]

There was no question that, under English law, Fisher was a traitor. He had not only openly opposed the royal supremacy, he had written to Charles V urging him to invade England and forcibly restore the authority of the pope. Yet because he had acted from conscience, and from a faith so deeply rooted that it commanded awe, Fisher seemed beyond the law. His age, his reputation as "the most holy and learned prelate in Christendom," his cardinalate all made him a grossly inappropriate object of the king's wrath—and no one hesitated to lay the execution directly to Henry's charge. Had Henry not reacted angrily to the news of Fisher's appointment as cardinal, announcing that he would give the bishop "another hat, and send the head afterwards to Rome for the cardinal's hat"?[3] Had Fisher not been a strong supporter of Katherine, and so among Henry's bitterest foes?

Royal enmity toward the old man had been building for years, an enmity so terrible it rode over Henry's tenderer feelings toward Fisher as his boyhood mentor and councilor. Contemporary opinion saw in Fisher's execution not judicial murder justified by state necessity but cruel vengeance, "the most cowardly, grievous and infamous" ever seen. It was not put down to leniency that the aged body, after a period of gruesome public display, was neither disemboweled nor quartered. Nor was Henry thought merciful for ordering the body buried almost at once; surely his intention was not to protect the dead man's dignity but to cheat the relic-hunters of their prizes. The final vengeance, though, belonged to the victim. Fisher's severed head, affixed to London Bridge, remained startlingly lifelike for days, its incorruptibility proof of the slain bishop's holiness.[4]

The outrage that erupted on Fisher's death was fed within days by another equally barbarous execution. Thomas More, the king's personal friend for decades and until 1532 his chancellor, followed Fisher to the scaffold, charged with treasonous refusal to swear assent to the succession. (Like Fisher, More opposed the Succession Act because he construed it to imply denial of papal power.) More was careful to go no further than to refuse the oath; beyond that he was silent. Yet there was no mistaking the impact of his silence, or of the longstanding opposition to the divorce which preceded it. For years More had served as a focal point for such opposition, with only the king's good will standing between him and persecution. In 1535, law and circumstances made his silence intolerable. Anything short of spoken assent was treason. "Though we should have no word or deed to charge upon you," Attorney General Christopher Hales told More at his trial, "yet we have your silence, and that is a sign of your evil intention and a sure proof of malice."[5]

In vain More's wife and children wrote to Henry, reminding him of the ex-chancellor's long and true service, and of the imperatives of conscience which impelled him in his stand. He acted not from malice but from "such a long-continued and deep-rooted scruple as passeth his power to avoid and put away," they wrote, and indeed the king knew well enough what More's scruples were. Years before, the two men had struck a bargain, with Henry assuring More that he would not have to handle what was distasteful to his conscience. More "should look first unto God," Henry said, "and after God unto him." More kept his part of the bargain to the end. Henry, who was hunting at Reading on the day of More's execution, had seen fit to ignore his.[6]

The shock wave that went out across Europe on More's death was as much a measure of the humanist's goodness as of his fame. Accounts of his trial and execution appeared in several languages, and in every European country his admirers recorded their grief in letters remarkable for their depth of feeling. More's candor, his urbanity, his all-pervasive kindness had won him a place in many hearts; men he had never met "lamented him as a parent or brother." "I have myself seen many shed tears for him who had never seen him or had anything to do with him," one humanist wrote from Paris. "My own tears fall unwillingly as I write this."[7]

While in the Tower More had concerned himself chiefly with preparing for death, he told his friends. But the casual writings he left and the notes he made in the margins of his books show broader interests. To lighten his sorrows he wrote songs. (More's enjoyment of singing in the choir once led Norfolk to scold him: "God body, God body, my lord chancellor, a parish clark, a parish clark! You dishonor the king and his office!") One song, "Lewis, the Lost Lover," began with the melancholy line "Fie, flattering fortune, look thou never so fair"; another, "Davy, the Dicer," was more lively.

Most of all More's Tower writings reveal the rare charity of spirit that was the hallmark of his character. Henry was often in his thoughts, yet he was without bitterness toward the man who had befriended him, then coerced him, then dispossessed him and put him at risk of his life. As he meditated on the verses in his prayer book More marked some to be repeated *"Pro rege"*—"For the king"—and apparently remembered Henry often in his devotions. "The king shall joy in his strength, O Lord; and in thy salvation greatly shall he rejoice!" "For the king trusteth in the Lord, and through the mercy of the Most High he shall not be moved," he prayed again and again, kneeling on the stone floor of his cell, until prayer drove out all resentment.[8]

The deaths of More and Fisher in 1535 marked the end of an initial positive stage in the English Reformation. In the first half of the decade

English men and women had in large part tolerated the alterations wrought by parliamentary statute, though in the north acceptance was much less widespread. Though the Commons had opposed the divorce, they embraced the break with Rome and the assault on clerical independence with remarkable compliance. Older views ascribing their acquiescence to political coercion have been discarded; it now appears that king and Commons alike viewed the church as a "shabby incubus" in need of radical reform.[9]

Among the populace at large there was much outspoken hostility toward the clergy and blasphemous contempt for sacred things. "Nearly all the people here hate the priests," Chapuys had written in 1529, and indeed the heavy taxation, the moral and material corruption of the clergy gave abundant cause for resentment.[10] Lollard doctrines centuries old rejecting the pope, the priests and the sacraments were reasserting themselves, adding to the religious tempest blown up by preachers of reform. Given every encouragement by Cromwell and by Archbishop Cranmer, a host of articulate evangelists headed by Hugh Latimer held forth against the overelaborate ritual of the church, its superstitious veneration of saints and its doctrine of purgatory. These teachings met with a good deal of counterargument, yet they were if anything less extreme than the anticlerical sentiments to be heard throughout the countryside. In one Sussex village the parishioners disdained holy statues as "idols and mammets," and dismissed the mass as no more meaningful than "the bleating of a cow to her calf." One man slandered the Virgin Mary with particular venom. "If our lady were here in earth," he was heard to say, "I would no more fear to meddle with her than with a common whore."[11]

But if the earlier 1530s had seen broad agreement between king and people on religious issues, by the middle of the decade the momentum of popular favor had ebbed. The deaths of More and Fisher signaled a cresting of opposition to all that the Reformation Parliament had accomplished. Now for every villager who scoffed at the mass there was another loudly proclaiming fidelity to it, and to the pope as well, and in order to contain the wave of reaction a means of enforcement was needed.

The new treason laws provided the legal framework, loyal subjects eager to denounce disloyalty the channel of information. All across the country ordinary men and women listened keenly to their friends, their neighbors, passers-by—even their relatives—to see whether they spoke ill of the king or queen, or criticized the royal supremacy. When evil words were detected, bystanders were called upon to swear to what they had heard. Then the informer went to the nearest knight or lord, who saw to it that the facts reached Cromwell. There were no spies or paid informers, yet the denunciations came in by the hundreds. Proclamations, official declarations, treatises, pamphlets, sermons, even ballads constantly warned the king's subjects of their duty to report treasonous words, and of the penalties they risked if they kept what they heard to themselves. Their response helped to spread a mantle of fear over the realm as Bishop Fisher and Thomas More went to their deaths.

This corrosive fear was fed by rumors of espionage on a grand scale and by the daily fact of arrests and denunciations. In actuality each report that reached Cromwell at court was weighed carefully to screen out accusations rooted in malice. Yet such scrutiny was small comfort to villagers and city-dwellers unnerved by stories of men seized for slight causes and held in prison on even slighter pretexts. "It is rumored," a correspondent wrote to the king's aunt Lady Lisle in 1535, "that a person should be committed to the Tower for saying that this month will be rainy and full of wet, next month, death, and the third month, war. He will be kept there till experience shows the truth of his prophecy."[12]

In their vigilance informers made no exception of words spoken by drunkards or the senile. A servant of the duchess of Northumberland was imprisoned for criticizing the king; he claimed to have been drunk beyond sense, and to have no memory of his offense. He was acquitted of the charge, yet was kept in prison, "in danger of his limbs," until his mistress had to intercede on his behalf.[13] When Cromwell heard that an absent-minded canon nearing his eightieth year had mistakenly prayed for "Katherine the queen" instead of Anne he did not press for punishment, but the bitter words of an "aged and wretched" Worcester husbandman were taken more seriously. Limping homeward through the mud one rainy market day the old man was overheard to curse the king as the cause of the bad weather that had plagued the countryside in recent years. Ever since Henry "began this business," the farmer muttered, the weather had been "troublous and unstable, and I ween we shall never have better weather while the king reigneth, and therefore it maketh no matter if he were knocked or patted on the head."[14]

Similar indifference toward the king's fate was shown by a more unique prisoner. John Bonde had been prior of Barton for sixty years when he came to the attention of the royal examiners for speaking "opprobious words" against the king and queen. They judged him to be over a hundred years old—he had been past his prime when Henry VII was a boy—but though his mind was "much enfeebled" his opinions were firm and critical. Bonde's jailers did not hesitate to seize his modest possessions and to imprison him, but they had no precedent to guide them in punishing so venerable an opponent of the king. They confined him to his house, allowing one servant to see to his needs and making certain he had warm meat and drink and enough firewood to keep off the chill, and then wrote to Cromwell for advice; his reply has been lost.[15]

The Tudor populace feared Cromwell and the spies they imagined him to have; they feared one another; they feared false accusations and excessive punishment. But most of all they feared the wrath of the king. In his fervor to protect his headship of the church Henry was sending holy and good men to their deaths—not only Fisher and More but Carthusian monks, hanged in their religious habits after suffering inhuman tortures in prison. His displeasure—many called it vengeance—seemed limitless. In the end it encompassed even the being he had once held dearer than his wife, his child, his peace of mind: Anne Boleyn.

To say that Henry was exceedingly dismayed at the birth of Elizabeth

Tudor in September of 1533 would far understate the depth of his disappointment. The baby was the culmination of years of eager expectation; it was to crown all of Henry's hopes, and some day to reign after him. The unforeseen arrival of a daughter instead of a son turned these hopes sour, and exposed the king to the mocking ridicule of all those who had opposed his marriage to Anne.

News of the birth of a girl to the queen led many to laugh inwardly at the king's expense. One who could not restrain himself was the bishop of Bath's secretary, who burst out his reaction at the bishop's dinner table. "By our Lord's body," he said with vehemence, "if he had lain with her he would have gotten a boy, or else he would have meddled with her till his eyes did start out of his head!"[16]

Henry's critics, his wife, even God himself had humiliated him—or worse. "God has forgotten him entirely," it seemed to Chapuys, "hardening him in his obstinacy to punish and ruin him." He had been cheated by both natural and supernatural forces, and this despite his longsuffering struggle against the pope, Katherine of Aragon's jurists, the weight of Catholic opinion. When Mary had been born seventeen years earlier the young Henry had made light of his disappointment, assuring solicitous courtiers that sons would surely follow. There was no such lightness now. In middle age the king's horizons were narrowing; what at twenty-five had seemed an infinite margin of time now loomed as a finite span of precious years, years in which his son and heir must be born, nurtured through infancy, trained through childhood to the tasks of rule. There was no time for mistakes. There must be no more daughters.

Henry was not present when Princess Elizabeth was christened in the silver font at Greenwich, and indeed he paid far less attention to his baby daughter than to the progress of Anne's second pregnancy, which followed almost immediately. By January of 1534 the queen was noticeably with child; a silver cradle was ordered for the hoped-for son, with roses entwined about its pillars and gleaming stones set in gold around the rim. The child miscarried, but by the time the royal hunting progress began in June Anne had "a goodly belly" once again, and hope revived briefly. When this third pregnancy too ended abruptly (probably in a miscarriage) Henry exploded in furious frustration.[17]

To distract himself he sought the company of new favorites: the pale, gentle Jane Seymour and another woman—a considerable beauty—whose name has been lost but whose partisan sympathy toward Katherine and Mary helped to improve their lot somewhat in the second half of 1534. Anne fought against these rivals, and against a third royal mistress, Margaret Shelton, whom her Norfolk relatives brought to court to tempt the king early in 1535. Yet the more Anne struggled to hold Henry's favor the more she drove him to others, and slipped further into a quicksand of insecurity. When Anne and her sister-in-law Lady Rochford conspired to send the unnamed beauty away from court the king stepped in and banished Lady Rochford instead. Deprived of her companion, Anne confronted Henry directly, but found him inured to her complaints. She should count herself lucky, he told her, for he had done much for her that "he would not do now if the thing were to begin."[18]

By his flirtations, his irritability, his wounding inattention to his wife Henry made his dissatisfaction clear. He had gone through a great deal to make Anne queen; she had not played her part. Like Katherine before her she appeared to be barren of sons. After two years of marriage, he repented his choice. Courtiers noted that, though she refused to resign herself to her situation, Anne had lost her old "pride and insolence," and now looked anxious and troubled.[19] Her distress would have turned to panic had she known that Henry was seeking an excuse to divorce her.

"Our greatest wish, next to having a son, is to see you again," Anne wrote to the queen of Navarre in 1535. Giving Henry an heir had become her consuming preoccupation, more important than outdistancing her rivals, more important than advancing the interests of her infant daughter. She paced the galleries of Hampton Court restlessly, recalling how in happier days she and Henry (and Lady Boleyn) had come to see the palace and its treasures just after Wolsey's death, full of hope for the future. Now everything around her reminded Anne of failure—the palace itself, the beautiful clothes and furnishings Henry had given her, the verses poets had written her wishing her "a son to be the living image of the king his father." According to a visitor to court Anne was never without a book in her hand—usually a French book—seeking "salutary remedies for this mortal life and consolations for the immortal soul." The songs in her music book too echoed the burden of sorrow she carried.[20]

> Come regrets, come all to my heart,
> Come swiftly, let none of you depart;
> Come care, come sorrow, and come tears,
> Come all that oppresses a lover's heart.

The king's urgent need for a son was underlined in 1535 when negotiations for the betrothal of Princess Elizabeth and a French prince ended in disagreement. Elizabeth had not only disappointed her father by being the wrong sex; doubts about her legitimacy (Cranmer's settlement of the nullity suit was not universally recognized outside England) made her useless to him as a diplomatic pawn as well. Anne became increasingly jealous of Henry's other children. Henry Fitzroy, now grown into "a most handsome, urbane and learned young gentleman" of sixteen, had married Norfolk's only daughter Mary, an alliance calculated to worsen the bad relations between Anne and her uncle. As for Henry's older daughter, no longer Princess Mary but plain "Lady Mary," Anne had long been her sworn enemy. "I am her death and she is mine," she said succinctly. Only one of them could survive the struggle she foresaw, and she meant to be the victor, even if she had to use poison.

Outsiders marveled that Mary and Katherine lived on despite the combined ill effects of confinement, isolation, recurrent sickness and constant fear for their lives. They were kept apart—allegedly because, as Henry said, Katherine might otherwise "raise a number of troops and make war as boldly as her mother Isabella had." They were for the most part kept in ignorance of one another's health and prospects, though each knew only too well the dangers the other faced. Katherine, aging now and growing less resistant to disease, was not expected to live long even if she escaped Anne's vengeance. Mary, who had been subject to chronic illness since adolescence, faded in and out of health though her strength of will remained unconquered. Mary's worst suffering was mental, for beyond her fear of Anne she had to endure extremes of cruel hostility and tempting offers of reconciliation from a father she had never ceased to adore.

By the spring of 1535 Anne was visibly in the grip of her fears. She tried to make light of her husband's infidelities, but her laughter was strained, and she confessed herself to be very near "ruined and lost." She felt she was under constant surveillance, and, what was worse, menaced by occult forces. According to popular prophecy a queen of England was to be burned at the stake; to deflect this fate from herself Anne tried to bring it on Katherine, telling Henry she was a traitor and rebel, more deserving of death than Fisher and More. Anne found an accommodating seer willing to swear to a miraculous vision. It had been revealed to him, he said, that as long as Katherine and Mary lived Anne could not conceive a child.[21]

The stratagem failed, and before too many months had passed Anne's swollen belly belied it. She had conceived again, and this time she had conceived a boy.

On January 8, 1536, Katherine finally died, still professing her love for Henry. Perhaps from callous bad taste, perhaps to brazen out a rush of disturbingly mixed feelings, Henry put on a bright suit of yellow satin and paraded ostentatiously before his courtiers as if rejoicing at the death. Anne too put on a yellow gown, though she remained in the background during the days of jousting and banqueting that followed. As eager as ever to distinguish himself in the lists, Henry ignored his middle-aged stoutness and his slowed reactions and ran course after course in the jousting; inevitably, he had an accident. Riding in full armor against an opponent, he fell to the ground, and seconds later his massive warhorse fell on top of him. For two hours he lay unconscious, while courtiers prayed and knitted their brows and planned what their first move ought to be once the king was pronounced dead.

When Norfolk informed Anne of the mishap, according to one account, she seemed indifferent to Henry's peril. A week later, though, when she miscarried her child she blamed the loss of the baby on the panic she felt at the news (and Norfolk's abrupt announcement of it). Henry's chagrin at the miscarriage turned to barely contained rage when he learned that the infant had "the appearance of a male."[22] Anne had become an intolerable source of frustration to him. Already estranged from her, he now sought to be relieved of her permanently, and to take a new wife.

Anne's fall was swift and dramatic. A royal commission was created to bring forward evidence of treason against her, and within days she and several others were imprisoned in the Tower. Anne was accused of adultery with five men—among them her own brother—and, with her lovers, of "encompassing the king's death." The identity of the five men (all closely tied to the Boleyn faction at court) has led to the suspicion that the accusations were as much the result of political intrigue as of marital disharmony.²³ Yet one fact overrode all: the king needed a male heir, and it seemed certain Anne could not provide one.

After summary trials the queen's convicted lovers—young Francis Weston, Henry's former page, William Brereton, another young man who had risen from page to gentleman of the privy chamber, Anne's brother George Boleyn, Henry's "favorite courtier" Henry Norris, who had been a trusted, intimate member of the royal household for twenty years, and the musician and dancer Mark Smeaton—were executed on May 17. Only one, Smeaton, confessed himself guilty of the crime alleged against him, and that after being put to the rack and tortured with hot irons. Anne swore she was entirely innocent, and showed a pathetic resignation in the face of death.

On May 19, less than a year after Bishop Fisher had mounted the scaffold, the Tower courtyard was once again filled with huge crowds. By one account, two thousand people came to watch Anne Boleyn die, to hear her profess her guiltlessness and announce readiness to "yield herself humbly to the will of the king." They watched as the furred mantle of her gray gown was removed, and her elaborate headdress laid aside. A maid handed her a plain linen cap and she carefully tucked her hair up into it, baring her neck. As she knelt by the block she paused to draw her gown over her feet, then called for a servant to bandage her eyes.

The French swordsman she had summoned from St. Omer struck off her head cleanly, and immediately one of her attendants took it and wrapped it in a white cloth. Anne's remains were buried in the Tower chapel of St. Peter in Chains, and Henry, as ready to note the passing of his second wife as of his first, put on a white suit for mourning.

33

A very grete wretche the mouldwarp sal be;
In every nede fast sal he fle.
And on him sall light, who so right redes,
The vengance of God for ald evill dedes.

IT was in the mid-1530s, the era of religious upheaval, of widespread terror and spectacular public executions, that the legend of Henry VIII took on a life of its own. The contours of that legend are familiar enough: an outsize man, at once stout and formidable, a royal satyr indulging his lusts and decapitating his discarded wives, a tyrannical ruler sweeping aside venerable institutions at his erratic whim. At root it is an image of power unleashed, of dark chthonic forces erupting into light—a Renaissance image of humanity unshackled.

And it is, of course, a grotesque caricature. The legend overlooks much that was vital to Henry's personality—his keen intellectuality, his debonair high spirits, the charm of his manner and the thick patina of chivalry that marked him as very much a product of the medieval past. Like all distillations of personality it is monochromatic: it ignores the lights and shadows of sanguine expectations and underlying fears, it masks a host of evanescent qualities—petulance, gaiety, combativeness, vanity, arrogance, spontaneity, affection, joking candor—that went together to make up the king courtiers and diplomats and household intimates struggled to comprehend. The legend obscures Henry's daring and his restless energy, characteristics Wolsey saw so clearly when he described his master as "a prince of royal courage" who would rather lose half his kingdom than abandon his undertakings.

Holbein's portraits crystallized the Henrician legend in visual form. The king gazes out in imperative splendor, his air of command intensified by the sheer bulk and weight of his broad chest and muscular arms and legs. His impassive, almost mindless expression takes away nothing from the impact of his wrestler's physique. It is an authority that overwhelms by sheer immensity, a majesty of size.

The portrait stereotype conveys a grossness and heaviness of spirit much at odds with Henry's alertness and quicksilver temperament, yet it captures something even more fundamental. To contemporaries the king was, throughout his reign, a superhuman figure, larger than life in person and psyche. In the early years of his reign he had seemed a resplendent, athletic hero; by 1536 he had taken on the appearance of a hulking, vindictive villain. Yet the hero was godlike, the villain monstrous; they were mirror-images alike in exaggeration.

To the country people who saw all events in the timeless light of prophecy and doom, Henry was more than superhuman; he was the dark anti-hero known as the Mouldwarp, whose coming had been foretold by Merlin hundreds of years earlier. According to the verse prophecy the sixth king (Henry was in fact the twelfth) after King John would be the Mole, or Mouldwarp, a hairy man with a hide like goatskin whose fate it was first to be greatly praised by his people, then "cast down with sin and with pride." After his fall the Mouldwarp was to "lead all his life/In war and in trouble and in much strife," condemned by the vengeance of God to wage a losing battle for his kingdom. In the end he would go down to defeat amid scenes of gore and destruction—his castles fallen, the rivers red with the blood of his vanquished armies, the very hills sundered in two with dread—and would flee like a coward to end his life in exile on a lonely island. England would be given over to the Mouldwarp's enemies, and would be known thereafter as "the land of conquest."[1]

Henry seemed to incarnate the Mouldwarp. Beloved by his people in youth, he had been brought low through the sin of his relations with Anne Boleyn and his prideful defiance of the pope. Though neither hairy nor goatlike he had become physically prodigious, a wonder of nature, and like the Mouldwarp of prophecy he faced enemies on every side. Beyond the unrelieved threat of war with France or the Holy Roman Empire— currently preoccupied with their own conflict—he had to contend with the everpresent menace of the Scots on the northern border and in particular with rebellion in Ireland. England might indeed become a "land of conquest"; invasion was more than a remote possibility, it was an imminent danger.

That Henry's subjects should apply the timeworn vision of the Mouldwarp to the king they had once adored as Great Harry was a measure of Henry's changing image in their eyes. Adoration had turned to disillusionment, then revulsion, and if the English never lost sight of their ruler as a vice-ridden man ("as for the king," one of them said in 1537, "an apple and a fair wench to dally withal would please him very well"), they saw in him at the same time a figure with a supernatural destiny.[2]

Sixteenth-century men and women had as eager a capacity for belief in the marvellous and the supernatural as their medieval ancestors. They routinely called down the powers of enchantment to aid them in their everyday affairs. There were charms to be spoken during childbirth and at the foaling of horses. Charms helped milk to churn more quickly and ale to brew. In time of sickness incantations were chanted to stop bleeding, and fevers and rheums were abated by a magical process called "casting of the heart." Country folk hung rue around their necks as an amulet against witchcraft, and put boughs of mountain ash and honeysuckle in their barns on the second of May to turn aside spells cast on their cattle. Hot wax from a paschal candle dropped between the beasts' horns and ears gave additional protection, while burying an aborted calf in the roadway prevented the cows from miscarrying.[3]

Occult lore figured prominently in one attempt on the king's life. A Yorkshire villager named Mabel Brigge, with the encouragement of a friend who paid her in wheat and linen, undertook "Saint Trinian's Fast," a murderous three-day period of abstinence said to leave the faster's enemies dead. Mabel tried the technique on one other occasion, and before the fast ended her victim's neck was broken. Convinced that she could kill both the king and the duke of Norfolk, she began the fast again, but word of her attempt reached the king's Council of the North and she was seized and, before long, executed.[4]

Save in the enormity of her crime, Mabel Brigge was in no sense unique. There were reputed to be five hundred conjurers in England, and many more fortunetellers, wizards and purveyors of white magic. In the later part of Henry's reign London was full of stories of the exploits of one "prophesyer," Robert Allen, who kept his crystals and potions and conjuring books in readiness in various places throughout the city to advise his large clientele. Known for his extraordinary skill as the "god of Norfolk," Allen told women their children's futures, told men how to win at dice, and how to gain the love of their sweethearts. It was said nothing was beyond the reach of his skill—he could find lost articles, he could tell when a man was lying and when he spoke the truth, he could advise on strategy at cards based on the positions of the stars. Allen was eventually committed to the Tower "for matters of astronomy and suspicion of calculation," but there were dozens of others to take his place.[5]

The occult arts were no less commonplace at the royal court than elsewhere in the country. It was widely believed that prominent courtiers owed their advancement to sorcery of some sort, and everyone who rose to importance around the king was suspected of using magic. During the years that Wolsey stood at the pinnacle of governmental power there were many stories of how he had made his way to favor. According to one account he had calculated the king's horoscope, then "made by craft of necromancy graven imagery, . . . wherewith he bewitched the king's mind, and made the king to dote upon him more than ever he did on any lady or gentleman." Others said the cardinal had a familiar demon in his service, still others that he had a magic ring—a traditional medieval talisman—with which he forced the king to do his will. (In 1538 a priest who had been in Wolsey's service admitted making his master "a ring with a stone that he wrought many things with."[6])

Among those who spread tales of Wolsey's powers were Norfolk and William Neville. The duke, always at odds with Wolsey, believed himself to be "sore vexed with a spirit" that the cardinal had set on him. He hired a priest to exorcise it, incidentally inquiring of the exorcist whether Wolsey himself had been enchanted by someone else. Neville took great interest in Wolsey's magic ring, and approached a conjurer to make him one like it. He had even more imaginative occult ambitions, however, and once tried to make himself a cloak of invisibility from linen and buckskin cloth treated with horse bones, skin, chalk, rosin and powdered glass.[7]

Henry shared his subjects' unquestioned acceptance of the pervasive influence of superhuman forces in everyday life. Believing natural phenomena to be charged with occult significance he crossed himself when it thundered, took seriously the import of unseasonable weather and other oddities of climate, and spent hours observing the heavens and talking over the meaning of celestial bodies with knowledgeable men. Astrology was to Henry both a constant fascination and something of a guide to life, but it accounted only in part for his interest in the skies. He enjoyed speculating on the nature and portent of comets, and made the Oxford astrologer and mathematician John Robyns his chaplain. Robyns dedicated his treatises on comets to the king in memory of discussions the two had had at Woodstock and Buckingham in the early 1530s— discussions in which Henry impressed his scholarly chaplain with his mathematical knowledge.[8]

When Henry complained, shortly before Anne Boleyn's disgrace, that he now realized she owed her years of influence over him to witchcraft, the respect he paid to the supernatural gave his statement weight. Yet to those who saw him as the cursed Mouldwarp he alone seemed squarely and brutally responsible for Anne's death, just as he bore the blood guilt for the deaths of Fisher and More and the butchered monks who died with them. From at least 1535 on, Henry's legend overshadowed him, obscuring the private, fallible man Henry Tudor as he struggled through midlife.

The diplomats and courtiers who dealt with the king from day to day were as baffled and exasperated by him as they were fearful of his displeasure. "Such are this king's fickleness and natural inclination to new or strange things," Chapuys wrote, "that I could not find words to describe it."[9] Having ordered one thing, he peremptorily commanded the opposite, and observers found it impossible to tell whether he had seriously reconsidered the matter or was simply indulging a contrary whim. He seemed to take a perverse delight in upholding the opposite side of any argument, creating disharmony where there had been agreement and reducing his advisers to helpless vexation.

"His natural inclination is to oppose all things debateable," Chapuys observed, "taking great pride in persuading himself that he makes the world believe one thing instead of another."[10]

Now capricious, now argumentative, now simply contrary, Henry often seemed villainously quixotic. The boasting and assertiveness that had always marked his relations with diplomats and foreign envoys turned to insulting bravado. He irritated Chapuys by talking disparagingly of the imposing quadrireme Charles V had built, with its twenty-seven benches of oarsmen. He meant to order one made with a hundred benches, Henry swore, adding that in any case his enviably strong fortresses at Calais and Dover made his realm secure even without it. Toward the emperor himself Henry showed patronizing scorn. "He is simple-minded, and knows no Latin," he said to a German envoy; in other conversations he took credit for gaining the throne of Spain and the office of emperor for Charles, and for winning the imperial victory at Pavia.[11]

"He never forgets his own greatness, and is silent as to that of others." The French envoy Castillon who sent this description of Henry to Francis I left out of it one essential fact: Henry was constantly measuring himself against his fellow-sovereigns and attempting to surpass them. Historians who have sought to account for the executions of 1535 have overlooked the highly influential circumstance that the continental rulers showed Henry the way. In the Netherlands Protestants were being burned and smothered and garroted by the hundreds in that year in accordance with recent harsh orders from the emperor. In France the king was exalting himself as the hammer of heretics, making himself the pious centerpiece of a macabre spectacle.

Late in January of 1535 a solemn procession wound through the narrow streets of Paris. Crowds massed as the word spread that the king himself was coming, and in time he came, not in state but walking, bareheaded, behind the bishop who carried the sacred host. Surrounding King Francis were his sons and the clergy, behind him the ladies of the court. Each of them carried a torch to light the fires under the heretics, enemies to God and the faith, that had been brought to suffer for their errors.

The procession halted, and the king put his torch to the dry wood at the base of the stake. The others followed his example, until within minutes the air was filled with thick smoke and with the stink of burning flesh. As the victims were consumed Francis gave thanks that he had been given the discernment to see and condemn the evil of false belief, and asked God to forgive him for having pardoned one or two of the heretics. With his subjects as witness he swore that from then on there would be no more leniency; every Protestant in Paris would be burned.[12]

Parisians talked for weeks of their king's reverential, determined assault on heresy, and of how he kept his word and came again soon afterward to burn more of the guilty. Word of the ceremonious public burnings reached England, and Henry, not to be outdone, determined "to do something new and strange to make people talk of him."[13] Before long the outrageous executions which brought him such infamy had begun.

The exasperating changeability, the self-glorification, the ceaseless bragging and open rivalry Henry showed were real enough, but they were in one sense a smokescreen. For behind his swaggering complacency was insecurity, behind his mercurial caprice an uncertainty that deepened as he matured.

His religious policies, which seem in retrospect monuments of decisive forethought, were at the time bold and potentially catastrophic experiments whose outcome could only be imagined. The popular reaction against enforcement of the Reformation statutes was deeply disconcerting to Henry—all the more so in that he believed himself to be divinely guided in the course he took. To these distressing worries were added background fears of war and rebellion. Henry was "wonderfully afraid," one courtier said, that he would have to withstand a military challenge from the continent; closer to home, the revolt in Ireland caused him equal if not greater anxiety. He was overheard to say in 1534 that he would much prefer to fight against Charles V "and another like him" than against the Irish.[14]

Nor was the war he feared likely to be an occasion for chivalric valor and heroism. If it came, it would be a contest of strategies and of defenses, with victory dependent on well-caulked ships and effective ordnance and fortress walls kept in good repair. Concern over these matters preoccupied Henry throughout the mid-1530s, along with the ever expanding details of a government he managed, essentially, on his own.[15]

More and more he had renounced the trust, if not the aid, of others in the essentials of rule. Like his father he narrowed the circle of his trust as he grew older, until even his intimates were excluded from it. Suspicious by nature, he was made more suspicious during the years of his divorce proceedings when many courtiers disguised their allegiance to Katherine under a cloak of support for his cause. The strain of those years hardened his mistrust, until it was said he was "so troubled in his brain about this matter that he does not trust any one alive." Still later he saw those in whom he had confided—particularly his chancellor Thomas More—betray his confidence (or so it seemed to Henry) and treasonously defy his laws. In the end he believed, with very little evidence, that his wife had not only cuckolded him but laughed with his gentlemen behind his back, slandered his potency, and conspired to take his life.[16]

To be sure, Henry still showed flashes of boyish affection and good humor. He was capable of tenderness (as he was of heartlessness) toward his beleaguered daughter Mary, and disarmed his advisers by his warmth and physicality. He liked to come up behind his courtiers, take them by the arm or sleeve and lead them off to a private conversation. With Chapuys he was often markedly affectionate, though the ambassador knew full well that the king's displays of fondness, like his displays of hostility or affronted dignity, were calculated in part to annoy or hearten the French ambassador. In December of 1535 Henry met Chapuys at Greenwich and, "after a most courteous and kind reception," he wrote, "put his hands around my neck, and walked for some time with me in the presence of all the courtiers."[17] Henry was still ready enough to laugh at whatever struck him as absurd, though either he laughed less frequently now or court observers noted it less often. A new fool, a story, a graphic letter full of news from the continent could send him into hearty laughter. He became "very merry" when he heard that Thomas Boleyn, in retirement in the countryside after his daughter's death, had written requesting a large sum of money.[18]

Yet his laughter at Boleyn's effrontery had more irony about it than mirth, and as time went by his mounting suspicion corroded his moments of lightheartedness. Without fully realizing it he was taking on many of his father's habits of life—his bad-tempered shouting, his eccentricity, above all his guardedness and fear. Torrigiano's portrait busts of Henry and his father were now kept in the king's study at Whitehall; it is tempting to think that the bust of Henry VII brought to his son's mind scenes he had witnessed in boyhood—scenes of loud bullying, of caprice and unpredictable behavior.

In the year Henry VII died his minister Edmund Dudley had written that the king's purpose had been "to have many persons in his danger at his pleasure." Henry VIII had executed Dudley in the first days of his reign. Now, it seemed, he had begun to incarnate the dead man's epitaph for his father.

34

Here take thy queene, our King Harry,
And love her as thy life,
For never had a king in Christentye,
A truer and fairer wife.

NOTHING could possibly interest him less, Henry said publicly after Anne Boleyn's execution, than to marry again. When the subject of his remarriage arose—as it did the very day after the king became a widower—he dismissed the possibility out of hand. The French ambassador offered him Francis I's daughter Madeleine, and almost before the words were out of his mouth Henry refused her, saying that at sixteen she was too young for him and that "he had had too much experience of French bringing up and manners" besides. The reference to Anne's Gallican education was unmistakable; the ambassador hastily withdrew the suggestion.[1]

The weeks of waiting while Anne and her accused accomplices were tried and executed had put Henry under little apparent strain. Just as he had separated himself from Wolsey and Katherine, suddenly and finally, he now cut himself off from Anne and the men he believed to be her lovers. To make certain no unpleasant confrontations arose he confined himself indoors during the day, coming out only to walk in the gardens of the palace. Late at night, though, he had himself dressed in silk and velvet and, sparkling with jewels, called for his bargemen to row him downriver to his evening's pleasures.

The courtiers who entertained the king during these weeks went out of their way to adorn their banqueting halls with beautiful women, and tried to smile good-humoredly while he loudly—some thought too loudly—slandered Anne for her transgressions, and enjoyed himself with conspicuous exuberance. He told anyone who would listen that Anne had betrayed him with a hundred men, that her faults were without number and her treason unforgivable. He behaved himself, one observer noted, as a man who had just rid himself of a "thin, old and vicious hack," and was looking forward to acquiring a new mount.

After showing the king lavish hospitality one evening, the bishop of Carlisle told Chapuys how Henry had displayed "an extravagant joy" as he dined, surrounded by ladies, and had unburdened himself at length about his misalliance with Anne. He had long expected to find his queen unfaithful, he said, and had gone so far as to compose a tragedy on the theme. So saying he took a little manuscript out of his pocket and offered

270

it to his host. The disconcerted bishop forbore to read the book, but Chapuys speculated later that it might have contained some of Henry's ballads—ballads Anne and her brother were accused, at their trials, of ridiculing.[2]

Henry's effusive merrymaking was meant to disguise his lingering misgivings about Anne's fate, and to distract him during the final suffering of the woman who was, after all, the great love of his life. His nightly revelry had another purpose as well: to deflect curiosity about what company he kept during the day. For by day he was making final arrangements enabling him to marry Jane Seymour.

"The king hath come out of hell into heaven," wrote one of Henry's privy chamber gentlemen when he heard Jane was to replace Anne, "for the gentleness in this and the cursedness and the unhappiness in the other." The contrast between the two women was indeed striking. Jane was fair, even pale, where Anne had been dark. Jane was well mannered, steeped in the courtliness Henry prized; Anne had been at best impertinent, at worst unmanageable. Anne had been wild, but Jane was tame— "the most virtuous lady and veriest gentlewoman that liveth"—and beyond her docility of temperament she seemed eminently fit for the chief queenly responsibility of bearing the king sons.

The Seymours were prolific. Jane was the eldest daughter in a family of ten, and her brother Edward fathered a dozen children. This enhanced Henry's liking for her, as did her modest refusal of his gifts and, in all probability, his advances. While Anne lived Jane behaved with demure respectability, though Henry's unmistakable attraction to her caused Anne "intense rage." But with Anne disgraced and awaiting death in the Tower the marriage plans went forward, and on May 20, the day following the queen's execution, Henry and Jane were formally betrothed.

Because the prospective bride and groom were both descended from Edward III (and thus were too near by blood to marry under church law), Archbishop Cranmer had to issue a dispensation permitting the marriage. There were none to object, however, as both the betrothal and the marriage were secret. Eleven days after Anne's death Henry married Jane in the queen's closet at York Place, and began to make elaborate plans for her coronation. She would be crowned in October, he decided, with the crown that had been Anne's and Katherine's, a heavy gold coronal set with sapphires and rubies and pearls. The festivities would outshine any yet seen, with the queen riding from Greenwich to the city in a huge ship built in imitation of the famous *Bucentaur* of Venice and saluted with pageantry and music of surpassing beauty.[3]

With the new alliance came changes in the succession. Three-year-old Elizabeth, less than unwanted now as the daughter of a traitress, was declared to be not the king's child at all, but the daughter of Anne and her convicted lover Henry Norris. (There were those who said she was not even Anne's child, but a supposititious baby represented as Anne's to disguise her childlessness.[4]) Twenty-year-old Mary was reconciled to her father, but not before she had undergone much agony of conscience. What had kept her sane during years of mistreatment had been her unshakable defense of her mother's marriage and her own right to the throne; now, to preserve her life, she swore an oath denying her legitimacy. Henry's old affection for his daughter returned, reinforced by their similarities in face and voice and strength of presence. But they were from now on tacit political enemies, and it was Mary's emerging purpose to undo all that her father was doing should she come to the throne.

By an irony of fate Henry's only surviving son died less than two months after Jane Seymour became queen. Henry Fitzroy had been unwell for some time; were it not for his illness, Cromwell said, the king "certainly intended to make [him] his successor, and would have got him declared so by Parliament."[5] As it was his death was untimely, for both Mary and Elizabeth had been declared ineligible to succeed and Jane had yet to conceive. To minimize uncertainty about the succession the king gave orders that his son's body should be transported into the country and buried secretly, and entrusted the delicate matter to Fitzroy's father-in-law Norfolk. Through the carelessness of Norfolk's servants the arrangements lacked both secrecy and dignity. In place of the closed cart the king ordered the corpse was borne in a wagon covered with straw, and there were no mourners save two attendants who followed at a distance.[6]

Hearing of this Henry was gravely displeased, and his anger fell on Norfolk, whose influence was in any case waning as that of the Seymours rose. A rumor reached the duke that the king meant to send him to the Tower. Norfolk was as fearful as he was enraged, and hurriedly wrote out his will before pouring out his feelings in a letter to Cromwell, written "with the hand of him that is full, full, full of choler and agony." He longed to challenge the rumor-monger who spread the story to a duel, the duke wrote, not only to "prove himself the more honest man" but because of the monstrous injustice of the accusation. The Tower was for traitors; Norfolk was the most steadfast servant the king had. "When I deserve to be there," he wrote with aristocratic contempt, "Tottenham shall turn French."

The rumor that troubled Norfolk was as much a product of the unsettled times as it was of the king's uncertain temper. The popular reaction to Henry's religious policies, to his vengeful executions, to the atmosphere of suspicion and fear fed by informers and presided over by the hated Cromwell was building to a climax. Even as the king and his new bride hunted together in the summer months, taking dozens of red deer in each park they visited and enjoying "good sport," the dissatisfactions grew unrestrained. Finally in October, as the hunting season ended, a season of rebellion began.

The risings that erupted in the fall of 1536 created the greatest single crisis Henry would face as king. Beginning in Lincolnshire in the early days of October rioting spread to the entire East Riding, then westward until the rest of the north was up. Altogether the rebels numbered at least twenty thousand—some said forty—while the king could send only eight thousand against them. The army of the discontented could not at first be overcome, merely held in check by a promise of royal pardon. Throughout the fall and into the winter of 1536–37, the northern men held undisputed sway over the king's lands and cities and castles, and came near to sparking a greater upheaval that might have brought invasion from the Scots border and from the armies of the continental powers as well.

It was afterward clear that the north country risings were less spontaneous than planned, less an explosion of popular disaffection than an organized bid for political power led by nobles and local gentry frustrated by increasing royal authority.[7] But to those who took part in it the rebellion had the character of a massive popular outcry against all that the king had purposed and done in the last decade—his repudiation of Katherine and her daughter, his transformation of the church, his harsh punishments for treasonous words and his reliance on unworthy, lowborn advisers such as Cromwell. Above all it seemed an outcry against the most recent and most visible of his assaults on the old religion: his dissolution of the monasteries.

A year and a half before the unrest in the north broke out an official scrutiny of the wealth and inner life of England's monastic institutions began. Royal investigators examined the estate books and accounts of the monks and nuns, noting with care the extent of their landed property, the profits of their rents and tithes, their mining and milling and fishing interests. At the same time, monastic visitors gathered evidence about the lives of the religious, inquiring into their observance of the monastic rule, their regard for holiness and wholesome surroundings, the sincerity of their vocations. The results of these investigations—which were by no means unprejudiced—were damning in the extreme. The decay, criminality and moral corruption documented by the examiners were appalling; to the king and his vicar general, Cromwell, they seemed to reaffirm the label one of Cromwell's correspondents had given the religious houses—"slaughterhouses of the conscience."[8]

The physical circumstances of many monasteries and convents bore witness to a way of life in decline. Clathercott, a house of Gilbertines, the visitors found to be "old, foul and filthy." At the Benedictine priory of Wymondham the mass vestments were in tatters, and the bread and wine too moldy and sour to be used in the eucharist. At Dorchester near Oxford the buildings were in an advanced state of dilapidation; the locks had disappeared from all the doors, and the church and cloister had become almost "a public highway." Poverty accelerated the deterioration. Often the monks had no money to make repairs or to replace worn furnishings or habits. The monks of Westacre were so impoverished, they told the king's representatives, that they had been forced to pawn one of their most revered relics—a piece of Saint Andrew's finger.[9]

If the external decay in the monasteries and convents was lamentable the decline in their spiritual lives was even more to be deplored. The inmates themselves gave eloquent testimony to the atmosphere of mean-spirited turbulence to be found in the cloister. A monk of Wynchelcomb wrote to Cromwell begging to be released from the monastic "prison" he had entered as a boy of thirteen. Holiness was foreign to his fellow-monks, he wrote. He had never seen less charity and more envy, less quietness and more disharmony than among his brethren. Strife and dissension were more common at Wynchelcomb than in the outside world, and the hypocrisy of men who professed goodness and practiced evil was almost more than he could stand. A similar pattern of hypocrisy was discovered among the nuns of Redingfield, where the sub-prioress had a vicious temper and struck the nuns, and at a Lincolnshire priory where the prioress kept her half-starved nuns in the stocks. Another monastic superior was reported to be "occasionally mad," and was given to drawing his sword against the monks.[10]

Corroboration for the examiners' findings about convent violence came from no less a partisan of the old regime than Thomas More, who knew at first hand of an incident concerning the prior of a religious house and a band of cutthroats he hired to commit murder and sacrilege. The evil was carried out at the prior's direction, but before the murderers began their work the prior paid an odd respect to his vocation by taking them into his cell and forcing them to pray on their knees to the virgin.[11]

Sexual sins accounted for the majority of monastic irregularities, according to the royal visitors. Monks with mistresses, nuns with bastard children, homosexuality and even incest were documented in abundance. Among the monks of Bath were some who kept ten mistresses, others who had nearly as many; at Farley the prior kept company with eight prostitutes, and immorality of many kinds was so commonplace, the royal deputies wrote, that "the place was a very brothel." When they came to the London house of the Crossed Friars they found the prior "in bed with his whore, both naked, about eleven o'clock in the forenoon upon a Friday." Rather than make excuses the prior leaped out of bed, knelt before the officials and begged them to accept thirty pounds and say nothing.[12]

Few religious sinned as ebulliently, though, as the abbot of Cerne, who let the lands and buildings of his house go to ruin while he cultivated an extravagantly secular life and indulged his monks when they followed his example. He kept concubines in the cellars, so the report ran, but brought them up to the refectory table to sit beside him at mealtimes, and squandered the abbey's income on supporting them and the children they bore him. The abbot tolerated similar lapses from saintliness in his monks, allowing them to gamble at dice and cards and to keep company with women, asking only that the female companions be out of the house by evensong so as not to hinder vespers.[13]

In actuality much that was reported about convent life was distorted by half-truths; some of the visitors' claims were either outright lies or the product of highly biased observation. Where the royal examiners saw vice others noted industriousness and dedication. The prior of Folkstone, condemned as lax by the monastic visitors, was in fact in process of repairing his house at his own expense when they arrived, laying down a new pavement, rebuilding the bakehouse and the monks' sleeping quarters, and buying new vestments.[14] The men sent to tear down the religious houses not infrequently noted contradictions between the official reports and what they found, and in the absence of systematic counterevidence the commissioners' findings must be read with some skepticism.

Nor were the commissioners themselves above suspicion. One of their

number, Dr. John London, led a thoroughly vice-ridden life and was even
accused of attempting to seduce the nuns in the course of his visitations.[15]
On balance, however, even the most sympathetic students of sixteenth-
century monasticism concede that the spiritual life of the religious had
become dulled, and that immorality, violence and excess corroded the
sacred observances. If the king's visitors overlooked evidence of re-
vivifying forces at work among the monks and nuns, they also found the
corruption they sought.

In the spring of 1536 Parliament approved the dissolution of all
monastic houses with incomes of less than two hundred pounds a year—
some three hundred institutions—condemning them for their "manifest
sin, vicious, carnal and abominable living." Some eighty houses bought
temporary exemptions from the king, and so staved off destruction for a
time, but for the rest the process of closure soon got under way. The
monks were given pensions and turned out (nuns received nothing); the
animals and tools were sold off, the chalices and plate and other treasure
removed, along with the furnishings. Eventually teams of skilled workmen arrived to tear down the ancient walls, and by the time they left the
cloisters were reduced to ruins of stone and shattered glass.

For the most part the work of destruction went smoothly, but some
resistance was encountered. When the royal commissioners in Northumberland arrived at the canonry at Hexham, they found the religious armed
and in harness, and prepared for a siege. As soon as they entered the town
of Hexham the common bell began to ring, signaling an emergency. Then
the great bell of the monastery was sounded, and as the town gates were
shut one of the canons appeared on the roof in full armor and informed the
commissioners that he and his twenty brethren were prepared to defend
their house to the death before they would turn it over peaceably for
destruction.

"Afore any of our lands, goods or house be taken from us," he
announced, "we shall all die, and that is our full answer." Rather than
challenge the canons' determination the commissioners left, but in the end
the king won out. The canons were "arrant traitors," Henry claimed, and
deserved to be treated as such; if they would not yield, then force would
have to be used, "for force is the chief rein [of] such sudden enterprises
and easethe them to be redressed." Finally, five months after the initial
confrontation, Norfolk succeeded in dissolving the monastery "with very
good exhortations to the inhabitants," ejecting the canons.[16]

Everywhere houses of contemplation became sites of public spectacle.
As the country people looked on in fascinated bewilderment, teams of
workmen demolished sacred buildings so old they seemed part of the
landscape. The destruction followed a common pattern. First carpenters
built scaffolding around the walls and laborers dug under the foundation
and shored it up with temporary wooden props. Then the props were set
on fire, and when they crumbled to ashes they brought the walls down on
top of them. Plumbers set to work at once salvaging the lead and carrying
it to a furnace where it was melted down and carted away, while smiths
sorted through the debris for useful scraps of iron and other metal.

Though many of them deplored the closing down of the religious houses the poor did not hesitate to share in the plunder. "The poor people thoroughly in every place be so greedy upon these houses when they be suppressed," an observer wrote, "that by night and day, not only of the towns, but also of the country, they do continually resort as long as any door, window, iron, or glass, or loose lead remaineth in any of them." Nothing went to waste, not even the books from the monastic libraries, whose pages could be used to light fires or scour candlesticks or rub muddy boots clean. Book pages had a more mundane use as well, as "a common servant to every man, fast nailed up upon posts in all common houses of easement."[17]

The king's efficient laborers tore down in a matter of days monuments to piety that had taken generations to erect, and the sight of such sudden, irreversible destruction was a wounding reminder of the extent of Henry's newfound power over his subjects' lives and faith. In Lincolnshire, where the number of smaller monasteries was unusually great, ruined cloisters marred the landscape, and underscored rumors of further tyrannical measures. It was said the king meant to introduce "Lutheranisms"—a suspicion arising from the conspicuous presence in London of representatives of several Protestant German states—and that the parish churches would soon be despoiled of their chalices and relics and ornaments just as the monasteries had been. More fantastic fears were expressed: that Henry intended "to have all the gold in the hands of his subjects to be brought to his tower to be touched, and all their chattels," and that before long no one would be allowed to eat pork or goose or capon, or even wheat or bread, without a royal license.[18]

These alarms, coupled with the presence of more than one set of royal commissioners in the north parts in 1536, were a backdrop to the revolt that engulfed the region in October. Many causes united the rebels. A great number wanted a return to the traditional religion, with the restoration of the abbeys and priories. Some sought redress against rapacious landlords, others lower taxes, still others reforms in parliamentary elections and restoration of Mary as heir to the crown. Many of the rebels simply followed their lords—the gentry and old feudal aristocracy—who summoned them to fight, and throughout most of the north it was noted that, where the men of substance backed away, the commons' resistance ended.

But if the underlying purposes of the rising were political, its tone was that of a millenarian peasant revolt. The name by which it came to be known, the Pilgrimage of Grace, had an archaic ring, and conveyed a poignant nostalgia for all that was passing in the rapid metamorphoses of the 1530s. The watchwords of the rebels too belonged to another era, though their urgency was as fresh as ever. "All commons stick ye together, rise with no great man [till] ye know his intent," one proclamation read. "Keep your harness in your own hands and ye shall obtain your purpose in all this North land. Claim ye old customs and tenant right to take your farms by a God's penny, . . . then may we serve our sovereign lord king Henry the VIIIth. God save his noble grace." "Wherefore now is time to arise," another manifesto read, "or else never, and go proceed with our Pilgrimage for Grace, or else we shall all be undone: wherefore, forward! Forward! Now forward in pain of death, forward now or else never!"[19]

The insurgents' staunch assertions of loyalty to the king were deceptive as well, for though they swore to preserve Henry's "person and issue," and took as their motto "God save the king, the church and the commonalty," they went out of their way to assault nearly every royal representative they could find. The bishop of Lincoln's chancellor, a former servant of Wolsey's, taken to be a spy for the king, the cook of one of the monastic visitors Dr. Legh—all were murdered for their connections with the court. Two of Cromwell's servants were dispatched with particular relish. One was hanged, the other wrapped in a bull skin and baited to death by dogs, the latter a punishment the rebels would have preferred to confer on the lord privy seal himself.[20]

At court the rebellion seemed ominous indeed—"the dangerest insurrection that hath been seen." A feudal revolt was one thing, but a rising of "persons of no reputation" threatened to unleash the nightmare of complete social disorder. What was more, the rebels were only fifty miles from the capital, and might well come south in force before adequate defenses could be prepared. Defense had already proven to be a troublesome issue. When the Pilgrims descended on Pontefract Castle in the first days of the revolt its defenders despaired, and sent word to the king that they were "in great danger and saw no means of resistance." The castle's well was dry, its bridge in disrepair, and its walls and ramparts "much out of frame"; there were few bows and arrows, no gunners and no powder, and in any case none of the guns was fit to be fired.[21]

In London no time was lost: a counterforce was mounted, and orders were sent to every lord and gentleman to "be ready with his power." Disturbing word came back from some of the notables that they could scarcely raise a quarter of the men they had counted on. Defection diminished the ranks as well; one force of five hundred fighting men led by Bessie Blount's second husband Lord Clinton turned as one man on their captain and joined the rebels. The large numbers of "sanctuary men" in the capital—debtors and criminals living immune from capture on church grounds—had to be imprisoned to prevent them from swelling the army of the Pilgrims, while idle workmen from every craft were recruited to help in the work of arming and equipping the soldiers of the king.

Weapons and harness and ordnance were taken out of the Tower armory for the use of the hastily organized levies. More armor was bought from the merchants of the city; still more came from storage at the Crowned Key in Southwark. Eighteen armorers were kept busy in the tiltyard at Greenwich scouring the rusty suits and fitting them with new leather, while laborers stood by day and night to load them into carts for the journey north.[22]

Two of the suits of armor were for the king, who was reported to be "in great fear" of the rebellion. In twenty-seven years on the throne he had not faced a popular revolt, and the Pilgrimage may well have stirred in him haunting childhood memories of his dark stay in the Tower during the dangerous rising of 1496. Publicly Henry boasted of the armed might he could put into the field against the rebels. He had enough men, he claimed, to form two great armies—armies so strong they could crush the Pilgrims and immediately afterward give battle to any royal army in Europe.[23] Privately he worried over whether to go north himself (Norfolk advised against it), over the excessive caution of his captains (whom he accused of being "afraid of their own shadows"), over erratic provisioning and disorderly maneuvers.

The handling of the ordnance had been particularly disorganized. Charles Brandon, who along with Norfolk was put in charge of leading the royal forces against the rebels, was promised artillery once he reached Huntingdon. He hurried his men eastward only to find that the needed weaponry had not arrived. The guns had indeed been found, but there were no horses to transport them northward. The lord mayor was ordered to provide some, but though he did his best to command the citizens of London to part with their mounts and draft horses—telling them, to forestall panic, that a foreign dignitary was arriving in need of horses for his retinue—he acquired relatively few. Some thirty-four cannon were finally loaded and dispatched, but before they had gotten far the horses began to founder and progress was halted. The cannon were unhitched, the teams reinforced, and twenty-one of the heavy guns rolled forward toward Huntingdon, leaving the thirteen others behind on the London road.[24]

"This matter hangeth like a fever," one courtier wrote as the Pilgrimage of Grace reached its zenith, "one day good, another bad." There was no decisive confrontation, no dramatic victory to be claimed by either side. The royal forces were too few to crush the rising, so Norfolk, on orders from Henry, negotiated with the Pilgrims, first at Pontefract and then at Doncaster early in December. He passed on to the rebel leaders a promise of pardon, and gave them the king's word that a parliament would be held in the north to look into their grievances. In all probability these were meant to be false guarantees; Henry was adopting the strategy of his medieval predecessors when faced with large-scale revolt—to delay indefinitely, until the initial impetus of the rebellion was lost and its adherents began to fall away out of frustration and weariness. As it turned out his good faith was not.put to the test, for with the beginning of the new year fresh insurrections broke out in Yorkshire. It was now possible to claim that the Pilgrims had not kept faith, and in response to the new unrest Norfolk was sent northward once again, this time with a sizable enough army to suppress the rebels.

Sixteenth-century rulers were accustomed to punish rebellion with thoroughgoing savagery, but Henry's vengeance against the north country rebels was truly awesome. "You must cause such dreadful execution upon a good number of the inhabitants," he wrote to Norfolk, "hanging them on trees, quartering them, setting the quarters in every town, as shall be a fearful warning." In Cumberland, where a peasant mob six thousand strong menaced Carlisle in February, Norfolk followed his master's orders with a vengeance. Seventy-four of the rebels were hanged, some "on trees in their own gardens"; elsewhere dozens more perished, to a total of something less than two hundred.

In the village squares, in churchyards and along the highroads of the north the corpses hung in chains from trees and gibbets. Many were poor men, some were rebellious monks and clergy whom Henry ordered slain "without pity or circumstance." Widows and other relatives came by night to steal the bodies away, burying them secretly in churchyards or in ditches by the side of the road. Some of the women kept their dead husbands wrapped in shrouds for days in their cottages, waiting to bury them until the firestorm of reprisal passed. While they waited, the putrefying corpses bred disease; when they were buried at last they left pestilence behind them.

As the grim panorama of retaliation was unfolding in the spring of 1537 the king was made aware of a new and great hope. Queen Jane was with child.

Nothing could have made for greater joy at the court, where talk of executions and quarterings gave way to happy anticipation of the birth of a prince. The queen's needs became pre-eminent, and to indulge her cravings Henry sent to Calais for quails—fat quails—by the dozen. The first few dozen arrived with record speed, sent by the king's uncle and governor of Calais Lord Lisle. They were tasty, but only moderately plump. Henry wrote again to say he and Jane were glad of them, "but would have them fatter." Lisle was to send to Flanders if need be for the choicest birds. Throughout the summer, as Jane remained at Windsor and Henry moved between his hunting lodges in the vicinity, Lisle continued to send quails, two or three dozen at a time. They were roasted on landing at Dover and rushed to the kitchens at Windsor in time for the queen's dinner and supper; she ate them along with the game sent to the castle from the royal hunt.[25]

But for his sore leg, which pained him a good deal, Henry was exultant as he awaited the birth of his child. "He useth himself more like a good fellow than a king among us that be here," one of his companions wrote, and his only anxiety appeared to be the danger to Jane from plague. To protect her he ordered that no one in disease-ridden London—where sickness was carrying off at least a hundred victims a week—could come near the court, yet his efforts did little to quiet Jane's fears. "Your Ladyship could not believe how much the queen is afraid of the sickness," Hussey wrote to Lady Lisle, in a letter sent to Calais along with a quail cage. When in September she retired to her apartments at Hampton Court to await her delivery Jane's proximity to the capital created fresh fears, and new orders were given to keep Londoners away from the palace. To reduce the household staff Henry retired to Asher, where he waited impatiently for news of the queen.[26]

After prolonged and painful labor Jane gave birth to a boy on October 12. He seemed lusty and comely, a child fit to grow and in time to govern. An explosion of pageantry and feasting was ordered to celebrate the birth, and in every church Te Deums of joyous thanksgiving were sung. Messengers were sent to all corners of the realm with this, "the most joyful news that has come to England these many years," but the greatest jubilation was in the capital. There the shooting of cannon and the ringing of church bells went on day and night, and in every street bonfires were made "in praise of God, and rejoicing of all Englishmen."

35

My lustes they do me leave,
My fansies are all fled;
And tract of time begins to weave
Gray heares upon my hed.

ON the day Prince Edward was christened the officers of court and household and other notables gathered at Hampton Court, in the presence lodging off the Council chamber, and took their places in the christening procession. Some had been staying in the palace since before Queen Jane's delivery; others came as soon as news of a liveborn prince reached them. But the assemblage was deliberately kept small, for plague was still rampant in London and the king meant to protect his son. The lord mayor and sheriffs saw to it that no one from the city entered the precincts of the court. Only those with special royal letters were allowed to attend the christening, with a minimum number of retainers—six for the dukes, four for the bishops and abbots, only two for the knights and squires.

Servants bearing lighted torches lined the way from the presence lodging through the king's great chamber and on through galleries and courts to the palace chapel. Here, on a raised platform, was the christening font of silver and gilt; the prince's three godfathers, the archbishop of Canterbury and the dukes of Norfolk and Suffolk, stood beside it awaiting their godson's arrival. Nearby four damask tapestries had been hung to form a traverse or withdrawing area within which the infant would be undressed and dressed again. A fire-pan of hot coals warmed this area, and basins of perfumed water kept it sweet-smelling.

When all was in readiness the procession began. The courtiers filed into the chapel two by two, first gentlemen carrying unlighted torches, then the lower household officers, the abbots and bishops, the royal councilors and peers and ambassadors. The four accessories of the ceremony—basin, taper, salt and chrism—were borne in, the taper carried by Thomas Boleyn and the chrism by the four-year-old Princess Elizabeth. Next, under a miniature canopy of estate, came the little prince himself, carried by the marchioness of Exeter and wrapped in a fur-trimmed mantle of crimson cloth of gold. The long train of his mantle fanned out like the coronation robes of a king, and had to be held by two peers. Behind Edward walked the nurse and midwife who delivered him, then his godmother, his half-sister Mary, followed by all the ladies of the court in order of rank.

The archbishop christened the prince, and as soon as he finished the gentlemen lit their torches and the Garter King at Arms stepped forward to proclaim his title and style: "God, of his almighty and infinite grace," he cried out, "give and grant good life and long to the right high, right excellent, and noble prince Prince Edward, duke of Cornwall, and earl of Chester, most dear and entirely beloved son to our most dread and gracious lord King Henry VIII!"

Trumpeters standing in the outer court began a fanfare, and continued to play throughout the singing of a Te Deum and on until the procession had reformed and wound its way back to its starting point. Then Prince Edward was returned to the king and queen, who were waiting in their palace apartments; they blessed him, and finally the king distributed alms to the poor men and women who had gathered in expectation of his largesse.[1]

For the first time in a quarter century there was a legitimate male heir to the Tudor throne—if he survived. The privy councilors, the officers and diplomats, the nurses and midwife all held their breaths, waiting to see whether the king's good fortune would last. To their relief the prince seemed to grow stronger day by day, "sucking like a child of his puissance," until in time they ceased to be anxious about him, and began to worry about his mother.

As Edward flourished Jane withered. She lay weak in her bed, unable to conquer the fever that attacked her soon after her son was delivered. In her delirium she threw off the warm furs that covered her and called for foods too rich for her delicate stomach. Overindulgent servants gave in to her whims; eleven days after giving birth she suffered an "unnatural lax"—a violent attack of diarrhea—and sank rapidly through the night. On the morning of October 24 she received extreme unction from her confessor, and by evening it was clear she could not live long. Norfolk wrote in haste to Cromwell, who was away from court, urging him to return as soon as he could "to comfort our good master, for as for our mistress there is no likelihood of her life, the more pity, and I fear she shall not be alive at the time ye shall read this."[2]

"If good prayers can save her," one of the saddened courtiers wrote, "she is not like to die, for never lady was much plained with every man, rich and poor." Despite the prayers of her loving subjects Jane died within hours of Norfolk's prediction, and the grieving king "retired to a solitary place to pass his sorrows," leaving the funeral in Norfolk's hands.

The duke oversaw the elaborate ritual—the first of its kind since the death of Elizabeth of York three decades earlier. The chapel where Edward had been christened was now hung with black cloth and "rich images" as a backdrop for the royal hearse. Banner-rolls showing Jane's noble descent ringed the hearse, while the number and status of her attendants bore witness to her own high rank. Priests, gentlemen ushers and officers of arms kept watch over the corpse by night; by day the official mourners, led by the Lady Mary, guarded Jane's remains until, "in presence of many pensive hearts," she was conveyed to Windsor and interred in the chapel. So that those who had prayed for her recovery might commemorate her passing, Norfolk ordered twelve thousand masses to be celebrated in the churches of London for the queen's soul.[3]

A few days after Jane was laid to rest Henry was reported to be "in good health and merry as a widower may be." No record survives of how he coped with the turmoil of feeling occasioned by the loss of his wife and the gain of an uncommonly precious son. Both events, though, were calculated to make him feel his age, and in fact he had recently begun to refer somewhat pointedly to his advanced years. Earlier in 1537 a French merchant had come to his court with lace trimmings and velvet headgear and other costly ornaments of dress—in particular, some elaborate embroidery. Henry waved the embroidery away at a glance, announcing to the Frenchman that he was "too old to wear such things." (Apparently he was not too old to buy a rich collar and visor, an elegant hat, a strip of fur and some fine linen, together with a mirror to admire them in.[4])

At forty-six Henry was well into the time of life his contemporaries called old age, when "the body beginneth to decrease." Beyond this, after age fifty, lay the wasteland of decrepitude, a region of life reached by an unenvied few. Most sixteenth-century men (and women surviving the mortal penalties of childbirth) died before they reached fifty; at thirty-five they counted themselves aged, on the threshold of the season when "dried-up old age tires the body's strength." Outliving these conventional limits was a dubious advantage, for longevity brought feebleness, disease, and everpresent pain.[5]

To be sure, some men not only lived into their sixth decade and beyond but earned their bread combating others thirty or forty years their juniors. Sixty was the common upper limit for military service, and a handful of hardy veterans served on into their seventies. Venetian records of the 1520s told of a eighty-year-old Spanish seaman who was the sole survivor of a harrowing adventure. En route to the Spice Islands his ship was seized by the Portuguese. Many in its Spanish crew were killed, and the rest were marooned "at a desert place," with nothing to sustain life. All the younger men perished, but the elderly mariner not only kept himself alive in the desert but contrived in time to board a Portuguese ship and to make his way back halfway around the world to Portugal. Lest his feat be forgotten he wrote an account of his entire journey, and when the king of Portugal read it he set the man free and sent him home to Spain.[6]

What lifespan Henry may have hoped for is unknown, but he employed the finest apothecaries and physicians he could find to sustain his health and strength for as long as possible. So far he had been spared many of the ailments common in his day—intermittent fevers, jaundice, vertigo, rheumatism, stones, the "green sickness," or chlorosis, the "choking tonsil" disease, or quinsy, worms, "gnawings in the belly," coughs and agues. But he was increasingly tormented by his painful leg ulcers, and suffered from time to time with headaches and other transitory complaints. To treat these he relied on a series of apothecaries, first Richard Babham, then Cuthbert Blackeden, whose advice and herbs helped to bring the royal household through the sweat of 1528 and who supplied many medicinal compounds for Henry's "use and behoove" in the 1530s, and finally Thomas Alsop, who as gentleman apothecary after 1540 headed a staff of assistants and presided over an increasing volume of pharmaceutical activity.[7]

Of the three classes of Tudor doctors the apothecaries stood midway between the physicians, who concerned themselves with the abstract theory and philosophy of medicine, and the surgeons, then thought of as vulgar manual laborers occupied "in staunching of blood, searching of wounds with irons and other instruments, in cutting of the skull in due proportion to the pellicules of the brain with instruments of iron, couching of cataracts, taking out bones, sowing of the flesh, lancing of boils, cutting of apostumes, burning of cankers, . . . letting of blood, drawing of teeth, with other such like."[8]

Physicians concerned themselves with Latin and Greek treatises on disease, with the theories of the four humors of mankind (sanguine, phlegmatic, choleric and melancholic) and with the astronomical lore governing the disease cycle and the taking of medicines. Henry's physician John Chambers, a dour octogenarian whose portrait by Holbein betokens grim senescence, informed the king that he was of sanguine temperament, cheerful and gamesome, insouciant and overly fond of women and drink; to avoid the constipation, headaches, restlessness and lustful dreams common to this temperament he must govern his eating and sleeping habits and take care not to put on too much weight. In addition to bleeding him five times a year as a preventive against sickness Henry's surgeons looked after his ulcerous legs, the condition having spread to both. One of the surgeons, Thomas Vicary, was credited with unusually efficacious treatment, but on the whole the court surgeons were of lower status than the apothecaries, whom Henry continued to patronize eagerly even though their medicines made him ill.[9]

In May of 1538 Henry very nearly died. The purulent fistulas in his legs became blocked, and "the humors which had no outlet were like to have stifled him." Perhaps a blood clot from the king's swollen legs traveled to his lungs, for he lay writhing and choking in agony, unable to speak and spending all his massive energy in gasping for breath. Time after time he came to the point of suffocation, his veins straining, his eyes protruding and his face turning red, then blue, then black. Then as his doctors looked helplessly on there came a gurgle of breath, then another, until finally the king's chest began to heave in a desperate rhythm and the deadly stranglehold was temporarily relaxed. For ten or twelve days this mortal torment continued. Henry was pronounced to be "in great danger," and the ambitious courtiers, expecting his imminent death, laid their political plans, some throwing in their lot with the party of the infant Prince Edward and others supporting Mary.[10]

To their amazement the king's attack ceased as suddenly as it had come. His recovery was equally swift. By the end of the month he seemed as good as new, and two months later he was riding southward on progress "to visit his ports and havens," his wounded legs returned to normal and his hearty lungs free of congestion. But the specter of mortality lingered, for even before the near-fatal incident in May an uncontrollable rumor had spread throughout the countryside that the king was dead.

From Nottinghamshire to Sussex, from Gloucestershire to Suffolk word of Henry's death went out, and neither the firm denials of his officials nor the punishing of those who repeated the rumor could gainsay it. Rumor-mongers were imprisoned, beaten, and forced to admit publicly that they had lied. A Reading man "was punished and set upon a pillory, his ears cut off from his head, and afterwards whipped naked." Local magistrates and other men of substance tried in vain to trace the rumor to its origin. Yet such measures did little to discredit a story which had caught deep hold on the popular imagination, and the king's brush with death in the spring very nearly made it come true.[11]

The eagerness with which courtiers and country folk seized on the possibility of his death confirmed Henry's distrust of their loyalty. He was particularly suspicious of the men and women of his court, who had been all too quick to look after their political interests in the face of a change of regime.

By now Henry and his courtiers—many of whom were as old as or older than he was—had lived together in uneasy equilibrium for nearly thirty years. They formed a family of sorts, if a perverse and rigidly patriarchal one. Opportunism, greed and political expediency held them together, but so also did familiarity and habit, and the shared bonds of experience formed during an era of tumultuous change. There was little unalloyed sentimentality between them, but there was a sense of commonality rooted in fearsome admiration for their awesome, dangerous sovereign.

It was a quarrelsome family. Privy councilors insulted one another; the king's gentlemen were full of "proud and opprobrious words," and as often as not words led to blows. Sometimes the king was able to mediate the dispute before the bad feeling had gone too far. Announcing that he would "have no grudge among his gentlemen," he separated the combatants like misbehaving schoolboys until they could be reconciled.

Yet he could not forestall all conflict. In April of 1538 a series of violent altercations erupted. One of Edward Seymour's servants fought a duel with a French dueling master, killed him, and took refuge in the Westminster sanctuary. Another assault, apparently unrelated to the first, left one of the lesser courtiers dead, and shortly afterward two of Fitzwilliam's servants came into conflict and one was found murdered. At this point Sir Gawen Carew and one of his retainers took on one of the sergeants of the household with his yeoman, and when the fighting ended the yeoman was dead and the sergeant gravely wounded. Carew was placed under arrest, but by this time the conflict had escalated to take in Cromwell's serving men, and the lords of the Council had become involved. A melee broke out, with some forty gentlemen and their servants warring with one another within the precincts of the court. The records are silent as to the final outcome, but it was almost certainly affrays of this kind that led Cromwell to undertake a complete reorganization of the royal household in the following year.[12]

Intermittent violence was perhaps inevitable in the constrained atmosphere of the court, where natural emotions had to be hidden behind
elaborate displays of gentility. The gilded life of lavish dress, frivo-
lous pastimes and sugared rivalries cloaked deep bitterness and cankered
hatreds. When Lord Hussey wrote Lady Lisle to tell her he had found
places for her daughters as waiting maids, he cautioned her that "the
court is full of pride, envy, indignation and mocking."[13] Continental
influences had increased its sophistication as well; the chivalrous manners
of the early years of the century were giving way to greater worldliness
and sensuality.

Here the king set the tone to an extent, for though Henry's fondness
for women was far less excessive than the gross lechery of Francis I or the
unconventional indulgences of other contemporary kings he had come a
long way from the boyish ruler of 1509 who "loved where he did marry."
His chief companion in waywardness was the one-eyed Francis Bryan,
reputedly the most dedicated philanderer in the realm and a familiar figure
at the French court. Bryan's speech was as cheerfully earthy as his
behavior; once while on a diplomatic embassy to Calais he wrote ahead
about his lodging, telling his correspondent "to make more ready for me a
soft bed than a hard harlot."

It was his aptitute for coarseness that led Henry to choose Bryan as his
foil when he decided to put his elder daughter's reputation for purity to
the test. The king had been told that Mary "knew no foul or unclean
speeches." To prove her he told Bryan to approach her at a masque and
find out whether or not she was truly innocent. Mary's genteel biographer
did not record the details of the encounter—what Bryan said or did,
whether Mary responded with modest blushing or angry dignity—but in
the end Henry was convinced that what he had been told was true. The
incident says much about the changed atmosphere of the court, once
hearty in its carnality, now verging at times on decadence.

The sort of sordid trick Henry played on Mary was indicative of a
community turned in on itself, where boredom bred overripe pleasures.
To alleviate their boredom the courtiers sought out and devoured novel-
ties of every sort—new fashions in kirtles and doublets, shoes and hats,
new games and pastimes, new faces. Newcomers to court were received
with eager scrutiny, especially if they were young and attractive. On one
occasion a treaty was to be signed, and among the ambassadorial deputa-
tion that came to conclude the arrangements was a handsome young man
of twenty-two. "He was of such appearance and beauty," an observer
wrote, "that everybody ran to see him."[14] Curiosities from the New
World also provided diversions. Exotic foods and plants, artifacts and
written accounts of the explorers were passed from hand to hand, and live
imports were especially sought after. In 1534 Lady Lisle received two
marmosets from Brazil, with detailed instructions for their care. They
were to be fed on nuts and apples, with a little warm milk, they were to be
taken out of their cages every day, and they were to be kept warm—the
smaller of the two "hung up at night near the chimney."[15]

To fill the hours between dawn and midnight, the accustomed times of rising and retiring, the courtiers ate. Breakfast, an early dinner, "drink-ings," supper, and a light evening meal were supplemented by "collations"—servings of food and drink that were less than hearty meals but more than mere refreshments. On feast days and other solemn occasions the banqueting went on without intermission for many hours; to celebrate a coronation or royal wedding or birth the feasting continued over several days. But even at the most modest court suppers the amount of food served and consumed was prodigious. When Henry Courtenay, marquis of Exeter, entertained the king and his hunting household at his manor of Horsley in 1533 his cooks prepared a simple meal: counting the ten desserts, there were more than twenty-five dishes. Henry himself was notably fond of game pies and haggis, and of artichokes. Intending to cross the Channel to Calais in 1534 he sent orders ahead to his provision-ers to ensure a supply of his favorite foods. "It is the king's special commandment," the dispatch read, that all the artichokes "must be kept for him."[16]

Presiding over the turbulent, volatile community of courtiers and household staff was no small challenge, yet Henry achieved it year after year, relying as much on charm as on coercion and belying the fearsome menace of his displeasure by his disarming manner. To be at court for any length of time was to learn that the king had an astounding capacity for detail, and that he kept strict account of the comings and goings of each of his courtiers. If he gave anyone permission to leave the palace he set an exact time for his return, and made his irritation plain if the appointment was not kept. In the same way he paid attention to minute details of dress on ceremonial occasions, and a lady or gentleman who failed to wear the right color or ride the right mount in a procession risked a reprimand.[17]

But if Henry was an exacting father to his courtly family he could be an ingratiating companion and host as well, and he had a talent for combining necessary duties with social occasions. When inspecting the *Great Harry* in 1540 he took a number of ladies with him, and gave a party for them on board. He took many of the lords of the court with him when he went to examine new ordnance recently arrived from Calais, pointing with special pride to a huge double cannon—so large no axletree could be found to move it—and telling them how he liked it "marvellous well."[18]

Above all he kept his aristocratic retinue in mind when planning and remodeling his palaces. He enlarged Hampton Court until it extended to a thousand rooms, making it the largest structure to be built in England since Roman times. There were nearly three hundred beds with silken sheets and soft wool blankets to accommodate the courtiers, and to feed them a second kitchen was added to the huge one constructed in Wolsey's time. Building preoccupied Henry throughout the 1530s. He ordered new tennis courts and an arena for cockfights at Westminster, and a "sumptu-ous wall" around the palace park, and began construction of St. James's Palace, "a magnificent and goodly house," which would not be completed until 1540. Wolsey's former residence at York Place was transformed into Whitehall Palace following Henry's architectural designs. "What a great charge it is to the king," Cromwell complained, "to complete his buildings in so many places at once. How proud and false the workmen be; and if the king would spare for one year how profitable it would be to him."

To Cromwell's dismay Henry undertook yet another building project in November of 1538, the fanciful, extravagant palace of Nonsuch in Surrey. "One could imagine everything that architecture can perform to have been employed in this one work," wrote a traveler who saw it during Queen Elizabeth's reign. "It may well claim and justify its name of Nonsuch, being without an equal." In design a fantasywork of carved turrets and crenellated battlements, with flags flying from every tower and cupola as on a ship, Nonsuch was intended as a hunting lodge, and its well-stocked, spacious parks covered over a thousand acres. Yet Henry clearly planned to have the lords and ladies of his court at hand while he hunted, for the forecourt of the palace was huge, "capable to receive all the nobility of the king, and horsemen in great numbers." A large banqueting house rose amid the expanse of parkland, and there were remarkable gardens for guests to walk in, full of groves and hidden dells and trellised paths. A "grove of Diana" showed the huntress in her bath. There were statues everywhere, and two fountains that spouted water "one round the other like a pyramid," while marble birds poured forth water out of their bills. Another marble device was "full of concealed pipes, which spurt upon all who come within their reach."[19]

Now playing pranks, now admonishing, now dazzling them with the commanding splendor of his presence, Henry kept his courtiers well in hand. "The king has a way of making every man feel that he is enjoying his special favor," More once wrote of him, "just as the London wives pray before the image of Our Lady by the Tower till each of them believes it is smiling upon her."

Certainly John Hussey, Lord Lisle's servant, believed he was being singled out for special favor at the presentation of New Year's gifts in 1538. He wrote to his master describing the scene in the presence chamber, where Henry stood leaning against a cupboard accepting his gifts. Behind him were two of his chamber gentlemen, and beside him Edward Seymour and Cromwell. His secretary Brian Tuke stood at the other end of the cupboard, scroll in hand, writing down a description of each present and the giver's name. When Hussey entered Cromwell looked pleased.

"Here cometh my lord Lisle's man," he said to Henry, who gave a cheerful reply Hussey could not hear, then smiled broadly as he accepted the gift Hussey presented. It seemed to Hussey that Henry spent more time talking with him than with anyone else, expressing his thanks, asking after the health of Lord and Lady Lisle, inquiring about their lives and welfare. All the while the gifts continued to stream in, paintings and velvet purses, carpets, coffers, dog collars and a dog hook of fine gold, embroidered shirts and hawks' hoods and six Suffolk cheeses. Charles Brandon brought a book garnished with gold, "having therein a clock," one of the earls gave a gold trencher, someone else a marmoset; there were many, many purses of coins.[20]

The scene remained long in Hussey's memory, an image to inspire fidelity and fondness. Yet like all those who frequented the court Hussey kept in mind another image of the king, as the stern monarch who had sent many to execution, the changeable lord who had sworn "that there was not a head so fine that he would not make it fly."[21]

In 1538 his wrath fell on his first cousin Henry Courtenay, marquis of Exeter, and on the relatives of Cardinal Reginald Pole. Exeter, his wife Gertrude Blount and their little son were imprisoned in the Tower, and the marquis was executed. Henry had suspected his cousin's loyalty for years, ever since he and his wife had given comfort and support to Katherine of Aragon. Now he believed the marquis guilty of conspiring to marry his son to Henry's daughter Mary, endangering Prince Edward's right to the throne, and of being in league with Reginald Pole's brother Lord Montague.

The Poles were under suspicion on several counts: Reginald Pole, in exile on the continent, was actively opposing the king and everything he stood for, and his brothers Henry and Geoffrey and his mother Margaret Pole, countess of Salisbury, were believed to be in communication with him. Henry Pole, Lord Montague, had no love for the king and had spoken treasonous words against him. In return for his testimony against his brother, Geoffrey Pole was allowed to go free, on condition that he leave England; Lord Montague, his young son, and his mother were imprisoned. Montague was executed along with Exeter. The aged countess was spared, though forced to remain in the Tower. No one ever saw the boy again.

Before the wave of executions ended sixteen persons had died. Of these, the Courtenays and Poles had undeniable, if somewhat remote, claims to the throne. They were undeniably conspirators, or would-be conspirators, though their ineptness made them innocuous.[22] That the heads of these Yorkist families should be kept under guard, perhaps even killed, was understandable. But only vindictiveness, it seemed, could account for the hounding of their womenfolk and young children.

A Protestant writer tried to make Henry the hero of the incident, describing in a treatise how God himself had warned the king against the evil done by the "arch-traitor" Pole and his allies. But such propaganda left the wary men and women of the court unconvinced. Many of them preferred to heed Lord Montague's sour warnings about Henry shortly before his execution. "He would be out of his wits one day," Montague had said, "for when he came to his chamber he would look angrily, and after fall to fighting."[23] The doomed courtier had seen at close range the dark side of the king's nature; he at least believed that Henry's ebullient exterior was losing ground to another self. Without knowing it Montague had foretold his own fate. "The king never made [a] man," he was overheard to say, "but he destroyed him again either with displeasure or with the sword."

36

Great was the crying, the running and riding,
Which at that season was made in that place;
The beacons were fyred, as need then required;
To hyde their great treasure they had little space.
Dub a dub, dub a dub, thus strike their drums;
Tantara, tantara, the Englishman comes.

ON the high towers and battlements of the medieval town of Aigues-Mortes in the Rhone delta soldiers of Francis I and Charles V kept careful vigil. Within the town their royal masters were meeting face to face for the first time in many years, to make peace.

Francis and Charles had been at war in earnest for two years, ever since the French had invaded the Savoy and Piedmont in the spring of 1536 and the imperialists had retaliated by overrunning Provence and Burgundy. The conflict had been inconclusive, and dispiriting. The French failed to secure Milan as they had hoped, and succeeded only in provoking a massive counterattack. Challenging Francis to personal combat, the emperor led an army of fifty thousand into the Languedoc, where his men burned and killed and tore down every object in their path. Peasants fleeing across their smoldering fields could find neither food nor refuge; their beasts slaughtered and their granaries emptied, they starved before they could make their way to safer ground.

Yet in the end the imperialists suffered even greater losses. The mighty army drew up before town after town, only to find them too well fortified to assault and too well provisioned to besiege. Before long the besiegers were themselves entrapped. They were short of food, and when they tried to draw water they found the wells poisoned. Raids and ambushes drew blood along the outskirts of the camp; within it dysentery was an even more effective scourge. With thousands dying and little hope of a major conquest Charles ordered his army to retreat, but the long march back across the frontier was fatal to many among his weakened troops. Two men in five died, and the dying were left by the wayside. "All the roads were strewn with dead and dying men," an eyewitness wrote, "with lances, pikes, arquebuses and other weapons, with horses abandoned because they could not keep up." Mounds of corpses, horses and men together, marked the route of retreat—a victory of sorts, if a costly one, for the ravaged French.

Years of such bruising yet futile combat left both sides enfeebled.

Francis had been cheated of his hoped-for gains in Italy, while Charles had been prevented from meeting major threats on the other frontiers of his wide empire. Turkish fleets menaced his holdings in Italy, and Turkish pirates raided the Barbary coast; Turkish armies pressed him on the eastern frontiers of his empire. The sultan, Suleiman, was in league with the French king, who wryly excused his unholy alliance on grounds of expediency. "When wolves fall on my flock," Francis said, "it is necessary to call upon dogs for help." Within the German-speaking lands of Charles V the Lutherans, also allied with France, were dominant everywhere but in the palatinate, Bavaria and the Austrian territories, and there was unrest at Ghent in the Netherlands.

The pressure for peace was great, yet no one could have foreseen the spectacle of amity the two sovereigns displayed at their historic meeting. They embraced as brothers. Charles showed tender affection for Francis' sons—one of whom, Henri, he had once kept as a hostage. "My brother," Francis exclaimed to Charles with extravagant mendacity, "I am your prisoner once again!" The oblique reference to the aftermath of the battle of Pavia was meant as a chivalrous compliment; the emperor returned it by removing from his own neck the collar of the Order of the Golden Fleece and placing it around the French king's throat. The negotiations were as amicable as the public politeness. In two days a ten-year truce was agreed to, with Charles and Francis pledging themselves to join forces against all those who opposed Christian unity—by which they meant Francis' allies the Turks and the Lutherans and, in all probability, the renegade king of England.

Aigues-Mortes had been built in the thirteenth century by the sainted Louis IX as a launching point for his crusades. The agreement reached there in 1538 had the aura of a crusade about it, for it symbolized the launching of an offensive by Catholic Europe. Hapsburg and Valois, the two great Catholic powers, seemed to be drawing together at last. The pope, Paul III, had summoned a General Council of the church to try to heal the religious schism, and was about to release the time-honored weapon of excommunication against Henry in an effort to return him to the fold. In December he issued a bull renewing the execution of the excommunication drawn up three years earlier. Henry was declared deposed, and his subjects were freed from all obligations to him. In the eyes of the Roman church, England was now forfeit to the pope's champion—a prize of conquest to be seized in the name of the faith.

As Henry stood by in isolation the battle lines were being drawn around him. What comfort he had taken from the divisions among his enemies now dwindled, and the prospect of invasion and incited rebellion, always a hovering possibility, began to loom as an immediate challenge. "The king is at present very much surprised, bewildered and perplexed at what has happened," Chapuys wrote to Charles V just after the Franco-imperial treaty was signed. "He has evidently lost a good deal of his former bravery and buoyancy of spirits, showing at present greater mildness of temper and even simplicity than was his wont before."[1] The imperial ambassador noted that worry glazed the king's eyes and doubt checked his air of command; the French ambassador Castillon recorded only his camouflage of hauteur and empty boasts. "The friendship will not last long," the king told him contemptuously. Surely some issue would arise to cloud the newfound accord—probably the much-debated issue of Milan, which had not been mentioned during the recent discussions at Aigues-Mortes. Actually, Henry told Castillon, the emperor had offered Milan to him, more than once, and had renewed the offer within the last few days.[2]

Such high talk was hardly credible; more important, it did nothing to increase England's security. Clearly what Henry needed was an ally, but which? Superficially at least the natural choice would seem to be the German Protestants. Despite the mutual invective of the 1520s—when Henry referred to Luther as "a great limb of the devil," and Luther dismissed Henry as a "damnable rottenness and worm"—there had been frequent contact, both political and theological, between England and the Lutheran principalities during the following decade. Henry was disappointed in his hope for Lutheran support for his marriage to Anne Boleyn (though for a brief, fantastic time England was allied with the thriving Protestant town of Lübeck and Henry was promised endorsement for his marriage to Anne, twelve gunships, and the crown of Denmark).[3] But there was extensive communication on doctrinal matters, and in 1536 English envoys at Wittenberg came to preliminary agreement with Lutheran leaders on a joint statement of faith. Meanwhile the Lutheran princes had been creating a vital Protestant political organization, the Schmalkaldic League, with its own officials and treasury, and its own troops. The more powerful the League grew, the more advantageous an alliance came to seem. All that remained was to achieve theological concord.

Here the Lutherans were to be disappointed. The theologians they sent to Henry's court in the summer of 1538 to draw up a definitive declaration of faith found compromise with their English counterparts impossible on several points. The English refused to take a stand against private masses, or to permit priests to marry. Nor had they moved toward the Lutheran practice of offering both bread and wine to the laity during the mass. Months of deliberation ended in a stalemate, and in the end the Germans returned home, their mission and the hopes of both parties for an alliance temporarily abandoned.

When the Lutherans presented detailed written arguments in defense of their views they were somewhat taken aback to receive replies written by the king himself. As earnest and vigorous a controversialist as he had been while his nullity suit hung in the balance, Henry devoted hours of labor to doctrinal questions. He read the drafts his bishops drew up line by line, phrase by phrase, critically assessing each word and noting alternative choices in the margins. Often he made dozens of corrections. On such major theological formulations as the Ten Articles, put forth as the benchmark of faith for the English people in 1536, Henry determined the very nature of belief, defining a middle ground between Catholic orthodoxy and the teachings of the reformers on baptism, penance and the eucharist and diverging sharply from Catholicism in omitting the remaining sacraments entirely.

As the author of his subjects' faith Henry had his disadvantages. His learning was impressive—he was able to detect errors in Bishop Tunstall's reading of Greek, and to inform him that in construing Chrysostom he had "gathered a wrong sense upon his words"—and his opinions were thoughtfully taken. But it was the learning of a gifted layman, a dilettante capable, as Archbishop Cranmer found to his dismay, of making the sort of alterations in a crucial passage that turned it into error or nonsense. What was more, though the king could argue with the overfine exactness of a medieval schoolman his religious mentality was Erasmian; caring more for the quality of belief than for its external signs, he preferred to define a range of tolerated opinions than to prescribe a single narrow path. And on some points he was simply idiosyncratic. Rejecting the existence of purgatory he found distasteful, and he held a peculiar view of the Christian's need for divine grace in order to be saved—a heretical opinion known to the early church as semi-Pelagianism.[4]

Whatever the vagaries of the king's personal religious taste his realm appeared to be squarely in the reform camp. Nowhere in Europe was the destruction of the old church so evident to the eye. By 1538 at least half the religious houses in the country had been emptied, dismantled and torn down, the greatest of them now going the way of the lesser. Visitors to London were struck by the transformation of the monastery churches, some partly destroyed, others converted to a startling variety of secular uses. The church of the Crutched Friars was serving as a quarry for stone to repair the Tower. A nobleman had bought the church of the Austin Friars in order to store his corn and coal supplies in the steeple, while his son, having sold off all the usable building materials, stabled his horses in the nave. Convent buildings housed factories, friary churches government storehouses. The king's hunting nets and tents were kept at the Charter-house, while St. Mary Graces was crammed with naval supplies, including huge ovens for baking biscuit for the seamen.[5]

A more recent outrage had been the despoiling of the holiest shrine in Christendom, the tomb of Saint Thomas Becket at Canterbury. Since the twelfth century pilgrims had come by the thousands to kiss the silver-encased skull of the martyr and to lay their offerings before the gilded coffin that held his remains. In gratitude for the miracles he had performed kings and nobles had brought jewels by the hundreds to be set into his shrine, many of them gems of extraordinary size and brilliance. Over time the tomb had become an incomparably dazzling monument to piety and wealth, the earthly riches of the saint echoing his heavenly merits. When the king issued a proclamation denying Becket's martyrdom at the hands of Henry II (the archbishop had been "slain in the throng," the document read, after provoking a violent quarrel) the public outcry was considerable; when he ordered the tomb stripped of its ornaments, the shrine demolished and the relics burned, the lamentation reached the Holy See. It was said that the cardinals in Rome were more horrified by the news from Canterbury than by the Turkish destruction of the Christian fleet, and their dismay at Henry's brutal sacrilege was shared by most of the Christian world.

But though evidence of England's breach with her Catholic past was everywhere, doctrinal change had been relatively slight. Having severed its ties to Rome, the new English church had entered a period of consolidation, and was in fact moving further to the right on points of belief. In May of 1539 the Ten Articles were superseded by another doctrinal formulary, the Six Articles, which marked a return to Catholic orthodoxy and a final rejection of Lutheran tenets. The conservative voices in the Council—chiefly Gardiner, bishop of Winchester, and Norfolk, men whose views paralleled the king's own—had won out over the Protestant moderates Cranmer and Cromwell. And as the Six Articles were to remain the official theology while Henry lived, their victory was permanent.

Those who opposed the new distillation of belief were subject to be hanged as felons; in particular, those who denied the authorized teaching of transubstantiation (the doctrine that the bread and wine of the mass are miraculously transformed into Jesus' body and blood when consecrated by the priest) were to be burned as heretics. To an extent these severe measures were called forth by the appearance of a new religious population. For the first time in 1538, sacramentaries, followers of Zwingli who denied transubstantiation, and Anabaptists, radical Protestants advocating re-baptism of adults, began to arrive from the continent. Unlike the Lutherans, these reformers had no stable leadership or traditional political organization. Even to moderate Protestants they seemed outcasts, dangerous carriers of spiritual and social anarchy. To Henry and his advisers they were intolerable, a scourge to be banished, exterminated, or, just possibly, persuaded of better views.

On a November afternoon in 1538 the king's great hall at York Place was readied for an unprecedented event. King Henry was to engage in theological debate a priest who dared to deny the miracle of transubstantiation. That the Supreme Head of the church should take note of the opinions of a renegade cleric was remarkable. As a rule, he confined his participation in doctrinal controversies to meticulous written glosses or commentaries, though when the Six Articles were being debated in Parliament six months later he joined in the discussions in person, "confounding them all with God's learning." When learned treatises came to his attention he customarily handed them over to one of his advisers to read, then to another "of an opposite way of thinking," and finally arrived at an opinion from their comments.[6] But if this debate was extraordinary it had a special purpose: to display with memorable formality the king's zeal for truth, and to refute utterly the radical teachings that threatened the Henrician church.

Scaffolding had been built up around the walls for the spectators, and at one end of the hall was a dais with a throne for the king. Colorful tapestries had been hung around the walls and behind the throne, and when Henry entered and mounted the dais, dressed from head to foot in white silk, he seemed to shine with an unearthly brilliance. Most of the lords and great churchmen were present, along with a battery of theologians and judges. All of these stood ready to support the king's arguments, which considering their source must after all be irrefutable. There was no one to speak for Henry's opponent, John Lambert, but himself, and given his isolation, the peril under which he stood and the pointed arguments of the king and his supporters it is amazing Lambert lasted as long as he did.

The arguing went on for hours, with Lambert upholding the view that it was impossible for the bread and wine of the mass to retain the outward appearance of bread and wine (their "accidents," in Aristotelian logic) after their essential nature (or Aristotelian "substance") had changed. No miracle takes place during the eucharistic celebration, he maintained, only a commemoration of Jesus' passion, enacted to encourage piety. Lambert's position was radical in the extreme, and it was a relatively easy task to cite the writings of both Catholic and moderate Protestant theologians against him. This the king did, "fulminating the most vehement articles" to confute his opponent's reasoning and "sundry times confounding him" by scripture as well.

Toward the close of the day Lambert began to falter, whether beaten down by the strength of his sovereign's arguments, or from hoarseness, or simply from fear of death it is impossible to say. Even so he refused to recant, and put himself at the king's mercy instead. Rising to his full majesty, his white doublet gleaming, Henry condemned him as a heretic and ordered Cromwell to sentence him immediately. Lambert was taken off to the Marshalsea, and six days later, along with three Flemish Anabaptists, he was burned at the stake at Smithfield.[7]

The alarm over extremist heresy, the growing conservatism of doctrine, the king's spectacular display of righteous erudition were all prompted by the fragile diplomatic situation. For the Franco-imperial accord reached at Aigues-Mortes had not evaporated, as Henry had hoped, but had grown stronger, and as the year 1539 opened England was a nation on the brink of war.

"The most pestilent idol and usurpator of princes, the bishop of Rome," so read letters summoning all the nobles and gentlemen of the realm to arms, "has moved, excited and stirred great princes and potentates of Chistendom, not alonely to invade this realm of England with mortal war, but also by fire and sword to exterminate and utterly to destroy the whole nation and generation of the same."[8] This vision of conquest followed by mass annihilation roused the English as no call to arms had done for half a century. In every corner of the kingdom troops were levied, weapons scoured, defense works thrown up. Every report of warlike movements spurred more activity. There was talk of a great fleet gathering in the Netherlands to carry French and German soldiers to the Channel coast. It was said all English ships in Flanders had been seized, and trade interrupted. In every coastal town the king's laborers were arriving to undertake the work of shoring up bulwarks, constructing blockhouses and erecting new fortresses where none had ever been before.

In February the Privy Council was sitting daily to try to meet the growing threat of war. Word reaching England from sources on the continent indicated that the invasion was coming closer; in mid-January Francis and Charles had signed yet another accord binding themselves to make no unilateral agreements of any kind—a customary preliminary to taking the field—and both sovereigns recalled their ambassadors in England. The pope had sent Cardinal Pole to put additional pressure on the French and the imperialists, as well as on James V of Scotland. King James had recently strengthened his country's traditional ties to France by marrying Marie de Guise, and this, coupled with his antipathy to Henry and the influence of Cardinal Beaton, newly arrived from the papal court and urging war, was expected to draw him into the conflict.

At times Henry sat among his councilors at their daily sessions, but as often he was at the seacoast supervising the fortifications. He seemed to be everywhere at once, at Calshot and Pendennis, Plymouth and Lyme. He oversaw the progress of repairs at Berwick and Tynemouth and a dozen other ports—and even at "Harry's Walls" in the faraway Scilly Islands—by letter and messenger. With his usual care for economy he directed that building stone from the razed monastaries be put to use in the defense works, with the result that Hurst Castle was constructed in part from the ruined walls of Beaulieu Abbey. He set his stamp on the structures as a commemoration and a warning; at St. Mawes a plaque proclaimed "Henry the Eighth, Invincible King of England, France and Ireland, Builded Me Here in Defense of the Republic to the Terror of his Enemies." At Dover he overcame the difficulties presented by restive workmen who had recently gone on strike for higher wages and who were known for their violence. And at Deal, where over fourteen hundred laborers were employed, he worried over the soundness of the bulwarks amid heavy seas and roaring winds—the greatest storms ever seen along the coast in early spring.[9]

While the ring of fortresses was taking shape the mustering of troops went forward. Levies from the southern and southeastern shires were put in readiness to withstand assault from the continent, and in the north, Norfolk summoned his militiamen to guard the Borderlands against the Scots. Faced with the present peril none shied from the king's service, not even the men of Lincolnshire who had rebelled in such numbers only two years before. Far from hanging back they swore to Suffolk, who had been sent to lead them, that they would eagerly spend their lives and goods to serve King Harry, and were only too glad to have a chance to redeem themselves in his eyes.[10] In some places townspeople not only formed themselves into armed bands but undertook to prepare their defenses on their own initiative. When the earls of Oxford and Essex arrived in Harwich to put the town on guard they found the entire population, including the women and children, shoveling dirt from two huge trenches and shaping it into bulwarks. All that the people of Harwich lacked were cannon, and these Henry supplied within days of their request.[11]

By March much of the work was finished, and the frenzied activity of the past few months gave way to a mood of watchful apprehension. There had been an unexpected gesture of rapprochement from France; having withdrawn his ambassador Castillon Francis sent a replacement, ostensibly an indication of a lessened threat of war. But an English spy in France sent word warning Henry and his councilors not to be deceived by this ruse, for in fact Francis was busy gathering men and materiel in secret, and had already assembled fifty warships—including his great ship the *Havre Neuf*—to send against the English coast. "Be on your guard," he concluded, "for the king intends harm, whatever good face the ambassador may show."[12] Armed with his informant's advice Henry gave orders for the final provisioning of his hundred and fifty warships and commanded that a watch be kept beside all the coastal beacons, to be set alight in case of sudden attack.

On April 2, Good Friday, the warning came. Fifty huge imperial ships had been seen lying off Marsdiep, ready to raise anchor. They would be at Dover by Easter Sunday. Thomas Cheyney, warden of the Cinque Ports, sent his swiftest messenger to the court, and received orders to send two boats to sea to confirm the report. All Easter day and night the English boatmen spent in mid-Channel, "in the trade where all great ships must pass," expecting at any moment to see the turrets of the vast imperial armada rising up before them out of the mist.

They did not come that day, nor the next, nor the day after, though the winds were favorable and the seas relatively calm. Finally on Wednesday the mariners caught sight of a massive fleet, sixty-eight sail in all, flying the black eagle of the Hapsburgs and making for the Downs. Cheyney ordered his fifteen hundred men to take up their positions on the ramparts of Dover Castle, loaded his ordnance, and prepared to fire.

Yet before giving the alarm he paused, recalling the king's insistence on absolute certainty. He decided once again to send small boats to approach the enemy warships, then kept an uneasy watch as he awaited their return.

For the next twelve hours Cheyney looked for a sign, either of hostility or reassurance. Meanwhile an alarming rumor spread that farther to the south the invasion had already begun, and that a companion fleet to the one originally sighted had landed troops on the island of Thanet off the Kentish coast. Reinforcements were sent southward immediately, but almost before they had been dispatched the English boatmen came ashore, looking relieved and smiling.

They told Cheyney that they had been taken aboard the imperial flagship and shown every courtesy by the admiral, who explained that his fleet was bound for Spain, not England, and that he meant no harm whatever to them or their coasts. If they doubted his word they had only to see for themselves how undermanned and poorly armed the ships were, equipped more like merchantmen than gunships, their holds bursting with provisions for the emperor's planned voyage to Constantinople. On boarding their own boats again the Englishmen received a final token of respect: a parting salute from the Hapsburg fleet's inadequate guns.[13]

With the passing of this crisis the tension began to lift, and in the following weeks, as no further peril showed itself, the war measures began to wind down. The ships returned to their docks and their crews went ashore. The London militia and the shire levies disbanded, their captains leaving for their country estates. Thomas Cheyney relaxed at his post, and heard to his extreme pleasure that he had been elected a Knight of the Garter. The king, who had on the whole rather enjoyed all the excitement, set off with a reduced household to spend the summer in his hunting parks, and turned his thoughts once again to matrimony.

37

This is all that women do,
Sit and answer them that woo;
Deck themselves in new attire,
To entangle fresh desire;
After dinner sing and play,
Or dancing, pass the time away.

ONE weapon Henry had not chosen to wield against his enemies during the critical months just past: the offering of his hand and throne in marriage. Had he done so he could easily have set his opponents at odds, for to take either a French or a Hapsburg bride would have renewed the longstanding distrust between Francis I and Charles V and might even have rekindled war between them. That Henry did not commit himself finally to marry was a measure of his faith in England's defenses should war come, and of the usefulness of his availability as a diplomatic drawing card. His private desires, though discernible, played on the whole a minor role in his choice.

For more than two years following the death of Queen Jane the king was the object of intense matchmaking by his councilors—particularly Cromwell. More than a dozen women were brought forward as possible brides, from Mary Skipwith and his former mistress Margaret Shelton, thought to be the most likely candidates among the ladies of the English court, to Francis I's daughter Marguerite, to the dazzling Christina, duchess of Milan, said to be the most beautiful woman in Flanders. Women of all ages and descriptions were suggested. The matronly widow of the earl of Egmond ("over forty, but does not look it") was recommended alongside a fourteen-year-old waiting maid at the Flemish court, who despite her youth was said to be "of goodly stature, virtuous, sad and womanly." The duke of Cleves' daughter Anne, thought by one writer to be "of no great praise either of her personage or her beauty," was nonetheless proposed for the sake of the diplomatic advantages which an alliance with the duchy would represent.[1]

While the merits of these and other potential mates were being debated Henry played the role of a sedate widower, understandably cautious about the prospect of entering on the "extreme adventure" of marriage a fourth time. If taking four brides was not exactly unheard-of—after all, Suffolk had done it, and he was not unique—it was far from customary; in marrying yet again Henry would be giving ample demonstration of the triumph of hope over experience.

Given his marital history the king might well be excused if he forswore matrimony altogether. Long after her death Katherine of Aragon was still causing him difficulties. He was eager to claim her estate, valued at some five thousand marks, as his by right, but the money was entangled in an unusually complex probate case. At issue was Katherine's legal status. If, as Henry had spent years of effort trying to show, she was not and had never been his wife, then her goods were not his to claim. As an unmarried woman she could have made a will naming her heir or heirs, yet because to her dying day Katherine held herself to be married she died intestate, which meant that her property had to be administered by her Spanish relatives. Doubtless the irony of the situation was not lost on Henry as he read with wry dismay the reports of his lawyers cautioning him against trying to seize assets legally due the crown of Spain.[2]

As for Anne Boleyn, he could only pray never to run across her like again. And even Jane Seymour, to all appearances a more than satisfactory wife save for her mortal delicacy, gave Henry some pause. Within a week of their marriage he had been overheard to regret his choice. Catching sight of two beautiful girls at court he "said and showed himself somewhat sorry that he had not seen them before he was married."[3]

Overall Henry took maximum advantage of his situation, allowing his advisers and diplomats to design any number of matrimonial schemes—several of them calling for multiple weddings for the king and one or more of his three children—while he professed no more than disinterested acquiescence in their plans. He had "framed his mind," he said publicly, "both to be indifferent to the thing and to the election of any person from any part that with deliberation shall be thought meet." That is, he would either marry or not, as led by his advisers; if they urged him to take a wife, he would accept any bride they recommended, wherever she came from. To this rather astounding declaration he added the offhand remark that the diplomats negotiating on his behalf "would have good sport to make him amorous at his age."[4]

Henry's wariness in the marriage market was real enough, but no one took seriously his claim to be indifferent about the choice of a bride. He would not be content with secondhand reports. He must see and speak with his intended before making a final decision. "The king my master," Cromwell announced to the German Protestants in 1538, "is not one to marry without having first seen and known the princess who is to be his companion for life."[5] As it turned out this crucial requisite was to be ignored, with fateful results.

Among the imperial candidates Henry's favorite by far was the duchess of Milan, preferred primarily for her claims to the duchy ruled by her late husband, Francesco Sforza, but also for her vast personal charms. A niece of Charles V, Duchess Christina had been married at thirteen and widowed a year later. She was now a blooming sixteen, and rumored to be "both widow and maid," as Katherine of Aragon had claimed to be when Henry married her. (Christina was of course Katherine's great-niece, which meant that she was related to Henry by affinity; had he cared about such things, this would have made her unsuitable.) The more Henry heard of Christina the more he was enchanted by her. She was said to be very tall, gentle of countenance and soft of speech. When she spoke she lisped, "which did nothing misbecome her," and when she smiled "there appeareth two pits in her cheeks and one in her chin, the which becometh her right exceedingly well." Though not so fair-skinned as Jane Seymour, Christina had exceedingly pretty features, and bore a strong resemblance to Margaret Shelton, whose attraction for Henry was beyond doubt.[6]

Henry sent Holbein to sketch a likeness of the dimpled duchess, and was so "singularly pleased" with the result that he began to act at once like a man in love. His spirits rose, he commanded his musicians to play all day long and far into the night, and he filled his evenings with masking—either a sign of budding romance, Chapuys commented, or a smokescreen intended to mislead the French.[7] On the English side at least there seemed to be nothing but enthusiasm for the match, yet the imperialists were cautious. Before he gave his niece to Henry the emperor would be certain to insist on a papal dispensation, an impossibility in anti-papal England. Christina herself, accounted to be "the wisest of the wise" despite her age and customary reticence, had her doubts about becoming queen of England. Her councilors were adamantly opposed to the idea, convinced as they were that any wife of Henry VIII would be certain to suffer an unnatural death. To a man they warned Christina "that her great-aunt was poisoned, the second was put to death and the third lost for lack of keeping her childbed."[8]

If one woman stood out among the Hapsburg candidates the French court abounded in potential brides. That "warren of honorable ladies," as Castillon termed it, yielded at least a half-dozen attractive women, any one of whom could be counted on to grace Henry's throne. If, as Francis was supposed to have said, "a court without ladies is like a year without springtime," then at the French court it was perpetual spring. "I never saw so many women," Francis Bryan wrote while on an embassy to France. "I would I had as many sheep to find my house whilst I live."[9] There were so many, in fact, that it seemed unreasonable to expect any suitor to approach each one individually. Would Francis agree to assemble seven or eight of them at Calais, Henry asked Castillon, "especially of the houses of Lorraine or Vendôme and Nevers," so that he could come there and make their acquaintances all at the same time?

The response was an abrupt no. "It is not the custom in France to send damsels of that rank and of such noble and princely families to be passed in review as if they were hackneys for sale," Francis replied haughtily. If Henry desired one of the women, he should send his envoys to report on her manner and appearance in the traditional way.[10] When Castillon told Henry much the same thing he got an emphatic reaction.

"By God!" Henry said. "I trust no one but myself. The thing touches me too near. I wish to see them and know them some time before deciding."

The ambassador answered, half laughing, "Maybe your Grace would like to mount them one after another, and keep the one you find to be the best broken in? Is that the way the Knights of the Round Table treated women in your country in times past?''

These pointed questions shamed Henry, Castillon wrote, ''for he laughed and blushed at the same time,'' and saw the indelicacy of his proposal. He hesitated before speaking again, and rubbed his nose, and shifted the conversation to the friendship between Francis and Charles.[11]

There was no mass gathering of French brides, but the portraits, descriptions and the reports of his envoys gave Henry much information without it. He liked best what he heard of Marie de Guise, whose ample proportions matched his own. (Henry's girth widened prodigiously in the late 1530s; his wardrobe accounts and other court records contain frequent payments to his tailors for letting out his doublets and jackets.[12]) Only two months after Queen Jane's death Castillon believed him to be so enamored of Marie that he would do nearly anything to gain her hand. He had been heard to express the rather unromantic sentiment that ''he was big in person and had need of a big wife''; ambassadorial reports had convinced him that Marie was just the right size. But she proved to be unavailable, having been promised to James V of Scotland many months before, and Henry was forced into the uncomfortable role of uncle by marriage to a woman he ''would have given half his kingdom to marry.''

Even more irritating was the fact that Marie was handed over to Henry's strapping, insouciant nephew, whose sexual arrangements were as disorderly as those of his aging mother Margaret. James's fragile French wife Madeleine had died after only six months of Scots cheer and Scots weather; Marie might well succumb to the same contagions. In any case Henry was expected to welcome her into the family with avuncular generosity, and he began to receive importunate letters from his sister asking for money and ''silver work'' to use in preparing for the wedding. Henry declined to send either, but received unbidden assurances from Margaret afterward that all had gone well, and that James and his new bride had ''great love between them.''[13]

Rather than lament the loss of Marie de Guise, Castillon told Henry, he ought to take comfort from the fact that she had two sisters. One of them, Renée, was said to be the beauty of the family but was intended for the religious life. The remaining girl, Louise de Guise, seemed perfect. A Scotsman who had seen both Louise and Marie pronounced the former to be ''the most beautiful creature that he ever saw,'' and the French ambassador underscored this impression. Louise was not only lovely and graceful, bred to please and obey the man she married, she was a virgin besides. ''Take her,'' Castillon advised lasciviously. ''She is still a maid; with her you will be able to shape the passage to your measure.'' Henry laughed at this, and clapped Castillon on the shoulder. Then, still smiling over the ambassador's earthiness, he dismissed him ''with a good countenance.''[14]

It was in September of 1539, when the immediate danger of invasion from the continent had passed and all pending marriage negotiations had cooled, that final arrangements were made to provide a fourth wife for the king. It was to be as much a match with a principality as with a woman.

The duchy of Cleves, whose Rhineland territories bordered the Hapsburg Netherlands, offered great strategic value in any future conflict between Henry and Charles V. The duke, whose full title was "William, Duke of Juliers, Gelders, Cleves and Berg, Count of Marchia, Zutphania and Ravensburg, and lord in Ravenstein," had recently come into possession of Gelderland, a region disputed by the emperor and a particular irritant at this time of political turbulence in the Low Countries. Cleves was also a prime recruiting ground for the much-sought-after German mercenaries who formed the core of most sixteenth-century fighting forces. Duke William was not a Lutheran but had close ties with the German Protestants whose aid Henry had solicited without success in recent years; though outside the Schmalkaldic League himself he was the brother-in-law of the Lutheran elector of Saxony and was closely connected to Philip of Hesse, both men leading members of the League.

Duke William's sister Anne seemed to fit Henry's personal requirements nearly as well as her brother fit his political ones. At twenty-four she was neither too young nor too old for him; though lacking the linguistic and musical attainments common among wellborn Englishwomen she was intelligent and capable of learning; of a gentle and undemanding nature, she was accustomed to a quiet life of needlework and gentility in the company of a rather strict and hovering mother.[15] There seemed no reason to doubt her fitness for motherhood. To Henry she appeared to be "of convenient age [and] healthy temperament" to bear him children, and he hoped they would produce sons together.

Prince Edward was now nearly two years old, and "one of the prettiest children of his age that could be seen anywhere." He had stood alone on his sturdy legs long before he was a year old, and would have walked, a visitor wrote, if his nurse had let him. Like his father he was good-natured yet shrewd, with "so earnest an eye as it were a sage judgement towards every person that repaireth to his grace."[16] The little prince was a continual comfort to his father, yet both the king and his subjects wished there were more sons; there were even some among the people who questioned Edward's right as heir on the grounds that Jane Seymour had not had a coronation. And as always there was the danger that the prince might die from a childhood disease or plague or as a result of some darker force. In 1538 a porter at the University of Oxford told of seeing a waxen replica of Edward—a doll used in sympathetic magic—with a knife through its heart.[17]

Of the health and nubility of Anne of Cleves there was no doubt, but her looks were another matter. The earliest ambassadorial descriptions were not only favorable but flowery. "Every man praises the beauty of the lady," Henry's envoy Christopher Mont wrote from the court of Cleves, "as well for the face as for the whole body, above all ladies excellent." Anne was said to excel the duchess of Milan, the beauty of all Flanders and Henry's particular favorite, "as the golden sun did the silver moon."[18] Yet until she became the object of Henry's attention Anne had never been spoken of as a beauty; candid appraisals had been less than flattering. English envoys sent to provide a fuller description came away

uncertain. They had been allowed to interview both Anne and her sister
Amelie, yet the "monstrous habit and apparel" in which the women were
swathed hid their faces and disguised their figures.[19]

Holbein's portraits dispelled all doubts. He painted Anne and Amelie
with his customary fidelity to feature and expression; the portrait of Anne
seems to have satisfied Henry, for within weeks of its arrival in August
negotiations with the Clevan representatives were under way, and by
early October the marriage treaty had been drawn up. A slight shadow
hung over the match. Anne had at one time been promised to a son of the
duke of Lorraine, and the English negotiators had to make certain this did
not stand as an impediment to her marriage to Henry. By October 6 they
were convinced, and the treaty was signed at Hampton Court.

The next two months were taken up with hurried preparations for the
reception of the new queen. She would travel overland to Calais, then
cross the Channel to Dover, it was decided. Her overanxious mother was
concerned that a sea journey in winter might "alter her complexion," not
to mention her health, and there was always danger from pirates and from
the imperial fleet. In Flanders news of the betrothal was already bringing
angry threats. It was widely believed there that Henry had actually
promised his throne to the duchess of Milan. If he intended to break his
promise, the Flemish insisted, they would at least see to it "he should
never enjoy the sister of the duke of Cleves."[20]

The English accepted the coming of the king's German bride without
demur, and the townspeople of Dover and Canterbury and Rochester set
to work planning official receptions for Anne when she passed through on
her way to London. At Henry's court the nobles and gentlewomen sent
for large quantities of cloth of gold and silk, and ordered their gowns for
the wedding and coronation. Painters and plasterers were brought in to
repair and decorate Hampton Court, especially the queen's apartments,
and to make it a honeymoon palace once again.

The task of ordering Anne's household and providing for her large
German retinue fell to Cromwell, who was only too pleased to smooth the
way for an alliance he had worked untiringly to promote. The number of
the new queen's English and German servants, the ordering of their
liveries, the assigning of their beds and their places at table occupied him
more and more as the day of Anne's arrival approached. And he had the
unenviable task of sifting among all the requests for places in Anne's
establishment from the women of the court. There could be only so many
ladies in waiting and privy chamber women and maids of honor; for every
petitioner Cromwell was able to satisfy he had to disappoint several
others.

The immediate challenge was to work out the arrangements at Calais,
where a large company of English courtiers would meet the Clevans
coming from Antwerp. Lodgings had to be procured for all the hundreds
of visitors, and halls and kitchens rented for them to eat in. How much of
the cost the king would bear was unclear—but until that was decided he
had to send money across the Channel in advance to secure space in the
houses and inns, and to begin the bargaining with innkeepers and stew-

ards. Where the English party was concerned no detail escaped his notice, not even the provision of dishes and napkins and tablecloths. The Germans were a different problem. There were to be some three hundred and fifty of them, including nearly a hundred of Anne's personal servants (her gentlewomen and household officers and their pages, her cook, physician, chaplain and secretary) and an escort of notables and ambassadors. There were thirteen trumpeters and "a man who plays upon two things as drums of a strange fashion." All of these people had to be looked after at least temporarily, though the majority of them were to return to Cleves once Anne was safely in English hands.[21]

Anne set out from Düsseldorf and made her way slowly to Antwerp, where the English merchants of the town, arrayed in velvet coats and heavy gold chains, rode out to greet her.[22] From there she traveled to the coast and down along it until, early in the morning of December 11, she and her party entered the English Pale. A military escort met them there, the officers of the Calais garrison and town, the captains of the adjoining fortress of Rysbank and of the newly formed King's Spears, and a contingent of liveried royal archers. Another welcoming party of a dozen English lords and nearly three hundred gentlemen and yeomen wearing the king's colors of red and blue rode up to the travelers a mile out of Calais, and as they led them into the town all the cannon boomed out again and again in greeting. The ships in the harbor too shot off their guns, the largest of them, the *Lion* and the *Sweepstake*, making "such a smoke that her train could not see one another."[23]

Anne and her retinue stayed in Calais for more than two weeks waiting for a favorable wind to cross to England. Though the weather was poor, jousts were held in her honor (while waiting for Anne to arrive the younger English knights had spent their time jousting for their own amusement), and in the evenings there were banquets and games. Thomas Wriothesley, lord admiral, taught Anne to play a card game that Henry liked, and perhaps she learned a little English as well. Overall she adjusted quickly to the strangeness of her surroundings and her new English companions. She was dignified without being haughty, amiable yet not overly familiar. Perhaps she felt at once the particular liking for the English she was later to show so strongly. "Her manner was like a princess," Wriothesley wrote to Henry, who was becoming impatient to see his fiancée. Lady Lisle described Anne as "good and gentle to serve and please," and wrote reassuringly to her daughter at Hampton Court that she and the other gentlewomen would have a good-natured mistress.

Finally two days after Christmas the crossing was made, amid stormy seas and driving rain. Another splendidly clad delegation was waiting to meet the visitors when they landed at Deal, and to ride with them to Dover and then on to Canterbury. The weather seemed to grow more foul each day, and Anne had to shield her complexion against heavy winds and hailstones. Her good spirits held up nonetheless. When after a long, wet day she was conducted to her chamber at Canterbury she found some fifty women of the town in velvet bonnets waiting for her there, and offering her service. "All which," Suffolk wrote to Cromwell, telling him to pass the news on to the king, "she took very joyously, and was so glad to see the king's subjects resorting so lovingly to her, that she forgot all the foul weather and was very merry at supper."[24]

At Greenwich Henry read each of the letters about Anne again and again, pacing the floor in vexation. Their formal meeting was five days away. How could he wait that long? Since mid-December he had been "not a little desirous" to have Anne by his side; now he found the waiting intolerable, especially since Suffolk had written that she too was "desirous to make haste" to join him.

At last, too restless to wait another hour, he made up his mind to act. Anne was to arrive at Rochester on New Year's Eve. He would surprise her there on New Year's Day, bursting in on her as in his youth he had burst in on Katherine and her maidens, disguised as Robin Hood. When she recovered her composure they would laugh together, and he would kiss her and give her gifts—sables for her neck and throat, and a furred muffler and cap.[25]

On New Year's Eve Henry and a few companions dressed themselves in modest coats and caps of gray velvet, and set off on their romantic errand. Henry rode hard for the coast, eager to see his bride at last, eager, as he confided to Cromwell before he left, "to nourish love."

38

You husbands, match not but for love
Lest some disliking after prove.

IT was after noon on New Year's Day when Henry and his party rode up to Rochester Abbey and dismounted in the courtyard. After riding so far the king must have been weary—he rode so rarely now that his stables had sadly declined—but he hardly paused to catch his breath before making his way to the rooms where Anne was lodged and walking in, unannounced. There she was, the woman compared to the sun in beauty, the face and form Holbein had ennobled with his lifelike portraiture. There she stood in the flesh, her tall body less than pleasing in its stiff, old-fashioned German robes, her complexion more brown than white, her face more regal than maidenly, with a shrewd and determined set to her features that did not promise obedience.

Henry caught his breath, "marvellously astonished and abashed," a companion wrote, by what he saw. He was thoroughly taken aback, but good manners forced him to go up to Anne and embrace her, and to give her a chaste kiss of welcome. His "discontentment and misliking of her person" could hardly be hidden, though, and after the briefest of conversations—excusably brief, given Anne's linguistic limitations—he left as suddenly as he had come.

Probably that first meeting was enough to make Henry rue his betroth-al. By the time Anne reached London two days later he could think of nothing but how to free himself. He made no secret of his dissatisfaction with Anne, telling John Russell, who went with him to Rochester, that "he saw no such thing in her as hath been showed unto him of her." He "liked her not," he told Russell plainly, and looked "sore troubled" as he said it.[1] It was equally clear to Suffolk that Henry "liked not the queen's person," and that he wanted nothing more than to be free of his obligation to her. To Cromwell, the man chiefly responsible for bringing Anne to England, Henry was blunt. Had he known beforehand what he knew now, he told the lord privy seal, she would never have set foot in England.[2]

Others besides Henry judged that Anne's attractiveness had been overrated. The French ambassador Marillac wrote candidly that she was "tall and thin, of middling beauty, with a determined and resolute countenance." She looked to be about thirty years old (well advanced in years for a sixteenth-century woman), and was on the whole a good deal less handsome than the English had been led to believe. The rather plain-featured waiting maids she brought with her only enhanced her unloveliness. They were scarcely admired by the English crowds that came to see the queen, but then they wore such "coarse and unsightly garb," Marillac conceded, "that they would be considered ugly through it even had they any personal attractions."[3]

Apparently Anne's German upbringing left her somewhat unpolished in courtly manners; one of her English waiting women, Lady Browne, confided to her husband that the king would find his new wife too uncultured to tolerate. "She saw in the queen such fashion and manner of bringing up," she said, "so gross that in her judgement the king should never heartily love her."[4] It was no wonder Henry felt misused as well as misled by his advisers. In a reflective moment he mused on the injustice of arranged marriages. The state of princes, he lamented, was far worse than that of poor men who could at least choose their wives for themselves.[5]

For the moment Henry gave no public sign that the wedding plans were being reconsidered. He carried out the elaborately formal welcoming arranged for Anne at the foot of Shooter's Hill near Greenwich, riding across Blackheath with a spectacular escort of six thousand attendants, "with marvellous silence and no confusion," to meet her. He was still an awesomely commanding figure on horseback—though it took a much stronger horse to carry him now—and as always he dressed for the crowd, his massive form outlined in jewels of incomparable size and brilliance. His coat of purple and gold was fastened with "great buttons of diamonds, rubies and Orient pearl"; around his neck he wore a collar of pearls and huge rubies; his sword and sword belt were ornamented with sparkling emeralds, and his bonnet and nightcap (worn because of the freezing weather and, perhaps, to hide his baldness) were "so rich of jewels that few men could value them."

Anne too was splendidly attired in a costly gown of cloth of gold, with a pearl-trimmed bonnet on her head and around her neck and chest "a partelet set full of rich stones which glistered all the field." She and her gentlewomen had been awaiting the king in a large golden pavilion, warmed inside with braziers and made sweet-smelling with incense and perfumes. As Henry approached she came into view at the door of the tent, mounted her palfrey and rode toward him accompanied by her footmen wearing the black lion of Cleves on their liveries. With "most lovely countenance and princely behavior" Henry took off his bonnet and saluted Anne, embracing her warmly "to the great rejoicing of the beholders." Then they rode together off the field, flanked by the merchants of the city, the lord mayor and aldermen, the bishops and nobles, the ladies and gentlewomen in their ranks.

At Greenwich Henry bade Anne "welcome to her own," their arrival at the palace marked by a great peal of guns, but as soon as he had left her at the door of her chamber he began a last-minute effort to forestall the wedding. He summoned Cromwell and ordered an immediate meeting of his privy councilors and the envoys of the duke of Cleves. The solemnization of the betrothal might be prevented on two grounds: either that the German envoys failed to bring an official commission from the duke authorizing them to conclude the legalities of the marriage, or that they could not provide written evidence that Anne's prior betrothal to the duke of Lorraine's son had been formally revoked. Both questions were raised at the Council meeting, and the Germans, "much abashed," had to admit that they could not produce the required documents. They offered to send for them, however, and Henry, realizing that at best this tactic could only postpone and not prevent the dreaded union, did not press the issue.

Recalling these events later the king's servants claimed that it had been Cromwell who, taking Henry aside and talking to him "secretly," at last persuaded him to go through with the wedding. Even so he made his reluctance obvious. "My lord," he said to Cromwell on his wedding morning, "if it were not to satisfy the world and my realm, I would not do that I must do this day for none earthly thing."

Henry showed his mood of heavy-hearted resignation in the way he prepared that morning for the ceremony, taking twice as long as usual to allow his chamberers to dress him in his wedding finery. At last he was ready, and walked as slowly as courtesy permitted to the gallery adjoining his chamber where Archbishop Cranmer was waiting to join him to his fourth wife. The sight of Anne in her rich pearl-studded wedding gown, her "fair, yellow and long" hair hanging to her waist and a jeweled coronal on her head did nothing to alleviate his forlorn mood. She cùrtsied to him three times "with most demure countenance"; he forced a wan smile in reply. The vows were exchanged, the bride given away by one of her attendants, the earl of Overstein. Within minutes the ceremony was over, and on Anne's finger was a gold wedding ring engraved with the words "God send me well to keep."[6]

For the rest of the day Henry dreaded the coming of night, and the hour of retiring, and the unavoidable moment when he and Anne must be alone. The day passed in masses and collations and banqueting, the evening in masks and "diverse disports." But then "the time came that it pleased the king and her to take their rest," and he led his wife to her bed.

Then began an ordeal of spirit as acute as any Henry had ever undergone. He had taken Anne to wife in all good conscience, expecting to force his body to the distasteful task of begetting sons by her. Yet though he "did as much to move the consent of his heart and mind as ever man did," his revulsion overcame his determination.

Time and again he tried, lying with Anne night after night yet ever "leaving her as good a maid as he found her." He was not reticent about her imperfections. He complained to his gentlemen that her breasts were loose and slack, her belly stretched and unmaidenly. He believed he had reason to suspect her virginity—while maintaining that he had never tested it—and the more he brooded on the issue the more he was "struck to the heart" by it and incapacitated for lovemaking. After several months of this he began to remark ruefully that he doubted he would ever have any more children, adding that "before God he thought [Anne] was not his lawful wife."[7]

Until Easter Henry was well advised to pretend, in public at least, that he was satisfied with his bride. His alliance with the duke of Cleves had had the predictable effect of making Charles V more insecure; as if in response to the new coalition the emperor had come northward from Spain to attend to his interests in the Low Countries and the Rhineland. A clash between Charles and Henry's brother-in-law of Cleves over the disputed area of Gelders seemed imminent, especially as, in the view of Henry's ambassador, Gelders meant more to the emperor than Milan, more even than all Italy. Charles was meanwhile displaying his friendship with Francis by sojourning in Paris, and as long as he stayed there Henry did not dare to suggest that his Protestant marriage was blemished by a fatal flaw.

The king might speak candidly to his intimates about his dubious wedded state but no one else must know: to all appearances the pulse of life at his court quickened with the coming of the new queen, with Anne presiding over "a great court of noblemen and gentlemen" engaged in tournaments and disguisings and similar diversions. Discerning courtiers might notice that the king's gaze rested too often on his wife's round little waiting maid Catherine Howard, but Anne herself said nothing, and professed to be perfectly happy with her situation. She sent word to her mother and brother thanking them for arranging for her "such a marriage that she could wish no better." That she was the king's wife in name only seemed a minor anomaly.[8] Members of Anne's retinue who left England in the aftermath of the wedding told no tales; overburdened with gilt cups and fat purses of coins from Henry's bounty, their wages and expenses paid from the English treasury, they carried back only stories of marital harmony and happiness.[9]

But as the spring wore on Henry's patience with his sham matrimony wore thin. What was more, the diplomatic situation which had compelled him to continue the nominal marriage was changing. The emperor left Paris, and soon afterward his relations with the French king showed increasing strain. His feud with the duke of Cleves lost much of its fervor, while Henry's need for the duke—and for his Lutheran colleagues in the Schmalkaldic League—dwindled. And there had been a shift in the legal status of the marriage. The documents sought for on Anne's arrival in England finally came to light many weeks later, and to the surprise of all concerned they showed that her precontract with the duke of Lorraine's son had in fact been a binding union, not merely a future promise to wed, revocable at need.

A way out of the regrettable marriage had shown itself. Cromwell must once again engineer a divorce—actually, as with Katherine of Aragon, a nullity suit—and smooth the way for a new queen.

By April Henry's infatuation with Catherine Howard was becoming a subject of scandal, though it was not yet clear that he meant her to replace Anne of Cleves as queen. She was thirty years his junior, with a charm of face and manner that beguiled the king the way her cousin Anne Boleyn had beguiled him many years before. He began to favor her with gifts— quilts and jewels and painted brooches—and spent more and more time with her. They met at Norfolk's London house, or at Gardiner's episcopal palace. Londoners became accustomed to the sight of Henry's barge as he rode up or downriver into the city from Greenwich or Richmond to see Catherine at all hours of the day or night. They gossiped about his adultery, never guessing that he held himself to be unmarried in the sight of God, and when at last they heard that he had separated from Anne of Cleves they presumed at once that Catherine Howard must be pregnant by the king.[10]

So the months passed, and still Cromwell delayed beginning the divorce proceedings. He could hardly do otherwise, given the dangerous choices he faced. To proceed with the nullity suit would have meant not only admitting the failure of his policy favoring the German Protestants but aiding the triumph of Catherine Howard's uncle, Cromwell's arch-rival Norfolk. To advise the king against a divorce was unthinkable—and futile. So Cromwell delayed, while attending to parliamentary bills, attempting to forestall an assault by Gardiner over the radical religious views of Robert Barnes, managing the day-to-day supervision of interna-tional affairs. Meanwhile his enemies grew stronger, and plotted his downfall.

By 1540 Cromwell was among the most hated men in England. Like his predecessor and mentor Wolsey he was hated by all sorts and conditions of the king's subjects, though where Wolsey had been despised for his arrogance and ostentation it was the inhuman ruthlessness of Cromwell's methods that drew down on him the people's wrath. Thousands of lives had been touched by his administration of the treason law; in person or through his agents he had sentenced hundreds of men and women to the pillory or to prison. More than five dozen of his victims had been hanged, drawn and quartered in chilling public executions.[11] Though his achievements in transforming royal administration were as remarkable as they were far-reaching they hardly counted to his contem-poraries in government, who saw in him only a lowborn opportunist who at last rose too high.

Among Cromwell's bitterest enemies was Cardinal Reginald Pole, who called him "the messenger of Satan" and looked forward to the time when his misdeeds would be punished. The day would come, Pole said, when the lord privy seal would feel the pains of all those he had sent to die, and on that day Londoners would witness one of the most joyous entertainments ever offered them.[12] (Pole's malevolence grew out of unbearable grief. Cromwell had sworn to make the cardinal "eat his heart"; when many of Pole's relatives were executed or imprisoned in 1539 Cromwell's oath was fulfilled.)

Next to Pole Norfolk bore most malice against Cromwell, and stood to gain most by his removal from government. Yet the king's favor had always shielded him from the duke. Though he mistreated and underesti-mated his chief servant Henry had thus far stood by him in his quarrels with his rivals. Henry never forgot that, no matter how great his genius, Cromwell was a commoner, unfit by birth "to intermeddle with the affairs of kings." He treated him like a page or a kitchen boy, raging at him frequently and "knocking him well about the pate" on occasion, though

Cromwell invariably shook off the blows and recovered his composure almost at once.[13] Yet the more the king abused him the more he esteemed him, to judge from the honors Cromwell accumulated. In April of 1540, when Henry's impatience over the nullity suit was mounting, he exalted Cromwell to the high rank of earl of Essex. To all appearances the king's commoner had reached the pinnacle of worldly success.[14]

Two months later, on June 10, Cromwell was seized without warning as he sat at the Council table and arrested as a traitor. Norfolk stood before him, stern and sardonic, relishing his revenge. He snatched the collar of the Garter from around Cromwell's neck and motioned to the captain of the guard to take his prisoner away. Bemused at first by the suddenness of these events Cromwell did not react, but as he regained himself he exploded in fury, snatching off his bonnet and slamming it to the floor. This time his protector had not intervened. He was beaten, and what slight hope he had of royal clemency was extinguished when he heard that his goods had been seized at once on his arrest. There was no need to await the verdict of his trial; his fate was clear.

Indeed there was no trial, only an overwhelmingly convincing (and unrecorded) denunciation to the king, who in the end was persuaded that the earl of Essex was a dangerous heretic, a source of contagion to the true belief and a sworn traitor besides. Cromwell espoused sacramentarian doctrines—the same doctrines Henry had personally confuted in his debate with John Lambert, who had been burned for holding them—and beyond that, Henry was told, he had committed himself to fight for these doctrines against any opponent, even the king. Henry must have heard from Cromwell's enemies how on one occasion he defended the erroneous teachings of Robert Barnes (who was in fact not a sacramentarian but a Lutheran), saying that if the king disavowed them he would "fight in his own person, with his sword in his hand, against him and all others." According to the story Cromwell had underscored his threat by drawing his dagger and swearing a high oath: "Or else this dagger thrust me to the heart, if I would not die in that quarrel against them all."[15]

It was a dramatic story calculated to offend the king's strong sense of orthodoxy while impressing itself on his chivalrous mentality as well. He allowed himself to be convinced, pushed toward conviction by his dissatisfaction over the nullity suit. He abandoned his brilliant servant to his enemies, and remained unmoved by Cromwell's desperate, pleading letters from his Tower prison, begging for "mercy, mercy, mercy!" He kept him alive, though, long enough to serve as a key witness in the divorce.

A month after Cromwell's arrest Henry was declared to be an unmarried man once again. After first sending Anne away to Richmond he set in motion the official chain of events culminating in the parliamentary declaration of nullity. There were no legal difficulties. The precontract was put in evidence, and with it Henry's testimony, backed up by the written recollections of his chamber servants and the former lord privy seal, that he had lacked the will and power to consummate the marriage. His inability was taken to show his lack of consent; he swore on his word as a gentleman that "if Anne brought maidenhead with her" to England, then as far as he was concerned she was still a maid.[16]

No account was taken of what Anne of Cleves might think of these proceedings, yet when she was formally notified of their outcome by a delegation of courtiers she received the news "without alteration of countenance," and showed herself to be almost perversely compliant with Henry's wishes. He had taken care to sweeten the sour news with a purse of coins, but the precaution was unnecessary. Without hesitation Anne sat down with her interpreter to read the letters Henry had written her, and afterward declared herself ready to give her consent to all that had been done—or rather undone. She wrote him a reply, accepting his judgment while acknowledging that "the case must be hard and sorrowful," and that only her "regard for God and his truth"—and her ever lively obedience—could persuade her to put aside her great love for the man she once thought to be her husband. She signed the letter "Your Majesty's most humble sister and servant," and to symbolize her change in status she sent Henry the wedding ring she had worn for six months, asking him to have it "broken into pieces as a thing which she knew of no force or value."[17]

The reasoning behind Anne's acquiescence, and her subsequent decision to spend the rest of her life in England, was not far to seek. If to Henry she was no more than a troublesome impediment to his fifth marriage to her brother in Cleves she had become a hated liability, an object of intense resentment and possible violence. She told the English courtiers in no uncertain terms that if she returned to her homeland her brother would kill her, and there can be no doubt that even if he spared her she would have faced an exceedingly uncomfortable future there as an unwanted, and probably unmarriageable, young dowager.[18] Caught between her cheerfully indifferent "brother" Henry and her vengeful natural brother Duke William, her choice was clear.

And it was well rewarded. After some negotiation—Anne was a clear-headed and practical woman—she agreed to accept a substantial yearly income, with the manors of Richmond and Bletchingly, a sufficient household of servants and furnishings, and a generous assortment of "most precious clothes," jewels and pearls. She kept her Dutch maids Katherine and Gertrude, her cook Schoulenburg, and an honorable title and place in the courtly hierarchy. She would be a marchioness, lower in rank than the king's wife and daughters but higher than any other woman in the realm. And she would occasionally enjoy the king's society as a friend, along with his perpetual gratitude.

Having dispatched Anne Henry had no further use for Cromwell, and on July 28 he went to the block at Tyburn. In his last moments he transcended the ignominy of a traitor's end. Wrongfully accused, condemned unheard, he made no reference to the injustice of his situation in his dignified speech. He repented his sins, and prayed for the king and his heir. Then he spoke his last prayer—not the prayer of a sacramentarian heretic, but that of a humanist and admirer of Erasmus.

Cromwell's death called for more bloodshed. To justify the accusation

that he had protected heretics three men were burned at Smithfield, one of
them the Lutheran Barnes whom Cromwell had indeed protected but who
had himself been a vigorous persecutor of sacramentaries. Barnes, William Jerome, vicar of the London parish of Stepney where Cromwell
lived, and another Lutheran preacher, Thomas Garrett, were brought to
the place of execution and tied to a single wooden stake. None of the men
knew why he was there; when Barnes asked the executioner to name his
crime the man admitted he could not.

Torches were put to the dry wood heaped about the stake, and in a
moment the flames leaped up around the victims' legs. A moment more
and they were overcome by smoke and pain, but before they died the
crowd that watched the horrifying spectacle took careful note of their
behavior. Their faces remained composed, their features neither twisted
in anguish nor contorted in pain. It was as if an unseen force shielded
them against all suffering, and when they spoke the spectators strained to
hear their last words, the words of martyrs in an extraordinary state of
grace.

As the reek of burning flesh rose over the field three other men were
led to their deaths: Thomas Abell, once Katherine of Aragon's chaplain,
Edward Powell, a cleric who had written in her defense years before, and
Richard Featherstone, former tutor to her daughter Mary. These Catholic
victims too were linked to the fall of Cromwell, creating a grotesque
balance of suffering that satisfied his opponents—not the king, who may
well have been ignorant of all these executions.

Yet if Henry knew nothing of these events his ignorance was perhaps
understandable. He was far away at Oatlands, enjoying the company of
the woman he had married the day Cromwell died, his "rose without a
thorn," Catherine Howard.

VI

Old Harry

39

Henry, our royall king, would ride a hunting
To the greene forest so pleasant and faire;
To see the harts skipping, and dainty does tripping:
Unto merry Sherwood his nobles repaire:
Hawke and hound were unbound, all things prepar'd
For the game, in the same, with good regard.

AT midsummer of 1541 Henry journeyed northward on progress to the most distant parts of his realm. He had never before traveled so far from London. Lincoln, Pontefract, York, Doncaster—these were only names to him, names he associated with rebellion and reaction. The places themselves he had only imagined, as he imagined the tall, taciturn men and resolute women of the north parts, his fearsome subjects who had never seen their king.

The royal progress was not a simple hunting party but a great traveling court, with some five thousand courtiers and servants making up the king's retinue. No town could house such a host; two hundred large tents and pavilions served as portable sleeping quarters and banqueting halls, kitchens and stables. On traveling days the great tents were folded and carried in carts from one camp site to the next, along with the rugs and hangings and chests of clothes and furnishings that made them seem less bare. On other days, when the king's itinerary called for an extended stay or when bad weather or poor roads caused delays, the tents stayed up, and the full ceremony and activity of court life was recreated within them.

To onlookers the itinerant court resembled an armed camp, for if King Henry took his councilors and courtiers with him he also took fighting men—armed knights and archers and halberdiers with full panoply. There were drummers and trumpeters and military heralds, and warhorses enough, it seemed, to engage battle. And as if this were not protection enough, there were cannon too, sent northward by sea and then upriver to a point near York. It was here, in the heart of the north country, that the royal party might expect to encounter resistance.

York had been a center of rebellion in what was euphemistically referred to as "the commotion time"—the Pilgrimage of Grace—five years earlier, and though the risings of that era had been thoroughly and savagely suppressed a new conspiracy had been uncovered there only recently. Yorkshire was a bastion of support for the remnants of the White Rose, the Poles and Courtenays and Nevilles whose Plantagenet blood put them at odds with Henry Tudor. It was largely to overawe these past and potential rebels that Henry journeyed northward, but he had a second purpose as well. His nephew James V of Scotland had promised to meet him at York in September. For a variety of reasons, ranging from French pressure to fear of capture by the English, James might choose not to honor his promise, but Henry was prepared to meet him if he did.

Because he meant to be away from London for at least three months Henry determined to remove all threat of revolt there by ordering the execution of several Tower prisoners of royal blood. There were a good many of them: Lord Leonard Grey, under suspicion for misconduct in Ireland; Lord Lisle, more incompetent than dangerous, who had been in the Tower for a year and whose prison robes were made by the king's tailor out of deference to his rank; the queen's cousin Lord Dacres, a young rake of twenty-three who with several companions had killed an old man in a brawl; Gertrude Blount, marchioness of Exeter, and Edward Courtenay, widow and son of the late marquis executed as a traitor in 1538; the aged matriarch Margaret Pole, countess of Salisbury and mother of the attainted Reginald Pole and of the condemned traitor Henry Pole, Lord Montague; and finally Montague's young son. (One other Plantagenet, John Neville, was under sentence of death though not in the Tower; it was he who had led the most recent disturbances in the north.)

Four of these prisoners—Grey, Dacres, Neville, and Margaret Pole—were hanged or beheaded, while the others remained imprisoned under strict guard. The deaths of Dacres and Pole caused a mild outcry. Despite his youth and high birth Dacres was dragged through the streets to Tyburn like any lowborn criminal and hanged—a death so ignominious it made his judges weep.[1] For his beheading of the enfeebled countess of Salisbury, butchered by inches by a clumsy novice executioner, Henry won nothing but contempt. Was his throne so insecure he must protect it by slaughtering old women? And was he so heartless as to forget his former respect and affection for his venerable kinswoman?[2]

If the deaths of these noble prisoners aroused pity the dozens of commoners executed along with them attracted relatively less comment. Though never indifferent to it Henry's subjects had become in recent years habituated to judicial violence on a large scale. "It is no new thing to see men hanged, quartered, or beheaded, for one thing or another," a visitor to London wrote in 1541, "sometimes for trifling expressions construed as against the king."[3] Thus the hanging of two archers of the royal guard, a customs controller, a Kentish gentleman, and two knights of Rhodes for offenses ranging from robbery to treason were recorded by court observers without comment. No particular popular reaction was noted when two men, one of them a groom of his chamber, died for counterfeiting the king's seal, or when men were hanged for eating meat on Friday.

One chronicler did note with pity the burning of a boy for heresy. He was only fourteen, far too young to comprehend the doctrines he was accused of perverting. Hearing his elders debate about the theology of the mass, he made the mistake of repeating their words. The bishop of

London heard of it, and condemned him to die; before the fire consumed him he repeated, in "childish innocence and fear," what the bishop's officers had taught him to say in praise of the orthodox belief.[4] But if the monstrous inappropriateness of this execution was perceived the burnings of other heretics were recounted without emotion. Chroniclers noted the burning of three heretics (an Italian painter, an anonymous Englishman and a French groom of Anne of Cleves) as matter-of-factly as they did the annual return of plague or the calling of the midsummer watch, just as the executions of some sixty followers of John Neville, two dozen of them churchmen, called forth neither regret nor revulsion.

This season of bloodshed was after all only an episode in a gory tale extending over several years. Fifty-three people had been attainted in 1539–40, and most of them had died. A dozen more had been burned or beheaded with Cromwell, many others in isolated executions. For some, such as Norfolk's half-brother Thomas Howard (imprisoned for aspiring to marry the king's niece Margaret Douglas), the filth and disease of the rat-ridden Tower brought death more swiftly than the headsman's sword.

The court, always a scene of partisan contention and rivalry, had taken on a darker tone of murderous conflict. Factions rose to power by devouring or annihilating their rivals, only to be in the end devoured themselves. Cromwell and his allies had hounded the great nobles out of power, then had fallen prey to the resurgent influence of Norfolk and his adherents. And as all pre-eminence was transitory, the Norfolk faction now looked for enemies everywhere, and the Privy Council chamber became an arena of snarling discord. "I do not recall having ever seen these people so morose as they are at present," Marillac wrote in 1541, "for they do not know whom to trust, and the king himself, having offended so many people, mistrusts everyone."[5]

Looming in menace over all the infighting was the suspicious, aging king, now riding roughshod over the factions, now using them for his own secret ends, occasionally used by them. His surface mastery of their wrangling concealed much "irresolution and despondency," according to Marillac; he was easily thrown into uncertainty about the loyalty of his courtiers and officials, and his solution was to "dip his hands in blood" again and again.

Henry's unpredictable, murderous wrath had come to be his most potent weapon against his irascible courtiers. When in a fury his reason and understanding deserted him entirely. He became, quite simply, "the most dangerous and cruel man in the world."[6] The violence he had done, the lives he had taken gnawed at him; though he never doubted the morality of his actions (which in many cases were politically justifiable) he was not immune to their corroding influence. In time the unrelenting carnage blighted his spirit and wore away at his judgment, making him more dangerous with every passing year. Henry had after all ordered the executions of a beloved wife, a dozen or more blood relatives and twice as many intimate friends and associates. He no longer hesitated, as he would have once, to order men and women to the block.

He seemed almost to take a macabre pleasure in exercising his life and death powers, occasionally sentencing men to die and then reprieving them at the last minute. He brought his intellect to bear as well, revolving in his mind reasoned justifications for his judicial murders and in one case setting them down in writing. Just as he had boasted of writing a play about Anne Boleyn in the days following her death, so he wrote a "little book"—apparently an imagined post-facto trial—about the deaths of the marquis of Exeter and Lord Montague just after they lost their lives.[7]

Such justifications may have soothed his conscience, but they did nothing to alter his worsening reputation. On the continent, news of Henry's executions met with incredulity, then disgust. "Let us cease to sing the praises of the English Nero," the Protestant leader Melanchthon wrote, regretting that he had flattered Henry and sought his alliance.[8] Within the realm there was profound unease and fear, and a sense that the times themselves were shifting. "Thy father's father never saw such a world," a Berkshire man remarked in amazement. Londoners grew accustomed to watching the gruesome display of severed heads on Tower Bridge; when they were taken down it was a sure sign the king had ordered a harvest of fresh heads to put in their place.[9]

"In England, death has snatched everyone of worth away, or fear has shrank them up," a foreigner commented, and the remark might have stood as an epitaph for the depleted court. To be sure, there were still men and women in abundance around the king, but few of them belonged to his generation; still fewer could recall the joyous early years when the youthful, sunny monarch had presided over a chivalrous court. A new group of young, ambitious courtiers now kept him company, but they could not replace men such as Edward Neville, who had so resembled his royal kinsman, or Henry Courtenay, who had been with the king since boyhood and slept in his chamber, or Nicholas Carew, the spectacular jouster and royal horse master who had been among Henry's inseparable companions. These and many like them had been swept away, tainted by treason, and though the king did not lack company they could not be replaced.

The losses were unusually conspicuous when the exclusive inner circle of courtiers, the Knights of the Garter, met on Saint George's Day to elect new members. The Order of the Garter was more to Henry than a mark of highest distinction and a sacred band of sworn companions: the order and its festivities were linked in a fundamental way with his reign itself. He had been proclaimed king on Saint George's Day in 1509. His regnal years were calculated from that day, and it was his royal birthday, a personal and sentimental occasion. With each annual meeting of the order the king, surrounded by the twenty-five Knights, ended an old cycle and began a new one.

Thus when the Knights Companions assembled at Windsor in 1540 to observe their feast it was dismaying to see how few of them were left. Keeping the records had become a problem, as so many of the names on the rolls belonged to men who had dishonored their place among the Companions by being executed or imprisoned as traitors. The matter had to be brought to the king's attention. Should the names of traitors continue to be carried on the rolls, or should they be blotted out, marring the immaculate appearance of the time-honored records? Henry thought for a while, then gave his judgment. Nothing would be blotted out; instead, opposite each unworthy name the words *"Vah! Proditor!"* — "Oh! Traitor!"—should be written in the margin.[10]

The one new companion who lightened Henry's heart was his young wife Catherine, his thornless rose, the rejuvenating comfort of his old age. Her good effect on him had been apparent from the earliest days of their marriage. It was hunting season, and the king set out each morning at daybreak for the fields, riding with the eager energy of a young man and working up a healthy appetite for an early midday dinner. He declared himself to be in excellent health (his physicians would hardly have agreed), and praised the benefits of country air and exercise in contrast to the pestilential fogs and indoor life of London. Certainly he seemed to have energy to spare, passing his evenings banqueting with the queen, limping through the newest French dances and complimenting his wife and her ladies on their fashionable French gowns.

It was said Henry spent more money on clothes and jewels for his fifth wife than he ever had for any of the others. Every day brought some new caprice to be satisfied, some new bauble purchased. There were chains of gold and ropes of pearls, jeweled crosses and necklaces of table diamonds. One day Henry presented Catherine with a black velvet muffler furred with sables and ornamented with rubies and hundreds of pearls, "betwixt every row of pearls small chains of gold, with also a chain to hang the same muffler containing thirty pearls."[11] Such expenditures were trifling, though, compared to the extravagant affection he lavished on her. "The king caresses her more than he did the others," Chapuys noted of Catherine; though she lacked the haunting, fey sensuality of Anne Boleyn, she awakened and satisfied Henry's desire to the full. Unauthenticated portraits said to be of Catherine do not bear out Marillac's judgment that she was "a lady of great beauty." Her brow and eyes were fair enough, but (if these portraits are to be trusted at all) she had inherited the large Howard nose, and her chubby cheeks and double chin gave her face a slightly bulbous look. In fact Catherine may well have borne an unfortunate resemblance to her uncle Norfolk, whose fishlike face and downward-slanting eyes must have made him one of the uglier men at the court.

To Henry Catherine's youth and vital carnality were what counted, and to celebrate their union he commissioned a French artisan to make a "pearl bed," its dimensions adequate to accommodate his bulk and its decoration a fantasywork of nacreous splendor.[12] How often he joined Catherine in this bed was a matter of public knowledge, attended by ceremony. Once his gentlemen had undressed him and put him to bed in his own chamber, he called for his night-robe and prepared himself for the excursion to the queen's apartments. An escort of grooms of the bedchamber and pages carrying torches accompanied him through the anterooms and passages connecting his apartments with hers, and left him at her door.

The frequency of these nocturnal visits led to the expectation that Catherine would soon become pregnant, but month after month passed and there was no word of a child. By January of 1541, after half a year of marriage, there was talk of the king's displeasure with his wife—most of it the result of Anne of Cleves' recent visit to the king and queen during the holiday season. A few months later, however, Catherine herself became "rather sad and thoughtful" at the possibility that Henry might divorce her and take Anne back, and his reassurances left her unconvinced.[13]

Henry and Catherine had been married nearly a year when the great progress northward began, and by this time they were reported to be somewhat estranged. Henry was behaving toward Catherine as he had toward Anne Boleyn when she seemed barren of sons, "avoiding as much as possible her company" and seeking distractions elsewhere. It was noted that the queen, who had once done nothing but "dance and amuse herself," now shut herself away in her apartments. What she did there only her confidante Lady Rochford knew.

Nearly three weeks after the king and his retinue of five thousand set out for the north he was tempted to abandon the excursion entirely and go home. Only a few miles out of London the caravan was halted by heavy rains. The tents were struck, and the travelers huddled inside them, shivering in the unseasonable cold. Day after day the stormy weather continued, until the fields lay under water and the roads became impassable bogs. The carts and baggage wagons sank into the mire, the courtiers grew bored and irritable, and as a last straw the queen fell sick.[14]

Somehow, toward the end of July the unwieldy cortège got moving again. Norfolk and Suffolk, who had gone ahead to prepare the way, had managed to find a safe route through the marshy fen country and to bargain for grain and other provisions undamaged by the flooding. The queen regained her health, and the courtiers recovered their good spirits in anticipation of the pageantry and hunting to come.

On August 9, a month behind schedule, the royal party arrived in Lincoln. To flatter his northern subjects Henry at first wore Lincoln green, though he had Catherine changed into robes of cloth of gold and silver for their formal entry into the town. The mayor and citizenry made their sovereigns a cheerful and colorful welcome, with orations in Latin and English and a celebration of thanksgiving in the cathedral. There seemed to be no evidence of disaffection, though Henry showed a prudent mistrust for all large gatherings of his subjects throughout his months away from London. Everywhere, in small towns and large, the reception was equally respectful. The citizens decorated the streets with rich cloths and hangings, there was singing and cheering and speechmaking, and then a procession. With the townspeople preceding him and a guard of eighty archers bringing up the rear, Henry and his nobles rode to their lodgings. Beside Henry rode Queen Catherine and his daughter Mary, the latter a much-beloved figure in the Catholic north.

Everywhere he rested the king hunted, and increased his popularity among the local gentry by sending them a portion of the deer and game he killed. Largely because of the size of the royal retinue, the hunting was on an unprecedented scale. Beasts were driven by the hundreds into enclosed areas where the king and his companions, standing in one spot, could shoot them. More slaughter than sport, this pastime pleased Henry partly because he imagined no continental ruler could imitate it. Marillac, who was present on the progress, described a "chase" made near Hatfield, where the well-stocked hunting grounds included not only woods but adjacent ponds and marshes. Here the huntsmen staged a spectacular display of venery. As the king and nobles shot some two hundred stags and does, boatmen swept the marshes for dozens of young swans and other river birds, while fishermen hauled in great quantities of pike and bream and sturgeon. Afterward the hunters dined on the spot, and Henry, who invited the French ambassador to join him in his tent, urged him not to forget to tell King Francis what he had seen that day. While they were eating the king pointed with pleasure to the surplus animals that had been left in reserve for the next day's hunt, some three hundred stags grazing "as near the company as if they had been domestic cattle."[15]

The high point of the progress came when the king confronted the men of Yorkshire who had risen against him in such numbers five years earlier. They came by the thousands to kneel before him and ask his pardon. "We your humble subjects," their spokesman cried out, "confess that we wretches . . . have most grievously, heinously and wantonly offended your majesty in the unnatural, most odious and detestable offenses of outrageous disobedience and traitorous rebellion." They begged Henry to rid his mind of any "relics of indignation" he might harbor against them, and swore that they would pray unceasingly for his preservation, and that of his queen and the prince, from then on. They presented the king with lengthy written submissions as well, and showed him such reverential deference that he could not but be moved.[16]

In his fondest expectation, though, Henry was disappointed. His nephew James failed to keep his appointment as promised, and remained in safety on the Scots side of the border. Much labor and expense was wasted. More than a thousand workmen had been employed to prepare a "great lodging"—a ruined abbey, restored to temporary usefulness—for the royal meeting, and all the hangings and plate and finery of the London court had been hauled north to ornament it. Post horses had been brought from the royal stables to carry messages between Henry at York and James at Berwick as final preparations were made. Yet even as the work went forward the Scots were riding across the border in the name of King James to harry the English, spoiling fields and burning barns and killing anyone who opposed them. And Henry, indignant at the insult, ordered his men on the borders to retaliate with "spoils, burnings and killings, three hurts for one."[17]

Reconciliation between the two kings seemed further off than ever, and Henry, who had already been away from the capital far longer than expected, turned for home.

The return journey took nearly a month. Henry arrived at Hampton Court in the last week of October, disgruntled over the murderous Scots and their unreliable king, yet exhilarated by his excursion in the country and satisfied that his appearance in the north had helped to secure his throne. He was unprepared for the jarring news that awaited him.

Prince Edward was seriously ill. He lay in his gilded bed, a chunky child of four, his face drained of color and his body glistening with sweat from a high fever. The king immediately summoned all the physicians he could reach by messenger, and one by one they came. They peered at the prince, they muttered to one another, they deliberated as a group. Publicly they recommended measures to be taken toward a cure; privately one of them told Marillac that Edward was in danger of his life.[18]

For days the prince remained in the grip of the fever, as his anxious father sought to get on with the business of government after his long absence. Then on November 2 Henry received much worse news. His wife, whose purity he had thought beyond reproach, was in fact an adulteress.

40

Of speech she is too bold,
Of carriage all too free;
Sir king, she hath within thy hall
A cuckold made of thee.

All frolick light and wanton
She hath her carriage borne:
And given thee for a kingly crown
To wear a cuckold's horne.

AT first Henry could not believe the report Cranmer brought him about Catherine. It was an account by an informer, based on a chance remark his sister made wondering "at the king's taking for queen one who had lived so incontinently before marriage." On the face of it the accusation was unworthy of notice, to be taken no more seriously than other slanderous insults reported to the Privy Council every week. Yet in accusing the queen the informer, John Lassells, was taking his life in his hands, and his sister, Mary Hall, had been in a position to know. Had Catherine Howard acted unwisely, and indiscreetly, as a girl? Either way the truth should be sought.

Piece by piece the unhappy tale came out. Catherine had indeed, as Mary Hall testified, been "light, both in living and in conditions." As a very young girl she had been infatuated with Henry Manox, an unprincipled music teacher who came to give her lessons on the virginals and stayed to teach her the facts of life. She had allowed Manox to kiss her and to "feel the secret parts of her body"; he might have gotten further except that Catherine passed into other hands, those of Francis Dereham. With Dereham she lived out an adolescent love fantasy, made all the more exciting by intrigue and midnight revelry and pledges of love and future marriage. Catherine was living in a large household of young people at Lambeth, under the lax supervision of the dowager duchess of Norfolk. She found it easy enough to steal her aunt's keys, let Dereham into her room, and welcome him into her bed.[1]

As more and more witnesses were examined it became clear that Catherine's behavior before coming to court had been far from secret. Her chamber servants at Lambeth, their friends, an old porter, several grooms and the duchess' chamber woman were all privy to the scandal Catherine had caused. Many of her female relatives knew of her past when she became queen, but kept a conspiratorial silence. The duchess maintained that she was ignorant of the entire affair, "holding up her hands and saying she was as innocent as the child newborn," but in the face of much counterevidence no one believed her.

Five days after Henry first heard of his wife's prior entanglements he came to a hard decision: sorrowfully and "with careful proceeding," he ordered that Catherine's household be disbanded, her coffers and chests sealed and her former possessions kept under guard. Proclamation was to be made at Hampton Court that, as she had forfeited her honor, so Catherine had now to forfeit her title of queen; henceforth she was to be plain Catherine Howard again, kept in confinement with "a mean number of servants" at Syon House until the law took its course against her.[2]

Given the extreme embarrassment and disgrace she had brought to him Henry was remarkably lenient. There was talk of sending her to a convent—eventually, after the marriage was declared null. (Nullity would be easy to prove. Dereham swore that he and Catherine had been pledged to one another; this plus consummation made them man and wife under church law. If Catherine was married to Dereham when she married Henry, the latter was no marriage.)

Catherine was suffering enough. There was no need to punish her further. When Cranmer went to see her he found her in a state "it would have pitied any man's heart to see." Remorse over her past, bitter regret that her indiscretions had come to light, even the king's mercy all brought her to tears. While the archbishop was with her the hour of six o'clock came, and with it a fresh flood of weeping. It was at that hour, she told Cranmer, that Hennage customarily brought her news of Henry.[3] With more thought for saving face than for taking vengeance Henry proceeded with as much dignity as he could in degrading Catherine, and resumed his usual pastimes with conspicuous nonchalance. He went out of his way to appear high-spirited and jovial, and to surround himself with ladies when he dined.

But by mid-November new shock waves ran through the court as the full scope of the queen's misconduct began to emerge, and the king left for the country "for the purpose of relieving his mind from the annoyance and troubles caused by late events."[4] To save himself, Dereham had revealed what only a few of the queen's women knew for certain: Catherine had a lover at court, Thomas Culpepper.

To Henry's utter dismay he now learned that his young wife had not only been repeatedly unfaithful to him, she had carried on her intrigues right under his nose. And she had chosen one of his closest intimates, a man who had been brought up in his chamber and who occasionally shared his bed. That Culpepper persisted in defending his innocence only made matters worse. The queen had sent for him, he swore, with Lady Rochford as go-between; when he came to meet her "at a retired place" she said she loved him and was "dying for his love" in return. He was blameless.

Throughout the summer and early fall, while the great northern progress ran its course, Catherine had flirted with Culpepper and more than likely seduced him. She was clearly the aggressor, not the victim, and in her blind desperation she failed to conceal her passion from her bedchamber women, who now testified against her. There could be no further leniency for one who had cuckolded the king.

Once all was known Henry, grief-stricken and humiliated, grew angry. Catherine had made a fool of him. His courtiers whispered to one another behind his back, and laughed at him. And the more he gave vent to his extremes of feeling, the more people talked, though they "thought more than they said," as Marillac put it. Henry alarmed his councilors by calling for a sword to kill Catherine, and by mumbling vengefully in the midst of their deliberations that "that wicked woman had never such delight in her incontinency as she should have torture in her death." Sometimes he seemed to forget himself entirely, suddenly rising in the midst of a Council meeting and calling for his horses, telling no one where he meant to go. And always he gave in at last to tears, weeping publicly over his ill fortune, declaring he would never marry again as long as he lived, wishing he had never seen Catherine and treating his councilors as if they and not the queen were to blame.[5]

On through December and January the ordeal of trials, condemnations and executions proceeded. On December 10 Culpepper and Dereham were executed, the former having "obtained the grace" of being beheaded rather than hanged and disemboweled as his sentence prescribed. Christmas came and went—Henry spent the holiday season at Greenwich and, with a small company, at country houses "seeking in pastimes to forget his grief"—and then the major indictments were brought. Toward the end of January Catherine Howard and Lady Rochford were attainted of treason, and shortly afterward they were brought to the Tower to prepare to die. Catherine had spent her last months making macabre cheer at Syon House, adorning herself with greater care than ever and ordering her few attendants about with imperious disdain. As the day of her execution approached this façade wore thin. She admitted her guilt, and expected no mercy, she said. Her only request was that her death be a private affair, not a public humiliation.

On the morning of February 13 Catherine was beheaded in the same place where Anne Boleyn and Buckingham had lost their lives. Afraid of disgracing herself before the spectators, she had rehearsed her role the night before, asking that the executioner's block be brought to her Tower room and placing her head on it for practice. When she faced the headsman the next morning her courage nearly failed her; she was "so weak that she could hardly speak," but managed to confess her guilt and to praise Henry's graciousness toward her before the axe fell.[6]

When Catherine's women had taken her body away, enshrouded in a black cloak, her accomplice Lady Rochford was led in to die. Her death put an end to months of grotesque suffering. Ever since her arrest she had been beside herself with apprehension. Her brain was affected by a "fit of frenzy," the doctors reported; by a quirk of the law she could not be tried for treason as long as her derangement lasted. With malicious irony Henry sent his physicians to visit her every day so that she might recover sufficiently to be executed. Yet she persisted in her hysterical state, and finally a parliamentary bill was enacted permitting punishment of traitors who had lost their reason. Then, when at last she came to die, Lady Rochford enjoyed a final hour of lucidity. On the scaffold she made a "long discourse" about her faults and prayed for Henry's welfare before submitting herself to her fate.[7]

To those who observed him at close range the king seemed to be nearly as affected by the recent revelations and their aftermath as the culprits themselves. "Ever since he heard of his late queen's misconduct," Chapuys wrote, "he has become sad and mournful, and I have scarcely spoken to him once without finding him low-spirited and dejected, sighing continually."[8] Others found him to be "not a little troubled with this great affair," and declared he was not the man he had been. Though it was midwinter he went hunting, trying in vain to improve his spirits and to escape from governmental labors which had come to seem intolerable. When bad weather confined him indoors he occupied himself with going over the statements of witnesses against Catherine, revising the legal documents in an attempt to confront in his mind what gnawed at his heart.[9]

Chapuys explained Henry's condition by analogy with a woman who mourned more for her tenth husband than for the other nine put together. Though all nine had been good men and faithful husbands, she had grieved over them the less because as each one died she had been certain of the next. With the loss of the tenth there was no new husband in view; in burying him she buried her hopes, and so mourned him the more bitterly. "Such is the case with the king," the ambassador concluded, who "does not seem to have any plan or female friend to fall back upon."[10]

Whatever the cause, there was no mistaking the physical change that had come over Henry in the months since he returned from the northern progress. He was noticeably older and grayer, and to Marillac at least he appeared to have lost his customary bellicosity. He resembled his grandfather King Edward in his fifties, the French ambassador said, in "loving rest and fleeing trouble." And he was daily becoming more and more mountainously fat.

Henry had been "very stout" for several years, the result of "marvellous excess" in eating and drinking. In 1536, the year he jousted for the last time and suffered the dangerous fall from his horse, the royal armorers measured him. His chest was forty-five inches, his waist thirty-seven inches—only a little larger than his measurements at age twenty-three. In 1541, his chest had grown to fifty-seven inches, and his waist, at fifty-four inches, was rapidly expanding to meet it. Catherine's disgrace and its bloody sequel sent him back to the dining table with renewed gluttony, until by the spring of 1542 he had transformed himself into a rotund colossus whose belly all but burst out of his doublets and who walked at a ponderous pace, limping unsteadily on his painful legs.

Such self-destructive excess was worrisome enough in itself, but Henry's councilors had another reason to worry. Only a year earlier they had witnessed an almost incapacitating cycle of mental and physical symptoms in the king, made worse, if not brought on, by his overindulgence. In the late winter of 1541 a tertian fever seized him, and instead of taking its normal course it affected his ulcerated legs. Ever since his brush with death in 1538 his physicians had kept the wound open; as long as the poisons were allowed to drain out he was safe. Now, abruptly, it closed. He was terrified. But the surgeons, Thomas Vicary in particular, had learned from the last experience and were able to unblock the passage, and restore their royal patient to health.

Yet the physicians had not been able to treat the altered state of his mind and spirits. As he lay on his sickbed the king lashed out verbally at his ungrateful subjects, at his advisers, at the bulwarks and walls of his coastal fortresses which had fallen into disrepair. His people were an unhappy lot "whom he would shortly make so poor that they would not have the boldness nor the power to oppose him." His councilors were a pack of lying flatterers, pretending to serve him yet caring only for their own profit. He knew full well, he ranted on, what they were plotting, "and if God lent him health, he would take care that their projects should not succeed." In his darkest moments Henry blamed his Council members—quite accurately—for deceiving him about Cromwell and maneuvering his execution; their false accusations had made him put to death "the most faithful servant he ever had."

So Henry had spoken of Wolsey's disgrace and death twelve years earlier, as a tragic result of malicious rivalries. Perhaps that old grief, and others, rose to torment him now, leading him to shut himself off from his courtiers, his wife (it was at this time that he saw little of Catherine, and there were strong rumors of divorce), and even his beloved music. He spent the Shrovetide season virtually alone, without music or other pastimes, with such a small household "that his court resembled more a private family than a king's train." Visitors who came to Hampton Court on business were received with brusque efficiency and sent away.[11]

The fit of violent dissatisfaction and isolated depression passed, but recurred the following winter, accompanying Catherine's disgrace. What his innermost thoughts were no one knew. He now had no wife to confide in; his son and younger daughter, at four and eight years old, could not share his moods. Even his daughter Mary, whom he now brought to court to act in place of a queen, was left out of his private ruminations.

Henry did leave some traces of his inner self in this period in a predictable place: the margins of his books. His printer delivered a long list of books to him in the early 1540s, devotional works, leatherbound Bibles with golden clasps and gilt ornamentation, scholastic texts from the twelfth and thirteenth centuries and a scattering of works by the Church Fathers. They were the purchases of a true bibliophile and humanist—and a man of deep and rather conservative piety.[12] In these years Henry heard mass daily and twice on feast days. On Good Friday he still "crept to the cross" from the chapel door to the altar in observance of a medieval custom, "his own person kneeling on his grace's knees," and served the priest at mass afterward.[13] However his moods and attitudes might shift, his faith was firmly grounded. He pored over his devotional books and studied their familiar texts again and again, writing "*nota bene*" beside particularly meaningful passages and incidentally illuminating the themes and issues he turned in his mind.

In one book, a contemporary translation of Proverbs called *The Bokes of Salomon,* Henry's annotations made in 1542 tell a good deal. In this book he marked verses about kingship ("Let mercy and faithfulness never go from thee . . ."), about those "desiring war" ("Cast down the people whose delight is to have battle"), about divine judgment and the vanity of worldly goods. But the overwhelming majority of passages he marked had to do with wives and harlots and punishment for sexual sins.

Next to the verse "be glad with the wife of thy youth" he wrote "for wyfves"—on the face of it an irony—and drew a marginal sign next to a passage paralleling Queen Catherine Howard's unhappy path of life. "That thou mayest be delivered also from the strange woman," the passage read, "which giveth sweet words, forsaketh the husband of her youth and forgetteth the convenant of her God. For her house is inclined unto death, and her paths unto hell."

Beside the verse "For the lips of a harlot are a dropping honeycomb, and her throat is softer than oil" the king made a double mark, continuing it as the passage went on, "But at the last she is as bitter as wormwood, and as sharp as a two-edged sword."[14]

Clearly the brooding depression Chapuys and Marillac noted went deep. Yet as always Henry made at least a show of gaiety and high spirits to cover his distress and, for a time, to escape from it. By now it had become almost a tradition with him to celebrate the deaths or discardings of disappointing wives. He had feasted with pointed rejoicing when Katherine of Aragon and Anne Boleyn died; with Anne of Cleves he had begun to celebrate his freedom in the company of Catherine Howard long before the nullity suit was concluded. So, on the day his fifth wife was condemned, he gave a supper and banquet, with twenty-six ladies at his own table and another thirty-five close by. The celebrating went on for many weeks. Henry gave banquets for his privy councilors and the lords of the court, for the men of law, and, one evening, for a select group of ladies, all of whom spent the night at the palace. On the morning of that banquet he devoted all his time to inspecting the preparations made for his guests. He went from one chamber to another, examining the furnishings and bedding and making certain the rugs and hangings were of the best.

When the women arrived he received them all "with much gaiety," and observers watched eagerly to see whether he showed special interest in any of them. Some thought they detected a new favorite: Lord Cobham's sister, a woman of both wit and beauty who, it was said, might well be disposed to follow Catherine Howard's model if given the chance. Several other names were put forward after the banqueting as possible sweethearts for the king, but were dropped almost as soon as they arose.[15] In fact, as Chapuys saw clearly, there were few women likely to covet the role of queen. Henry was aging, he was physically unlovable, he was subject to raging irritability. And his wives seemed to be accursed. Parliament had recently added another impediment. Any woman marrying the king would henceforth be required to declare, on pain of death, that no charge of misbehavior could be brought against her. And if she lied, others who knew the truth had to come forward or face imprisonment for life.[16]

Two months after Catherine Howard's execution there was still no sign of a new love. Henry continued to surround himself with ladies, but more from long habit than current interest. His councilors saw his widowed state as a lost opportunity, and urged him to remember that he had only one son, and that one a fragile child. Only months earlier Edward's life had been in danger, and in the spring of 1542 his doctors were predicting that he was "not of constitution to live long."[17] Despite the ill fortune that had attended the last two royal marriages, Henry was under some pressure to take his happiness in his hands and try once again.

One woman at least knew exactly whom Henry should marry—or rather re-marry. Anne of Cleves could hardly have been more delighted at the news of her successor's disgrace. She ordered her household to move immediately to Richmond in order to be nearer the king, and it was noted that "gentlemen of the duke of Cleves" were present at the trial of Dereham and Culpepper. Anne had kept herself discreetly visible ever since Queen Catherine's accession, dining occasionally at court, exchanging gifts with her former husband and behaving so disarmingly toward the new queen that Catherine welcomed her as a friend. On one occasion Anne supped with Catherine and Henry, then stayed after the king had gone to bed to dance and talk with Catherine far into the night.[18] When Catherine's jewels were inventoried after her imprisonment it was found that one of her rings was missing, whose stone was said to possess "some virtue against spasms." She had given the ring to Anne; so that the inventory might be complete Henry sent some of his privy councilors to get it back.[19]

Henry's subjects saw remarriage to Anne of Cleves as only right and humane. Though mistreated and cast aside she had accepted her lot graciously, they said; she had grown "more beautiful than she ever was," and besides, she had borne the king's child. The false rumor of Anne's pregnancy was widespread. Two men were bold enough to repeat it to the royal officers. The fall of Queen Catherine, they said, was God's judgment against Henry for deserting Anne, "since she was known to have gone away in the family way from the king, and had actually been confined."[20] Anne was more pitied by the people than Katherine of Aragon had ever been, Marillac wrote. Everywhere she was praised as "the sweetest, most gracious and kindest queen" England had ever known. How could Henry possibly refuse to take her back?[21]

The people's hopes rose when they heard that the king and his former wife exchanged gifts at New Year's. Anne had sent him some valuable cloth, and had received some glass pots and flagons in return. As Henry moved about the countryside near London during the holiday season it was said he would come to Richmond and stay with Anne, and so begin a new courtship. Instead he took "quite a different route," and stayed well out of Anne's way until long after the new year began.

41

Father, you are an aged man,
Your head is white, your bearde is gray;
It were a shame at these your yeares
For you to ryse in such a fray.

IN the queen's privy closet at Hampton Court, Henry VIII stood before Bishop Gardiner and repeated his marriage vows. He spoke the words as the bishop said them, though by now he knew them so well he needed no prompting.

"I, Henry, take thee, Catherine, to my wedded wife, to have and to hold from this day forward, for better for worse, for richer for poorer, in sickness and in health, till death us depart, and thereto I plight thee my troth."

The protonotary who recorded all that happened at the ceremony wrote that the king spoke his vows "with a joyful countenance," and that when the bishop asked if anyone present knew of any impediment to the marriage—a very grave question, considering the recent laws governing royal wives—there were no voices raised in opposition. Indeed the small group of relatives and courtiers in attendance seemed only too pleased to see their king married. More than any previous ceremony this had the air of a family wedding, with Henry's daughters Mary and Elizabeth, his niece Margaret Douglas, his brother-in-law Edward Seymour all present (Prince Edward did not attend), along with several of the new queen's relatives.

The woman who stood beside Henry as he made his pledge, holding his hand, steadying him a little was a mature, good-natured widow of thirty-one, Catherine Parr. She had been married twice before—once as a very young girl to an elderly lord who died "very old and distracted of memory" when she was seventeen, and once to John Neville, an aged Yorkshire knight who left her his substantial fortune and his three children on his death in this year of 1543. Catherine Parr was neither a beauty nor a coquette. Though she had a "lively and pleasing appearance," she was a serious, thoughtful woman whose intellectual tastes matched Henry's own. Wriothesley's view of Catherine as "a woman in my judgement, for virtue, wisdom and gentleness, most meet for his highness" was widely shared; "sure I am," he wrote, "his majesty had never a wife more agreeable to his heart than she is."[1]

That she was willing to take on the irascible king in his declining years—and his precocious, oddly-assorted children—said much for Catherine's capability and courage. "A fine burden Madame has taken on herself," Anne of Cleves remarked with contemptuous vulgarity when she heard of the marriage. Though the remark was meant literally, as a crude reference to Henry's bulk, in a broader sense Anne spoke the truth. Henry VIII's sixth queen put her life at risk, apparently willingly, with few rewards in view beyond the name of queen and the satisfaction of filling a difficult role with exceptional competence. Her cheerful sacrifice was all the more remarkable in that, when the king approached her, another man had already won her heart. Thomas Seymour, Jane Seymour's irrepressible, attractive brother, had proposed to Catherine. But for Henry's intervention she would have accepted him.

Yet there she stood on her wedding day with her corpulent sovereign beside her, glad enough to take him as her third husband and lord.

"I, Catherine, take thee Henry to my wedded husband," she recited, "to have and to hold from this day forward, for better for worse, for richer for poorer, in sickness and in health, to be bonair and buxom in bed and at board, till death us depart, and thereto I plight thee my troth." There were no second thoughts. A week after the wedding Catherine wrote to her brother William Parr that her position as the king's wife was "the greatest joy and comfort that could happen to her."

A member of Catherine's household once told her that her "rare goodness" made "every day a Sunday." It was a dubious compliment, but it would be a mistake to see in the queen either a tight-lipped, overserious churchgoer or a moralizing prude. Catherine's goodness was unmistakable, but so was her humanity. She kept no ascetic regimen, and was not overly conspicuous in her charities or other good works. She paid loving attention to everyday things, decorating her chamber with fresh flowers each day and tending to her greyhounds. She dressed gaily in French gowns and Venetian sleeves and pleats and shoes with gold trim. She saw to it that her stepchildren were equally well dressed. At Christmas of 1544 she ordered Prince Edward's tailor to make him a doublet and coat of crimson velvet with gilt buttons and gold braid, and a velvet cap with a feather.

Queen Catherine's piety showed itself not in austerity but in serious study. To her belief and religious devotion were matters worthy of much thought and concentration, and she labored to put her spiritual gleanings into written form. In her *Prayers or Meditations,* published in 1545 and exceedingly popular, she expressed in mystical language her search for illumination. "Send forth the hot flow of thy love to burn and consume the cloudy fantasies of my mind," she wrote. "Gather, O Lord, my wits and the powers of my soul together in thee and make me to despise all worldly things and by thy grace strongly to resist and overcome all motions and occasions of sin."[2] Throughout her marriage to Henry Catherine would be composing her most ambitious work, *The Lamentation of a Sinner,* in which she "bewailed the ignorance of her blind life" and described her awakening to a holier way. The *Lamentation* gave much of the credit for her enlightenment to Henry, who like Moses had led England out of "captivity and bondage" to Rome and into a purified faith. It also went beyond prevailing orthodoxy in upholding the primacy of faith in an almost Lutheran sense; this strain in Catherine's religious thinking, combined with her patronage of Protestant reformers, made her vulnerable to attack by the conservatives at court.

Henry married Catherine Parr on July 12, 1543. Only three weeks earlier he had delivered a thundering ultimatum to the French ambassador. Unless the French acceded to his (impossible) demands, England and France would be at war within twenty days.

Since 1540 the breach between Charles V and Francis I had been widening. The French had made common cause with the Turks, and this alliance, scandalous in its cynical disregard for the safety of Christendom, had put Hapsburg lands in peril on several fronts. Emboldened by Turkish support Francis went to war with Charles once more in the spring of 1542, and Charles, ever heedful of the possibility of an Anglo-French alliance, began to woo his uncle Henry. Not long afterward the English and imperialists came to terms, and war plans were made. After years of preparing his forces and reinvigorating his own belligerence, Henry was more than ready to go into battle.

Recent successes in Scotland had whetted his appetite for military glory. In November of 1542 Norfolk had defeated a Scots army twenty thousand strong at Solway Moss, and in the aftermath of victory Henry had felt confident enough to try to consolidate his hold over the Scots by persuasion and politics rather than by force of arms. Organized opposition seemed to have vanished. The king, James V, died within weeks of the battle, leaving his throne to a girl child (Mary Stuart) six days old. James's mother, Margaret, had died in 1541. There was no locus of power, only warring factions and ambitious figures such as the earl of Arran, heir presumptive, who was eager to cooperate with the English. For the last six months, as he negotiated an alliance with the emperor Charles V and made final plans to go to war with the French, Henry bargained with Arran, arriving at what he believed to be a conclusive peace with the Scots on July 1. Under its terms, Prince Edward would marry the infant Princess Mary when she reached the age of ten, securing by a dynastic link the sovereignty Henry would exert in the interim.

With Scots affairs in order, the king was free to live up to the challenge he had made to the French. His timetable called for immediate invasion, and in fact the signing of the Scots treaty coincided with the departure of the first contingent of English troops bound for Calais. Almost immediately, however, his arrangements in the north came unraveled. The forces opposing the English treaty and favoring Scotland's time-honored ties to France rose in strength to threaten Arran's shaky primacy. French arms and ships and munitions reinforced the opposition, and in December of 1543 a formal alliance between Scotland and France was signed.

"Under the sun live not more beastly and unreasonable people than be here of all degrees," Henry's envoy Sadler wrote from Edinburgh, and the king agreed. The treachery of the Scots forced postponement of the invasion and created a dangerous second front on the northern border.

Such a betrayal deserved nothing less than massive retaliation. In May of 1544, as soon as the harsh weather ended and campaigning season began, Edward Seymour, earl of Hertford, went northward with an army to punish the Scots. The orders the king gave him were cruel. He was to reduce Edinburgh and other towns to ruins, laying waste their structures "so that the upper stone may be the nether and not one stick stand by another." Men, women and children were to be slain. Hertford's argument for moderation—which he saw as strategically preferable to ruthless destruction—was ignored, and he carried out Henry's commands with punishing exactness. Most of the capital was burned to the ground.

This time the Scots were less resilient in defeat. For the time being at least, Hertford's devastation prevented a resurgence of opposition, and allowed the French invasion plans to move ahead.

During April and May of 1544 the fighting men were summoned and equipped, and the paraphernalia of war assembled. Baking and brewing equipment was ordered, with large quantities of wheat and malt and hops. There were ovens made to be carried on wagons and mills "which grind as the wagon moves," and cohorts of bakers, brewers and underbrewers and their assistants to operate them. Fodder for the horses and meat for the soldiers was purchased and stored at warehouses beside the ports where the men would embark and across the Channel at Calais. Iron, lead, copper, saltpeter—all the raw stuff of weaponry—were on hand in good supply, and at the Tower, the mint was in operation day and night, turning silver plate and other precious ornaments from the plundered abbeys into coins to pay the provisioners and soldiers. Long lists of necessities were drawn up, with the word "dispatched" written beside items attended to. Many of the details were referred to the king himself, as there was no single administrator to oversee everything, as Wolsey had done in the 1513 campaign. Thus it was often left to Henry to worry over the supplies of axes and mattocks for the laborers, yokes and chains for the thousands of oxen that would pull the carts and wagons and provide fresh meat, harnesses and bellybands for the horses, sickles and scythes for clearing the grass and bushes at the gun sites, balances and weights for weighing out the charges of gunpowder, and leather buckets for carrying it to the guns, and dozens of other sundries needful on campaign. The quantities assembled far surpassed those required by any earlier military undertaking, and were reminiscent of that other immense invasion of France, the meeting of Henry and Francis I at the Field of Cloth of Gold. Hundreds of chests of arrows and barrels of bowstrings. Six thousand horseshoes and three hundred thousand horseshoe nails and other sorts of nails. Six thousand pounds of rope and twenty thousand suits of armor.

The scale of the undertaking was no more staggering than the minuteness of its requirements. Exact instructions had to be drawn up for the royal armorers as to the filing and engraving of armor, the trimming of javelins and the gilding of buckles, the burnishing of the king's own panoply in the privy armory under the supervision of his armorer Erasmus Kyrkenar. As the mustering proceeded there was a huge demand for arms in London, and to prevent merchants and "covetous persons" from gouging the soldiers official price lists were circulated. No more than one shilling and eightpence could be charged for a pair of jointed gauntlets or for a Flemish halbert "of the best sort," and for a full complement of arms and armor, with demy-lance, cuirass, vambrace, and headpiece, forty-five shillings at most.[3] Offending suppliers were imprisoned and fined ten pounds.

Providing sufficient horseflesh for the army was a considerable task in itself. Draft horses, seven abreast, were needed to pull carts and ordnance, and for hauling food and drink. It was calculated that 420 horses were required to carry five days' supply of biscuit for twelve thousand men; 315 more were needed to carry their cheese, and six hundred their beverage. Beyond these, large numbers of riding horses were needed, and strong warhorses to bear armed knights.

Scores of letters went out from the court to landholders in the countryside, commanding them to provide as many mares and geldings "meet for draught and carriage" as they could spare "without disfurniture of necessary tillage and husbandry." Hundreds of horses had to be imported from the continent as well, and hundreds more brought from the private stables of the king and nobles. For several years, Marillac noted, Henry and his courtiers had been turning their parklands into stud farms. Parliamentary acts now required every lord to keep a number of horses available in proportion to his rents, and these, plus the royal farms on the Welsh border and in Nottinghamshire, yielded a good number of mounts. In addition Henry had two stables of a hundred horses each—a change from the late 1530s when his stables had been markedly reduced. Horses were among the least replaceable necessities of war, and to ensure that they suffered no damage in crossing the Channel particular specifications were drawn up for the ships that would carry them to Calais. For balance, the ships were to be designed to carry horses on both sides of their holds; their beams were to be high enough for the horses to stand under them, "for if they be too low the horses' backs shall be marred."

Henry devoted more time and attention to fortifications and armaments than to anything else. For years he had been employing expert engineers from all over Europe to design and build his bulwarks and repair his castles and fortresses; a Sicilian builder helped to improve England's coastal defenses in the late 1530s, while in 1541, a Portuguese was brought in to direct the rebuilding of fortifications at the important outlying fortress of Guînes in the Calais Pale. The latter had the misfortune to disagree with his royal employer about the prospects for defense. After looking over the town and castle he came to England to report to Henry and his privy councilors. It would be impossible to fortify Guînes in an efficient manner, he said. Two high hills in the vicinity looked directly down into the town; its streets were easy targets for any attackers gaining control of the hilltops.

Henry grew angry as he listened to the man, bursting at length into a storm of abuse. He himself had gone beyond such preliminary observations months before, and had found a way to overcome the logistical problems. Two thousand men were already at work at Guînes, shoring up the walls and constructing new bulwarks; an entire settlement near the town had been uprooted so that the ruins of its houses and churches could provide building materials for the fortifications. Henry had not committed his men to this labor to listen to an incompetent foreigner counsel despair. Calling the Portuguese a fool and an ass who knew nothing of his profession, he declared the interview to be at an end.[4]

Henry delegated the work of fortress-building to others with some reluctance, and kept a close watch on the plans and progress of every major defense work. In the spring of 1542 he inspected his works at Dover, and would have crossed the Channel to view the corresponding fortifications within the Pale of Calais had he been able to keep his embarkation secret.[5] Where possible he took a hand in the engineering of the works himself. Calais, which Marillac called in 1541 "the strongest town in Christendom," owed some of its invincibility to the king, whose design for improved firing apertures giving a wider field of fire was adopted in its construction. At the seaside town of Ambleteuse between Boulogne and Calais his contribution was even more fundamental. He drew up a plan for a pentagonal fort to be built at Ambleteuse, and succeeded in convincing his chief English engineers John Rogers and Richard Lee that his design was feasible. The diagrams which illustrated his plan—possibly done by the king himself—reveal not only considerable expertise in military architecture but familiarity with the most up-to-date Italian models of fortress design.[6]

All the time he was strengthening his defenses Henry was striving for improvements in England's offensive power as well. He accumulated trunks and pots of wildfire, and materials for making it. He built oared ships "according to a model of which he himself was the inventor." He brought Flemish and German armorers to England to devise new types of mortars and shells, and to cast huge guns that, with their iron bolts and chains, weighed two tons.[7] And he eagerly sought out experimental devices, however fantastic, that might give him a tactical advantage.

A seventy-year-old Italian arrived at the English court with a plan for a marvelous invention. He would make a huge mirror, haul it to the top of Dover Castle and affix it there, then adjust it to reflect the French coast. Any ship leaving Dieppe harbor could be seen in the mirror, he assured Henry, long before it approached English shores. When he heard of this Marillac could not take it seriously, yet to the ambassador's amazement Henry not only seemed persuaded of the soundness of the project but was willing to back up his conviction with money. The old man left for Dover with full pockets, but no further word was ever recorded concerning his great mirror.[8]

Another invention was somewhat more practical. It was a mortar that shot a fearsome "artificial bullet" which flew into the air "spouting fire on every side." On its descent the burning mass actively "leapt from place to place, casting out fire," and shot forth a hundred missiles with a noise like a volley of musket fire. The English envoys in the imperial camp who saw this incendiary device were unsure of what damage it inflicted, but they felt certain it would please the king, and engaged the master gunner who invented it to come to England as soon as Charles V could spare him.[9]

There had never been any doubt in Henry's mind that he would lead the invading army himself. The joint agreement with the emperor signed in December of 1543 suggested tactfully that Henry "would wish to be in person in the said army" and that his presence "would be most important." Charles committed himself to lead his own troops, though he was gouty and beginning to age, and this commitment, coupled with the successes he had recently won on campaign in Italy, was enough to challenge Henry to do likewise.

As the campaigning season drew nearer, however, the emperor became alarmed that Henry's health might prove to be a liability. At the end of March his familiar complaint set in. His legs swelled and throbbed with pain, confining him to his bed. He developed a fever, and for two days his physicians worried over him until it passed. In all he was ill for eight days, and "a little indisposed" for some time afterward. How would he fare in France, facing the rigors of harsh weather and long marches, the sudden stresses of battle and the demands of leadership? To remind the emperor that he too had an agonizing complaint, and that its "proper season" was autumn, when the fighting would be at its height, did not alter the argument against Henry's taking the field. On the contrary, it made it all the more imperative that at least one of the armies should be led by a younger man, a vigorous commander in his prime, who if need be could assume leadership of the entire combined invasion.

But there was no dissuading Henry. His honor, his courage in arms, his memories of battlefield glory on the plains of Picardy thirty years earlier all impelled him to risk his health and go ahead. He was after all assembling the greatest expedition force in a century—contemporaries believed it to be the greatest ever—and his imperial ally too was strong. His people were docile, the Scots quiescent, the French ripe for defeat. He might not live to see such an opportunity again. He must rise to the challenge, heedless of his contrary legs and ungainly bulk.

At the end of June Suffolk crossed the Channel to join his men, who had been gathering for weeks in the vicinity of Calais. He and Norfolk would each command one body of the English forces, under Henry's overall generalship. Suffolk was now in his sixties, and looked elderly. His once splendid physique sagged with age, and like Henry he walked with a limp. Before he left for France he made his will, knowing he might never see his young wife Catherine again.

As Henry made ready to follow his venerable lieutenant a crowd of difficulties arose to delay him. French spies were abroad in England, counting ships and men, watching activity at the port cities and sending war news to Francis I; they had to be captured and relieved of their information on the rack. Despite her promises, the regent of Flanders, Charles V's sister Mary, had provided too few horses and wagons for the use of the English. Then, when Henry took matters into his own hands and purchased two hundred Flemish mares, she impounded them at Dunkirk. Finally, only days before the king's scheduled departure, she consented to release them. Other last-minute crises appeared: the bakers were unpaid and dissatisfied, there were too few munitions wagons with Norfolk's host already in France, and, most serious of all, money was becoming scarce.

With unusual dispatch the king and his privy councilors took action. Orders went out for the bakers to receive their wages immediately, and Norfolk was instructed to send to Flanders for a thousand wagons, and to bear the inconvenience patiently, seeing that "it would be a much greater prejudice if there should be any lack at the coming over of the [king's] army." As to the shortage of money, the Antwerp loan would temporarily have to serve. Henry approached a number of merchants in secret, asking them to stand surety for him to borrow another huge sum from the Flemish bankers, and in the meantime he managed to raise twenty thousand pounds in London, using his rents as security.[10]

To Chapuys these transactions—which were concluded at exorbitant rates of interest—seemed ominous, and in fact Henry's last days in England were clouded by fiscal difficulties. But by mid-July he put all worries behind him as he boarded the ship that would carry him to Calais, confident that no cost was too high for the winning of the highest prize of kings, victory in war.

42

Behoulde the figure of A Royall Kinge,
One whom sweet victory did ever attende:
From every parte wher he his power did bringe,
He homewarde brought ye Conquest in ye end.

HENRY VIII, "armed at all pieces upon a great courser," rode out of the gates of Calais into French territory on Friday the twenty-fifth of July, 1544. Across his saddle he carried a heavy musket with a long iron barrel; an officer riding behind him carried his headpiece and great lance. The gun and lance were afterward preserved in the Tower armory. A visitor who saw them there in Queen Elizabeth's reign was impressed by their huge size, and marveled that merely to lift the lance took all his strength.

In the king's immediate company that day rode drummers and trumpeters to herald his coming, the officers of arms, and the royal henchmen. But these dozens of attendants were only a tiny part of his army, some forty-eight thousand strong. In an age of relatively small populations the army was almost incomprehensibly vast. It was an armed mass equal to two-thirds of the population of London, an itinerant community three times the size of any provincial English town. As in 1513, it was organized along feudal lines into three parts: the vanguard, rearguard and "king's battle." In the latter unit marched nearly thirteen thousand horsemen and footmen, with the hundreds of noncombatants—butchers, herdsmen, millwrights, bargemen, coopers, smiths, bricklayers, armorers, mortar makers, surgeons and priests—needed to feed and serve them and keep them battle-worthy.[1]

As Henry advanced southward toward Boulogne the main body of his army fell into place around him—the earl of Essex, chief captain of the men of arms, with a great number of horsemen, then the lightly armed horsemen, then the archers and gunners on foot, then a host of pikemen, "the king being in the midst." At Sandingfield a body of guardsmen joined the host, bringing up the rear "with banners displayed," and behind them, strung out for miles along the line of march, were the heavy wheeled mills and bake ovens and brewing vats, the wagons of flour and malt, and the great herds of cows and bullocks and sheep whose mooing and lowing nearly drowned out the martial sound of the trumpets and drums. By the end of the day the entire force straggled into Marquison, near Boulogne, and made camp for the night.

Engravings made from contemporary paintings of the camp at Marquison survive, corroborating graphically the written records of the campaign. They show a hastily erected temporary settlement, a confusion of tents and wagons and milling soldiery, with little evidence of organization or command. Military textbooks of the time taught officers to draw up camp with ordnance and munitions in a large outlying circle, surrounding the vulnerable sleeping tents and beasts and provisions inside. At Marquison there were heavy guns and carts of pikes and cannon shot everywhere, with the mouths of the cannon pointing directly at the tents and barrels of gunpowder all too near the cooking fires. Instead of long, orderly rows of tents, separated by regularly spaced firebrakes and marked by banners, there was a jumble of large and small pavilions, some collapsing under the force of the wind. (Insubstantial as they were, tents were preferred quarters, for officers only; ordinary soldiers had to take refuge in whatever structures they could devise, or in peasant huts or woods or thickets. In winter campaigns, or in the storms and early frosts of a northern summer, they froze.)

Every soldier in Henry's army was entitled to at least a pound of biscuit, a pound of beef and a gallon of beer a day, if not more. But if the provisions wagons went astray, or if the camp animals died of disease or the supply route was blocked by the enemy, or if irresponsible purveyors failed to meet their quotas, food grew scarce. In the 1544 campaign the English soldiers ate their way through the countryside around Boulogne until everything edible had been consumed. They stole chickens and ducks, shot hares and wildfowl, drove pigs and sheep to the camp to be slaughtered. The Irish soldiers went after beef, tying up bulls and making them bellow until all the cows in the vicinity had been attracted within range of the camp. Within a very few weeks the thousands of soldiers brought famine to the peasants of Picardy. A veteran of the campaign who left an account of his experiences wrote how an old countrywoman came to the camp begging bread. A kindhearted soldier offered her a few coins.

"God in heaven!" she said, throwing up her hands, "what should I do with money, or anything else but bread, and only a little of that, so that we can eat it now, because we do not dare to store it for fear of the wild men, who, if any of them get any bread or money from any of us beat and batter us."[2]

The king himself ate well, indeed on a princely scale. Among the officers traveling with him "for the provision of his diet" were men to staff a bakehouse, cellar, buttery, wafery, confectionery, boiling house, pultry and acatery—the last a storage larder for fresh foods that spoiled easily. Two hundred people made up the itinerant kitchen and provisioning departments, all of them equipped to fight if needed. Another large contingent of serving men "appertaining to the King's Majesty's tents, hales and pavilions" saw to his housing; among them were bedmakers, coffermakers, and matmakers.[3]

Camp followers were in evidence in the engravings of Marquison, though not in the numbers they were later to achieve. By early September, when the campaign was seven weeks old, the camp was reportedly "troubled with a sort of light women which daily do repair out of

England." So that this population would cease to grow, the lord mayor of London was ordered not to permit any woman to leave the city for any port near the capital, and the officials of Dover and Portsmouth and other port towns were given similar instructions.[4] Deserters were another sizable problem. The Marquison engravings show a soldier hanged, probably for desertion, within full view of his living fellows, a macabre reminder of each man's primary duty to his sovereign, to stay at his post.

The camp was under fire from the fortress of Boulogne, and men are shown scrambling to evade flying missiles and hugging fresh wounds. On the night of the twenty-sixth a party of French skirmished briefly with the English, creating work for the camp surgeons. Military surgeons in this period had developed considerable skill in amputating limbs—usually with one swift cut and three strokes with a saw—and could replace them with artificial substitutes, but severe chest or intestinal wounds were beyond their skill. There was little to be done for Treasurer Cheyney's son, wounded in the side by an arquebus shot "by reason whereof his guts do come out," but to make him as comfortable as possible while he lay "in great jeopardy of death." Given the low survival rate following treatment soldiers might be forgiven for preferring death to the excruciating pain of surgery without anesthetics (save for alcohol, and, possibly, herbal infusions to induce a drugged sleep). Still, many endured the digging and slicing of the crude pointed probes and tweezers and scissorlike instruments of the time, and the agony of cautery—the burning of the flesh around a wound thought to help prevent infection.

By the time Henry arrived in France his troops were already deployed, with two objectives. The majority of the men were besieging Boulogne, "the chief propugnacle of all France" whose strong ramparts and thick double walls the French considered invulnerable to artillery. A smaller force under Norfolk was besieging Montreuil several miles to the south. This was the lesser effort, with smaller likelihood of success; in the words of a contemporary the siege of Montreuil was a diversion made "so that the king and his host might take their ease and sleep more easily in their beds in the camp around Boulogne."[5]

In planning his strategy Henry was departing from the agreed battle plan arrived at by English and imperial negotiators months earlier. The ultimate goal, they had agreed then, was Paris; the English were to strike through Picardy, the troops of Charles V through Champagne, then a combined Anglo-imperial force was to seize the French capital. In besieging Boulogne and Montreuil, Henry said, he was reducing the two strongest Picard fortresses as a preliminary to marching on Paris. (The emperor was in fact doing the same thing on his front, besieging the fortresses of Luxembourg and St. Didier.) Yet in actuality Boulogne, not Paris, was the prize Henry sought, and the longer he stayed in France the more he wanted it. To the emperor's dismay, the "Enterprise of Paris" was transmogrified in Henry's mind to the "Enterprise of Boulogne," and as the campaigning season went on Charles' expansive territorial ambitions dwindled as his ally narrowed his aims.

Boulogne in the mid-sixteenth century was a hilltop town surrounded by high walls and ramparts, with the castle commanding its eastern wall. Below the fortified settlement, between the hills and the harbor, was Basse Boulogne, a separate town with its own inferior fortifications. High on a cliff at the harbor mouth was the most distinctive monument in the region: the "Tour d'Ordre," a Roman tower built by Caligula and equipped by the French with cannon. The English called the tower the "Old Man," and when Henry arrived they had just captured it and turned out its defenders, fourteen men and a boy. Suffolk, who was in command of the siege, pointed with pride to this success when the king made his appearance, and to the English seizure of Basse Boulogne as well. The French had left behind some treasure in military stores in Basse Boulogne; they had tried to burn the town to cheat the English of their spoils, but without success.

Henry threw himself tirelessly into the siege effort, spurred perhaps by the sight of the redoubtable old Brandon, who did not spare his aged body and was more courageous than many of the younger men. Suffolk was reportedly so heedless of his own safety that he leaped into trenches where men lay dead from recent enemy fire, and was so contemptuous of the artillery in the high town that "he enforceth others to be hardy whether they will or not."[6] Henry now took charge of directing the offensive. He ordered earthworks erected, and deployed his ordnance and troops for a three-pronged assault.

By the twenty-ninth, only three days after he arrived in Boulogne, the heavy English siege guns had done a good deal of damage to the castle, and Henry was confident that the town would soon be his. When Chapuys appeared in the English camp to talk with the king—a painful errand for the old ambassador, for his gout crippled him and he had to be carried everywhere in a sedan chair—Henry was already looking ahead to his next conquests.

As soon as Boulogne and Montreuil fell, he confided to Chapuys, he intended to order his army forward at once, further into French territory, and he meant to lead the men himself. He had heard a rumor that Montreuil had already been taken, he added; even if the rumor proved false it was undoubtedly prophetic. "I never found the king so joyous and so light-hearted as when my colleague and I saw him," Chapuys wrote. "Even if he had had positive news of the taking of those two towns by his men, I doubt whether he would have been in such buoyant spirits."[7]

In fact Henry was gloating. He seemed near to gaining his objectives, while his ally Charles V was making little headway toward his. Charles and his army had been unsuccessfully besieging St. Didier since the beginning of July, hampered by French ambushes and fearful of a large-scale counterattack. Bad weather impeded siege maneuvers. "We have had so much rain and such cloudy days," an English diplomat wrote from the imperial camp, "that we can scant see the sun once a day to look by our dials what it is o'clock."[8] The emperor himself rode out about midnight one night with a picked force, intending to engage the enemy, but returned frustrated. His spies had reported that French reinforcements would be attempting to enter the town in the dead of night, but none were found. Overall the imperial forces were achieving so little that Charles became fearful that Henry might desert him and treat with the French for peace.

Francis had indeed written to Henry offering peace terms, but had received a brusque and negative reply, full of knightly indignation. In his letter Francis implied that he, Henry, had been the one to make peace overtures, the king wrote back. Francis ought to realize that he would never betray his ally the emperor by making peace on his own. The suggestion "greatly touched his honor," Henry wrote, which, "having always guarded inviolably to this present, he would never consent in his old age that it should be anyway distained."[9]

Nothing pleased Henry more than an opportunity to prove his good faith. Here on the field of honor, with the single focus of a great enterprise in progress, he was in his element. It was, to him at least, a simpler, chivalrous world, free of the murky ambiguities of statecraft, its ethical bounds refreshingly clear. Here he could gain unequivocal victories and win undisputed esteem. Here he could pursue once again knightly ideals cherished since boyhood, in all their anachronistic innocence.

Physically and mentally, he flourished. There were no dark moods, no savage violence, only courtesy to friends and chivalrous gestures toward the enemy. Chapuys was amazed at Henry's vitality and stamina. He was not only in excellent health, but working much harder than anyone would have expected. Edward Seymour pronounced him to be "merry and in as good health as I have seen his Grace at any time this seven year."[10] He rose at daybreak and was active until evening, supervising the laborers, checking on incoming supplies and ordering others, observing the conduct and morale of the soldiers.

He sent to Antwerp for two thousand arquebuses (two hundred arrived, many of them antiquated models lacking firelocks that had to be lit with matches), eighty-five wagonloads of powder, and twenty-two hundred pikes of ash wood with iron heads; two hundred of these, intended perhaps for the royal guard, were gilded and trimmed with velvet.[11] He consulted with the Italian artist and engineer he had engaged to design the siege works, Girolamo da Treviso, becoming more and more mistrustful of the latter's expertise. Treviso was well-intentioned and enthusiastic, but his ideas were more the product of abstract theorizing than proven success. In the opinion of the seasoned campaigner and privy councilor John Russell the Italian was plainly "inexperienced in sieges"; when Norfolk heard him recommend sending laborers armed with mattocks to seize an entrenched wooden outwork of Montreuil Castle he remarked dourly that Treviso "spake not as a man very skillful in such things."[12] Henry, who had become disgusted with his Portuguese engineer at Guînes and equally dissatisfied with a German, Stefan von Haschenperg, whom he had brought to conduct the works at Carlisle, looked with skepticism on Treviso and where possible made his own decisions.

Henry was skeptical too of his soldiers. Siege warfare made for idleness and boredom, and after some weeks of it he suspected his men were becoming soft. To test them—specifically, to "make sure of their good behavior in case of assault"—he devised a trial. He planned to have one of the explosive charges under the castle wall exploded prematurely, without warning, in order to observe the "temper and disposition" of the men in a sudden crisis.[13]

The outcome of this trial is not recorded, but whether because of his soldiers' temper or from other causes Henry lost a little of his buoyant optimism during July. By the middle of the month neither Boulogne nor Montreuil had fallen to the besiegers, while to the king's shame Charles V had seized two fortresses and taken fifteen hundred enemy prisoners. The news from Montreuil seemed to grow worse day by day. There were too few English troops to surround the town, too few even to stop up both of the town gates; men and supplies went in and out of one of the gates as the English watched helplessly from their entrenched position before the other.[14] Food was running low. On July 5 Norfolk wrote to Suffolk from Montreuil that there had been no beer in the camp for ten days. "Send us a dozen or twenty tun of good English beer, for us old fellows to drink," he pleaded, though he added that the soldiers bore their deprivation with surprisingly "little grudging."[15]

Every sort of hindrance and disruption marred the progress of English aims in France: inaccurate military information, insufficient supplies of food and equipment, incompetence and dishonesty. The unseasonable rains drowned the low grounds and spoiled grain that would have provided fodder for the horses and cattle. Greedy soldiers seized double and triple rations, and could not be disciplined. Crowds of hangers-on gathered in the camps, stealing food and drink and, when they had drunk their fill, brawling like madmen. "Ingraters" stole on a larger scale, boarding the supply ships from England as soon as they docked in the French ports and buying up their cargoes to resell to the royal purveyors at a profit. Worse still, there was fighting between the English and the German mercenaries hired to serve alongside them. Much of the violence went on out of sight of the officers, but some incidents came to their attention. Norfolk received word that one of the Germans struck an English soldier "with a boar spear in the throat, without any occasion given"; the culprit was shielded by his compatriots, and could not be found.[16]

The rain, which at first had been dismissed as an untimely inconvenience, soon became an enmiring disruption in itself. The English tried to remind themselves that the almanacs forecast fair weather, but as the wet days dragged by they began to believe the prognostication they heard from the old women of the region: rain on July 3 meant rain for forty days thereafter.[17]

On September 8 Henry dictated a letter to his wife Catherine, who was serving as regent in his absence. He apologized for not writing in his own hand, "but that we be so occupied, and have so much to do in foreseeing and caring for everything ourself, as we have almost no manner rest or leisure to do any other thing."[18] He thanked her for the venison she sent him, and informed her in some detail of the good progress of the bombardment of Boulogne. He expected the town would fall in two or three days, he said; but for a shortage of gunpowder it would already be in ruins. (By this time Henry had used up not only all powder originally provided for the siege, but all of another shipment from Flanders and every bit from the reserve stores at Calais and Guînes; on the day he wrote Catherine he was looking for more powder from England—"what may be spared out of castles and bulwarks within the survey of the Cinque Ports," and any that might be found in the ships on the Thames.[19])

The outworks were already in English hands, and Henry's men were contending with the defenders "hand to hand" for the inner ramparts. Even more gratifying to Henry was the imminent arrival of a peace delegation from King Francis, made up of men of such high rank and status that they complimented his own honor considerably. (Chapuys found him "proud and vainglorious" on the subject.) Doubtless he hoped to be able to impress the French when they arrived, and to this end he stepped up the bombardment. At the bottom of the dictated letter Henry added a paragraph in his own hand. This day, he wrote, "we begin three batteries, and have three mines going, besides one which hath done his execution in shaking and tearing off one of their greatest bulwarks." Even as he wrote, he said, the castle dike had been stormed, and was "not like to be recovered by the Frenchmen again." "No more to you at this time, sweetheart," he concluded, "both for lack of time and great occupation of business, saving we pray you to give in our name our hearty blessings to all our children." After final greetings to Catherine's ladies and his councilors, he signed the letter "with the hand of your loving husband, Henry R.," and went back to his labors.

The good news pleased Catherine, who was nearly as busy with the business of government as Henry was with the business of war. It fell to her (through the royal lieutenant of the north and the Privy Council) to make certain the Scots did not rekindle war on the northern border, and to coordinate the shipment of needed supplies to France. A few weeks earlier she had gotten word of the capture of a Scots ship carrying letters toward France. In sending on the more important of the letters to Henry she wrote that their capture was clearly ordained by God to show the "crafty dealing and juggling" of the Scots, and to further Henry's righteous struggle on the battlefield. Her own letters to him are filled with her immediate concerns and occurrences at court, but there were personal passages too. She missed Henry very much, she was impatient for his letters, indeed she could not endure to be separated from him were it not in a good cause, Catherine wrote. "God, the knower of secrets, can judge these words not to be only written with ink, but most truly impressed in the heart," she added, signing herself "your Majesty's humble obedient loving wife and servant" Catherine the queen.[20]

On September 11, the day the first member of the French delegation, the bishop of Arras, arrived at camp before Boulogne, Henry mounted his final assault. The English hurled themselves through openings in the breached walls, and there was much bloodshed on both sides. The chief attack, though, was to come from an elaborate mining operation directed by Girolamo da Treviso. With one vast explosion the castle was to be destroyed, and Henry made certain that he and his companions were at a good vantage point when the order to fire the mines was given. There was a deafening blast. The castle walls cracked and heaved, and great gaps appeared as heavy blocks of stone and mortar fell on the heads of the fighting men. The impact sent stones flying everywhere, and when the dust settled many of the besiegers lay dead, among them the unfortunate Treviso.[21]

Though the castle was badly damaged the walls still held, and the defenders turned back the assault. Henry was mortified at first, but to his great relief the next day the French commander opened negotiations to deliver the town, and two days later the formal surrender took place. Some two thousand of the townspeople of Boulogne filed out of the town gates and past the watching English soldiers, taking the road toward Montreuil, their scrawny horses pulling carts piled high with their possessions. Following them came the soldiers of the garrison, whole and wounded, walking five abreast, to the number of another two thousand and more. The town had been undermanned, and its defenders short of gunpowder; Chapuys gave it as his opinion that, had they been adequately supplied, the English losses would have been much higher.[22]

Henry rode in triumph as a conqueror through the gates of Boulogne on September 18. It was a sentimental entry, which must have brought back memories of his formal entry into Tournai, and later into Lille, as a young man. His treasured objective had been won. He had taken the town he said was more important to him than Paris—more important than ten Parises, as he put it later.[23] He called Boulogne "our daughter," and referred to himself proudly as "The King's Highness of Bolloign," and as he rode through the rubble-strewn streets trumpeters standing precariously on the broken walls saluted him with a royal fanfare.

During the next ten days he made himself familiar with every tower and wall of the town—from the inside. Having destroyed much of the place while it was in French hands, he now faced the challenge of rebuilding it into a strong English fortress. He planned the reconstruction of the works, ordering a high defensive mound built on the ruins of a church and appointing a master mason, master carpenter, chief smith and surveyor of the works to carry out his instructions. There was much civilian rebuilding to be done as well, as nearly every structure in the town had been damaged or destroyed in the final bombardment. In addition, there were a great many survivors of the siege, most of them "aged, sick, and hurt persons" who had to be cared for in some fashion.

Harsh news came while the king was savoring his triumph: Charles V had made peace with the French. Without consulting his English ally he had come to terms the very day Henry entered Boulogne, leaving the English to fight on alone as best they could.

"Silent and pensive," Henry hastily revised his plans in the light of the emperor's defection. With Boulogne in order, its restoration under way, he marched to Montreuil, which was still in enemy hands, and mustered the men under Norfolk's command to see how they fared. It was a dismal spectacle. Inside the town the starving French, having eaten all the larger four-footed beasts, including their horses, were now "glad to eat of a cat well larded and call it dainty meat." Outside, in the besiegers' camp, the shortage was nearly as severe. The countryside for twelve miles around had been denuded; every ear of corn and blade of grass had vanished. The horses were dying, and at least twenty men died each day of disease.[24] There was no choice but to lift the siege and retreat, though Henry feared to seem dishonored. To his bitter regret the costly siege engines, portable mills and brewhouses had to be burned to keep them from the enemy.

It was the last distasteful act of a frustrating campaign. There would be no further assaults, no further prizes. The fall rains had set in—distinguishable from the summer rains only in their tempestuous violence—and the campaigning season was at an end. Henry delayed his departure until the English had, miraculously, retreated safely from Montreuil. Then on the last day of September he embarked for home, concerned for the disesteem the retreat had brought him yet "quite buoyant and joyful" overall. He left Boulogne in the hands of his commanders Norfolk and Suffolk, instructing them to guard it well.

There was one last obstacle to be surmounted. Plague raged at all the Channel ports, and in London; after much planning and advice from the queen and Privy Council an itinerary was mapped "by which his Majesty might, most safely for sickness and most commodiously for his travel, return within the realm."[25] Late on the evening of September 30 the King's Highness of Boulogne was back in England, "to the great rejoicing of all his loving subjects."

43

The wrinkles in my brow,
The furrowes in my face
Say, Limping age will lodge him now,
Where youth must geve him place

ONCE he was back in England the battlefield vitality that had so reinvigorated Henry waned, and he began once again to be weighed down by his heavy, unresponding flesh. Chapuys thought him "much broken" since his return, and the king himself said early in 1545 that he had felt "ten times better" in France than he had since.[1]

Now and then he displayed a sort of mental calcification—an almost obsessive narrowing of mind that was not precisely senility but was very much the product of advancing age. When talking with ambassadors he had less and less tolerance for "interpretations"—a term he used repeatedly, and by which he meant the deceitful rationalizations of those who were against him. He would only speak of straightforward, unambiguous things: of honor and dishonor, honesty and dishonesty, candor and guile. In his last years he dwelt with pathetic redundancy on his own high-minded virtues and the malignant faults of others, on his fidelity to his friends despite their betrayals, on his chivalry and others' churlishness. These were none other than the high-minded ethics that had brought Henry esteem in his young manhood, yet where before they had been the heartfelt ideals of youth they were now the platitudes of a spent old man, whose long and bloody rule spoke eloquently against his claims to virtue.

It was as if, in order to comprehend men and events, he had to reduce them to moral absolutes; the everyday middle ground of ambivalent motivations and nuanced meanings was becoming intolerable to him. And as he struggled to reduce all to light and dark, good and evil his sharp anger returned. In the midst of discussions with his councilors and foreign envoys his temper would flare, and a torrent of recriminations would put an end to all conversation. His advisers were forced to make apologies for him (sometimes, as Chapuys reported, "in a joking, semi-shamefaced fashion") even as they feared his wrath; he alone ruled, but as always he could be swayed, and his anger could be turned to advantage by an adroit councilor who approached him at the right moment.

The challenges to the realm increased rather than diminished after Henry returned from France. England and France remained at war, with the French attempting to recover all that they had lost in recent months. Within days of the king's departure they attacked Boulogne—left all but undefended by Norfolk, who withdrew his troops to Calais contrary to Henry's last command—and fell on the small English garrison in Basse Boulogne on the night of October 9. Many of the English, including women and noncombatants, were slaughtered as they slept, and the town that had symbolized victory now became a watchword for defeat. The English defenders of the high town, though, held it against the attackers and were still resisting a French siege the following spring.

Meanwhile Charles V, having ceased to be an ally of the English, began behaving like an enemy. He ordered all English ships and property in the Low Countries to be seized—including crown merchandise intended to be used as repayment to Antwerp merchants for Henry's large loans. And he refused to come to England's aid even when, by the late spring of 1545, it looked as though the French might invade the island in force.

By now the English residents of the coastal towns were accustomed to setting out and tending the beacons that were to warn of enemy approach and to summon "all gentlemen, burgesses and peasants to be ready with arms to join the standards." The watch fires were laid, at three-mile intervals, all up and down the coast, with three beacons in every valley near the sea and two on adjoining hills, visible to seaward and landward. "Wise and vigilant persons" kept watch. If enemy ships were sighted, one lowland beacon was to be set alight. At the sight of ships carrying soldiers and making for shore two lowland and one hilltop beacon were to be fired—the signal for a general muster. And if the landing force was evidently more numerous than the men assembled to resist it, all three lowland fires were to be lit "in haste," and every man was to run to the nearest high place, prepared to fight for his king and his life.[2]

This year the dreaded invasion came. On the afternoon of July 18, as Henry sat at dinner aboard his venerable flagship the *Great Harry* in Portsmouth harbor, a French fleet "in great force" sailed menacingly into view at the harbor mouth. The king hurriedly left his ship, and the English fleet weighed anchor at once and began to fire on the enemy. Though the French were too wary of the English cannon to approach very closely the English ships too were at a disadvantage. They were windbound, and could not leave the harbor to give chase.

But though there was no engagement there was a major catastrophe. The huge English ship the *Mary Rose,* having fired all her cannon on one side, hove about to fire those on the other. All her gunports were open, and when a sudden gust of wind caught her sails and rolled her over the lowest row of openings dipped below the water line. The ship foundered and sank, too quickly for the crew of five hundred mariners and the captain, Vice-Admiral George Carew, to escape. It was a sobering loss, for besides her large crew and skilled captain the *Mary Rose* had carried much "goodly ordnance" and other valuable equipment. Attempts were made to raise her, with heavy cables tied to her masts, but the foremast broke under the strain and in the end the ship could not even be dragged up into shallow water.[3]

As soon as the French fleet was sighted the warning beacons were lit, and men mustered in expectation of a landing. Two days later some

French troops were landed on the Isle of Wight, where they burned some houses and skirmished with the English, yet when the number of defenders reached three thousand or so the Frenchmen retreated, and finally took ship again the next day. Fifteen hundred French arquebusiers and pikemen came ashore farther eastward along the coast at Seaford, confirming the English judgment that an invasion in force was imminent (the French fleet was very large, and carried both soldiers and hundreds of horses, with provisions for two months), but this contingent too embarked after burning a few poor cottages. Three hundred Englishmen of the neighborhood, including twenty archers, gathered to oppose them, and so "plucked up their courage" that they slew a hundred of the French.[4]

As it turned out there was no large-scale confrontation either by land or by sea. The two fleets faced one another in mid-August, but bad weather prevented the English from attacking and gave the French the cover they needed to retreat homeward, satisfied to have disrupted the sending of supplies to Boulogne and to have forced Henry to the expense of maintaining some thirty thousand men under arms and twelve thousand mariners at sea over several months. To the English it seemed a dubious victory. They spoke sarcastically of the weather as the "French God," and grumbled at the damage to their ships and to their disease-ridden crews. A mysterious epidemic struck nearly every English vessel, seemingly the result of "the great heat and the corruption of their victual," which rotted uneaten in the steaming holds. The sailors suffered from swollen heads and limbs and from diarrhea, and many who came to collect their pay bore in their faces the marks of plague. As the common mariners died the officers neglected them and quarreled among themselves, and on the whole the navy "decayed very sore," as the admiral expressed it.[5]

The king, who had watched the first naval engagement and the fighting on the Isle of Wight from his vantage point in Portsmouth, was pleased with his subjects' stouthearted valor and talked expansively of his "great joy that he had been able to measure his strength against that of his enemy." So great was his confidence in the "valor and affection of his subjects" (and in God's favor in his just quarrel) that he had kept up his accustomed summer pastimes throughout the conflict, Henry told the imperial ambassador, but his cocksure unconcern was only a pose.[6] If he hunted during the day he read letters and dispatches and conferred with his advisers when he returned from the chase, and kept himself perfectly informed about the course of the war.

He watched with particular interest the activities of Ludovico da l'Armi, a roguish adventurer and nephew of Cardinal Campeggio whom he had sent to Italy to recruit a force of six thousand mercenaries for the coming campaigning season. Da l'Armi was on the whole unsuccessful (and ended his life the following year on a Venetian scaffold), and another venture of Henry's in Italy also went awry. He had sent a man there to buy a number of arquebuses, and to send them to England disguised as a shipment of sugar, packed in barrels. The guns got as far as Antwerp, but there a customs official opened one of the barrels, discovered the fraud, and confiscated them all.

If the military consequences of the 1544 campaign brought further hazard to England, its economic consequences brought disaster. By one estimate the expedition cost some £800,000—three times what had originally been calculated and many times the annual income of the crown. Boulogne had been won at a cost of £600,000; to defend and supply it, during the first two years following its capture, cost another £400,000 and more.[7] When the costs of the Scots wars are added to expenses in France the total amounts to well over two million pounds, a sum all but incalculable in an age when an ordinary subject of the king could get by on five pounds a year. And given the inefficiency of sixteenth-century warfare it was inevitable that much of this money should be wasted—on mercenaries who performed badly or not at all, on fortifications that at best stood intact for a few years, then had to be rebuilt, on paying grasping ingraters. Food spoilage was exceptionally costly; the Boulogne accounts for September, 1545, listed the sum of £11,191 for "waste and loss of victuals."[8]

For a king forced to finance his government, as his feudal predecessors had done, from a fixed income to find such sums was impossible. Higher taxes were one answer, but an inadequate one; though the English paid much more in taxes during the 1540s than ever before, the gap between the king's debts and his income grew wider every year. "Benevolences"—money gifts made to the crown by wealthy subjects without expectation of repayment—brought in perhaps one quarter of the needed income, but they led to much grumbling. It was said that Henry had to leave the capital to "avoid hearing those who would complain that they are assessed too grievously."

Every possible expedient was attempted. Lands which came to the crown from the dissolving of the monasteries were sold off, raising revenues by some £90,000 a year, and the lead from their roofs was used as collateral for loans. Foreign borrowing, at interest rates as high as thirteen percent, brought in about another £100,000. Since the late 1520s Henry had been subsidizing the search for precious metal within England. A German expert was brought in to conduct mining operations in 1529, and in the 1540s English miners were licensed to seek out and work "mines of silver, gold and copper" throughout Cornwall.[9]

If precious metals could not be found, perhaps they could be created. In 1539 Henry licensed two alchemists, John Misselden and his son Robert, to transmute "unperfect metal" into the "perfect metal" from which he could make coins. Having lived for many years abroad, Misselden claimed to have acquired the "craft or science of philosophy" called alchemy, through which he could replicate any ore the king desired. The two men set to work, keeping in mind Henry's command that they must not use "necromancy," but only "plain science of philosophy." Had they succeeded at their task the 1540s might have been a very different decade.[10]

Short of bankruptcy, only one workable solution presented itself: debasement of the currency. The coining of money could be turned to profit in several ways. The price of gold could be raised, and the coins made smaller and lighter. (Wolsey had adopted both these measures in the 1520s.) Or the amount of base metal in each coin could be increased, with the excess precious metal going into the royal treasury. It was this policy that Henry and his councilors adopted, first to a small extent in 1542 and, in 1544, on a massive scale. New mints were set up to increase the output of the new coins, and before long the expedient was working so well that Thomas Wriothesley, lord chancellor, was referring to the mint as "our holy anchor."

Total collapse of government finance was forestalled—but at immense cost to the people. As the coins were lowered in value, prices rose (though more slowly than the coins lost worth), until by 1547 they had gone up some twenty-five percent and were continuing to mount rapidly. The sudden and, to most people, inexplicable dislocations in their economic lives were unsettling. No one could foresee what lay ahead; perhaps the current fluctuations were only a foretaste of worse to come.

To rural laborers on the margin of subsistence, for whom coins were an incidental and occasional means of exchange, the fluctuations brought only indirect harm. Those with plots of earth ate what grew in them, and dressed in cloth made at home. Merchants, particularly cloth merchants, and the thousands dependent on them actually prospered for a time, for the falling value of English coins meant that English wool was in greater demand than ever in Flanders. But such short-run prosperity was more than undercut later on, while to even modest landowners dependent for their income on their rents the inflation was punishing.

Bad money made everyone insecure, and from the early 1540s on the pennies and groats and shillings looked less and less like good silver and more and more like the copper it was mixed with. When they first left the mint the coins were given a thin coat of silver, yet the disguise was ineffective. The silver wash wore away unevenly but unmistakably from the design stamped on the coins—King Henry's face—leaving his prominent nose a coppery red. "Old Copper-Nose" became at once a royal nickname and a byword for popular mistrust of the king and his money.

In Henry's later years the disaffection of his angry, unruly people reached new heights. For twenty years they had lived with the consequences of their ruler's desires and aspirations, suffering war when he sought a knightly challenge, enduring economic hardship when his coffers were empty, shifting their religious beliefs to answer to his theology. His taxation and his costly warmaking made them indignant; his treasured prize Boulogne they called "the new Milan," referring to the city that caused such futile conflict between the emperor and the French king. His multiple marriages embarrassed them, while the uncertain health of his only male heir made them uneasy. His vengeful executions filled them with both fear and sorrow, and did much to numb the natural allegiance he called forth from them as king.

In tampering with their faith Henry had won particular opprobrium from his people. The ordinances, injunctions and oaths of allegiance he had imposed on them had attempted to uproot their traditional beliefs without substituting any firm, consistent doctrines in their place. Instead there had been a series of royal prescriptions for belief, each contradicting the one that came before. The most recent of these formulations, the "King's Book" of 1543 (*A Necessary Doctrine and Erudition for Any*

Christian Man), turned the faith still further in the direction of Catholic orthodoxy—a direction very evident in the Six Articles of 1539—though it stopped short of restoring the Catholic doctrines and practices Henry's most conservative advisers wanted. Outwardly Catholic, the King's Book contained Lutheran phraseology and left room for compromise on matters the Protestant reformers considered essential; like all pronouncements of the Henrician church, it was both eclectic and ambivalent.

In this it was a mirror of the king's own ill-assorted faith. Henry himself wrote the preface to the King's Book, and its contents grew out of discussions he held with his theologians. As usual, drafts of the document were covered with Henry's amendments and Archbishop Cranmer's annotations on them.[11] Any attempt to determine the nature of the king's faith from his actions in the 1540s comes up against contradictions. To judge from the King's Book, he was moving further and further away from reform, while retaining his Erasmian distaste for "superstition." The ascendancy of religious conservatives—chiefly Norfolk and Bishop Gardiner—in the Privy Council gave added evidence of this, as did the Act for the Advancement of True Religion, which restricted to upper-class men the reading of the English Bible. To the reformers Bible-reading was a cornerstone of true doctrine, necessary for all believers, yet to religious conservatives such as Norfolk it mattered little. "I have never read the Scripture, nor never will read it," he told an exchequer clerk in an argument over clerical marriage. "It was merry in England afore the New Learning came up; yea, I would all things were as hath been in times past."

Yet if in some respects Henry was Catholic and conservative, in other ways he seemed to side squarely with the Protestants. He sanctioned the use of Cranmer's English liturgy (though not his English communion service) in 1544, and in the following year a book of prayers in English was authorized by royal proclamation. He turned over the education of his son Edward to the reformers Richard Cox and John Cheke, thereby all but ensuring a Protestant inclination at court in the next reign. And, if Cranmer is to be believed, he even contemplated the radical step of abolishing the mass.

According to the archbishop, in 1546 Henry and Francis I negotiated an alliance whose terms called for nothing less than "within half a year to have changed the mass into a communion," and Francis agreed to deny the authority of the pope within his realm as well.[12] There were even plans to include the Catholic emperor in the scheme, though the negotiations never reached this stage. Nothing whatever came of these discussions, which were after all diplomatic, not theological. Probably they were no more in earnest than the hints of a reconciliation between Henry and the pope recorded at about the same time. In all, the evidence about the king's belief points in contradictory directions, and his subjects were understandably baffled about the nature of their own and England's faith.

A Warwickshire curate summed up the frustration his parishioners felt at the king's ever changing doctrine and the overly wordy official documents that proclaimed them. "By God's bones I have read this out to you a hundred thousand times," he cried out as he was reciting the Injunctions of 1538 to the faithful, "and yet ye be never the better." The Injunctions were not only ineffectual in promoting virtue, they were needlessly enmeshed in verbiage. "By God's flesh," the priest swore, "here is a hundred words in these Injunctions where two would serve, for I know what it meaneth as well as they that made it." To ask learned churchmen to puzzle out the royal doctrinal formulas was one thing, but to expect ordinary men and women to be instructed by the same longwinded prescriptions was another. "A vengeance upon him that printed these Injunctions!" the angry curate concluded. "By God's bones there is never one in Westminster Hall that would read thus much for twenty nobles!"[13]

Henry's subjects were conspicuously devoted to the outward forms of religion—to hearing daily mass, to saying their rosaries and Paternosters, to reciting the holy offices. Many were anticlerical, a tiny minority were completely alienated from religion. But the vast majority—including most of those who hated the clergy—were believers, though their belief consisted chiefly of memorized teachings and semi-mystical lore. They learned the fourteen articles of faith, the Ten Commandments, the two precepts of the gospel, the seven works of mercy, the seven deadly sins and the seven sacraments of grace. They envisioned God the way he was portrayed in the mystery plays—as a bearded cleric in a tiara, a white cope and gloves. They came to know the names and wonder-working virtues of dozens of saints, and they mastered the prayers and other time-honored formulas thought to trigger release of divine benefits.

When in the 1530s this pious scaffolding began to be dismantled these comfortable habits of belief were lost. To be sure, efforts at understanding the new formulas were made. One humanist preacher sent out from the court to familiarize the people with the king's doctrines told how, after his sermons, parishioners crowded around him "lamenting their long ignorance," and desiring him to repeat the arguments he had made.[14] Yet if some arrived at newfound certainty in the 1530s (as many who adopted the doctrines of the reformers did), others remained in confusion and uncertainty. The overriding verities which had once governed their lives were now in flux; even the religious conventions accompanying birth and death were being redefined. Now when they made their wills English men and women added to the number of masses to be said for their souls the cautious proviso "if the law will suffer it," hoping all the while that the law would not imperil their salvation.

An investigation of the religious practices of Archbishop Cranmer's Kentish parishioners in 1543 revealed an odd combination of traditional Catholicism, radical reform doctrines, superstition and occult lore. One vicar, nine years after the Act of Supremacy was made law, had yet to inform his flock that the king and not the pope was head of the English church. Another vicar neglected to read out from his pulpit the royal injunctions and proclamations, and allowed the people of his parish to continue in their old ways, ignorant of the changes decreed by the court. Protestantism had taken deep root in Kent, and many men and women influenced by reform teachings protested loudly against the old-fashioned ceremonies—creeping to the cross, showing special devotion to the saints, fasting and the keeping of the holy days—their fellow parishioners observed. When protests failed they turned to violence, seizing religious pictures and smashing them and breaking statues and crucifixes. One woman let it be known "that images in the church were devils and idols," and "wished the church and they were set on fire." A man boasted of "hewing in pieces" a statue of the Virgin Mary, and made a point of reading the Bible aloud to whoever would listen, including several women, thought to be least able to interpret it for themselves.

Many in Cranmer's flock were unconcerned with tenets of faith and practice, but used holy things, as their ancestors had for centuries, to work magic and promote healing. In thunderstorms the villagers of Northgate reportedly ran to their church for holy water to sprinkle in their houses to exorcise evil spirits. The vicar of Feversham recommended holy water and "other sorcery" as a remedy for piles, while in the parish of St. Mildred, an old woman with a grievance against a younger one spoke of using a holy candle to enchant her victim, to "make the cule [anus] of the said maid to divide in two parts."[15]

If the investigation showed the uneven impact of the Reformation on the common people it also revealed their hostility to the king. The clerics who refused to instruct believers in the new doctrines, the individuals who refused to learn the Lord's Prayer and Creed in English, clinging to the Latin they had learned in youth, the staunch Protestants who rejected the royal injunctions because they stopped short of a thoroughgoing break with the past—all these people defied the king. There were even those who, despite the dangers of outspokenness, expressed their contempt for all to hear. When asked his view of the religious regulations sent down from London one Thomas Hasylden of the village of Elmstead remarked laconically, "A fart for them." "Why should I do more reverence to the crucifix than to the gallows?" he asked, and backed up his bitter words by throwing down the crucifix that hung above the altar of his parish church. Hasylden knew the punishment for what he did, and had no doubt that he would be reported to the authorities, yet so rancorous were his feelings that he could not contain them.[16]

"If the king knew every man's thought," a Kentish man said to a friend, "it would make his heart quake."[17] Hundreds of reports reaching the Privy Council gave substance to this chance remark. A Buckinghamshire man said in open court that the king was nothing but a knave whose crown was fit to play football with; another man called him a tyrant more cruel than Nero; another, told to keep the peace in the king's name, cried out "A turd for the king!"[18] A gunner serving on one of the king's ships disparaged King Henry's royal blood. "If the king's blood and mine were both in a dish or saucer," he told a seaman, "what difference were between them, or how should a man know the one from the other?" His loyalty to the king was no greater than could be measured in coins, he added. If the Great Turk would pay him a penny a day more than Henry paid, he would gladly serve the infidel.[19]

Yet no matter how much they maligned him—and examples of slanderous speech are very numerous—Henry's subjects had other feelings for their king as well. When he was on campaign in France they needed little encouragement to repeat the official prayer for the safety of a monarch who "endangereth himself" at war, and who, with his soldiers, "bent himself to battle for God's cause and our defence."[20] They came by the thousands to see him as he rode through the capital, or passed by on the river in his barge. Through some ancestral fellow-feeling beyond conventional sentiment they shared his hopes and griefs. For nearly forty years his awesome presence had overshadowed their lives, inspiring a unique tangle of emotions defying clarification. He was godlike yet infinitely manly, a prince of the church yet, in many minds, a very great sinner. He was as far above the common people as the angels were above mankind, yet at times he seemed no more remote than a distant relative, irascible yet beloved, who happened to hold the fate of the kingdom in his hands.

Great Harry had now become Old Harry to his people. For years some of them had wished him dead; now few among them expected him to live long. This urgent awareness of the king's mortality gave particular meaning to the speech he made to Parliament in 1545.

It was the day before Christmas, and Parliament was assembled to hear the lord chancellor speak for the king, as custom required, before the session ended. To the surprise of all present Henry indicated that on this occasion he meant to speak in his own behalf, "to set forth his mind and meaning, and the secrets of his heart."[21]

He began by thanking "his well beloved commons" for their subsidy in support of the war, and for putting at his disposition (to be dissolved) more church property, chiefly private chapels or chantries where masses for the dead were performed. He went on to speak of Boulogne, "that fortress which was to this realm most displeasant and noisome, and shall be, by God's grace hereafter, to our nation most profitable and pleasant." But these were only preliminaries. He warmed now to his main theme.

"Now since I find such kindness on your part toward me," he went on, speaking, one observer noted, in a tone as fatherly as it was kingly, "I cannot choose but love and favor you, affirming that no prince in the world more favoreth his subjects than I do you, nor no subjects or commons more love and obey their sovereign lord than I perceive you do me." He would not spare either his treasure or his person to defend them, Henry said, and his recent exploit gave weight to his words. Yet this "perfect love and concord" which bound ruler and subjects was marred by conflict among the people themselves. "Charity and concord is not amongst you," Henry said reproachfully, "but discord and dissension beareth rule in every place."

Here Henry became a sententious, if paternal, preacher. He preached to the clergy: "Behold then, what love and charity is amongst you, when the one calleth the other, heretic and Anabaptist, and he calleth him again Papist, hypocrite, and Pharisee? Be these tokens of charity amongst you? Are these the signs of fraternal love between you?" He accused them of preaching against one another, of refusing to compromise their views, of lacking forgiveness and understanding, so that "all men almost be in variety and discord, and few or none preach truly and sincerely the word of God."

He preached to the laity then, reproving them for failing to keep "good order and Christian fraternity," and for slandering priests and bishops, and "rebuking and taunting" preachers in their pulpits. They took it upon themselves to judge the clergy by the sole light of their "phantastical opinions and vain expositions," and turned their newfound knowledge of the Bible to use as an anticlerical weapon. "Although you be permitted to read holy Scripture," Henry told his Commons, "you must understand that it is licensed you so to do, only to inform your own conscience, and to instruct your children and family, and not to dispute and make Scripture, a railing and a taunting stock against priests and preachers." He had given the people the Bible in their own tongue to enlighten them; instead "that most precious jewel the word of God is disputed, rimed, sung and jangled in every alehouse and tavern." What had been offered in fatherly kindness was being abused by wanton children.

The speech was having its effect. The hardened men in the Parliament chamber were moved by the king's words, and by the sight of their aged sovereign, his body enfeebled yet his eyes as animated as ever in his fleshy face. He mingled blame and fondness with the skill of a loving parent, and those who were not accustomed to hearing him speak were deeply affected by the power of his presence. "To us, that have not heard him often," one member wrote, it "was such a joy and marvellous comfort as I reckon this day one of the happiest of my life." Many in the audience were in tears, among them the king's closest advisers, as he concluded:

"Therefore, as I said before, be in charity one with another, like brother and brother; love, dread and serve God (the which I, as your supreme head and sovereign lord, exhort and require you) and then I doubt not but that love and league that I spake of in the beginning shall never be dissolved or broken between us."

In that rare moment, by the force of his sincere affection, Henry succeeded in creating the unity he sought. But the moment passed, the Parliament was dissolved, and before long the old king himself began to wear toward his end.

44

In erthly things there is no surete,
For unstabil and transitory they be;
But for a tyme to the they ar lent,
To forsake them thou must be content,
For here thou may not allway remayne;
Vanitas vanitatum *all that is but vayne.*

HENRY VIII spent the last months of his life in a rather small room. The privy chamber in each of his palaces was of modest size, with tapestries on the walls, a carpeted floor, and a chair of estate for the king to sit in. Other furniture was rather sparse. The privy chamber at Greenwich had a walnut breakfast table, two other tables, one covered in black velvet, a cupboard for dishes and goblets, a few chairs and some musical instruments. At Hampton Court the furnishings were exactly the same, with the addition of a black leather desk, a clock stand and a pair of fire irons, and a "thing artificial" set into the wall, enshrining an alabaster fountain.[1]

Here, served by two dozen gentlemen and grooms, his barbers, his page and his physicians, Henry lived out his days. He dressed, ate and transacted business in the relative privacy of the small chamber, as outside in the vast, high-ceilinged presence chamber with its splendid brocade throne dozens of courtiers and suitors waited to see him or to present their petitions. It was in the privy chamber that Henry talked with his ambassadors and advisers, and with the queen; more than likely he compounded his medicines here as well, and underwent the treatments prescribed for his ailments.

Apart from the unfinished palace of Nonsuch, which the king visited rarely, Whitehall was the chief royal residence, and the privy chamber at Whitehall was in a block of apartments running parallel to the river. In the guard chamber nearby fifty gentlemen pensioners were in constant attendance, their poleaxes at the ready, should anyone try to disturb the king. Outside in the presence chamber a shadow court held sway. Reverence was paid to the empty throne; steaming dishes of meat were served at the empty dining table, and then respectfully removed. In deference to the king's symbolic presence courtiers and servants alike went bareheaded, and in every other way behaved as if their master's eye were upon them.

In the 1530s Whitehall had been almost unimaginably grand. Its long, elegant galleries had ceilings "marvellously wrought in stone and gold," and wainscots of carved wood "representing a thousand beautiful figures." The high windows looked out over blooming gardens and orchards, the tiltyard, and the river. Inside, beyond magnificent hangings and gold-fringed furnishings the palace held "many and singular com- modious things, pleasures and other necessaries," as Henry ordered, "most apt and convenient to appertain only to so noble a prince, for his singular comfort, pastime and solace."

By the 1540s, however, the grandeur was tarnishing. The tiltyard had grown over with weeds, the privy kitchens were in a sad state of disrepair, and the queen's apartments were in need of renovation. In the indoor tennis courts the tapestries that lined the walls were worn and motheaten, and had to be taken down, while in the palace itself the hangings had become "foul and greasy" at the ends and had to be replaced.[2]

Much had been made new when Catherine Howard became queen, yet a stigma hung over the palace. Among the new furnishings were many confiscated from the estates of executed traitors. Load after load of goods "from sundry persons attainted" was delivered to the king's receivers, who distributed their contents among the royal residences. There were purple velvet bedcoverings trimmed in cloth of gold from Nicholas Carew, embroidered cushions that had belonged to Lord Montague, bedchamber furnishings from the estate of Edward Neville. Robes from the wardrobe of the marquis of Exeter now came to his royal cousin, and rich goods that had been Cardinal Wolsey's, many of them still bearing his arms, were everywhere.

Whenever he left the privy chamber Henry was surrounded by remind- ers of the past, reminders of the men he had outlived. In recent months more deaths dismayed him. Thomas Audley, an uncommonly loyal ser- vant and since 1533 lord chancellor, died in 1544. The commander of Boulogne, Lord Poynings, died the following year, as did Henry's longtime physician Dr. Butts. More wounding was the death of Charles Brandon, who succumbed while his lifelong friend the king was away from court on progress.[3]

Henry himself was sinking unwillingly into the semi-retired life of an elderly invalid. The intervals between his bouts of disease were becoming shorter, his periods of convalescence longer. He refused to compromise with his infirmities, shaking off illness as quickly as he could and driving himself by sheer force of will to keep up his accustomed pursuits. But more and more often sickness overcame him, and he was forced to keep to his bed or at least to his privy chamber, where he passed the time playing cards with Edward Seymour and John Dudley and the chamber gentlemen until he was well enough to resume his regular pastimes. In Chapuys' view it was remarkable that he could get about at all, for he had "the worst legs in the world," and was in far weaker condition than other men who were permanently bedridden.[4] He could no longer walk up and down stairs, and kept to the lower floors of his palaces; even there he had to be carried from room to room in a "tram," or traveling chair, when his legs were weak. An inventory of Henry's houshold furnishings listed two of these trams, one upholstered in gold velvet and silk, the other in russet, each of them complete with two embroidered footstools for the king to rest his legs on.[5]

Much of the time now Henry's life was in thrall to his physicians. They were always to be found around him, easily distinguishable from the courtiers by their long, fur-sleeved gowns and black velvet caps, and by the bladder-shaped flasks they carried for inspecting their patient's urine. This they did frequently, measuring carefully the amount eliminated against the amount of liquid the king drank to make certain the two remained in balance. They inspected the contents of his "close stools" or portable toilets as well, and gave him enemas to counteract fever and purge his bowels.

Henry seems to have been fortunate in his doctors. The methods of many Tudor physicians ranged from the exotic to the brutal. "Fustigation," or beating, was a ubiquitous remedy of the age; other cures were often so harsh they led to new disorders. One doctor, Richard Smith, did such harm to his patients in the 1530s that they made an official complaint against him to Cromwell. Smith gave one man a purge, telling him it would cure him within two days; it made him so sick he was in bed for a month and a half. Smith demanded a large fee to cure a woman of three "impostumes" which he said would kill her otherwise. When she told him she had only five shillings he took that, gave her a potion to drink, and sent her home. She collapsed on the way, and it was six months before she walked again. Another case was reported posthumously. Dr. Smith examined a sick man and, setting his mind at ease about his condition, told him to drink a special preparation and all would be well. Four days later the patient was dead.[6] The court physicians attending the king avoided such drastic remedies, as they did the sort of occult or magical cures adopted by one Cambridge doctor reputed to do wondrous things with a "quintessence" which made old men young again.[7]

The physicians were if anything subordinate to the apothecaries, who increased in numbers and importance at court toward the end of the reign. Additional men were hired in 1540 and again in 1546 to assist the gentleman apothecary, Thomas Alsop, and from time to time professional apothecaries from outside the court were brought in to prepare concoctions for the king. One summer in the late 1530s a man was commissioned to harvest roses at the peak of their bloom to use in preparing medicinal compounds: oil of roses, vinegar of roses, rose water, conserve of roses, syrup of roses, julep of roses, and half a dozen more.[8]

These aromatic elixirs were doubtless a good deal more appealing than most of the potions and plasters Henry used. He was given eyebright, caprifoil water, and rhubarb pills. He took "pills of Rasis" to fend off plague, gargled with "gargarisms" for his throat, used unguents for his belly and "fomentations for the piles." He was provided with herbal mixtures sewn into bags to be applied to the head or neck or feet or spleen—wherever it hurt—and for internal disorders the apothecaries cooked drugs and spices into "dreges," or medicinal comfits. They made up a mixture of herbs, musk and civet for the baths Henry was accustomed to take, particularly in the fall, for his sore leg, and they probably supplied the herbs and other ingredients he used in preparing his own ointments and decoctions.[9]

Among the king's personal contributions to the apothecarial art were a plaster "to ease pain and swelling about the ankles," an ointment "to dry excoriations and comfort the member," and another "to take away itch," and some thirty other medicines. One, "the Kinges Majesties Own Plaster" for sore legs, was made from marshmallows, linseed, oxide of lead, silver, red coral and dragon's blood mixed in oil of roses, rose water and white wine. This mixture was to be "boiled in a pan," then, when cooled, made into "rolls" and wrapped in parchment. "This plaster resolves humors where there is swelling in the legs," the recipe concludes.

Yet another of Henry's plasters "to heal ulcers without pain" called for a mixture of pearl and "lignum guaiacum"—a hard wood from the New World also called lignum vitae, still used as a remedy for chronic sore throat and gout.[10] Guaiacum had been introduced into Europe in the early years of the sixteenth century as a cure for syphilis, but was known to ease nonvenereal leg pains as well. The wood was ground into sawdust and drunk, mixed with water. It was very widely used; Charles V took it for his gout, and Francis I was known to be taking either guaiacum or a similar substance called "Chinese wood" for a septic groin infection which his physicians believed to be syphilitic. An English surgeon who recommended it for Henry swore he had "known divers in England healed with it," and indeed had never known it to fail.[11]

Henry's sickroom expenses during 1546 included perfumes to freshen his rooms and scent his sheets, repairs to his old close stools and the cost of a new one, upholstered in black velvet, with a down seat, "elbows and side pieces" and black silk fringe. He also had "two pair of large slippers newly devised" to warm his feet, though the rest of his wardrobe retained its traditional elegance. Hose of white leather and crimson satin, velvet nightcaps and hats, gold lace, and feathers for trim were among the items supplied for the king by his milliner in the last two years of his life. His jewels were more dazzling than ever. To his dozens of rings set with diamonds and rubies and emeralds he now added gems from the dissolved monasteries: precious stones of all kinds removed from gold crosses and altar ornaments, a huge amethyst, and "the Great Sapphire of Glastonbury." There were so many of these loose jewels that he had to order a new coffer, "with drawers to put stones in," from his cabinetmaker.[12]

Henry's intellectual curiosity did not dim as his physical activity decreased. He ordered new books and a locking coffer to carry them in, calendars and almanacs for the year 1546, and plenty of writing paper. He read with spectacles now, which he ordered ten pair at a time. They helped him to make out the names on a globe he commissioned, and to read his numerous clocks, among them timepieces "fashioned like books," or set in crystal and adorned with rubies and diamonds.[13]

For amusement Henry had his fools, who made faces while he dined, sang him bawdy songs, ridiculed everyone and everything, and created diverting anarchy at his command. When his old jester Sexten grew feeble with age in the mid-1530s a replacement had been found, a boy then no more than fifteen with a remarkable gift for comic invention.[14] But the favorite fool remained Will Somers, who for twenty years both made

Henry laugh and acted as a confidant. In his green doublet and cap with multicolored fringe, carrying his monkey or, as in one portrait, a horn, Somers was a figure of mockery yet not of frivolity. He was as treasured by his master as the favored musicians who played for Henry in his privy chamber; as a companion he was indispensable. The artist who illustrated Henry's personal psalter in 1540 chose to portray the king seated on a chest, his legs crossed at the ankle, playing a small Welsh harp. Beside him was Will Somers, his hands clasped before him, his attention elsewhere. Bald and with a beard more white than red the king looks old in the painting, yet Somers, despite his wrinkles, looks puckish and boyish.

When his health permitted Henry walked in his gardens, where in 1546 he ordered his gardeners to plant four thousand rosebushes. He grew there the large artichokes he loved to eat, and employed men skilled in grafting to create new plants and care for the rarer species. He gave much time to his animals as well: his canary birds, his ferrets, his beagles and hounds and spaniels. There were still some eighty riding horses in his stables, including four "Barbary horses," or Arabians, but Henry could no longer ride them.

Hawking had become a serious passion of Henry's, and he paid as much attention to the great gerfalcons and peregrines as another man might have paid to his children. He sent a hawks master to Ireland to collect good hunting birds, in a ship fitted out with a special cabin for conveying them back to England. He officially prohibited his subjects from taking hawks' eggs or young birds to raise at home, lest their numbers in the wild be reduced, and made certain his eleven falconers dosed the birds with sugar candy, horehound water, and rhubarb, and with special pills when they were molting. The apothecaries' records for 1545 listed "diverse medicines for hawks of ten sundry sorts in silver boxes, by order of the king," and among Henry's personal expenses at the same time were hawks' hoods and bells, silk hawking bags and gloves.[15]

Court pastimes continued as they always had, with music and dancing, masking and revelry at the appointed seasons, and entertainers such as the two brothers, "keepers of the king's bears," who amused the courtiers with the bloody spectacle of bear-baiting. Ferocious dogs tore at the legs and belly of a tethered bear, maddening him with pain and rage so that he lashed out at them with his claws and maimed or killed them. No one thought the sport inappropriate for children, and Prince Edward had his own bears and bearward just as his father had. Edward played a key role in the ceremonial reception of the French admiral Claude d'Annebaut, the last large-scale display of pageantry of the reign. With Cranmer and his uncle Edward Seymour, the prince rode to meet the admiral at Hounslow, escorted by eight hundred yeomen of the guard. He was not yet nine years old, but his horsemanship was so flawless it would have done credit to his father, and the speech he made—perhaps in his excellent schoolboy Latin, as he had only recently begun to study French—was full of "high wit and great audacity." Throughout the days of celebrations that followed the prince often took his father's place, carrying out his responsibilities with precocious gravity and royal composure.

Yet even as they went about their accustomed duties the household servants watched and waited for the king to die, and in the midst of their pleasures the courtiers maneuvered for primacy of place around the king, and calculated their chances of retaining power in the new reign.

Of the leading councilors, many were newly come to influence. William Paget, principal secretary of state since 1543, was the unglamorous but highly competent administrator overseeing the ordinary work of government. John Dudley, who had been given Arthur Plantagenet's title Lord Lisle and was raised to the earldom of Warwick in 1546, was among the fastest-rising of the younger men; his distinguished military and naval reputation (he was lord admiral), his close alliance with Edward Seymour and his ability to divert the invalid king as a partner at cards all helped his political fortunes. In 1542 died William Fitzwilliam, who had succeeded Cromwell as lord privy seal and who, in Chapuys' view, understood Henry's "nature and temper better than any man in England."

Fitzwilliam had been a reassuring presence for Henry—a companion, if not an intimate, since boyhood, an honest soldier who died fighting the Scots, a man who never triggered his suspicions. Thomas Wriothesley, who succeeded Audley as chancellor in 1544 and, three years later, was given Fitzwilliam's title earl of Southampton, was another sort of man entirely. Like Cromwell, through whose favor he rose in the mid-1530s, Wriothesley combined extreme capability with an awesome capacity for accomplishing virtually anything he set out to do. He had neither powerful family connections nor the customary professional background (in either law or the church) for holding high office, yet by 1542 an observer at court wrote in amazement that Wriothesley "almost governed everything," and he was still far from achieving all his ambitions.

It was the chancellor's chief ambition to keep himself in favor with the king while actively moving against his rivals, and in the last months of the reign Wriothesley joined Gardiner in an extensive campaign to search out and prosecute Protestant "heretics." Factional struggles as much as zeal for the faith had prompted efforts to expose those who held unorthodox theological views throughout the 1540s, but in the summer of 1546 the campaign took a particularly vicious turn when the queen herself was the target of attack.

Catherine Parr was as earnest a reformer as the humanists Henry had patronized as a young man, and her dedication to purifying the church was as persistent as it was sincere. She and her ladies devoted themselves to daily religious discussions, and in the aftermath of these sessions she often took up the same themes with her husband, who on the whole enjoyed their debates. Her influence on the king was considerable—or so her opponents believed—and there was no doubt of its direction. Catherine's personal faith was probably not outside the ever shifting bounds of orthodoxy, but her views ran perilously close to those of outspoken heretics such as Anne Askew, a prominent London reformer given financial support by two at least of Catherine's ladies.

At her every opportunity the queen urged Henry "zealously to proceed in the reformation of the church," pushing him occasionally past the verge of annoyance. On one occasion, according to the Protestant martyrologist John Foxe, Catherine's oppressive godliness and urgent pressure for reform led Henry to cry out in anger after she left his presence.

"A good hearing it is, when women become such clerks," he said sarcastically to Gardiner, "and a thing much to my comfort, to come in mine old days to be taught by my wife!" The bishop was only too pleased to feed the king's anger, offering to show him evidence of Catherine's errors, and to prove to him "how perilous a matter it is to cherish a serpent within his own bosom." According to Foxe, the king actually gave Gardiner permission to draw up "certain articles" against the queen, and signed them, and told one of his physicians that he meant to have her charged with heresy.

If court gossip is to be trusted, Catherine was already in peril. Four or five months earlier the imperial ambassador Van der Delft had reported hearing rumors that Henry was seriously thinking of taking a new wife. The talk had spread to Antwerp, where it was even more widespread; there, wagers "that the king's majesty would have another wife" were commonplace.[16] Charles Brandon's widow Catherine, now in her late twenties, was said to be the probable next queen. She was "much talked about," and "in great favor"; as she had borne Brandon two sons, she was known to be fertile, while Catherine Parr had yet to conceive.

Though reportedly "somewhat annoyed at the rumors," Queen Catherine kept her dignity despite this humiliation. But when, according to Foxe, she heard news of her imminent arrest as a heretic, she fainted dead away. Eventually, summoning all her courage—for she knew full well that once evidence had been brought against two of Henry's former queens they were doomed—Catherine went to the king and asked his pardon. She was appropriately subservient, deferring to his higher authority as a man, as her husband and lord, and as "supreme head and governor here in earth, next under God, to lean unto."

"Not so, by Saint Mary," the king is said to have replied. "You are become a doctor, Kate, to instruct us (as we take it), and not to be instructed or directed by us."

It took all of the queen's intelligence and her three years of experience with Henry to turn aside his indignation. In the end, though, she convinced him of her sincere submissiveness and lack of learned pretensions. He was mollified.

"And is it even so, sweetheart," he said finally, "and tended your argument to no worse end? Then perfect friends we are now again as ever at any time heretofore."

The next day, as Henry and Catherine were walking in a garden at Whitehall, Wriothesley appeared with an escort of forty men, intending to arrest the queen and take her to prison as planned. The chancellor approached the king; they had words. The next thing Wriothesley knew Henry was shouting insults at him. Clearly there had been some mistake.

Wriothesley backed off and led his men away, bewildered, the king's words—"Knave! Arrant knave! Beast! And fool!"—still ringing in his ears.

That Henry should go to such lengths and put his wife at such peril merely in order to embarrass his ministers and assert his primacy over them seems, on the face of it, implausible. Yet three years earlier, when Cranmer had come under attack, Henry had warned, forearmed, and rescued the archbishop just as he did Catherine, and to the same purpose. Cranmer's accusers were given the same treatment Wriothesley received, with the same clear meaning: only the king could read the king's thoughts, and guess his actions. Keeping those around him surprised and off balance had long been a hallmark of Henry's personal politics; in his old age it took on sinister outlines.

One victim Henry chose not to rescue at the last moment: his sour, irascible lieutenant Norfolk. The duke, having twice survived his king's severe indignation, little expected a third crisis. Following the disgrace of his niece Catherine Howard Norfolk had escaped the wrath that fell on his family; to preserve his own standing he had ranged himself with Henry against Catherine, saying loudly that she deserved to be burned for her crime and staying away from court on his country estates while his wife, his sister and many of his relatives and servants were imprisoned.[17] He had avoided punishment a second time when, after the capture of Boulogne, he failed to provide adequately for the town's defense. Now, suddenly on December 12, 1546, he was arrested and taken to imprisonment in the Tower.

It was his son's treasonous misconduct that Norfolk's enemies used to bring him down. Henry Howard, earl of Surrey and heir to the ducal title, was an arrogant lordling who though not yet thirty had made a brilliant name as a soldier and poet and a more dubious reputation as a quarrelsome troublemaker. Tall and lanky, with the jaunty bearing and style of a born egotist, Surrey won Henry's admiration for his wit and poetry, his air of command, and his excellence as a jouster and soldier. That he was exceedingly hot-tempered and given to rowdy midnight excursions through the London streets, breaking windows, assaulting honest citizens and shooting at prostitutes, was an annoyance to be overlooked.

But when it was discovered that Surrey was guilty of much more than this, that he had actually altered his arms to indicate a strong claim to the throne, and this at a time when the end of the reign loomed near, he began to seem dangerous. He was arrested, and his father with him, and it was Edward Seymour, earl of Hertford and bitter enemy to both men, who was put in charge of Surrey's trial.

To many, the arrests of Norfolk and Surrey seemed inexplicable. Whether like Cranmer and the queen they were victims of the devouring power-hunger of their enemies in the Council, or whether it was the king's fateful disapproval that fell on them at last, remains uncertain.

Certainly Henry involved himself in Surrey's trial, poring over the legal documents at his desk in the privy chamber and making notes on the nature of the earl's offenses. In Henry's apocalyptic imagination at least both Norfolk and Surrey were guilty of a monstrous plot to assassinate the entire Council and take control of Prince Edward, ensuring their dominance in the next reign.[18] At the very least they deserved death. Surrey was executed in January of 1547; no one doubted that his father would soon end his life in the same way. Edward Seymour, who had served his king well as chief of the commissioners who condemned Surrey, now read through the inventories of the confiscated Howard wealth in anticipation of all that would come to him.

45

He that dieth with honour liveth for ever,
And the defamed dead recovereth never.

SEYMOUR did inherit the bulk of the Howard wealth and possessions in time, but as the year 1546 ended he had a larger prize well within his grasp. With his allies Dudley and Paget, the privy chamber gentlemen Anthony Denny and William Herbert, Seymour had a firm grip on the Council, the king and the future. As head of the chamber gentlemen and Henry's close intimate Denny was able, to an extent, to control who the king saw and what he heard. With Wriothesley, who had shifted his allegiance to the Seymour faction once they seemed likely to prevail, Paget oversaw government. Council meetings from December 1546 to early January 1547 were held at Seymour's London house. And, most important, Denny and his servants were keepers of the "dry stamp," the official instrument which for the last fifteen months had replaced the king's manual signature on all state papers. The dry stamp impressed a replica of the signature on paper; a clerk then traced the outline in ink. To a large extent command of the stamp meant command of the country, and it is a strong indication of the alertness and continuing power of the aged king that Seymour was cautious about abusing it.

Throughout the summer and into the fall of 1546 Henry was alternately indisposed and unexpectedly active. He spoke of undertaking an extensive progress to the far corners of the realm, and though nothing came of this he did manage a fair amount of hawking. He was ill in July, and, for a time, shut himself away in marked depression. But the ambassadors took this to be a reaction to recent events (peace had been made with France, but the French continued to build fortifications and there was fear of renewed warfare), and wrote in their dispatches that he was "very well."[1]

On September 4 the king left for his customary fall hunting tour. He planned to visit "houses remote from towns," he said; he did not intend to alter his itinerary because of possible ill health. He went first to Oatlands, where great stags were driven within range of hunters shooting from fixed standings. Henry took his turn among the hunters; according to a man who watched the hunt the king actually coursed with greyhounds and rode down the stags on horseback as well, shooting at them with darts and spears. Three days later he was still spending long hours in the fields, "always at the chase," but soon afterward he paid for his excess. He became seriously ill, and though visitors to the itinerant court were told that it was only a cold Van der Delft found out from his informants that in fact he was in "great danger."[2] Yet once again he recovered, and by early October was at his hunting again, and receiving ambassadors with his accustomed air of majesty.

To the last the king spoke with keen and well-informed interest about military and governmental matters, directing diplomatic maneuvers so baffling in their intricacy that his underlying aims are impossible to discover. As often as he was able he talked for hours to Van der Delft and the new French ambassador Odet de Selve; as in the past, the envoys noted that his eyes lit with excitement when he sensed intrigue, and that any hint of dissimulation or deceit made him indignant.

Yet after October it became more and more difficult to obtain an audience with Henry. Either he was indisposed, or he had retired to take his medicines and prepare himself for his healing baths, or he had gone hoarse with a cold. Sometimes when he was said to be ill he was in fact abroad hunting, but as the holidays approached he succumbed to what was to be his last illness.

In London all the talk was of the king's fragile health, of Prince Edward who would soon be king (though some thought his sister Mary might after all succeed), and of the shifting status of the men in power. There was much talk of treason, and of suspicion of treason; the lord mayor was commanded to "inquire secretly" for such as spoke against the king or knew of conspiracies against him.[3] It was known that the men of the Privy Council were plotting one another's destruction, and that at least once they had come to blows. Little political sophistication was needed to realize that, as Van der Delft wrote to Charles V, Henry's death "would plunge everything here into confusion."

The king spent Christmas in the capital, in the utmost seclusion. The queen had been sent away to Greenwich, with most of the court and household; only the councilors and a few chamber gentlemen attended Henry. Ostensibly, it was the arrest and disgrace of Norfolk and Surrey that prompted this isolation. Yet Henry had never before been away from his spouse at Christmas, and the imperial ambassador suspected that in fact the king was dying. Earlier in the month he had wrestled with a fever for some thirty hours, and ever since then his complexion had been sallow and his body "greatly fallen away." He managed to get out of bed and dress, but he could do little or nothing, and as the new year opened Seymour was more and more in command of affairs.

Though he knew his life to be ebbing Henry still forbade his family to gather at his bedside. The queen remained at Greenwich, the royal children at country houses far from court. The physicians governed all, torturing the king's bloated legs with cautery and swabbing the sweat from his fevered torso. As they worked over him they frowned and muttered to one another, fearing to pronounce the king's imminent death (which was treason), yet fearing to give false hope lest they be blamed when the end came. For several weeks, from late December to mid-January, no one was allowed in to see Henry and there was no word of his condition. Rumor had it that he was dead; whatever his state, the French ambassador wrote, "it can only be bad and will not last long."[4]

It seems odd that, in his last days, Henry did not summon his nine-year-old son to his bedside to instruct and encourage him for the responsibilities he was soon to inherit. It may be that, against all reasonable hope, Henry believed he could find the strength to throw over his diseases yet again. All his life he had fled from disease, and looked on death and reminders of death with an exaggerated abhorrence. Probably he chose now to ignore the finality of his circumstances, and in any case he had always avoided final partings.

Prince Edward was at Ashridge, much in doubt for his father's health and without the comfort of his stepmother or half-sisters. Young as he was he knew he was expected to toughen himself against grief and the dread of becoming king. As he waited in the wintry country house for news from the court he wrote in elegant Latin formal letters of thanks for his New Year's gifts. He wrote to his father, promising to strive to follow his example "in virtue, wisdom and piety." He wrote to the queen, thanking her for the double portrait of herself and Henry that she had sent him, and received a reply urging him to "meditate upon the distinguished deeds of his father," as he gazed at the portrait he liked so well.[5]

On January 16 de Selve was admitted to Westminster to see the king. He found him "fairly well," and spoke to him of continental affairs. Henry's thoughts were of fortifications and military supplies, of the artillery and powder and armor being sent north to defend the Scots border, of the impoverished soldiers defending Boulogne. He spoke competently, but relied a good deal on Paget, who occasionally spoke for him and who seemed much the better informed of the two.

Henry now turned to Paget for help as he had never turned to anyone. The two men spent entire nights in conversation—or so Paget later claimed—presumably working out the details of the new government that would soon come to power.[6] Eventually Seymour joined them, and still later the other councilors, until at last the shape of the regency that would govern for Edward became clear.

In 1540 Henry had written to Norfolk that, given his regal destiny and ancestry, "his progenitors afore him emperors in their own realm and dominions," he had no doubt that he would leave his kingdom "in as good case to his son as his father before left it unto him, and better."[7] In fact the realm was in an exceedingly unhealthy state, its currency eroded and its credit all but gone, its people alienated, its military standing insecure. For a generation after Henry VIII's death his successors would wrestle with the conflicts and crises he had created, seeking in vain to impose stability and permanency on a realm in flux. In time Henry's younger daughter, her strength and force of character as striking as her father's and her personal fortunes favorable, would preside over calmer times. But for the next few years there would be hardship and unrest on a massive scale, extremism in government, and, in the royal Council, men who enriched themselves with a calculating rapacity that would have astonished the old king as much as it enraged him.

The design for the successor government was embodied in Henry's will, drawn up in final form (but not signed) in late December and altered, to benefit Seymour and his allies, either in Henry's last hours or in the early days of the new reign.[8] Sixteen councilors were to guide Edward through his minority, among them Seymour, Dudley, Paget, Herbert, and Denny. Among the sixteen were diplomats, jurists, administrators and two churchmen—the ancient Cuthbert Tunstall, who had served Henry since the early years of his reign, and Archbishop Cranmer. It would have seemed a balanced group of men, save for the evident mastery of Seymour, Paget and Dudley. Of their political opponents, Gardiner had been excluded by the king himself, who declared to Denny that "surely, if he were in my testament, and one of you, he would cumber you all and you would never rule him, he is of so troublesome a nature." And Norfolk lay in the Tower, awaiting his sentence of death.

Henry's will directed that he be buried at Windsor, "midway between the stalls and the high alter," in a tomb "now almost finished" (Wolsey's tomb). Queen Jane's bones were to be placed alongside his; the will did not specify Queen Catherine's eventual resting place. Beside the tomb an altar was to be furnished "for the saying of daily masses while the world shall endure," and to complement this divine commemoration Henry instituted a human one. Thirteen poor men were to be selected to form a new order of knighthood, the Poor Knights, each to receive a daily stipend and, every year, a long gown of white cloth as the livery of their order. Beyond this, forty pounds a year was to be given in alms to the poor, though not to "common beggars," if avoidable.[9]

On January 27 Henry gave the order which would send Norfolk to his death the next morning. By evening, though, it appeared that he might not outlive the duke. He suffered a relapse, and sank weakly down into his pillows as if for the last time. The doctors shook their heads, and Denny, of all the men in the room least fearful of his master's anger, told him gravely that "in man's judgment" he had not long to live.

It was the last hour of human reckoning, the time when on the brink of promised immortality mortal man must wrestle with his conscience and his God. What Henry's thoughts were in that hour no one ever knew: whether in his extremity he doubted his past judgment, or glimpsed in a moment of insight the pain and terror he had brought to those who loved and feared him. Whatever his ruminations, his faith did not waver in the face of death. The mercy of Christ, he declared to those about him, was "able to pardon all his sins, though they were greater than they be."

He was urged to call a priest. He wanted only Cranmer, Henry replied, but not yet. "I will first take a little sleep, and then, as I feel myself, I will advise upon the matter."

He slept, and then, waking, sent for the archbishop, who came from Croydon as fast as he could ride, shivering in the midnight cold. As he waited for Cranmer Henry was overcome by a paralyzing weakness. By the time the archbishop arrived he could not speak. He fought for consciousness. There was no time for the last rites, no possibility of confession, but the king still had some power of movement. Cranmer asked him for a sign of his faith in the redemptive grace of Christ. With an effort he seized Cranmer's hand and wrung it with all his remaining strength. Soon afterward, at about two o'clock in the morning of January 28, he died.

There was at first no announcement, no immediate mourning, only secrecy and planning by the councilors who now held power. But one man guessed the truth. In the Tower, the time appointed for Norfolk's execution came and went, and he lived on. Had Henry personally intervened to save him he would have heard of it. The silent reprieve—or was it merely a postponement?—could mean only one thing: the old king was dead, and the duke's fate and England's had passed into new hands.

Notes

ABBREVIATIONS

BIHR

Bulletin of the Institute of Historical Research.

Brown, ed., *Four Years*

Brown, Rawdon, ed. and trans., *Four Years at the Court of Henry VIII,* 2 vols. London: Smith, Elder and Co., 1854.

Byrne

Byrne, Muriel St. Clare, ed., *The Letters of King Henry VIII.* London: Cassell, 1936.

EconHR

Economic History Review.

EETS

Early English Text Society.

EHR

English Historical Review.

L.P.

Letters and Papers, Foreign and Domestic, of the Reign of Henry VIII, ed. J. S. Brewer, R. H. Brodie and James Gairdner, 21 vols. London: Her Majesty's Stationery Office, 1862–1910.

Mil. Cal.

Calendar of State Papers and Manuscripts, Existing in the Archives and Collections of Milan, ed. Allen B. Hinds, Vol. I. London: His Majesty's Stationery Office, 1912.

Sp. Cal.

Calendar of Letters, Despatches, and State Papers, relating to the Negotiations between England and Spain, preserved in the Archives at Vienna, Simancas, Besançon and Brussels, ed. Pascual de Gayangos, G. A. Bergenroth, M. A. S. Hume, Royall Tyler, and Garrett Mattingly, 13 vols. London: His and Her Majesty's Stationery Office, 1862–1954.

TRHS

Transactions of the Royal Historical Society.

Ven. Cal.

Calendar of State Papers and Manuscripts, Relating to English Affairs, Existing in the Archives and Collections of Venice, and in Other Libraries of Northern Italy, ed. Rawdon Brown and Allen B. Hinds, 38 vols. London: Longman and Co., 1864–1947.

References to *L.P., Sp. Cal., Ven. Cal.* and similar collections are to page numbers, not document numbers.

373

PART ONE
YOUNG HARRY

Chapter 1

1. *The Reign of Henry VII from contemporary sources,* ed. Albert F. Pollard, University of London Historical Series, No. 1, 3 vols. (London, 1913–14), I, 106.
2. Gladys Temperley, *Henry VII* (Boston and New York, 1914), 67.
3. *Ibid.,* 123.
4. Pollard, ed., *Reign of Henry VII,* I, 220.
5. Nicholas Harris Nicolas, ed., *Privy Purse Expenses of Elizabeth of York: Wardrobe Accounts of Edward the Fourth* (London, 1830), 219.
6. Temperley, 122.
7. Pollard, ed., *Reign of Henry VII,* II, 232; Nicolas, ed., *Privy Purse Expenses of Elizabeth of York,* 198; A. F. Pollard, *Henry VIII,* new ed. (London, 1951), 19.
8. Temperley, 383–84.
9. Charlotte Augusta Sneyd, trans., *Relation or rather a true account of the island of England; . . . about the year 1500,* Camden Society, Old series, XXXVII (London, 1847), 85.

Chapter 2

1. Frank Arthur Mumby, *The Youth of Henry VIII: A Narrative in Contemporary Letters* (London, 1913), 3.
2. F. M. Salter, ed., "Skelton's *Speculum principis,*" *Speculum,* IX, No. 1 (January 1934), 25–37.
3. Percival Hunt, *Fifteenth Century England* (Pittsburgh, 1962), 76–79.
4. Quoted in Ruth Kelso, *The Doctrine of the English Gentleman in the Sixteenth Century,* University of Illinois Studies in Language and Literature, Vol. XIV (Urbana, Illinois, 1929), 157.
5. *Ibid.,* 157.
6. Edith Rickert, ed., *The Babees' Book: Medieval Manners for the Young* (New York and London, 1908), 252.
7. Kelso, 80–81.

Chapter 3

1. Temperley, 379–80 and note.
2. Nicolas, ed., *Privy Purse Expenses of Elizabeth of York,* 37.
3. *Ibid.,* 3.
4. Pollard, ed., *Reign of Henry VII,* II, 4.
5. *Ibid.,* I, 219.
6. E. M. G. Routh, *Lady Margaret, Mother of Henry VII* (London, 1924), 103.
7. *Ibid.,* 25.
8. *Ibid.,* 92.

Chapter 4

1. *Sp. Cal.* I, 318.
2. Mumby, 47–48.
3. Nicolas, ed., *Privy Purse Expenses of Elizabeth of York,* xciii.

Chapter 5

1. Pollard, ed., *Reign of Henry VII,* I, 238–39.
2. *Ibid.,* I, xxiii.
3. *Ibid.,* I, 205–6; J. R. Hale, *Renaissance Europe* (New York, 1973), 165.
4. Pollard, ed., *Reign of Henry VII,* II, 5.
5. *Ibid.,* I, 238–39.
6. Temperley, 391.
7. Pollard, ed., *Reign of Henry VII,* I, lxii; Temperley, 311.
8. Temperley, 340.
9. *Sp. Cal.* I, 406–7.
10. Pollard, ed., *Reign of Henry VII,* I, 238.

Chapter 6

1. James Gairdner, ed., *Memorials of King Henry VIII,* Rolls Series, No. 10, 2 vols. (London, 1858), II, 124.
2. *Correspondencia de Gutierre Gómez de Fuensalida, embajador en Alemania, Flandes é Inglaterra (1458–1509)* (Madrid, 1907), 449.
3. *Ibid.*
4. *L.P.* XIII:ii, 318.
5. Gairdner, ed., *Memorials,* II, 128.
6. Frederick Chamberlin, *The Private Character of Henry the Eighth* (New York, 1931), 105; S. B. Chrimes, *Henry VII* (Berkeley and Los Angeles, 1972), 314 and note.
7. *Sp. Cal.* II, 15.
8. Pollard, ed., *Reign of Henry VII,* I, 330 points out that the later tradition that Henry died on April 22 was in error.

Chapter 7

1. *L.P.* I, 31.
2. *Correspondencia de Fuensalida,* 518ff.
3. *Sp. Cal.* II, 14.
4. Edward Hall, *The triumphant reigne of King Henry the VIII,* ed. Charles Whibley, 2 vols. (London, 1904), I, 5.

Chapter 8

1. *Sp. Cal.* II, 40–41.
2. *Ven. Cal.* II, 30.

3. *Sp. Cal.* II, 42.

4. *L.P.* I, 35, 42, 44, 129.

5. Many of the verses to Henry VIII's early songs, preserved in "Henry VIII's MS," are printed in John Stevens, *Music and Poetry in the Early Tudor Court* (Lincoln, Nebraska, 1961), 386–425.

6. Hall, I, 15.

7. *Sp. Cal.* II, 44.

8. *L.P.* I:i, 284.

9. *State Papers of Henry VIII,* 11 vols. (London, 1830–1852), I, 95.

10. *Ven. Cal.* II, 5.

11. *Ibid.,* 21.

12. B. P. Wolffe has re-evaluated the extent of the fortune Henry VII left to his son. The young king began his reign with only a moderate surplus, though in an age of royal insolvency this made him remarkable.

13. James Anthony Froude, *Life and Letters of Erasmus* (London, 1894), 98.

14. *Ibid.,* 97.

Chapter 9

1. *L.P.* I:i, 178.

2. *Sp. Cal.* II, 38.

3. *Ibid.,* Supplement to Vols. I and II, 40.

4. *Ibid.*

5. *State Papers,* I, 45–46.

6. J. S. Brewer, *The Reign of Henry VIII: from his Accession to the Death of Wolsey,* ed. James Gairdner, 2 vols. (London, 1884), I, 45.

7. *L.P.* I:i, 370.

PART TWO
GREAT HARRY

Chapter 10

1. *L.P.* I:ii, 919, 1495.

2. This account of the fighting at Agincourt is based in part on John Keegan, *The Face of Battle* (New York, 1976), 79–116.

3. Arthur B. Ferguson, *The Indian Summer of English Chivalry* (Durham, North Carolina, 1960), 68, 160–62.

4. *Ven. Cal.* II, 95–96.

5. Denys Hay, ed., *The anglica historia of Polydore Vergil, 1485–1537,* Camden Society, Third series, LXXIV (London, 1950), 161, 197.

6. Froude, ed., *Life and Letters,* 225. I concur with Froude's judgment that in Erasmus' usage the term *cordatissimus* exceeds it conventional meaning; "high-heartedness" or "fullness of heart" are close approximations.

7. *Ibid.,* 244–46.

8. *Sp. Cal.* II, 69–70.

9. *L.P.* I:ii, 1489–90.

10. Froude, ed., *Life and Letters,* 171.

11. *Ven. Cal.* II, 54.

12. *L.P.* I:i, 423–24.

13. *Ibid.,* 675.

14. *Ibid.*

15. *Ibid.,* 580; *L.P.* I:ii, 949.

16. *Sp. Cal.* II, 96.

17. *L.P.* I:i, 831.

18. *Ibid.,* 798.

19. Nicholas Harris Nicolas, ed., *Privy Purse Expenses of King Henry the Eighth, from November 1529 to December 1532* (London, 1827), 351–52, 362.

20. *L.P.* II:ii, 1461; *Ven. Cal.* II, 105.

21. *L.P.* I:ii, 945.

Chapter 11

1. Keegan, 91, 98; C. H. Firth, "The ballad history of the reigns of Henry VII and Henry VIII," *TRHS,* Third series, II (London, 1908), 30–31; Charles W. C. Oman, *A History of the Art of War in the Sixteenth Century* (New York, 1937), 382–83.

2. *L.P.* I:i, 814.

3. *Ibid.,* I:ii, 1003, 1184.

4. *Sp. Cal* II, 148.

5. *Ven. Cal.* II, 83.

6. *L.P.* I:ii, 880.

7. *Ibid.,* 923, 965.

8. *Ibid.,* 1058.

9. *Ibid.,* 942, 944, 1057.

10. *Ibid.,* 1322–23, 1554–56.

11. Hall, I, 62.

12. *L.P.* I:ii, 972.

13. Henry's biographers disagree about his involvement in the Battle of the Spurs. While it is true that he was not among the English knights who rode against the French at Guinegate, according to the military historian Charles Oman he led his footsoldiers in the direction of the French camp as soon as the panic retreat of the French began, thus joining the pursuit albeit at a considerable distance. Oman, *Art of War,* 292.

Chapter 12

1. *L.P.* II:ii, 1457; Ernest Law, *England's First Great War Minister* (London, 1916), 97–98.

2. *L.P.* I:ii, 954.

3. *Ibid.,* 1060; *Mil. Cal.* I, 414–15.

4. *Ven. Cal.* II, 142.

5. *L.P.* I:ii, 1048.

6. *Mil. Cal.* I, 402, 415; *L.P.* I:ii, 395.

7. *L.P.* I:ii, 1349.

8. *Mil. Cal.* I, 402.

9. *Ven. Cal.* II, 92.

10. *L.P.* I:ii, 1015.

11. *Ibid.,* 977.

12. *Ibid.,* 974.

13. *Mil. Cal.* I, 410.

14. *Sp. Cal.* II, 146.

15. *L.P.* II:ii, 1459.

16. *Ibid.,* I:ii, 1040, 1086.

17. *Ibid.,* 1027. Additional proof that Katherine was advancing northward with an army comes from *L.P.* I:ii, 1230, where among the ordnance stores listed in spring, 1514, were guns "which should have gone northward with the queen's grace" in the previous year.

18. *Ibid.,* 1014.

Chapter 13

1. This account of the May Day festivities in 1515 is taken from the dispatches of Giustiniani, in Rawdon Brown, ed. and trans., *Four Years at the Court of Henry VIII,* 2 vols. (London, 1854), I, 79–81, 90–93.

2. *Ibid.,* 90–91.

3. *Ibid.,* 86–87.

4. *Ibid.,* 85–86.

5. *Ibid.,* 80.

6. *The Antiquarian Repertory: A Miscellany, intended to Preserve and Illustrate Several Valuable Remains of Old Times,* 4 vols. (London, 1775–84), II, 181.

7. *L.P.* I:ii, 532.

8. The following is based on *L.P.* IV:i:ii, 861ff.

Chapter 14

1. *Ven. Cal.* II, 524–25, 529.

2. Edward Guildford may also have been included in the upheaval of 1519, and it was believed at the French court that there were others. *L.P.* III:i, 82.

3. *L.P.* II:i, 871.

4. *Ven. Cal.* II, 561.

5. *L.P.* II:ii, 1045.

6. *Ven. Cal.* II, xxxi.

7. Brewer, I, 200–201.

8. Hugh Rhodes, *The boke of Nurture for men, servantes and children* (London, 1545), 164, 215.

9. Paul V. B. Jones, *The Household of a Tudor nobleman,* University of Illinois Studies, Vol. VI (Urbana, Illinois, 1917), 74; Rhodes, 173.

10. Rhodes, 166–69.

11. *Ibid.,* 125ff, 204.

12. Brewer, I, 109; *L.P.* II:i, 295.

13. Brown, ed., *Four Years,* II, 192–93.

14. *L.P.* II:ii, 1479 and *passim.*

15. *Ibid.,* III:i, 499.

16. Hall, I, 28.

17. Cited in John Dover Wilson, *Life in Shakespeare's England* (Cambridge, England: Cambridge University Press, 1911), 150, 155–57.

18. *L.P.* I:ii, 1484.

19. Hunt, p. 66.

20. *L.P.* II:ii, 1246, 1249, 1252.

21. *Ven. Cal.* III, 515.

22. Stevens, *Music and Poetry,* 298–99.

23. *L.P.* II:i, 411, 423.

24. Stevens, *Music and Poetry,* 276.

25. *L.P.* II:ii, 1473.

26. Hall, I, 170–71.

27. Brewer, I, 229–30.

28. *L.P.* II:ii, 1517.

29. *Ibid.,* 1509; Hall, I, 585.

30. *Ven. Cal.* II, 211.

31. Quoted in Hale, *Renaissance Europe,* 113.

32. Sneyd, trans., *Relation,* 125–28.

33. *Ven. Cal.* II, 210, 178.

34. *L.P.* II:ii, 1473, 1504.

Chapter 15

1. Brown, ed., *Four Years,* I, 101; *Ven. Cal.* II, 450.

2. Nicolas, ed., *Privy Purse Expenses of Henry VIII,* 334.

3. P. S. Allen, H. M. Allen and H. W. Garrod, eds., *Opus Epistolarum Desiderii Erasmi Roterodami,* 12 vols. (Oxford, 1906-1958), VIII, 129–30.

4. *Ibid.,* III, 547.

5. *L.P.* II:i, 716.

6. Froude, ed., *Life and Letters,* 224.

7. *Ibid.,* 111, 114.

8. Allen *et al.,* eds., *Erasmi Epistolae,* III, 583.

9. Percival Hunt, *Fifteenth Century England* (Pittsburgh, 1962), 93ff; *L.P.* III:i, cxci.

10. Froude, ed., *Life and Letters,* 43–44, 105–7.

11. Allen *et al.,* eds., *Erasmi Epistolae,* IV, 525–26.

12. Froude, ed., *Life and Letters,* 111–14.

Chapter 16

1. *L.P.* I:ii, 1050, 1053, 1205.

2. *Ibid.,* 1270–72, 1279.

3. *Ven. Cal.* II, 196; *L.P.* I:ii, 1415.

4. *L.P.* II:i, 74.

5. *Ibid.*, 26.

6. *Ibid.*, 73–75.

7. *L.P.* II:ii, 1465, 1467.

8. *Ibid.*, II:i, 111.

9. *Ibid.*, 117.

10. *Sp. Cal.* II, cxiii.

11. *Ven. Cal.* II, 399.

12. *Ibid.*, 400.

13. *L.P.* III:i, 64.

14. *Ibid.*, 413.

15. Nicolas, ed., *Privy Purse Expenses of Henry VIII*, Index, 298–99.

16. The following is taken from *Ven. Cal.* II, 162.

PART THREE
"THE MAN MOST FULL OF HEART"

Chapter 17

1. *L.P.* II:ii, 1118–19.

2. *Ibid.*, 1468, 1472, 1522; R. C. Clepham, *The Tournament* (London, 1919), 107.

3. Brown, ed., *Four Years*, I, 116.

4. A. F. Pollard, *Wolsey: Church and State in Sixteenth-Century England*, new ed. (London, 1953), 313–14.

5. George Cavendish, *The Life and Death of Cardinal Wolsey*, ed. Richard S. Sylvester and Davis P. Harding (New Haven and London, 1962), 62.

6. *L.P.* II:i, 835; Neville Williams, *The Royal Residences of Great Britain* (New York, 1960), 120; Cavendish, 20.

7. Pollard, *Henry VIII*, 87.

8. *L.P.* II:ii, 1130.

9. *Ibid.*, 1364; *Ven. Cal.* II, 521.

10. *L.P.* II:ii, 1154.

11. *Ibid.*, 957.

12. *L.P.* I:ii, 952–53, 974–75; Charles W. C. Oman, "The Personality of Henry VIII," *Quarterly Review*, CCLXIX (July 1937), 91.

13. *L.P.* II:i, 291–92.

14. *Ibid.*, III:ii, 595, 909.

15. *Ibid.*, 717.

16. *L.P.* II:ii, 1249.

17. *Ibid.*, 294.

18. *Ven. Cal.* II, 30.

19. *L.P.* III:i, 227.

20. Brown, ed., *Four Years*, I, 30.

21. *Ibid.*, 47. Just before Louis XII's death plans were discussed for a meeting of the two sovereigns "at a place about Ardes." *L.P.* I:ii, 1432.

22. *L.P.* II:i, 332, 446.

23. Brown, ed., *Four Years,* I, 84, 88 note 4.

24. "Combat de François Premier contre un sanglier," cited in W. L. Wiley, *The Gentleman of Renaissance France* (Cambridge, Mass., 1954), 58–59.

25. Brown, ed., *Four Years,* II, 170.

26. *L.P.* II:i, 342.

27. *Ibid.,* 573.

28. *Ibid.,* III:i, 285.

29. *Ibid.,* 611.

30. *Ibid.,* 291.

31. *Ven. Cal.* III, 15.

Chapter 18

1. *Ven. Cal.* III, 23; *L.P.* III:i, 312.

2. *Ven. Cal.* III, 50.

3. Brown, ed., *Four Years,* I, 49.

4. *Ven. Cal.* III, 69.

5. *Ibid.,* 67.

6. *Ibid.,* 25 and *passim.*

7. *Ibid.,* 64.

8. *L.P.* III:i, 286.

9. *Ven. Cal.* III, 77.

10. *Ibid.,* 71, 72, 77.

11. *Ibid.,* 82–83.

12. *L.P.* III:i, 126–29.

Chapter 19

1. J. J. Scarisbrick, *Henry VIII* (Berkeley and Los Angeles, 1968), facing p. 66, citing BM Add. 1938 f.44; Scarisbrick assigns this letter to c.1520.

2. Brown, ed., *Four Years,* II, 69ff., 74–75n. *L.P.* II:ii, 1045.

3. Hall, I, 165.

4. *Ven. Cal.* II, 412.

5. *L.P.* II:ii, 1142–43.

6. *Ibid.,* 1179

7. Brown, ed., *Four Years,* II, 130–31

8. *Ven. Cal.* II, 428.

9. *Ibid.,* 430, 436.

10. *L.P.* II:ii, 1257–58.

11. *Ibid.,* III:i, 490ff.

12. *Ven. Cal.* III, 119.

13. *Ibid.,* 124–25.

14. *L.P.* III:i, 514.

15. *Ibid.,* 492.

16. *Ven. Cal.* III, 122.

17. *Ibid.,* 4.

18. *L.P.* III:i, 494.

19. Hall, I, 149.
20. *L.P.* III:i, 421.
21. *Ibid.,* II:i, 325.
22. *Ibid.,* III:i, 421.
23. *Ibid.,* II:i, 49, 871; III:i, 494.

Chapter 20

1. *L.P.* II:i, 454.

2. *State Papers,* I, 1–2.

3. In July, 1524, Margaret Tudor was led to believe that her son James would marry the princess and become king of England as well as Scotland. *L.P.* IV:i:ii, 240, 241.

4. Elizabeth Francis Rogers, ed., *The Correspondence of Sir Thomas More* (Princeton, New Jersey, 1947), 159n.

5. Hale, *Renaissance Europe,* 17. The humanist John Colet was the only surviving child of a mother who gave birth twenty-two times. Froude, ed., *Life and Letters,* 105.

6. The suggestion that Katherine may have been rhesus-negative was disputed by Ove Brinch, "The Medical Problems of Henry VIII," *Centaurus,* V, Nos. 3–4 (1958), 351, who pointed out that with this characteristic her pregnancies would have followed a pattern of one or two natural births, followed by unvarying stillbirths.

7. *Ven. Cal.* II, 559; III, 61; *L.P.* III:i, 306.

8. *L.P.* III:i, 494.

9. J. C. Flügel, "The Character and Married Life of Henry VIII," in Bruce Mazlish, ed., *Psychoanalysis and History* (New York, 1963), 131, has pointed out that "the idea of sterility as a punishment for incest is one that is deeply rooted in the human mind." If so, a strong atavistic belief may have reinforced Henry's fear of divine punishment. Though they lie outside historical documentation, Flügel's elaborate and intriguing speculations on Henry's sexual nature offer food for thought.

10. *L.P.* III:i, 424.

11. Froude, *Life and Letters,* 49.

12. Neville Williams, *Henry VIII and His Court* (London, 1971), 66. If Jane was the same "Joan Popingcourt" who was one of Elizabeth of York's servants, she may have been somewhat older than Henry. Nicolas, *Privy Purse Expenses of Elizabeth of York,* 217. It may be that a 1513 reference to Henry "who for love of a lady, clad himself and his court in mourning" in France reveals the existence of yet another love. *Ven. Cal.* II, 152.

13. *L.P.* II:ii, 1471, 1502.

14. *Ibid.,* IV:i:i, cxlv–cxlvi.

15. *Ibid.,* III:ii, 1539. Brewer dates the marriage 1520; Paul Friedmann, *Anne Boleyn: A Chapter of English History 1527–1536,* 2 vols. (London, 1884), I, 324, dates it 1521.

16. *L.P.* III:ii, 1396.

17. *Ibid.,* IV:i:i, ccxxi note. Henry told one Symon Grynaeus in 1531 that he had not slept with Katherine for seven years.

18. Brinch, 342; *L.P.* IV:i:i, cxli.

19. Henry's confessor Longland claimed the divorce issue was first raised with him in 1522 or 1523. Rumors that Henry contemplated a divorce as early as 1514 (Betty Behrens, ''A Note on Henry VIII's divorce project of 1514,'' *BIHR*, XI, No. 33 [February 1934], 163–64) were without foundation. Garrett Mattingly, *Catherine of Aragon* (Boston, 1941), 452; Scarisbrick, 151.

20. *L.P.* III:ii, 1552.

21. *Ibid.*, IV:i:ii, 433–34.

22. Rogers, ed., *Correspondence of Thomas More*, 311–14.

23. *L.P.* IV:i:i, ccxx and note.

24. *Ibid.*, XII:ii, 48, 341–42.

25. *Ibid.*, IV:i:ii, 327.

26. *Ibid.*, 724.

27. *Ibid.*, 490.

28. *Ibid.*, 506.

29. *Ibid.*, 694.

30. *Ibid.*, 638–39; *Van. Cal.* III, 454.

31. *L.P.* IV:i:ii, 673, 676–77, 687.

32. *Ven. Cal.* III, 448.

33. *L.P.* IV:i:i, cxliii.

Chapter 21

1. *L.P.* I:ii, 167, 1238.

2. *Ibid.*, II:i, 259, 376–77.

3. Brown, ed., *Four Years*, I, 194.

4. *Ibid.*, II, 63–67.

5. Law, *England's First Great War Minister*, 231.

6. *Ven. Cal.* II, 438.

7. *L.P.* III:ii, 624.

8. *Ibid.*, III, 1, cclxxxv note.

9. Rogers, ed., *Correspondence of Thomas More*, 289–95.

10. *L.P.* III:ii, 1164–65.

11. Rogers, ed., *Correspondence of Thomas More*, 300–301.

12. *L.P.* IV:i:i, ii–iii.

13. *Ibid.*, III:ii, 1295.

14. *Ibid.*, III:i, 437.

15. *Ibid.*, III:ii, 1271.

16. *L.P.* IV:i:ii, 9.

17. *Sp. Cal.* II, 610–11.

18. *L.P.* IV:i:ii, 283.

19. *Sp. Cal.* III:i, 62.

20. *Ibid.*, 82.

Chapter 22

1. *Sp. Cal.* III:i, 8.

2. *Ibid.*, 108.
3. *Ven. Cal.* III, 178–80.
4. *Sp. Cal.* III:i, 100–102.
5. *Ibid.*, 134.
6. *Ibid.*, 284.
7. *L.P.* IV:i:ii, 574.
8. *Ibid.*, IV:i:i, lxxi.
9. *Ibid.*, IV:i:ii, 579.
10. *Ibid.*, 580.
11. *Sp. Cal.* III:i, 174.
12. *L.P.* IV:i:ii, 579.
13. Hall, II, 38.

PART FOUR
"DIEU ET MON DROIT"

Chapter 23

1. Cavendish, 27–30; *Ven. Cal.* IV, 3–4. Cavendish's dramatic account of this memorable banquet was, as Brewer, II, 107n. pointed out, "interspersed with other reminiscences."
2. *L.P.* IV:i:i, cxli.
3. *State Papers,* I, 26.
4. *L.P.* IV:ii, 1411.
5. Nicolas, ed., *Privy Purse Expenses of Henry VIII,* xxii.
6. *Mil. Cal.* I, 451.
7. *Ibid.*, 451, 459.

Chapter 24

1. Refuting Friedmann's contention (Friedmann, I, xxxvii) that Anne was born in 1502 or 1503, Brewer (Brewer, II, 170) argued that the true date of her birth was probably 1507, and most writers adopt his conjecture. The seventeenth-century writer Camden gave 1507 as Anne's birth year, and the contemporary biographer of Mary Tudor's gentlewoman Jane Dormer concurred. It was not Anne but her older sister Mary Boleyn who accompanied Henry VIII's sister Mary to her wedding in France in 1514. Anne followed her sister to the French court in 1519, returning either in late 1521 or early 1522.
2. *L.P.* X, 181.
3. Though found in the works of Catholic propagandists, the evidence for Wyatt's confession cannot be dismissed entirely. Kenneth Muir, *Life and Letters of Sir Thomas Wyatt* (Liverpool, 1963), 20ff.; *Collected Poems,* ed. Kenneth Muir (London, 1949), x. "It is impossible to be sure of what really happened," Muir concludes, "not because of any lack of evidence, but because what facts there are appear to be inextricably mingled with gossip and legend." Scarisbrick, 148–49, places the possible affair in 1522.

4. *L.P.* IV:ii, 1411.

5. *Ibid.*, 1228.

6. *Ibid.*, IV:i:ii, 846.

7. *Ibid.*, IV:ii, 1375, 1402.

8. Cavendish, 71–74.

9. Hall, II, 80–81.

10. *Sp. Cal.* III:ii, 178.

11. *Ibid.*, 192–93.

12. Hall, II, 79.

13. *Sp. Cal.* III:ii, 26.

14. *Ibid.*, 107.

15. *Ibid.*, 194; III:i, 108, 1018–19; *L.P.* IV:i:i, cxliv.

16. *L.P.* II:ii, 1210.

17. *Ibid.*, IV:i:ii, 453.

18. *Sp. Cal.* III:ii, 109–10.

Chapter 25

1. *Sp. Cal.* III:ii, 276.

2. *L.P.* V, 476, 500; XI, 272; VII, 8. More called Longland "another Colet" for his goodness and preaching. Philip Hughes, *The Reformation in England,* 3 vols. (New York, 1951–1954), I, 228.

3. I cannot agree with Scarisbrick's contention that an inquiry about Henry's marriage from the French envoy Gabriel de Grammont, bishop of Tarbes, would have been inconceivably tactless. In addition, in questioning the merits of the story he mistakenly asserts that the bishop did not come to England until April, a "few weeks" before the secret court met at Westminster. In actuality the bishop seems to have come twice, one earlier in the year. Brewer, II, 163; Geoffrey de C. Parmiter, *The King's Great Matter: A study of Anglo-Papal Relations 1527–1534* (London, 1967), 2.

4. Reginald Pole, *Pro Ecclesiasticae Unitatis Defensione,* Book 3, fol. lxxvi, cited in Parmiter, 3–4.

5. *L.P.* IV:ii, 1433.

6. *Ibid.*, IV:i:ii, 332.

7. *Ibid.*, IV:ii, 1434, 1470–71.

8. *State Papers,* I, 212.

Chapter 26

1. The order and dates of Henry's surviving love letters to Anne are conjectural. Muriel St. Clare Byrne, ed., *The Letters of King Henry VIII* (London, 1936), is followed here.

2. *L.P.* IV:ii, 1496, 1504, 1525; IV:iii, 2541.

3. *State Papers,* I, 222; Cavendish, 66–67.

4. Cavendish, 63.

5. *Sp. Cal.* III:ii, 303, 345–46.

6. Cavendish, 50–51.

7. Hall, II, 96, 107.

8. *State Papers*, I, 230; *L.P.* IV:ii, 1466–67.

9. *L.P.* II:ii, 933.

10. Francesco Vettori, cited in T. C. Price Zimmermann, "A note on Clement VII and the divorce of Henry VIII," *EHR*, LXXXII, No. 324 (July 1967), 548–49.

11. The final verdict was postponed, Giovio wrote, "in order to nourish the controversy for awhile as a means for maintaining in obedience the disposition of the kings." Cited in P. S. Crowson, *Tudor Foreign Policy* (New York, 1973), 94.

12. Byrne, 57–59.

13. *Ibid.*, 61.

14. *L.P.* IV:ii, 1740.

15. *Ibid.*, 1764–65.

16. *Sp. Cal.* III:ii, 432–33.

17. *L.P.* IV:ii, 1808–9.

18. *Ibid.*, 1741; Parmiter, 41.

Chapter 27

1. *L.P.* IV:ii, 1970.

2. *Ibid.*, II:i, cclxxx–cclxxxiv.

3. *Ibid.*, IV:ii, 1678–79.

4. Hall, II, 110–11; *Ven. Cal.* III, 121.

5. *L.P.* IV:ii, 1893–94.

6. *Ibid.*, 1900.

7. *State Papers*, I, 304.

8. *L.P.* IV:ii, 1942–43.

9. *Ibid.*, IV:i:i, ccxxii; Byrne, 71.

10. *L.P.* IV:ii, 1892, 2087, 2116.

11. *Ibid.*, 2043–44.

12. *Ibid.*, 1932; Nicolas, *Privy Purse Expenses of Henry VIII*, 79.

13. *L.P.* IV:ii, 1931.

14. *Ibid.*, IV:iii, 2606.

15. *Ibid.*, IV:ii, 1931.

16. Byrne, *passim*, especially 75–79.

17. *Ibid.*, 82–83; *L.P.* IV:ii, 2020–22.

18. Parmiter, 62n.–63n.

19. Byrne, 84.

Chapter 28

1. *L.P.* IV:ii, 1909.

2. *Ibid.*, 1953.

3. Byrne, 82.

4. *L.P.* IV:ii, 1913–14.

5. *Sp. Cal.* III:ii, 789.

6. *Ibid.*, 819.

7. Parmiter, 51.

8. *L.P.* IV:ii, 2158; *Ibid.*, IV:iii, 2356.

9. *Ibid.*, IV:ii, 2101, 2203.

10. *Sp. Cal.* III:ii, 861.

11. *Ibid.*, 846.

12. *Ibid.*, 208; *L.P.* IV:iii, 2702.

13. *Ven. Cal.* IV, 185, 293.

14. Hall, II, 145–47.

15. *Sp. Cal.* III:ii, 803.

16. *L.P.* IV:ii, 2158. Although there is good reason to believe that Henry left Katherine's bed permanently in the mid-1520s, his official representatives made conflicting statements about the couple's relationship during the later years of the decade. Thomas Boleyn testified before the legatine court that the king and queen had continued to cohabit until 1527, when Longland advised Henry to break with his wife so as not to offend his conscience (*L.P.* IV:iii, 2580ff.). At Saragossa in April, 1529, English diplomats assured the imperialists that since his doubts first arose Henry had "not touched her," yet the following month the king's delegates in Rome swore that he "eats and dines and sleeps with his wife, and gives her the due [has intercourse with her], so that she does not know he no longer holds marital affection for her." (*L.P.* IV:iii, 2412, 2446. See also *Sp. Cal.* III:ii, 861.) Like the issue of Henry's cohabitation with Anne, the story of his waning relations with Katherine is beclouded by contradictory evidence.

17. *Sp. Cal.* III:ii, 861.

18. *Ibid.*, 845.

19. *L.P.* IV:ii, 2163.

20. *Ibid.*, IV:iii, 2281; *Sp. Cal.* III:ii, 889.

21. *L.P.* IV:iii, 2320, 4322.

22. *Ibid.*, 2354, 2410.

23. *Correspondance du Cardinal Jean du Bellay*, ed. R. Scheurer (Paris, 1969), I, 48.

24. *L.P.* IV:iii, 2576ff.

25. Hall, II, 153.

Chapter 29

1. *L.P.* IV:iii, 2743; Edward Lowinsky, "A music book for Anne Boleyn," in *Florilegium Historiale: Essays Presented to Wallace K. Ferguson,* ed. J. G. Rowe and W. H. Stockdale (Toronto, 1971), 170; *Ven. Cal.* IV, 287; *L.P.* IV:iii, 2509. Many contemporary comments suggest that it was common knowledge that Henry and Anne were cohabiting. A proposal was made in the Roman consistory to warn Henry "not to cause scandal by his intimate intercourse with his lady friend" (*L.P.* IV:iii, 3059). Anne herself reportedly bewailed her "lost honor" during the years of waiting for a favorable papal judgment (*L.P.* IV:iii, 3035). Charles V received information from Rome in December of 1531 that Anne had miscarried (*L.P.* V, 281). In the previous month Katherine referred to her husband's having "married another woman without obtaining a divorce" (*Sp. Cal.* IV:ii:i, 291). On the other hand, in January of 1531 the imperial diplomat Mai wrote to the emperor saying there was "no positive proof of adultery, none having yet been produced

here at Rome, but on the contrary several letters proving the contrary" (*Sp. Cal.* IV:ii:i, 8). But Mai was far from actual events in England.

2. *L.P.* V, 10–11.

3. *Ibid.,* IV:iii, 3035; V, 27–28.

4. *Ibid.,* V, 28.

5. Nicolas, *Privy Purse Expenses of Henry VIII,* 4, 88, 133, 90, 183, 13, 101, 97.

6. *Ibid.,* 77.

7. Friedmann, I, 37–38.

8. *Ven. Cal.* IV, 304.

9. Nicolas, 188, 6, 25, 68; *L.P.* IV:i:ii, 846; IV:iii, 2358.

10. Nicolas, 10.

11. *Ibid.,* 17, 36–37, 115.

12. *Ibid.,* 64, 43, 125, 96, 80, 106, 117, 184, 188 and *passim.*

13. *L.P.* I, 54; II:i, 176, 875, 326; Nicolas, *Privy Purse Expenses of Henry VIII,* 150, 40, 93; *L.P.* II:ii, 1467, 1461.

14. *L.P.* IV:iii, 2812.

15. Scarisbrick, 176 and note.

16. *L.P.* IV:iii, 2895, 2922, 2946, 2987, 3192; *Sp. Cal.* IV:i, 696.

17. *Sp. Cal.* IV:i, 352.

18. *Ibid.,* 359.

19. Stevens, *Music and Poetry, passim.*

20. *L.P.* IV:iii, 2683.

21. *Ibid.,* 2781.

22. *Ibid.,* 2849.

23. *Ibid.,* 2729.

24. *Ibid.,* 3035, 3054.

25. *Sp. Cal.* IV:i, 351.

26. *L.P.* IV:iii, 3035.

27. *Ibid.,* IV:ii, 2253.

28. Chamberlin, 269–71 and *passim;* Arthur S. MacNalty, *Henry VIII: A difficult patient* (London, 1952), *passim.* Attempts to prove that Henry's infected thigh was a secondary symptom of syphilis are unconvincing. An alternative diagnosis is osteomyelitis—a chronic septic infection. Scarisbrick, 485n.

29. Stevens, *Music and Poetry,* 61.

30. *L.P.* IV:iii, 2834.

31. *Ibid.,* V, 21.

32. *Ibid.,* IV:iii, 2757.

Chapter 30

1. *L.P.* VI, 243; *Sp. Cal.* IV:ii:i, 609.

2. *Ibid.,* 167.

3. *Ibid.,* 230–31.

4. *Ibid.,* 167.

5. *Ibid.,* 224, 244.

6. *Sp. Cal.* IV:ii:i, 214. Anne's slander may have been rooted in Brandon's courtship and subsequent marriage (after the death of his third wife Mary Tudor) to the young heiress, Catherine Willoughby, who had been betrothed to his son.

7. *L.P.* VI, 167.
8. *Ibid.,* 266.
9. *Ibid.,* V, 425; VI, 328, 674.
10. *Sp. Cal.* IV:i, 475; IV:ii:i, 412.
11. *Ven. Cal.* IV, 335.
12. *Sp. Cal.* IV:i, 368–69.
13. Thomas, 401–2.
14. *Sp. Cal.* IV:i, 852.
15. *Ven. Cal.* IV, 357–58, 377.
16. *L.P.* VI, 397.
17. *Ibid.,* 420, 444.
18. *Ibid.,* 450.
19. *Ibid.,* V, 244.

PART FIVE
THE MOULDWARP

Chapter 31

1. *L.P.* VIII, 230–31.
2. Elton, *Reform and Reformation,* 132, 135–36.
3. However, Chapuys wrote that Cromwell was "remarkably fond of pomp and ostentation in his household and in building." *Sp. Cal.* V:i, 569.
4. *L.P.* XII:ii, 12.
5. *Ibid.,* VII, 485.
6. Elton, *Reform and Reformation,* provides the best current guide to the controversies concerning the 1530s. Many interpretive issues remain unsettled. As Elton has written, the years between 1529 and 1534 continue to be "a very difficult sector" of Tudor history, in which "while most of the facts are reasonably agreed, interpretations differ widely."
7. *L.P.* VII, 540; VIII, 403; X, 370.
8. *Ibid.,* XII:ii, 313; VI, 241.
9. *Ibid.,* VIII, 214–15.
10. *Ibid.,* XII:ii, 243; p. 491 gives another version of the story.
11. *Ibid.,* IV:iii, 2851–52.
12. *Ibid.,* VIII, 357.
13. *Ibid.,* VII, 95, 541.
14. *Ibid.,* X, 307.
15. *Ibid.,* VIII, 320–21; Friedmann, I, 10.
16. *L.P.* X, 295.

Chapter 32

1. *L.P.* VII, 583.
2. *Ibid.,* VIII, 388–89.
3. *Ibid.,* 345.
4. *Ibid.,* 429.

5. Thomas Stapleton, *The Life and Illustrious Martyrdom of Sir Thomas More,* trans. P. E. Hallett (London, 1928), 192.

6. *L.P.* VII, 592; VIII, 391.

7. *Ibid.,* VIII, 430.

8. Louis L. Martz and Richard S. Sylvester, eds., *Thomas More's Prayer Book: A Facsimile Reproduction of the Annotated Pages* (New Haven and London, 1969), 47–48.

9. William W. Macdonald, "Anticlericalism, Protestantism, and the English Reformation," *Journal of Church and State,* XV, No. 1 (Winter 1973), 31–32; Elton, *Reform and Reformation,* 121; Parmiter, 116; Parker, 19.

10. *Sp. Cal.* IV:i, 367.

11. Elton, *Policy and Police* (Cambridge, England, 1972), 88.

12. *L.P.* VIII, 290.

13. *Ibid.,* 12.

14. *Ibid.,* 98; IX, 21–22.

15. *Ibid.,* VII, 506.

16. *Ibid.,* VI, 493.

17. *Ibid.,* VII, 22, 44, 615. The surviving evidence makes it difficult to be sure about Anne's medical history in 1534, but see Chamberlin, 160–63.

18. *L.P.* VII, 465.

19. *Ibid.,* 485.

20. Lowinsky, 182, 188–90, 231, 232.

21. *L.P.* VIII, 15, 61; VII, 282; VIII, 169.

22. *Sp. Cal.* V:ii, 39.

23. E. W. Ives, "Faction at the Court of Henry VIII," *History,* LVII, No. 190 (June 1972), *passim.*

Chapter 33

1. J. Hall, ed., *The Poems of Laurence Minot,* 3rd ed. (Oxford, 1914), 110–11; Thomas, 399–400. The Mouldwarp prophecy was originally applied to Henry IV.

2. *L.P.* XII:i, 340.

3. John Brand, *Observations of Popular Antiquities,* arr. and rev. Henry Ellis, 3 vols. (London, 1813), II, 582.

4. *L.P.* XIII:i, 177–79, 267.

5. John G. Nichols, ed., *Narratives of the Days of the Reformation,* Camden Society, Old series, LXXVII (London, 1859), 173–75, 319–31.

6. Cited in George Lyman Kittredge, *Witchcraft in Old and New England* (Cambridge, Mass., 1929), 109–10.

7. *L.P.* IV:ii, 2222; Elton, *Policy and Police,* 50.

8. Lynn Thorndike, *A History of Magic and Experimental Science,* 8 vols. (New York, 1923–1958), V, 320–21.

9. *Sp. Cal.* V:ii, 568.

10. *L.P.* XI, 21.

11. *Ibid.,* VIII, 316; Friedmann, I, 10–11.

12. *L.P.* VIII, 55, 64–65.

13. *Ibid.,* 257.

14. *Ibid.,* VII, 222, 448.

15. *Ibid.*, VIII, 13, 139; X, 513.

16. *Ibid.*, VIII, 102; VI, 560.

17. *Sp. Cal.* V:i, 596.

18. *L.P.* XI, 334.

Chapter 34

1. *L.P.* X, 377; *Sp. Cal.* V:ii, 574.

2. *L.P.* X, 378, 380, 385.

3. *Sp. Cal.* V:ii, 122. The queen's crown is described in a 1532 inventory of jewels in *L.P.* V, 737.

4. *L.P.* X, 380; *Sp. Cal.* V:ii, 121; *L.P.* X, 104.

5. *L.P.* XI, 64.

6. *Ibid.*, 97, 102.

7. Elton, *Reform and Reformation*, 262–70. Scarisbrick, 339–48, adheres to the traditional view of the revolt as fundamentally, though not exclusively, religious.

8. *L.P.* XI, 404.

9. *Ibid.*, IX, 149; Hughes, *Reformation in England*, I, 53ff.; *L.P.* XIII:i, xii.

10. *L.P.* VII, 518–19; Hughes, *Reformation in England*, I, 53ff., 57.

11. Cited in Froude, 154.

12. *L.P.* IX, 11, 376.

13. *Ibid.*, VIII, 46.

14. *Ibid.*, IX, xxviii.

15. Hughes, *Reformation in England*, I, 285.

16. *L.P.* XI, xiv, 274; XII:i, 256.

17. Margaret Aston, "English Ruins and English History: The Dissolution and the Sense of the Past," *Journal of the Warburg and Courtauld Institutes*, No. 36 (1973), 240, 245.

18. *L.P.* VII, 467–68; Paul L. Hughes and James F. Larkin, eds., *Tudor Royal Proclamations* (New Haven and London, 1964), I, 244.

19. *L.P.* XII:i, 64.

20. *Ibid.*, XI, xxi.

21. *Ibid.*, 269.

22. *Ibid.*, 229–30, 266.

23. *Ibid.*, 404.

24. *Ibid.*, xxii.

25. *Ibid.*, XII:i, 579, 582–83.

26. *Ibid.*, XII:ii, 123, 296.

Chapter 35

1. *L.P.* XII:ii, 311; John Leland, *Antiquarii de Rebus Brittanicis Collectanea*, 6 vols. (London, 1770), II, 670–77; IV, 302.

2. *L.P.* XII:ii, 139.

3. *Ibid.*, 364, 372–74, 388.

4. *Ibid.*, XII:i, 24–25.

5. Creighton Gilbert, "When Did Renaissance Man Grow Old?" *Studies in the Renaissance,* XIV (1967), 12; Hale, *Renaissance Europe,* 17; Thomas, 5, 6n.

6. *Ven. Cal.* III, 276–78, 526.

7. Leslie G. Mathews, "Royal Apothecaries of the Tudor Period," *Medical History,* VIII, No. 2 (April 1964), 171–73; Nicolas, *Privy Purse Expenses of Henry VIII,* 79, 124, 165.

8. *L.P.* III:ii, 1562.

9. *Sp. Cal.* VI:i, 430, 446.

10. *L.P.* XIII:i, 368.

11. *Ibid.*, XII:ii, 454; Elton, *Policy and Police,* 73–74.

12. *L.P.* XIII:i, 265.

13. *Ibid.*, XII:ii, 114.

14. *Ven. Cal.* II, 397.

15. *L.P.* VII, 555.

16. *Ibid.*, 372.

17. *Ibid.*, XII:ii, 479; Oman, "Personality," 90.

18. Nicolas, *Privy Purse Expenses of Henry VIII,* 351; *L.P.* XII:ii, 483.

19. Williams, *Royal Residences,* 152–53; John Dent, *The Quest for Nonsuch* (London, 1962), 56; Elizabeth Burton, *The Pageant of Early Tudor England* (New York, 1976), 258.

20. *L.P.* XIII:i, 9.

21. *Ibid.*, IV:ii, 2145.

22. Elton, *Reform and Reformation,* 279–81. Margaret Pole had been under suspicion since the time of the trial of the duke of Buckingham, though Henry in 1535 called her "a fool, of no experience," and could hardly have looked on her as a dangerous conspirator. Brewer, I, 384; *L.P.* VIII, 101.

23. *L.P.* XIII:ii, 318.

Chapter 36

1. *Sp. Cal.* VI:i, 24.

2. *L.P.* XIII:ii, 9; *Sp. Cal.* VI:i, 28.

3. *L.P.* VIII, xiiff.

4. *Ibid.*, XIII:ii, xxii; A. G. Dickens, *The English Reformation,* 7; Scarisbrick, 403ff.

5. E. Jeffries Davis, "The Transformation of London," in *Tudor Studies presented by the Board of Students in History in the University of London to Albert Frederick Pollard,* ed. R. W. Seton-Watson (London, 1924), 305ff.

6. *L.P.* XIV:i, 475; XII:ii, 130.

7. *Ibid.*, XIII:ii, 355–56, xxviii.

8. *Ibid.*, XIV:i, 438–39.

9. Richard Bruce Wernham, *Before the Armada: the Growth of English Foreign Policy, 1485–1588* (London, 1966), 143–44; Crowson, 115; *L.P.* XIII:ii, 116; XI, 135; XIV:i, 401.

10. *L.P.* XIV:i, 362.

11. *Ibid.*, 241, 339.
12. *Ibid.*, 165.
13. *Ibid.*, xxxiv–xxxvi.

Chapter 37

1. *L.P.* XIII:i, 9; XII:ii, 414–15.
2. Margaret Bowker, "The Supremacy and the Episcopate: The Struggle for Control, 1539–1540," *Historical Journal,* XVIII, No. 2 (June 1975), 241.
3. *L.P.* XI, 10.
4. *Ibid.*, XII:ii, 348; XIII:i, 285.
5. *Sp. Cal.* V:ii, 531.
6. *L.P.* XII:ii, 419; XIII:i, 109.
7. *Sp. Cal.* V:ii, 520.
8. *L.P.* XIII:i, 251; XIV:ii, 141.
9. *Ibid.*, XIII:i, 367, 451.
10. *Sp. Cal.* VI:i, 6.
11. *Ibid.; L.P.* XIII:ii, 28–29.
12. *L.P.* XIV:ii, 77.
13. *Sp. Cal.* V:ii, 574; *L.P.* XIII:i, 415, 558.
14. *L.P.* XIII:i, 425, 367.
15. *Ibid.*, XIV:ii, 9.
16. *Sp. Cal.* V:ii, 509; *L.P.* XIII:ii, 120.
17. *L.P.* XV, xix; Elton, *Policy and Police,* 57.
18. *L.P.* XIV:i, 213.
19. *Ibid.*, 430.
20. *Ibid.*, XIV:ii, 135.
21. *Ibid.*, 203, 231.
22. This account of Anne of Cleves' coming to England is taken from *L.P.* XV, 4–5; XIV:ii, 246–47.
23. *Ibid.*, XV, 4.
24. *Ibid.*, XIV:ii, 283.
25. *Ibid.*, XV, 389, 422 and Historical Manuscripts Commission, *Report on Manuscripts in the Welsh Language,* Vol. I (London, 1898), viii.

Chapter 38

1. *L.P.* XV, 422.
2. *Ibid.*, 389, 422.
3. *Sp. Cal.* VI:i, xi–xii.
4. *L.P.* XV, 423.
5. *Ibid.*
6. *Ibid.*, 391, 423; Hall, II, 302.
7. *L.P.* XV, 391, 423.
8. *Ibid.*, 87.
9. *Ibid.*, 27, 307.
10. *Ibid.*, 447.

11. Elton, *Reform and Reformation,* 191–92.

12. Hughes, *Reformation in England,* I, 224.

13. *L.P.* XIII:i, 368, 171.

14. *Ibid.,* XV, 243.

15. Elton, *Reform and Reformation,* 293–94; Stanford E. Lehmberg, "Parliamentary Attainder in the reign of Henry VIII," *Historical Journal,* XVIII, No. 4 (December 1975), 694–95.

16. *L.P.* XV, 395.

17. *Ibid.,* 417, 457.

18. *Ibid.,* 446.

PART SIX
OLD HARRY

Chapter 39

1. *L.P.* XVI, 466.

2. *Ibid.,* 507.

3. *Ibid.,* 272.

4. Hall, II, 311.

5. *L.P.* XV, xvi–xvii.

6. *Ibid.,* XIV:i, 53.

7. *Ibid.,* 31.

8. *Ibid.,* XV, 493.

9. *Ibid.,* XIV:i, 379; XVI, 411.

10. *Ibid.,* XV, 312.

11. *Ibid.,* XVI, 636.

12. *Ibid.,* XV, 321.

13. *Sp. Cal.* VI:i, 305, 328.

14. *L.P.* XVI, 482.

15. *Ibid.,* 533.

16. *Ibid.,* 532–34.

17. *Ibid.,* 558.

18. *Ibid.,* 598.

Chapter 40

1. *L.P.* XVI, 608–9, 615–16.

2. *Ibid.,* 611, 613, 630.

3. *Ibid.,* 610.

4. *Sp. Cal.* VI:i, 396.

5. *L.P.* XVI, 620, 631, 666.

6. *Ibid.,* XVII, 44, 50.

7. *Sp. Cal.* VI:i, 408; J. D. Mackie, *The Earlier Tudors 1485–1558* (Oxford, 1952), 419; *LP.* XVII, 44, 50.

8. *Sp. Cal.* VI:i, 505.

9. *L.P.* XVI, 665.

10. *Sp. Cal.* VI:i, 410–11.

11. *L.P.* XVI, 284.

12. *Ibid.,* XVIII:ii, 108–10.

13. *Ibid.,* XV, 57; XIV:i, 448.

14. Michael Hattaway, "Marginalia by Henry VIII in His Copy of the Bokes of Salomon," *Transactions of the Cambridge Bibliographical Society,* IV, No. 2 (1965), 166–70.

15. *L.P.* XVII, 40, 717.

16. *Sp. Cal.* VI:i, 473.

17. *L.P.* XVII, 119.

18. *Ibid.,* XVI, 217.

19. *Sp. Cal.* VI:i, 471.

20. *Ibid.,* 413–14. In Flanders an opposite rumor circulated, to the effect that Anne was given to sensual excess and was as deserving of Henry's wrath as Catherine Howard. Or perhaps in his fear that Henry might remarry the Protestant Anne, Chapuys exaggerated the story. *Ibid.,* 408.

21. *Ibid.,* 549; *L.P.* XV, 446.

Chapter 41

1. *L.P.* XVIII:i, 490.

2. William P. Haugaard, "Katherine Parr: The Religious Convictions of a Renaissance Queen," *Renaissance Quarterly,* XXII, No. 4 (Winter 1969), 354–55.

3. *L.P.* XIX:i, 390–91.

4. *Sp. Cal.* VI:i, 315–16.

5. *L.P.* XVII, 198.

6. L. R. Shelby, *John Rogers, Tudor Military Engineer* (Oxford, 1967), 79.

7. *L.P.* XIV:ii, 368; XVI, 481; *Sp. Cal.* VI:i, 343.

8. *L.P.* XVI, 339.

9. *Ibid.,* XVIII:ii, 175, 197.

10. *Ibid.,* XIX:i, 487.

Chapter 42

1. C. S. L. Davies, "Provisions for Armies, 1509–1560: A Study in the Effectiveness of Early Tudor Government," *EconHR,* XVII, No. 2 (December 1964), 234; *L.P.* XIX:i, 145ff., 163.

2. Davies, "Provisions," 244.

3. *L.P.* XIX:i, 164–65.

4. *Ibid.,* XIX:ii, 101.

5. Cited in Davies, "Provisions," 244n.

6. *L.P.* XIX:i, 578.

7. *Sp. Cal.* VII, 262–63.

8. *L.P.* XIX:i, 592.

9. Byrne, 364. Henry expressed a similar sentiment to De. Courrières. *Sp. Cal.,* VII, 284.

10. *Sp. Cal.* VII, 286; *L.P.* XIX:ii, 89.
11. *L.P.* XIX:ii, 65.
12. *Ibid.,* XIX:i, 601.
13. *Sp. Cal.* VII, 335.
14. *L.P.* XIX:i, 601.
15. *Ibid.,* 529–30.
16. *Ibid.,* XIX:ii, 134.
17. *Ibid.,* XIX:i, 610.
18. Byrne, 365–68.
19. *L.P.* XIX:ii, 101.
20. *Ibid.,* XIX:i, 606, 611.
21. *Ibid.,* XIX:ii, xxv and note, 124, 241; Shelby, 54.
22. *L.P.* XIX:ii, 241–42; *Sp. Cal.* VII, 285, 341–42.
23. *L.P.* XIX:ii, 99, 206.
24. *Ibid.,* 119, 127.
25. *Ibid.,* 132.

Chapter 43

1. *Sp. Cal.* VIII, 2.
2. *Ibid.,* 130; *L.P.* XX:i, 24.
3. *Sp. Cal.* VIII, 190; *L.P.* XX:ii, 17, 39.
4. *Sp. Cal.* VIII, 204.
5. *L.P.* XX:ii, 6, ix, 104, 154.
6. *Sp. Cal.* VIII, 236, 237.
7. Elton, *Reform and Reformation,* 310–11. Estimates of the cost of the campaign of 1544 vary. See Scarisbrick, 453, and Frederick Dietz, *English Public Finance, 1485–1641* (New York, 1964).
8. *L.P.* XX:ii, 258.
9. Pollard, 196n.; *L.P.* XVII, 649.
10. *L.P.* XIV:i, 108.
11. *Ibid.,* XVIII:i, 351.
12. T. M. Parker, *The English Reformation to 1558* (London, 1966), 94.
13. Elton, *Policy and Police,* 259.
14. *L.P.* XII:i, 331.
15. *Ibid.,* XVIII:ii, 300, 307, 308.
16. *Ibid.,* 307.
17. *Ibid.,* XIV:i, 551.
18. *Ibid.,* VIII, 114; Elton, *Policy and Police,* 363; *L.P.* XII:i, 271.
19. *L.P.* XIV:ii, 48.
20. *Ibid.,* XIX:ii, 238.
21. The following account of Henry's last speech to Parliament is taken from Byrne, 418–22.

Chapter 44

1. Roy Strong, *Holbein and Henry VIII* (London, 1967), 29–32.
2. *L.P.* XVI, 203–4; XV, 321; XIV:ii, 41.

3. *Sp. Cal.* VIII, 241.

4. *Ibid.,* VII, 164; *L.P.* XIX:i, 326. Chamberlin, 191, gives the document in full.

5. Chamberlin, 210n. There is no evidence that Henry was moved about by mechanical means; when in 1546 Bess Holland said that he was let up and down stairs by a "device," she was almost certainly referring to the tram or traveling chair.

6. *L.P.* XV, 524.

7. *Ibid.,* I, 279.

8. Leslie G. Matthews, "Royal Apothecaries of the Tudor Period," *Medical History,* VIII, No. 2 (April 1964), 172–73; *L.P.* XII:ii, 176.

9. *L.P.* XII:ii, 394 lists the goods the apothecaries supplied in 1546–47. Further details, including information on Henry's own remedies, are in Blaxland Stubbs, "Royal Recipes for Plasters, Ointments and other Medicaments," and Howard Bayles, "Notes on Accounts Paid to the Royal Apothecaries in 1546 and 1547," both in *The Chemist and Druggist,* CXIV, Special issue (June 1931), 792–96.

10. Brewer, I, 233 and note.

11. *L.P.* XX:i, 70; *Sp. Cal.* VIII, 219–20; *L.P.* XIV:ii, 142.

12. *L.P.* Add. I:ii, 610, 564; XII:ii, 474; XV, 383.

13. *Ibid.,* XXI:ii, 400; XIV:ii, 317; Add. I:ii, 611.

14. *Ibid.,* X, 64.

15. *Ibid.,* XIV:ii, 344; XV, 159; XVII, 120; XXI:ii, 395.

16. *Sp. Cal.* VIII, 318; *L.P.* XXI:i, 169.

17. *L.P.* XVI, 628; *Sp. Cal.* VI:i, 412, 452.

18. *L.P.* XXI:ii, 294.

Chapter 45

1. *Sp. Cal.* VIII, 426.

2. *Ibid.,* 475.

3. *L.P.* XXI:ii, 185.

4. *Ibid.,* 360.

5. *Ibid.*

6. *Sp. Cal.* IX, 30–31.

7. Byrne, 418.

8. Elton, *Reform and Reformation,* 331–32. On the controversy over the royal will see Scarisbrick, 488–95, Lacey Baldwin Smith, "The Last Will and Testament of Henry VIII: A Question of Perspective," *Journal of British Studies,* II (November 1962), 14–27, and Mortimer Levine, "The Last Will and Testament of Henry VIII: A Reappraisal Reappraised," *Historian,* XXVI, No. 4 (August 1964), 471–85.

9. *L.P.* XXI:ii, 320–22.

Select Bibliography

ORIGINAL SOURCES

Allen, P. S. and H. M., eds. *Letters of Richard Fox, 1486–1527*. Oxford: Clarendon Press, 1929.

———, H. M. Allen and H. W. Garrod, eds. *Opus Epistolarum Desiderii Erasmi Roterodami*. 12 vols. Oxford: Clarendon Press, 1906–58.

Arber, Edward, ed. *Tottel's Miscellany: Songes and Sonnettes by Henry Howard, Earl of Surrey, Sir Thomas Wyatt, the Elder Nicholas Grimald and Uncertain Authors*. Westminster: A. Constable and Co., Ltd., 1903.

Bacon, Francis. *History of the reign of King Henry VII*, ed. J. Rawson Lumby. Cambridge, England: Cambridge University Press, 1902.

Blundeville, Thomas. *The Fower chiefest offices belongyng to horsemanship. Part II: The Arte of Riding*. London: Wyllyam Seres, 1565.

Boorde, Andrew. *A compendyous regiment or a dyetary of Helth*, ed. F. J. Furnivall. Early English Text Society, Extra series, X. London: Trübner, 1870.

Brown, Rawdon, ed. and trans. *Four Years at the Court of Henry VIII*. 2 vols. London: Smith, Elder and Co., 1854.

Bullett, Gerald, ed. *Silver Poets of the Sixteenth Century*. London: Dent and New York: Dutton, 1966.

Byrne, Muriel St. Clare, ed. *The Letters of King Henry VIII*. London: Cassell, 1936.

Calendar of Letters, Despatches, and State Papers, relating to the Negotiations between England and Spain, preserved in the Archives at Vienna, Simancas, Besançon and Brussels, ed. Pascual de Gayangos, G. A. Bergenroth, M. A. S. Hume, Royall Tyler, and Garrett Mattingly. 13 vols. London: His and Her Majesty's Stationery Office, 1862–1954.

Calendar of State Papers and Manuscripts, Existing in the Archives and Collections of Milan, ed. Allen B. Hinds. Vol. I. London: His Majesty's Stationery Office, 1912.

Calendar of State Papers and Manuscripts, Relating to English Affairs, Existing in the Archives and Collections of Venice, and in Other Libraries of Northern Italy, ed. Rawdon Brown and Allen B. Hinds. 38 vols. London: Longman and Co., 1864–1947.

Campbell, William, ed. *Materials for a history of the reign of Henry VII*. Rolls Series, No. 60. 2 vols. London, 1873.

Cavendish, George. *The Life and Death of Cardinal Wolsey,* ed. Richard S. Sylvester and Davis P. Harding. New Haven and London: Yale University Press, 1962.

Foxe, John. *The Acts and Monuments of John Foxe,* ed. George Townsend and S. R. Cattley, 8 vols. London: R. B. Seeley and W. Burnside, 1837–41.

Fuensalida, Gutierre Gómez de. *Correspondencia de Gutierre Gómez de Fuensalida, Embajador en Alemania, Flandes é Inglaterra (1458–1509).* Madrid: El Duque de Berwick y de Alba, 1907.

Gairdner, James. *Memorials of King Henry VII.* Rolls Series, No. 10. 2 vols. London, 1858.

Great Britain, Historical Manuscripts Commission. *Report on Manuscripts in the Welsh Language.* Vol. I. London: Eyre and Spottiswoode, 1898.

The Great Tournament Roll of Westminster: A Collotype Reproduction of the Manuscript. Oxford: Clarendon Press, 1968.

Hall, Edward. *The triumphant reigne of King Henry the VIII,* ed. Charles Whibley. 2 vols. London: T. C. and E. C. Jack, 1904.

Hall, Joseph, ed. *The Poems of Laurence Minot.* Oxford: Clarendon Press, 1914.

Hall, Richard. *The Life of Fisher,* ed. Rev. Ronald Bayne. Early English Text Society, Extra series, CXVII. London: Humphrey Milford and Oxford University Press, 1921.

Harpsfield, Nicholas. *A Treatise on the Pretended Divorce between Henry VIII and Catherine of Aragon.* Camden Society, New series, XXI. London: Nicholas Pocock, 1878.

Hay, Denys, ed. *The anglica historia of Polydore Vergil, 1485–1537.* Camden Society, Third series, LXXIV. London: Butler and Tanner, 1950.

Herbert of Cherbury, Edward, Lord. *The life and raigne of King Henry the Eighth.* London: Andrew Clark, 1672.

Hughes, Paul L. and James F. Larkin. *Tudor Royal Proclamations.* Vol. I. *The Early Tudors (1485–1553).* New Haven and London: Yale University Press, 1964.

Hume, Martin A. S., trans. *Chronicle of King Henry VIII of England.* London: George Bell and Sons, 1889.

Kingsford, C. L., ed. *The First English Life of Henry the Fifth.* Oxford: Clarendon Press, 1911.

Leland, John. *Antiquarii de Rebus Brittanicis Collectanea.* 6 vols. London: Gul. and Jo. Richardson, 1770.

Lemon, Robert, comp. *Catalogue of a Collection of Printed Broadsides in the possession of the Society of Antiquaries of London.* London: Society of Antiquaries of London, 1866.

Letters and Papers, Foreign and Domestic, of the Reign of Henry VIII, ed. J. S. Brewer, R. H. Brodie and James Gairdner. 21 vols. London: Her Majesty's Stationery Office, 1862–1910.

Madden, Frederick, ed. *Privy Purse Expenses of the Princess Mary, daughter of King Henry the Eighth, afterwards Queen Mary: with a Memoir of the Princess, and Notes.* London: William Pickering, 1831.

Martz, Louis L. and Richard S. Sylvester, eds. *Thomas More's Prayer Book: A Facsimile Reproduction of the Annotated Pages.* New Haven and London: Yale University Press, 1969.

Muir, Kenneth and Patricia Thomson, eds. *Collected Poems of Sir Thomas Wyatt.* Liverpool: Liverpool University Press, 1969.

————. *Life and Letters of Sir Thomas Wyatt.* Liverpool: Liverpool University Press, 1963.

Mumby, Frank Arthur. *The Youth of Henry VIII: A Narrative in Contemporary Letters.* London: Constable, 1913.

Nichols, John Gough, ed. *Chronicle of the Grey Friars of London.* Camden Society, Old series, LIII. London: J. B. Nichols and Son, 1852.

————. *Inventories of the Wardrobes, Plate, Chapel Stuff, etc., of Henry Fitzroy, Duke of Richmond, and of the Wardrobe Stuff at Baynard's Castle of Katherine, Princess Dowager.* Camden Society, Old series, LXI. London: J. B. Nichols and Son, 1854.

Nicolas, Nicholas Harris, ed. *Privy Purse Expenses of Elizabeth of York: Wardrobe Accounts of Edward the Fourth.* London: William Pickering, 1830.

————. *The Privy Purse Expenses of King Henry the Eighth from November MDXXIX, to December MDXXXII.* London: William Pickering, 1827.

Percy, Thomas, ed. *Reliques of Ancient English Poetry.* 3 vols. London: Swan Sonnenschein, 1885, reprinted George Allen and Unwin, 1927.

Persons, Robert. *Certamen Ecclesiae Anglicanae.* Assen: Van Gorcum and Co., 1965.

Pisan, Christine de. *The Book of Fayttes of Armes and of Chyvalrye,* trans. William Caxton. ed. A. T. P. Byles. Early English Text Society, Original series, CLXXXIX. London: Oxford University Press, 1932, reissued 1937.

Poole, H. E. *The Wisdom of Andrew Boorde.* Leicester: E. Backus, 1936.

Rhodes, Hugh. *The boke of Nurture for men, servantes and children . . . very utyle and necessary unto all youth.* London: Thomas Petyt, 1545.

Rickert, Edith, ed. *The Babees' Book: Medieval Manners for the Young. Done into Modern English from Dr. Furnivall's Texts.* New York and London: Duffield and Co., Chatto and Windus, 1908.

Rogers, Elizabeth Francis, ed. *The Correspondence of Sir Thomas More.* Princeton: Princeton University Press, 1947.

Roper, William. *The Life of Sir Thomas More,* ed. Richard S. Sylvester and Davis P. Harding. New Haven and London: Yale University Press, 1962.

Salter, Emma Gurney. *Tudor England Through Venetian Eyes.* London: Williams and Norgate, 1930.

Scheurer, R., ed. *Correspondance du Cardinal Jean du Bellay.* Paris: Klincksieck, 1969.

Slavin, Arthur J., ed. *Thomas Cromwell on Church and Commonwealth: Selected Letters 1523–1540.* New York: Harper and Row, 1969.

Sneyd, Charlotte Augusta, trans. *Relation or rather a true account of the island of England; with sundry particulars of the customs of these people . . . about the year 1500.* Camden Society, Old series, XXXVII. London: John Bowyer Nichols and Son, 1847.

Stapleton, Thomas. *The Life and Illustrious Martyrdom of Sir Thomas More,* trans. P. E. Hallett. London: Burns, Oates and Washburn, 1928.

Starkey, Thomas. *England in the reign of Henry VIII.* Part I: *Starkey's Life and Letters,* ed. Sidney J. Herrtage. Early English Text Society, Extra series, XXXII. London: Trübner, 1878.

Stevens, John, ed. *Music at the Court of Henry VIII. Musica Britannica*, Vol. XVIII. London: Stainer and Bell, 1962.

Thomas, William. *The Pilgrim: A Dialogue on the Life and Actions of King Henry the Eighth*, ed. J. A. Froude. London: Parker, Son, and Bourn, 1861.

Tyndale, William. *Expositions and Notes on Sundry Portions of the Holy Scriptures together with the Practice of Prelates*, ed. Rev. Henry Walter. Cambridge: Cambridge University Press, 1849.

Wyatt, Thomas. *Collected Poems*, ed. Kenneth Muir. London: Routledge and Kegan Paul, 1949.

SECONDARY AUTHORITIES

Adair, Edward R. "English Galleys in the Sixteenth Century." *English Historical Review*, XXXV, No. 140 (October 1920), 497–512.

Allen, Don Cameron. *Doubt's Boundless Sea: Skepticism and Faith in the Renaissance*. Baltimore: Johns Hopkins Press, 1964.

Anglo, Sydney. *Spectacle, Pageantry and Early Tudor Policy*. Oxford: Clarendon Press, 1969.

The Antiquarian Repertory: A Miscellany, intended to Preserve and Illustrate Several Valuable Remains of Old Times. 4 vols. London: Francis Blyth, 1775–84.

Archaeologia: or Miscellaneous Tracts Relating to Antiquity. 102 vols. London: Society of Antiquaries, 1773–1969.

Aston, Margaret. "English Ruins and English History: The Dissolution and the Sense of the Past." *Journal of the Warburg and Courtauld Institutes*, No. 36 (1973), 231–55.

Ban, Joseph D. "English Reformation: Product of King or Minister?" *Church History*, XLI, No. 2 (June 1972), 186–97.

Baskerville, Geoffrey. *English Monks and the Suppression of the Monasteries*. New Haven: Yale University Press, 1937.

Baumer, Franklin Le Van. *The Early Tudor Theory of Kingship*. New Haven: Yale University Press and London: Oxford University Press, 1940.

Bayles, Howard. "Notes on Accounts Paid to the Royal Apothecaries in 1546 and 1547." *The Chemist and Druggist*, CXIV, Special issue (June 1931), 794–96.

Behrens, Betty. "A Note on Henry VIII's divorce project of 1514." *Bulletin of the Institute of Historical Research*, XI, No. 33 (February 1934), 163–64.

Berry, Boyd M. "The First English Pediatricians." *Journal of the History of Ideas*, XXXV, No. 4 (October–December 1974), 561–77.

Blench, J. W. *Preaching in England in the Late Fifteenth and Sixteenth Centuries*. Oxford: Basil Blackwell, 1964.

Bowker, Margaret. "The Henrician Reformation and the parish clergy." *Bulletin of the Institute of Historical Research*, L, No. 121 (May 1977), 30–47.

———. "The Supremacy and the Episcopate: The Struggle for Control, 1539–1540." *Historical Journal*, XVIII, No. 2 (June 1975), 227–43.

Bowle, John. *Henry VIII: A Biography*. London: Allen and Unwin and Boston: Little, Brown, 1964.

Brand, John. *Observations of Popular Antiquities: Chiefly Illustrating the Origin of Our Vulgar Customs, Ceremonies, and Superstitions*, arr. and rev. Henry Ellis. 3 vols. London: F. C. and J. Rivington, 1813.

Brewer, J. S. *The Reign of Henry VIII: from his Accession to the Death of Wolsey*, ed. James Gairdner. 2 vols. London: John Murray, 1884.

Brinch, Ove. "The Medical Problems of Henry VIII." *Centaurus*, V, Nos. 3–4 (1958), 339–69.

Bruce, Marie Louise. *Anne Boleyn*. London: Collins, 1972.

———. *The Making of Henry VIII*. New York: Coward, McCann and Geoghegan, 1977.

Burton, Elizabeth. *The Pageant of Early Tudor England 1485–1558*. New York: Charles Scribner's Sons, 1976.

Bush, M. L. "The Lisle–Seymour Land Disputes: A Study of Power and Influence in the 1530's." *Historical Journal*, IX, No. 3 (1966), 255–74.

———. "The Tudors and the Royal Race." *History*, LII, No. 183 (February 1970), 37–48.

Byman, Seymour. "Suicide and Alienation: Martyrdom in Tudor England." *Psychoanalytic Review*, LXI, No. 3 (Fall 1974), 355–73.

Callender, Geoffrey A. R. "The Evolution of Sea Power Under the First Two Tudors." *History*, New series, V, No. 5 (October 1920), 141–58.

Capes, William Wolfe. *The English Church in the Fourteenth and Fifteenth Centuries. A History of the English Church*, ed. Rev. W. R. W. Stephens and Rev. William Hunt, Vol. III. London and New York: Macmillan, 1900.

Challis, C. E. "Currency and the Economy in Mid-Tudor England." *Economic History Review*, XXV, No. 2 (May 1972), 313–22.

———. "The Debasement of the Coinage, 1542–1551." *Economic History Review*, Second series, XX, No. 3 (December 1967), 441–66.

———. *The Tudor Coinage*. Manchester: Manchester University Press, 1977.

Chamberlin, Frederick. *The Private Character of Henry the Eighth*. New York: Ives Washburn, 1931.

Chambers, D. S. "Cardinal Wolsey and the Papal Tiara." *Bulletin of the Institute of Historical Research*, XXXVIII, No. 97 (May 1965), 20–30.

Chapman, Hester W. *Anne Boleyn*. London: Jonathan Cape, 1974.

Childe-Pemberton, William S. *Elizabeth Blount and Henry VIII*. London: Eveleigh Nash, 1913.

Chrimes, S. B. *Henry VII*. Berkeley and Los Angeles: University of California Press, 1972.

Clebsch, William A. *England's Earliest Protestants 1520–1535*. New Haven and London: Yale University Press, 1964.

Clepham, Robert Coltman. "The Military Handgun of the Sixteenth Century." *Archaeological Journal*, Second series, LXVII, No. 265, XVII, No. 1 (March 1910), 109–50.

———. *The Tournament*. London: Methuen and Co., 1919.

Cooper, J. P. "Henry VII's Last Years Reconsidered." *Historical Journal*, II, No. 2 (1959), 103–29.

Crabitès, Pierre. *Clement VII and Henry VIII*. London: G. Routledge, 1936.

Cripps-Day, Francis Henry. *The History of the Tournament in England and in France*. London: Bernard Quaritch, 1918.

Crowson, P. S. *Tudor Foreign Policy.* New York: St. Martin's Press, 1973.

Cruickshank, Charles Grieg. *Army Royal: Henry VIII's Invasion of France, 1513.* New York and Oxford: Oxford University Press, 1969.

————. *The English Occupation of Tournai 1513–1519.* Oxford: Clarendon Press, 1971.

————. "Henry VIII and Tournai." *History Today,* XXI, No. 9 (January 1971), 3–13.

Davies, C. S. L. "The Administration of the Royal Navy under Henry VIII: The Origins of the Navy Board." *English Historical Review,* LXXX, No. 315 (April 1965), 268–88.

————. "The Pilgrimage of Grace Reconsidered." *Past and Present,* XLI (December 1969), 54–76.

————. "Provisions for Armies, 1509–1560: A Study in the Effectiveness of Early Tudor Government." *Economic History Review,* XVII, No. 2 (December 1964), 234–48.

Davis, Eliza Jeffries. "The Transformation of London." In *Tudor Studies presented by the Board of Students in History in the University of London to Albert Frederick Pollard,* ed. R. W. Seton-Watson. London: Longmans, Green and Co., 1924.

Dent, John. *The Quest for Nonsuch.* London: Hutchinson, 1962.

Derrett, J. Duncan M. "Henry Fitzroy and Henry VIII's Scruple of Conscience." *Renaissance News,* XVI, No. 1 (Spring 1963), 1–9.

————. "The Trial of Sir Thomas More." *English Historical Review,* LXXIX, No. 312 (July 1964), 449–77.

Dickens, A. G. *The English Reformation.* London: B. T. Batsford, 1964.

Dietz, Frederick. *English Public Finance, 1485–1641.* 2nd ed. 2 vols. New York: Barnes and Noble, 1964.

Dillon, Viscount. "Barriers and Foot Combats." *Archaeological Journal,* LXI, Second series, XI, No. 1 (1904), 276–308.

————. "Tilting in Tudor Times." *Archaeological Journal,* LV, Second series, No. 5 (1898), 296–339.

Dodds, Madeline Hope. "Political Prophecies in the Reign of Henry VIII." *Modern Language Review,* XI, No. 3 (July 1916), 276–84.

————, and Ruth Dodds. *The Pilgrimage of Grace, 1536–1537, and the Exeter Conspiracy, 1538.* 2 vols. Cambridge: Cambridge University Press, 1915.

Doernberg, Erwin. *Henry VIII and Luther: An Account of their Personal Relations.* Palo Alto, California: Stanford University Press, 1967.

Dolmetsch, Mabel. *Dances of England and France from 1450 to 1600.* London: Routledge and Kegan Paul, 1949.

Douce, Francis. *Illustrations of Shakespeare, and of Ancient Manners: with Dissertations on the Clowns and Fools of Shakespeare; on the Collection of Popular Tales Entitled Gesta Romanorum; and on the English Morris Dance.* 2 vols. London: Longman, Hurst, Rees and Orme, 1807.

Du Boys, Albert. *Catherine of Aragon and the Sources of the English Reformation,* ed. and trans. Charlotte M. Yonge. 2 vols. London: Hurst and Blackett, 1881, republished New York: Burt Franklin, 1968.

Dunham, William Huse, Jr. "Regal Power and the Rule of Law: A Tudor Paradox." *Journal of British Studies,* III, No. 2 (May 1964), 24–56.

Edwards, H. L. R. *Skelton: The Life and Times of an Early Tudor Poet*. London: Jonathan Cape, 1949.

Elton, G. R. "Henry VII: a restatement." *Historical Journal,* IV, No. 1 (1961), 1–29.

———. *Henry VIII: An Essay in Revision*. Historical Association Pamphlet, General series, No. 51. London: Routledge and Kegan Paul, 1962.

———. "Henry VII: Rapacity and remorse." *Historical Journal,* I, No. 1 (1958), 21–39.

———. "Informing for profit: a sidelight on Tudor methods of law enforcement." *Cambridge Historical Journal,* XI, No. 2 (1954), 149–67.

———. *Policy and Police*. Cambridge, England: Cambridge University Press, 1972.

———. "The Political Creed of Thomas Cromwell." *Transactions of the Royal Historical Society,* 5th series, VI (1956), 69–92.

———. *Reform and Reformation: England 1509–1558*. Cambridge, Mass.: Harvard University Press, 1977.

———. *Reform and Renewal: Thomas Cromwell and the Common Weal*. Cambridge, England: Cambridge University Press, 1973.

———. "Sir Thomas More and the Opposition to Henry VIII." *Bulletin of the Institute of Historical Research,* XLI, No. 103 (May 1968), 19–34.

———. *The Tudor Revolution in Government: Administrative Changes in the Reign of Henry VIII*. Cambridge, England: Cambridge University Press, 1962.

Erickson, Carolly. *Bloody Mary*. Garden City, New York: Doubleday and London: Dent, 1978.

Ferguson, Arthur B. *The Articulate Citizen and the English Renaissance*. Durham, N.C.: Duke University Press, 1965.

———. *The Indian Summer of English Chivalry*. Durham, N.C.: Duke University Press, 1960.

Ferguson, Charles W. *Naked to Mine Enemies: The Life of Cardinal Wolsey*. Boston and Toronto: Little, Brown, 1958.

Firth, Charles H. "The ballad history of the reigns of Henry VII and Henry VIII." *Transactions of the Royal Historical Society,* Third series, II (1908), 21–50.

Flügel, J. C. "The Character and Married Life of Henry VIII." In Bruce Mazlish, *Psychoanalysis and History*. New York: Grosset and Dunlap, 1963.

Friedmann, Paul. *Ann Boleyn: A Chapter of English History 1527–1536*. 2 vols. London: Macmillan, 1884.

Froude, James Anthony. *History of England, from the Fall of Wolsey to the Death of Elizabeth*. 4 vols. New York: Charles Scribner's Sons, 1881.

———. *Life and Letters of Erasmus*. London: Longmans, Green and Co., 1894.

Gairdner, James. *Henry the Seventh*. London: Macmillan, 1892.

Gilbert, Creighton. "When did Renaissance man grow old?" *Studies in the Renaissance,* XIV (1967), 7–32.

Gould, J. D. "F. J. Fisher on Influenza and Inflation in Tudor England." *Economic History Review,* Second series, XXI, No. 2 (August 1968), 361–68.

———. *The Great Debasement: Currency and Economy in Mid-Tudor England*. Oxford: Clarendon Press, 1970.

Greenslade, S. L. "The Morean Renaissance." *Journal of Ecclesiastical History,* XXIV, No. 4 (October 1973), 395–403.

Greenwald, Isidor. "The supposed 'Syndrome of Anne Boleyn' (Goiter and Polydactylism)." *Bulletin of the History of Medicine,* XXXVIII, No. 3 (May–June 1964), 271–75.

Gregg, Pauline. *Black Death to Industrial Revolution: A Social and Economic History of England.* London: Harrap Books, 1976.

Hale, John R. *The Art of War and Renaissance England.* Washington: Folger Shakespeare Library, 1961.

———. *Renaissance Europe: Individual and Society, 1480–1520.* New York: Harper and Row, 1971.

Harrison, Eric. "Henry VIII's gangster: The affair of Ludovico da l'Armi." *Journal of Modern History,* XV, No. 4 (December 1943), 265–74.

Hattaway, Michael. "Marginalia by Henry VIII in His Copy of the Bokes of Salomon." *Transactions of the Cambridge Bibliographical Society,* IV, No. 2 (1965), 166–70.

Haugaard, William P. "Katherine Parr: The Religious Convictions of a Renaissance Queen." *Renaissance Quarterly,* XXII, No. 4 (Winter 1969), 346–59.

Heal, Felicity and Rosemary O'Day, eds. *Church and Society in England: Henry VIII to James I.* London and Basingstoke: Macmillan, 1977.

Heath, Peter. *The English Parish Clergy on the Eve of the Reformation.* London: Routledge and Kegan Paul and Toronto: University of Toronto Press, 1969.

Hoffman, Ann. *Lives of the Tudor Age, 1485–1603.* New York: Barnes and Noble, 1977.

Hogrefe, Pearl. "Legal Rights of Tudor Women and their Circumvention by Men and Women." *Sixteenth Century Journal,* III, No. 1 (April 1972), 97–105.

———. *Women of Action in Tudor England: Nine Biographical Sketches.* Ames, Iowa: Iowa State University Press, 1977.

Holderness, B. A. *Pre-Industrial England: Economy and Society 1500–1700.* London: Dent and Totowa, N.J.: Rowman and Littlefield, 1976.

Hoskins, William George. *The Age of Plunder: The England of Henry VIII, 1500–1547.* London and New York: Longman, 1976.

Hughes, Philip. *The Reformation in England.* 3 vols. New York: Macmillan, 1951–54.

Hume, Martin. *The Wives of Henry the Eighth and the Parts They Played in History.* New York: McClure, Phillips and Co., 1905.

Hunt, Percival. *Fifteenth Century England.* Pittsburgh: University of Pittsburgh Press, 1962.

Ives, E. W. "Faction at the Court of Henry VIII: The Fall of Anne Boleyn." *History,* LVII, No. 190 (June 1972), 169–88.

James, M. E. "Obedience and Dissent in Henrician England: The Lincolnshire Rebellion, 1536." *Past and Present,* XLVIII (August 1970), 3–78.

Jones, Whitney R. D. *The Mid-Tudor Crisis 1539–1563.* London and Basingstoke: Macmillan, 1973.

———. *The Tudor Commonwealth 1529–1559.* London: Athlone Press, 1970.

Jorgensen, Paul A. *Shakespeare's Military World.* Berkeley and Los Angeles: University of California Press, 1956.

Kelly, Henry Ansgar. *The Matrimonial Trials of Henry VIII.* Palo Alto, California: Stanford University Press, 1975.

Kelso, Ruth. *The Doctrine of the English Gentleman in the Sixteenth Century.*

University of Illinois Studies in Language and Literature, Vol. XIV. Urbana, Illinois: University of Illinois Press, 1929.

Kittredge, George Lyman. *Witchcraft in Old and New England*. Cambridge, Mass.: Harvard University Press, 1929.

Landler, J. R. "Bonds, Coercion and Fear: Henry VII and the Peerage." In *Florilegium Historiale: Essays Presented to Wallace K. Ferguson,* ed. J. G. Rowe and W. H. Stockdale. Toronto: Toronto University Press, 1971.

Law, Ernest. *England's First Great War Minister*. London: George Bell and Sons, 1916.

––––––. *A Short History of Hampton Court Palace in Tudor and Stuart Times*. London: George Bell, 1929.

Lehmberg, Stanford E. "Parliamentary Attainder in the reign of Henry VIII." *Historical Journal,* XVIII, No. 4 (December 1975), 675–702.

Levine, Mortimer. "Henry VIII's use of his spiritual and temporal jurisdictions in his great causes of matrimony, legitimacy, and succession." *Historical Journal,* X, No. 1 (1967), 3–10.

––––––. "The Last Will and Testament of Henry VIII: A Reappraisal Reappraised." *Historian,* XXVI, No. 4 (August 1964), 471–85.

––––––. *Tudor England 1485–1603*. Conference on British Studies Bibliographical Handbooks. Cambridge: Cambridge University Press, 1968.

Loades, D. M. "The Press Under the Early Tudors: A Study in Censorship and Sedition." *Transactions of the Cambridge Bibliographical Society,* IV, No. 1 (1965), 29–50.

Lodge, Edmund. *Illustrations of British History*. 3 vols. London: G. Nicol, 1791.

Logan, F. Donald. "The Henrician Canons." *Bulletin of the Institute of Historical Research,* XLVII, No. 115 (May 1974), 99–103.

Lowinsky, Edward. "A Music Book for Anne Boleyn." In *Florilegium Historiale: Essays Presented to Wallace K. Ferguson,* ed. J. G. Rowe and W. H. Stockdale. Toronto: University of Toronto Press, 1971.

MacDonald, William W. "Anticlericalism, Protestantism, and the English Reformation." *Journal of Church and State,* XV, No. 1 (Winter 1973), 21–32.

Mackie, John Duncan. *The Earlier Tudors, 1485–1558*. Oxford: Clarendon Press, 1952.

Maclennan, Hector. "A Gynaecologist Looks at the Tudors." *Medical History,* XI, No. 1 (January 1967), 66–74.

MacNalty, Sir Arthur S. *Henry VIII: A difficult patient*. London: Christopher Johnson, 1952.

Mason, John E. *Gentlefolk in the Making*. Philadelphia: University of Pennsylvania Press, 1935.

Mathew, David. *The Courtiers of Henry VIII*. London: Eyre and Spottiswoode, 1970.

Matthews, Leslie G. "Royal Apothecaries of the Tudor Period." *Medical History,* VIII, No. 2 (April 1964), 170–80.

Mattingly, Garrett. *Catherine of Aragon*. Boston: Little, Brown, 1941.

Mazlish, Bruce. *Psychoanalysis and History*. New York: Grosset and Dunlap, 1963.

Mitchell, Margaret. "Works of Art from Rome for Henry VIII." *Journal of the Warburg and Courtauld Institutes,* XXXIX (1971), 178–203.

Morison, Stanley. *The Likeness of Thomas More: An Iconographical Survey of Three Centuries,* ed. and supplemented by Nicholas Barker. New York: Fordham University Press, 1963.

Morris, Christopher. *The Tudors.* New York: John Wiley and Sons, 1967.

Morrison, N. Brysson. *The Private Life of Henry VIII.* London: Robert Hale, 1964.

Nelson, William. *John Skelton, Laureate.* New York: Columbia University Press, 1939. rev. ed., 1964.

Newton, A. P. "Tudor Reforms in the Royal Household." In *Tudor Studies presented by the Board of Students in History in the University of London to Albert Frederick Pollard,* ed. R. W. Seton-Watson. London: Longmans, Green and Co., 1924.

Nuttall, Geoffrey F. "The English Martyrs 1535–1680: A Statistical Review." *Journal of Ecclesiastical History,* XXII, No. 3 (July 1971), 191–97.

O'Malley, C. D. "Tudor Medicine and Biology." *Huntington Library Quarterly,* XXXII, No. 1 (November 1968), 1–27.

Oman, Charles W. C. *A History of the Art of War in the Sixteenth Century.* New York: E. P. Dutton and Co., 1937.

———. "The Personality of Henry VIII." *Quarterly Review,* CCLXIX (July 1937), 88–104.

Outhwaite, R. B. *Inflation in Tudor and Stuart England.* London: Macmillan, 1969.

———. "The Trials of Foreign Borrowing: The English Crown and the Antwerp Money Market in the Mid-Sixteenth Century." *Economic History Review,* Second series, XIX, No. 2 (August 1966), 289–305.

Pardoe, Julia. *The Court and Reign of Francis the First, King of France.* 3 vols. New York: James Pott and Co., 1901.

Parker, T. M. *The English Reformation to 1558.* 2nd ed. London: Oxford University Press, 1966.

Parmiter, Geoffrey de C. *The King's Great Matter: A Study of Anglo-Papal Relations 1527–1534.* London: Longmans, Green and Co., 1967.

———. "A Note on Some Aspects of the Royal Supremacy of Henry VIII." *Recusant History,* X, No. 4 (January 1970), 183–92.

Paul, John E. *Catherine of Aragon and Her Friends.* New York: Fordham University Press, 1966.

Pinchbeck, Ivy and Margaret Hewitt. *Children in English Society,* Vol. I. *From Tudor Times to the Eighteenth Century.* London: Routledge and Kegan Paul, 1969.

Plucknett, Theodore F. T. "The Lancastrian Constitution." In *Tudor Studies presented by the Board of Students in History in the University of London to Albert Frederick Pollard,* ed. R. W. Seton-Watson. London: Longmans, Green and Co., 1924.

Pollard, Albert F. *Henry VIII.* new ed. London: Longmans, Green and Co., 1905, 1951.

———. *The reign of Henry VII from contemporary sources.* University of London Historical Series, No. 1. 3 vols. London: Longmans, Green and Co., 1913–14.

———. *Wolsey: Church and State in Sixteenth-Century England.* new ed. London: Longmans, Green and Co., 1929, 1953.

Powell, C. L. *English Domestic Relations, 1487–1653: A Study of Matrimony and*

Family Life in Theory and Practice as revealed in the Literature, Law and History of the Period. New York: Columbia University Press, 1917.

Pugh, Ralph B. *Imprisonment in Medieval England.* Cambridge, England: Cambridge University Press, 1970.

Pyne, William Henry. *The History of the Royal Residences of Windsor Castle, St. James's Palace, Carlton House, Kensington Palace, Hampton Court, Buckingham House and Frogmore.* London: A. Day, 1819.

Rabb, Theodore K. and J. E. Siegel. *Action and Conviction in Early Modern Europe: Essays in Memory of H. E. Harbison.* Princeton: Princeton University Press, 1969.

Raleigh, Sir W., ed. *Shakespeare's England: An Account of the Life and Manners of His Age.* Oxford: Clarendon Press, 1916, reissued 1932.

Ramsey, Peter Herbert, ed. *The Price Revolution in Sixteenth-Century England.* London: Methuen, 1971.

Reynolds, E. E. *Saint John Fisher.* rev. ed. Wheathampstead: Anthony Clarke Books, 1972.

Richardson, Walter C. *Mary Tudor: The White Queen.* London: Peter Owen, 1970.

Ridley, Jasper. *Thomas Cranmer.* Oxford: Clarendon Press, 1962. reissued 1967.

Routh, E. M. G. *Lady Margaret, Mother of Henry VII.* London: Oxford University Press, 1924.

Rowe, J. G. and W. H. Stockdale, eds. *Florilegium Historiale: Essays Presented to Wallace K. Ferguson.* Toronto: University of Toronto Press, 1971.

Rupp, Ernest G. *Studies in the Making of the English Protestant Tradition. Mainly in the reign of Henry VIII.* Cambridge, England: Cambridge University Press, 1947.

Salter, F. M. "Skelton's *Speculum principis.*" *Speculum,* IX, No. 1 (January 1934), 25 37.

Scarisbrick, J. J. *Henry VIII.* Berkeley and Los Angeles: University of California Press, 1968.

Seton-Watson, R. W. *Tudor Studies presented by the Board of Students in History in the University of London to Albert Frederick Pollard.* London: Longmans, Green and Co., 1924.

Shelby, L. R. *John Rogers, Tudor Military Engineer.* Oxford: Clarendon Press, 1967.

Shore, Miles F. "Henry VIII and the Crisis of Generativity." *The Journal of Interdisciplinary History,* II, No. 4 (Spring 1972), 359–90.

Shrewsbury, J. F. D. "Henry VIII: A Medical Study." *Journal of the History of Medicine,* VII, No. 2 (Spring 1952), 141–85.

Slavin, Arthur Joseph. "Parliament and Henry VIII's Bigamous Principal Secretary." *Huntington Library Quarterly,* XXVIII, No. 2 (February 1965), 131–43.

———. *The Precarious Balance: English Government and Society.* New York: Knopf, 1973.

———, ed. *Thomas Cromwell on Church and Commonwealth: Selected Letters, 1523–1540.* New York: Harper and Row, 1969.

———, ed. *Tudor Men and Institutions: Studies in English Law and Government.* Baton Rouge: Louisiana State University Press, 1972.

Smith, H. Maynard. *Pre-Reformation England.* London: Macmillan, 1938.

Smith, Lacey Baldwin. "English Treason Trials and Confessions in the Sixteenth Century." *Journal of the History of Ideas,* XV, No. 4 (October 1954), 471–98.

———. *Henry VIII: The Mask of Royalty.* Boston: Houghton Mifflin, 1971.

———. "A Matter of Conscience." In *Action and Conviction in Early Modern Europe: Essays in Memory of E. H. Harbison,* ed. Theodore K. Rabb and J. E. Siegel. Princeton: Princeton University Press, 1969.

———. *A Tudor Tragedy: The Life and Times of Catherine Howard.* London: Jonathan Cape, 1961.

Stevens, John. *Music and Poetry in the Early Tudor Court.* Lincoln, Nebr.: University of Nebraska Press, 1961.

Strong, Roy. *Holbein and Henry VIII.* London: Routledge and Kegan Paul, 1967.

———. *Tudor and Jacobean Portraits.* 2 vols. London: Her Majesty's Stationery Office, 1969.

Stubbs, Blaxland. "Royal Recipes for Plasters, Ointments and other Medicaments." *The Chemist and Druggist,* CXIV, Special issue (June 1931), 792–94.

Taylor, Eva Germaine Rimington. *The Mathematical Practitioners of Tudor and Stuart England.* Cambridge, England: Cambridge University Press, 1967.

Temperley, Gladys. *Henry VII.* Boston and New York: Houghton Mifflin and Cambridge: Riverside Press, 1914.

Thomas, Keith. *Religion and the Decline of Magic.* New York: Charles Scribner's Sons, 1971.

Thomson, Patricia, ed. *Wyatt: the Critical Heritage.* London and Boston: Routledge and Kegan Paul, 1974.

Thorndike, Lynn. *A History of Magic and Experimental Science.* 8 vols. New York: Columbia University Press, 1923–58.

Tucker, Melvin J. *The Life of Thomas Howard: Earl of Surrey and Second Duke of Norfolk, 1443–1524.* The Hague: Mouton, 1964.

"Two Papers Relating to the Interview between Henry the Eighth of England, and Francis the First of France: Communicated by John Caley in a Letter to Henry Ellis." *Archaeologia: or Miscellaneous Tracts Relating to Antiquity,* XXI (1827), 175–91.

Wagner, Bernard M. "New Songs of the Reign of Henry VIII." *Modern Language Notes,* L, No. 7 (November 1935), 452–55.

Wernham, Richard Bruce. *Before the Armada: The Growth of English Foreign Policy, 1485–1588.* London: Jonathan Cape, 1966.

Wiley, W. L. *The Gentleman of Renaissance France.* Cambridge, Mass.: Harvard University Press, 1954.

Williams, C. H. *William Tyndale.* London: Nelson, 1969.

Williams, Neville. *The Cardinal and the Secretary: Thomas Wolsey and Thomas Cromwell.* London: Weidenfeld and Nicolson and New York: Macmillan, 1975.

———. *Henry VIII and His Court.* London: Weidenfeld and Nicolson, 1971.

———. *The Royal Residences of Great Britain.* New York: Macmillan, 1960.

Williams, Penry. "A Revolution in Tudor History?" *Past and Present,* No. 25 (July 1963), 3–56.

Wilson, Derek. *A Tudor Tapestry: Men, Women and Society in Reformation England.* Pittsburgh: University of Pittsburgh Press, 1972.

Woodward, G. W. O. *The Dissolution of the Monasteries*. New York: Walker and Co., 1967.

Youings, Joyce. *The Dissolution of the Monasteries*. London: George Allen and Unwin, 1971.

Zimmermann, T. C. Price. "A note on Clement VII and the divorce of Henry VIII." *English Historical Review*, LXXXII, No. 324 (July 1967), 548–52.

Index

Abell, Thomas, 313
Abergavenny, Lord, 151
acateries, royal, 98
Act for the Advancement of True Religion, 354
Act of Annates, First (1532), 250
Act in Restraint of Appeals (1533), 250, 253
Act of Succession (1534), 250, 256
Act of Supremacy (1534), 250
Agincourt, battle of (1415), 72
Aigues-Mortes, truce of (1536), 289
alchemy, 34, 46, 352
Alençon, duchess of, 206
Allen, Robert, 266
Alsop, Thomas, 283, 361
Amicable Grant (tax levy), 170, 173–74, 175
Ammonio, Andrea, 44, 118, 127, 149
Anabaptists, 293
André, Bernard, 28
Anne Boleyn (ship), 190
Anne of Cleves, 298, 302–12, 322, 331, 333
  betrothal of, 303
  description of, 302–3, 307
  divorce of, 309, 310, 311–12
  earlier marriage contract of, 303, 309, 311
  Henry's disappointment in, 306–7, 308
  retirement of, 312
  wedding of, 308
apothecaries, 261–62, 283, 363
apprentices, riots by, 146–47, 148, 150, 154
ap Rhys, Griffith, 227, 228
archery, military use of, 80–81
architecture, Henry's enterprises in, 182, 235, 286–87, 336–37, 344, 347
Ardres, French town of, 131, 141, 142
armor, 71, 191, 233, 335, 340
  for Field of Cloth of Gold tournament, 136
  Henry's expenditures on, 79
arms, armaments, 132
  in 1513 campaign, 71, 75–76, 80–81
  in 1543 campaign, 335–37, 344
  inventions in, 337
Arran, earl of, 334
Arras, bishop of, 346
Arthur, prince of Wales, 23, 25, 26, 27
  death of, 41
  Henry's relationship with, 23
  marriage of, 39–41
Aquinas, Saint Thomas, 116
Askew, Anne, 364
astrology, 138, 201, 266–67
astronomy, Henry's interest in, 183, 267
Audley, Thomas, 360
Ayala, Spanish ambassador, 35

Babham, Richard, 282
Badoer, Venetian ambassador, 58, 61, 72, 76, 82, 114
Bainbridge, Cardinal, 76
Barbaristo (Henry's horse), 127
Barnes, Robert, 310, 311, 313
Basilisk (gun), 132
"Battle of the Spurs" (1513), 87–88, 93
Bayard, Chevalier, 87
bear-baiting, 363
Beaton, David, Cardinal, 295
Beauchamp, Richard, earl of Warwick, 73
Beaufort, Margaret, *see* Margaret, countess of Richmond
Becket, Saint Thomas, tomb of, 292
beer, supplied to military, 79
Bellarmine, Robert, 234
Benevolences, 352
Berners, Lord, 72
Bible:
  divorce issue and, 234
  law on reading of, 354, 356, 358
  translations of, 117, 251, 354, 358
Biel, Gabriel, 116
Blackeden, Cuthbert, 282

Blackfriars, 56
Blount, Bessie, 159, 277
Blount, Gertrude, marchioness of Exeter, 280, 288, 318
Blount, William, Lord Mountjoy, 27, 61, 62, 118, 155
boar hunting, 184
Bokes of Salomon, The, 330
Bolenger, John, 235
Boleyn, Anne, 187, 188, 191, 198, 216, 245, 270–71, 299
  ancestry of, 231
  coronation of, 239, 241
  correspondence of, 203, 204, 208–9, 218–19
  courtiers' reactions to, 240, 241–42
  description of, 187
  early affairs of, 189–90
  fall and death of, 262–63
  feelings for Henry of, 204, 220
  at French court, 187, 270
  Henry's alienation from, 243, 259–62
  Henry's love for, 186, 190, 195, 204, 209, 217, 220, 223, 231, 238
  hostility of populace toward, 231–32, 241–42
  musical gifts of, 187–88, 235
  pregnancies of, 239, 260, 262
  status of, before marriage, 210, 212, 230, 231
  wedding of, 240
  witchcraft attributed to, 267
  Wolsey and, 189, 190, 201, 210, 220, 236
Boleyn, Geoffrey, 231
Boleyn, George, 209, 223, 262, 263
Boleyn, Mary, *see* Carey, Mary Boleyn
Boleyn, Thomas, earl of Wiltshire, 105, 148, 159, 173, 187, 201, 203, 206, 215, 232, 269, 280
  Anne's relations with, 240, 241
  created Viscount Rochford, 163, 189
  daughters as pawns of, 188–89
Bonde, John, 259
Bonnivet, French admiral, 143
Boothe, William, 112
Bordeaux, English in, 131
Bosworth Field, battle of (1485), 33, 35
Boulogne, city of, 353
  in English hands, 347–48, 349–50
  in 1523 campaign, 167
  1543 English siege of, 340–47, 352
  1545 French siege of, 350
Brandon, Catherine, 245, 338, 365

Brandon, Charles, 55, 59, 67, 78, 82, 90, 112, 144, 152, 159, 173, 189, 201, 203, 229, 278, 280, 287, 305, 306, 322
  as Anne Boleyn's enemy, 241
  created duke of Suffolk, 121
  death of, 360
  in 1523 campaign, 167, 168
  in 1539 campaign, 295
  in 1543 campaign, 338, 343, 348
  as Henry's intimate friend, 29–30, 92, 121, 125
  as Henry's jousting partner, 125–26, 233
  Henry's marriage plans for, 122–23
  Henry's suspicions of, 148
  marriage complications of, 121, 124, 162, 199–200
  marriage to Catherine Willoughby of, 245
  marriage to Mary Tudor of, 124–25
  succession issue and, 158
  as Viscount Lisle and marshal of army, 80, 121
Brandon, Frances, 162
Brandon, Henry, earl of Lincoln, 156, 214
Brandon, Mary, *see* Mary, duchess of Suffolk
Brandon, William, 30
Brantôme, Seigneur de, 188
Brereton, William, 105, 263
Brigge, Mabel, 266
Brody, John, 169
Brown, Anne, 144–45
Brown, Anthony, 144, 203
Brown, John, 75
Brown, Weston, 144
Browne, Anne (servant), 112
Browne, Anne (wife of Charles Brandon), 121
Bryan, Francis, 103, 105, 112, 144, 159, 217, 285, 300
Buckingham, Edward Stafford, duke of, 65, 82, 105, 109, 152, 154, 157
  execution of, 151
  Henry's suspicions of, 148, 150–51
  wardrobe inventory of, 114
Butler, Agnes, 23
Butler, James, 189
Butts, Dr., 216, 360

Cajetan, Cardinal, 234
Caligula, 343
campaign of 1513, 71–93
  battle of Guinegate ("Battle of the Spurs") in, 87–88, 93

in Calais, 80
  deployment of army in, 82
  in France, 82–93
  Henry's living conditions in, 86
  monetary costs of, 92
  outcome of, 92–93
  preparations in England for, 71–79
  siege of Thérouanne in, 86–88, 89, 92
  siege of Tournai in, 88, 89, 92
  "statutes of war" in, 89
  troops' reactions in, 83–86, 89–90
campaign of 1523, 167–70
  financing of, 168–69, 170, 174
  Henry's motives questioned in, 169–70
  launching of, 167
  popular resentment of, 168–69
  preparations for, 167
  strategies in, 167–68, 169
  territorial claims on France in, 170
campaign of 1539, 294–97
  end of, 296
  popular response to, 294
  English preparations for, 294, 295–96
campaign of 1543, 334–52
  action in France in, 340–48
  Charles's reversal in, 350
  Charles's role in, 342, 343–44, 345, 347,
    350
  English preparations for, 335–39
  financing of, 338–39, 350, 352
  Francis's peace envoys in, 344, 346
  Henry's condition in, 338, 344
  after Henry's return to England, 349–51
  invasion plans of, 334, 335, 337, 338
  Marquison campsite in, 340–42
  provisioning of, 340, 341
  reversals in, 345, 348
  size of English army in, 340
Campeggio, Lorenzo, Cardinal, 116, 165,
    218, 220–23, 225, 226, 351
  character of, 221
  created bishop of Salisbury, 221
  legatine divorce court in England and,
    209, 221–22, 227–29
camp followers, 341–42
Canicida (Henry's horse), 127
Capua, bishop of, 169
Carew, Edward, 86
Carew, Elizabeth Bryan, 105
Carew, Sir Gawen, 284
Carew, George, 350
Carew, Nicholas, 103, 105, 112, 126, 144,
    320, 360

Carey, Mary Boleyn, 159–60, 188, 189, 190,
    207, 215
Carey, William, 144, 159–60, 215
Carlisle, bishop of, 270
Carmeliano, Pietro, 44, 118
Caroz, Spanish ambassador, 58, 59–60, 64,
    65
Carthusian monks, persecution of, 259
carvers, royal, 97, 107
Castiglione, Count Baldassare, 32
Castillon, French envoy, 267, 290–91, 295,
    300–301
castles, changes in structure of, 152
Cavendish, George, 132–33
Cecily, Princess, 40
Chambers, John, 217, 283
Chapel, Giles, 144
Chapuys, imperial ambassador, 234, 242,
    252, 254, 258, 267, 271, 290, 328, 349,
    364
  1543 campaign and, 330, 339, 343, 344,
    346, 347
Charles V, Holy Roman Emperor, 47, 122,
    166–67, 190, 214, 309
  doctrinal questions and, 354
  Henry and, 139–40, 146, 171, 172–73, 190,
    206, 300
  Henry's hostility to, 191, 193–94, 254, 267
  Katherine of Aragon and, 140, 171–72,
    194, 195, 199, 206, 208, 222, 224–25, 238
  marriage to Isabella of, 173
  peasants' revolt and, 172, 174–75
  pensions to English nobility by, 171
  persecution of Protestants by, 268
  relations with France of, 167, 170, 171,
    172–73, 289–91, 295, 309, 334, 338,
    342–45, 347, 350
  Rome captured by, 200
  Wolsey and, 171–73
  see also England; Holy Roman Empire
Charles VIII, king of France, 22
charms, belief in, 265
Cheke, John, 354
Cheyney, Thomas, 296, 297
Chieregato, papal nuncio, 133, 149
Chièvres, minister of Charles V, 156
children:
  buying of, by Henry, 112
  hazards to, 26
chivalry, 60, 73
  Henry's ideals of, 28–29, 72–74, 88, 89,
    165–66, 334
  training in, 28–29, 31–32

choir, royal, 110–11
Christina, duchess of Milan, 298, 299–300
Christopher (royal milliner), 232
Chronicles (Froissart), 72
Chrysostom, 291
Claude, queen of France, 137, 143, 144, 145, 187
cleanliness (personal hygiene), 25–26, 31
Clement VII, Pope, 200–201, 206
    death of, 252
    Henry's divorce suit and, 208, 210–11, 220, 226, 233, 238, 243
    Henry's threats to leave church and, 211
clergy:
    Colet's denigration of, 119
    Cromwell's opposition to, 251
    Henry vs., 250, 252, 254, 357–58
    popular reactions to, 258, 355
    royal investigations of, 273–75
    sexual irregularities of, 274
    Wolsey's fall and, 250
Cleves, Anne of, *see* Anne of Cleves
Cleves, duchy of, strategic value of, 302, 309
Cleves, duke of, 302, 307, 312
Clinton, Lord, 277
clocks, 182, 362
clothing:
    colors and materials of, 113
    elaborateness and costliness of, 113–14
    Henry's opulent style in, 56, 75, 114, 232, 282, 307, 362
    Italianate style of, 44
    for masks, 112–13
    of priests, 119
    royal, care of, 98–99, 113
    sumptuary laws on, 75, 113
Codrus, king of Athens, Henry compared to, 92
coin, shortages and debasement of, 173, 352–53
Colet, John, 100, 118–19
colors of Tudor dynasty, 71
Compton, William, 29, 59, 65, 82, 152, 161, 189
    as court favorite, 105
    death of, 215
conspiracies, *see* court, court life
Constable, Robert, 162
constable of Dover, Henry's title of, 23
cordatissimus, Henry described as, 73–74
Cornish, William, 111, 112
Cornish rebellion (1497), 21–22

Costopolegrino, Bartholomew, 109
Council, royal, 104, 354
    Charles Brandon condemned by, 125
    hostility to 1523 campaign of, 169
    mortal discord in, 319, 366–67, 368, 369, 370
    opposition to Henry by, 76
    power shifts in, 125
    Wolsey's power in, 132
Courtenay, Edward, 29, 318
Courtenay, Henry, 29, 156, 163, 203, 286, 288, 320, 360
Courtenay, Katherine, 29, 43
Courtenay, Margaret, 26, 29
court, court life:
    advantages gained by Henry's attendants in, 100, 104
    banqueting in, 97–98, 106–8, 286
    conspiracies in, 21–22, 24, 34, 44, 148, 150–54, 288, 319, 366, 369
    courtiers' roles in, 106
    decadence of, 285–86
    discomforts of, 25
    festivities in, 24, 25, 40–41, 94–95, 96, 112–13, 179–83, 191–92, 363
    French fashions at, 103–4
    French vs. English manners in, 188
    Henry's favorites in, 103–6, 189
    in Henry's later years, 267, 269, 284–87, 319, 320, 359, 363–64
    Henry's reformation of (1519), 103–4
    Italian influences in, 44–45
    learned elite as favorites in, 115, 118, 119
    marriage irregularities in, 161–62
    murderous conflict in, 319, 366–67, 368, 369
    personal adornments in, 113–14
    romantic concepts in, 60
    royal household arrangements and, 96–102
Cox, Richard, 354
Cranmer, Thomas, archbishop of Canterbury, 240, 271, 280, 308, 326, 363
    church reform and, 258, 292, 293, 354
    in Edward's regency, 371
    Henry's rescue of, 366
Crécy, victory of (1346), 73
Croke, Richard, 234
Cromwell, Thomas, 237, 259, 284, 286, 287, 329, 364
    arrest for heresy of, 311
    character and background of, 251–52

church reform and, 251, 258, 293
in divorce proceedings against Anne of
    Cleves, 309, 310–11
as earl of Essex, 311
execution of, 312
Henry's relations with, 252, 254, 310–11
matchmaking by, 298, 299, 303, 306, 307,
    308
Norfolk as enemy of, 273, 310, 311
unpopularity of, 272, 273, 310
crusades, 38, 72, 74–75, 165–66
Culpepper, Thomas, 326–27

Dacres, Lord, 318
da l'Armi, Ludovico, 351
da Leze, Zuam, 111
da Lodi, Paolo, 90–91
dancing, Henry's ability in, 41, 91, 112
Darcy, Lady, 23
Daubeney, Captain, 21–22
de Athequa, Jorge, 227
de Augustinis, Augustin, 236
de Bornemacker, Jacotyn, 127
Defender of the Faith, Henry's title of, 166
de Foix, Françoise, 188
de la Baume, Étienette, 91
de la Pole, Edmund, 36, 77, 87
dc la Polc, Richard, 36, 77, 87, 111, 138–39,
    156, 168
de la Pole family, claim to English throne of,
    77, 156
de Longueville, duc, 89, 106, 128, 159
Denny, Anthony, 368, 371
de Opitiis, Benedict, 111
de Pescara, Marqués (Fernando Avalos),
    170
de Praet, imperial ambassador, 171, 193
de Puebla, Spanish ambassador, 46, 47, 48,
    50
Derby, earl of (Edward Stanley), 148
Dereham, Francis, 325, 326, 327
de Selve, Odet, 369, 370
des Prés, Josquin, 188
de Victoria, Ferdinand, 155, 195
d'Ewes, Giles, 28
dice:
    fortunetelling with, 110
    gambling at, 109
Dick (king's fool), 24
Diego (king's jester), 24
disguisings (mummeries), 25, 40, 57, 112,
    180–81

divorce of Henry VIII and Katherine of
    Aragon:
    Biblical citations in, 234
    bigamy as alternative to, 207, 222, 223
    Charles V and, 171–72, 194, 195, 199, 206,
        208, 222, 224–25, 238
    church establishment affected by, 250–51
    "decretal commission" in, 222
    English legatine court and, 199, 200, 209,
        221–22, 226–29
    Henry's canonical studies relating to, 218,
        222, 233–34, 238, 250
    Henry's draft bulls and, 207
    Henry's motives in, 197–98, 224
    invalidity of marriage declared (1533), 240
    More's opposition to, 256
    as nullity suit, 199
    papal action on, 207, 208, 209, 210–11,
        218, 220–22, 226, 233, 238
    papal marital dispensation as issue in, 42,
        53, 199, 200, 221, 226
    popular reaction to, 206, 222–23, 224,
        241–42, 252
    scholarly disputes on, 234–35
    status in 1530 of, 234
    succession issue and, 197, 222, 224
    trade disruptions due to, 214
    Wolsey and, 200–201, 205, 206–7, 211,
        218, 221, 225–26, 228
Douglas, Archibald, earl of Angus, 199
Douglas, Margaret, 319, 332
dry stamp, royal, 368
Du Bellay, French ambassador, 218, 222,
    225, 230, 238
Dudley, Edmund, 269
Dudley, John, duke of Northumberland,
    148, 360, 364, 368, 371
Duque, Hernán, 44, 46

carl marshal of England, Henry's title of, 24
economy:
    coin supply and, 173, 352–53
    in 1520s, 173, 213
    financing of campaigns and, 92, 168–69,
        170, 174, 338–39, 350, 352
    inflation and, 213, 353
    nobles affected by, 152
    wool industry and, 214, 353
Edmund, Prince, 26
Edward, earl of Warwick, 34, 36, 157
Edward III, king of England, 33, 72
Edward IV, king of England, 33, 36, 50, 77

Edward VI, king of England (Prince Edward), son of Henry VIII, 302, 332, 363, 369
  betrothed to Mary Stuart, 334
  birth and christening of, 279, 280–81
  education of, 354
  factions supporting, 283
  frail health of, 324, 331
  Henry's last days and, 369, 370–71
  regency planned for, 370–71
  royal responsibilities undertaken by, 363–64
  succession of, 369
Eleanor of Castile, 52
Elizabeth, countess of Suffolk, 36, 77
Elizabeth, Princess, 23
Elizabeth I, queen of England, daughter of Henry VIII, 259–60, 280, 332, 370
  birth of, 245
  legitimacy of, 261, 271
Elizabeth of York, mother of Henry VIII, 23, 25, 26, 29, 41, 45, 77
  death of, 42–43
  descriptions of, 21, 36
  family life of, 36
  lineage of, 36
  piety of, 35, 42
  popularity of, 21, 35, 36
Eltham Palace, 27, 127
engineers, in war services, 336–37, 344
England:
  condition of, at Henry's death, 370
  in fifteenth century, 44
  in 1511 Holy League, 75–93
  in 1523 alliance with Charles V against France, 167–70
  in 1527 alliance with France, 191, 192, 198, 205
  in 1539 campaign against France and Empire, 290–91, 294–97, 309, 334
  1543 alliance with Charles V against France, 334–52
  France as traditional enemy of, 29
  nobles vs. king in, 151–52
English church, see Reformation, English
entertainment and games, 29, 230, 363–64
  Henry as patron of, 56–57, 106–14
epidemics, 51–52, 83, 86, 149–50, 212–18, 348, 351
  healers and miracle-workers and, 149
Erasmus of Rotterdam, 29, 36, 61–62, 73–74, 75, 78, 120, 158, 185, 189, 221, 237, 312

  consulted on marriage issue, 160, 162–63, 197
  critics of, 116, 117
  New Testament translation of, 117, 251
  view of Henry's intellect by, 27–28, 116, 118
  wish for residence at Henry's court, 117–18
Essex, earl of, 295, 340
Evil May Day (1517), 148–49, 154
ewerers, 97

Falier, Venetian ambassador, 223
Famagosta, bishop of, 75
famine, 1527–28, 213–14
Featherstone, Richard, 313
Fécamp, abbot of, 60–61
Felipe, Francisco, 199
Ferdinand, king of Spain:
  Henry VII and, 39, 42, 46, 47, 48, 49
  Henry VIII and, 58, 59, 64, 81–82, 173
  in Holy League against France, 77, 81–82, 92
Fernández, Diego, 63, 64, 66
Feron, Robert, 249–50
Field of Cloth of Gold (1520), 131–46
  Anglo-French relations and, 131, 138–39, 145–46
  atmosphere and mood at, 139, 145–46
  common people at, 142–43, 146
  competitive events in, 143–44
  consequences of, 146
  events in London during, 146–47
  exchange of gifts at, 145
  food supplies for, 135–36
  pavilions at, described, 141–42
  planning and negotiations for, 135–36
  precedence issues in, 136, 143
  rules of combat in, 136
Fisher, John, bishop of Rochester, 37–38, 58, 118, 198–99, 202, 224, 228, 234
  execution of, 255–56, 267
Fitzroy, Henry, natural son of Henry VIII, 159, 215, 222
  death of, 272
  marriage plans for, 194
  marriage to Mary Howard of, 261
  as possible successor, 160, 163–64, 194
  titles bestowed son, 163
Fitzwilliam, William, 364
Flanders, 338, 339
  gunnery making in, 71, 75

Henry as viewed in, 243
trade relations with, 214, 353
Fleuranges, French knight, 144
Flodden, English victory at (1513), 93
food:
  pageantry in, 107, 191–92
  preparation and serving of, 97–98, 106–8
  sumptuary laws on, 106, 153
fools:
  Henry's favorite, 362–63
  musicians as, 111, 363
foreigners, hatred of, 146–47, 148, 150,
  192–93
fortifications, building of, 336–37
fortunetelling, 110
Fox, Richard, bishop of Winchester, 23, 58,
  60, 76, 82, 132, 133
Foxe, Edward, 209, 210–11, 220, 250
Foxe, John, 365
France, 29
  in alliance with Empire, 289, 290, 294–97,
    309, 334
  in alliance with Turks, 290, 334
  Charles V as enemy of, 139, 146, 205, 206,
    214, 289–90, 334–52
  court manners in, 188
  English claims in, 71–73, 170
  English partisans of, at Henry's court,
    103–4
  famine relief to England from, 214
  1513 campaign against, 71–93
  1520 relations with England of, 131,
    138–39, 145–46
  1523 campaign against, 167–70
  in 1527 alliance with England, 191,
    192–93, 198, 205
  1539 campaign against, 294–97
  1543 campaign against, 334–52
  1546 alliance with England of, 354, 368
  papacy vs., 74–93
  ties with Scotland of, 87, 295, 301, 318,
    334, 344, 346
  Venice and, 166, 167
  see also Charles VIII; Francis I; Louis XII
Francis I, king of France, 104, 111, 161, 166,
  203
  bellicosity of, 138
  as captive of Charles V, 170
  character of, 137–38, 188
  doctrinal questions and, 354
  at Field of Cloth of Gold tournament,
    131–46

Henry and, 136, 137, 138–39, 142, 143,
  144, 145–46, 184, 254, 300–301
  Henry compared with, 95, 137
  Mary Tudor and, 123, 125
  persecution of Protestants by, 268
  see also France
Froissart, Jean, 72
Fuensalida, Spanish envoy, 50, 51, 53
fustigation, as remedy, 361

gambling, 29, 108–10
  Henry's pleasure in, 108–9, 232
  as "king's largesse," 90
Gardiner, Stephen, bishop of Winchester,
  209, 210–11, 217, 220, 293, 310, 332,
  354, 364, 371
  Catherine Parr opposed by, 365
Garrett, Thomas, 313
Gelderland (Gelders), 302, 309
Gigli, Silvestro, 44
Giovacchiono (Joachim), French agent, 172
Giovio, Paolo, 208
Giustiniani, Venetian envoy, 94, 109, 126,
  133, 134, 138, 166
Goose, John, 24
Governatore (Henry's horse), 127–28
grace, as noble quality, 32
Great Harry (Henri Grâce à Dieu) (Henry's
  flagship), 78, 141, 286, 350
Great Sapphire of Glastonbury, 362
Greek, study of, 116, 117
Greenwich, "highest library" at, 116
Grey, Elizabeth, 121
Grey, Lord Leonard, 146, 318
Grysacre, Anne, 162
guaiacum (lignum vitae), 362
Guildford, Edward, 55, 127
Guildford, Henry, 103, 104, 112, 180, 240
Guînes, 131, 141, 142, 336–37
Guise, Louise de, 301
Guise, Marie de, 295, 301
Guise, Renée de, 301
Guislain, Guillaume de, 90
Gyldon, Thomas, 154

hair styles, 114
Hale, John, 249–50, 252
Hales, Christopher, 257
Hall, Edward, 54, 103, 104, 149, 154, 175,
  192
Hall, Mary, 325

Hampton Court, 179, 181, 286
    as Wolsey's gift to Henry, 182
handguns, use of, 80–81
Hapsburg dynasty:
    in alliance with Valois, 290
    Tudor family ties with, 47, 167
Harlock, William, 242
Harris, Ann, 98
Haschenperg, Stefan von, 344
Hastings, Anne, 215
Hastings, Sir George, 65
Hasylden, Thomas, 356
hawking, 363
Hély, mistress of Francis I, 203
Hennage, Thomas, 209–10, 217, 326
Henry, infant son of Henry VIII, 66–67
Henry V, king of England, 71–72, 73, 89
Henry VII, king of England, 21–25, 41, 53,
    174
    alchemy as interest of, 34, 46
    alliance with Philip of Castile by, 47
    angry outbursts of, 51
    court life of, 24–25, 27, 34, 45
    death of, 52
    death of wife and, 42–43
    descriptions of, 34–35
    diplomatic style of, 46–47
    French military engagements of, 22
    genealogy of, 33
    heretics persecuted by, 46
    influence of mother on, 37
    Italianate tastes of, 44–45
    Katherine of Aragon and, 48–49
    monarchy exalted by, 45
    personality of, 34–35
    piety of, 34–35, 46
    plots and rebellions against, 21–22, 34, 44
    popular view of, 33–34, 35, 44
    relic collections of, 34, 46
    royal matches for his children arranged
        by, 45–49
    son Henry and, 35, 46, 51, 185, 253, 269
    wealth of, 45
Henry VIII, king of England:
    amorous excesses attributed to, 252–53,
        285
    anger as diplomatic tool of, 185, 269, 319
    architectural enterprises of, 182, 235,
        286–87, 336–37, 344, 347
    art of government studied by, 44, 46–47
    birth and christening of, 23
    boyhood restrictions on, 50–52
    carefree life criticized in, 57–58, 103
    ceremonial titles of, 23–24
    childhood hazards to, 21–23
    chivalric glory sought by, 28–29, 72–74,
        88, 89, 165–66, 334
    clothing of, 56, 75, 98–99, 113, 114, 232,
        282, 307, 362
    complex personality of, 115, 120, 184,
        264, 268, 269
    conscience of, 197–98, 218, 254
    court favorites of, in early life, 103–6, 115,
        118, 119
    creative power of, at peak, 235
    crusading ambitions of, 71, 74–75, 165–66
    dancing ability of, 41, 91, 112
    dark side of, 183–85, 217, 237–38, 288,
        319–20, 328–29, 366–67, 369
    death fears of, 43, 150, 217, 370
    death of, 371–72
    dependants supported by, 233
    descriptions of, 21, 50, 54, 91, 95, 157,
        223, 264–65, 301
    as duke of York, 24–35
    education of, 27–32
    as example for subjects, 74, 242
    excesses in eating and drinking of, 328–29
    father as seen by, 35
    fellow-sovereigns' effect on, 268
    fighting ardor of, 29, 59, 60–61, 72–79, 82,
        86, 90, 170, 233, 338
    gambling by, 108–9, 232
    grandmother's influence on, 28, 36–38, 53,
        58
    Henry V as heroic model for, 83, 89,
        172–73
    horses of, 127–28, 232–33, 363
    hunting as pleasure of, 24, 30–31, 184–85,
        217, 233, 322–23, 363, 368
    illnesses of, 237, 238, 282–83, 338, 359,
        360–62, 368–69
    infidelities of, 65, 158–60, 188, 190, 243,
        252, 260
    jousting by, 59–60, 90–91, 125–27
    judicial violence of, 318–20
    language abilities of, 115–16
    last months of, 359–71
    legendary aspects of, 264–65, 267, 357
    mother's death and, 43
    musical ability and interests of, 24, 57,
        106, 110, 235
    physicality of, 30, 50, 56, 59, 90–91, 232
    poetry and songs created by, 57, 58–59,
        110, 235, 238
    portraits of, 21, 185, 264, 363, 370

practical nature of, 134–35, 185, 237, 286, 295, 335–37, 368, 369, 370
as prince of Wales, 41–52
religions beliefs of, 62, 119, 165–66, 198, 217–18, 329–30, 354
resemblance to father of, 185, 253, 269
royal manner in early years of, 46, 56–63, 90–91, 101, 103–4
royal manner in mature years of, 103, 114, 185, 253–54, 267–69, 285–87
royal manner in old age, 329, 349, 357–58, 368
self-doubts of, 183, 217, 268
self-image of, 166, 253–54, 349
subjects' attitude toward, 54–55, 89–92, 151, 154, 168–69, 173–74, 243, 249–50, 253, 254, 259, 264–65, 267, 284, 320, 353, 356–57, 371
suspiciousness of, 269, 288, 319
tomb of, 217, 371
ulcerous legs of, 237, 282, 283, 329, 338, 360
violence of, 318–21, 335
wealth of, 61, 109, 114
will of, 217, 370–71
see also specific persons and topics
Herbert, William, 368, 371
heresy, 46
　　Erasmus accused of, 117
heretics, 46
　　persecution in Europe of, 268
　　see also Reformation, English
Hetherington, William, 162
hippocras wine, 108
Hispaniola, 194
Hobbes, Emily, 23
Holbein, Hans, 264, 283, 300, 303, 306
Holland, Bess, 161–62
Holy Land, see Jerusalem
Holy League (1511), 75–93, 119
Holy Roman Empire:
　　England and, see England
　　France and, see France
　　in Holy League, 77, 81, 82, 92
　　unrest in, 172, 174–75, 268, 290
　　see also Charles V; Flanders; Maximilian I; Netherlands
Hopkins, Nicholas, 151
horsemanship, 30–31
　　Italianate style of, 126–27
　　Spanish style of, 128
horses:
　　Henry's love of, 127–28, 232–33, 363

royal accommodations for, 98, 127
as royal gifts, 127, 128, 145
for war service, 336, 338
household, royal, 96–102
　　categories of service staffs in, 96–99, 235
　　eating arrangements of, 97–98, 106–8
　　guests' retinues and, 101
　　hangers-on in, 101-2
　　Henry's supervision of, 101, 102
　　moving of, 98
　　officers of, 97–98
　　outdoor services for, 98
　　in personal service to king, 98–100
　　pros and cons of service in, 100–101
　　vice and petty criminality in, 102
Howard, Catherine:
　　adultery of, 324, 325–29
　　degrading of, 326
　　description of, 321
　　effect on Henry of, 321–22
　　execution of, 327
　　family's desertion of, 366
　　Henry's estrangement from, 322
　　Henry's infatuation with, 309–10
　　wedding of, 313
Howard, Edward, 55, 67, 76, 78
Howard, Elizabeth Stafford, duchess of Norfolk, 161–62
Howard, Henry, earl of Surrey, 366–67
Howard, Thomas, 2nd duke of Norfolk, earl of Surrey, 55, 76, 93, 103, 125
Howard, Thomas, 3rd duke of Norfolk, earl of Surrey, 79, 161, 193, 201, 203, 214, 215, 223, 236, 251, 266, 272, 280, 282, 319, 322
　　Anne Boleyn and, 188–89, 231, 240, 241
　　Cromwell and, 251, 273, 310, 311
　　in 1539 campaign, 295
　　in 1543 campaign, 338, 339, 342, 344, 345, 347, 348, 350
　　imprisonment and trial of (1546), 366, 371, 372
　　rebels fought by, 278
　　as religious conservative, 293, 354
　　royal ambitions of, 366
humanism, 312, 354
　　attitude to chivalry and war in, 73, 119
　　church vs., 116
　　Henry and, 61, 73–74, 118
　　More and, 357
　　as New Learning, 117
　　Reformation and, 292–93, 354, 355, 364

humanism, *(cont.)*
  see also Erasmus of Rotterdam
Hundred Years' War, 29, 72
hunting:
  court life and, 24–25, 30–31, 98, 106
  Henry's skill and enthusiasm in, 24, 30–31, 184–85, 217, 233, 322–23, 363, 368
Hurst Castle, 295
Hussey, John, 279, 285, 287–88

Injunctions (1538), 354–55
Ireland, rebellion in, 265, 268
Isabella, queen of Spain, 42, 47, 74
Isabella of Portugal, 173
Isle of Wight, French landings on (1545), 351
Italy, 351
  art of the manage (horsemanship) in, 126–27
  imperial ambitions in, 172
  influence in England of, 44–45
  as locus of competition (mid-1520s), 170
  Renaissance in, 73

James IV, king of Scotland, 22, 87, 93
  marriage to Margaret Tudor of, 45
James V, king of Scotland, 295, 301, 318, 323
  death of, 334
  as prince, 156
  wife Madeleine of, 301
  wife Marie de Guise of, 295
Jaspar, Stephen, 56
Jerningham, Richard, 144
Jerome, Saint, 117
Jerome, William, 313
Jerusalem, 72
  Henry's aid to, 74, 165
  under Ottoman Turks, 165
jewelry, Henry's taste in, 114
Joachim (Giovacchiono), French agent, 172
Joanna, queen of Castile, 47–48
John of St. Martin, Friar, 74
jousts and tourneys, 24, 55, 233, 304
  at Field of Cloth of Gold (1520), 131–46
  Henry's ardor for, 59–60, 90–91, 125–27
  spectacular feats in, 126
Julius II, Pope, 166
  in Holy League against France, 74–75, 77, 81, 82

Katherine, countess of Devonshire, 233

Katherine of Aragon:
  accused of treachery, 225
  campaign against Scots supervised by, 87, 92, 93
  Charles V and, 140, 171–72, 194, 195, 199, 206, 208, 222, 224–25, 238
  court intrigues and, 105
  death of, 262
  descriptions of, 40, 54, 66, 94, 144
  dispossession of (1533), 240
  divorce issue and, 160, 195, 196–97, 198, 200, 202, 204, 206, 207, 211, 221–22, 224–26, 227–28, 234, 235, 238; *see also* divorce of Henry VIII and Katherine of Aragon
  estate of, disputes over, 299
  exile of, 261–62
  Field of Cloth of Gold and, 139, 143, 144, 145
  first marriage question and, 42, 53, 157, 160, 162–63, 197, 207, 226, 227, 228
  first son and, 66–67
  Fitzroy and, 164
  Henry's behavior toward, 49, 64, 66, 156, 160–61, 195, 203, 204, 210, 217, 224, 225–26, 230, 244, 260
  Henry's betrothal to, 48
  Henry's first meeting with, 39–40
  intellectual abilities of, 117
  isolation among English of, 194
  marriage to Arthur of, 39–41
  marriage to Henry of, 53–55
  piety of, 66, 163, 194
  popularity of, 40, 223, 227
  pregnancies of, 63–65, 66, 71, 155–56
  as "princess dowager," 244
  as regent, in 1513 campaign, 71, 76, 87
  succession issue and, 155–56, 157, 163, 194–95, 197
  widowhood of, 48–49
  Wolsey and, 171, 194, 195, 196
Kebet, William, 233
King's Book (1543), 353–54
"king's riding boys," 98
Kingston, William, 144
king's ward, makeup of, 82
kissing, English custom of, 158
Knevet, Anthony, 105, 144, 232
Knevet, Charles, 151
Knevet, Henry, 105
Knevet, Thomas, 67
Knight, William, 207
knighthood, ideals of, 60

Knight of the Bath, Henry's title of, 24
Knights of the Garter, 96, 320-21
  Henry's title of, 24
Kratzer, Nicholas, 182
Kyrkenar, Erasmus, 335

Lambert, John, 294
Lamentations of a Sinner, The (Parr), 333
Lancaster, house of, 23, 33, 36, 317-18
Lassells, John, 325
Latimer, Hugh, 258
Latin:
  as diplomatic language, 116
  in translation of New Testament, 117, 354,
    358
learning (scholarship):
  conflictatiunculae and, 116
  Henry's abilities in, 27-28, 115-18, 362
  Henry as patron of, 61-62, 115, 118, 235
  religious doctrine and, 116-18, 234
Lee, Richard, 337
le Negro, Peter, 109
Leo X, Pope, 90, 165
life expectancies, 282
Linacre, Thomas, 118
Lisle, Lady, 279, 285, 287, 304
Lisle, Lord, governor of Calais, 279, 287, 318
liturgy in English, 354
Lollard doctrines, 258
London:
  riots against foreigners in, 146-47, 148, 150
  sweating sickness in, 51, 149, 212-18, 279,
    280
London, John, 275
Longland, John, bishop of Lincoln, 161,
    197, 206
lord lieutenant of Ireland, Henry's title of,
    24
Louis XII, king of France, 60, 66, 81, 95
  disinclination for fighting of, 83
  Henry's belligerence toward, 60-61
  marriage to Mary Tudor of, 123
  as schismatic, 74-75
Louise of Savoy, 138, 143, 144, 145, 201
love, English view of, 159
Luke, Ann, 23, 233
Luther, Martin, 172, 174, 200, 251
  Henry and, 238, 291
  Henry's book against, 218
  Katherine supported by, 238
Lutherans, 290, 293, 311
  in doctrinal differences with Henry, 291,
    293

persecution in England of, 313
political alignments of, 291, 302

Madeleine, daughter of Francis I, 270
magic and occult, 172, 262, 361
  court intrigues and, 22, 34-35, 46
  Henry as focus of, 265-67
  marvels and, 242-43
  religious objects used for, 356
  Wolsey and, 154
magnanimity, as noble quality, 32
majesty, ideal qualities of, 31-32
manage (horsemanship), 126-27
manners (civility and courtesy), 29, 31-32
Manox, Henry, 325
Mantua, marquis of, 127-28
Margaret, countess of Salisbury, *see* Pole,
  Margaret
Margaret, queen of Scotland, sister of
    Henry VIII, 23, 24, 25, 26, 27, 301, 334
  as Arthur's heir, 41
  marriage to James IV of, 45
  second and third husbands of, 199
Margaret (Beaufort), countess of Richmond,
    28, 33, 40, 244
  death of, 58
  Henry as heir of, 37
  influence on Henry of, 28, 36-38, 53, 58
  intellectual abilities of, 37-38
  piety of, 38
  as "rightful queen of England," 37
Margaret of Angoulême, 45
Margaret of Savoy, 53, 66, 81, 88, 91, 227
  Charles Brandon and, 122-23
Marguerite, daughter of Francis I, 298
Maria, niece of Charles V, 194
Marillac, French ambassador, 306-7, 319,
    323, 330, 337
marshal, royal household, 102, 108
martial training, 29, 30-31, 59-60
Mary, duchess of Suffolk, sister of Henry
    VIII, 23, 26, 27, 112, 144, 241
  daughter Frances of, 162
  death of, 245
  Francis I and, 123, 125
  galley named for *(Virgin Mary)*, 108
  Henry's fondness for, 150
  marriage plans for, 48, 122, 123
  marriage to Charles Brandon of, 123,
    124-25
  as queen of France, 123
  son Henry born to, 155
Mary, regent of Flanders, 338

Mary I, queen of England, daughter of
    Henry VIII, 222, 280, 281, 322, 332
  birth of, 155
  factions in support of, 283
  Henry's feelings for, 157, 184, 192, 260,
    269, 271–72, 285
  isolation of, 261–62
  Katherine's pride in, 194
  as "Lady Mary," 261
  legitimacy of, 198, 224, 272
  marriage plans for, 167, 173, 191, 198, 205
  as pawn in divorce proceedings, 226
  as "Princess of Wales," 163
  return to court of, 329
  succession of, possibilities for, 158, 160,
    163, 164, 369
masks, 112–13
  as mirror of court life, 113
  see also disguisings
Maximilian I, Holy Roman Emperor, 77, 81,
    82, 92
  crusades and, 74, 165
May Day festivities, 94–96, 192–93
medicine, 283, 361–62
  Henry's preparations of, 361–62, 363
medieval institutions, 152, 250
medieval scholasticism, 116, 233, 234
Melanchthon, 320
Memo, Dionysius, 103, 111, 150
Menaechmi (Plautus), 182
Mendoza, imperial ambassador, 193–94,
    195, 221, 223, 224
mercenaries, 80, 111, 169, 302, 345, 351
Merlin legends, 265
Milan, city of, 289, 291
Mirror of Naples diamond, 123, 125
Misselden, John and Robert, 352
monasteries (religious houses), 292
  corruption in, 273–75
  dissolution of, 275–76
  see also clergy
Mont, Christopher, 302
Montreuil, English siege of, 342, 344, 345,
    347–48
More, Blind, 111
More, Thomas, 27, 40, 83, 115, 117, 118,
    139, 161, 163, 267, 274
  as chancellor, 235
  execution of, 256–57
  Henry's reliance on, 120, 269
Mortimer, Margaret, 121, 162
Most Christian King, Henry's title of, 75
Mouldwarp (Mole), Henry as, 265, 267

Mountjoy, Lord (William Blount), 27, 61,
    62, 118, 155
Mouton, Claude, 188
mummeries, see disguisings
music, musicians:
  at court, changes in, 235
  foreign, at court, 111, 235
  Henry's interest and ability in, 24, 57, 106,
    110, 235
  in royal household, 110–12, 235

Nagel, Hans, 111–12
navy, English, 141
  artillery in, 108
  enlargement of, after 1513, 132
  in 1513 campaign, 71, 76, 77–78
  in 1523 campaign, 167
  in 1543 campaign, 350–51
Necessary Doctrine and Erudition for Any
    Christian Man, A, 353–54
Netherlands, 268, 290
  see also Margaret of Savoy
Neville, Edward, 55, 59, 103, 104–5, 112,
    181, 320, 360
Neville, John (executed 1541), 318
Neville, John (husband of Catherine Parr),
    332
Neville, William, 266
New Learning, see humanism
New Testament, translations of, 117, 251,
    354, 358
New World, interest in, 194, 285
New Year's Boy, 66–67, 155
nobles:
  conspiracies and, 21–22, 24, 34, 44, 148,
    150–54, 288, 319, 366, 369
  Henry vs., 150, 151–52
  housing conditions of, 25
  mortal conflicts among, 319, 366–67, 368,
    369
  see also court, court life
Nonsuch Palace, 287
Norfolk, dukes of, see Howard
Normandy, English claims to, 72
Norris, Henry, 105, 112, 263, 271
Nowell (royal minstrel), 235

"Old Copper-Nose" (Henry's nickname),
    353
"On Preserving Marriage" (De servando
    conjugio), 162–63
Order of the Garter, see Knights of the
    Garter

Order of the Golden Fleece, 47
Orio, Venetian ambassador, 163, 164
Ottoman Turks, 165, 290
Our Lady of Friendship (proposed church), 145, 146
Oursian, Nicolas, 182
Overstein, earl of, 308
Oxford, earl of, 295

Pace, Richard, 116, 117, 118, 134, 156, 207–8
pages, royal, 99
Paget, William, 365, 368, 370, 371
Pallet, Edward, 29
papacy:
    authority question of, 354
    corruption of, 207–8
    dispensations in marriage arrangements by, 42, 53, 199, 200, 221, 226
    Henry's break with, 250–51, 252
    Henry's commitment to, 75, 165–66
    Wolsey's ambitions and, 132, 173, 205
    see also divorce of Henry VIII and Katherine of Aragon; and individual popes
Parliament:
    dissolution of monastic houses by, 275–76
    1523 campaign and, 169, 170
    Henry's 1545 speech in, 357–58
    law on queen's behavior by, 330–31
    Reformation, 250, 258, 354
Parr, Catherine, 369, 370, 371
    background of, 333
    character of, 332, 333
    in orthodoxy question, 364–66
    piety of, 333–34
    as regent, in 1543 campaign, 345, 346
    wedding of, 332–33
Parr, Thomas, 105
Parr, William, 105, 333
Pasqualigo, Venetian envoy, 94, 95–96
"Pastime with Good Company" (song by Henry VIII), 110
Patch (king's fool), 24
Paul III, Pope, 295, 354
    Henry excommunicated by, 290
Pavia, victory at (1525), 170, 290
peasants' revolts:
    in England, 173–74, 175, 276–77
    in imperial territories, 172, 174–75
Pechy, John, 55, 58, 103, 104, 139
Penys, Lord, 77
Percy, Henry, 189–90, 236
Pérez de Almazán, Miguel, 52

Pero (royal minstrel), 235
Perpoynte, William, 112
Philip I, king of Castile, 47
Philip of Hesse, 302
physicians, 261, 262, 283
Pilgrimage of Grace rebellion (1536), 276–79, 317
    basis of, 272–73, 276
Plantagenet dynasty, 29, 47, 317–18
Plautus, 182
plays and pageants, 182–83, 192
poetry and song, Henry's creations in, 57, 58–59, 110, 235, 238
Pole, Geoffrey, 77, 288
Pole, Henry, Lord Montague, 77, 105, 288, 318, 320, 360
Pole, Margaret, countess of Salisbury, 36, 105, 157, 288, 318
Pole, Reginald, Cardinal, 51, 77, 151, 198, 254, 288, 295, 310, 318
Poor Knights, 371
"Pope July" game, 230
Popenruyter, Hans, 75
Popyncort, Jane, 159
posset, described, 108
Powell, Edward, 313
Poynings, Lord, 360
Poyntes, Elizabeth, 67
Poyntz, Edward, 103, 104, 112
Praise of Folly, The (Erasmus), 117
Prayers or Meditations (Parr), 333
precious metals, search for, 352
pretenders to throne, 22, 24, 34, 36, 44, 77, 111
privy chamber, royal, 99
progresses, royal (traveling court), 22, 317, 322–23
prophecies:
    concerning Henry and Anne, 242, 265
    of Mouldwarp, 265
Prosopopoeia Britanniae (Erasmus), 27–28
Protestants, strains among sects of, 293

Radclyf, Roger, 58
Rainsford, Humphrey, 203
Ratto, Giovanni, 127–28
rebellions, 21–22, 34, 44, 148–49
    against Amicable Grant, 173–74, 175
    peasants', 172, 173–75, 276–77
    as Pilgrimage of Grace (1536), 272–73, 276–79, 317
    trade disruptions as cause of, 214

Reformation, English:
  Catholic orthodoxy and, 291, 293, 354
  church reorganization and, 250–51, 252,
    253–54
  clergy and, 250–52, 254, 258, 273–75, 355,
    357–58
  doctrinal changes and, 291, 293–94,
    354–56
  general theory of sovereignty and, 252
  Henry's doctrinal knowledge and, 291–92,
    293–94, 354
  Henry's excommunication and, 243, 290
  Henry's supremacy of English church
    and, 250–54, 259
  persecutions resulting from, 255–59, 267,
    268, 293, 294, 313, 318–19, 364–66
  popular reactions to, 258–59, 268, 272,
    273, 276, 354–56
  religious houses destroyed in, 273–75, 292
  roots of, 258
relics, 34, 75, 145
religious doctrine:
  on baptism, 293
  Holy League and, 119
  learned disputations on, 116
  popular practices vs., 355–56
  on transubstantiation, 293–94
  see also Bible; clergy; Henry VIII;
    heresy; heretics; humanism; Luther,
    Martin; Lutherans; papacy; Protes-
    tants; Reformation, English
Renaissance, influence in England of, 56, 73
Renée, daughter of Louis XII, 206
residences:
  of king, see specific palaces
  of nobility, 25
Richard, duke of York, 22
Richard III, king of England, 30, 33, 36, 237
Richards, Gryffyn, 58
Richmond Palace, 36
Robin Hood legend, 94–95
Robyns, John, 267
Rochford, Lady, 260, 322, 326, 327–28
"Rockers," 23
Rogers, John, 337
Rome, fall to Charles V of, 200–201
Round Table, romantic ideal of, 60
Rovezzano, Benedetto da, 201
Roy, Peter, 109
Russell, John, 243, 306, 344
Ruthal, Thomas, bishop of Durham, 58, 76,
    82, 108
  Council position of, 125, 132

  as lord privy seal, 132
Rutter, John, 132

sacramentaries, 293, 311, 313
Sadler, English envoy, 334
Sagudino, Niccolo, 94, 138
St. James's Palace, 286
St. John, John, 29
"Saint Trinian's Fast," 266
Sandys, William, 180–81
Saxony, elector of, 302
Scarpinello, Milanese ambassador, 185
Scaticia, Giovanni, 127
Schmalkaldic League, 291, 302, 309
Scot (king's fool), 24
Scotland, 295, 323
  cost of 1540s wars with, 352
  in 1542 peace treaty, 334
  rebellions in, 92, 93, 265
  renewal of hostilities in 1543 of, 334–35
  ties with France of, 87, 295, 301, 318, 334,
    344, 346
  see also James IV; James V
Scotus, John Duns, 116
Selim I the Grim, 165
semi-Pelagianism, 292
"Seven Sisters" (guns), 93
sewers, royal, 97, 105, 107
Sexton (Henry's jester), 362
Seymour, Edward, earl of Hertford, 287,
    332, 335, 344, 360, 363, 364
  Edward's regency and, 370–71
  Howard trial and, 366–67
  power and wealth of, 368, 369
Seymour, Jane, 260, 299, 371
  death of, 281–82
  family background of, 271
  marriage of, 271
  son Edward born to, 279
Seymour, Thomas, 333
Sforza, Francesco, 299
Sheen, palace of, 21, 22–23
Shelton, Margaret, 260, 298
Simnel, Lambert, 36
Six Articles (1539), 293, 354
Skelton, John, 28, 73, 112, 153
Skipwith, Mary, 298
Smeaton, Mark, 235, 263
Smith, Richard, 361
social order:
  from medieval to humanist view of, 73
  peasants' revolt and, 174–75
  waning of feudal powers and, 152

Somers, Will, 362–63
Song of the Lady Bessy, The, 36
Spain, *see* Ferdinand, king of Spain
spies, spying, 76, 111–12, 139, 296, 338
sports, *see specific sports*
Stafford, Anne, Lady Hastings, 65, 158
Stafford, Edward, *see* Buckingham, duke of
Stafford, Elizabeth (Buckingham's sister), 65
Stafford, Elizabeth, *see* Howard, Elizabeth Stafford, duchess of Norfolk
Stanley, Lord Thomas, 33
Stanley, Sir William, 22
Star Chamber, 154
Stewart, Henry, 199
Stokesley, John, 118
Stuart, Mary, 334
succession, problem of, 154, 155–64, 183
    Anne Boleyn and, 191, 260, 261, 263
    candidates in, 156, 158, 163–64, 194, 271–72
    diplomacy and, 158
    English law on, 158, 250
    Henry's aging and, 260, 261
    Henry's divorce from Katherine and, 197, 222, 224
    Prince Edward and, 281, 302
    solution of, upon Henry's death, 370–72
    Succession Act and, 250
Suffolk, duke of, *see* Brandon, Charles
Suleiman, Sultan, 290
sumptuary laws, 75, 106, 153
surgeons, 283, 342
sweating sickness, 51–52, 83, 149–50, 212–18, 243
    as God's punishment, 51, 212
    preventives and cures claimed for, 149, 212, 213, 216
syphilis, 362

Taberet, Peter, 235
Talbot, captain of Calais, 86
Talbot, Mary, 190
Talboys, Gilbert, 159
Ten Articles (1536), 291, 293
tennis, 109, 182, 232
Thérouanne, siege of, 86–88, 89, 92
Third Order of Saint Francis, 194
time, variations in reckoning of, 182
Torrigiano (sculptor), 44, 185
Tour d'Ordre ("Old Man"), 343
Tournai:
    English sale to French of, 137

sieges of, 73, 88, 89, 92
Tower of London, 21, 42, 319
transubstantiation doctrine, 293–94
treason laws, English Reformation and, 258–59, 293, 310
Treviso, Girolamo da, 344, 347
Tudor-Lancaster relationship, 23, 36, 77n, 317–18
Tuerdus, Baltasar, 134
Tuke, Brian, 212, 216, 217, 287
Tunstall, Cuthbert, bishop of Durham, 158, 193, 225, 292, 371
Turenne, comte de, 191
Twelfth Night festivities, 25
"Twelve Apostles" (guns), 71

ushers, gentlemen, 97

Val Doré, 1520 tournament at, 131
Valois dynasty, 290
Van Arcle, Gerrard, 98
Van der Delft, imperial ambassador, 365, 368, 369
Vannes, Peter, 44, 118
Venice, 166, 167
Vergil, Polydore, 44
Vicary, Thomas, 283, 329
Vives, Juan Luis, 163, 224, 227, 234

Walsingham shrine, 67
war:
    arms and equipment for, 71, 75–76, 80–81, 335–37, 344
    changing role of nobles in, 152
    costs of, 92, 168–69, 170, 174, 338–39, 350, 352
    as diplomatic alternative, 82
    execution of deserters in, 342
    humanists' attitude toward, 73, 119
    as knightly ideal, 72–73
    lack of standing armies and, 152
    mercenaries in, 80, 111, 169, 302, 345, 351
    religious doctrine and, 119
    see also specific campaigns
Warbeck, Perkin, 22
warden of the Cinque Ports, Henry's title of, 23–24
warden of the Scottish Marches, Henry's title of, 24
wardrobe servants, royal, 98–99
Warham, William, archbishop of Canterbury, 53, 76, 118, 132, 174, 202, 224, 225

Warwick, earl of (false), 34
Webbe, William, 253
Weston, Francis, 235, 263
Whitehall Palace, 286
  as chief royal residence, 359–60
William (queen's fool), 36
Willoughby, Catherine, *see* Brandon, Catherine
wines, 107–8
Wingfield, Richard, 123, 136, 138
Wodehouse, Hugh, 235
Wolsey, Gardiner, 236
Wolsey, Thomas, Cardinal, 41, 80, 82, 104, 105, 118, 150, 156, 216, 244, 329, 352, 360
  Amicable Grant and, 170, 175
  Anne Boleyn and, 189, 190, 201, 210, 220, 236
  as chancellor, 132
  Charles V and, 171–73
  conspiracies and, 148, 149, 150, 141
  Council position of, 125, 132
  crusades and, 165
  death of, 237
  in diplomatic negotiations, 166, 167, 193, 205–7
  in divorce proceedings, 200–201, 205, 206–7, 211, 218, 221, 225–26, 228
  Field of Cloth of Gold and, 135, 142, 143, 145
  in 1523 campaign, 167–70
  French negotiations of, 171, 172, 205–7
  indictment and exile of, 235–36
  influence on Henry of, 92, 103, 132, 133, 207, 251
  Mary Tudor and, 123, 124, 125
  on mission to free Clement VII, 201–2, 205–6

  nobles' enmity and, 152–53, 237
  occult powers attributed to, 154, 266
  as opponent of Katherine of Aragon, 171, 194, 195, 196
  papal ambitions of, 132, 172, 205
  as papal legate, 196, 199
  personality of, 132–34
  populace's hatred of, 154, 175, 192, 193, 201, 206, 214, 237
  power of, 132–33, 135, 153, 180, 201
  tomb of, 201, 371
  treaty of universal peace sought by, 137, 205–6
  wealth and display of, 133, 142, 153, 179–80, 181, 191
women:
  court life of, 29, 179, 188
  doctrinal issues and, 365
  Henry's attitude toward, 38, 252–53
  treatment in war of, 90
Woodville, Elizabeth, 36
wool industry, 214, 353
Worcester, bishop of, 138
Wriothesley, Thomas, 304, 332, 353, 364, 365–66, 368
Wyatt, Thomas, 189, 190

Yardeley, John, 203
York, duke of, Henry's title of, 24
York, duke of (false), 22, 24
York dynasty, 23, 33, 36, 288, 317–18
York Place (Wolsey's palace), 153, 286
Yorkshire, Henry's progress to, 317, 322–23

Zinzano, Hannibal, 232
Zwingli, Ulrich, 200, 293